Human-Computer Interaction Series

Human-Computer Interaction is a multidisciplinary field focused on human aspects of the development of computer technology. As computer-based technology becomes increasingly pervasive – not just in developed countries, but worldwide – the need to take a human-centered approach in the design and development of this technology becomes ever more important. For roughly 30 years now, researchers and practitioners in computational and behavioral sciences have worked to identify theory and practice that influences the direction of these technologies, and this diverse work makes up the field of human-computer interaction. Broadly speaking, it includes the study of what technology might be able to do for people and how people might interact with the technology.

In this series, we present work which advances the science and technology of developing systems which are both effective and satisfying for people in a wide variety of contexts. The human-computer interaction series will focus on theoretical perspectives (such as formal approaches drawn from a variety of behavioral sciences), practical approaches (such as the techniques for effectively integrating user needs in system development), and social issues (such as the determinants of utility, usability and acceptability).

For further volumes:
http://www.springer.com/series/6033

Christian Müller-Tomfelde
Editor

Tabletops - Horizontal Interactive Displays

 Springer

Editor
Christian Müller-Tomfelde
CSIRO-ICT Centre
Cnr Vimiera & Pembroke Rd
Marsfield NSW 2122
Australia
Christian.Mueller-Tomfelde@csiro.au

ISSN 1571-5035
ISBN 978-1-84996-112-7   e-ISBN 978-1-84996-113-4
DOI 10.1007/978-1-84996-113-4
Springer London Dordrecht Heidelberg New York

British Library Cataloguing in Publication Data
A catalogue record for this book is available from the British Library

Library of Congress Control Number: 2010922803

Printed on acid-free paper

Springer is part of Springer Science+Business Media (www.springer.com)

Foreword: From Furniture to Interaction Substrate

Norbert A. Streitz

Introduction

Tables are elements that provide basic functions in a wide range of environments by supporting and enabling living, working, eating, entertainment, leisure and many more activities, indoors and outdoors. Very often they are prominent and eye-catching examples of well-designed furniture. Their function is to provide a usually horizontal surface (supported by legs) for putting and displaying objects. This supportive function can be available at different heights, sometimes even in an adjustable way. There are also tilted tables, e.g., drafting tables, drawing boards or lecterns (deviating a bit from the prototypical table instances). The materials are manifold: wood, metal, plastic, cardboard and many other combinations. In a specific context, "tables" is a general name given to a class of board games similar to backgammon, e.g., "tavli" in Greece. Tables games are among the oldest known board games played in the world. We come back to the combination of tables and games. In a different meaning and context, "tables" are a means of displaying information in a matrix, e.g., as a mathematical table, or they demote a set of data elements (values) in a data base.

Table-Based Scenarios

Tables are used by individuals and by groups. In an office environment, a person sits at a table or its transformation into a desk and uses it for writing or typing. Members of a project team are sitting around a table in a meeting room taking notes of the discussion and/or looking at material (e.g., an architectural floor plan) displayed on the table. The surface of the table/desk and the information displayed or created there by an individual is a primarily personal/private space, while in the meeting room most of the table surface is public and only some limited territory can be considered private. Working in a group sitting around a table was and still is often complemented by another public, this time vertical display as, e.g., a flip chart or a white board which usually has no connection to the table and the content shown on it. A different case is having a computer-projection from a laptop.

The objects displayed on a table can take multiple forms. In meetings, it is still very often printed paper although its content was originally created on a computer. The content can also be a "table", but now in the mathematical sense, showing, e.g., the budget of a project. Then, we have a "table" on the table. Most often, the computer-generated contents are subject of frequent changes or dynamic in nature.

It is a logical consequence to avoid the detour and the inherent media break by transforming the surface of the table into a display able to show media that are active and can be computer-generated and computer-controlled. At the same time, it is desirable to maintain the inherent features and affordances of working with the objects and the contents while sitting or standing around a table.

Electronic Meeting Rooms

On the basis of these and other elaborate considerations, we started to design in 1992/1993 an electronic meeting room in Darmstadt at GMD-IPSI (later Fraunhofer IPSI). The setup of our custom-built DOLPHIN-System consisted of a "traditional" large rectangular wooden table with four physically integrated workstation-like computers with flat screens. This set-up was complemented by linking a large vertical pen-operated interactive display, at that time the first LiveBoard outside of Xerox PARC (two of which I was able to get to Darmstadt after my stay at Xerox PARC in 1990). Our DOLPHIN software combined the pen-based interaction hardware of the LiveBoard with our multi-user cooperative hypermedia system and allowed public as well as private spaces.

While the DOLPHIN-System supported group work as, e.g., brain storming and idea generation, creating and processing informal structures as well as formal argumentation structures and shared document processing across all devices in the meeting room, the table component did not have all the required interaction characteristics. For example, there were still keyboard and mouse involved, accessible in drawers at the side of the table.

The InteracTable as Part of Roomware Environments

In a later project starting in 1997, we reflected again on it but with a more foundational intention of designing pervasive computing and ambient communication environments. The guiding principle was "The Disappearing Computer" involving questions like: How can we move from human-computer interaction to designing human-information, resp. human-artefact interaction and support human-human communication and cooperation by exploiting the affordances of existing artefacts in our environment? We extended from "boards" to "walls" and integrated other artefacts as, e.g., tables and chairs, into the overall setting initially called i-LAND. This resulted in our Roomware® components DynaWall®, InteracTable®, CommChairs®, ConnecTables® which were developed in several generations, the first in 1998, the second in 1999 and 2000. The application was inspired by the idea of creating the i-LAND environment, an interactive landscape for creativity and cooperation and was governed by the BEACH software. Our InteracTable (in 1998 still projection-based) and subsequent versions (starting 1999 using plasma displays) were interactive by having a touch-sensitive surface to be operated by finger or pen. Using an incremental gesture recognition, we provided a modeless interaction. We also addressed having different perspectives when standing on opposite sides of the table from the very beginning of our work.

It has to be noted, that – in contrast to many others – we designed interactive tables always as integral parts of a larger ensemble of smart artefacts (walls, chairs, lecterns, etc.) as in the i-LAND setting. We also facilitated the intuitive transfer of digital information between roomware artefacts without media breaks via the Passage mechanism by using arbitrary physical objects. An example is the combination and coupling of the horizontal InteracTable with the vertical interactive DynaWall. This comprehensive view was always important for us and provided additional perspectives on the role, functionality and design of interactive tables in contrast to focusing only on the table as a single artefact.

We also used the InteracTable and other subsequent table- and board-like artefacts for developing new types of games. Here, our goal was to facilitate new experiences by taking the best of both worlds, traditional tabletop games (real) and computer games (virtual). The result was a set of Interactive Hybrid Games (2003) that preserved the social situation, e.g., a group of friends sitting around a table in contrast to isolated computer console gamers, but also enhancing the situation by integrating parameters and contexts from the real and the virtual world.

Interaction Substrate

So far, interactive tables are most often table-like shaped artefacts with integrated displays or projections from above or below. This is falling short of what we envision within the context of new paradigms like pervasive computing and ambient intelligence in combination with rapid developments in material science. Future personalized individual as well as collective services will exploit new qualities of infrastructures and components situated in smart environments. They are based on a very large number of "invisible" small computing devices embedded into our environment and use a corresponding infrastructure of sensors and actuators. It is anticipated that economics will drive this technology to evolve from a large variety of specialized components to a small number of universal, extremely small and low-cost components that can be embedded in a variety of materials. Thus, we will be provided with a computing, communication, sensing and interaction "substrate" for systems and services which we can then characterize as "smart ecosystems". In this scenario of a not-so-distant future, we will have at our disposal, e.g., interactive wallpaper and interactive smart tablecloth that we can buy by the meter in a department store. This type of tablecloth and wallpaper will then take over the role currently played by interactive screens or projections but, of course, in a much more flexible and adaptive fashion. We anticipate this will lead to new interaction paradigms including a more intuitive handling and exploitation of the content produced and consumed leading also to a new generation of "prosumers". As our roomware components in the past, these ensembles of smart materials providing new interaction substrates will be the constituting elements of future smart buildings (smart bricks) and – at a global level – of hybrid smart cities.

The contributions in this book provide the reader with an excellent and comprehensive overview of the state of affairs in this domain. The editor Christian Müller-Tomfelde succeeded in bringing together an inspiring collection of papers. I am convinced it will become a flagship publication and important reference work when discussing the area of tabletop interactive horizontal displays. I therefore wish the book a wide distribution and reception by the scientific community.

November 2009   Norbert Streitz
Smart Future Initiative
Cologne, Darmstadt
Germany
www.smart-future.net
norbert.streitz@smart-future.net

Preface

This book is an attempt to bring together current research in the domain of interactive horizontal displays. The book integrates and summarises findings from the most important international tabletop research teams. It provides a state-of-the-art overview and allows for the discussion of emerging and future directions in research and technology of interactive horizontal displays.

In the early 1990s Mark Weiser's vision of Ubiquitous Computing redefined the notion of Human Computer Interaction. Interaction was not anymore considered to happen only with desktop computers but also with other elements of the environment. This is documented for tabletop research by the early works of Pierre Wellner and Hiroshi Ishii and who envisioned the interaction and collaboration in tabletop settings with their seminal research prototypes DigitalDesk and ClearBoard. In the following years, research led to the development more prototypes such as the Active Desk, Augmented Surface and the Roomware component InteracTable. Recent developments of various technologies such as affordable large display panels, reliable multi-touch detection and software toolkits open up new possibilities and refuel the interest in Human Computer Interaction on horizontal interactive displays. At the same time researchers aim for a better understanding of social aspects of interaction and group work practice around tabletops in order to successfully deploy tabletops in work, education and entertainment environments.

Today we may witness the beginning of the last phase of a long process from the concept of interactive tabletops and lab prototypes to a sustainable business. Looking back to nearly 20 years of research, commercially available tabletop systems are on the brink of becoming part of our everyday interaction and collaboration environments. Tabletop systems appear in semi-public spaces, the hospitality business and the domestic environment but also in office environments for which tabletop were initially envisioned. However, the relevance of the research in this book remains independent of the domain of deployment of future tabletops as horizontal interactive displays.

Structure of the Book

The book is structured in three parts: "under", "on and above" and "around and beyond" tabletops. These parts are associated with different research disciplines such as Hardware/Software and Computer Science, Human Computer Interaction (HCI) and Computer Supported Cooperative Work (CSCW). The associations with the research areas are not strict and also the notion of the specific location for each part of the book should not be understood and interpreted too literally. All of the 18 book chapters reflect and underline the interdisciplinary character of tabletop research. Furthermore, the introductory chapter about the short history of tabletop research, technologies and products precedes the book parts. This historical review over a period of nearly 20 year informs the analysis of the research activities, the development of technologies and commercial products. Three *transitions*, marking distinct shifts in the evolvement of tabletops are identified. They are discussed and integrated into a synoptic landscape of tabletop research, technologies and products to set up the context for the chapters.

The part *under tabletops* covers various topics, starting with practical considerations when building multi-touch surfaces. The part comprises the review of major tabletop systems, including a classification scheme. Aspects of high-resolution displays for tabletops are presented comprehensively. The implications of view-dependent information display on tabletops are discussed and possible applications presented. The part concludes with insights into hand and object recognition and applications, which lead and connect to the next book part.

On and above tabletops addresses surface and interaction related aspects and is commenced by two chapters discussing tangibility for interactive surfaces, whether the objects are passively illuminated or physically actuated. Furthermore, interaction styles for tabletops are explored focussing on high fidelity when compared to those in the real world. The decomposition of tabletop actions into basic components complements this research in tabletop interaction styles. This book part also provides a discussion of the fundamental limitations of direct touch interaction before it *takes-off* the surface and finishes with a taxonomy of 3D tabletop systems.

The part *around and beyond tabletops* focuses on the understanding of how interactive tabletops shape the way users collaborate and socially interact. Implications of interaction techniques on individuals as well as on groups are discussed, followed by the presentation of a solution for the basic operation of accessing personal files at tabletops. Empirical and theoretical investigations in the concept of spatial territories further the understanding of social practice around tabletops. Tabletop systems in work and public environments are examined in the context of collaborative information visualization. Aspects *beyond tabletops* become discussed in detail presenting research on an experimental setting with shared remote tabletops. Finally, links are explored and established between tabletop research in real-world settings and the research domains of Ubiquitous Computing and Media Spaces.

Common Themes

Aside entering the book through one of its parts, the reader may want to approach the rich body of documented research from a different perspective. In the book particular topics are discussed in multiple chapters from various angles. These topics are called *common themes* of the book since they are not limited to one of the three book parts and may be subject of multiple research areas such as Computer Science, HCI and CSCW. In Table 1 the common themes of the book are listed against the three parts of the book and the chapters are classified accordingly:

Table 1 Book content matrix of parts and common themes, marked are the chapters

Common theme	Part 1: under	Part 2: on and above	Part 3: around and beyond
Multi-touch interaction technologies	2, 3	7, 10, 11	
Display and surface technologies	2, 3, 4, 6		17
Gesture interaction on and above surfaces	3, 4, 5, 6	8, 9, 10, 11, 12	13, 17
Tangible interaction on surfaces	5	7, 8, 9, 12	
Organisation of spaces on the surface	5	9	13, 14, 15, 18
Collocated collaboration at tabletops			13, 14,15
Distributed shared tabletops		8	17, 18

Audience

The book addresses fellow researchers who are interested in this domain and practitioners who consider deploying interactive tabletops in real-world projects. The structure of the book also facilitates access to the newest findings in tabletop research for interested readers from other research disciplines. Finally, the book will be useful for the academic curriculum and hopefully stimulate new research leveraging on the documented works to advance the knowledge about tabletops as horizontal interactive displays.

Sydney, Australia   Christian Müller-Tomfelde
October 2009

Acknowledgements

I would like to thank all authors for their excellent and outstanding contributions to this book. Without their effort documenting their research and preparing the manuscripts the book would not have been possible. I would like to express my sincerest gratitude to the author of the foreword for this book, Norbert A. Streitz, for sharing his viewpoints, ideas and thoughtful insights.

I would also thank the reviewers who helped to review and select the chapters for the book. The reviewers contributed to the high quality of the book through their invaluable advice and comprehensive, constructive feedback to the authors. Without this help from acclaimed members of the research community, the book would not have reached this high standard. The reviewers are, in alphabetical order:

Morten Fjeld, Chalmers University of Technology (Sweden)

Michael Haller, Upper Austria University of Applied Sciences (Austria)

Yasauaki Kakehi, Keio University (Japan)

Hideki Koike, University of Electro-Communications (Japan)

Gregor McEwan, University of Saskatchewan (Canada)

David Pinelle, University of Saskatchewan (Canada)

Stacy D. Scott, Waterloo University (Canada)

Norbert A. Streitz, Smart Future Initiative (Germany)

Sriram Subramanian, University of Bristol (UK)

Masahiro Takasuka, University of Sydney (Australia)

Brygg Ullmer, Louisiana State University (USA)

Andy Wilson, Microsoft Research (USA)

I would also like to thank Beverly Ford, Helen Desmond and Natasha Harding from the Springer-Verlag for their outstanding help and support. Finally, my special thanks goes to my partner Uta Daur for proofreading parts of the book and her constant support and encouragement during my time preparing and editing this book.

Sydney, Australia   Christian Müller-Tomfelde
November 2009

Contents

Contributors

Jason Alexander Department of Computer Science, University of Bristol, Bristol BS8 1UB, UK, jason@cs.bris.ac.uk

Dzmitry Aliakseyeu User Experiences Group, Philips Research Europe, 5656AE Eindhoven, The Netherlands, dzmitry.aliakseyeu@philips.com

Mark Ashdown Thales Research and Technology, Reading RG2 0SB, UK, mark@ashdown.me

Tom Bartindale Culture Lab, Newcastle University, Grand Assembly Rooms, Kings Walk, Newcastle upon Tyne NE1 7RU, UK, tom@bartindale.com

Hrvoje Benko Microsoft Research, One Microsoft Way, Redmond, WA 98052, USA, benko@microsoft.com

Jan Borchers Media Computing Group, RWTH Aachen University, 52074 Aachen, Germany, borchers@cs.rwth-aachen.de

Peter Brandl Media Interaction Lab, Upper Austria University of Applied Sciences, 4600 Wels, Austria, peter.brandl@fh-hagenberg.at

Andreas Butz University of Munich, Munich, Germany, butz@ifi.lmu.de

Sheelagh Carpendale Department of Computer Science, University of Calgary, Calgary, AB T2N 1N4, Canada, sheelagh@ucalgary.ca

Anthony Collins School of Information Technologies, University of Sydney, Sydney, NSW 2006, Australia, anthony@it.usyd.edu.au

Florian Echtler Technical University of Munich, Munich, Germany, echtler@in.tum.de

Morten Fjeld Department of Computer Science and Engineering, Chalmers University of Technology, SE-412 96 Gothenburg, Sweden, morten@t2i.se

Kentaro Fukuchi Japan Science and Technology Agency, Bunkyo-ku, Tokyo 112-0002, Japan, Japan, fukuchi@gegaui.net

Tovi Grossman Autodesk Research, Toronto, ON M5A 1J7, Canada,
tovi.grossman@autodesk.com

Carl Gutwin Department of Computer Science, University of Saskatchewan,
Saskatoon, SK S7N 5C9, Canada, gutwin@cs.usask.ca

Mark Hancock Department of Computer Science, University of Calgary, Calgary,
AB T2N 1N4, Canada, mshancoc@ucalgary.ca

Otmar Hilliges Microsoft Research Cambridge, CB3 0FB Cambridge, UK,
otmarh@microsoft.com

Uta Hinrichs Department of Computer Science, University of Calgary, Calgary,
AB T2N 1N4, Canada, uhinrich@ucalgary.ca

James D. Hollan Distributed Cognition and Human-Computer Interaction Lab,
Department of Cognitive Science, University of California, San Diego, CA 92093,
USA, hollan@hci.ucsd.edu

Jonathan Hook Culture Lab, Newcastle University, Grand Assembly Rooms,
Kings Walk, Newcastle upon Tyne NE1 7RU, UK, j.d.hook@newcastle.ac.uk

Masahiko Inami Graduate School of Media Design, Keio University, Yokohama,
Kanagawa, 223-8526 Japan, inami@computer.org

Petra Isenberg Department of Computer Science, University of Calgary, Calgary,
AB T2N 1N4, Canada, petra.isenberg@ucalgary.ca

Shahram Izadi Microsoft Research Cambridge, Cambridge CB3 0FB, UK,
shahrami@microsoft.com

Yasuaki Kakehi Keio University, Fujisawa, Kanagawa 252-8520, Japan,
ykakehi@sfc.keio.ac.jp

Judy Kay School of Information Technologies, University of Sydney, Sydney,
NSW 2006, Australia, judy@it.usyd.edu.au

Hideki Koike University of Electro-Communications, Chofu, Tokyo 182-8585,
Japan, koike@acm.org

Andreas Kunz Department of Mechanical and Process Engineering, Swiss
Federal Institute of Technology, CH-8092 Zurich, Switzerland,
kunz@iwf.mavt.ethz.ch

Regan Mandryk Department of Computer Science, University of Saskatchewan,
Saskatoon, SK S7N 5C9, Canada, regan@cs.usask.ca

Nima Motamedi Simon Fraser University, Burnaby, B.C., Canada V5A 1S6,
nimam@sfu.ca

Christian Müller-Tomfelde CSIRO ICT Centre, Marsfield NSW 2122, Australia,
Christian.Mueller-Tomfelde@csiro.au

Miguel A. Nacenta Department of Computer Science, University of Calgary, Calgary, AB T2N 1N4, Canada; Department of Computer Science, University of Saskatchewan, Saskatoon, SK S7N 5C9, Canada, miguel.nacenta@ucalgary.ca

Takeshi Naemura University of Tokyo, Bunkyo-ku, Tokyo, Japan, naemura@nae-lab.org

Wataru Nishikawa University of Electro-Communications, Chofu, Tokyo 182-8585, Japan, wataru@vogue.is.uec.ac.jp

Kenton O'Hara Microsoft Research Cambridge, Cambridge CB3 0FB, UK, v-keohar@microsoft.com

Patrick Oliver Culture Lab, Newcastle University, Grand Assembly Rooms, Kings Walk, Newcastle upon Tyne NE1 7RU, UK, p.l.olivier@newcastle.ac.uk

David Pinelle Medical Imaging, College of Medicine, University of Saskatchewan, Saskatoon, SK S7N 0W8, Canada, david.pinelle@usask.ca

Jan Richter Wearable Computer Lab, School of Computer and Information Science, University of South Australia, Mawson Lakes, SA 5095, Australia, jan.richter@wcl.ml.unisa.edu.au

Peter Robinson Computer Laboratory, University of Cambridge, Cambridge CB3 0FD, UK, peter.robinson@cl.cam.ac.uk

Toshiki Sato University of Electro-Communications, Chofu, Tokyo 182-8585, Japan, den@vogue.is.uec.ac.jp

Dominik Schmidt Lancaster University, Lancaster LA1 4WA, UK, schmidtd@comp.lancs.ac.uk

Johannes Schöning German Research Center for Artificial Intelligence (DFKI), D-66123 Saarbruecken, Germany, johannes.schoening@dfki.de

Stacey D. Scott Department of Systems Design Engineering, University of Waterloo, Waterloo, ON N2L 3G1, Canada, s9scott@uwaterloo.ca

Norbert A. Streitz Smart Future Initiative, Belvedere Str. 78, D – 50933 Köln (Cologne), Germany, norbert.streitz@smart-future.net

Sriram Subramanian Department of Computer Science, University of Bristol, Bristol BS8 1UB, UK, sriram@cs.bris.ac.uk

Maki Sugimoto Graduate School of Media Design, Keio University, Yokohama, Kanagawa, 223-8526 Japan, sugimoto@kmd.keio.ac.jp

Bruce H. Thomas Wearable Computer Lab, School of Computer and Information Science, University of South Australia, Mawson Lakes, SA 5095, Australia, bruce.thomas@unisa.edu.au

Philip Tuddenham Computer Laboratory, University of Cambridge, Cambridge CB3 0FD, UK, philip.tuddenham@cl.cam.ac.uk

Ulrich von Zadow Archimedes Solutions GmbH, Saarbrücker Str. 24 10405, Germany, uz@archimedes-solutions.de

Malte Weiss Media Computing Group, RWTH Aachen University, 52074 Aachen, Germany, weiss@cs.rwth-aachen.de

Daniel Wigdor Microsoft Corporation, One Microsoft Way, Redmond, WA 98052, USA, dwigdor@microsoft.com

Andrew D. Wilson Microsoft Corporation, One Microsoft Way, Redmond, WA 98052, USA, awilson@microsoft.com

Chapter 1
Introduction: A Short History of Tabletop Research, Technologies, and Products

Christian Müller-Tomfelde and Morten Fjeld

Abstract This chapter presents a brief history of scientific research into interactive tabletops, associated emerging technologies, and commercial products. It summarizes and visualizes a body of scientific work, identifies major advances during the past 15 years, and thereby draws a picture of the research landscape to date. Key innovations during this period are identified and their research impact is discussed. We synthesize historical information into a synoptic landscape including research highlights, enabling technologies, prototypes, and products. On top of this landscape, we point out and trace innovations as they stimulated and triggered key transitions in research and technology. These innovations have also played a major role in leveraging ideas from a conceptual level to widespread adoption and use. Finally, the chapter examines possible future trends of tabletop research, technologies, and applications.

Introduction

The rise of personal computers (PC) in the 1980s provided individuals with computational power on the desk in front of them rather than on a central mainframe. Interface designers structured and simplified user access to and interaction with data and information stored in these *desktop computers*. They turned the physical desktop into a metaphor for the Graphical User Interface (GUI) rendered on the vertical computer screen. In this manner the physical desktop itself shaped the way computers and information technology became integrated into everyday life. The idea that physical desktops play a central role when it comes to reviewing, organizing, and creating information that is not only paper-based, stems from the 1940s. This was when Vannevar Bush envisioned Memex, an electromechanical device for storing and reviewing information [1]. While technologies have changed dramatically since

C. Müller-Tomfelde (✉)
CSIRO ICT Centre, Marsfield, NSW 2122, Australia
e-mail: christian.mueller-tomfelde@csiro.au

C. Müller-Tomfelde (ed.), *Tabletops – Horizontal Interactive Displays*,
Human-Computer Interaction Series, DOI 10.1007/978-1-84996-113-4_1,
© Springer-Verlag London Limited 2010

then, his concept was later to be picked up and refined by Pierre Wellner when he presented the DigitalDesk in 1993 [2]. With this work, the computer display ultimately became a desktop, or as Wellner put it, "[no] desktop metaphor is needed because [the display] is literally a desktop" [2]. While the merger he suggested was consistent and compelling, research in the late 1990s showed that this interface would particularly add value to the work practice of small teams. This was also the period when various devices with new form factors such as laptops and Personal Digital Assistants (PDAs) became available. The advent of these devices in the early 1990s marks the onset of the era that Mark Weiser calls "ubiquitous computing" [3]. This trend has continued into recent times with the emergence of smart phones as well as netbooks.

The term *tabletop* stands in the tradition of earlier terms, such as *desktop* and *laptop*, highlighting the location of the computer or display. Tabletops distinguish themselves by being suitable as group interfaces and by the fact that their horizontal display is the interface where the user directly interacts with digital information rather than using the keyboard and mouse. In that sense, the tabletop is one of the interfaces where even the computer disappears, not only for the end-users [4, 5], but also for researchers exploring new forms of hand and gesture interaction, tangible interfaces, and novel interactive visualizations. This understanding of the term tabletop was first used in research literature around 2001 by Dietz and Leigh [6] and Tandler et al. [7].

Tabletop interfaces still maintain a notion of physicality as they rely on users' mental models of traditional tables. In contrast to virtual environments, where all sensory presentation is synthetic and most interaction is three-dimensional, tabletop interfaces are two-dimensional and better described as hybrid environments. Users combine the advantages of the physical environment with the possibilities of the digital information space. Rather than being dogmatic about which sort of reality or space users should work in, designing hybrid environments enables users to fluidly switch between and navigate physical and digital workspaces in an opportunistic way. Viewing a tabletop as a surface with electronic sheets of paper is an inadequate understanding of it as merely a horizontal display. Researchers and application designers will have to transcend this traditional user perception and take advantage of the possibilities that make interactive tabletops unique and fascinating. Inspired by Hollan and Stornetta [8], who question the efficacy of digital media replication of face-to-face communication, we see a need to "develop tools that go beyond" the work at traditional tabletops.

The first section of this chapter examines tabletop research in terms of Human Computer Interaction (HCI), Ubiquitous Computing (Ubicomp), and Computer Supported Cooperative Work (CSCW). The section goes on to present seminal research publications, enabling technologies, and commercial products. This is followed by a second section tracing key transitions driven by research and development since the late 1990s. Then, a third overview section graphically visualizes and contrasts selected landmarks of research, technologies, and products. The fourth and final section presents trends, again in terms of research, enabling technologies, and commercial products. The chapter ends with a discussion and summary.

Tabletops: From Prototypes to Products

This section first gives an overview of tabletop research in terms of key scientific publications. Then, it presents a set of important enabling technologies and how they benefited the design and realization of interactive tables. Finally, the section reviews commercial products from the last 15 years.

Research

Research into interactive tabletops and horizontal displays originated from and continues to be conducted within a few different research domains. Among the most important ones are Human Computer Interaction (HCI) and Computer Supported Cooperative Work (CSCW). HCI addresses individual user actions and performance at the tabletop interface level. The desktop metaphor of GUIs, as introduced in the early 1980s (e.g. Xerox Star), was a leading paradigm for simplifying interaction with computer resources. Interactive tabletops allowed for the opportunity to experiment with new forms and challenges of the user interface. In contrast, the CSCW domain addresses how computers can mediate and support group collaboration and social interactions. Each of these two domains provides an ideal community and forum to successfully "balance between good social processes and procedures with appropriately structured technology" [9].

In the early 1990s traditional HCI was inspired by Mark Weiser's paradigm of Ubiquitous Computing [3] (Ubicomp), which gained widespread prominence. Computer displays started to move beyond the form factors of traditional desktop environments, which had dominated until then. In Weiser's vision the yard-sized displays (36 inch or 91 cm) for collaboration were predominantly vertical, accompanied by foot-sized shared mobile displays (12 inch or 30 cm) and personal handheld displays (2 inch or 5 cm). However, by the end of the 1990s horizontal yard-sized displays also appeared as part of ubicomp scenarios for collaboration. In that sense Ubicomp inspired research into interactive tabletops. Finally, a key affordance [10] of horizontal displays is that their surface supports any physical object, making them an ideal setting for the seamless integration of tangible interaction on tabletops. Such integration is studied in the research domain of Tangible User Interfaces (TUIs). Hence, the four domains HCI, CSCW, Ubicomp, and TUIs constitute the scientific foundation and framework for tabletop research.

While the measures of task performance are well defined in the HCI domain for traditional desktop settings, measures such as object manipulation and movement times can also be used for interactive tabletop settings. However, tabletop task performance also involves more recent issues such as touch selection, physical reach, turn-taking, and verbal/non-verbal communication. In this sense, tabletop research is located in the CSCW category of *face-to-face interaction* [9]. Such collaborative work is diametrically opposed to, for instance, web-based approaches where spatially distributed users interact asynchronously. Another major characteristic of tabletop collaboration is that teams are typically small, seldom consisting of more than four people. Sugimoto's Caretta urban design system combining a tabletop with handheld PDAs [11] is a good demonstration of such small team collaboration. His system enabled its users to switch between private stylus-based sketching and shared tabletop planning. For larger groups, basic ergonomic issues emerge such as visibility and reachability of elements on the table.

As tabletop research is part of the larger HCI and CSCW communities, the most relevant publishers are the Association for Computing Machinery (ACM) and the Institute of Electrical and Electronics Engineers (IEEE). The ACM hosts the Special Interest Group on Computer–Human Interaction (SIGCHI) whose Conference on Human Factors in Computing Systems (ACM CHI) is a major annual international conference started in 1982. This conference is highly competitive and very relevant for the development of the tabletop research community. The ACM also hosts the CSCW conference, which was started in 1994 and is an important biannual conference addressing the collaborative aspects of interactive tabletops. Since 2006, the IEEE has hosted the International Workshop on Horizontal Interactive Human-Computer Systems (IEEE Tabletop). From 2009, the ACM supports this research activity by hosting the International Conference on Interactive Tabletops and Surfaces (ACM ITS). In 2007, the related ACM-hosted International Conference on Tangible, Embedded, and Embodied Interaction (ACM TEI) was launched.

To provide further insights into the body of research in the domain of interactive tabletop settings, we carried out a search on the Google Scholar web page accessed via the "Publish or Perish" program.[1] The search query terms were "tabletop," "interactive table," and "horizontal display," thus covering all publications including early ones that may not have used the term, "tabletop." For instance, Wellner's seminal work from 1993 [2] refers only to a "computer display [that] is projected on the desk" and does not use the term, "table," at all. The *top-ten* landmark publications listed in Table 1.1 cover a time period of over 10 years, and the number of citations ranges from 260 to 792.

While the citation figures may be read as indicators of relevance, they must also be considered with care since they come from only one database and do not reflect the length of time that has passed since publication. Also, these publications may have been cited for reasons other than tabletop research. The publications up to 1997 present experimental lab systems such as ClearBoard [18], DigialDesk [2], Bricks [12], and metaDESK [15]. From around 1998 onwards the key publications concentrate on systems for work environments with multiple users, such as the InteracTable in the i-LAND project [13], or introduce new technologies for the detection of multi-touch user input, as by the DiamondTouch in 2001 [6], SmartSkin [17], and then later by Han's 2005 work on FTIR [19]. It is a noteworthy that the publication about multi-user touch technology introduced by Dietz and Leigh in 2001 [6] is already at the third position only eight years after its publication (see Table 1.1). This is a clear indicator of the importance of multi-touch technologies for tabletop research.

---

[1] http://www.harzing.com/pop.htm

Table 1.1 Top-ten most-cited research publications on interactive tabletops. Citation numbers are based on a Google Scholar query carried out (4.8.2009)

Citations	Author(s)	Title	Year
792	Wellner	Interacting with paper on the DigitalDesk [2]	1993
532	Fitzmaurice et al.	Bricks: Laying the foundations for graspable user interfaces [12]	1995
517	Dietz and Leigth	DiamondTouch: A multi-user touch technology [6]	2001
479	Streitz et al.	i-LAND: An interactive landscape for creativity and innovation [13]	1999
422	Rekimoto and Saitoh	Augmented surfaces: A spatially continuous work space for hybrid computing environments [14]	1999
352	Ullmer and Ishii	The metaDESK: Models and prototypes for tangible user interfaces [15]	1997
329	Kato et al.	Virtual object manipulation on a table-top AR environment [16]	2000
314	Rekimoto	SmartSkin: An infrastructure for freehand manipulation on interactive surfaces [17]	2002
309	Ishii and Kobayashi	ClearBoard: A seamless medium for shared drawing and conversation with eye contact [18]	1992
260	Han	Low-cost multi-touch sensing through frustrated total internal reflection [19]	2005

To further understand the development of the interactive tabletop research domain we investigated the number of publications in the proceedings of the major ACM conferences, CHI, CSCW, and User Interface and Software Technology (UIST), from 1998 until 2008 as well as the tabletop workshops (IEEE Tabletop) held from 2006 until 2008. While the ACM TEI conference is not investigated here, we note that its 2010 call for submissions explicitly mentions interactive surfaces. A search with the logical disjunction of the three query terms "tabletop," "interactive table," and "horizontal display" was executed using an off-the-shelf file search tool[2] based on the Lucene[3] indexing and retrieval software. The results of this search query organized by conference and year are represented in Fig. 1.1. The figure shows number of publications, also referred to as hits. Each resulting publication is accounted for only once.

---

[2] Aduna AutoFocus 5, http://www.aduna-software.com

[3] http://lucene.apache.org/

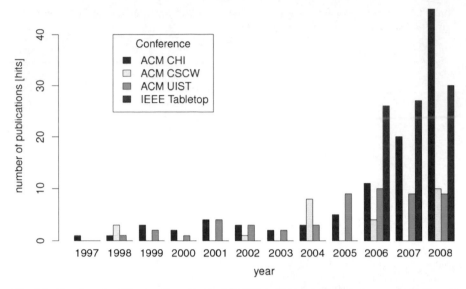

Fig. 1.1 Number of publications found in the ACM Digital Library. The query term was "tabletop" OR "interactive table" OR "horizontal display". Since 2005 the number of hits has increased for all major conferences, which is particularly visible for the proceedings of the ACM CHI conference

We assumed that all contributions to the proceedings of the workshop relate to tabletop research. Figure 1.1 reveals that from 2005 until 2008 the numbers of publications at ACM CHI has consistently increased. At the same time, the hits for ACM UIST increased from around three to nearly ten hits per conference. The IEEE Tabletop workshop, started in 2006 and turned into the ACM ITS in 2009, follows this trend as well. Another interesting observation is that the biannual ACM CSCW conference peaked in 2004 with seven publications, which is 15% of the proceedings. A detailed review of these hits revealed that these are highly relevant works in the area of interactive tabletops. The increase of publications in the proceedings of the ACM CHI conference could correlate simply with an increase of total accepted publications for the archives. However, a detailed analysis reveals that the hits represent 5% of all contributions in ACM CHI 2005, a percentage that increases yearly until 2008 when the hits were over 25%. However, it is not clear from the results whether a hit refers to a work of genuine tabletop research or the publication only refers to tabletops as part of related work. Extending the file repository with the proceedings of future conferences will better illuminate the historical trend in research and may give initial indications about future trends.

Enabling Technologies

Enabling technologies for tabletop systems can be identified in the areas of touch, display, and software, all of which are required to successfully build a tabletop system. Without a direct-touch device a system would be just a large screen; without a display the device would be no more than a graphic tablet; without appropriate software, interaction would be no more than what is offered by a simple pocket calculator. Early research systems used a large variety of general-purpose technology, such as video cameras and tethered tracking systems, to develop the prototypes. As time went by the technologies were further refined and some were adopted that were originally developed for other domains.

The origin of direct-touch devices can be traced back to 1971 when Samuel Hurst of the University of Kentucky invented the touch screen [20, 21]. He developed the first computer display that incorporated a transparent surface sensitive to touch. His guiding design principle was the precise detection of the location of a touch on a screen so that the display and input device could be used at the same time. Ivan Sutherland had demonstrated this earlier in 1963, however, in his prototype a pen or stylus was proposed to interact with the displayed information. Hurt's approach using the touch of the bare finger can be considered a very important step towards enabling touch screens and consequently tabletop systems. At the beginning of the 1990s large interactive wall displays were envisioned [3] and reliable touch detection became available. However, these touch technologies were rather basic and provided only a single point of interaction. From then on the refinement and development of exciting new touch detection technologies has had a significant role for tabletop settings. At the same time, stylus-based interaction on graphic tablets had been developed fulfilling similar requirements, only using a dedicated device. Various touch technologies have been developed based on resistive, capacitive, or acoustic sensors, optical triangulation using cameras or lasers, and computer vision using infrared image capturing. Key performance factors of touch technologies with relevance to interactive tabletop settings are:

- applicability to large display space (> 40 inch or 102 cm)
- reliable real-time multi-user touch capability
- low spatial requirements when integrating direct-touch devices into displays

Of particular interest in the near future may be the flexibility of the sensor technology with respect to the screen, that is, whether it needs to be planar or can be applied to, for example, curved surfaces [22, 23]. For widespread adoption in the market, low production costs are key. Data projectors, which became affordable in the late 1990s, allowed for a computer display that was similar to traditional slide shows and could be used on any flat surface. These projectors can be considered an important technology enabling the development of early, though bulky tabletop systems (see Fig. 1.2).

The development of large but sleek displays for the domestic entertainment market also stimulated research into HCI. Plasma Display Panels (PDP) with single touch overlay frames became commercially available around 1999 and were popular because of their large display size. This became the first alternative to large touch displays based on bulky rear projection, even when used in a horizontal tabletop setting [13].

Fig. 1.2 A typical example
of tabletop system based on
double-mirrored rear
projection and a single touch
interactive 1,024 by 768 pixel
display. The InteracTable was
developed as part of the
i-LAND project in 1999 [13]
and was further refined in
collaboration with an
industrial partner [24] with a
Plasma Display Panel
(Courtesy of
Frauhofer-IPSI/GMD-IPSI)

PDPs have since then been outperformed by Liquid Crystal Display (LCD)
technology [25], but they may experience a comeback if they can be developed
into thinner form factors. Due to improved mass fabrication, LCDs have recently
become available in sizes of up to 42 inch or 107 cm. These have been dominat-
ing the domain of large or yard-sized displays for small-group collaboration around
a table. In combination with infrared video cameras for capturing hand movement
and sensing touch interaction, these LCDs have the potential to become mainstream
technology just as data projectors used to be. An important upcoming stimulus that
may emerge from consumer electronics is the innovation of Organic Light Emitting
Diodes (OLEDs). OLED technology enables slimmer displays combined with high
contrast and better viewing angles [25]. The integration of the light emission into the
pixel rather than using a backlight, as in LCDs, allows for thin display devices and
new applications that were neither conceivable with PDPs nor LCDs. In general, display technology is a driving force in the development of tabletop systems, as new
features such as depth and resolution allow for novel applications in combination
with multi-touch and multi-user interaction technologies. A particularly innovative combination of hybrid display and light-based tracking was seen in Olwal's
Lightsense [26]. In his work, a mobile phone was used as a "handheld lens" to
examine layered map information on the tabletop.

Software and protocol standards also play an important role for the development of interactive tabletop systems. Standard user interfaces based on the paradigm of Windows, Icons, Mouse, and Pointer (WIMP) were not and are still not designed to support touch, multi-touch, and multi-user interaction. Still, this has been achieved, for instance, in pen input devices with special pen- or tablet-PC editions of operating systems. Furthermore, multi-touch pads have become standard for portable devices and are already supported by operating systems. However, while these extensions are rather moderate, supporting the characteristics of tabletop settings poses particular challenges for the software development. In some respects it requires solutions that are similar to groupware settings, as multiple users interact at the same time. Furthermore, while orienting the display horizontally the dedicated sides (left, right, top, and bottom) of the display change their significance. This has implications for how the software handles the display of information. Display areas may need to be rotated to an arbitrary angle to accommodate the perspectives of users around the table, just like it can be done with a sheet of paper. Early software solutions to offer such rotation were seen in BEACH [27] and DiamondSpin [28]. Today, similar solutions are achieved using hardware independent solutions such as OpenGL, Quartz, and DirectX. Other solutions, such as Simple DirectMedia Layer (SDL) and Windows Presentation Foundation (WPF), are more abstract at the price of reduced performance.

A variety of new approaches and solutions for tabletop software have been presented since 2000. Earlier research prototypes addressed the topics of collaborative work [27] and multi-user touch [28]. These highlighted the unique requirements of software for tabletop systems such as rotation and multi-user interaction and demonstrated possible solutions at the application level. At the input device level, the integration of single touch input into the software architecture of applications was as simple as with a computer mouse. With the introduction of multi-touch and multi-user input, event handling had to be redesigned to assure correct processing of the events at the application level. Also, aspects of multimodal interfaces became relevant for multi-touch input processing. Detecting a user's hand gestures requires applying the concept of fusion of multiple user input streams, for instance, for tracking two or more touch points of one or two hands, detecting object rotation or scaling gestures. These gestures became a standard component of the software of integrative table settings. Programming libraries such as touchlib and WPF have been developed to provide reliable access to the multi-touch detection technologies [29].

Furthermore, protocol standards, such as TUIO [30], emerged to propagate the touch interaction information through the level of layered software architecture [31]. An ultimate focal point of these efforts would be to make multi-touch input events an inherent part of the operation system. This would provide an environment that would be abstracted from the device layer, as is currently the case with the standard keyboard and mouse, to the application programmer. So far, research groups, direct-touch device hardware providers, and commercial application developers all use dedicated prototypes, tools, and drivers with limited applicability to the wider community of researchers and developers. Recently, systems were made commercially available allowing the development of tabletop applications where all required components come from one provider including hardware, operating system, and high level application software development kits (SDK) [32, 33]. While this may provide wider access to the development of tabletop applications, these systems are tailored for dedicated components and do not include generic software interfaces to the hardware and the operating system. These systems are designed for markets such as entertainment, sales, and education.

Commercial Products

Commercial products providing an interactive horizontal display have been developed over the past 10–15 years, but they have not yet reached the mass market. In fact, the early efforts in commercializing the concept of interactive tabletops were done by small enterprises in cooperation with research organizations or initiatives. These efforts cornered a niche market and garnered public attention. Only recently have larger companies with substantial research and development and public relations departments engaged themselves with interactive tabletops and developed products for the entertainment, education, and domestic domains. Interactive tabletop prototypes have also often served as an attraction at fairs and exhibitions.

One of the earliest products was the outcome of the Ontario Telepresence Project (OTP) [34], a Canadian research program for academic and industry studies into "sociological issues associated with the deployment of computer and video supported cooperative work systems." Among other results, the Active Desk and the Hydra picture phone system [35] were developed from 1992 onwards as part of this government research program. The "Active Desk [was] a large horizontal desktop surface" slightly tilted at a 30-degree angle and designed jointly by the OTP and a Toronto based company called Arnott Design Group [36]. It was also the device on which Fitzmaurice et al. did their seminal work on tangible Bricks, that is, Graspable User Interfaces [12]. Out of the Arnott Design Group's work grew another Toronto based company called Input Technology Inc. (ITI). Their patented VisionMaker product "[combined] the functionality of the graphics tablet and pen, with a computer monitor, making the two a single seamless entity" [37, 38]. The seminal work on the metaDESK by Ullmer and Ishii [15], in turn, built upon ITI's Visionmaker product.

In the mid-1990s the products of another Canadian-based company called SMART Technologies became increasingly important. The product line was called SMART Board, which was essentially interactive whiteboards. It took several years from their initial introduction until around 1997 before the large-sized interactive whiteboard became popular. They also introduced the first SMART Board for PDPs in 1999. Recently they presented a coffee table-sized multi-touch tabletop system for the educational domain: the SMART Table Model 230i [32]. However, eight years earlier the Germany-based office furniture company, Wilkhahn and later the spin-off *foresee*, started to distribute the second generation InteracTable [24], an office table based on the same technologies. This product was the outcome of a joint research and industry collaboration with the German research institute GMD-IPSI in 1999 [13, 39].

In 2001 researchers at the Mitsubishi Electric Research Laboratories (MERL) in Boston, Massachusetts developed the first multi-touch and multi-user tabletop device for collocated collaboration [6]. This research prototype was distributed to universities and fellow researchers in order to conduct research and develop applications. The device, DiamondTouch, was not commercially available until in 2009 when a company called Circle Twelve took over its commercial distribution [6, 40]. The years of active usage in the research community yielded a rich body of work from many researchers in various labs. Then, in 2005 researchers from Barcelona, Spain developed reacTable*, a tangible tabletop interface to control synthesizer software for live electronic music performances [41]. While this system may not be considered a typical consumer product, it has become popular within a niche market. It became famous as part of the 2007 live show of the Icelandic pop singer, Björk. Playing the reacTable* is compelling to the audience when observing the interactions of the musicians on the table while listening to the sound generated in real-time.

In 2005, Jeff Han presented a multi-touch technology [19] that was very inspiring and heavily broadcasted in 2006. He founded the New York City-based company, PerceptivePixel, to commercialize the Multi-Touch Collaboration Wall for use in broadcasting and medical visualization. From then on, various new companies emerged either by refining and integrating exciting devices and technologies or by building on a patented approach for multi-touch detection. The Helsinki-based spin off company, Helsinki Institute for Information Technology, began selling MultiTouch in 2008 making it the first commercially available multi-touch device integrated into a large LCD. Originally these "MultiTouch LCD Cells" were designed to form a multi-touch display wall, however, turned on its side a cell can act as a tabletop system [42]. A Swedish company, FlatFrog, recently introduced a multi-touch device based on a patented technology called Planar Scatter Detection [43]. It is unclear whether this technology has the potential to further improve the touch interaction experience, however, its close integration into LCD may allow the construction of a significantly less bulky device [42, 19]. Various other small start-up companies have been formed in Europe and the USA to serve a potential market for interactive tabletop systems.

To date, there are two companies distributing a comprehensive tabletop solution: Microsoft and SMART Technologies. While the latter company serves the educational market with its product, Microsoft targets the hospitality and entertainment industries. Both technologies are quite similar in their core specifications, but the design and style of the products are different. Both systems were launched around 2008, but the product development must have begun some years earlier. A key benefit for Microsoft might be that basic multi-touch capabilities can be realized in future releases of their operating systems: .NET and Windows 7. These systems are significant mostly because of the fact that end-users can purchase an all-inclusive solution that includes the hardware platform, software API, and, presumably, support. However, the core technology in these rear-projection systems with infrared, multi-touch capturing is challenged by cost-effective solutions adopted by Han in 2005 [19]. These technologies are currently being refined at universities and smaller start-up companies with the potential to construct new interactive tabletop systems.

Key Transitions

This section gives an overview of major developments and seminal publications marking significant shifts in tabletop research, technologies, and products. With the term *innovation* we refer to a seminal publication or an innovative technology that inspired and shaped the way research and development evolved from that point on. While innovations are usually marked by discrete events such as inventions and publications, we understand a *transition* as an abstract shift from the prevailing approach or paradigm to a new one. They may have either a more scientific or more technical character; as in most HCI-related fields, the cross-pollination of ideas constitutes a dynamic force for innovation. In the following, we identify and trace three such key transitions. They are not exclusive; we acknowledge that other less prominent transitions in this field may have occurred as well.

From Lab Prototypes to Real World Collaborative Applications

The emphasis of the early works investigating the use of horizontal displays and new approaches for computer interaction was on technical prototypes developed in labs. Projects such as DigitalDesk, Active Desk, metaDESK, Bricks, and ClearBoard realized technically challenging features and concentrated on novel applications. In retrospect, the importance of these works lies in the fact that research trends such as augmented reality, tangible interfaces, and distributed collaboration drove their development. At the end of the 1990s these research ideas were picked up and transformed into a new research context. Rather than sitting in labs as prototypical set-ups, novel approaches emerged, first for office and then domestic environments. Since that time it also became apparent that a tabletop setting is a piece of groupware. The BUILD-IT system from 1998 [44] and the InteracTable of the i-LAND project from 1999 [13] represent this transition in the direction of research. Both projects featured more than mere technical solutions; they also embodied new work practices using ICT. Work scenarios became envisioned that were grounded in real world collaborative activities such as planning and discussing. This included the identification of the tabletop setting as a highly suitable solution for small groups whether the team members are standing or sitting. More specifically, one aspect of the BUILD-IT project was the realization of real-time tabletop interaction with a connected simulation software system (SIMPLE++) [45]. Hence, collaborative production planning could be taken from individuals' PCs to the tabletop [46].

While application scenarios for interactive tabletop systems were originally identified for office environments, domestic and entertainment applications were later developed as well as systems for public spaces. As part of the Living Memory Project [47] in 2000, Philips Design created an interactive table situated and tailored for use in a café. In 2004 the Drift Table [48] was developed to investigate playful activity in the domestic environment. Interactive tabletop systems have also been deployed in various museums offering public new collaborative ways to explore exhibitions.

From Single Touch to Multi-touch and Tangibility

The first touch-based devices connected to computer systems essentially replaced mouse-based input and, as such, the processing of input events was done in the same manner. So while different physical input devices were developed, such as the touch screen and the pen or stylus, the input event processing in the operating system was not changed accordingly. Rather than tracking a particular point of input, TUIs empowered the interface by mediating objects that maintain natural tangibility. Reliable multi-touch capability was introduced with the Diamond Touch in 2001, targeting the requirement that the device "allows multiple, simultaneous users to interact in an intuitive fashion" [6]. The work addressed the drawback, at the time, of existing touch technologies that did not support concurrent touch interaction for co-located collaborative work at interactive tabletops. In 2004 this multi-touch device was complemented with a software toolkit for the "prototyping of and experimentation with multi-person, concurrent interfaces" at MERL [28].

However, single touch point interaction in a multi-user context still followed the pointing paradigm of manipulation in a graphical user interface. The pointing and touching gesture is only one possibility from the rich set of hand gestures than humans are capable of. Apart from earlier works [49], gestures in single user multi-touch tabletop interaction were recently popularized by the works of Wu and Balakrishnan [50] and Han [19]. Their demonstration of the abilities of multi-touch interaction broadened the interest in underlying technology and stimulated the research of gesture interaction on interactive tabletops complementary to the collaboration research domain. Along with this extension from multi-user to gesture-based interaction, TUI research received further stimulation. Although highly physical prototypes, such as metaDESK [2] and BUILD-IT [44, 51], had been developed in the late 1990s, tangibility became of interest again due to novel methods of tracking objects on the horizontal surface and the incorporation of ubicomp scenarios using mobile phones or other portable devices.

From Projection to Direct Display Technology

One of the crucial factors when considering the construction of a tabletop system is the display technology. Without a sufficiently large, hi-resolution, and bright display, tabletop systems may not fulfill basic requirements such as visibility and accessibility. The development of powerful data projectors in the 1990s stimulated research into user interaction with large displays beyond the traditional use of bulky and heavy CRT monitors. While early tabletop systems used front-projection, most systems thereafter applied rear-projection to avoid the occlusion of the display by the users' hands and forearms. Rear-projection also allowed for the particular illumination of objects placed on the screen. Outdoor usage is another challenge, as large displays are sometimes built into malls and street facades.

The consumer electronic market's focus on large affordable flat display systems for home entertainment was and still is a major contributor when it comes to suitable display technologies for tabletop systems. By the end of the 1990s, PDPs became commercially available with sizes of up to 52 inch (132 cm) and a chassis depth of around 4 inch (10 cm). The first interactive tabletop that used this novel display technology was the second generation InteracTable [52] equipped with a SMART Technology touch frame. At the same time, LCDs with a size of around 17 inch (43 cm) became an affordable replacement for CRT monitors. However, LCDs have only recently become available in sizes of up to 42 inch (107 cm) and with a 2-megapixel resolution. At this size and resolution, horizontal displays in tabletop systems significantly reduce the space required "behind the display" as compared to rear-projection systems. However, while these displays have the depth of a few inches, certain multi-touch technologies may still require as much space as rear-projection displays do in order to capture the interaction on the screen with an infrared camera such as in MultiTouch [42]. Recent research projects, such as TViews, Thinsight, and MightyTrace [53–55], highlighting the use of LCDs and novel technologies, e.g., as presented in [43], aim at the development of multi-touch interaction devices with reduced space behind the LCDs. For some niche applications on interactive tabletops, rear-projection, or even front-projection systems may still be the most suitable solution. However, in the foreseeable future effective multi-touch technologies may be integrated into flat displays without compromising the overall slim form factor of the system.

Synoptic Landscape

In this section we visualize landmark publications, enabling technologies, research prototypes, and industrial products in a synoptic landscape (Fig. 1.3). The visualization is inspired by the so-called *tire-track charts* as used in a US National Research Council report [56] to illustrate the impact of government-sponsored IT research and development on the economy. The clustering of the historical landmarks in the figure is primarily based on temporal proximity and secondarily on the categorization of research and products. We chose to visualize the three key transitions (yellow bars) rather than emphasizing technology transfer from research labs (red areas) to industry (blue areas). Contemporary research has not yet reached a high enough level of maturity, as based on citation ranking (Table 1.1), to constitute substantial

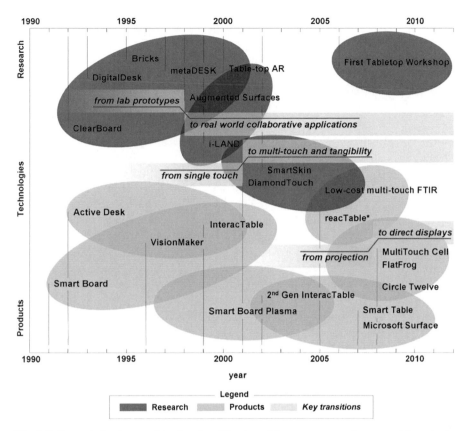

Fig. 1.3 Synoptic landscape of landmark publications, lab prototypes, and commercial products. For each of three key transitions traced and visualized we imposed a saddle point nearby landmark publications and products (1998, 2001, and 2008)

contribution to science. It is up to future investigation to find out what the research landmarks are after 2005.

Key transitions, marking when new concepts and ideas inspired and triggered new directions in research and development, are highlighted in Fig. 1.3. However, we are aware that early pioneering work always precedes the mainstream. For instance, TUIs had been introduced in the mid-1990s and were explored in early tabletop research work by Ullmer and Ishii [15] and Rauterberg et al. [44]; however, it was only in conjunction with multi-touch interaction technologies introduced in 2001 and 2005 [6, 19], that the tangibility aspect became popular in the tabletop research community.

In his article, "The Long Nose of Innovation," Bill Buxton argues that product innovation is "low-amplitude and takes place over a long period" [57]. In his claim to focus "on refining existing as much as on the creation" of new technologies, he recalls the history of the mouse pointing device. It was invented in the mid-1960s and developed into a ubiquitous and integral part of desktop computing by the mid-1990s. Indeed, the National Research Council (USA) states in their 2003 report on "Innovation in Information Technology" that there is a "long, unpredictable incubation period between initial exploration and commercial deployment" [56]. The council's report goes on to say that this incubation period needs "steady [research] work and funding." We apply their concept of a gestation or incubation period of up to 30 years to our synoptic landscape (Fig. 1.3) assuming that interactive tabletop systems will eventually hit the mass market. Marking the origin of the interactive tabletop landscape as Wellner's seminal work in the early 1990s, it may only be around 2020 that we will see the widespread use of tabletop systems. However, until then, early adopters in niche markets will be the first buyers of this technology and will stimulate the industrial development.

In retrospect, initial technology transfer from research lab to industry has already occurred but only on a modest scale. Government-funded research initiatives, such as the Ontario Telepresence Project [34, 36] of the early 1990s, enabled the landmark publication of Fitzmaurice et al. [12] in 1995, based on the Active Desk prototype, distributed in 1996 as a product by ITI, Canada. Another example is the collaboration between a German government research agency (GMD-IPSI, and later Fraunhofer-IPSI) and an industrial partner started in 1999, which led to the development of the second generation InteracTable [52, 24] distributed as a product by Wilkhahn/foresee, Germany in 2002. As a final example, in 2009, eight years after the landmark publications about the DiamondTouch [6], MERL decided to commercialize and distribute the technology via Circle Twelve, USA [40].

In the second phase of product development, larger companies such as SMART Technologies and Microsoft developed multi-touch tabletop systems that have been commercially available since 2008 (Fig. 1.3, lower right). It is notable that in-house research and development preceding these products may have started about 5 years earlier. In a similar way, smaller start-ups have directly taken over prototypes and engineered them into on-demand, small-scale production [41, 42] or built on their patented technology [43]. For example, Touchtech AB of Sweden develops novel tabletop solutions for fairs, stores, and offices. These solutions often also include a suite of tailored software and a software API for developing multi-touch applications.

Tabletop Trends

The research domain and community around tabletop systems was established in the early 1990s and has since developed steadily. Then, in 2006, an annual international workshop (now a conference) was established to serve as a formal forum for this research. It began in Adelaide, Australia, then headed to the USA, Europe, and finally to Canada. Initial government-sponsored research programs and laboratory research carved out early tabletop research directions such as distributed collaboration [18, 58], tangible interfaces [12, 15] and collaborative interaction at the tabletop [44, 13]. Since then major companies have developed and commenced selling tabletop products, indicating that the research domain and its technologies have matured enough to be a prosperous and profitable business. At the same time, mainstream media visibility of tabletop systems and applications has grown consistently since 2005. All these observations may signal a completion of technology transfer from research labs to industry. From now on, companies and their research departments will develop and refine products for broader end-user communities. This phase of product development may ultimately lead to a stable economy of a yet unknown volume, as demonstrated by inventions such as the GUI, the PC, and the Internet [56]. This phase may last another decade until the market has reached a sustainable volume.

Trends in Research

When the industrial development of tabletop systems started, the research community extended the focus of their conference from tabletops to "tabletops and interactive surfaces." This may have been done to address a broader scientific audience and partly to enlarge the research community. However, it can be observed that other conferences with related topics, such as the recently launched International Conference on Tangible, Embedded, and Embodied Interaction (TEI), might overlap with this extended topic. This observation also indicates the trend that new directions may be required to maintain a viable and innovative field of research. Novel directions are important to maintain interest and attract government funding, which restarts the cycle of investigating a broad set of ideas that, in turn, trigger the development of new commercial products. By now, the research area of multi-touch interaction on large display surfaces has demonstrated its potential to be a driving force in the creation of new prototypes and systems. It has the potential to stimulate a new range of exploratory research and embrace novel technologies as yet unknown. New opportunities may arise from novel form factors of displays and cost-effective production of multi-touch device technologies. Outcomes in these areas have the potential to refuel the development and redesign of tabletop products.

Since the 1990s the investigation of TUIs has been on the research agenda of Hiroshi Ishii. New research into tangibility has recently arisen from the affordance of horizontal tabletop surfaces in the same manner that multi-touch research evolved from single touch interaction in tabletop systems. This research trend is even followed in ubicomp scenarios where users interact with an ecology of artifacts, that is, in an environment augmented by various devices such as mobile phones and digital cameras, as well as laptops and netbooks. In that sense, tabletop research bears the potential to unify various interaction and interface paradigms in the concrete scenario of co-located collaboration of a small group around an interactive table.

So far, user studies with tabletop systems have been conducted predominantly in labs and controlled environments. When systems become affordable and available, thus finding their way into the real world, new research opportunities may arise. Researchers might, for example, run longitudinal studies on the adoption of this new collaborative interface and its impact on work processes, social interactions, and domestic activities.

Trends in Enabling Technologies

Novel display technologies tend to influence the physical design of tabletop systems. A transition from data projection systems to direct displays such as LCDs is occurring. Display manufacturers present future trends at technical fairs by showcasing prototypes with extraordinary characteristics such as Organic Light Emitting Diodes (OLEDs). These can form displays that are flexible and bendable compared to the rigid construction of LCDs, and, at the same time, OLED displays are significantly thinner than both LCDs and PDPs [25]. It is predicted that OLED displays can also be produced more cost-effectively. Using a similar technology as that which is used to print ink on paper, OLEDs can be printed so as to constitute a display. So far, OLED technology has been used and deployed for small-sized displays, but it is a matter of time before larger displays become available. The consequences for tabletop systems are not completely foreseeable, but a thinner display basically allows augmenting every existing horizontal surface without compromising the design of the supporting table. This rising technology is driven by the demand in the consumer electronic market for large and thin home television sets.

Combining OLED displays with thin multi-touch devices are the next step towards the ultimate tabletop system, but these new technologies have yet to be fully developed. Recent research has presented new, cost-effective methods of producing multi-touch devices [22, 23]. The physical form factors of these touch sensor matrices match up with those of OLED display matrices, while at the same time efficient production seems conceivable. Alternatively, projects such as Thinsight and MightyTrace aim to reduce the bulkiness of current systems by replacing the infrared sensor with an array of discrete sensors that allows for a lower profile [54, 55]. The ultimate goal of these efforts is the convergence of the touch-sensing device and a thin, flexible display matrix into one integrated element that can be efficiently manufactured at a large size of 40 inch (107 cm) or more.

Optimal hardware set-up is a key challenge to the practice of tabletop system design. Another challenge will be the development of an appropriate application and software environment to leverage on the advanced hardware technologies. The development of new software technologies seems to require a longer incubation time than hardware.

To date, modern computer operating systems as well as standard applications such as text editors and spreadsheet programs are single-user applications. On interactive tabletops the applications have always been dedicated software developments or research prototypes. However, in order to facilitate and simplify building genuine tabletop applications two requirements must be fulfilled. Firstly, multi-touch input devices must become standardized in accordance with other peripheral interaction devices such as the mouse, keyboard, and single-point touch screen, which operate and communicate with applications regardless of the manufacturer. Secondly, standard operating systems must be extended or modified to handle specific multi-touch and multi-user input events. Like in tablet-PC editions, *multi-touch editions* of popular operating systems may become available as commercial or open source products. The fulfillment of these two requirements would allow a larger user community to experience interactive tabletops.

The demand for multi-user support originates from research into collaborative group work, and the requirements of multi-touch and multi-user interfaces resemble those of Single Display Groupware (SDG) as described by Stewart et al. in 1999 [59]. While discrete interactions such as clicking a button or lifting the finger from a button may be simple to handle in multi-user applications, more continuous interaction requires rethinking interface widgets, such as scroll bars and sliders, to avoid interference [60] and improving groupware interface via so called coordination policies [61, 62]. Ultimately, the operating system should register and trace the identity of users in order to allow for individualized input commands. The capability of identifying the originator of a touch event has been realized in the DiamondTouch system [6], but this has not been addressed by later projects.

There is a tendency to pursue a more moderate strategy for introducing multi-touch features. It has become popular to support a single user's hand gestures by mapping them into the traditional event processing of a computer system. Examples include a dual-touch sliding gesture used to scroll and a pinching gesture to control the zoom feature. While providing new features for the user, this development approach is rather moderate since it is based on the PC paradigm and does not require the substantial modifications of the computers operating system to provide multi-user input event processing [63].

Trends in Commercial Products

In the near future we expect affordable commercial products to be introduced in shops, public spaces, and the educational environment. Tabletops may also come to be bought for laboratory studies as alternatives to specialized experimental set-ups. Since the development of a comprehensively and continuously supported product requires a long period of time, there is a potential for small companies to emerge. Large-scale production of a tabletop system may require standard solutions, hindering the fast adoption of new technology and allowing only smaller improvements. Hence, younger companies tend to be better poised to adjust to and integrate late-breaking technology into their production line. We are currently witnessing this diversification in the commercial domain and in the future the consumers will have the choice to buy either fully developed products or one of a kind, specialized products employing cutting-edge technologies.

Discussion and Summary

We have presented a short historical overview of more than a decade of research in the area of interactive tabletops, enabling technologies, and commercial products. In doing so, we have described the phenomenon of interactive tabletops as an example of how innovation and technologically oriented research in the domains of HCI, CSCW, and Ubicomp may turn into a prosperous business. We have pointed out that an incubation period from early research works to stable economy may be up to 30 years. Current product lines from major companies mark the completion of technology transfer from research labs to the industry. However, it may take another 10 years until the business becomes sustainable. We have exemplified how government-sponsored research in various countries has played a significant role in the early periods of this history. Also, we have shown how the various enabling technologies, such as displays and touch sensors, were and still are important factors for tabletop systems. The direct and unobstructed experience these technologies offer may, to some extent, explain the general fascination with them throughout research and end-user communities.

Based on our review of research, technologies, and products, we have identified and traced three transitions in terms of research and development caused by innovative systems and applications. The first transition, from lab prototypes to real world collaborative applications, was motivated by the research questions of the CSCW domain. The second transition, from single touch to multi-touch and tangibility, can be associated with the research domain of HCI. The third transition, from projection to direct display technology, was stimulated by recent advances in consumer electronics. For each of the transitions traced and visualized in the synoptic landscape, we imposed a saddle point nearby landmark publications and products.

Finally, we presented plausible and foreseeable trends which may spur transitions in tabletop research and affect future user interaction. Looking back on more than a decade of activity, tabletop research has reached a certain level of maturity. This activity has led to the establishment of tabletops as a valid alternative to PCs and interactive whiteboards as a tool for collaboration in small teams. However, successfully integrating tabletops into the current practice and culture of our work places as well as in the public and domestic spaces is still on the agenda.

Acknowledgments We are greatly thankful to Erik Tobin who helped in making the text more enjoyable to read.

References

1. Bush V (1945) As we may think. The Atlantic Monthly 176(1):101–108, doi: 10.1145/227181.227186, http://www.theatlantic.com/doc/194507/bush
2. Wellner P (1993) Interacting with paper on the DigitalDesk. Communications of the ACM 36(7):87–96, doi: 10.1145/159544.159630
3. Weiser M (1991) The computer for the 21st century. Scientific American 265(3):94–104, http://www.ubiq.com/hypertext/weiser/SciAmDraft3.html
4. Cooperstock JR, Tanikoshi K, Beirne G, Narine T, Buxton WAS (1995) Evolution of a reactive environment. doi: Proceedings of the SIGCHI conference on human factors in computing systems (CHI '95), ACM Press/Addison-Wesley Publishing Co., New York, pp 170–177, doi: 10.1145/223904.223926
5. Streitz N, Nixon P (2005) The disappearing computer. Communications of the ACM, Special Issue 48(3):33–35
6. Dietz P, Leigh D (2001) DiamondTouch: A multi-user touch technology. In: Proceedings of the 14th annual ACM symposium on user interface software and technology (UIST '01), ACM Press, New York, pp 219–226, doi: 10.1145/502348.502389

7. Tandler P, Prante T, Müller-Tomfelde C, Streitz N, Steinmetz R (2001) Connectables: Dynamic coupling of displays for the flexible creation of shared workspaces. In: Proceedings of the 14th annual ACM symposium on user interface software and technology (UIST '01), ACM Press, New York, pp 11–20, doi: 10.1145/502348.502351

8. Hollan J, Stornetta S (1992) Beyond being there. In: Proceedings of the SIGCHI conference on human factors in computing systems (CHI '92), ACM Press, New York, pp 119–125, doi: 10.1145/142750.142769

9. Ellis CA, Gibbs SJ, Rein GL (1991) Groupware: Some issues and experiences. Communications of the ACM 34(1):39–58

10. Gibson J (1979) The ecological approach to perception. Houghton Mifflin, London

11. Sugimoto M, Hosoi K, Hashizume H (2004) Caretta: A system for supporting face-to-face collaboration by integrating personal and shared spaces. In: Proceedings of the SIGCHI conference on human factors in computing systems (CHI '04), ACM Press, New York, pp 41–48, doi: 10.1145/985692.985698

12. Fitzmaurice GW, Ishii H, Buxton WAS (1995) Bricks: Laying the foundations for graspable user interfaces. In: Proceedings of the SIGCHI conference on human factors in computing systems (CHI '95), ACM Press, New York, pp 442–449, doi: 10.1145/223904.223964

13. Streitz NA, Geißler J, Holmer T, Konomi S, Müller-Tomfelde C, Reischl W, Rexroth P, Seitz P, Steinmetz R (1999) i-LAND: An interactive landscape for creativity and innovation. In: Proceedings of the SIGCHI conference on human factors in computing systems (CHI '99), ACM Press, New York, pp 120–127, doi: 10.1145/302979.303010

14. Rekimoto J, Saitoh M (1999) Augmented surfaces: A spatially continuous work space for hybrid computing environments. In: Proceedings of the SIGCHI conference on Human factors in computing systems (CHI '99), ACM Press, New York, pp 378–385, doi: 10.1145/302979.303113

15. Ullmer B, Ishii H (1997) The metaDESK: Models and prototypes for tangible user interfaces. In: Proceedings of the 10th annual ACM symposium on user interface software and technology (UIST '97), ACM Press, New York, pp 223–232

16. Kato H, Billinghurst M, Poupyrev I, Imamoto K, Tachibana K (2000) Virtual object manipulation on a table-top AR environment. In: Proceedings of the international symposium on augmented reality (ISAR 2000), IEEE Computer Society, Los Alamitos, CA, pp 111–119, doi: 10.1109/ISAR.2000.10013

17. Rekimoto J (2002) SmartSkin: An infrastructure for freehand manipulation on interactive surfaces. In: Proceedings of the SIGCHI conference on human factors in computing systems (CHI '02), ACM Press, New York, pp 113–120, doi: 10.1145/503376.503397

18. Ishii H, Kobayashi M (1992) ClearBoard: A seamless medium for shared drawing and conversation with eye contact. In: Proceedings of the SIGCHI conference on human factors in computing systems (CHI '92), ACM Press, New York, pp 525–532, doi: 10.1145/142750.142977

19. Han JY (2005) Low-cost multi-touch sensing through frustrated total internal reflection. In: Proceedings of the 18th annual ACM symposium on user interface software and technology (UIST '05), ACM Press, New York, pp 115–118, doi: 10.1145/1095034.1095054

20. Ellis N (2007) Sam Hurst touches on a few great ideas. Berea College Magazine 77(4): 22–27, http://www.berea.edu

21. Saffer D (2008) Designing gestural interfaces: Touchscreens and interactive devices. O'Reilly Media, Inc., North Sebastopol, CA

22. Chang WY, Fang TH, Yeh SH, Lin YC (2009) Flexible electronics sensors for tactile multi-touching. Sensors 9(2):1188–1203, doi: 10.3390/sensors90x0000x, http://www.mdpi.com/1424-8220/9/2/1188

23. Rosenberg I, Grau A, Hendee C, Awad N, Perlin K (2009) IMPAD – an inexpensive multi-touch pressure acquisition device. In: Proceedings of the 27th international conference on human factors in computing systems (CHI '09), ACM Press, New York, pp 3217–3222, doi: 10.1145/1518701.1518779

24. Wilkhahn (2001) InteracTable. http://www.roomware.wilkhahn.com/, accessed 10.03.2007
25. Godlewski J, Obarowska M (2007) Organic light emitting devices. Opto-Electronics Review 15(4):179–183, doi: 10.2478/s11772-007-0020-x
26. Olwal A (2006) Lightsense: Enabling spatially aware handheld interaction devices. In: Proceedings of the 2006 5th IEEE and ACM international symposium on mixed and augmented reality (ISMAR'06), IEEE Computer Society, Washington, DC, pp 119–122, doi: 10.1109/ISMAR.2006.297802
27. Tandler P (2004) The BEACH application model and software framework for synchronous collaboration in ubiquitous computing environments. Journal of Systems and Software 69(3):267–296, doi: 10.1016/S0164-1212(03)00055-4, http://www.sciencedirect.com/science/article/B6V0N-49R5K3S-3/2/f79c8450d75025be4b3d9d6af450516d, ubiquitous computing
28. Shen C, Vernier FD, Forlines C, Ringel M (2004) DiamondSpin: An extensible toolkit for around-the-table interaction. In: Proceedings of the SIGCHI conference on human factors in computing systems (CHI '04), ACM Press, New York, pp 167–174, doi: 10.1145/985692.985714
29. Touchlib (2009) A multi-touch development kit. http://www.nuigroup.com/touchlib/, accessed 01.02.2009
30. Kaltenbrunner M, Bovermann T, Bencina R, Costanza E (2005) TUIO – a protocol for table based tangible user interfaces. In: Proceedings of the 6th international workshop on gesture in human-computer interaction and simulation (GW '05), Vannes, http://mtg.upf.edu/files/publications/07a830-GW2005-KaltenBoverBencinaConstanza.pdf
31. Echtler F, Klinker G (2008) A multitouch software architecture. In: Proceedings of the 5th Nordic conference on human-computer interaction (NordiCHI '08), ACM Press, New York, pp 463–466, doi: 10.1145/1463160.1463220
32. SMART Technologies (2009) SMART Table. http://smarttech.com/table, accessed 05.02.2009
33. Microsoft (2009) Surface_berlin_datasht_fnl. http://download.microsoft.com/download/7/2/9/729fc97d-692d-4231-abf3-20b6a1de8a43/Surface_Berlin_Datasht_fnl.pdf, accessed 05.02.2009
34. Riesenbach R (1994) The Ontario telepresence project. In: Conference companion on human factors in computing systems (CHI '94), ACM Press, New York, pp 173–176, doi: 10.1145/259963.260217
35. Sellen A, Buxton B, Arnott J (1992) Using spatial cues to improve videoconferencing. In: Proceedings of the SIGCHI conference on human factors in computing systems (CHI '92), ACM Press, New York, pp 651–652, doi: 10.1145/142750.143070
36. Ontario Telepresence Project (1995) www.dgp.toronto.edu/tp/techdocs/Final_Report.pdf, accessed 13.07.2009
37. Input Technologies Inc (1998) The company. http://web.archive.org/web/19980121101249/www.iti-world.com/profile/, accessed 04.08.2009
38. Arnott J (1996) Rear projection display apparatus. http://www.patentlens.net/patentlens/structured.cgi?patnum=US_5521659, accessed 18.09.2009
39. Streitz NA, Tandler P, Müller-Tomfelde C, Konomi S (2001) Roomware: Towards the next generation of human-computer interaction based on an integrated design of real and virtual worlds. In: Carroll JM (ed) Human-computer interaction in the new millenium. ACM Press, New York
40. Circle Twelve (2009) DiamondTouch. http://www.circletwelve.com/, accessed 05.02.2009
41. Jordà S, Kaltenbrunner M, Geiger G, Bencina R (2005) The reacTable*. In: Proceedings of the international computer music conference (ICMC 2005), Barcelona, Spain
42. MultiTouch (2009) Modular MultiTouch Cell. http://multitouch.fi/, accessed 05.02.2009
43. Eliasson JOP, Wagenblast J, Østergaard S (2008) System and method of determining a position of a radiation emitting element. http://www.patentlens.net/patentlens/structured.cgi?patnum=7442914, accessed 09.09.2009
44. Rauterberg M, Fjeld M, Krueger H, Bichsel M, Leonhardt U, Meier M (1998) BUILD-IT: A planning tool for construction and design. In: Proceedings of the SIGCHI conference on

human factors in computing systems (CHI '98), ACM Press, New York, pp 177–178, doi: 10.1145/286498.286657

45. Fjeld M, Jourdan F, Bichsel M, Rauterberg M (1998) BUILD-IT: An intuitive simulation tool for multi-expert layout processes. In: Engeli M, Hrdliczka V (eds) Fortschritte in der Simulationstechnik (ASIM) [Advances in simulation], vdf Hochschulverlag AG, Zürich, pp 411–418

46. Fjeld M, Morf M, Krueger H (2004) Activity theory and the practice of design: Evaluation of a collaborative tangible user interface. International Journal of Human Resources Development and Management 4(1):94–116, http://inderscience.metapress.com/link.asp?id=mmw2dund214hnbnk

47. LiMe (2000) Dedicated to the living memory project. http://www.living-memory.org, accessed 04.07.2009

48. Gaver WW, Bowers J, Boucher A, Gellerson H, Pennington S, Schmidt A, Steed A, Villars N, Walker B (2004) The drift table: Designing for ludic engagement. In: CHI '04 extended abstracts on human factors in computing systems (CHI '04), ACM Press, New York, pp 885–900, doi: 10.1145/985921.985947

49. Buxton B (2009) Multi-touch systems that I have known and loved. http://www.billbuxton.com/multitouchOverview.html, accessed 15.04.2009

50. Wu M, Balakrishnan R (2003) Multi-finger and whole hand gestural interaction techniques for multi-user tabletop displays. In: Proceedings of the 16th annual ACM symposium on user interface software and technology (UIST '03), ACM Press, New York, pp 193–202, doi: 10.1145/964696.964718

51. Fjeld M, Lauche K, Bichsel M, Voorhorst F, Krueger H, Rauterberg M (2002) Physical and virtual tools. Activity theory applied to the design of groupware. Computer Supported Cooperative Work 11(1):153–180, doi: 10.1023/A:1015269228596

52. Streitz NA, Prante T, Müller-Tomfelde C, Tandler P, Magerkurth C (2002) Roomware the second generation. In: CHI '02 extended abstracts on human factors in computing systems (CHI '02), ACM Press, New York, pp 506–507, doi: 10.1145/506443.506452

53. Mazalek A, Reynolds M, Davenport G (2006) TViews: An extensible architecture for multiuser digital media tables. IEEE Computer Graphics & Applications: Special Issue on Interacting with Digital Tabletops 26(5):47–55, doi: 10.1109/MCG.2006.117

54. Hodges S, Izadi S, Butler A, Rrustemi A, Buxton B (2007) Thinsight: Versatile multi-touch sensing for thin form-factor displays. In: Proceedings of the 20th annual ACM symposium on user interface software and technology (UIST '07), ACM Press, New York, pp 259–268, doi: 10.1145/1294211.1294258

55. Hofer R, Kaplan P, Kunz A (2008) MightyTrace: Multiuser tracking technology on lc-displays. In: Proceeding of the 26th annual SIGCHI conference on human factors in computing systems (CHI '08), ACM Press, New York, pp 215–218, doi: 10.1145/1357054.1357091

56. Computer Science and Telecommunications Board of the National Research Council (2003) Innovation in information technology. http://www.nap.edu/openbook.php?isbn=0309089808, accessed 07.03.2009

57. Buxton B (2008) The long nose of innovation. http://www.businessweek.com/innovate/content/jan2008/id2008012_297369.htm, accessed 26.08.2008

58. Ishii H, Kobayashi M, Grudin J (1992) Integration of inter-personal space and shared workspace: ClearBoard design and experiments. In: Proceedings of the conference on computer-supported cooperative work (CSCW '92), ACM Press, New York, pp 33–42, doi: 10.1145/143457.143459

59. Stewart J, Bederson BB, Druin A (1999) Single display groupware: A model for co-present collaboration. In: Proceedings of the SIGCHI conference on human factors in computing systems (CHI '99), ACM Press, New York, pp 286–293, doi: 10.1145/302979.303064

60. Zanella A, Greenberg S (2001) Reducing interference in single display groupware through transparency. In: Proceedings of the 7th European conference on computer supported cooperative work (ECSCW '01), Kluwer Academic Publishers, Norwell, MA, pp 339–358

61. Morris MR, Ryall K, Shen C, Forlines C, Vernier F (2004) Beyond "social protocols": Multi-user coordination policies for co-located groupware. In: Proceedings of the 2004 ACM conference on computer supported cooperative work (CSCW '04), ACM Press, New York, pp 262–265, doi: 10.1145/1031607.1031648
62. Morris MR, Cassanego A, Paepcke A, Winograd T, Piper AM, Huang A (2006) Mediating group dynamics through tabletop interface design. IEEE Computer Graphics and Applications 26(5):65–73, doi: 10.1109/MCG.2006.114
63. Hutterer P, Thomas BH (2007) Groupware support in the windowing system. In: Proceedings of the eight Australasian conference on user interface (AUIC '07), Australian Computer Society, Inc., Darlinghurst, pp 39–46

Part I
Under Tabletops

This first part of the book addresses aspects of Hardware/Software and Computer Science of tabletop systems. The positioning of the chapters topics *under tabletops* may not be taken too literally. In a boarder sense the chapters of this part refer to topics "hidden from and invisible to the user" and to core tabletop technology and its evolvement. The part introduces basic technical topics and provides a system classification as well as more specific aspects such as high-resolution and object recognition.

Schöning et al. begin this book part with a comprehensive and detailed overview and documentation to build a multi-touch surface system. Beyond practical technical details, this team of authors also provides insights into the complexity of technologies and software for tabletop systems. In the following chapter Kunz and Fjeld offer a classification of tabletop interaction input devices and tracking technologies and work out systematically the characteristic features of prominent tabletop systems. Then Ashdown et al. present work on high-resolution tabletop displays focusing on the applications that require detailed graphics and text. The topic is presented with comprehensive background information from related disciplines and describes future trends in various directions. The chapter from Kakehi and Naemura presents an optical design approach for tabletop systems that provides a view-dependent display of information and possible interactive applications. Even objects held over the surface can become part of the tabletop display. The final chapter in this part of Koike et al. discusses the possibilities of a vision-based hand and object recognition for tabletop systems. This work is centered on the unique optical characteristics of current Liquid Cristal Display technologies and showcase applications on tabletop systems.

Chapter 2
Building Interactive Multi-touch Surfaces

Johannes Schöning, Jonathan Hook, Tom Bartindale, Dominik Schmidt, Patrick Oliver, Florian Echtler, Nima Motamedi, Peter Brandl, and Ulrich von Zadow

Abstract Multi-touch interaction with computationally enhanced surfaces has received considerable attention in recent years. Hardware implementations of multi-touch interaction such as Frustrated Total Internal Reflection (FTIR) and Diffuse Illumination (DI) have allowed for the low cost development of surfaces. Although many of these technologies and associated applications have been presented in academic settings, the practicalities of building a high quality multi-touch enabled surface, both in terms of the software and hardware required, are not widely known. We draw upon our extensive experience as developers of multi-touch technology to provide practical advice in relation to building, and deploying applications upon, multi-touch surfaces. This includes technical details of the construction of optical multi-touch surfaces, including: infrared illumination, silicone compliant surfaces, projection screens, cameras, filters, and projectors, and an overview of existing software libraries for tracking.

Introduction

Multi-touch technology has opened up a wide range of opportunities for interaction design. Relatively simple and inexpensive hardware and software configurations allow the development of interfaces with expressive gestural control and fluid multi-user collaboration. The underlying technology has existed in different forms since the late 1970s and multiple patents [1–5] demonstrate how multi-touch surfaces can be constructed. However, it was Han's 2005 presentation [6] of a low-cost camera-based multi-touch sensing technique, based upon Frustrated Total Internal Reflection (FTIR), which truly highlighted the potential for multi-touch interaction in the development of the next generation of human computer interfaces. Han's system was both cheap and easy to build, and was creatively applied to illustrate

J. Schöning (✉)
German Research Center for Artificial Intelligence (DFKI), D-66123, Saarbruecken, Germany
e-mail: johannes.schoening@dfki.de

C. Müller-Tomfelde (ed.), *Tabletops – Horizontal Interactive Displays*,
Human-Computer Interaction Series, DOI 10.1007/978-1-84996-113-4_2,
© Springer-Verlag London Limited 2010

a range of novel interaction techniques. Indeed, his YouTube demonstration captured the imagination of experts and laymen alike, and as a result, we have seen an explosion of interest in multi-touch interaction. Hardware implementations of multi-touch interaction such as FTIR and DI have allowed for the low cost development of surfaces and enabled much research exploring the benefits of multi-touch interaction [7–13]. Unsurprisingly, multi-touch surfaces have also found their way into the Hollywood's futuristic visions of human-computer interaction (e.g. "James Bond – Quantum of Solace" and "The Day the Earth Stood Still" [14]).

Although many the multi-touch technologies, and associated applications, have been presented in an academic context, the practicalities of building a high quality multi-touch enabled surface, both in terms of the software and hardware required, are still not widely known. In this chapter we draw upon our extensive experience as developers of multi-touch technology to provide practical advice as the development and deployment of such systems. This includes technical details of the construction of optical multi-touch surfaces, including: infrared illumination, silicone compliant surfaces, projection screens, cameras, filters, and projectors, and an overview of existing software libraries for tracking. Our goal is to enable researchers to embrace multi-touch by providing the basic knowledge required to "build your own" multi-touch surface. Many of the established technologies, such as resistance, capacitance, or surface wave-touch screens, require industrial fabrication facilities beyond those available even to the academic research. In contrast, we focus exclusively on optical approaches to multi-touch sensing which can be developed and integrated with an interactive application by a moderately competent hobbyist. Optical approaches to multi-touch use image processing to determine the location of interactions with the surface. Typically using infrared illumination, their simple set-up means they have the potential to be extremely robust. Although not described here, in addition to FTIR and DI there are a number of less widespread, but related, approaches including Laser Light Plane and Diffused Screen Illumination (see [15]). In addition there are other upcoming techniques and directions as presented at CHI 2009 [16, 17] also not covered in this chapter.

In this chapter we give step-by-step instructions as to how to build interactive multi-touch surfaces, discuss the pros and cons of the different approaches and try to help the reader avoid the traps, which a novice may fall into when developing their first surface.

The arrival of large consumer multi-touch surfaces is eagerly anticipated. Similarly, display, projection and other technologies on which optical multi-touch systems depend continue to advance apace. As a result the practical "shelf-life" of our contribution would appear rather short. However, we see our account as more than simply a detailed documentation of a critical point in time for user interface software and technology. Whilst many of the details that we describe provide a context to current academic research in multi-touch (far more than the conventions of academic publishing normally allow) we see considerable value in human–computer interaction researchers continuing to develop their own underlying hardware. Indeed, multi-touch as a paradigm is still very much in its infancy. The production of commercial systems has the potential to simultaneously promote the emerging status quo as to what a multi-touch interface is, and frustrate further development. So long as researchers shape and control the underlying hardware the opportunity for more fundamental innovation remains open.

Non-optical Multi-touch Approaches

Before describing optical multi-touch systems in more detail its appropriate to review alternative technologies. There is no fundamental characteristic that makes optical approaches superior to the alternatives. Indeed, many of these alternatives have already found their way into consumer products, albeit in smaller interactive surfaces (e.g. mouse pads on laptops and touch-screens in phones). However, as already described, the principal drawback is that resistance, capacitance, or surface wave-touch screens, require industrial fabrication facilities.

Resistance-Based Touch Surfaces

Resistance-based touch panels generally consist of two clear sheets coated with transparent conductive substances such as indium tin oxide [18]. These surfaces are separated by an insulating layer, typically tiny silicon dots. The front of the panel is often made of a flexible hard coated outer membrane while the back panel is typically a glass substrate. A controller alternates between the layers, driving one with a specific (electric) current and measuring the current of the other. When users touch the display, the conductive layers are connected, establishing an electric current that is measured both horizontally and vertically (by the controller) to resolve the exact position of a the touch event. Such touch surfaces have the advantage of low power consumption, are used in mobile devices such as the Nintendo DS, mobile devices and digital cameras, and can be operated using fingers or a stylus. However, resistance-based technologies generally yield low clarity interactive surfaces (i.e. 75–85%) and additional screen protection cannot be added without significantly impacting on their sensitivity. More detailed information about classical resistance based (multi-) touch surfaces can be found in [19].

Capacitance-Based Touch Surfaces

Capacitance based (multi-) touch surfaces can be broadly subdivided into two classes depending on the underlying sensing mechanism: (1) Surface Capacitance; and (2) Projected Capacitance. Both technologies were originally developed for single touch interaction, and one advantage of capacitive touch surfaces over competing technologies is their high clarity; making capacitive touch surfaces very suitable for use where the display and touch sensitive surface are integrated (i.e. beyond simple touch pads). Capacitive touch screens are generally durable, reliable and can be operated by any conductive device and hence are not limited to finger based interaction. However, they are relatively expensive to manufacture and are therefore usually reserved for use in rugged environments such as in public displays and industrial applications.

Although it is possible to manufacture capacitive multi-touch surfaces, typically the number of simultaneous touches is limited by firmware and/or by the design of the controller. Furthermore, accuracy decreases when performing touches with more than one object, although a number of capacitance-based technologies have been developed that overcome many of these restrictions in order to allow many simultaneous touches (e.g. MERLs DiamondTouch [7]).

Surface Capacitive Touch Surfaces

Surface capacitive touch panels consist of a uniform conductive coating on a glass layer. Compared to resistive technologies, a much higher clarity can be achieved by again using indium tin oxide [18] as the conducting material (it is transparent as well as colourless when used in very thin layers). From each side of the touch panel electrodes maintain a precisely controlled store or electrons in the horizontal and vertical directions thereby setting up a uniform electric field across the conductive layer. As fingers (and other conductive objects) are also electrical devices capable of storing charge and supporting electric fields, touching the panel results in a small transport of charge from the electric field of the panel to the field of the touching object. Current is drawn from each corner of the panel; this process is measured with sensors located in the corners, and a microprocessor interpolates an exact position of the touch based on the values measured. Panels based on surface capacitive technology can provide a high positional accuracy.

Projected Capacitive Touch Surfaces

Of all the technologies we describe projected capacitive touch devices are the most expensive to produce. Their performance is also rather worse than competing technologies; however, they afford superb mechanical resilience. Projected capacitive surfaces can also be covered by a non-conductive material (up to a maximum thickness of approximately 20 mm) without significantly impacting on their functionality. When used for (multi-) touch displays, as described by Rekimoto [11] a very thin grid of microphone wires is installed between two protective glass layers. When touched, the capacitance between the finger and the sensor grid, and the touch location can be computed based on the electrical characteristics of the grid layer. The accuracy of projected capacitive technology is similar to that of surface capacitive technology although light transmission is often better since the wire grid can be constructed such that it is nearly transparent. The technology is also very suitable for rugged environments such as public installations, as a protective layer (such as thick glass) may be added without drastically decreasing the sensitivity. Finally, compared to surface capacitance technology, multiple simultaneous touches can be more easily interpreted.

Surface Acoustic Wave Touch Surfaces (SAW)

In surface acoustic wave surfaces transmitting and receiving piezoelectric transducers, for both the X- and Y-axes, are mounted on a faceplate, and ultra-sonic waves on a glass surface are created and directed by reflectors. By processing these electronic signals and observing the changes when the faceplate is touched, it is possible to calculate the position of that interaction. Most SAW systems can support dual-touch.

Optical Based Touch Surfaces

Optical approaches to multi-touch use image processing to determine the location and nature of interactions with the surface. These systems typically use infrared illumination, and due to their simple set-up have the potential to be very robust. Han's work in 2005 [6], which utilized the principle of FTIR in multi-touch interaction, can be seen as the turning point in both the interest and development of such optical systems. The FTIR approach is based on optical total internal reflection within an interactive surface. Electromagnetic waves transmitted inside a transparent surface are completely reflected if: (1) the inner material has a higher refractive index than the outer material; and (2) the angle of incidence at the boundary of the surface is sufficiently small.

The most common FTIR configuration involves the use of a transparent acrylic pane into which infrared light is injected using strips of LEDs around its edges (see Fig. 2.1 (left)). When the user touches the acrylic, the light escapes and is reflected (due to its higher refractive index) and is reflected by the finger that is in contact with the surface. An infrared-sensitive camera aligned perpendicular to the surface can then clearly sense these reflections. A basic set of computer vision algorithms is applied to the camera image to determine the location of the contact point. As the acrylic is transparent a projector can be located behind the surface (near to the camera) yielding a back-projected multi-touch display (see Fig. 2.1 (left)).

Diffuse Illumination (DI) systems have a similar configuration, with both a projector and an infrared sensitive camera placed behind the surface. However, for DI,

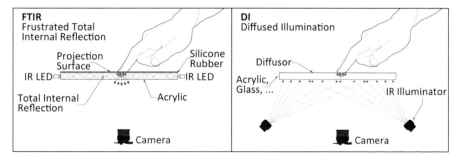

Fig. 2.1 General set-up of a FTIR system (*left*) and a DI system (*right*)

infrared lighting is placed behind the projection surface; causing the area in front of the surface to be brightly lit in the infrared spectrum. As a result the camera is capable of detecting the infrared reflections of fingers and objects on, or in close proximity to, the surface (see Fig. 2.1 (right)). Touch detection exploits the fact that a projection surface (placed on the front of the surface) diffuses light, blurring objects at a distance. The main advantage of FTIR is that it allows very robust tracking of fingers, however, DI has the additional advantage that it allows easier tracking of physical objects, which can be identified either by their shape or through the use of fiducial markers [20] (easily recognizable markers usually in the form of a distinctive pattern) on the base of the objects. DI also has the potential to support hovering gestures, and any transparent surface (such as safety glass) can be placed between the projection screen and the user since sensing does not rely on surface contact.

Building Optical Multi-touch Surfaces: Step-by-Step

In this section we divide the challenges faced in designing and building an optical multi-touch surface into those relating to the hardware and the software; our goal is to provide practical advice based on our own experiences of developing robust tabletop systems. The hardware of an optical multi-touch system comprises: infrared illumination sources, silicone compliant surfaces, projection screens (or LCD screens), cameras, filters, and projectors. In the following sections we describe the desirable characteristics of each of these components and provide step-by-step advice on how they should be used. For a more detailed overview of the material used refer to [21].

Step 1: Frame

The surface's frame is the foundation of the whole system. For tablet-based surfaces it needs to be stable enough to support the wall covers, the surface, and all interior components; the projector being the heaviest of these. Crucially the rigidity of the structure is an important factor to consider when designing a frame, as components will need to stay in place when the table is moved either for transportation or maintenance. Further considerations in relation to the frame material include ease of assembly (as well as disassembly in case of tables that need to be transported) and weight, which is in particular important for larger structures. We suggest the use of an aluminium profile system[1] as it allows the realization of a range of different structure and the profile itself is available in various thicknesses and lengths. Aluminium is easy to handle and craft, and is easily cut using a miter saw. In addition, a large range of flexible connection elements are available that allow the profile to be attached together in different configurations and for other components, such as projector or camera, to be easily mounted on the structure (see Fig. 2.2).

---

[1] http://www.alluminium-profile.co.uk

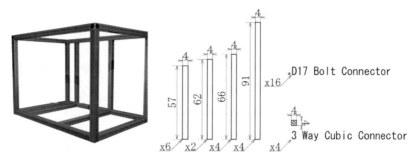

Fig. 2.2 Aluminium struts form a solid base structure for the interactive table. Due to the flexible connection system, components and walls can be easily mounted in any position. Twelve aluminium struts form the table's cuboidal main frame. Four more struts are inserted at the bottom and back to support the projector

Displaying the GUI: Projectors and LCD Screens

An important issue, which must be considered when creating an optical multi-touch surface, is how the graphical user interface itself will be displayed upon the screen. The choice is usually between two technologies; using a digital projector, or using a modified LCD screen.

Step 2: Projector

A digital projector is used to project the interface image on the projection screen from behind the surface. Care must be taken to ensure that the projector has the appropriate resolution, throw and brightness, and the lag between input and output (in addition to sensing lag) is appropriate for the target application (see Fig. 2.3).

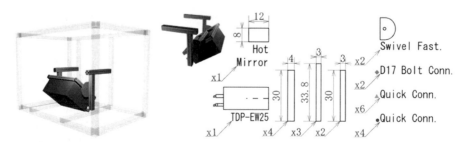

Fig. 2.3 With a single mirror, the 720 p short-throw projector generates an image of about 107 cm in diagonal at a table height of only 70 cm. A hot mirror mounted in front of the projector's lens removes infrared emissions. The projector is held by two swivel fastenings attached to a supportive frame to allow for easy adjustments

Projection Based Systems

Projection-based systems utilize a digital projector to display the interface upon a projection screen. As optical multi-touch surfaces commonly use transparent acrylic, it is possible to rear-project directly onto the interaction surface; preventing problem of occlusion that arises when projecting from the front. The use of a projector provides several advantages. Firstly, projection-based systems are technologically simple to configure, with the projector being either pointed directly at the rear of the surface, or at the surface via a system of mirrors (see Fig. 2.3 for a range of configurations). Secondly, digital projectors are relatively cheap and can display a very large image. They are therefore an extremely cost affective solution for the creation of large interactive surfaces. Finally, as the image is projected onto the interaction surface, the use of appropriate optical filters means that a projection-based system will not interfere with the underlying sensing technology.

Projection-based systems do however have a number of limitations. Firstly, digital projectors generally do not display an image at resolutions greater than XGA (1,024 × 768). An image of this resolution, when projected over a large area, can lead to a low quality visual presentation, for example, one on which small or diagonally oriented text is difficult to read. High definition projectors are now commercially available, but are currently significantly more expensive than the mass consumer models. Another issue, which a developer employing a projector-based system will face, is *throw*; the distance between the projector and projection surface which is required to display an image of a specified size. When multi-touch surfaces are to be built in table forms or embedded in walls, this can be a significant challenge.

Projector throw: As described above, projector throw describes the distance from which the projector must be positioned from the projection surface for an image of a specified size to be displayed. The throw of a projector is an important element of its specification, and is typically given as two angles from which the size of the image (horizontally and vertically) at a given distance can be calculated. A standard digital projector (such as those for office use) will normally have a horizontal throw angle of no more than 35°. To project an image upon a 1,024 × 768 mm multi-touch table using a projector (which displays an image with an aspect ratio of 4:3 with a throw angle of 35°) the projector must be placed at least 1,624 mm away from the surface; this presents a problem as an average tabletop surface is only around 770 mm above the ground.

To address this we can simply use ultra short-throw projectors, which will project large images at very small distances; although again, the process can be prohibitive. A more cost affective alternative is to shorten the physical distance the projector must be placed from the surface by folding the projector's throw using a single, or series of, mirrors. When designing a system of mirrors a developer is likely to encounter two problems. Firstly angled mirrors can lead to distortion of the projected image (as seen in Fig. 2.3). This distortion can be corrected using the *key-stone* function found on many projectors, although this can often lead to a lower quality image as pixels are stretched to counter the misshapen image. In most cases

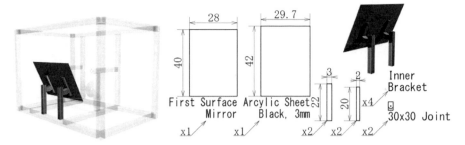

Fig. 2.4 Mirror: a front surface mirror redirects the projector's light without causing a shadow image

it is best to avoid such distortion by placing mirrors as close as possible to each other at right angles to, or 45° angles to, the projector (see Fig. 2.5). Secondly, a shadow image can result from light being reflected from not only the mirror itself, but also from the glass layer, which protects it. Such shadow images can be avoided by using a front surface mirror (which has no glass front) (see Fig. 2.4); these can be expensive and therefore the use of a mirror with a very thin front layer of glass is cheaper alternative, this will reduce, but not remove, the shadowing affect.

Brightness: In most applications the projector must be able to produce an image, which is clear enough to be easily viewed by users even in a well lit room or in an environment where there is significant natural light. As a rule of thumb projectors need to have a brightness of at least 1,500 lumens. In addition to brightness, the contrast ratio of a projector should be carefully considered, as more contrast allows for an image of similar clarity to be produced with a less bright projector (high contrast is particularly important for back-projected optical multi-touch surfaces).

Resolution: The images produced by a standard XGA projector may not be of a high enough resolution to present certain content (such as text) when used for larger multi-touch surfaces. Therefore it is preferable when creating a multi-touch surface, which requires such content to (a) reduce the size of the surface; or (b) choose a projector with a greater resolution image; currently, the use of such high definition projectors is unlikely to be cost effective. A alternative solution, which has been demonstrated by Tuddenham and Robinson, is to use an array of lower resolution projectors to create a very high resolution image [22] (see also Chapter 4).

Lag: A final issue, which must be considered when choosing a projector for a multi-touch surface, is the projector's lag. Usually, an important quality of a multi-touch interfaces a sense of responsiveness to the user through the provision of an almost instant response to their interactions with the surface. Certain models of projectors can exhibit a slight delay in displaying the image upon the screen, when combined with the time delays introduced within the sensing pipeline this can contribute to an unresponsive interface. Schöning et al. [15] present an approach for measuring this time lag which can be used when choosing a projector for a multi-touch surface.

Step 3: Mirror

If a back projection is used, a mirror (of set of mirrors) may be used to fold the throw of the projector and thereby achieve a reduced table height. The use of a front surface mirrors to redirect the projector's light circumvents the problem of shadow images (see Fig. 2.4).

LCD Based Systems

Using an LCD display instead of a projector has a number of advantages including the achievable DPI, sharpness, cost and size, but due to nature of current LCD technology, these benefits come at the expense of a reduced size of display region. Detailed information can be found in [23].

Choosing the Right LCD: Almost any LCD screen (not Plasma or OLED) can be used in a multi-touch system, and although all LCD panels are in practice transparent to infrared light, two factors should be taken into account when selecting the device to use. Firstly, it is best to use a display with DVI or VGA input to avoid pixel information being lost when the video image quality is down-graded (for example with an LCD TV). Secondly, the aspect ratio should match to physical qualities of the system that you are intending to produce; widescreen LCD screens are now much more common and affordable.

Fitting the LCD: In order to use an LCD screen in a multi-touch display, the LCD glass panel inside the unit needs to be removed; it should consist of a thin sheet of black glass with a number of delicate circuit boards along one or two edges. It is important to handle the panel with great care, so as not to scratch or chip this surface. Along with this panel, a control circuit, power supply and other boards may need to be removed and cables retained for later use. Sandwiched in-between layers in the display will be a number of optical sheets, including a Fresnel lens, diffusion and reflection layers; these should be saved these for re-fitting. Particular care must be taken when removing the backlights from the screen as they may contain harmful materials, and the control board may have a persistent high voltage charge. Once the LCD panel is removed, it can be fitted on the surface of a multi-touch display by supporting the surrounding edges firmly, and making sure all electronics are to the side and not in line of sight to the camera below.

Back Light: Unlike OLED displays, LCD displays only modulate visible light passing through them, so a source of white light is needed behind the display. Around 2,500 lm of visible light is needed; this light must be diffused as much as possible behind the display to avoid unattractive bright spots. This light source can be produced using the cold cathode tubes from the original display, traditional household lighting sources such as fluorescent tubes or LEDs. In all cases (except LEDs), it is important to be aware that most light sources produce ambient IR light, which may interfere with the tracking process. Some light sources may produce bright spots, so it is important to experiment with combinations of optical layers taken from the original LCD placed under the surface of the LCD to find the best diffuse light source without interfering with camera focus. Painting the inside of the unit white and removing large objects from the inside of the unit will also help to remove dark shadows from the displayed image, as when the screen is displaying white, it is effectively transparent. When using LEDs, the first thing to do is calculate how many will be needed in order to produce the desired luminosity (price also may be a consideration). Depending on the type of backlight in the original display, the perspex light box (with engraved or painted reflection tiles on one side) can be used against the underside of the LCD, experimentation will ascertain if the chosen camera setup will be able to focus through the backlight to the surface above.

Tracking Solutions: Due to the way in which LCDs are manufactured, IR light emitted from behind the display will reflect off its rear and not pass through in enough quantity to allow use of diffuse illumination, but any method of tracking with produces reflections of IR light from above the surface (e.g. FTIR) will produce the desired tracking effect. When calculating luminosity levels for infrared LEDs or lasers, be aware that the brighter the reflected image, the easier it will be for the camera to be over-exposed as the contrast ratio will be very small due to ambient radiation from the backlight. In order to track markers on an LCD based surface, the markers should be either active (contain a light source) or optically reflecting light from outside the unit through the display.

Tracking User Input: Cameras, Lenses and Filters

Optical multi-touch systems use cameras to track a user's interactions with the surface. In the case of FTIR and DI the camera captures the bright infrared light reflected from the users fingers as they make contact with the surface. In the case of tangible object-based interaction the camera tracks the fiducial markers on the underside of objects.

Step 4: Camera

User interactions are detected using a camera viewing the surface from below. The camera "sees" infrared light reflected by finger and objects touching the surface. The resulting image is then processed using computer vision software for touch detection. The projector and mirror are adjusted to produce an undistorted image, which fills the complete surface. While the camera is able to capture the whole surface area it does not suffer from interference from the projected image (see Fig. 2.5).

Choosing the Right Camera

Due to the important role the camera plays in an optical system, choice of the correct model is one of the most important design decisions. In the following sections we consider the impact of resolution, frame rate, sensor type, lenses and synchronisation of the camera.

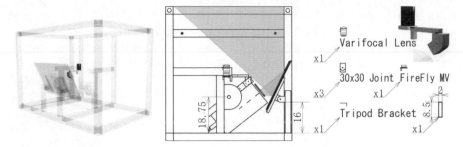

Fig. 2.5 Equipped with a wide-angle lens, a high-speed black and white camera can capture the whole surface at once. A band pass filter removes all visible light; only infrared light used to illuminate objects on the surface can pass

Resolution: A camera must have a high enough resolution in order to allow it detect the small blobs of light which indicate that a user is making contact with the multi-touch surface. When designing a surface which will track touch interactions alone we have found that a camera with 640 × 480 pixel image will suffice for surfaces even as large as 1,000 × 1,000 mm. When attempting to track tagged tangible objects however a much greater camera resolution is required to capture the detailed patterns of the fiducial markers. In this case we recommend a camera resolution of 1,024 × 768 pixels (as a minimum). Camera resolution can impact on performance and responsiveness though; as camera resolution increases the time taken by tracking software to process the image also increases.

Frame rate: The frame rate of the camera directly affects the temporal sensing resolution of an optical multi-touch surface. Therefore if the surface is to feel responsive to the user then a camera with a frame rate of at least 30 frames per second (30 Hz) is required. Increasing the frame rate of the camera will of course lead to a more responsive surface; for example, a camera which provides a frame rate of 60 Hz will give a temporal sensing resolution similar to that of a mouse. Performance increases resulting from an increased camera frame rate may however be limited by the speed at which the tracking software can process the camera image.

Sensor type: As optical multi-touch surfaces are generally based around infrared illumination a camera with a sensor, which can satisfactorily detect light in this range, is crucial. Two decisions must be taken when selecting a camera, which can detect infrared light. Firstly, many digital video cameras are fitted with a filter designed to block infrared light. Consumer web-cams commonly have such filters, which are often difficult to remove, or are painted directly onto the lens. Therefore we recommend the choice of either an industrial grade camera as these generally have no such filters, or a camera with a filter that is easy to remove. Secondly, a sensor must be chosen which is sensitive to the bandwidth of infrared light emitted by the illumination source of the multi-touch surface (typically this will be 850 or 880 nm). The data sheets of both the illumination source (such as the LED used) and the camera sensor will usually provide enough information to determine if the light emitted is within the range captured by that particular sensor.

Lenses: A camera must be selected with a field of view, which can capture the whole interaction surface from the distance allowed by the systems physical design. In many cases, such as when a camera is placed below a large interactive tabletop, this may be difficult to achieve with a standard lens; there are two solutions to this problem. Firstly the camera can be fitted with a replacement lens with a wider field of view; many consumer web-cams do not allow for lens replacement and hence an industrial grade camera may be required. It should be noted however that such *wide-angle* lenses lead to a degree of fish-eye distortion of the image, which can prove problematic, especially when attempting to track fiducial markers. Secondly, as already described, a system of mirrors can be used to fold the distance required for the camera to view the required area.

Filters: Optical multi-touch systems can suffer from interference from environmental and other infrared light sources. The most problematic interference is created by the image displayed on the multi-touch surface (such as those from the projector). Also, ambient light from sources such as direct sunlight can be a significant problem. Such interference can be reduced by placing a filter over the camera which blocks unwanted light of specific wavelengths. Indeed, if a band-pass filter is used this will block out all light of a frequency outside a narrow band encompassing the wavelength of the illumination source. Such band-pass filters are often expensive and so a cheaper alternative can be to use a low-pass filter which blocks only visible light from the camera. A visible light filter can be constructed cheaply from either a film negative, which has been exposed or from black acrylic. Although this will prevent inference from the projected image, problems may still arise if the surface is to be used in a room, which has bright natural or artificial light.

Camera Synchronization: An alternative (or complementary) approach to the reduction of interference from ambient light is to synchronize the camera shutter with a pulsed illumination source [24]. By operating the illumination source with short pulses, higher currents can be passed through the LEDs resulting in greater light emission. Also, by only opening the camera shutter for the short period during which the LEDs are illuminated, the amount of ambient infrared light, which reaches the sensor, can be drastically reduced and distinguished from the overall ambient level. Unlike a band-pass filter, this approach even reduces interference from ambient infrared light of the same wavelength as the illumination source. To utilize this approach however a camera, which can be controlled by a trigger signal, is required in addition to a configurable shutter speed.

Infrared Illumination

Step 5: Illumination

In the DI setup, infrared light sources emit light, which passes through the surface and is reflected by objects on top of (or even approach) the surface, thus making them visible to the camera. Using this principle, arbitrarily shaped objects and visual

markers can be detected in addition to finger touches. In the FTIR set-up infrared
light is injected into an acrylic surface around its edges. Fingers touching the surface
will cause light to escape, resulting in bright and clearly visible touch points (see
Fig. 2.6).

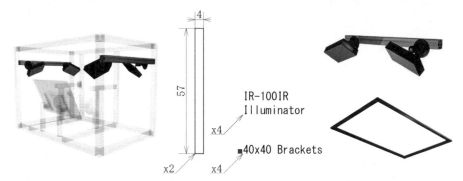

Fig. 2.6 Four infrared LED arrays are mounted in the table's corners, pointing downwards in order
to diffuse the light and avoid overexposed areas

Both FTIR and DI require an infrared light source. Achieving the right infrared
illumination can be challenging and requires a knowledge of both the different methods of illuminating a surface and different the types of IR LEDs (5, 3 mm, SMD)
that are available commercially. Almost all existing IR-based set-ups employ light-
emitting diodes (LEDs) as light sources. Two commonly used types of IR LEDs
are Osram SFH4250 (SMD) and Osram SFH485 (5 mm). Whether SMD devices or
standard LEDs are more appropriate depends on a number of factors, for example,
if the LEDs have to be mounted to the rim of an acrylic glass plate, this is easier to
achieve with SMD sources, as it is possible to simply attach them to the rim with
instant glue. After hardening, instant glue is chemically identical to acrylic glass
creating a very strong, transparent bond. Mounting standard LEDs requires holes to
be drilled into the material, which can be a time-consuming and error-prone process,
and should be undertaken with care.

One major problem for both FTIR and IR systems is their sensitivity to ambient
IR light from the external environment. This can be mitigated by adding a small
electronic circuit to the set-up, which supplies short high-current pulses instead
of a continuous low current. The pulse current can be set high enough such that
under sustained operation, the LEDs would be likely to suffer permanent damage
after a few seconds. Typically, these pulses are given a duration of between a hun-
dred microseconds and a few milliseconds. The high current level, which is possible
during the short pulses, results in a much higher light output.

The pulse duration and the following cool down period should be kept as close
to the manufacturer's specification as possible to prevent overheating of the LEDs.
As modern computers are usually not equipped with the hardware or software to

undertake such real-time control tasks, we suggest using a simple microcontroller (e.g., PIC or AVR) or the venerable 555 timer for pulse generation. A second-level switching element is also necessary, to handle the high currents which flow through the LEDs. Field-effect transistors (FETs), such as the IRF512 logic-level FET, are particularly easy to integrate with logic circuits and we suggest using these as second-level switches. A final precaution against LED damage is an ordinary fuse. A fuse with a *lower* rating than the expected pulse current should be inserted in series with the LEDs. Although more current will flow through the fuse than it is rated for, it is unlikely to blow during pulsed operation.

Pulsing the LEDs significantly increases total light output, but this in itself does not produce enough contrast with ambient light levels. As already described, the pulses need to be synchronized with the camera in such a way that: (1) one pulse is emitted for each camera frame, and (2) each pulse's duration is equivalent to the camera's exposure time. As the LEDs are usually brighter by approximately one order of magnitude during the pulse, the contrast ratio with respect to environmental light is also significantly higher. If the camera exposure time is longer than a single pulse, stray light from the environment is accumulated during the cool down period between pulses, decreasing the contrast ratio. However, in the continuous mode, the brightness of the background is approximately 160 (when the LED is displayed with a maximum brightness – 255 in 8-bit mode), whereas in the pulsed mode, the background values are approximately 20, an 8-fold difference.

Surface: Material, Projection Screens and Compliant Surfaces

Step 6: Surface

In both FTIR and DI set-ups, a diffuser is required (in addition to the base acrylic sheet) to make the projector's image visible, i.e. serving as a back projection screen. Depending on the illumination technique applied, additional layers of different materials may have to be added (see Fig. 2.7).

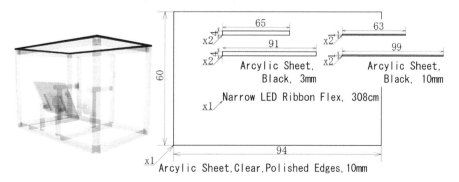

Fig. 2.7 A 1 cm thick, transparent acrylic sheet forms the surface of the table in the DI set-up

Surface Materials for DI

DI requires a material that diffuses the light on the surface. This can be achieved by having the surface itself is as a diffuser or using a transparent surface with an additional diffuser. Plexiglas RP makes a good diffuse surface as in contrast to traditional Plexiglas, it has small micro-lenses embedded in the acrylic sheet that distribute the light evenly across the surface. The resulting projected image has no visible hotspot since the surface smoothes the light. Additionally, the gray surface allows for a good contrast with natural colors, and the material is scratch resistant and therefore well suited to direct touch interaction (Fig. 2.8).

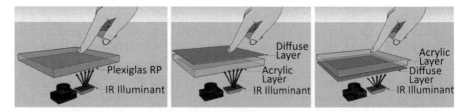

Fig. 2.8 The simplest DI setup uses the diffuse Plexiglas RP material (*left*). For Front DI setups, the diffuser is placed on top of the acrylic (*middle*). Rear DI needs the diffuser beneath the acrylic base layer (*right*)

As an alternative to Plexiglas RP a transparent surface material can be used combined with an additional diffuser. In this case a transparent acrylic plate is typically used as sturdy base layer (a common choice is a 5 mm thick plate). In order to allow projections on the surface and to distribute the IR light, the additional diffuser is used. The diffuser can be a rear-projection foil or simply tracing paper. Any material used as a diffuser must allow enough IR light pass through so as to create a visible reflection on objects near the surface. The diffuser can be applied in front (front DI) or behind the acrylic (rear DI). If it is applied in front, the touch experience is generally more pleasant since the acrylic itself causes a high surface friction for dragging movements. However, the glossy backside of the acrylic results in hotspots due to the rear-mounted IR illuminators, which interfere with the vision tracking. If the diffuser is applied on the backside of the acrylic, this effect can be decreased, since the IR light is already diffused before it reaches the acrylic.

Diffused Surface Illumination (DSI) is a variation on the standard DI setup. DSI uses a transparent acrylic called EndLighten that is a commercial lighting and presentation product. EndLighten has many embedded colourless diffuser particles, which distribute the IR light evenly across the surface. Instead of rear-mounted IR illuminators, DSI set-ups use an IR-LED frame similar to FTIR setups. The light from the LEDs is distributed and emitted uniformly over the entire surface. This results in a DI effect but with a FTIR light setup.

Surface Materials for FTIR

Tables that use FTIR for tracking the user's input are generally composed of a transparent acrylic plate augmented with a frame of IR-LEDs. The acrylic acts as a sturdy base layer that enables the FTIR effect. Additionally, the set-up needs a projection layer that is applied on top of the acrylic plate. Such an approach can negatively impact on its sensitivity and users have press hard on the surface in order to trigger the FTIR effect. Additionally when dragging a finger on the surface, such as in the performance of a motion gesture, friction may reduce the FTIR effect. As a result, many people use an additional layer (compliant surface layer) on top of the polycarbonate material to improve the sensitivity of the surface. These compliant surfaces are usually a soft and transparent material, which is placed between the polycarbonate sheet and a diffuse (projection screen) layer. Figure 2.9 highlights the relevant layers of a commonly used composition. When pressure is applied on the surface, the coupling of the diffuse layer and the polycarbonate surface triggers the FTIR effect; the compliant surface layer intensifies this effect.

Finding the correct material for a compliant surface is crucial. When experimenting with different materials we noticed two different problems that can occur with the layer: either it does not set off a strong-enough FTIR effect or it sticks to the surface, constantly triggering the FTIR effect even after a finger has been removed. Very practical materials come in the form of SORTA-Clear™ 40 and ELASTOSIL® RT 601 silicone, both materials being relatively hard (Hardness Shore A>40), non tacky and very clear. Once hardened, both silicone layers can easily be removed from and re-attached to the polycarbonate surface. Using silicone as a compliant surface poses one problem however as the material comes as a gel which must be poured evenly over the surface. This can prove a difficult task. ELASTOSIL® RT 601 is less viscous and hence easier to pour, resulting in fewer bubbles in the vulcanized layer. As an alternative to silicone for the compliant layer, a thin layer of latex also works well. This also has an advantage over silicone layers as it does not have to be poured, reducing production time for the combined layer set-up significantly. Additionally latex is easier to handle, faster and cheaper

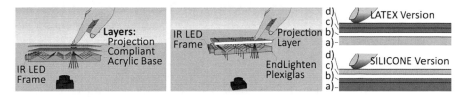

Fig. 2.9 The EndLighten Plexiglas distributes the IR light from the LED frame across the surface, which creates a light emitting layer that can be used for DI tracking (*left*). The three layers needed to track the finger touches. The acrylic plate is covered with a compliant surface layer and a diffuse projection layer on top (*middle*). With the latex version, the projection (d) and the latex layer (c) must be combined; the gap (b) is between these two and the polycarbonate plate. In the silicone version, the gap (c) is between the projection surface (d) and the combined silicone (b) polycarbonate (a) layer (*right*)

to produce and more easily accessible as a mere off-the-shelf component. Moreover, latex does not stick to neighboring layers, as with other alternative compliant surface materials, so latex can be combined with a wider variety of projection screens. However, in contrast to silicone, latex must be combined with the projection layer; with an air gap between the latex and the polycarbonate base plate, whereas in the silicone version we have exactly the opposite requirement. Figure 2.9 shows this difference between the latex and silicone layer construction.

Depending on the compliant material (silicone or latex), it is possible to use different layers as the projection screen. The main requirements are to achieve a result that allows for an air gap between the correct two layers and the triggering of the FTIR effect. Rigid PVC is optimal for FTIR yielding a high contrast touch point. Comparable tracking can be achieved using tracing paper, but with a lower image quality and less robust characteristics. Materials such as Rosco translucent result in touch points that are either too dark, or showed permanent traces on the silicone. Other materials completely stuck to the silicone (HP backlit UV), are all considered not to be suitable for FTIR. For the latex version, HP Colorlucent Backlit UV is an effective option. HP Colorlucent Backlit UV foil was originally designed for use in back lighted signs. Similar to rear-projection screens it generates an even diffuse image without any hotspots from the projector, making it an ideal rear-projection surface. Because of its glossy backside, it cannot be used with the silicone version (as it sticks to the silicone). Rosco screens can also be combined with latex, since the latex sticks well to the screen.

Software

With the hardware in place, the next challenge is the selection and configuration of software components, with the goal being to set up a pipeline of image processing operators that transform a camera image into user interface events.

FTIR Tracking Pipeline

Figure 2.10 shows the canonical imaging pipeline of an FTIR set-up. Images captured by a camera are first pre-processed to remove any unchanging parts using history subtraction. A connected components algorithm (described e.g. in [25]) finds bright regions in the pre-processed image; these are determined to be areas where a surface contact has been made. Post-processing involves finding corresponding touches in different camera frames (temporal correlation) and transforming the camera coordinates to screen coordinates.

DI Tracking Pipeline

DI tracking is a more complex process but allows for proximity as well as touch to be sensed. DI Touch detection exploits the fact that objects at a distance from

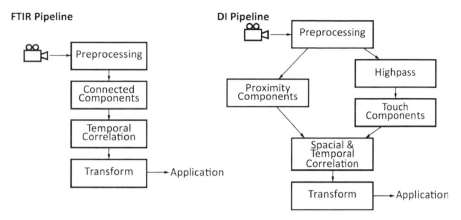

Fig. 2.10 FTIR tracking pipeline (*left*). DI tracking pipeline (*right*)

the surface appear blurred. reacTable [26] does this by adaptive thresholding based on the curvature of the luminance surface (see [27] for a detailed description of the algorithm). The multimedia platform *libavg*,[2] used in the *c-base MTC*, pioneered the use of a high-pass filter to achieve the same effect.

Figure 2.10 shows images generated in a typical DI tracking pipeline. As can be seen, the image pipeline is split and the connected components algorithm is run twice, once each for touch and once for proximity sensing. Touch sensing involves an additional high-pass filter to isolate areas very close to the surface. After the regions have been found, touch and proximity information can be correlated. The bottom right image in Fig. 2.10 shows the result of this process: Fingers touching the surface have been identified and associated with hands.

Interface Considerations

The tracking pipeline provides higher-level software layers with information about finger and hand positions.

The TUIO protocol [28] uses Open Sound Control over UDP to transmit this information in a format, which can be interpreted easily by a wide variety of tools and languages. By default, Touchlib, and many other libraries, come with the functionality to send TUIO events over the popular OpenSound Control (OSC)[3] protocol. OSC libraries are available for many modern programming languages such as C\#, Adobe Flash (Actionscript 3), Java, Max/DSP, Processing, Pure Data, Python and Visual Basic. When using Flash UDP packages have to be converted to TCP using the Flosc tool, which acts as a proxy. Other software packages which provide tracking and TUIO (or similar) output include TouchLib (and its successor,

---

[2] http://www.libavg.de/

[3] http://www.cnmat.berkeley.edu/OpenSoundControl/

Community Core Vision), VVVV, OpenTouch, OpenFTIR, T-Labs multi-touch lib, libavg and libTISCH. For a more detailed overview please refer to [15].

Work is in progress to provide higher-level interfaces such as widget libraries *libavg, NUI Suite Snowflake,*[4] *libTISCH* [29]. *libavg* includes event processing that correlates touches to a hierarchy of on-screen widgets. *libTISCH* provides a hierarchy of layers such as tracking, calibration, interpretation of gestures and display of widgets [30]. This corresponds to the mouse event handling that window systems provide and hence affords the basis for robust implementation of classical GUI widgets like buttons and scrollbars. Both libraries support emerging gesture standards that allow for dragging, rotating and scaling of GUI elements through window-system-like event processing.

When an application uses the OSC protocol, it is only able to receive events containing properties of the detected blobs. It is for example not possible to adjust the settings of *TouchLib* from within the application. However, since OSC uses the UDP network protocol to transfer data it makes it possible to create a set-up in which a dedicated system provides blob tracking and transfers the data to another system, which provides the visualization.

Lessons Learned and Outlook

The steps involved in building a high quality multi-touch enabled surface are not trivial. We hope that by sharing our knowledge and experience of developing multi-touch technologies with the wider community we can inspire the development of new tabletop interfaces, which embrace the possibilities, posed by this exciting interaction technology (Fig. 2.11). Of course there are a lot of other helpful tutorials on the web that summarize knowledge on how to build multi-touch surface (one example is the Wiki book of the NUI group[5]). In this chapter we try to summarize all key information needed to build your own multi-touch surfaces and this chapter as a good starting point for multi-touch newbies. More advanced topics will be covered later in this book (e.g. bringing tangible interface onto multi-touch surfaces).

Of course, despite the technologies described in this paper many fundamental questions for researchers still remain, including: What are the practical benefits of multi-touch systems over single-touch systems? What can graphics and interaction design practitioners "do" with multi-touch surfaces? Which applications is multi-touch input appropriate, viable and useful? Are there more than interaction possibilities than "just" rotating and scaling photos or zooming into maps? Is rotating a picture really a natural gesture? We hope that our description of the realities of building optical multi-touch surfaces will enable more people (experts and laymen alike) to engage in answering these questions and help then build more useful and interesting applications of interactive multi-touch surfaces.

---

[4] http://natural-ui.com/solutions/software.html

[5] http://nuicode.com/projects/wiki-book

Fig. 2.11 A self-made interactive multi-touch table (*left*) and multi-touch applications on a vertical and horizontal multi-touch surface (*middle, right*). The application in the middle is described in more detail in [32]. The application on the *right*, is the GlobalData application by Archimedes Products. The application was part of GlobalData application was part of the Science Express Germany Exhibition

Multi-touch is probably here to stay, but as Bill Buxton said of the mouse: "Remember that it took 30 years between when the mouse was invented by Engelbart and English in 1965 to when it became ubiquitous" [31]. To speed this passage from invention to adoption we would like to encourage developers to design interfaces that help users forget the dominant WIMP paradigm of desktop computing, by producing designs that can only be operated using multi-touch gestures. More than this they should take their newly built interactive surfaces outside the lab and engage with users "in the wild". Many of the most interesting and exciting observations as to the true utility of multi-touch has resulted from real-world observation of their use as in the City Wall project [10] or the multi-touch wall "Hightech Underground" [32].

As mentioned in the introduction, building interactive multi-touch surfaces and letting researchers shape and control the underlying hardware, gives the opportunity for more fundamental innovation.

Acknowledgements We would like to thank Florian Daiber, Otmar Hilliges, Markus Löchtefeld, Laurence Muller, Tim Roth, Daivd Smith, Urich von Zadow, David Hollmann and Antonio Krüger for their help with the Multi-touch Bootcamp 2008 in Amsterdam in conjunction with IEEE Tabletops and for their comments and help (e.g. graphics and feedback) on this chapter.

References

1. Johnson RG (1972) Touch actuable data input panel assembly. US Patent http://www.google.com/patents?vid=USPAT3673327
2. Kasday LR (1984) #4,484,179: Touch position sensitive surface. US Patent http://www.google.com/patents?vid=USPAT4484179
3. Mallos JB (1982) #4,346,376: Touch position sensitive surface. US Patent http://www.google.com/patents?vid=USPAT4346376
4. Mueller RE (1974) #3,846,826: Direct television drawing and image manipulation system. US Patent http://www.google.com/patents?vid=USPAT3846826
5. White RM (1987) #4,484,179: Tactile sensor employing a light conducting element and a resiliently deformable sheet. US Patent http://www.google.com/patents?vid=USPAT4484179

6. Han JY (2005) Low-cost multi-touch sensing through frustrated total internal reflection. In: Proceedings of the 18th annual ACM symposium on user interface software and technology (UIST '05), ACM Press, New York, pp 115–118

7. Dietz P, Leigh D (2001) DiamondTouch: A multi-user touch technology. Proceedings of the 14th annual ACM symposium on user interface software and technology, pp 219–226

8. Kin K, Agrawala M, DeRose T (2009) Determining the benefits of direct-touch, bimanual, and multifinger input on a multitouch workstation. In: Proceedings of graphics interface 2009 (GI '09), canadian information processing society, Toronto, Ontario, Canada, pp 119–124

9. Moscovich T (2006) Multi-touch interaction. In: CHI '06 extended abstracts on human factors in computing systems (CHI '06), ACM Press, New York, pp 1775–1778

10. Peltonen P, Kurvinen E, Salovaara A, Jacucci G, Ilmonen T, Evans J, Oulasvirta A, Saarikko P (2008) It's mine, don't touch!: Interactions at a large multi-touch display in a city centre. In: Proceeding of the twenty-sixth annual SIGCHI conference on human factors in computing systems (CHI '08), ACM Press, New York, pp 1285–1294

11. Rekimoto J (2002) Smartskin: An infrastructure for freehand manipulation on interactive surfaces. In: Proceedings of the SIGCHI conference on human factors in computing systems (CHI '02), ACM Press, New York, pp 113–120

12. Schöning J, Hecht B, Raubal M, Krüger A, Marsh M, Rohs M (2008) Improving interaction with virtual globes through spatial thinking: Helping users ask "why?". In: Proceedings of the 13th international conference on intelligent user interfaces (IUI '08), ACM Press, New York, pp 129–138

13. Valli A, Linari L (2008) Natural interaction sensitivetable. In: CHI '08 extended abstracts on human factors in computing systems (CHI '08), ACM Press, New York, pp 2315–2318

14. Schöning J, Krüger A, Olivier P (2009) Multi-touch is dead, long live multi-touch. CHI 2009: Workshop on Multi-touch and Surface Computing, April 4 – March 9, Boston, MA, http://www.dfki.de/~jschoen/website/Publications_files/SchoeningMultiTouchisDead.pdf, accessed 11.03.2010

15. Schöning J, Brandl P, Daiber F, Echtler F, Hilliges O, Hook J, Löchtefeld M, Motamedi N, Muller L, Olivier P, Roth T, von Zadow U (2008) Multi-touch surfaces: A technical guide. Technical report, Technical University of Munich

16. Harrison C, Hudson SE (2009) Providing dynamically changeable physical buttons on a visual display. In: Proceedings of the 27th international conference on human factors in computing systems (CHI '09), ACM Press, New York, pp 299–308

17. Rosenberg ID, Grau A, Hendee C, Awad N, Perlin K (2009) Impad: An inexpensive multi-touchpressure acquisition device. In: CHIProceedings of the 27th international conference extended abstracts on human factors in computing systems (EA '09), ACM Press, New York, pp 3217–3222

18. Wikipedia (2009) Indium tin oxide — Wikipedia, The Free Encyclopedia, accessed 10.07.2009

19. Downs R (2005) Using resistive touch screens for human/machine interface. Technical Report, Texas Instruments Incorporated, Texas Instruments, Post Office Box 655303, Dallas, Texas 75265

20. Costanza E, Robinson J (2003) A region adjacency tree approach to the detection and design of fiducials. Vision, Video and Graphics (VVG), pp 63–70

21. Schmidt D (2009) Design and realization of an interactive multi-touch table. Technical Report, Lancaster University

22. Tuddenham P, Robinson P (2007) Distributed tabletops: Supporting remote and mixed-presence tabletop collaboration. In: Horizontal Interactive Human-Computer Systems, 2007. TABLETOP'07: Proceedings of the 2nd annual IEEE international workshop, pp 19–26

23. Motamedi N (2008) Hd touch: Multi-touch and object sensing on a high definition lcd tv. In: CHI '08 extended abstracts on human factors in computing systems (CHI '08), ACM Press, New York, pp 3069–3074

24. Echtler F, Sielhorst T, Huber M, Klinker G (2009) A short guide to modulated light. In: Proceedings of the 3rd International Conference on Tangible and Embedded Interaction (TEI ' 09), ACM Press, New York, pp 393–396
25. Han Y, Wagner R (1990) An efficient and fast parallel-connected component algorithm. Journal of the ACM (JACM) 37(3):626–642
26. Kaltenbrunner M, Bencina R (2007) reacTIVision: A computer-vision framework for table-based tangible interaction. Proceedings of the 1st international conference on Tangible and embedded interaction pp 69–74
27. Costanza E, Shelley S, Robinson J (2003) Introducing audio d-touch: A tangible user interface for music composition and performance. Proceedings of the 6th IntÖl Conference on Digital Audio Effects (DAFX), pp 63–70
28. Kaltenbrunner M, Bovermann T, Bencina R, Costanza E (2005) TUIO: A protocol for table-top tangible user interfaces. Proceedings of the 6th IntÕl Workshop on Gesture in Human-Computer Interaction and Simulation
29. Echtler F (2008) TISCH: Tangible Interactive Surfaces for Collaboration between Humans. http://tisch.sourceforge.net/, accessed 23.09.2008
30. Echtler F, Klinker G (2008) A multitouch software architecture. In: Proceedings of the (NordiCHI '08), ACM Press, New York, pp 463–466
31. Buxton B (2008) The long nose of innovation. http://www.businessweek.com/innovate/content/jan2008/id2008012_297369.htm, accessed 26.08.2008
32. Daiber F, Schöning J, Krüger A (2009) Whole body interaction with geospatial data. Smart Graphics, pp 81–92

Chapter 3
From Table–System to Tabletop: Integrating Technology into Interactive Surfaces

Andreas Kunz and Morten Fjeld

Abstract Teamwork for generating new ideas is typically done on vertical or horizontal interaction spaces in order to capture volatile ideas by generating digital content that can be used during ongoing work. While many products are available for vertical interaction spaces, tabletop interaction is still subject to ongoing research and development. The following article gives a classification of existing tabletop systems according to the type of interaction, the means of tracking and identification, and the method of displaying images. Then, the challenges faced by researchers and the motivations behind their endeavors are discussed. We describe the evolution of this technology by citing important projects and their significance in the overall development of interactive tabletop surfaces. Finally, we give an outlook on future trends in this research field.

Introduction and Classification

The difference between a horizontal and a vertical interaction space is much more than an angle of 90°. The orientation has a significant impact on the user's behavior as well as on the employed technology.

Vertical interaction spaces utilize the metaphor of a whiteboard, and so, are typically designed as a single user interface. Their main purpose is to disseminate information and, as such, only one user with a single interaction device will work with the system at a time. The most common interactions on these spaces are writing and sketching. In both cases, the user touches the surface with the pen's tip at one point at a time, which can be detected by various technologies. In addition, the interaction devices need only be detected and tracked for the duration of interaction, since they

A. Kunz (✉)

Department of Mechanical and Process Engineering, Swiss Federal Institute of Technology, CH-8092, Zurich, Switzerland
e-mail: kunz@iwf.mavt.ethz.ch

C. Müller-Tomfelde (ed.), *Tabletops – Horizontal Interactive Displays*,
Human-Computer Interaction Series, DOI 10.1007/978-1-84996-113-4_3,
© Springer-Verlag London Limited 2010

cannot remain on the surface without any user interaction. Also, vertical interaction spaces have less challenging demands regarding the content orientation on the screen. Standard drop-down menus can be used, since all users will have the same perspective on the visible information.

Horizontal interactive spaces behave much differently. Tabletop systems are not primarily used to disseminate information, but to elaborate it by a single user or a small group gathered around the table. They are used to generate, manipulate, and display digital objects, which are carriers of information and thus the basis of discussion within a team. A horizontal surface also imposes new challenges in terms of system design. Within a typical tabletop interaction scenario, users stand or sit around the table and have very different views on the displayed content (see Figs. 3.8, 3.9, 3.10, 3.11, and 3.12). So, typical interaction menus such as drop-down menus are not suitable since they are difficult to read from most positions around the table. Moreover, many devices are placed on the table that are partially meant for interaction. However, there are also devices on the table that are neither related to the system nor to the task at hand. From a technical point of view, this results in multiple points on the interactive surface that either need to be tracked and identified or ignored. In the act of writing, for example, users want to interact with the tip of the stylus, but they also touch the interactive surface with their hands and fingers. In this situation, the system should detect only the stylus and ignore the hand. However, in the next moment the user might use their fingers to move a virtual piece of paper around, which requires that the system now detect the fingers. Additionally, the stylus may be used for pointing at certain objects. In this case, the system should detect the stylus even if it does not touch the tabletop's surface, but hovers a short distance above it.

During interaction on the table, the user frequently interferes with the light path that is required by most systems for image display and vision-based tracking. This results in either shadow casting by the user or non-ergonomic working positions when sitting at the table. These challenges must be addressed within the fields of interaction, tracking and identification, image display, and software, which are described in more detail in the following paragraphs.

Interaction

Since a tabletop system is both a display and a direct input device, it must accept natural hand gestures and other intuitive devices as input [1]. This will improve the fluidity and reduce the cognitive load of the user–system interaction. Thus, the tabletop system must be able to distinguish between intended input using fingers and other devices, and unintended input by other objects on the table. Furthermore, tabletop systems must be able to detect multiple devices simultaneously, no matter if one or multiple users are interacting with the system. Figure 3.1 shows a classification of the types of interaction with a tabletop system.

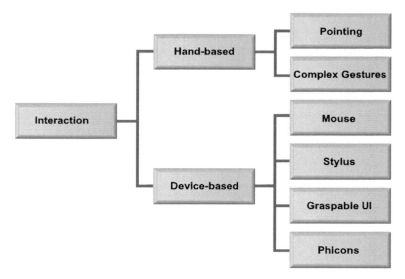

Fig. 3.1 Classification of tabletop interaction

In order to enable intuitive interaction with the content that is visible on the tabletop, devices other than the mouse and keyboard must be used. There is a class of devices that are easily identifiable by their inherent function known as "physical icons" or phicons [2]. In this case, each device usually has a static association so that the tabletop system is able to detect its identifier (ID) and not just its position. Once the device's ID is known to the system, the underlying functionality is also defined since the association cannot be changed. However, other tabletop systems have a dynamic association that allows for simpler detection algorithms. In the latter case, the devices have a more general character and so the intuitiveness is only guaranteed by the displayed content, i.e. the graphical user interface (GUI). The dynamic association is user-triggered and follows predefined steps. These steps may require some learning on the part of the user.

Tracking and Identification

Tabletop systems must be able to detect the position of an interaction device and, in case of phicons or other specialized input devices, their ID. While the position of a device is important for the interaction in a global context to be displayed on the tabletop's surface, the ID is relevant for integrating a device's specialized functionality into a specific application.

Although tracking has been well researched in the field of virtual reality, it is still quite a delicate task even on a 2D tabletop surface. More degrees of freedom (DOF) than given by planar interaction become relevant. For instance, the z-coordinate may be used to distinguish between writing and pointing in pen-based interaction.

Additionally, the tracking and detection system's latency should be below the user's perceptual threshold, otherwise user irritation may occur.

An even more critical task for the tracking and identification system is distinguishing between objects meant for interaction, such as a finger, and objects not meant for interaction, such as coffee mugs or the side of a user's hand. During normal operation on a tabletop system, various objects may be placed on the surface which are not meant for interaction, but which could cause irritations to the tabletop system, e.g. by shadowing effects.

Unlike a mouse, which is a relative pointing device (i.e. the travelling distance and orientation are detected), all tracking systems for tabletop systems allow, so-called, absolute pointing, i.e. the object's detection is at the place where the user puts the device. Below, Fig. 3.2 depicts the various types of tracking and detection that can be used.

Beside interaction and tracking, a third, more technical way of classifying tabletop systems exists. By taking the position of the individual technical components and other general aspects into account, such as multi-user capability, touch detection, TUI interaction, ID, and state (such as passive, idle, active, mode of use, etc.), a classification matrix (see Fig. 3.3) can be established.

The above matrix template will be used in section "Milestones on the Way to an Integrated System" to give a quick overview of systems' capabilities along with a brief description of key research results in the past decade.

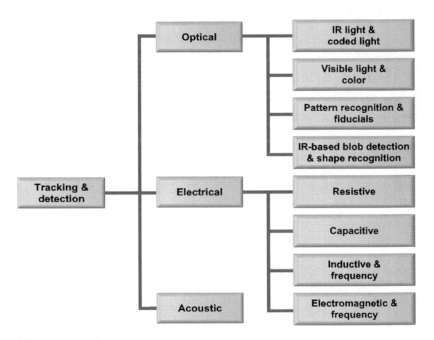

Fig. 3.2 Types of tabletop tracking

Fig. 3.3 Classification
matrix of tabletop systems

	multi-touch	touch	multi-TUI	TUI	State
over					
in					
under					

Image Display

In principle, two basic ways of displaying information exist: front- and back-projection. While front-projection refers to when the user and the image source are on the same side of the interaction plane, back-projection is when they are on different sides of the plane. In both cases, projectors are most frequently used, but some back-projection systems already employ flat screens based on liquid crystal display (LCD) or plasma technology. Figure 3.4 gives an overview of the employed technologies.

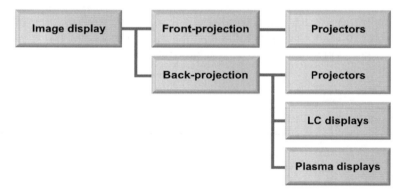

Fig. 3.4   Display technologies for tabletop systems

Technical Challenges and Motivation

Tabletop interaction strongly depends on the involved technology. Various kinds of tracking technologies, projection systems, and sophisticated interaction devices have been realized and combined into new groupware for collocated multi-user environments. Most of these systems suffer from technical imperfections either in tracking, identification, interaction, or image display. They also suffer from the fact that a light-path is required for the projection and the camera's image acquisition.

Resolving these problems and realizing a table where a user can actually sit comfortably imposes requirements on the display as well as on all the other technical systems involved.

During the past decade tabletop research has often been focused on supporting collaborative teamwork, in particular brainstorming and creativity sessions. In such phases of teamwork, intuitive handling of the devices sitting on a table is crucial. Supporting team-oriented idea gathering through tabletop interaction implies that all participants are able to interact simultaneously. Even when simultaneous user input does not take place, the system should be able to detect and identify multiple objects on the surface. Here, tabletop systems must overcome the single user principle and the underlying idea of controlling the system by one single interaction device.

Realizing tabletop systems differs completely from implementing typical interaction behaviors on vertical interactive surfaces, where multiple commercial solutions already exist. While vertical interactive surfaces follow the so-called whiteboard metaphor, relying on a single-user presentation and single-device pen-based input, the tabletop metaphor is inherently a multi-user system, triggered by intended and unintended input. For instance, simple writing, which is not typically problematic on a vertical whiteboard, turns out to be a delicate task on a horizontal tabletop. This is because tabletop users typically touch the interaction surface at multiple points with their hand and not only at the intended interaction point of the device. So, the system should be able to distinguish between intentional and unintentional input in order to generate correct results. This situation becomes even more complex if users consciously use their fingers in addition to devices to interact with the system. For this situation, systems must be able to combine tangible user interfaces with touch input on the same surface.

In order to meet the technical challenges mentioned above, continuous work on improving registration, display, and system technology for tabletop interaction is required. Another goal is to integrate all the technical components from above and below the tabletop into the tabletop itself, thus realizing a system that is more intuitive to handle and more ergonomic to work with. The following section presents milestones from the past decade on the way to such integrated systems.

Milestones on the Way to an Integrated System

For about 20 years, tabletop interaction has inspired researchers all over the world. While the technology required was placed "over the tabletop" in the early systems, recent research focuses on the integration of all components "under the tabletop" or even "in the tabletop". The following overview presents some important milestones on the way to realizing an intuitive tabletop system.

DigitalDesk – 1991

In 1991, Wellner [3] recognized that the electronic desktop on the screen is separated from the user's physical desk. He pointed out the basic motivation for doing tabletop research in general: electronic documents lack many properties of physical paper, while physical paper lacks many useful properties of electronic documents. With DigitalDesk, he created a system that allows interacting with digital (projected) paper with a bare finger. The system uses a front-projection as well as a front image acquisition of the user's hand and finger. In order to achieve a reasonable update rate, the camera's image was first configured with a low resolution when detecting the positions of the finger and hand. Once this was detected, a second high-resolution image with a close-up view could detect the characters of the underlying document. Using this optical tracking and recognition system, the underlying application was capable of reading numbers from a piece of paper and entering them into a digital calculator application (see Fig. 3.5).

Normal daylight and office lighting conditions caused problems. Also, a frame rate of 25–30 frames per second created irritating latencies. At this point, the system did not require any additional interfaces than the fingers.

Active Desk – 1995

In 1995, Fitzmaurice et al. [4] introduced Active Desk, which allowed using interaction devices other than the fingers. Using a back-projected digitizing board, it was also possible to interact with a stylus. Fitzmaurice also introduced the term, graspable user interface, which is the physical representation of the graphical user interface, having the same abbreviation of GUI. This required the ability to use tools

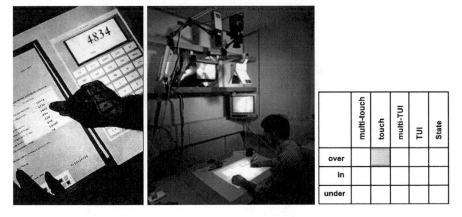

	multi-touch	touch	multi-TUI	TUI	State
over					
in					
under					

Fig. 3.5 DigitalDesk Transferring content from analogue paper to a digital application [3]

A. Kunz and M. Fjeld

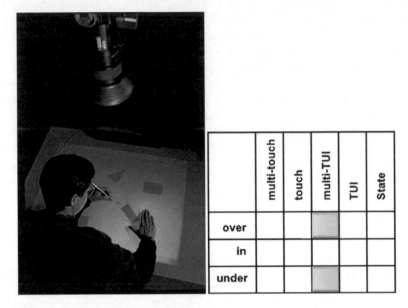

	multi-touch	touch	multi-TUI	TUI	State
over					
in					
under					

Fig. 3.6 Bimanual interaction on Active Desk [4]

other than the stylus to interact with the system. The graspable user interface was dynamically associated to a virtual object if it was placed upon it. In order to release it, the user had to lift the GUI away from the surface. Finally, to retrieve information about the bricks' positions, an electromagnetic tracking system was used with its receiving antennae serving as a brick for interaction. The receivers were cable-bound and could mechanically interfere with each other. Thus, mainly bimanual interaction was supported, as shown in Fig. 3.6.

Unlike DigitalDesk, Active Desk uses a back-projection onto the tabletop. Thus, the tabletop system's active components are above the tabletop (tracking) as well as under the tabletop (projection).

The metaDESK – 1997

In 1997, metaDESK was introduced by Ullmer et al. [5]. It addressed the problem that interaction with either fingers only or a dynamic assignment of interaction bricks to virtual objects did not allow sufficient interaction capabilities. Also, the interaction bricks were not intuitive to handle. Thus, Ullmer et al. introduced the term Tangible User Interface (TUI). These interfaces disclose their inherent functionality and influence the tabletop system by their shape. Employing shapes known to users from their daily life makes the handling of tabletop systems more intuitive (see Fig. 3.7).

The metaDESK employs a vision-based tracking system using infrared (IR) light, which is back-projected onto the tabletop's surface together with the visible image.

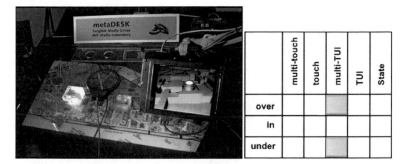

	multi-touch	touch	multi-TUI	TUI	State
over			▓		
in					
under			▓		

Fig. 3.7 Typical TUI within metaDESK [5]

Since the objects will reflect the infrared light, they are visible to the camera, which is also mounted underneath the tabletop. In addition, an electromagnetic tracking system is used for the lens and the position of an additional liquid crystal (LC) screen in order to provide a 3D-view of the scenery.

Again, to reinforce the fact, the system's components are above and below the tabletop.

The BUILD-IT System – 1998

The BUILD-IT system was introduced in 1998 by Fjeld et al. [6]. This system uses a front-projection onto a tabletop and a reflective IR tracking system. Applying computer-vision technologies to the acquired camera image allows multiple physical handles – the so-called bricks – to be detected on the table, which serves as a passive projection screen. Thanks to a combination of bricks that reflect IR light and a camera with an IR filter, the bricks are the only objects on the tabletop's surface that are visible to the camera. They are dynamically associated to the virtual objects. Releasing the bricks is done by interrupting the free line-of-sight between the brick and the camera (see Fig. 3.8).

Like metaDESK, the BUILD-IT system also offers a quasi-3D view on a vertical screen (see Fig. 3.8), allowing a perspective view of a 3D scene. For this system, all active components are located above the table, allowing for comfortable work in a sitting position.

The Magic Table – 2003

In 2003, Bérard [7] introduced the Magic Table, consisting of a regular whiteboard on which a user can write and sketch using regular ink. For special commands, such as copy, cut, or rotate, colored tokens are used which are recognized by the camera above the table. Special gestures with the tokens are interpreted triggering another

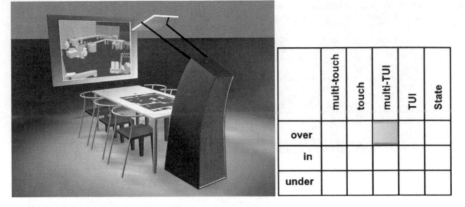

	multi-touch	touch	multi-TUI	TUI	State
over					
in					
under					

Fig. 3.8 The BUILD-IT system [6]

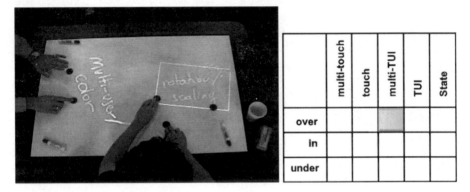

	multi-touch	touch	multi-TUI	TUI	State
over					
in					
under					

Fig. 3.9 The Magic Table [7]

camera to perform a high-resolution scan of the sketches on the table. Next, a copy is projected over the original version, which can now be moved, rotated, or deleted (see Fig. 3.9).

The tabletop system's components are placed above the surface, requiring a free line-of-sight for the optical tracking.

SenseTable – 2000–2002

SenseTable was presented by Patten et al. [8] in 2001. The system uses two WACOM Intuos tablets, which allow inductive sensing. Since this kind of sensing is only capable of tracking two devices, these were designed in such a way that the integrated coil is randomly switched on and off. This allows for a greater number of devices to be used, but results in a significantly lower update rate of about 1 Hz. The so-called pucks were dynamically associated to a virtual object by placing the puck

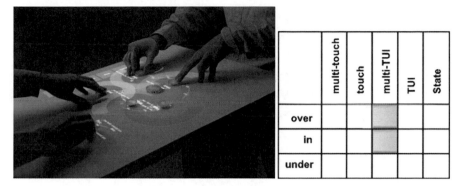

	multi-touch	touch	multi-TUI	TUI	State
over			�©		
in			▣		
under					

Fig. 3.10 SenseTable with interactive puck [8]

next to it. The object is released again by shaking the puck or removing it from the interactive surface.

The system uses a front-projection, and the information is also partly visible on the surface of the pucks. This allows clear identification of a puck's functionality, since this cannot be derived from its shape (see Fig. 3.10).

SenseTable was also the first approach to integrate part of the tabletop system's technology into the tabletop, namely the tracking system. The system still uses a front-projection, which is partly camouflaged when the user interacts with the puck. Thus, a part of the technology is still located above the tabletop.

DiamondTouch – 2001

In 2001, DiamondTouch was introduced by Dietz et al. [9]. Much like SenseTable, this system uses a front-projection above the tabletop and has a tracking system integrated into the tabletop. However, the tracking system works electronically, i.e. a high-frequency signal is transmitted from the table through the user and is detected by receivers in each user's chair. Thus, the table can detect multiple touches from different users, while objects on the surface do not interfere with normal operation. When the user touches the table, a capacitive coupled circuit is closed. This circuit runs from the transmitter through the touch point on the table's surface, through the user to the user's receiver, and back to the transmitter (see Fig. 3.11).

Since the system is designed to detect multiple users' touches, no additional tools are available (TUI) for the intuitive operation of more complex functions.

SmartSkin – 2002

Rekimoto introduced SmartSkin in 2002 [10]. Like DiamondTouch, it is a system that is able to detect multiple finger touches on a tabletop using capacitive sensing.

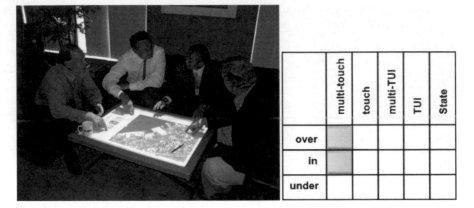

	multi-touch	touch	multi-TUI	TUI	State
over					
in					
under					

Fig. 3.11 DiamondTouch [9]

In this case, the tracking system is again integrated into the tabletop, consisting of a mesh of transmitter and receiver electrodes. The resolution of the system also allows detecting gestures by interpreting the relative positions of detected blobs. Thus, gestures like grasping or zooming in/out can be detected by the system. Although the system cannot be influenced by most of the other objects on the table, there are some TUIs – so-called capacitance tags – available. However, as these tags are electrically grounded, they are not detected until the user touches them. Since the tags have a unique pattern, they can be unequivocally differentiated from normal finger touch patterns (Fig. 3.12).

SmartSkin was one of the first systems that integrated both TUI and touch into the tabletop. In addition, the system was able to distinguish between several TUIs by interpreting their shape. However, the system still uses a front-projection and so, does not completely integrate all components into the tabletop.

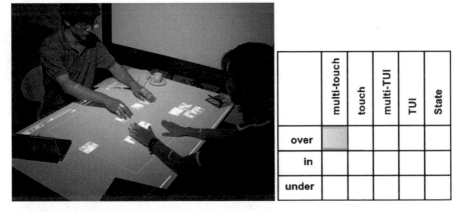

	multi-touch	touch	multi-TUI	TUI	State
over					
in					
under					

Fig. 3.12 SmartSkin [10]

reacTable – 2003–2007

The reacTable is a comparatively long project whose final system was presented by Jourdà et al. [11]. This tabletop system is capable of detecting TUIs and touch, but all of its components are located below the tabletop's surface. The system uses a back-projection as well as an optical tracking of fiducials from underneath the tabletop's surface. The TUIs are applied with fiducials that can be unequivocally detected by the camera. These also allow detecting orientation, which supports inter-action capabilities. Since the tabletop is back-illuminated with IR light for detecting the fiducials, finger touch can also be easily detected. This allows modifying and adjusting preset parameters given by the TUIs (Fig. 3.13).

The TUIs are statically associated to a function (for a music application), but they do not show their inherent functionality intuitively by their shape. Thus, users need some training time in order to operate the system.

PlayAnywhere – 2005

In 2005, PlayAnywhere was introduced by Wilson [12]. It is a front-projected, computer-vision based interactive tabletop system. Both the wide-angle projection and the IR-based tracking system are located above the tabletop. The IR illumina-tion is used to generate shadows, which can be seen by the camera (see Fig. 3.14). Detecting the size of the shadow can determine not only a finger's position but also whether the finger touches the surface or hovers above. So, PlayAnywhere is capa-ble of taking the z-axis into account, that is, it is possible to distinguish between pointing and touching. If objects are applied with a visual code, they can also be detected by the system. Thus, it is also possible to integrate TUIs into the underlying application.

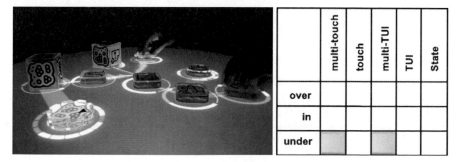

	multi-touch	touch	multi-TUI	TUI	State
over					
in					
under					

Fig. 3.13 Interacting with TUIs on the reacTable [11] (courtesy to Xavier Sivecas)

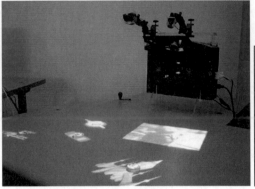

	multi-touch	touch	multi-TUI	TUI	State
over	▨				
in					
under					

Fig. 3.14 Working with PlayAnywhere [12]

FTIR – 2005

Multi-touch IR-based technology was introduced by Han [13, 14] in 2005. The system uses a back-projection onto the tabletop's surface and an IR-based tracking system, which also requires a camera underneath the tabletop. Again, all components are below the tabletop. Unlike reacTable, the IT-light is not realized in a back-illumination but is coupled into an acrylic overlay from the side. Within the acrylic, the IR light is completely internally reflected. At the position where a finger is pressed onto the tabletop's surface, the total internal reflection is distorted and some IR light is coupled out. This amount of light can be seen by a camera, which is applied with a special IR pass-through filter (see Fig. 3.15).

The system was designed to support multi-touch, but, due to the physical working principle, other objects on the tabletop's surface cannot be detected unless they are coated with a silicone layer, which is also able to couple out light from the acrylic tabletop. The camera image is used for blob detection, which gives information about the fingers' positions.

	multi-touch	touch	multi-TUI	TUI	State
over					
in	▨				
under	▨				

Fig. 3.15 The FTIR system [13, 14]

Ortholumen – 2007

Ortholumen is a light pen based tabletop interaction system that can employ all the pen's spatial degrees of freedom (DOF). The pen's light is projected from above onto a horizontal translucent screen and tracked by a webcam sitting underneath, facing upwards. The system output is projected back onto the same screen (see Fig. 3.16). The elliptic light spot cast by the pen informs the system of pen position, orientation, and direction. While this adds up to six DOFs, Piazza et al. [15] used up to four at a time.

In order to better separate input and output light, they employed polarizing filters on the webcam and the projector lens. Two applications, painting and map navigation, were presented. Ortholumen can be expanded to track multiple pens of the same or different colors. This enabled multi-pointer input, collaboration, and placed pens as external memory. Visible light, as opposed to infrared or radio, may be perceived more directly by users. Ortholumen employs only low-cost parts, making the system affordable to home users.

InfrActables – 2005

In 2005, Ganser et al. [16] proposed the InfrActables system. Within this system, all components are underneath the tabletop's surface; it uses back-projection as well as image acquisition from underneath. The devices are active, that is, they are triggered by an IR synchronization-flash and respond with a device-specific bitcode. Based on this principle several interaction devices were realized such as stylus, eraser, ruler, caliper, ink dwell, etc. (see Fig. 3.17).

While a device's position on the tabletop can be determined by blob detection, ID and mode can only be determined by evaluating five subsequent camera frames. This means that the overall refresh frequency is divided by the number of bits being used for unequivocally determining the identity of each device. In the presented version, seven different devices with three states each could be detected.

	multi-touch	touch	multi-TUI	TUI	State
over					
in					
under					

Fig. 3.16 Ortholumen: Light-based navigation of Google Earth [15]

	multi-touch	touch	multi-TUI	TUI	State
over					
in					
under			▩		▩

Fig. 3.17 Working with InfrActables [16]

MightyTrace – 2008

In 2008, MightyTrace was introduced by Hofer et al. [17]. This system focuses on integrating all technical components into the tabletop. The display and the tracking system are integrated into a single housing, and thus, it is possible to realize an ergonomic table that people can actually sit at.

Figure 3.18 shows an early prototype of MightyTrace, which employs IR sensors, being integrated into an LC-screen for tracking multiple devices on the tabletop. The tracking system consists of an array of IR-sensors that are placed behind the LC-matrix. The TUIs actively emit IR-light when being triggered by a synchronization flash. The emitted IR-light of the TUIs goes through all components of the LC-screen and is only marginally influenced by the content being displayed on the screen. The prototype reaches a resolution of 3 mm with an update rate of at least 100 Hz. However, it only allows interaction using specialized active devices such as a stylus or interaction bricks.

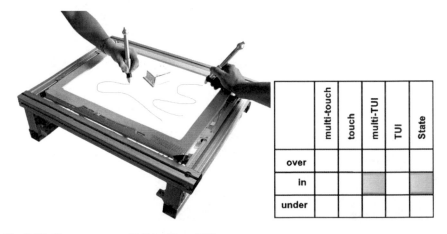

	multi-touch	touch	multi-TUI	TUI	State
over					
in			▩		▩
under					

Fig. 3.18 First prototype of MightyTrace [17]

FLATIR – 2009

An adaptation of the FTIR technology to an LC-screen was suggested by Hofer et al. [18]. This system, again, integrated all components into the tabletop. As in MightyTrace, IR-sensors behind the LC-matrix are used. In addition, the LC-screen is equipped with an FTIR-overlay, which allows multi-touch detection (see Fig. 3.19).

	multi-touch	touch	multi-TUI	TUI	State
over					
in					
under					

Fig. 3.19 FLATIR: FTIR multitouch detection on an LC-screen [18]

Now, the blobs generated by the finger touches (visualized as red circles in Fig. 3.19) can be analyzed and then used for an underlying application. However, it is no longer possible to distinguish between individual fingers, and so finger touch can mainly be used for controlling a mouse pointer. After a dynamic association with a virtual object or functionality, the finger can also be used for performing and controlling more complex functions.

Summary and Outlook

This article classifies research activities within the field of tabletop interaction. In order to illustrate the tendency of more intuitive systems and technology completely integrated into the tabletop, several of the most relevant research results have been briefly introduced. While in the past larger interactive spaces could only be realized with projection systems, today's flat screen technology – in particular LCD technology – offers interesting alternatives as it becomes increasingly affordable.

Using LCD technology in tabletop systems has become more ergonomic, since functional tables can now be realized. It is now possible to actually sit at the table, because cameras and projectors are no longer in the way. Although this was possible using systems with the technology "above the tabletop," disturbing shadow casting that typically exists in front projection systems can now be avoided.

While current research into this new generation of tabletop systems supports either finger touch or TUI interaction, future research works, such as TNT [19], will be able to integrate both, making tabletop systems even more intuitive to handle. In addition, future operating systems such as Windows 7 will support multiple mouse pointers, which will pave the way for new applications that benefit from multi-touch tabletop systems as described above.

References

1. Shen C, Ryall K, Forlines C, Esenther A, Vernier F, Everitt K, Wu M, Wigdor D, Morris M, Hancock M, Tse E (2009) Collaborative tabletop research and evaluation: Interfaces and interactions for direct-touch horizontal surfaces. In: Dillenbourg P, Huang J, Cherubini M (eds) Interactive artifacts and furniture supporting collaborative work and learning, Springer Science and Business Media, New York, pp 111–128, doi: 10.1007/978-0-387-77234-9_7
2. Ishii H, Ullmer B (1997) Tangible bits: Towards seamless interfaces between people, bits and atoms. In: CHI '97: Proceedings of CHI '97; ACM Press, New York, pp 234–241, doi: 10.1145/258549.258715
3. Wellner P (1991) The DigitalDesk calculator: Tactile manipulation on a desktop display. In: UIST '91: Proceedings of the ACM symposium on user interface software and technology (UIST '91), ACM Press, New York, pp 27–33
4. Fitzmaurice G. Ishii H, Buxton W (1995) Bricks: Laying the foundation for graspable user interfaces. In: CHI '95: Proceedings of CHI 1995, ACM Press, New York, pp 442–449, doi: 10.1145/223904.223964
5. Ullmer B, Ishii H (1997) The metaDESK: Models and prototypes for tangible user interfaces. In: Proceedings of UIST '97, ACM Press, New York, pp 223–232, doi: 10.1145/263407.263551
6. Fjeld M, Bichsel M, Rauterberg M (1998) BUILD-IT: An intuitive design tool based on direct object manipulation. In: Wachsmut I, Fröhlich M (eds) Gesture and sign language in human-computer interaction, Lecture Notes in Artificial Intelligence, Vol. 1371, Springer Berlin Heidelberg, New York, pp 297–308, doi: 10.1007/BFb0053008
7. Bérard F (2003) The magic table: Computer-vision based augmentation of a whiteboard for creative meetings. In: Proceedings of IEEE international conference in computer vision, Nice, France
8. Patten J, Ishii H, Hines J, Pangaro G (2001) SenseTable: A wireless object tracking platform for tangible user interfaces. In: Proceedings of CHI '01 ACM Press, New York, pp 253–260, doi: 10.1145/365024.365112
9. Dietz P, Leigh D (2001) DiamondTouch: A multi-user touch technology. In: Proceedings of the 14th annual symposium on user interface software and technology UIST 2001, ACM Press, New York, pp 219–226, doi: 10.1145/502348.502389
10. Rekimoto J (2002) SmartSkin: An infrastructure for freehand manipulation on interactive surfaces. In: Proceedings of CHI 2002, ACM Press, New York, pp 113–120, doi: .org/10.1145/503376.503397
11. Jourdà S, Geiger G, Alonso M, Kaltenbrunner M (2007) The reacTable: Exploring the synergy between live music performance and tabletop tangible interfaces. In: Proceedings of the 1st international conference on tangible and embedded interaction, ACM Press, New York, pp 139–146, doi: 10.1145/1226969.1226998
12. Wilson A (2005) PlayAnywhere: A compact interactive tabletop projection-vision system. In: Proceedings of the 18th annual ACM synposium on user interface software and technology UIST 2005, ACM Press, New York, pp 83–92, doi: 10.1145/1095034.1095047
13. Multi-Touch Interaction Research, http://cs.nyu.edu/~jhan/ftirtouch, accessed 12.03.2009

14. Han JY (2005) Low-cost multi-touch sensing through frustrated total internal reflection. In: Proceedings of UIST 2005, ACM Press, New York, pp 115–118, doi: .org/10.1145/1095034.1095054

15. Piazza T, Fjeld M (2007) Ortholumen: Using light for direct tabletop input. In: Proceedings of IEEE TableTop 2007, IEEE Computer Society, Los Alamitos, CA, pp 193–196, doi: 10.1109/TABLETOP.2007.23

16. Ganser C, Kennel T, Birkeland N, Kunz A (2005) Computer-supported environment for creativity processes in globally distributed teams. In: Proceedings of the international conference on engineering design ICED 2005, Sydney, Australia, pp 109–110

17. Hofer R, Kunz A, Kaplan P (2008) MightyTrace: Multiuser tracking technology on LC-displays. In: Proceedings of CHI 2008, ACM Press, New York, pp 215–218, doi: 10.1145/1357054.1357091

18. Hofer R, Naeff D, Kunz A (2009) FLATIR: FTIR multi-touch detection on a discrete distributed sensor array. In: Proceedings of the 3rd international conference on tangible and embedded interaction TEI '09, ACM Press, New York, pp 317–322, doi: 10.1145/1517664.1517730

19. Hofer R, Kunz A (2009) TNT: Touch 'n' TUI on LC-displays. In: Proceedings of the 8th international conference on entertainment computing ICEC '09, Paris, pp 222–227, doi: 10.1007/978-3-642-04052-8_24

Chapter 4
High-Resolution Interactive Displays

Mark Ashdown, Philip Tuddenham, and Peter Robinson

Abstract Tabletop displays are mostly used for casual applications that do not require intricate graphics or precise manipulation. Browsing photographs and maps are common applications. A higher resolution is required to support work involving detailed graphics and text. A display the size of a desk, with the resolution of a typical LCD monitor, will have around 14 megapixels. Tabletop displays are usually constructed from projectors, and the only way to achieve this size and resolution is to combine multiple projectors. We present techniques from multi-projector display walls and adapt them for tabletops. These high-resolution displays also require high-resolution input, and although touch is simple and natural, better accuracy can generally be achieved using a pen. We also review technologies for pen input on tabletops.

Introduction

Large displays have compelling benefits. For individuals they allow materials to be spread out and perused as on a physical desk, thus exploiting the kinaesthetic sense and styles of working used in traditional workspaces; they facilitate multitasking; and they have been shown to have cognition and productivity benefits [1]. For groups they allow participants to work together while adhering to social protocols of personal space without formal turn-taking, and support consequential communication: allowing users to remain aware of the actions of others through their peripheral vision.

Most tabletop displays have low resolution. In recent years there has been much research interest in tabletop displays, and hardware of various forms has been constructed. One of the key features of tabletop displays is that they have diagonal sizes

M. Ashdown (✉)
Thales Research and Technology, Reading, RG2 0SB, UK
e-mail: mark@ashdown.me

C. Müller-Tomfelde (ed.), *Tabletops – Horizontal Interactive Displays*,
Human-Computer Interaction Series, DOI 10.1007/978-1-84996-113-4_4,
© Springer-Verlag London Limited 2010

of around 30–80 inchs, much larger than a conventional monitor. Most designs use a single-projector front- or rear-projected display, which enables the large size, but typically have low resolution in terms of pixels per inch. This is adequate to enable the standard tabletop demo application, photo browsing, but there are many applications that would benefit from a tabletop implementation but require high resolution to show detailed graphics.

Many applications require high-resolution to display the necessary information. Examples for which people currently use their desktop computers include document review, data analysis, and computer-aided design. Applications that have been implemented on a tabletop to demonstrate the use of high resolution include web browsing (the text must be legible), collaboration over documents (text and written annotations must be legible), programming (a typical integrated development environment display is very dense), unmanned aerial vehicle control (air-traffic control displays are dense), and command and control (maps with roads, buildings, symbols) [2]. Chapter 16 discusses information visualization on tabletops, which is another application that will benefit from high resolution.

This chapter describes techniques that have been used to achieve high-resolution output and input for tabletop displays. In particular, the tiling of projectors using techniques developed for multi-projector display walls, which has proved to be a powerful approach, and pen input, which complements touch input by providing more precision.

Background

Work on tabletop displays at the University of Cambridge Computer Lab started with the DigitalDesk [3], and continued with Origami [4], Escritoire [5], and T3 [2]. A common goal in these projects is the creation of a human–computer interface like a traditional desk, where items are arranged freely over a large surface and modified using a pen, as with traditional pen and paper. The goal has always been to provide high resolution displays to enable detailed work [6]. Many other tabletop systems have been constructed. Continuing advances in display technology, in particular the commoditisation of digital projectors, have brought such displays within the reach of researchers interested in the implications for human–computer interaction.

Resolution

As described in the introduction above, most tabletop displays have relatively low-resolution output. If they provided high resolution, new classes of applications could be implemented, and subjected to the research on novel multi-touch and pen-based interfaces that is being conducted on tabletops.

The Display Resolution section defines what we mean by low and high resolution. It defines a lower limit by considering the resolution necessary to display detailed content, and an upper limit by considering the properties of human vision and the more realistic resolutions of current LCD monitors. It then presents an analysis of how this range of resolutions can be provided by combining projectors, with particular attention to the cost of the hardware.

Display Wall Techniques

Since DigitalDesk [7] introduced the idea of projecting down onto a table to produce a "tabletop display", many researchers have explored this type of computer interface, and the use of projectors as personal displays rather than devices for making formal presentations to an audience. Despite some issues such as lack of privacy, and generation of noise and heat, this new use for projectors has been shown to have benefits for individual work and collocated collaboration [8].

Improvements in calibration techniques and the falling cost of projectors have led to the construction of many multi-projector display walls for scientific visualization. They tend to be large expensive installations. The Princeton Scalable Display Wall [9] was one of the first large scale walls, which demonstrated a 4×2 projector array, followed by a 6×4 (24 projector) array on custom-made adjustable bases, driven by a cluster of PCs. Various other multi-projector display walls have followed [10].

When combining multiple projectors, the aim is to make a single seamless display. Achieving seamlessness involves compensating for two types of problem: geometric and photometric [10]. Geometric compensation fixes the position of every pixel in the display, while photometric compensation fixes its colour. Compensation techniques such as perspective warping, edge blending, automatic calibration using computer vision, and intensity and full-colour radiometric measurement and compensation have been studied extensively in the context of display walls.

Compared to display walls, tabletop displays have a different emphasis: the display of as many pixels as possible from a single computer, in a self-contained horizontal form. However, many of the techniques from display walls can also be applied to tabletops with either front or rear projection. The Multi-Projector Display Techniques section reviews these techniques, shows how some of them have been applied to tabletops, and lists others that could be applied.

Input

An important aspect of the allure of tabletop displays is the naturalness and simplicity of direct input, rather than indirect control with a mouse or touch pad. In particular, touch and multi-touch input are driving many of the new interfaces that are being created. Frustrated total internal reflection (FTIR) and diffuse illumination have been used in many tabletop displays because they are simple, robust, and combine well with rear projection. Other sensing technologies based on resistance, capacitance, and computer vision, have also been developed. These touch input technologies are described in Chapters 2 and 3.

A high-resolution display is best exploited with an accurate input method. Chapter 11 discusses the issue of inaccuracy in touch input and proposed interaction techniques to alleviate that problem. The High-Resolution Input section below addresses another approach to the issue – giving the user a pen to allow accurate input and writing. It lists pen-input technologies, followed by descriptions of the issues intrinsic to pen input on tabletops.

Display Resolution

Before delving into techniques for creating high-resolution displays, we must define what resolution is, and how high we wish it to be. The resolution of a display is the number of pixels it has per unit distance. We assume a regular grid of square pixels, and state resolutions in pixels per inch (ppi), which is the convention for monitors and printers (1 inch = 25.4 mm). In this section we derive a resolution range for which to aim in new devices, and compare this to existing display devices and tabletop systems.

Minimum Resolution

A lower bound on the resolution that is required of a display can be defined by experimenting with various types of graphical content. Photographs degrade gracefully as resolution is reduced, but text imposes a hard limit, below which it is illegible.

Text on the Web has typically been displayed using a 10pt or 12pt font [11], and these are also typical font sizes for printed documents. A resolution of at least 2 pixels/mm (48 ppi) has been shown to be required to read 12pt text [2], which corresponds to approximately 60 ppi for 10pt text. Tullis et al. [12] imposed a minimum font size of 6pt on Microsoft Windows. Assuming the default 96 ppi, this is equivalent to a 10pt font at 57.6 ppi, thus roughly agreeing with the previous 60 ppi figure. We will therefore use 60 ppi as a lower limit on the resolution required on a tabletop display.

Maximum Resolution

To define an upper bound on the resolution of a display, one can consider human visual acuity. This results in a resolution above which it is pointless to go, because a human viewer will not be able to tell the difference.

"Normal" human visual acuity is widely taken to be 1.0 arc min [13], that is, a person can discern a grating test pattern when the distance between the lines is 1 arc min (1/60 of a degree). Actually, the acuity of most young observers is somewhat higher, at 0.59 arc min [14]. This angle corresponds to one cycle of the grating, which requires two pixels. Assuming that a tabletop display is used at arm's length, which is approximately 2 ft (61 cm), this leads to spatial resolutions of around 300–500 ppi.

The lower figure of 300 ppi is the standard resolution for professional printing. Note that printers often have higher dots-per-inch (dpi) ratings, because they use halftoning to display grey levels using patterns of binary dots. One might wish to create the ultimate display by matching the upper figure of 500 ppi, but this would probably be a waste of resources because most people would not be able to distinguish such fine detail. This prompts us to consider the desired resolution required for typical content.

Resolution of Monitors

Calculating the desired resolution of a display directly from the limit of visual acuity results in a somewhat excessive resolution. A more realistic one is obtained by matching commonly available computer monitors. Monitors display images via a regular grid of coloured pixels. The actual resolution of a monitor depends on the hardware, and is typically not known automatically by the software. The computer's operating system therefore assumes a certain number of pixels per inch so that it can display items, such as a word processed document, at "life size". Mac OS assumes the print standard of 72 ppi, the X Windows System defaults to 75 ppi or 100 ppi, and Microsoft Windows and Ubuntu Linux assume 96 ppi.

LCD monitors currently (2009) on the market have diagonal sizes of 15–30 inches, and display resolutions between $1,024 \times 768$ and $2,048 \times 1,152$. Resolutions, also known as *dot pitch*, are between 80 and 110 ppi. Rather than go above 110 ppi, manufacturers choose to increase the physical size of the display. We therefore choose 110 ppi as the practical upper limit of resolution that will be useful for a tabletop display, rather than the higher value in the subsection above, which is derived from the limit of human visual acuity.

Resolution of Projectors

The term resolution is used in two ways regarding projectors. One is *native resolution*, which states the number of pixels in the imaging element. The other is the density of pixels on the screen. In this section we will consider only the native resolution, because the pixel density is determined by the throw distance and is therefore dependent on a particular physical configuration.

The two main values that characterize the output of a projector are the native resolution (number of pixels), and the light output (brightness). For creating tabletop displays we are interested in good price-performance for both.

Table 4.1 Common native resolutions of projectors

Name	Width (pixels)	Height (pixels)	Megapixels
SVGA	800	600	0.48
XGA	1,024	768	0.79
WXGA (720p)	1,280	720	0.92
SXGA+	1,400	1,050	1.47
UWXGA (1080p)	1,920	1,080	2.07

The native resolutions available in reasonably priced projectors are dictated by market forces. For a long time the only options were 800 × 600 and 1,024 × 768. Table 4.1 below shows the most popular resolutions that are available now, with their names, width and height in pixels, and resulting number of megapixels. For example, an XGA projector has 1,024 × 768 = 786,432 pixels = 0.79 megapixels.

Figure 4.1 illustrates the relationship between native resolution, brightness, and current (2009) market price, of a representative set of projectors from 20 manufacturers. Almost all the projectors had one of the five native resolutions listed in Table 4.1. The remaining few were near the centre of the distribution, so they were

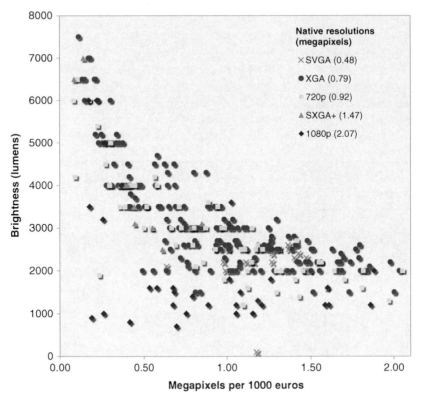

Fig. 4.1 Brightness of projectors against megapixels-to-price ratio. Native resolutions are listed in Table 4.1

omitted to simplify the graph. Brightness of projectors is measured in ANSI lumens [10].

The horizontal axis of Fig. 4.1 indicates the pixel economy of the projectors, with higher numbers of megapixels per 1,000 euros indicating better economy. The concave curve of the points shows that there is a trade-off between projector brightness and pixel economy. To make a good-value high-resolution display, one should use projectors on the right of the graph, which means there is a brightness limit of around 2,500 lm. Until recently XGA projectors offered the best pixel economy. These have now been joined by 720p and 1080p projectors, due to the demand for these resolutions driven by the uptake of high-definition television (HDTV). The graph shows that the most economical projectors, purely in terms if pixels, are the XGA, 720p and 1080p ones, with higher resolutions giving slightly lower brightness.

A native resolution of 1080p has more than twice as many pixels as 720p, and almost three times as many as XGA. Because there is a per-projector overhead in creating a multi-projector display, including the cost of graphics cards, cables, physical space, and calibration complexity, 1080p is a good choice. It provides good pixel economy while minimising the number of projectors. Given that 1080p projectors will be used, the number required to make a tabletop display is then determined by the size of the table and the desired resolution.

Resolution of Existing Tabletops

Table 4.2 below lists some tabletop systems that state their size and resolution attributes in their associated publications. The resolutions are calculated along the diagonal to even out any variation between horizontal and vertical.

The tabletop systems in Table 4.2 have resolutions between 21 and 106 ppi, with most of them below our 60 ppi lower limit. This reflects the fact that most tabletop displays to date have been designed for informal graphical tasks such as photo browsing, or fun tasks, such as simple games, that do not display detailed information. The availability of higher resolutions will allow more serious applications.

Several systems have combined projectors to achieve higher resolutions. Escritoire [24] used overlapping projectors to create a display with a high resolution region near the user for detailed work, and a much larger, low-resolution periphery (Fig. 4.2a, b). Baudisch's focus-plus-context screen [25] achieved a similar result in a vertical form. A system called i-m-Top [19, 26] enhanced this concept by using a steerable projector to create a moving fovea that can follow the user's input (Fig. 4.2c).

T3, the TableTop Toolkit [2], is an open-source software toolkit for creating multi-projector tabletop displays. Figure 4.3a shows a 3×2 XGA projector configuration with a total of 4.72 pixels, as listed in Table 4.1. Figure 4.3b shows an application that exploits the resolution. The DViT tabletop at the University of

Table 4.2 Size and resolution of some tabletop displays. Values are rounded to the nearest integer, excluding megapixels. These displays have between one and six projectors each. The "front/rear" column indicates front or rear projection

Tabletop system	Native (pixels)				Physical (inches)				Res.
	Front/rear	Horiz	Vert	Diag	Horiz	Vert	Diag	Mpxl	(ppi)
DigitalDesk [7]	F	1,120	780	1,365	18	12	22	0.87	63
DigiTable [15]	F	1,024	768	1,280	34	26	42	0.79	30
DViT Table (med. res.) [16]	F	2,048	1,024	2,290	60	48	77	2.10	46
DViT Table (high res.) [17]	R	2,800	2,100	3,500	60	48	77	5.88	63
Escritoire (fovea) [18]	F	1,024	768	1,280	17	12	20	0.79	63
Escritoire (periphery) [18]	F	1,024	768	1,280	48	36	60	0.79	21
i-m-Top (fovea) [19]	R	1,280	720	1,469	12	8	14	0.92	106
i-m-Top (periphery) [19]	R	1,280	768	1,493	47	32	57	0.98	26
InteracTable [20]	R	1,024	768	1,280	33	26	42	0.79	30
Lumisight [21]	R	1,024	768	1,280	16	16	22	0.79	57
Origami [4]	F	1,024	768	1,280	16	12	20	0.79	64
Surface [22]	R	1,024	768	1,280	26	15	30	0.79	43
T3 [23]	F	3,072	1,536	3,435	48	36	60	4.72	57

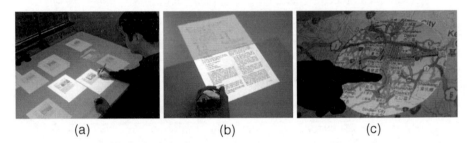

(a)   (b)   (c)

Fig. 4.2 Focus-plus-context tabletop displays. (**a**) Escritoire full view, (**b**) Escritoire fovea, (**c**) i-m-Top fovea

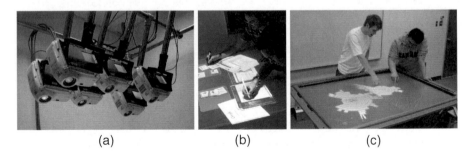

(a)   (b)   (c)

Fig. 4.3 Tiled tabletop displays. (**a**) Six-projector T3 display, (**b**) collaborative web browsing using WebSurface on T3, and (**c**) four-projector DViT display

Calgary [16] tiled two projectors to create a 2.1 megapixel tabletop display, and a second-generation model [17] uses four projectors to create a 5.88 megapixel display (Fig. 4.3c).

Tabletop Resolution Guide

A tabletop display should be a self-contained system where the projectors are driven from a single PC, using the best value projectors to achieve a good price-performance. The analysis of the resolution of projectors above advocates using 1080p projectors, which will have around 2,000 lm. Modern PCs can have four PCI express slots, each of which can hold a graphics card with two digital outputs, allowing eight projectors to be driven from a single PC.

The number of projectors determines the total number of pixels on the display, and the resolution varies as the reciprocal of the size. Figure 4.4 illustrates the relationship between resolution and diagonal size, assuming the display is composed of 1080p projectors. Our minimum and maximum resolutions of 60 ppi and 110 ppi are shown, as are the typical size of various types of tables, such as a small coffee table, or an eight-person conference table. For a small coffee table (30-inch diagonal) one projector is sufficient, three are ample. For a six-person conference table, six to eight projectors are required. Note that the calculations that were used to generate Fig. 4.4 are only based on tabletop area. Given a particular projector aspect ratio, a regular

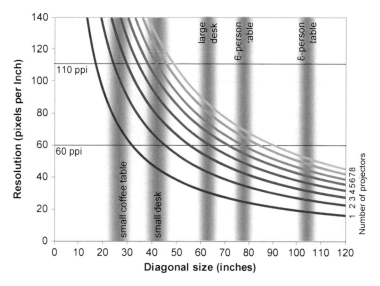

Fig. 4.4 Tabletop display resolution against size, assuming 1080p projectors. The *horizontal lines* show suggested minimum and maximum resolutions. The *vertical regions* show sizes of typical tables

array of projectors, and minimal projector overlap, only certain shapes of tabletop display are actually possible.

A tabletop display should have a resolution of at least 60 ppi to show detailed content, such as text. 110 ppi is a reasonable upper limit. Eight projectors can be driven from a single PC, which allows acceptable resolutions on tabletops up to a six-person conference table. As an example, Fig. 4.4 indicates that a large desk with a diagonal of 60 inches (1.52 m) using eight 1080p projectors will have a resolution of 78 ppi, which is comparable to the lower end of LCD monitor resolutions. The cost of the projectors for this display, using the best-value 1080p projector from Fig. 4.1 with a cost of 1.88 megapixels per 1,000 euros, will be 8,823 euros. This places large high-resolution tabletop displays within the reach of research projects on the applications and interaction techniques suitable for such displays. Consumers will have to wait a bit longer for such devices to become affordable products, but we can work on the software now, in anticipation of the availablility of the hardware.

Multi-projector Display Techniques

Multiple projectors can be combined to create a large high-resolution display, but this requires more than simply placing the projectors next to each other. The projectors must be calibrated so their combined output appears as a single seamless display. Various techniques have been developed over the last decade to address this issue in vertical cinema-style multi-projector displays walls, and many of these can be directly applied to tabletops.

The techniques for calibrating multi-projector displays address two fundamental problems: geometric misalignment and colour variation [10]. When projectors are combined, and are not precisely mechanically aligned, perspective distortion occurs. This can be removed by warping the graphics before displaying them by passing them all through the 3D graphics card, in a process called *geometric compensation*. Colour variation due to variation in output within and between projectors is addressed by *photometric compensation*. These two processes are described below, and between them is a description of *edge blending*, which has both geometric and photometric aspects. This section is concluded with some system issues.

The methods described in this chapter are equally applicable to front and rear projected displays, both of which have been used in various tabletop systems (Table 4.2). Front projection means the space under the display is free, as with a normal table, and can be used with sensing technologies comprising an opaque tablet. Rear projection hides the projectors inside the device to create a more self-contained unit, and avoids occlusion of the projection by the hands of the users. Some of these methods can also be used in tabletops made from other display technologies, such as LCD panels.

Many of the concepts in this section are covered in detail in Practical Multi-Projector Display Design by Majumder and Brown [10]. The interested reader might also want to consult Spatial Augmented Reality by Bimber and Raskar [27], and review the proceedings of the IEEE International Workshop on Projector-Camera Systems (PROCAMS),[1] which started in 2003.

The text below assumes precise meanings for several terms: *characterization* is the measurement of how a device actually performs; *compensation* is the modification of inputs to the device so that the system as a whole behaves as an ideal device; and *calibration* is the combination of the previous two steps.

Geometric Compensation

If a projector is not perfectly aligned to its projection surface, the resulting display will not appear as a perfect rectangle, and will instead be distorted. For a single projector, small distortions are not a problem for people viewing the display, but when projectors are combined their outputs must align precisely with one another. For this reason, multi-projector displays originally required precise and laborious mechanical alignment [9], but now commodity graphics hardware can be used to compensate for the distortions.

Projective Transformation

A projector is the inverse of a camera. It contains an imaging element and a lens, but the light travels out rather than in. By assuming central projection, the model of a pin-hole camera, we can compensate for the distorting effects of oblique projection by taking the original image to be displayed, and warping it before it is projected [28].

If the projection surface is flat, two-dimensional (2D) points in the projector correspond to 2D points on the surface, and the relationship between these two sets of points is a projective transformation which can be represented by a planar homography [29]. Geometric compensation is achieved by applying a homography to the original image, using the equation

$$\mathbf{x}' = \mathbf{H}\mathbf{x}, \tag{1}$$

where $\mathbf{H}$ is a 3×3 matrix and the vectors $\mathbf{x}'$ and $\mathbf{x}$ are two-dimensional points in homogeneous form [29]. Different forms of matrix H produce different types of transformation (Fig. 4.5).

Projection from a very acute angle will produce not only geometric distortions, but also differences in focus across the surface. A projective transformation can remove the geometric distortions but the blurring caused by a projector's finite focal depth is more difficult to remove, so this effect should be avoided where possible.

---

[1] http://www.procams.org/

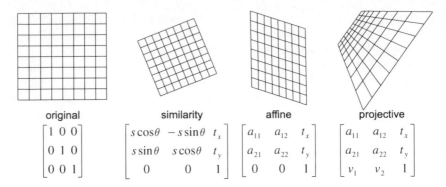

original

$$\begin{bmatrix} 1 & 0 & 0 \\ 0 & 1 & 0 \\ 0 & 0 & 1 \end{bmatrix}$$

similarity

$$\begin{bmatrix} s\cos\theta & -s\sin\theta & t_x \\ s\sin\theta & s\cos\theta & t_y \\ 0 & 0 & 1 \end{bmatrix}$$

affine

$$\begin{bmatrix} a_{11} & a_{12} & t_x \\ a_{21} & a_{22} & t_y \\ 0 & 0 & 1 \end{bmatrix}$$

projective

$$\begin{bmatrix} a_{11} & a_{12} & t_x \\ a_{21} & a_{22} & t_y \\ v_1 & v_2 & 1 \end{bmatrix}$$

Fig. 4.5 Transformations and their homography matrices [29]. Value S is a scale, θ is a rotation angle, and (t_x, t_y) is a translation. The other variables are other degrees of freedom. The *bottom right* element is normalized to 1 because the matrix is defined only up to a scale

Characterisation

In the geometric case, characterisation is also known as registration, and consists of measuring the transformations between various two-dimensional spaces. Ashdown [5] uses four such spaces: device-dependent pen input co-ordinates, device-independent tabletop co-ordinates, pixel locations in the projected image, and pixel locations in the texture on the graphics card. For ease of implementation, registration can be performed by selecting a series of projected points using the pen input device, and then the software can calculate a linear least-squares solution for the homography matrix in equation (4.1). If a calibrated camera is present, calibration of the projector can be performed automatically by projecting patterns such as dots or lines, and using image processing to locate them within the camera image [10].

Graphics Hardware

A very efficient way to perform a projective transformation on a typical computer is to put the original image into a texture on the graphics card, and draw it as a polygon. The transformations in Fig. 4.5 can be performed by manipulating the vertices of a polygon drawn with DirectX or OpenGL [5].

Modern windowing systems such as Windows Aero and Linux Compiz pass all graphical user interfaces through the 3D card, in a process known as *compositing*. When compositing is used, any of the transformations shown in Fig. 4.5 can be added to the transformation stack and performed on all content that is displayed with virtually no extra computational cost.

Even if projective transformations to compensate for projector alignment are not required, using compositing still offers a significant advantage. In particular, because tabletops are horizontal and people can stand around the outside of them, the ability to reorient content to the viewer is necessary. Orientation has been found to be important in collaborative tabletop use, affecting how individuals comprehend information, how collaborators coordinate their actions, and how they mediate communication [30]. The ability to rotate windows has not been required in conventional window managers, so it has not been implemented, and must be added as an extra feature in tabletop interfaces. Compositing allows the use of similarity transformations (Fig. 4.5) to arbitrarily rotate and translate any item, without incurring any extra processing overhead. Other transformations and effects can easily be added, such as scaling, alpha blending, and 3D effects.

Further Methods

Content–Dependent Transformation

Transforming rasterized content reduces the effective resolution of the result, but in some cases it is possible to alleviate the loss by tailoring the transformation to the content being transformed. When the projective transformation for geometric compensation is close to a simple translation, Hereld and Stevens apply a transformation to text that translates individual words separately [31], and Tuddenham and Robinson [32] have used this on a tabletop display.

Nonlinear and Nonparametric Methods

The projective transformation is a simple linear transformation on homogeneous points, and is typically sufficient for compensating for projection onto a planar surface. Other options are piecewise linear transformations [33], in which the screen is divided into a triangular mesh and each triangle is warped independently, and general nonlinear transformations, which can be implemented in the graphics card using fragment shaders [10].

Nonplanar Screens

Tabletop displays are generally planar (flat) surfaces. However, other options are available, such as parametric surfaces. General three-dimensional objects can be augmented with computer graphics via *two-pass rendering* [27] whereby the known 3D shape is first rendered from the viewpoint of the projector, then the result is projected onto the object, but this beyond the scope of this chapter.

Edge Blending

When geometric compensation is used, projectors can be positioned casually and graphics are aligned in software following calibration. In general, the projected images will not be exactly rectangular due to keystoning, and will be partially overlapped to avoid gaps between them. Figure 4.6 shows a typical configuration. The issue here, is that the resulting output will be much brighter in the overlap regions, because more than one projector is contributing.

Fig. 4.6 Arrangement of six projectors. The images are not rectangular, so two or more projectors overlap at some points

Binary Masking

The most obvious solution to this problem is to use only a single projector at any point, with the other(s) displaying black. This is the approach used by Escritoire [5] which displays a small high-resolution *fovea* inside a large low-resolution *periphery*, and simply displays a black rectangle in the region of the periphery that is overlapped by the fovea.

Blending

In T3, which supports tiled arrays of projectors as shown in Fig. 4.6, Tuddenham uses an edge blending technique for multi-projector displays described by Raskar et al. [34] and applies it to a multi-projector tabletop display [2]. For each projector i and two-dimensional pixel location $\mathbf{x}$, an alpha mask $\alpha(i, \mathbf{x})$ is multiplied by the projector's pixel value to obtain its edge-blended value. The values of the masks are constrained by $0 \leq \alpha(i, \mathbf{x}) \leq 1$ and $\sum_i \alpha(i, \mathbf{x}) = 1$, and are defined as

$$\alpha(i, \mathbf{x}) = \frac{dist(i, \mathbf{x})}{\sum_m dist(m, \mathbf{x})}, \qquad (2)$$

where $dist(i, \mathbf{x})$ is defined as the Euclidean distance on the projection surface of point $\mathbf{x}$ from the nearest edge of projector i.

Using this alpha blending approach, the projector arrangement in Fig. 4.6 results in the blending masks in Fig. 4.7. The result is shown in Fig. 4.8.

Further Methods

Smoother Blending Function

The simple linear edge blending function in equation (4.2) can be replaced with smoother one, such as one that has a continuous first-order derivative [35].

Fig. 4.7   Edge blending masks corresponding to the six-projector configuration in Fig. 4.6, from T3 [23]

Projector Brightness Variation

Having the blending functions sum to unity assumes that all projectors have the same brightness, that is, the same white level. This condition can be met, at least approximately, by manually adjusting the brightness of the projectors so they look the same. A more precise result can be obtained by allowing brightness to vary spatially, limited by a perceptual threshold on the gradient. Many projectors leak light when they are displaying black [36], so the black level will be increased in the overlap regions. This can also be addressed using a perceptual uniformity method, or simply by raising the lower limit of all parts of the display. This is a much less severe effect than the increased white level, so only a small amount of contrast need be sacrificed.

Photometric Compensation

Colour output can vary considerably between projectors, which can lead to visible variation over a multi-projector display. Colour matching can be attempted by adjusting the image settings commonly found on monitors and projectors: brightness, contrast, colour balance (between "warm" and "cool"), and individual controls for the red, green, and blue channels. However, these are crude controls, and matching them is a laborious manual process. Photometric compensation methods aim to alleviate this problem. They require an understanding of some colour spaces that are briefly introduced in the subsection below.

Additive Colour

Projectors, like monitors, use additive colour. The default colour of the display surface is black, light is added by the projector to display a pixel, and the light

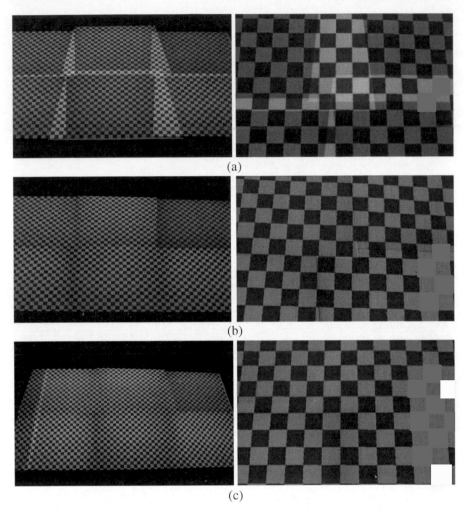

Fig. 4.8 (a) Geometric compensation ensures the *squares line* up, (b) blacking out the overlap region leads to visible seams, (c) using alpha blending the seams are no longer visible

combines additively. Humans see in three-dimensional colour, so displays usually use three primary colours. The standard primaries are red, green and blue (RGB, see Fig. 4.9). A pixel in an image is stored by a computer as an RGB value: a tuple of three numbers between 0 and 1 that are sent to the projector to be displayed.

RGB values are device-dependent. The exact colour of the three primaries varies between projectors, because of variations between manufacturers and models, and also because the output of a projector bulb will vary as it ages [37]. This means that compensation for this variation is necessary.

Fig. 4.9 Additive colour.
Three primaries are used: *red*,
green, and *blue*. All three
together produce white

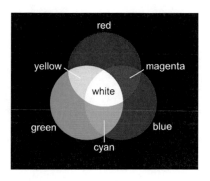

Characterization

To compare the output of multiple projectors we should use a device-independent
colour space, and the standard one is CIE XYZ-space [38]. In an additive colour
space the final colour is a linear combination of the primaries, so to characterize
the range of possible outputs of the projector we need only measure the minimum
and maximum values of each of the primaries, that is, the colour produced by RGB
inputs (0,0,0), (1,0,0), (0,1,0) and (0,0,1). This results in a three-dimensional *gamut*
in XYZ-space (Fig. 4.10a), which is often displayed in two-dimensional xy-space
(Fig. 4.10b), by ignoring luminance, and only considering chrominance (also known
as chromaticity coordinates [38]).

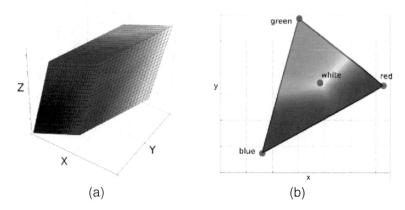

(a)   (b)

Fig. 4.10 Display device colour gamut in (**a**) XYZ-space and (**b**) xy-space

The gamut is a bound on the colours that a device can produce, but it does not
fully define the mapping from RGB input to colour output. The relationship between
each of the RGB channels and the intensity of its associated primary is called its
transfer function. The original computer displays were cathode ray tubes (CRTs),

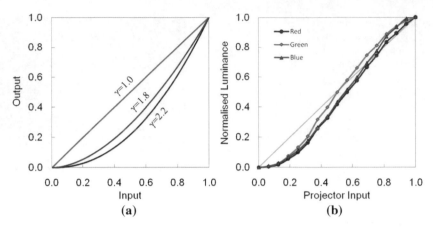

Fig. 4.11 (a) Gamma functions. The *lines* show γ=1.0 (linear), γ=1.8 (used by Mac OS), and γ=2.2 (used by Windows and the sRGB standard). (b) Response measured from a projector with gamma correction

which had gamma curves for transfer functions. That is, the intensity of a pixel I was related to the input value V by

$$I \propto V^\gamma. \tag{3}$$

Different values of γ produce differently shaped curves (Fig. 4.11a). LCD monitors and projectors now emulate the gamma curve, for the sake of backwards compatibility, so measuring the shape of this curve is also required during characterization. Some display devices have a mode designed to linearise their response and emulate $\gamma = 1$, but this may not be sufficient, as shown in Fig. 4.11b, which shows the transfer function of a projector (Sanyo LP-XP45) measured with a colorimeter (Minolta CS-100). The curves for the three primaries are more linear than a typical gamma curve, but still noticeably curved at the top and bottom.

In addition to a per-projector gamut and transfer function for each RGB channel, Majumder and Stevens measure the maximum luminance achievable at each pixel on the display, so spatial variation can be removed [39]. The luminance is generally higher near the centre of a projected image than at the side, and much higher where projectors overlap.

The full photometric characterization can be measured using a calibrated camera. An uncalibrated camera can also be used, given some assumptions about the response of the camera.

Compensation

The response of each projector is linearised by inverting the transfer functions. For each RGB channel there are only 256 possible inputs, so the inverted function is stored in a lookup table.

Intra-projector variation in RGB primaries can be addressed using a colour mixing matrix: a 3×3 matrix multiplied by the original RGB values. This can be chosen to match all the projectors to a device-independent colour standard like sRGB, or just to match the projectors with each other.

The spatial variation of maximum achievable luminance can be addressed by applying a luminance attenuation map [39] to darken parts of the display that are too bright. This is implemented in the same way as the edge blending masks previously introduced (Fig. 4.7), and the two methods can be combined. To avoid wasting projector luminance, the limit of contrast sensitivity in human vision can be exploited to allow display brightness to vary spatially without the user's noticing [40].

Further Methods

Irregular Gamuts

Some DLP projectors use a colour wheel with a white component in addition to the red, green, blue components. This boosts the lumens rating of the projector at the expense of distorting the gamut from the parallelepiped in Fig. 4.10a to a more complex shape [36]. This could be addressed with more complex colour matching, or by sacrificing the extra brightness.

Intra-Projector Variation

The compensation method described above assumes that it is only a projector's luminance that varies spatially, which is a good approximation when using a dedicated projection surface [41]. If projectors are used to create a display on a patterned wall or table, compensation for the pattern can be implemented by using a spatially-varying gamut [42].

Content-Dependent Compensation

The luminance attenuation maps described in the Compensation section hide the spatial variation in display brightness at the expense of some loss of contrast. The greatest possible contrast can be attained by allowing luminance clipping, bounded by a perceptual threshold, and performing content-dependent compensation [43]. However, a case must be made to justify this trade-off of computational complexity for display contrast.

System Integration

Tabletop displays have a different emphasis from typical multi-projector display walls in that they ought to be smaller, cheaper, more manageable systems. All of the geometric and photometric techniques described above can be implemented in a commodity 3D graphics card. PC motherboards are now available with four PCI-express slots, so with two digital outputs per graphics card, eight projectors can be driven from a single PC, which is enough even for a large multi-user tabletop display (Fig. 4.4).

Managing Multiple Graphics Cards

Current graphics cards now commonly have a gigabyte of memory, but even that large amount must be managed carefully if many high-resolution tiles (the tabletop display's analogue of windows) are to be stored as textures. Also, graphics card drivers may limit textures to sizes such as 1,024 × 1,024 or 2,048 × 2,048 pixels.

T3 splits a large tile into smaller sections, stores the sections in separate textures, and draws them as an array of polygons [2]. The textures are only stored on the graphics cards on which the corresponding sections are currently visible, thus reducing the memory requirements, and the time to update the textures when the tile content changes. This happens transparently to the user of the toolkit, freeing the application programmer from such considerations, and presenting a single large display device that supports tiles of any size.

Synchronisation of the updates of all projectors is also required. T3 addresses this simply by first preparing the double-buffered output for all projectors, then switching all of the buffers as quickly as possible. In practice synchronisation has not been a problem.

Rendering Performance

Modern graphics cards are designed to render thousands of texture mapped polygons per second, so they can easily handle projective transformations with almost no latency, or load on the CPU. The performance of T3 was tested with 200–800 tiles, with approximately 10,000 pixels each, being continuously transformed and redrawn on a four-projector display. This resulted in between 32 and 22 frames per second (fps). The Buffer Framework [44] also addresses this issue, and achieves similar performance [45].

Graphics cards are optimised for drawing many textured polygons, but not as optimised for updating those textures. T3 achieves 20 fps while updating a 1 megapixel texture spanning four projectors without compression. As in any graphical interface, it is good practice to design screen repainting code to only repaint what has changed.

Further Methods

Distributed Rendering

Chromium [46] intercepts OpenGL calls to present an existing application on a multi-projector display wall. However, scene complexity is generally not an issue for tabletop displays because the number of polygons is small, and it is desirable to perform all the rendering on a single PC, so distributed rendering should not be necessary.

Distributed Calibration

The iLamps of Raskar et al. [47] are a combination of a projector with a camera, wireless networking, a tilt sensor, and onboard computing, to form devices that calibrate with each other to create an ad-hoc multi-projector display. If such devices were mass produced, they could be used to create a large high-resolution display without the need for a high-end PC to drive it.

High-Resolution Input

Touch input is suitable for casual applications such as photo browsing, but basic input with the fingers is rather imprecise. If detailed work such as military command and control using maps is to be performed on a tabletop, more precise input is required. This can be provided in two ways: enhance touch input with new interaction techniques; or put a tool in the user's hand to provide more precision, with the most obvious tool being a pen. Another option for input is tangible interaction, that is, the interaction of multiple physical objects with the tabletop display. That is not discussed here because it is the focus of Chapters 7 and 8. Touch input technology will not be covered here because it is described in detail in Chapter 2. Issues with touch input are mentioned briefly, followed by the technology and issues of pen input.

Touch Input Issues

Fingers are not very accurate for pointing on high-resolution displays. This is because of two issues. The first is occlusion. The finger is often wide compared to the items being manipulated, so information is occluded in what is known as the "fat finger problem". The second issue is precision. On a mouse pointer, the exact point of interaction, at the tip of the arrow, is obvious, but the location of the "hot spot" within the area of a finger is not so obvious. These two problems increase as display resolution increases. Various approaches have been developed, particularly for small mobile devices, and they can be adapted for tabletop displays. Chapter 11 describes the problems and potential remedies.

Pen Input Technology

People practise writing and drawing with pens from an early age. This type of natural free-form input has long been available on desktop and handheld computers.

Below is a list of technologies that allow input with a pen, also known as a stylus, on a tabletop display.

Acoustic

Acoustic devices emit ultrasound from the stylus which is detected by microphones in a bar along the side of the display. Mimio is such a device. It is relatively inaccurate and is designed only to track a single stylus at a time [5], but it can easily be added to an existing display simply by attaching the bar with the microphones. Multiple bars and styli have been combined to form a very large pen-input surface [48].

Electromagnetic

Various sizes of electromagnetic tablets are available, from the graphics tablets by Wacom, to the large-format "digitisers" by GTCO CalComp which have sizes up to 60 × 44 inch (74-inch diagonal). These devices provide accurate positioning and robust hardware, but they are large expensive devices and are only suitable for front-projection. They have been used in several tabletop displays [5, 2]. N-trig has recently released a display overlay that combines capacitive multi-touch input with an electrostatic pen, which has important implications for tablet computers, and possibly tabletops.

Optical Pen

Anoto pens use a camera inside the stylus to detect its position on a surface printed with a special dot pattern. This provides high accuracy and precision. The coordinates are streamed over Bluetooth, and multiple styli can be used concurrently. Haller et al. [49, 50] demonstrated a front-projected tabletop interface using these pens, and they were also used in T3 [23]. Recently these pens have been combined with rear projection and FTIR touch input [51]. This technology provides an economical way to make a surface of any size with any number of pens, although the hardware required in the pens makes them fairly bulky and requires them to be recharged regularly.

Lateral Cameras

SMARTBoard DViT overlays, designed for wall displays, use infra-red LEDs and cameras mounted at the table edge to provide sensing over a large area [52] and have been used in several tabletop systems [16, 17]. They can support one touch reliably, and two maximum. The overlay is added to an existing display, or incorporated into the bezel around the edge. It works equally well for pen or finger, but it is not as accurate as the graphics tablet or digital pens listed above. A limitation is that the user must not lean on the surface, or put any objects on it, because this obscures the cameras.

Rear Camera

InfrActables [53] uses a camera behind a rear-projection screen to track multiple pens. The pens signal their id and state to the camera using a binary code from an LED in the tip. MightyTrace [54] replaces the single camera with an array of infrared sensors, which allows the technique to be used in an LCD panel in a similar manner to how ThinSight [55] allows touch input on an LCD panel. There is more information about InfrActables and MightyTrace in Chapter 3.

6DOF Tracking

Six-degree-of-freedom tracking provides continual updates for the pose of a tracked device: three distances specify a position, and three angles an orientation. Ashdown used a Polhemus FastTrak to provide remote pointing for linked tabletop and wall displays [5]. Parker et al. [56] studied the efficiency of, and preference for, different pointing methods. Pointing from a distance allows users to interact with both close and distant items on a tabletop display without having to change modes or devices. To interact with a close object the user simply touches the stylus to the table. A disadvantage of the Polhemus technology is that it uses a magnetic field for tracking, so it is affected by metal objects and its accuracy degrades as the distance between the emitter and stylus increases.

Pen Input Issues

Although mouse, touch, and pen input are, at their most basic, simply ways to point to positions on the display, they allow different types of interaction, which affects the design of interfaces.

   Using a pen instead of touch input largely solves the problem of precision, but some occlusion remains. The hand holding the pen can occlude information near the pen, depending on whether the user is left or right handed. A conventional scrollbar on the right may be problematic for a left-handed user, who needs to reach across to use it, thus occluding the information that is being scrolled. A conventional pop-up menu that appears to the bottom right of the cursor may be problematic for a right-handed user, because it appears underneath the user's hand. A pen-based interface should take account of occlusion by the hand, and could benefit from knowledge of which hand is being used, if this can be detected automatically. Brandl et al. [57] have implemented a circular menu that avoids occlusion by rotating automatically based on the positions of the hand and pen.

   Buxton defines three input device states: *tracking*, *dragging* and *out of range* (OOR) [58]. A conventional mouse has the tracking state, plus one dragging state for each button. Touch input has OOR and tracking states (for each finger). A pen potentially has all three states. The Mimio, DViT, and Anoto mentioned above have the tracking state when they are touching the surface, and the OOR state. The GTCO CalComp digitizers have all three states: tracking is enabled when the pen is within about 2 cm of the surface, and they have multiple buttons giving multiple dragging states. Other tablet technologies may also offer continuous pressure and tilt information in addition to position. The Polhemus 6DOF tracker cannot simply be taken out of range at will, so that state should not be required in any interaction technique.

These differences in device capabilities mean that an interface must be targeted at a specific input type, or adapted to work with a lowest common denominator. For instance, having different effects for "hovering" over an item versus selecting it, as is common with mouse interaction, is not suitable for touch input or some pen input types, because there is no way to distinguish between hovering over an item and selecting it. A conventional graphical user interface ported to a system with touch or pen input may emulate the mouse, but what happens when the device goes out of bounds? Having the mouse cursor stay where it is may cause unwanted hover effects. Having it disappear may trigger unwanted mouse exit events. Similarly, ergonomic differences mean that performance will be different with different input types [59]: entering handwriting is easy with a pen, much more difficult with a finger or mouse.

We offer no ready-made solutions to these problems, but an awareness of the issues will allow them to be considered carefully at the design phase. Moving an application to a tabletop is not simply a matter of displaying an existing GUI on the display device.

Tabletops have typically provided either touch or pen input but not both simultaneously. Future systems should exploit the benefits of both. Guiard provides a model of bimanual action [60] that can inform the design of such input techniques. He gives handwriting as an example of bimanual action: the non-dominant hand successively repositions the paper, and the dominant hand then does all the writing within a relatively small portion of the table. More generally, the non-dominant hand acts first, it acts more coarsely in time and space, and it sets up a frame of reference in which the dominant hand works. Think of threading a needle, or hammering a nail. Brandl et al. [61] have embodied these ideas in a set of principles for two-handed input, and implemented some specific techniques that combine pen and touch input. We believe that, like multi-touch, pen-plus-touch calls for more research on interaction techniques, and convergence on interface conventions just as has occurred with graphical user interfaces controlled with a keyboard and mouse.

Future Trends

This section lists our predictions for the future of high-resolution interactive displays.

Smaller Cheaper Projectors

It seems that projector native resolutions will remain at 1080p (1,920×1,080 pixels) for now, because this is the standard for high-definition television. Projectors have steadily been getting cheaper and smaller for many years, and several manufacturers are now producing *pico projectors*, which are about the size of a mobile phone, and easily fit in a pocket. These devices use LEDs or lasers as the light source, and although native resolutions are not up to 1080p yet, they are increasing. Moreover, laser projectors do not use traditional optics and can be made with an infinite focal depth, thus removing focussing problems for short-throw and tilted surfaces. This continues the trend that is making multi-projector displays more convenient and economical.

Vector Graphics

Graphics displayed on tabletops are typically prepared in an off-screen raster image, and then subjected to one of the transformations shown in Fig. 4.5 to scale, reorient, and perform geometric compensation. This resampling causes aliasing, and reduces the effective resolution of the display. Systems should transition to specifying graphics in a vector format like postscript, display postscript, Cairo,[2] or SVG. They will then be able to combine all necessary transformations into a single stack, and perform rasterisation in a single step.

Flat Panels

Projectors are currently useful for building tabletop displays in order to investigate the technical details, individual use, and collaborative use of tabletop displays. However, they make the systems unwieldy because of the throw distance required for projection, so before tabletop displays become mass-market products, the projectors should be replaced by flat panels.

Lambda Table [62] is an example of a tabletop display composed of an array of LCD panels. Figure 4.12 shows that in this case the seams between the panels are very apparent, but the technology already exists to increase the visual area of such panels using a special lens so that they can be abutted with no visible seams.

In future, LCD panels will be replaced by organic light-emitting diode (OLED) displays, which have a better brightness, contrast, and colour gamut than LCDs, or by electrophoretic displays, which have much lower power consumption and can be viewed under bright light.

Some of the techniques described in the section on multi-projector displays will still be applicable to tabletop displays composed of flat panels. Geometric transformations will be required to reorient content for multiple users, colour calibration may be required when multiple panels are used, and rendering will probably still be distributed over multiple graphics cards.

---

[2] http://cairographics.org/

(a)   (b)

Fig. 4.12 A variant of Lambda Table [62]. (**a**) Multiple panels form a tabletop display. (**b**) Objects are tracked to create a tangible user interface. Images courtesy of Jason Leigh

Combined Sensors and Displays

Current systems typically combine separate input and output technologies to form an interactive tabletop display: either front projection with an off-the-shelf input device, or rear projection with FTIR. Future systems will combine input and output into a single self-contained device, as has been prototyped in ThinSight [55] and MightyTrace [54]. Ideally, each pixel of the display will provide both input and output, possibly by augmenting the conventional red, green, and blue components of each pixel with two more: an infra-red emitter and an infra-red sensor. The challenge will then be to create table-sized versions of these devices, or make ones with no bezels so they can be tiled to cover large areas.

Combined Touch and Pen

The ease of touch should be combined with the precision of pen input. This will allow interactions like the use of paper on a traditional desk, and will allow users to exploit the naturalness and efficiency of bimanual interaction.

Conclusion

Tabletop displays have typically provided low resolution output, which has limited the applications that have been possible. Resolutions between 60 and 110 ppi are desirable, but many of the systems listed in Table 4.2 are below 60 ppi.

Most tabletop displays have been made using projectors, and the most economical native resolution for projectors has now improved from $1,024 \times 768$ to the HDTV standard of $1,920 \times 1080$, which provides slightly over 2 megapixels per projector. This means that one or two projectors are sufficient to create a high-resolution coffee-table-sized display, and four are sufficient for a large desk.

Various techniques that have been developed for multi-projector display walls are directly applicable to front or rear projected tabletop displays, making it possible to tile projectors seamlessly. The most useful and practical of these are: geometric compensation using projective transformations to align the images from multi projectors; edge blending using a simple alpha function to hide the overlaps between projectors; and photometric compensation for inter-projector variation. Over time, tiled projectors will be superseded by tiled flat panels that support both input and output, but some of multi-projector techniques described here will still be applicable. For example, applying transformations to reorient content for multiple users will be necessary.

The switch to high-resolution output also prompts the use of more accurate input, which could be achieved by augmenting touch with techniques to tackle occlusion and precision, or by adding pen input. We believe that touch and pen input should be combined for bimanual action because they are complementary.

References

1. Czerwinski M, Smith G, Regan T, Meyers B, Robertson G, Starkweather G (2003) Toward characterizing the productivity benefits of very large displays. In: Proceedings of the IFIP Interact 2003, IOS Press, Amsterdam, pp 9 16
2. Tuddenham P (2008) Tabletop interfaces for remote collaboration. PhD thesis, University of Cambridge, Technical Report UCAM-CL-TR-734, December 2008
3. Wellner PD (1993) Interacting with paper on the DigitalDesk. Communications of the ACM 36(7):87–97
4. Robinson P, Sheppard D, Watts R, Harding R, Lay S (1997) A framework for interacting with paper. In: Proceedings of the Eurographics '97, vol 16, Budapest, Hungary, http://www.cl.cam.ac.uk/research/origami/Origami1997c/
5. Ashdown M (2004) Personal projected displays. PhD thesis, University of Cambridge, Technical Report UCAM-CL-TR-585
6. Robinson P (1995) Virtual offices. http://www.cl.cam.ac.uk/~pr10/publications/rsvr95.pdf, Proceedings of the royal society discussion meeting on virtual reality, July 1995, British Telecom Publication number SRD/R5/1
7. Wellner PD (1994) Interacting with paper on the DigitalDesk. PhD thesis, University of Cambridge Computer Laboratory, Technical Report UCAM-CL-TR-330
8. Bishop G, Welch G (2000) Working in the office of "Real Soon Now". IEEE Computer Graphics and Applications 20(4):76–78
9. Li K, Chen H, Chen Y, Clark DW, Cook P, Damianakis S, Essl G, Finkelstein A, Funkhouser T, Housel T, Klein A, Liu Z, Praun E, Samanta R, Shedd B (2000) Building and using a scalable display wall system. IEEE Computer Graphics and Applications 20(4): 29–37
10. Majumder A, Brown MS (2007) Practical multi-projector display design. A. K. Peters, MA
11. Bernard ML, Chaparro BS, Mills MM, Halcomb CG (2003) Comparing the effects of text size and format on the readability of computer-displayed Times New Roman and Arial text. International Journal of Human-Computer Studies 59(6):823–835
12. Tullis TS, Boynton JL, Hersh H (1995) Readability of fonts in the Windows environment. In: Proceedings of the CHI' 95 conference companion, ACM Press, New York, pp 127–128
13. Kaiser PK (2009) The joy of visual perception: A web book. http://www.yorku.ca/eye/acuity.htm, accessed 22.06.2009

14. Boff DR, Lincoln JE (1988) Engineering data compendium of human perception and performance. http://www.dtic.mil/dticasd/edc/EDCSec01/e01-0602.html, accessed 22.06.2009
15. Coldefy F, Louis-dit-Picard S (2007) DigiTable: An interactive multiuser table for collocated and remote collaboration enabling remote gesture visualization. In: Proceedings of the PROCAMS 2007, Minneapolis
16. Scott SD (2005) Territoriality in collaborative tabletop workspaces. PhD thesis, University of Calgary
17. Isenberg P, Carpendale S (2007) Interactive tree comparison for co-located collaborative information visualization. IEEE Transactions on Visualization and Computer Graphics 13(6):1232–1239 (Proceedings of Visualization/Information Visualization 2007)
18. Ashdown M, Robinson P (2005) Escritoire: A personal projected display. IEEE Multimedia 12(1):34–42, doi: 10.1109/MMUL.2005.18
19. Hu T, Chia Y, Chan L, Hung Y, Hsu J (2008) i-m-Top: An interactive multi-resolution tabletop system accommodating to multi-resolution human vision. In: Proceedings of the TABLETOP 2008, Amsterdam, The Netherlands, pp 177–180
20. Streitz NA, Geißler J, Holmer T, Konomi S, Müller-Tomfelde C, Reischl W, Rexroth P, Seitz P, Steinmetz R (1999) i-LAND: A interactive landscape for creativity and innovation. In: Proceedings of the CHI '99, Pittsburgh, pp 120–127
21. Kakehi Y, Iida M, Naemura T, Shirai Y, Matsushita M, Ohguro T (2005) Lumisight table: An interactive view-dependent tabletop display. IEEE Computer Graphics and Applications 25(1):48–53
22. Microsoft Surface Datasheet (2008) http://download.microsoft.com/download/2/3/b/23b22-82e-9562-40ee-910c-ad721b57217d/MicrosoftSurfaceDatasheet.pdf, accessed 22.06.2009
23. Tuddenham P, Robinson P (2007) T3: Rapid prototyping of high-resolution and mixed-presence tabletop applications. In: Proceedings of the IEEE TABLETOP 2007, Newport, Rhode Island, USA. pp 11–18
24. Ashdown M, Robinson P (2003) The escritoire: A personal projected display. In: Proceedings of the 11th international conference in central Europe on computer graphics, visualization and computer vision (WSCG 2003), Pilsen, Czech Republic, pp 33–40
25. Baudisch P, Good N, Stewart P (2001) Focus plus context screens: Combining display technology with visualization techniques. In: Proceedings of the UIST 2001, Orlando, FL, pp 31–40
26. Hsiao CH, Chan LW, Hu TT, Chen MC, Hsu J, Hung YP (2009) To move or not to move: A comparison between steerable and fixed regions of high-resolution projection in multi-resolution tabletop systems. In: Proceedings of the ACM CHI 2009, ACM Press, New York, pp 153–162
27. Bimber O, Raskar R (2005) Spatial augmented reality: Merging real and virtual worlds. A. K. Peters, available as a free download from http://www.uni-weimar.de/medien/ar/SpatialAR
28. Sukthankar R, Stockton RG, Mullin MD (2001) Smarter presentations: Exploiting homography in camera-projector systems. In: IEEE Proceedings of the ICCV 2001, IEEE Computing Society, Washington, DC, pp 247–253
29. Hartley R, Zisserman A (2003) Multiple view geometry in computer vision, 2nd edition. Cambridge University Press, Cambridge
30. Kruger R, Carpendale S, Scott SD, Greenberg S (2003) How people use orientation on tables: Comprehension, coordination and communication. In: Proceedings of the ACM GROUP '03, ACM Press, New York, pp 369–378
31. Hereld M, Stevens R (2005) Pixel-aligned warping for multiprojector tiled displays. In: Proceedings of the IEEE Conference on Computer Vision and Pattern Recognition (CVPRW'05), IEEE Computer Society, p 104
32. Tuddenham P, Robinson P (2007) Improved legibility of text for multiprojector tiled displays. In: Proceedings of the PROCAMS 2007, IEEE Computer Society, pp 1–8, doi: 10.1109/CVPR.2007.383464

33. Brown MS, Seales WB (2002) A practical and flexible tiled display system. In: PG '02: Proceedings of the 10th Pacific conference on computer graphics and applications, IEEE Computer Society, Washington, DC, p 194

34. Raskar R, Brown M, Yang R, Chen WC, Welch G, Towles H, Seales B, Fuchs H (1999) Multi-projector displays using camera-based registration. In: Proceedings of the IEEE visualization '99, San Francisco, pp 161–168

35. Harville M, Culbertson B, Sobel I, Gelb D, Fitzhugh A, Tanguay D (2006) Practical methods for geometric and photometric correction of tiled projector displays on curved surfaces. In: Proceedings of the IEEE international workshop on projector-camera systems 2006, New York

36. Stone MC (2001) Color and brightness appearance issues in tiled displays. IEEE Computer Graphics and Applications 21(5):58–66

37. Hereld M, Judson IR, Stevens RL (2000) Introduction to building projection-based tiled display systems. IEEE Computer Graphics and Applications 20(4):22–28

38. Wyszecki G, Stiles WS (1982) Color science: Concepts and methods, quantitative data and formulae, 2nd edition, Wiley, New York

39. Majumder A, Stevens R (2002) Lam: Luminance attenuation map for photometric uniformity in projection based displays. In: Proceedings of the ACM virtual reality and software technology, ACM Press, New York, pp 147–154

40. Majumder A, Stevens R (2005) Perceptual photometric seamlessness in projection-based tiled displays. ACM Transactions on Graphics 24(1):118–139

41. Majumder A, Stevens R (2004) Color nonuniformity in projection-based displays: Analysis and solutions. IEEE Transactions on Visualization and Computer Graphics 10(2):177–188, doi: 10.1109/TVCG.2004.1260769

42. Grossberg MD, Peri H, Nayar SK, Belhumeur PN (2004) Making one object look like another: Controlling appearance using a projector-camera system. In: Proceedings of the CVPR 2004, IEEE Computer Society, Washington, DC, pp 452–459

43. Ashdown M, Okabe T, Sato I, Sato Y (2006) Robust content-dependent photometric projector compensation. In: Proceedings of the IEEE international workshop on projector camera systems (PROCAMS) 2006, IEEE Computer Society, Washington, DC, doi: 10.1109/CVPRW.2006.172

44. Isenberg T, Miede A, Carpendale S (2006) A buffer framework for supporting responsive interaction in information visualization interfaces. In: Proceedings of the 4th international conference on creating, connecting and collaborating through computing (C5'06), IEEE Computer Society, Washington, DC, pp 262–269

45. Miede A (2006) Realizing responsive interaction for tabletop interaction metaphors. Master's thesis, Otto-von-Guericke-Universit¨at Magdeburg

46. Humphreys G, Houston M, Ng R, Frank R, Ahern S, Kirchner P, Klosowski J (2002) Chromium: A stream processing framework for interactive rendering on clusters. ACM Transactions on Graphics 21(3):693–702

47. Raskar R, van Baar J, Beardsley P, Willwacher T, Rao S, Forlines C (2003) iLamps: Geometrically aware and self-configuring projectors. In: Proceedings of the ACM SIGGRAPH 2003, ACM Press, New York, pp 809–818

48. Summet J, Somani R, Abowd G, Rehg J (2002) Interactive walls: Addressing the challenges of large-scale interactive surfaces. Technical Report git-gvu-02-35, Computer Science Department, Georgia Institute of Technology

49. Haller M, Brandl P, Leithinger D, Leitner J, Seifried T, , Billinghurst M (2006) Shared design space: Sketching ideas using digital pens and a large augmented tabletop setup. Advances in Artificial Reality and Tele-Existence 4282/2006:185–196

50. Haller M, Brandl P, Leithinger D, Leitner J, Seifried T (2007) Large interactive surfaces based on digital pens. In: Proceedings of the 10th international conference on humans and computers (HC-2007), University of Aizu, Japan, pp 172–177

51. Leitner J, Powell J, Brandl P, Seifried T, Haller M, Dorray B, To P (2009) Flux: A tilting multi-touch and pen based surface. In: CHI '09 extended abstracts, ACM Press, New York, pp 3211–3216, doi: 10.1145/1520340.1520459

52. Morrison GD (2005) A camera-based input device for large interactive displays. IEEE Computer Graphics and Applications 25(4):52–57, doi: 10.1109/MCG.2005.72
53. Ganser C, Steinemann A, Kunz A (2006) InfrActables: Multi-user tracking system for interactive surfaces. In: Proceedings of the IEEE virtual reality conference, Alexandria, Virginia, USA, pp 253–256, doi: 10.1109/VR.2006.86
54. Hofer R, Kaplan P, Kunz A (2008) Mighty Trace: Multiuser technology on lcds. In: Proceedings of CHI'08, ACM Press, New York, NY, USA, pp 215–218, doi: 10.1145/1357054.1357091
55. Hodges S, Izadi S, Butler A, Rrustemi A, Buxton B (2007) Thinsight: Versatile multi-touch sensing for thin form-factor displays. In: Proceedings of the UIST, ACM Press, New York, pp 259–268, doi: 10.1145/1294211.1294258
56. Parker JK, Mandryk RL, Inkpen KM (2006) Integrating point and touch for interaction with digital tabletop displays. IEEE Computer Graphics and Applications 26(5):28–35
57. Brandl P, Leitner J, Seifried T, Haller M, Doray B, To P (2009) Occlusion-aware menu design for digital tabletops. In: CHI 2009 extended abstracts, ACM Press, New York, pp 3223–3228, doi: 10.1145/1520340.1520461
58. Buxton W (1990) A three state model of graphical input. In: Diaper D et al. (eds) Human-computer interaction – INTERACT '90. Elsevier Science Publishers B.V., North-Holland, pp 449–456
59. Forlines C, Wigdor D, Shen C, Balakrishnan R (2007) Direct-touch vs. mouse input for tabletop displays. In: Proceedings of the CHI'07, ACM Press, New York, pp 647–656, doi: 10.1145/1240624.1240726
60. Guiard Y (1987) Asymmetric division of labor in human skilled bimanual action: The kinematic chain as a model. Journal of Motor Behaviour 19(4):486–517
61. Brandl P, Forlines C, Wigdor D, Haller M, Shen C (2008) Combining and measuring the benefits of bimanual pen and direct-touch interaction on horizontal interfaces. In: Proceedings of the AVI 08, ACM Press, New York, pp 154–161
62. Krumbholz C, Leigh J, Johnson A, Renambot L, Kooima R (2005) Lambda table: High resolution tiled display table for interacting with large visu-alizations. In: Proceedings of the workshop on advanced collaborative environments (ACE), Redmond, Washington

Chapter 5
Optical Design of Tabletop Displays and Interactive Applications

Yasuaki Kakehi and Takeshi Naemura

Abstract Embedded electronic tabletop displays are useful for individual projects or group discussion. Our own approach to tabletop display design centers on our belief that not all information needs to be visualized. Instead, we want to create a natural and intuitive interaction environment that provides information in appropriate ways. To achieve these goals, we believe that an optical design of the hardware can make a new paradigm for novel information presentations and intuitive interactions on the tabletop. For example, when we use a normal screen on the tabletop, the display can show just single image on it. However, by adopting special materials and an optical design, the display can work as a view-dependent display or show images on not only the tabletop screen but also physical objects held over the tabletop. In this chapter, we focus on and describe the novel optical designs under tabletops and interaction design on them.

Introduction

Since embedded electronic tabletop displays are useful for individual projects or group discussions, various researchers have tried to develop the optimal interactive table. There are various approaches to tabletop display design; we believe that not all information needs to be visualized. Instead, it is desirable to create a natural and intuitive interaction environment that provides information in appropriate and discriminate ways.

To achieve these goals, various types of tabletop display software have been proposed. However, we believe that a hardware system optical design can provide a new paradigm for novel information presentations and intuitive interactions on

Y. Kakehi (✉)
Keio University, Fujisawa, Kanagawa 252-8520, Japan
e-mail: ykakehi@sfc.keio.ac.jp

C. Müller-Tomfelde (ed.), *Tabletops – Horizontal Interactive Displays*,
Human-Computer Interaction Series, DOI 10.1007/978-1-84996-113-4_5,
© Springer-Verlag London Limited 2010

the tabletop. In this chapter, various tabletop displays adopting diverse optical systems are described. Then, the possible interactive applications of these systems are introduced.

As examples of functions that optical systems enable, two topics are here targeted:

- View-dependent display for multiple users
- Projection images onto the tabletop physical objects and interactions using them

View-Dependent Display for Multiple Users

The first topic is a display design for multiple users. When used as a shared display for multiple users, the tabletop display should function to present the appropriate information to each user. Kruger et al. examined the fact that orientation of displayed information plays a significant role in the establishment and maintenance of personal and group workspaces [1]. However, since most tabletop displays for multiple users have a single view, there is a problem when people try to share information that has orientations. In other words, the information on the table is meant to be shared among all users, but there is only one privileged direction for viewing the displayed information. In addition, for competition scenarios, such as playing a card game or running a negotiation around a tabletop system, privacy protection is obviously an indispensable requirement. For this purpose, single view tabletop displays are not suitable because all information must be shared all the time and it is difficult to hide information from other players or negotiators. In such cases, tabletop displays need to have the capability to display both private and shared information at the same time.

Some tabletop display software enables the users to rotate the displayed information in either direction so that the information can be easily read and manipulated by everyone around the table. When the tabletop has a single view, this function may be helpful, but sometimes it may be inadequate [1]. As a possible solution to these problems, we considered the concept of providing multiple views on a single common tabletop by adopting optical hardware design.

Tangible Interaction Using Tabletop Physical Objects

The second topic is tangible interactions on the tabletop. A tabletop display system should be easy to use. Usually, physical objects are located on the table and our hands, arms, 3D vision, and ears are used to manipulate these objects and communicate with each other. To realize natural and intuitive input methods in the case of tabletop displays, many systems are capable of manual operation or recognizing the tabletop placement of physical objects for interaction.

To realize such interactions, projector-camera systems are often used; however, most systems attach projectors and cameras above the table, which increases the size of the system. To make the system design more compact and avoid shadow problems caused by top projection, we considered the installation of devices inside the table. By adopting special materials and optical design, the system can sense users' input on the tabletop space while projecting images on the tabletop screen. Moreover, it can show images not only on the tabletop screen but also on physical objects placed on the tabletop.

In this chapter, the optical design under the tabletop systems are described, as well as the interactions on them. First, related works concerning the optical design of tabletop display and interfaces are introduced. Then, we describe details of the design through our previous research.

Background

In this section, works related to the research field of tabletop display and optical designs for interactive displays are introduced.

Tabletop Displays for Multiple Users

In the field of CHI (Computer Human Interaction), CSCW (Computer Supported Cooperative Works), and MR (Mixed Reality), there have been many studies that combine the advantages of computers and tables through the development of table-top displays. When used as a shared display for multiple users, the tabletop display should be able to present appropriate information to each user. In some existing tabletop systems, developers have tried to solve this problem by means of software on a single-view display [1].

As an alternative solution, we contemplated providing multiple views on a single tabletop. Very few tabletop systems are able to show different images to each user surrounding the display. Some systems can provide shared and private views by using additional displays, such as PDA (Carreta [2]) and head mounted displays (Magic Cup [3]). However, when each user has his/her own display, it becomes difficult to share non-verbal modalities such as gestures and lines of sight.

Compared to these previous related works, display systems adopting optical design enables physically single but visually multiple displays.

Interaction Using Tabletop Physical Objects

There are several approaches to displaying images onto tabletop physical objects for intuitive interaction. DigitalDesk [4] and Urps [5] are representative systems, resulting from prior research into how to arrange physical objects on the desktop and how to display images on the physical objects. Shader Lamps [6] and Illuminating Cray [7] are precursors in regard to projecting images not only onto horizontal surfaces but also onto the vertical planes of tabletop objects. These systems use a projector mounted on the ceiling to project images directly onto both the tabletop itself and the objects placed on it. However, this method has the following problems: shadows from the users' hands and other objects obstruct the images, and the amount of equipment required, including the ceiling, is large. Some systems, such as BlockJam [8], display information on small electronic displays embedded in the physical objects. These systems are reliable, but because they require special devices, it is difficult for users to create or modify the objects.

As for the tabletop interaction technology that determines the objects with which the user is interacting, various methods have been developed. Pioneering research of a tangible interface with specialized sensing technologies is found in metaDESK [9] and Sensetable [10]. Compared to other approaches, a camera-based approach allows greater interaction versatility and fits the optical-based systems.

In the next section, several approaches to light control are described.

Optical Design for Emerging Display Technologies

Transparency Control Approach

Some research has applied a time-sharing approach to change the appearance of the screen. The IllusionHole [11] can simultaneously provide 3D stereoscopic images for three or more users moving around the system. By controlling the position of the image drawing area for each user according to the user's viewpoint, each user can see the stereoscopic image pairs in an individual area of the display system with shutter glasses. Single Display Privacyware [12] and Snared Illumination [13] can also provide different images to each user standing around the display. This system rapidly displays multiple images on a single common surface. Users wear shutter glasses that are clear for only a short moment. This allows for collaboration, cooperation, and communication for large and small user groups.

In SecondLight [14], users need not wear any electronic devices. In this system, the shutter device is attached to the tabletop surface. When the shutter is closed, the projection light from the bottom of the table diffuses on the surface. When the shutter is open, the light can pass through the tabletop screen and reach a handheld screen over the tabletop. Multi-layered information is displayed on the tabletop surface and handheld screen in a typical application of this system.

In addition, to controlling the user's view, polarization plates are also often used. In the FairyFinder-table of the Colobockle [15], users normally observe only white light on the tabletop surface. However, when the user holds plates that are made of a polarization material over the surface, hidden images can be seen through the plate. In the tabletop system of Sakurai et al. [16], polarization plates have been utilized as a handheld interface. This system shows projection images on the tabletop surface.

Moreover, when the user wears polarization glasses or holds polarization plates onto the tabletop surface, different projection images can be observed on the common surface.

Light Direction Control Approach

The second approach is controlling light direction using various types of lenses. Lenses are often used for developing 3D displays without wearing glasses.

In the Toshiba flatbed-type auto-stereoscopic display [17], an array of micro lenses is attached to an LCD monitor. This display can show different 3D images depending on the users' viewpoints. The dual view LCD display [18] manufactured by Sharp has also realized a view-dependent display function. In this system, two different 2D images are shown on a common surface depending on the viewpoints.

Another example of a display system that uses optical lenses effectively is a spatial image display. The spatial image is created by a special optical mechanism with a couple of Fresnel lenses and LCD monitors. The user standing in front of the LCD monitor can observe the images virtually projected in the air.

Kato et al. [19] have proposed a new MR system using a spatial image display. The proposed system uses a mirror and optical systems for displaying spatial images. The mirror is placed between two spatial images of virtual objects; one is the front view and the other is the reflected rear view of the objects. It is expected that this configuration is effective for natural viewing of spatial images and the seamless arrangement of physical and virtual objects. In the system of Li-Wei Chan et al. [20], a privacy-enhanced tabletop system was developed using two types of displays, a projection image on the tabletop surface and a spatial image emerging on the tabletop surface. The large tabletop surface is used as a public display, while the spatial image is used to display private information to the user facing the monitor.

The next section introduces our own approach for a tabletop system design using optical mechanisms.

Optical Design for a View-Dependent Display System

Optical Design Using View Control Film

Our approach focused on a view control film. This film controls the transmission of light on the basis of the incident angle. Specifically, the light transmission becomes transparent or opaque depending on the viewing direction. Sumitomo Chemical has developed such a functional film named Lumisty. Figure 5.1 illustrates optical property examples of the currently marketed Lumisty film.

We have developed several types of special tabletop screen systems by combining these films and Fresnel lenses. In our systems, the opaque direction of the screen is utilized as the back-projection screen. When an image is projected onto

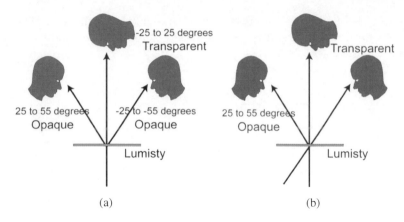

(a)   (b)

Fig. 5.1 Optical properties of lumisty film. (**a**) MFZ-2555. (**b**) MFY-2555

the screen from the opaque direction, it is diffused onto the screen. As one of the characteristics of this projection system, the directions of diffused light are limited and a user can observe the image only when he/she stands in front of the projector.

On the other hand, the screen maintains high transparency in the other directions, while the opaque directions are used for projection. In other words, incoming light in these transparent directions can pass through the screen. These transparent directions can be utilized for sensing user input or image projection toward the space above the tabletop while allowing all electronic devices (e.g., projectors, cameras) to be attached inside the table (see Fig. 5.2).

Figure 5.3 illustrates how the display looks according to the viewing position when a projection light comes from the backside in a diffusive angle. First, note the change in the appearance of the projected image in accordance with a horizontal change in the user's viewing position. As the viewing position moves, the projected white image begins to look gradually dimmer, as shown in Fig. 5.3. Thus, we can say that the display works well inside the range from approximately −10° to +10°. This means that a user can only see the image intended for him/her. Moreover, considering the size of the table and the display, it can be said that this display is capable of corresponding to slight head movements of the users as long as they sit at fixed positions. As for the vertical positions, the range at which the user can see an image properly is much wider than that of the result of horizontal movement. From

Fig. 5.2 A view from a
camera inside the table

Fig. 5.3 Appearance of the display

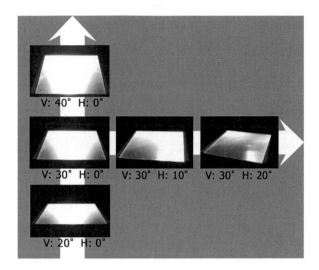

these observations, it is apparent that it is not necessary to consider the effect of the user's height.

In addition, a Fresnel lens is installed below the Lumisty films in this screen system. Since the range of the angle at which the Lumisty film becomes opaque is limited, it is desirable that the projected light be regarded as parallel light rays in order to improve the image quality. With the use of the Fresnel lens, this function can be realized without enlarging the scale of the system.

In this chapter, four types of tabletop display systems using this view-control screen system are introduced. In all of these systems, multiple projectors and cameras are installed inside the table as seen in Fig. 5.4.

(a) Lumisight Table [21]: This system can show different images to each user surrounding the table. Furthermore, hand gestures and tabletop physical objects can be used for interaction.
(b) through the looking glass [22]: This system can show different images to the tabletop screen and the screen in a mirror. A physical object is used for controlling a puck.
(c) Tablescape Plus [23]: This system can interactively show different images both to the tabletop surface and of tabletop physical objects.
(d) UlteriorScape [24]: This system can simultaneously show different images to the tabletop surface and tabletop physical objects. In addition, it works as a view-dependent display.

All these systems have some common characteristics, as follows:

• Users can observe and interactively manipulate images without wearing electronic devices.
• All equipment can be installed inside the table.

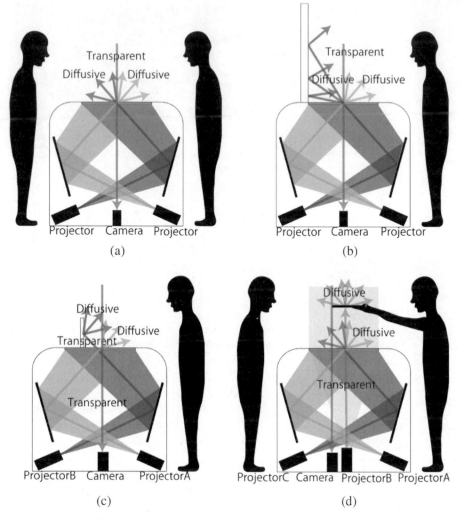

Fig. 5.4 Optical designs of our tabletop display systems. (**a**) Lumisight table. (**b**) Through the looking glass. (**c**) Tablescape Plus. (**d**) UlteriorScape

In the following sections, the detailed designs of each tabletop display and their applications are described.

Lumisight Table: An Interactive View-Dependent Display for Multiple Users

System Overview

The focus of this project is on tabletop displays for multiple users for meetings, gaming, and so on. To facilitate such face-to-face communication and collaboration, various tabletop displays that allow people to share an electronic display on the tabletop have been developed. The tabletop display can be used not only as a personal display, but also as a shared display for multiple users. However, since most tabletop displays for multiple users have a single view, a common problem arises when people try to share information that has a specific orientation.

As a possible solution to this problem, we considered providing multiple views on a single tabletop. In addition, a table-based system should be easy to use. The goal of this project is to provide a versatile platform for various interactive applications among multiple users. Two specific contributions are here presented.

One contribution is to develop an interactive display system that allows users to stay close enough to maintain verbal and nonverbal communication while they are watching their own computer output. For this purpose, we have developed a horizontal tabletop display that is physically single but visually multiple. The system combines these films and a lens with projectors to display four different images, one for each user's view. In addition, appropriate input methods are required for this kind of display media. In the current state of the project, computers can be controlled by placing physical objects on the display or by placing our hands over the display. This screen system also makes it possible to use a camera to capture the appearance of the tabletop from inside of the system.

The other contribution is to develop attractive and specialized applications on the Lumisight Table, including games and applications for CSCW environments. The projected images can be completely different from each other, or partially identical and partially different. Users can share the identical parts as public information, since all the users can see this part of the image. They can still exploit the different parts as private information, since this part is visible to only one user.

Thus, a method for mixed and integrated display of shared and private information on a single screen can be a new paradigm in human–computer interaction. This section describes the mechanism of the Lumisight Table and provides examples of its applications.

Hardware Configuration of Lumisight Table

Figure 5.5 shows the overview of the system. Cameras and projectors are installed under the table. The special screen system allows multiple images to be projected simultaneously.

In order to share one screen with equal visibility, the system should provide different images to every user around the tabletop screen. It is important to realize this function without the use of addition user-wearable devices. The tabletop screen should have a function that filters out image selectively in accordance to each user. In the Lumisight Table, the opaque direction is utilized as the back-projection screen. Several layers of Lumisty film thus allow us to present different images in different directions. Specifically, when four users intend to use the system, two Lumisty films are attached on the Fresnel lens, one film orthogonal to the other (see Fig. 5.5, right).

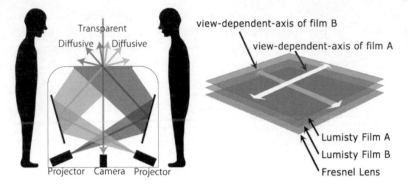

Fig. 5.5 System design (*left*) and screen design (*right*) of lumisight table

As mentioned earlier, the camera inside the system captures manual interactions with real objects. Since the Lumisty film is transparent in a certain direction, the camera inside of the system can capture the images of the tabletop, while projectors present images onto the screen. Moreover, projection of infrared rays and use of retro-reflective materials are effective for recognizing what is happening on the tabletop.

Implementation of Lumisight Table

A prototype system with a square tabletop was developed, intended for the use of four individuals surrounding the table. Presently the scale of the system is 850 mm (Width) × 850 mm (Depth) × 1,050 mm (Height). The screen size is 400 mm × 400 mm. Four projectors and a CCD camera are installed inside the table.

Figure 5.6 shows how the images are seen by each user surrounding the table. Each user can see a similar image but characters in the image are suitably rotated to the user. These images can be completely different from each other. However, they can also be completely identical or partially different. Users can share the identical part as public information; that is, all of the users can see this part of the image. Users employ the different parts as private information, since each of these parts is visible exclusively to one user. For this purpose, four projector images should be geometrically adjusted on the screen.

The camera input can be used to control the system and this system can recognize the existence of hands or physical objects with simple image processing and feed it back to the projected images. Figure 5.7 shows an example scene in which the projected images are controlled by physical objects on the screen.

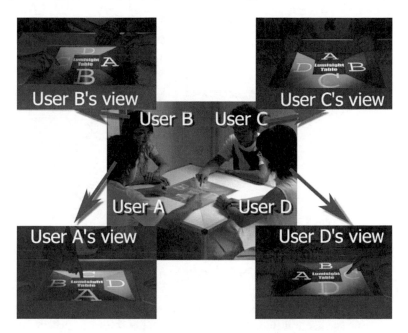

Fig. 5.6 Lumisight table

Fig. 5.7 Interaction with
physical objects

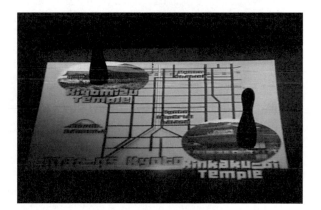

Applications of Lumisight Table

This system can freely control the orientation of the information presented to each
user. In addition to this function, the projected images can also be completely identical with the use of calibration techniques. By utilizing these functions, we have

Fig. 5.8 Map application

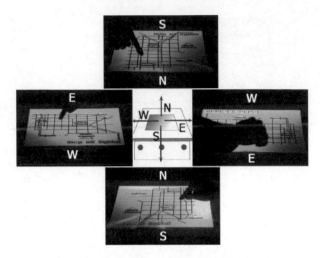

implemented some applications. The projected images can be partially different and each user can see a different image upon a single screen as private information, while all users can share the identical image as public information. Figure 5.8 shows an example of a map application. The map image is the shared public information, while the text and symbols on the map are not. The directions of the text and symbols can be optimized for each user.

When discussing a map, we often point and focus on a certain location. That is, the information on the map becomes the target of our gaze and gestures. As such, map information needs to be held in common. It is displayed in relatively different orientations to all users. On the other hand, site names are displayed with the same orientation to each user, i.e., their absolute orientations are different from one another, so that each user can easily read the names. In addition, when you put a physical object on a shared map, you will see the detailed information of the target location. The detailed information, typically pictures, is displayed in the appropriate position and direction for each user. These features are useful for facilitating cooperative work.

The Lumisight Table makes it possible to create multiplayer video games that can't easily be duplicated on today's video game consoles. Poker is an example of a popular game whose game play is hampered by current interfaces. When playing poker with the Lumisight Table, a player can see his or her own cards but not those of the other players (see Fig. 5.9). The Lumisight Table offers many innovative functions to increase the pleasure of playing games while sharing a single tabletop. In this application, users can choose the cards by putting their hands on the screen. As for chess, physical chess pieces can be manipulated while the Lumisight Table acts as a computerized chessboard on which you can see both a shared public game board and a private display of hints. Gaming is surely an attractive application for the Lumisight Table.

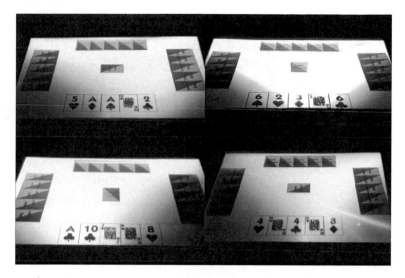

Fig. 5.9 Card game application

Through the Looking Glass

System Description

The Lumisight Table mentioned above is designed for multiple users. However, the function of the view-dependent display could be applied for other purposes. We have developed an interactive art piece named "through the looking glass (TLG)" using this view-dependent display.

The concept of our interactive system named "through the looking glass" is that the user can play against his or her own reflection. It is taken for granted that a looking glass accurately reflects the world in front of it. TLG can overturn this common sense and provide a totally new experience. Please examine Fig. 5.10 carefully. While a projection screen is placed in front of a looking glass, the screen image reflected in the looking glass and the image you see directly on the screen are not symmetrical. Thus, you can interact with your own reflection through the looking glass and the screen images.

In the field of Mixed Reality and Media Art, many research studies and art works have used the metaphor of a looking glass [25, 26]. Most of these systems, however, have not used an ordinary looking glass. For example, some of them use special equipment (e.g., HMD) or a computer display as a virtual looking glass. On the other hand, in our proposed TLG system, another world can be seen through a completely ordinary looking glass without any equipment.

Fig. 5.10 Different images
are observed on the screen

Hardware Configuration

Figure 5.11 (left) illustrates the system design. In order to show different images on
the screen inside and outside of the looking glass, this system employs the mechanism of the Lumisight Table. Two projectors and an infrared camera are attached
underneath the tabletop screen, which is made of a Lumisty film and a Fresnel
lens.

On the horizontal screen beside the vertical looking glass, a user can see only the
images projected from the Projector A. On the other hand, the Projector B is angled
to face the looking glass. The user can see the images from the Projector B reflected
in the looking glass. Thus, the reflected images can be different from what the user

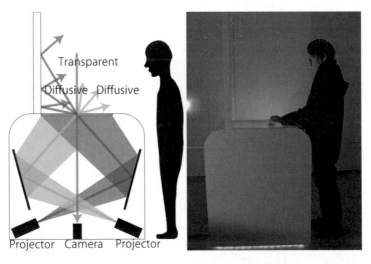

Fig. 5.11 System design of through the looking glass

sees in front of the looking glass. This is accomplished without wearing any special equipment.

In addition, users can control the system by putting real objects on the tabletop. The camera installed in the system captures the images of the tabletop.

Application of Through the Looking Glass

Figure 5.11 (right) shows the system we have developed. This system enables people to experience an entirely new kind of interaction by separating him/herself from his/her reflection in the looking glass. This application uses a set of a square screen and its reflection as a rectangular screen, in which a player plays an air hockey game against his/her own reflection (see Fig. 5.12). A video puck travels back and forth through the looking glass, and the player hits the puck to compete with his/her own reflection. The player has to think quickly enough to control the worlds both inside and outside of the looking glass. If the player hits the puck hard, his/her opponent has to scramble to return it. However, the player is also his/her own opponent; therefore, the player simultaneously wins and loses.

Fig. 5.12 Air hockey application on TLG system

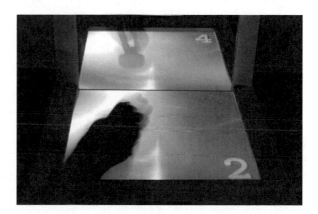

Tablescape Plus: An Interactive Table Theater Using Physical Objects

System Description of Tablescape Plus

A table is a versatile tool with a unique characteristic: it provides a surface where people can place physical objects. To offer intuitive and fluid interaction, tabletop displays must support this familiar practice. Since many interactive systems use the placement of physical objects on a tabletop as an input tool, there are several methods for sensing their positions. For the purpose of human-centered tabletop computing, however, more attention should be paid to the objects themselves.

When a tabletop physical object is used as an interface device, there are at least two requirements to be met: identifiability and versatility. Identifiability means that the object's form and function can be easily distinguished. To meet this requirement, the appearance of the object should have a concrete meaning. Versatility requires that the object should be applicable for different situations. To meet this requirement, the design of the object needs to be flexible and convey several meanings. It is difficult to satisfy these two requirements simultaneously.

To solve this problem, we consider using tabletop objects as an input tool while incorporating a projected image on the table for information display. The projected images have concrete meanings, which make it easy to see and understand the object's current purpose. In addition, by changing the projection image, the same object can be used as a tool in multiple and different situations. Small electronic devices may be used as this kind of object. However, we believe that for human-centered tabletop computing, the object should be as simple as possible, like a small-sized screen without electronic structure.

This section introduces the system, Tablescape Plus, which we implemented based on the considerations described above. Tablescape Plus can project different images onto both a table surface and vertical objects. We also achieved interactivity on Tablescape Plus by means of computer vision methods to recognize objects placed on the tabletop. The following section describes the optical design of Tablescape Plus, an input method that uses marker recognition.

System Configuration and Implementation

The system is designed so that all of the devices can be installed inside a table (Fig. 5.13). Because of this feature, the system is compact in size and reduces occlusion by the users' hands. For this purpose, we have developed a tabletop screen system that selectively filters out images according to the projection orientation.

Figure 5.3 shows the relevant optical property of the Lumisty film used in Tablescape Plus. It is diffusive from one privileged direction and has high transparency to incoming light from other directions. This feature is exploited for Tablescape Plus' special screen system and diffusive direction is utilized for the tabletop screen. As shown in Fig. 5.13, an image from projector A diffuses onto this screen, and consequently, the user can see the image on the tabletop. Furthermore, by projecting images from the transparent direction, this system can also show images on the surface of vertically placed objects.

In order to capture the users' interaction with physical objects, we installed two cameras inside the system. Since Lumisty film is transparent from a vertical direction, cameras inside the system can capture the images on the tabletop at the same time as the projectors display the images on the table's surface.

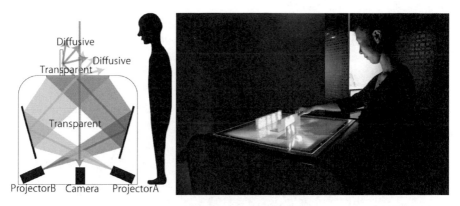

Fig. 5.13   System design of tablescape plus

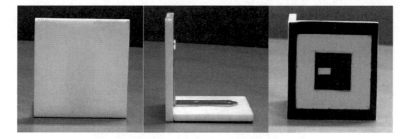

Fig. 5.14   Basic structure of the tabletop object

Figure 5.14 shows the basic structure of a tabletop object, which consists of a vertical screen and a paper marker attached on the bottom surface. To efficiently detect markers, an infrared light was installed at the bottom of the table oriented toward the tabletop and a filter was placed around it to shut out the visual light on each camera. Furthermore, a retro reflective material was utilized for the paper marker in order to reflect the infrared light. Consequently, the marker region appears brighter to the cameras than the other regions. In addition, the ARToolKit Library [27] is used to recognize the position, orientation, and ID of each marker.

Applications of Tablescape Plus

Tablescape Plus holds a lot of potentialities to open up new type of tabletop interactions. This section shows just three examples of future applications to demonstrate its significant advantage in human-centered computing.

Digital Kiosk Application

Tabletop vertical objects are useful for displaying supplemental information on a
horizontal tabletop image. In this application, the initial tabletop screen display is a
map of a city. By placing vertical objects on the image, users can see additional photographs or weather forecasts related to the mapped region, as shown in Fig. 5.15a.

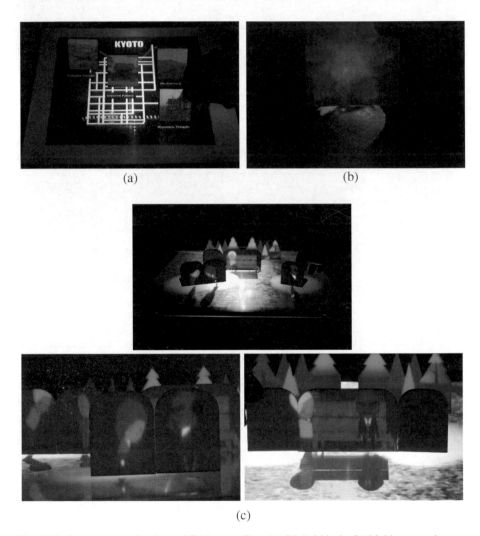

(a)   (b)

(c)

Fig. 5.15 Interactive applications of Tablescape Plus. (**a**) Digital kiosk. (**b**) Multi-aspect viewer.
(**c**) Tabletop theater

Multi Aspect Viewer Application

A tabletop vertical object can also be useful for intuitive viewing of different aspects of complex data displayed on the horizontal tabletop display. In this application, the user can see various cross-sections of solid objects, such as fruits, when he or she slides a tabletop object over the plane view initially displayed on the tabletop screen. As shown in Fig. 5.15b, the cross section images change according to the position of the tabletop object.

Tabletop Theater Application

A tabletop upstanding object can also provide an amusing way to control the table-top world, as in the tabletop theatre application. As seen in Fig. 5.15c, the tabletop screen initially displays a miniature park. When the user adds vertical objects to the scene, animated characters appear on them. The user can control the characters and tabletop theater by physically moving the objects. The actions of these characters change according to the positional relationship between each character as well as their motion. A character walks according to the moving direction of a screen object. When the users bring two characters close together, they start chatting. Furthermore, we have implemented other character behaviors in the tabletop theater application.

UlteriorScape: Interactive Optical Superimposition on a View-Dependent Tabletop Display

System Description

As mentioned above, in Tablescape Plus, tabletop objects could serve as miniature displays as well as input tools. However, Tablescape Plus was designed for single users because of its optical hardware design. With UlteriorScape, introduced in this section, multiple users can access their own object displays simultaneously, because, as in the Lumisight Table, UlteriorScape is capable of view-dependent multi-user interaction.

The main features of UlteriorScape are as follows:

- This system can simultaneously show separate images on tabletop and handheld screens.
- Cameras installed inside the table recognize the positions of handheld screens or placed objects, so their placement can be used for input.
- This tabletop display also works as a view-dependent display, allowing users around the table to see different images on the table or on inclined surfaces of a triangular tabletop object.

In this section, the hardware design and implementation of UlteriorScape is explained and examples of some of its interactive applications are presented.

Hardware Design

In order to elucidate how the functions mentioned above were achieved, we have divided the explanation of UlteriorScape's hardware design into three parts.

To display images on the screens held over the tabletop, a special projection system was developed. Figure 5.16 shows the basic configuration of this system, which utilizes at least two internal projectors, a layer of Lumisty film, and a Fresnel lens. The transparency or opacity of the Lumisty film depends on the angle at which light strikes it. By projecting light at an oblique angle, the opaque Lumisty film can be used to turn the table into a back surface projection screen. The user then sees the image from the projector (Projector A) on the table's surface. By placing a second projector (Projector B) that shines perpendicular to the tabletop inside the table, we can pass an image through the table's surface, and have it diffuse on a handheld screen. Thus, users can see different images on the tabletop screen and the handheld screens simultaneously (Fig. 5.16, right).

The Fresnel lens was added to improve the clarity of the projected images. While the Fresnel lens improves the quality of Projector A's image, the image from Projector B also benefits from the aligning properties of the Fresnel lens because the handheld image remains consistent even as the user raises or lowers the screen object.

The special characteristics of the Lumisty film were also used to locate tabletop objects. As shown in Fig. 5.17, upright cameras installed inside the table can capture the tabletop scene since perpendicular light rays pass through the filmed surface. When a paper marker is attached to the bottom of an object, the system can identify the object and determine its position and rotation. The marker tracking software for this current implementation uses the ARToolKit Library.

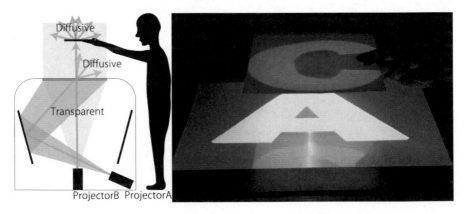

Fig. 5.16 Hardware for optical superimposition

Fig. 5.17 Camera system

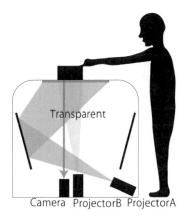

UlteriorScape was designed to accommodate the needs of multiple users. To accomplish this innovation, we designed a mountain-shaped triangular object, which can display separate images on each side (Figs. 5.18 and 5.19). With paper markers attached to the mountain's base, this system can track the object's movements in real-time. When a third projector (Projector C) is added, the tabletop can also be turned into a view-dependent display. The principle of view-dependent image projection is the same as the principle of the Lumisight Table. In the current implementation, this system was designed for two users. However, in principle, it can be adapted for more users. For example, by installing two more projectors at different angles, this table can show different images toward four directions.

Interactive Applications on UlteriorScape

The hardware for UlteriorScape has been implemented with a screen size 50 cm^2. In addition, several interactive applications that demonstrate the capabilities of UlteriorScape have already been developed. The first applications that will be

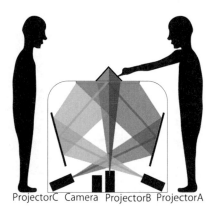

Fig. 5.18 System for
multiple users

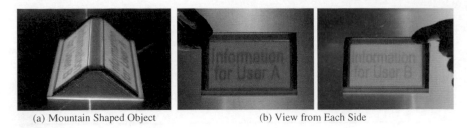

(a) Mountain Shaped Object   (b) View from Each Side

Fig. 5.19 View-dependent image projection

discussed are for single users using flat handheld screens. The second set of applications is designed for multiple users using mountain-shaped objects.

Single User Application

As mentioned above, this system can show separate images on the tabletop display and handheld screens. When related information is projected from each projector, the handheld screen works as a window to additional detail. Figure 5.20 shows an example of this application. The user designates which portions of the aerial photograph will appear in the map view by placing paper screens over parts of the image. In this application, sensing devices, such as cameras, are unnecessary. Users can interact with tabletop images just by holding screens of any shape or size. This simple interaction is suitable for educational tools and a digital kiosk.

Our second application uses camera input and flat handheld screens. This "Pick up and Move" application, allows users to look at digital photos in the same way they would analog photographs. Setting the screen object on the tabletop causes the tabletop photo image under the covered area to be copied onto the screen object. Users can then move and look at the picture from any angle they desire (Fig. 5.21).

Fig. 5.20 Map application

Fig. 5.21 "Pick up and Move" application

Multi-user Applications

As an example of a multi-user application, Fig. 5.22 depicts a multilingual digital kiosk. This application is designed for two users reading different languages. Each user can see identical map information on the horizontal tabletop display. When the users put a mountain-shaped object on the map, the place names appear in the appropriate language on each side of the object.

Figure 5.23 shows a tabletop theater application. Different character images are projected on each side of the triangular shaped objects. For example, when one user sees the front side image of the character on an object, the other user can see the backside of the character on it. In addition, users can control the characters with intuitive manipulations.

Fig. 5.22 Multilingual digital kiosk

Fig. 5.23 Tabletop theater application

Future Trends

So far, we described several interactive tabletop displays adopting optical designs. By adopting the optical design approach, various types of image presentations are realized. However, the possibilities of this approach are not limited on the tabletop display. In this section, we mention the future visions of this approach.

Recently we have tried to adopt optical designs not only for tabletop displays but also other targets around tables. For example of future trends on this research field, we introduce several types of tangible interfaces. By utilizing special materials on tabletop physical objects, tabletop interactions get more sophisticated. For example, we introduce two tangible interfaces working on our view-control screen systems. One is a transparent tangible interface [28]. The other one is a tangible interface with force distribution sensing [29]. In these systems, we utilized transparent heat insulating film as a marker for vision tracking.

Transparent Tangible Interfaces

When tabletop images are controlled using physical objects, inconveniences may result, such as the following:

- Physical objects equipped with electronic devices, markers, etc. restrict user's natural interactions.
- Physical objects placed on the surface of the table obstruct the view of the image on the display.

To resolve these problems, a transparent tabletop interface is proposed. Based on the technology of the view control screen system, a transparent tabletop interface for multiple users is presented, with the features listed below:

- The interface appears transparent to the users around the table, so the image on the tabletop screen is not obstructed.

- The camera installed inside the table can recognize the positions of the objects, so their placement can be used for input.

To implement objects that are invisible to the user but can be detected by the camera, this system uses a transparent heat insulating film that allows visible light to pass but absorbs light in the infrared region, so an infrared camera can recognize them.

The configuration of this system is illustrated in Fig. 5.24 (right). First, this implementation assumes the ceiling above the table to be evenly illuminated with infrared light. Inside the table, an infrared camera is placed facing directly upwards. When markers made of transparent heat-insulating film in known shapes are placed on the table, the markers block the infrared light that is reflected from the ceiling. The markers thus appear as dark shapes to the infrared camera and can be recognized in real time by image processing.

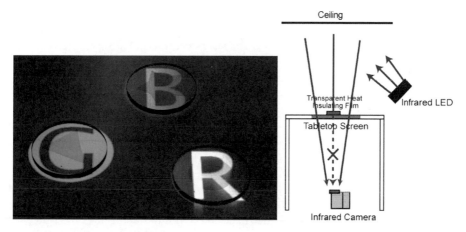

Fig. 5.24   Transparent tangible interface

This time, Reftel (type ZC-05G) [30], a highly transparent, heat insulating film produced in sheet form by TEIJIN was used, since markers are easily made from it. As shown in Fig. 5.24 (left), displayed images are changed depending on positions, IDs of each transparent interface. We can observe the displayed images through the interface.

ForceTile: A Tangible Interface with Force Distribution Sensing

The overall goal of this project is to increase the interactivity of tabletop tangible interfaces. To achieve this goal, a novel tabletop tangible interface named

Fig. 5.25 ForceTile

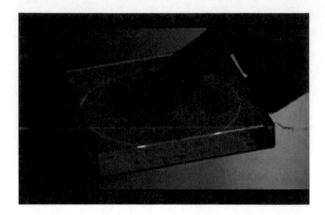

"ForceTile" is proposed [29]. This interface can detect the force distribution on its surface as well as its position, rotation, and ID using a vision-based approach. In our previous optical force sensor "GelForce" [31], an elastic body and cameras are fixed together. Contrarily, in this system, users can place and freely move multiple tile-shaped interfaces on the tabletop display. Furthermore, users can interact with projected images on the tabletop screen by moving, pushing or pinching the ForceTiles (see Fig. 5.25).

In our ForceTile, we offer core technical innovations, as follows.

One innovation is the design of the interface and the table-based camera system to detect the force distributions of each of the tiles on the tabletop. The tile interface consists of a transparent acrylic case filled with an elastic body, two layers of markers attached within the body for force distribution sensing, and a marker attached underneath the case for position sensing. Inside the table, cameras and IR light emitters are installed underneath. When users put ForceTiles on the tabletop, the system detects their locations and ID by the shape of the position marker. Furthermore, to calculate the force vectors on the surface, we adopt the GelForce method. When forces are applied on the surface of the ForceTile, this system derives the force vectors by detecting the internal strain of the body through the movement of the force markers. Note that no electronic devices are attached on the tabletop interfaces and users need not wear any special equipment for interaction.

Secondly, this system can show images on the tabletop screen and ForceTile surfaces. The basic optical design for displaying images on tabletop objects is same as UlteriorScape. By making a force marker with a transparent heat insulating material that allows the visible incoming light to pass and blocks the infrared incoming light, this system adopts a back projection so that the interface bodies and user's hands do not disturb the projection light.

The third innovation is a software architecture design for recognizing users' actions and generating projection images. According to various input information such as position, rotation, ID of tiles, and the intensity and direction of forces applied on them, users can control projected images in real-time.

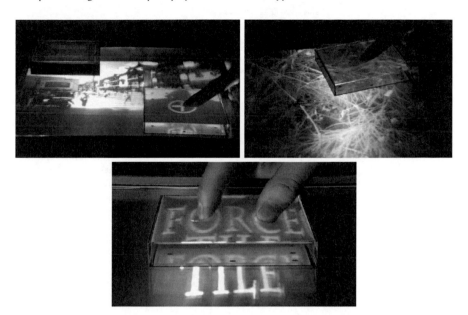

Fig. 5.26 Interactive applications using ForceTiles

While ForceTile offers brand new interactions on the tabletop, it can simultaneously integrate several functions of previous interfaces, such as touch panel, pointing device (i.e. mouse, trackpad), tangible physical interface, and small-sized screen. Some of these interactive applications have already been implemented (see Fig. 5.26).

Conclusions

In this chapter, we described optical designs for tabletop display systems. By adopting special materials and optical designs, the display system enables various functions on a physically single screen. As typical examples of this approach, we introduced several types of interactive tabletop displays developed by our research group. These display systems solved various problems on tabletop. For example, on Lumisight Table, each user around the table can read information such as characters in the appropriate direction. Moreover, public and private information can be displayed on the display simultaneously. The TLG system provides a novel experience of entertainment using a real mirror. In the Tablescape Plus, we can use tabletop physical objects not only input tools but also small-sized displays. It provides quite intuitive interactions. In the UlteriorScape, the functions of the Lumisight Table and the Tablescape Plus are integrated in a packaged tabletop display. In addition, note that users need not wear any electronic devices in these systems.

In the future, the technical know-how for view-control tabletop displays could be applied for other types of display systems such as ceiling displays, floor displays and wall displays. Furthermore, tabletop interactions using users hands and physical objects will be also more sophisticated by adopting optical designs.

References

1. Kruger R, Carpendale S, Scott SD, Greenberg S (2003) How people use orientation on tables: Comprehension, coordination and communication. In: Proceedings of the ACM Group 2003 Conference, ACM Press, Sanibel Island Florida, pp 369–378, doi: 10.1145/958160.958219
2. Sugimoto M, Hosoi K, Hashizume H (2004) Caretta: A system for supporting face-to-face collaboration by integrating personal and shared spaces. In: CHI'04: Proceedings of ACM CHI2004, ACM Press, Vienna, pp 41–48, doi: 10.1145/985692.985698
3. Kato H, Tachibana K, Tanabe M, Nakajima T, Fukuda Y (2003) A city-planning system based on augmented reality with a tangible interface. In: ISMAR2003: Proceedings of the 2nd International Symposium on Mixed and Augmented Reality MR Technology Expo, IEEE/ACM Press, Washington, DC, pp 340–341
4. Wellner P (1991) The DigitalDesk calculator: Tangible manipulation on a desk top display. In: UIST'91: Proceedings of ACM symposium on user interface software and technology, ACM, Hilton Head, South Carolina, United States, pp 27–34, doi: 10.1145/120782.120785
5. Underkoffler J, Ishii H (1998) Illuminating light: An optical design tool with a luminous-tangible interface. In: CHI'98: Proceedings of the ACM conference on human factors in computing systems, ACM Press, Los Angeles, CA, pp 542–549, doi: 10.1145/274644.274717
6. Raskar R, Weich G, Low KL, Bandyopadhyay D (2001) Shader lamps: Animating real objects with image-based illumination. In: EGWR2001: Eurographics workshop on rendering, London, pp 89–102
7. Piper B, Ratti C, Ishii H (2002) Illuminating clay: A 3-d tangible interface for landscape analysis, In: CHI'02: Proceedings of conference on human factors in computing systems, ACM, Minneapolis, MN, pp 355–362, doi: 10.1145/503376.503439
8. Newton-Dunn H, Nakano H, Gibson J (2003) Blockjam: A tangible interface for interactive music. In: NIME2003: Proceedings of 2003 international conference on new interfaces for musical expression. National University of Singapore, Montreal, Quebec, pp 170–177
9. Ullmer B, Ishii H (1997) The metaDESK: Models and prototypes for tangible user interfaces. In: UIST'97: Symposium on user interface software and technology, ACM Press, Banff, Alberta, pp 223–232, doi: 10.1145/263407.263551
10. Patten J, Ishii H, Hines J, Pangaro G (2001) A wireless object tracking platform for tangible user interfaces. In: CHI'01: Proceedings of the ACM conference on human factors in computing systems, ACM Press, Seattle, Washington, pp 253–260, doi: 10.1145/365024.365112
11. Kitamura Y, Konishi T, Yamamoto S, Kishino F (2001) Interactive stereoscopic display for three or more users, In: SIGGRAPH2001: Proceedings of the 28th annual conference on computer graphics and interactive techniques, ACM Press, Los Angeles, CA, pp 231–240, doi: 10.1145/383259.383285
12. Shoemaker GBD, Inkpen, KM (2001) Single display privacyware: Augmenting public displays with private information. In: CHI'01: Proceedings of the ACM conference on human factors in computing systems, ACM Press, Seattle, Washington, pp 522–529, doi: 10.1145/365024.365349
13. McDowall I, Bolas M (2004) Snared illumination. In: ACM SIGGRAPH2004 emerging technologies, ACM Press, Los Angeles, CA, p 24, doi: 10.1145/1186155.1186180
14. Izadi S, Hodges S, Taylor S, Rosenfeld D, Villar N, Butler A, Westhues J (2008) Going beyond the display: A surface technology with an electronically switchable diffuser. In: UIST 2008: Proceedings of the 21st annual ACM symposium on user interface software and technology, ACM Press, Monterey, CA, pp 269–278, doi: 10.1145/1449715.1449760

15. Hachiya K (2006) FairyFinder 03, http://www.petworks.co.jp/~hachiya/works/FairyFinder. html (in Japanese)
16. Sakurai S, Kitamura Y, Subramanian S, Kishino F (2009) A visibility control system for collaborative digital table, personal and ubiquitous computing, Special issue on interaction with coupled and public displays, Springer, London, doi: 10.1007/s00779-009-0243-6
17. Hirayama Y, Saishu T, Fukushima R, Taira K (2006) Flatbed-type autostereoscopic display systems using integral imaging method. In: ICCE2006: Digest of IEEE international conference on consumer electronics, Las Vegas, NV, pp 125–126, doi: 10.1109/ICCE.2006.1598342
18. About SHARP Technology, http://www.sharp-world.com/products/device/about/lcd/dual/, accessed 12.03.2010
19. Kato N, Naemura T (2006) Mixed reality environment with a mirror. In: SIGGRAPH2006: ACM SIGGRAPH2006 research posters, ACM Press, Boston, MA, no. 155, doi: 10.1145/1179622.1179801
20. Chan LW, Hu TT, Lin JY, Hung YP, Hsu J (2008) On top of tabletop: A virtual touch panel display. In: TableTop2008: Proceedings of 3rd IEEE international workshop on horizontal interactive human computer systems, IEEE, Amsterdam, Netherland, pp 169–176, doi: 10.1109/TABLETOP.2008.4660201
21. Kakehi Y, Iida M, Naemura T, Shirai Y, Matsushita M, Ohguro T (2005) Lumisight table: An interactive view-dependent tabletop display. In: IEEE computer graphics and applications, IEEE, vol. 25, no.1, pp 48–53, doi: 10.1109/MCG.2005.14
22. Kakehi Y, Naemura T (2005) Through the looking glass – you can play against your own reflection. In: ACE2005: Proceedings of the 2005 ACM SIGCHI international conference on advances in computer entertainment technology, ACM Press, Valencia, Spain, pp 373–374, doi: 10.1145/1178477.1178555
23. Kakehi Y, Naemura T, Matsushita M (2007) Tablescape plus: Interactive small-sized vertical displays on a horizontal tabletop display. In: Tabletop 2007: Proceedings of 2nd annual IEEE international workshop on horizontal interactive human-computer systems, IEEE, Newport, RI, pp 155–162, doi: 10.1109/TABLETOP.2007.25
24. Kakehi Y, Naemura T (2008) UlteriorScape: Interactive optical superimposition on a view-dependent tabletop display. In: Tabletop 2008: Proceedings of 3rd IEEE international workshop on horizontal interactive human computer systems, IEEE, Amsterdam, Netherland, pp 189–192, 10.1109/TABLETOP.2008.4660205
25. Iwai T (1993) Another time, another space, Antwerp Central Station, Belgium
26. Maes P, Darrell T, Blumberg B, Pentland A (1995) The ALIVE system: Full-body interaction with autonomous agents. In Proceedings of computer animation '95, IEEE Press, Geneva, pp 11–18, doi: 10.1109/CA.1995.393553
27. Kato H, Billinghurst M (1999) Marker tracking and HMD calibration for a video-based augmented reality conferencing system. In: IWAR 99: Proceedings of the 2nd IEEE and ACM international workshop on augmented reality, IEEE, San Francisco, CA, pp 85–94
28. Kakehi Y, Hosomi T, Iida M, Naemura T, Matsushita M (2006) Transparent tabletop interface for multiple users on lumisight table. In: TableTop2006: Proceedings of the 1st IEEE international workshop on horizontal interactive human-computer systems, IEEE, Adelaide, pp 141–148, 10.1109/TABLETOP.2006.34
29. Kakehi Y, Jo K, Sato K, Minamizawa K, Nii H, Kawakami N, Naemura T, Tachi S (2008) ForceTile: Tabletop tangible interface with vision-based force distribution sensing. In: ACM SIGGRAPH2008 new tech demos, ACM Press, Los Angeles, CA, Article No. 17, doi: 10.1145/1401615.1401632
30. TEIJIN, Reftel, http://www.teijin.co.jp/english/about/reftel/default.htm, accessed 12.03.2010
31. Kamiyama K, Kajimoto H, Vlack K, Kawakami N, Mizota T, Tachi S (2004) GelForce. In: SIGGRAPH2004 emerging technologies, ACM Press, Los Angeles, CA, p 5, doi: 10.1145/1186155.1186161

Chapter 6
Hand and Object Recognition on Liquid Crystal Displays

Hideki Koike, Toshiki Sato, Wataru Nishikawa, and Kentaro Fukuchi

Abstract Most traditional tabletop systems use video projectors to display large images on the tabletop. However, the projectors require long distance to project large images. What is worse, the images are often dark and it is not comfortable to be used in bright environment. On the other hand, Liquid Crystal Displays (LCDs) provide much brighter images, and they are getting larger, thinner, lighter, brighter, and less expensive. We have been using LCDs in our experiments as a horizontal tabletop, and there are some interesting characteristics of the LCD tabletop systems when it is used with some optical films. In this chapter, we describe a vision-based approach for hand and object recognition on an LCD tabletop system.

Introduction

Currently, considerable research is being devoted to tabletop systems that use a horizontal tabletop as an information display device [1]. In traditional tabletop systems, video projectors are mostly used. One of the issues in such projector-based tabletop systems is that the projected images are often dark. Although recent projectors provide much brighter images than earlier ones, they are still too dark to be used in a bright environment. The other issue is that projection-based systems require much effort and space to be set up. In a front-projection system, the projector must be mounted on the ceiling or a similar tall surface. In order to obtain a larger image, a high ceiling or a surface mirror is required. In a rear-projection system, the carefully designed optical hardware must be deployed under the table, and as a result the table becomes a big box with no usable space beneath it. Similar issues were discussed in detail in [2].

H. Koike (✉)
University of Electro-Communications, Chofu, Tokyo 182-8585, Japan
e-mail: koike@acm.org

C. Müller-Tomfelde (ed.), *Tabletops – Horizontal Interactive Displays*,
Human-Computer Interaction Series, DOI 10.1007/978-1-84996-113-4_6,
© Springer-Verlag London Limited 2010

On the other hand, an LCD is becoming larger, thinner, lighter, brighter, and less expensive, and it is attaining higher resolution. By using such a large LCD as a table-top, the issues in the projection-based systems, such as the brightness issue and the space issue, are solved. The resolution of the LCD High-Definition TV is 1,920 × 1,080, and that of a high-end LCD such as Apple's Cinema Display is 2,560 × 1,600. It would be very expensive to get such resolution by using projectors. For these reasons, tabletop systems using an LCD are becoming more and more popular.

In order for such an LCD to be used as a tabletop, what should be considered on an LCD tabletop system is how to sense a user's input and how to recognize real objects on the table. Although there have been many research results on sensing a user's input and recognizing objects on projector based tabletop systems, most of them are unable or hard to be used with the LCDs as we described in the later sections.

This chapter focuses on methods for recognizing hand and object on the LCD tabletop and shows our prototype systems.

Background

Related Work on Sensing User's Input

Touch panels are the most popular input devices for direct pointing on a computer display. There are many variations in touch panels, such as resistive touch panels, surface acoustic wave, capacitive touch screens, and optical imaging. The touch panel enables precise pointing and it can be applied to an LCD. It is, however, rather difficult to interact with using multiple fingers or gestures. And there are other issues, such as how to differentiate hands and other objects such as arms or real objects on the table when the LCD is used as a tabletop.

Pen-based input devices, such as Mimio, are sometimes used in tabletop systems. Mimio can be used with an LCD. However, it can sense only a single input. Even if it is extended to allow simultaneous multiple pointing, it is still hard to recognize users' rich interaction such as gestures. It requires other devices or methods to recognize and identify objects on the table.

DiamondTouch [3] is often used as an input device for tabletop systems. It allows multiple simultaneous inputs and it also identifies each user. However, it can be used only with front projection systems. SmartSkin [4] detects shapes of objects that are close to the surface. However, it requires special hardware below the surface, so it cannot be used with an LCD. ThinSight [5] is a multi-touch sensing device. The advantage of ThinSight is that it can be used with the LCD. The authors also showed how to identify visual markers. However, one of its disadvantages is its frame rate. It tracks hands or fingers at a rate of 10 frames per second. On the other hand, our approach described later can track hands and fingers at a rate of over 600 frames per second when it is used with a high-speed camera [6].

A near infrared camera is sometimes used for tabletop systems. In HoloWall [7], near infrared LEDs are illuminated from behind the screen, and a CCD camera with an infrared filter behind the screen captures the light that is reflected by the object in front of the screen. Han [8] proposed a similar approach for the tabletop system. Such approaches cannot be used with an LCD because there is no space behind the screen to equip the camera and the LED lights.

Koike et al. [9] developed a real-time hand/finger recognition method by using a far infrared camera. This method segments the hand/finger region from the projected image by capturing the radiation heat of the hand. After the segmentation, a template is applied that matches normalized correlation to detect finger positions precisely. This method, however, is hard to use with an LCD because the LCD itself becomes warm during its use.

To summarize, a touch panel is not sufficient for research and development of rich interaction on the tabletop. Most of the other methods developed for the tabletop cannot be used with the LCD.

Related Work on Object Recognition

In order to recognize objects on the table, some researchers use wireless tags such as RFID. Such physical tags, however, must be embedded to each object and it is rather difficult to identify positions of the objects by the RFID readers.

A much easier and more popular method is to use barcodes or markers. For example, Rekimoto developed a 2-D marker named CyberCode and also developed some applications for it [10, 11]. AR Toolkit [12] is often used by augmented reality systems, because it runs on multiple platforms, and it is easy to make 2-D markers called AR markers. The reacTIVision [13] uses its original 2-D markers called amoeba fiducials. In recent Japan, a 2-D barcode called QR Code [14] is very popular and is widely used. Most of the mobile phones in Japan are equipped with a QR code reader. By capturing the code with a camera of the mobile phone, users can obtain information encoded in the code such as a URL address. A common issue in these marker-based systems is the unnatural appearance of the marker. The black and white pattern, which means nothing to humans, spoils the appearance of the objects.

There are some work on invisible markers [15–17]. However, these approaches are common in using IR light. They require an IR camera and an IR light source and are not easily integrated into the LCD tabletop system.

There are a few methods that do not use the marker. For example, Nishi et al. [18] proposed a real-time object recognition method based on a color indexing algorithm. Since it uses color information from the object, it does not spoil the appearance of the object. It is, however, a sensitive to environmental light conditions.

To summarize, the marker is easy to use and robust for object recognition and identification. A major issue is its appearance.

Hand and Object Recognition on an LCD

LCD and Polarization

Light is electromagnetic waves with the direction of oscillation perpendicular to the direction of the waves' travel. Natural light oscillates to any direction. Polarized light is polarized to a specific direction. A polarized plate (i.e., polarizer) is a device that creates light with a single linear polarization such as that shown in Fig. 6.1.

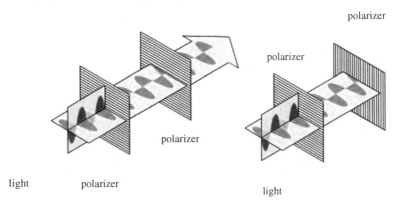

Fig. 6.1 Light and two polarizers

In an LCD, liquid crystal molecules are interleaved by two polarizers whose axes of transmission are perpendicular. As a result, the light from the LCD is polarized (Fig. 6.2).

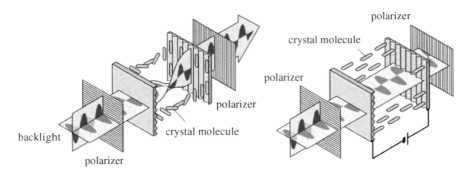

Fig. 6.2 Liquid crystal display

Blocking an LCD Image with a Polarizer

When the image from the LCD is captured with a normal camera, the image is clearly visible as shown in Fig. 6.3 (left). On the other hand, when a polarizer

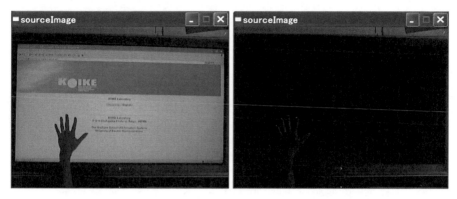

Fig. 6.3 Blocking the image from an LCD. A view captured by a camera without a polarizer (*left*). A view with the polarizer (*right*). The background image cannot be seen by the camera, while the hand on the table is still visible

is attached to the camera and its plane of polarization is perpendicular to that of polarized light from the LCD, the image from the LCD is blocked by the polarizer (Fig. 6.3, right).

Meanwhile, a hand (or any other object) on the LCD is still visible to the camera. By using this optical phenomenon, it is easy to segment the image of the hand on the table from the background image without any calculation by a computer.

Canceling the Image Blocking with Optical Films

Optical films are devices that transmit, reflect, or absorb light. The polarizer described previously is a kind of such optical films.

In the previous section, we described how a polarizer blocks the light from another polarizer when their planes of polarization are perpendicular to each other. On the other hand, the image blocking by the polarizer is canceled when a certain type of optical film including the polarizer is placed on the LCD. Figure 6.4 (left) shows how the LCD and the film are seen by humans or by the camera without a polarizer. On the other hand, Fig. 6.4 (right) shows how they are seen by the camera with a polarizer.

As one can see, the region outside of\the film is black. However, the image inside the film passes through the polarizer attached to the camera. This is because the polarized light from the LCD is polarized to a different direction by the optical film on the LCD (Fig. 6.6). Figure 6.5 summarizes the description above.

- Center arrow: the image from the LCD is blocked by the polarizer.
- Left arrow: the light from the hand or from objects on the LCD is extended to the camera.
- Right arrow: the image within the optical film is extended to the camera.

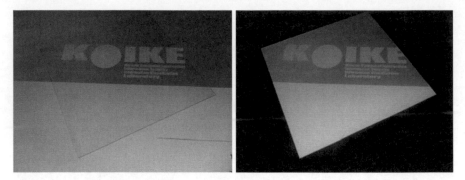

Fig. 6.4 Canceling the image blocking with an optical film. The *left figure* shows how the LCD and the film are seen by the user. The *right figure* shows how they are seen by the camera with a polarizer. The image blocking by the polarizer is canceled by the film

Fig. 6.5 The relation between light from an LCD and a polarizer attached to the camera

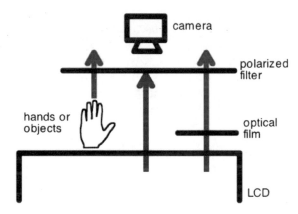

Hardware Set-Up

Figure 6.6 shows a typical hardware set-up of the LCD tabletop system. We used a 46-inch LCD (SONY KDL-46X1000) as a tabletop. An acrylic panel was placed on the LCD to protect the LCD. A CCD camera (PointGrey Dragonfly Express) was mounted on the ceiling to capture the entire image of the tabletop. In addition, a polarizer (Kenko PL filter) was attached to the camera, as its plane of polarization is perpendicular to that of the LCD. This camera can capture the image at a speed of over 600 frames per second. When recognizing high-speed gestures, it is helpful to reduce the cost of image processing by using the polarizer.

We used OpenCV [19] library for general image processing. To generate images on the table, OpenGL and SDL [20] were used.

Fig. 6.6 Hardware setup

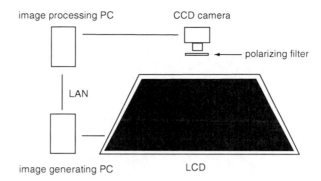

Hand Recognition: High Speed Gestures

Image Segmentation

As is described in [9], detecting hand or finger region from background image is computationally more expensive. This is because the background image is dynamically changing and it is more difficult to use normal background subtraction method.

This issue is easily solved by using a polarizer on the camera. As is described in the previous section, the background image of the LCD is blocked by using the polarizer without any computation.

Once the hand image is segmented, the finger recognition algorithm proposed by Oka [21] is applied to the image in order to identify precise finger positions. This is a simple, low-cost, and effective technique for detecting hands, fingers, and even objects on the LCD.

Recognizing High Speed Gestures

We also developed fast gesture recognition method as follows. At first, an input image from the camera is binarized and continuous regions are extracted. Regions whose size is larger than a certain number of pixels are recognized as arms temporary. Then the system scan search arm region to find an enclosed region of dark pixels as shown in Fig. 6.7. If the enclosed region's size is in a certain range (e.g. 1–10 cm^2), the surrounding temporal arm region is recognized as an arm.

When an arm region is newly recognized, the system tracks its two positions. One is the centroid of the arm region, and the other is the centroid of the enclosed region. Unlike Wilson's pinching gesture recognition [2], our technique does not calculate the posture of the enclosed region, but the direction from the arm to the enclosed region is used as the orientation of the pinch (Fig. 6.8). The system tracks the users' hands by tracking the position of the arm regions using a simple cost minimization analysis: calculates distances between an arm position detected in the

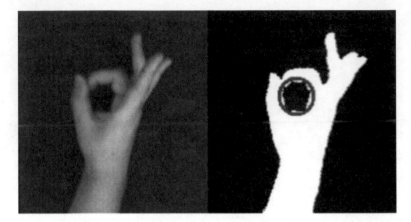

Fig. 6.7 Image segmentation by the polarizer (*right*), and binarization (*left*)

Fig. 6.8 Estimating direction
of the hand

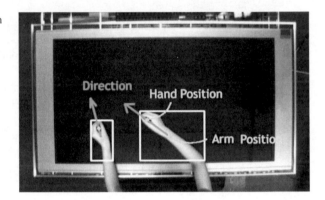

current frame and positions in the previous frame, and choose the closest previous arm. The application receives the positions and orientations of the hands from the system continuously.

When the previously recognized arm region has no enclosed region in the current frame, the system recognizes it as the user opened his fingers, and when an enclosed region is detected again, it is recognized as the user closed the fingers again. These opening and closing events are sent to the application.

The entire recognition process is finished in less than 10 ms by using the high-speed video camera that enables low-latency interaction.

Application

By using this fast gesture recognition method, we developed a shooting game on the LCD tabletop system as shown in Fig. 6.9. The system tracks high speed gestures

Fig. 6.9 A shooting game
named PAC–PAC

of up to 20 people's both hands in real time. The system was demonstrated at
SIGGRAPH Asia 2008 in Singapore [22].

Object Recognition: Transparent Marker

Basic Principle

By utilizing characteristics of polarization of the LCD and optical films, we developed a transparent marker on the LCD tabletop system [23]. That is, since the image
from the LCD is blocked by the polarizing filter attached to the camera, it is seen as
black. On the other hand, the image passed through the optical film on the LCD is
extended to the camera. If we put transparent (i.e., optically isotropic) films that do
not change the polarization of the LCD and polarizing films one after the other, a
marker that is mostly invisible to human sight but has a black-and-white pattern to
the camera is obtained.

Figure 6.10 shows the transparent marker we developed. The regions of the transparent film are captured as black by the camera with the polarizing filter, and the
regions of the polarizing film are captured as bright colors as seen in Fig. 6.11(left).
By subtracting the background image (Fig. 6.11, middle) from the captured image,
the black-and-white image is obtained as seen in Fig. 6.11 (right). For marker
recognition, existing software such as AR Toolkit can be used.

Rotation Variance Issues

The previous section described a basic idea of transparent markers using a polarization film. However, when the normal polarizing film is used for the marker, the
marker is rotation variant, and the camera cannot detect the marker in each rotation
by $\pi/4$ radians as shown in Fig. 6.12.

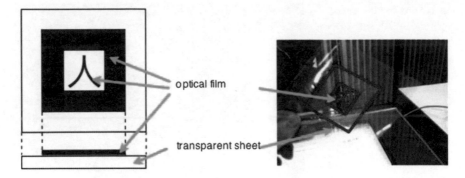

Fig. 6.10 Image processing to obtain *black-and-white* pattern from the captured image

Fig. 6.11 Image processing

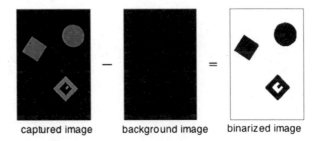

captured image   background image   binarized image

Through the experiments of various types of optical films, we found a solution to add rotation invariance to the transparent markers. That is to use two half-wave plates as the optical film.

A wave plate is an optical film that can change the polarization state of light. A quarter-wave plate and a half-wave plate are most popular. They shift the phase of the light $\pi/2$ and $\pi/4$, respectively. When the polarized light enters the half-wave plate whose fast axis is rotated θ with respect to the polarization direction of the light, the output light is rotated 2θ (Fig. 6.13). In Fig. 6.13 (Ex, Ey) and (E'x, E'y) are the Jones vectors of the input and output light to/from the first half-wave plate, respectively.

Fig. 6.12 A transparent marker without rotation invariance

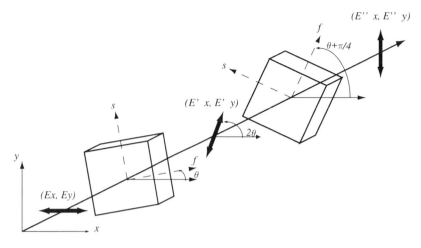

Fig. 6.13 Two half-wave plates and polarization directions of the light

As we described previously, if the angle between the polarization direction of the LCD and the fast axis is θ, the output light from the half-wave plate is rotated 2θ. When another half-wave plate is placed by rotating $\pi/4$ radians with respect to the first half-wave plate as shown in Fig. 6.13, the polarizing direction is rotated $2(\theta+\pi/4)$ radians. As a result, the polarization direction of the light from the second plate is always rotated $\pi/2$ radians with respect to the polarizing direction of the LCD (Fig. 6.13). In Fig. 6.13 ($E''x$, $E''y$) is the Jones vector of the output light from the second half-wave plate. That is, the LCD image always reaches the camera regardless of θ. Figure 6.14 shows the result. The marker can be seen as transparent when it is rotated.

Applications

Typical applications that clearly demonstrate the natural and intuitive character of our transparent marker are tangible transparent Magic Lenses. The original Magic Lenses were developed by Bier et al. [24], but this is a system in a window environment. Billinghurst et al. extended this idea to the AR environment and developed AR Magic Lenses [25, 26], which use AR markers and head-mounted displays (HMD).

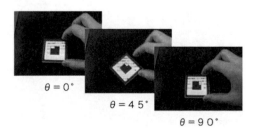

Fig. 6.14 Transparent marker with rotation invariance

Although AR Magic Lenses proposed an interesting idea, the visible markers are obtrusive. The visual effect can be seen only by the users wearing HMDs.

We developed three applications by utilizing transparent markers. In these applications, the markers are mostly invisible to users. Moreover, it does not require any special devices such as HMDs to view its visual effect. Everyone around the table can see and manipulate the visual effect just by moving the sheet.

Translator Application

Figure 6.15 shows a translator application. When a user put a transparent sheet with a transparent marker on the English sentences, the Japanese translation of the sentences is shown inside the transparent sheet. If the user uses other sheets with different markers, he or she can see other translation such as Spanish, French, etc.

Geographic Application

Geographic applications, such as Google Map or Google Earth, are popular. In such applications, users can see different layers of information such as normal map, satellite image, 3-D view, and so on. However, it is difficult to apply one or more visual effects to any specific areas. Figure 6.16 shows the geographic application of the tangible transparent Magic Lenses. In this figure, a satellite image is displayed on the LCD, but the normal map is shown inside the region of the transparent sheet. It is also possible to show other information on the different sheets. For example, one sheet may display traffic jam information and another may display the location of stores. It is important to notice that such sheets can be overlapped.

Image Filter Application

There are a variety of image filters, such as a binarizing filter, a dither filter, and so on. It is an important characteristic of such image filters that most of them are

Fig. 6.15 A translator application

Fig. 6.16 A map browser application

Fig. 6.17 An image filter application

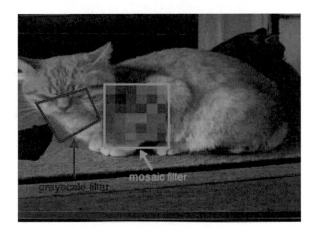

linearly applied. Using our tangible transparent Magic Lenses, intuitive operation of such image filters is possible. Figure 6.17 shows an example where two sheets are placed on the LCD. One is a grey scale filter, and the other is a mosaic filter. Each image filtering algorithm is applied to the region inside each sheet. When the user laps one sheet over the other, two filtering algorithms are applied to the region.

Future Trends

Advantages and disadvantages of the hand and object recognition are described in [6] and [23], respectively. In this section we describe future trends of the LCD tabletop system.

An interesting research topic with relation to the hand recognition is 3-D hand recognition on the LCD tabletop. For example, the hand recognition shown in here could be easily extended to a stereo camera by adding polarizers to two cameras. In case of the projector-based tabletop system, the room should be relatively dark and therefore the vision-based systems sometimes do not work correctly. On the other hand, in the case of the LCD tabletop, the room can be bright and therefore the vision-based system, particularly the stereo vision system work better than with the projector-based tabletop. The 3-D hand recognition has an ability to provide more natural and intuitive interaction on the tabletop.

The LCD and its polarization will show other interesting phenomena. For example, when the transparent elastic materials are placed on the LCD and deformed by the user's finger, they will show so-called photoelastic effect. The region deformed by the user is captured as bright region by the camera with a polarizer. By using this phenomenon, the tangible transparent interfaces are developed. This will provide a novel 2.5-D or 3-D interaction method that cannot be done with the normal 2-D surface.

Conclusion

This chapter described hand and object recognition on an LCD tabletop system. By utilizing the polarization of the LCD and a polarizer attached to the camera, it is possible to segment hand or object regions from the background image. Since it does not require any computational effort, fast gesture recognition became possible. Next, by using optical films, it became possible to make transparent markers on the LCD. Through experiments with various kinds of optical films, we showed two half-wave plates make the marker rotation invariant.

Finally, we describe the applicability of these methods to other displays such as plasma displays or organic light-emitting diode (OLED) displays. The light from these displays is not polarized. However, if the display is covered by a large polarized film, it is possible to polarize the light from the display. Therefore, these methods will also work with such displays.

We believe the LCD or such flat panel displays will become more and more popular as the tabletop in the future. The hand and object recognition methods shown in here will help other tabletop researchers or users.

References

1. Microsoft (2006) Microsoft surface. http://surface.microsoft.com, accessed 02.05.2009
2. Wilson A (2006) Robust computer vision-based detection of pinching for one and two-handed gesture input. In: UIST '06: Proceedings of the 19th annual ACM symposium on user interface software and technology, ACM Press, New York, pp 255–258
3. Dietz P, Leigh D (2001) DiamondTouch: A multi-user touch technology. In: UIST '01: Proceedings of the 14th annual ACM symposium on user interface software and technology, ACM Press, New York, pp 219–226
4. Rekimoto J (2002) SmartSkin: An infrastructure for freehand manipulation on interactive surfaces. In: CHI '02: Proceedings of the SIGCHI conference on human factors in computing systems, ACM Press, New York, pp 113–120

5. Hodges S, Izadi S, Butler A, Rrustemi A, Buxton B (2007) ThinSight: Versatile multi-touch sensing for thin form-factor displays. In: UIST '07: Proceedings of the ACM symposium on user interface software and technology, ACM Press, New York, pp 259–268

6. Sato T, Fukuchi K, Koike H (2006) Implementation and evaluations of vision-based finger flicking gesture recognition for tabletops. In: TABLETOP 2008: Proceedings of IEEE international workshop on horizontal interactive human computer system, IEEE, Amsterdam, The Netherlands, pp 137–144

7. Matsushita N, Rekimoto J (1997) HoloWall: Designing a finger, hand, body, and object sensitive wall. In: UIST '97: Proceedings of the 10th annual ACM symposium on user interface software and technology, ACM Press, New York, pp 209–210

8. Han JY (2005) Low-cost multi-touch sensing through frustrated total internal reflection. In: UIST'05: Proceedings of the 18th annual ACM symposium on user interface software and technology, ACM Press, New York, pp 115–118

9. Koike H, Sato Y, Kobayashi Y, Tobita H, Kobayashi M (2000) Interactive textbook and interactive venn diagram: Natural and intuitive interface on augmented desk system. In: Proceedings of human factors in computing systems (CHI'2000), ACM Press, New York, pp 121–128

10. Rekimoto J, Nagao K (1995) The world through the computer: Computer augmented interaction with real world environments. In: UIST '95: Proceedings of the 8th annual ACM symposium on user interface and software technology, ACM Press, New York, pp 29–36

11. Rekimoto J, Saito M (1999) Augmented surfaces: A spatially continuous work space for hybrid computing environments. In: Proceedings of the ACM conference on human factors in computing system (CHI'99), ACM Press, New York, pp 378–385

12. Kato H, Billinghurst M (1999) Marker tracking and HMD calibration for a video-based augmented reality conferencing system. In: Proceedings of the 2nd international workshop on augmented reality (IWAR '99), San Francisco, CA, pp 85–94

13. Kaltenbrunner M, Bencina R (2007) reacTIVision: A computer-vision framework for table-based tangible interaction. In: TEI '07: Proceedings of the 1st international conference on Tangible and embedded interaction, ACM Press, New York, pp 69–74

14. Denso Corp QR Code. http://http://en.wikipedia.org/wiki/QR Code, accessed 12.03.2010

15. Kakehi Y, Hosomi T, Iida M, Naemura T, Matsushita M (2006) Transparent tabletop inter face for multiple users on lumisight table. In: Proceedings of 1st international workshop on horizontal interactive human-computer systems (TABLETOP 2006), IEEE Computer Society, Washington, DC, pp 141–148

16. Shirai Y, Matsushita M, Ohguro T (2003) HIEI projector: Augmenting a real environment with invisible information. In: Proceedings of the 11th workshop on interactive systems and software (WISS2003), Ishikawa, Japan, pp 115–122

17. Park H, Park JI (2004) Invisible marker tracking for AR. In: Proceedings of 3rd IEEE and ACM international symposium on mixed and augmented reality (ISMAR 2004), IEEE/CS, IEEE Computer Society, Washington, DC

18. Nishi T, Sato Y, Koike H (2001) SnapLink: Interactive object registration and recognition for augmented desk interface. In: Proceedings of IFIP international conference on human–computer interaction (INTERACT'01), IOS Press, Amsterdam, pp 240–246

19. Open Source Computer Vision Library http://www.intel.com/technology/computing/opencv/

20. SDL: Simple Directmedia Layer http://www.libsdl.org/, accessed 12.03.2010

21. Oka K, Sato Y, Koike H (2002) Real-time tracking of multiple fingertips and gesture recognition for augmented desk interface system. IEEE Computer Graphics and Its Applications 22(6):64–71

22. Sato T, Mamiya H, Koike H, Fukuchi K (2008) An augmented tabletop video game with pinching gesture recognition. ACM SIGGRAPH Asia Emerging Technologies (also at http://pac-pac.org)

23. Koike H, Nishikawa W, Kentaro F (2009) Transparent 2-D markers on an LCD tabletop system. In: Proceedings of human factors in computing systems (CHI'2009), ACM, New York, pp 163–172
24. Bier EA, Stone MC, Pier K, Buxton W, DeRose TD (1993) Toolglass and magic lenses: The see-through interface. In: SIGGRAPH '93: Proceedings of the 20th annual conference on computer graphics and interactive techniques, ACM, New York, pp 73–80
25. Billinghurst M, Grasset R, Looser J (2005) Designning augmented reality interfaces. ACM SIGGRAPH Computer Graphics 39(1):17–22
26. Looser J, Grasset R, Billinghurst M (2007) A 3D flexible and tangible magic lens in augmented reality. In: ISMAR 2007: Proceedings of the 6th IEEE and ACM international symposium on mixed and augmented reality, IEEE, Washington, DC, pp 51–54

Part II
On and Above Tabletops

This part of the book is preoccupied with topics and aspects of Human Computer Interaction research. *On tabletops* refers to interactions on the surface, namely by direct touch input and gestures, while mediating tangible objects on the tabletop extend this notion of surface interaction. The area *above tabletops* addresses topics of interactions performed more distant to surfaces while still being attributed to them.

The following chapter of Weiss et al. introduces tangible general purpose control objects for surface interaction that can be dynamically changed in their optical appearances by illumination via the tabletop display. The authors provide scenarios and share details about user studies. Then Inami et al. presents research on tangible objects that are physically actuated, allowing them to move on tabletop surfaces remotely controlled. Hilliges et al. are exploring tabletop interaction styles and present an interaction model to achieve high fidelity to gestures and tangible input in the physical world. In the following chapter Aliakseyeu et al. present a review of existing tabletop interaction techniques to further the understanding of the underlying basic user interactions. They provide design recommendations for the various atomic actions. The chapter of Benko and Wigdor is preoccupied with the fundamental limitations of direct touch input. They identify seven problems of touch-based interfaces and offer a set of solutions based on current research. Finally, Grossman and Wigdor extend the notion of surface interaction into the area *above tabletops*. They present a taxonomy of 3D tabletop systems that use interactive volumetric display over horizontal surfaces.

Chapter 7
Augmenting Interactive Tabletops with Translucent Tangible Controls

Malte Weiss, James D. Hollan, and Jan Borchers

Abstract Multi-touch surfaces enable multi-hand and multi-person direct manipulation interfaces. However, they lack haptic feedback. Tangible interfaces (TUIs) are a promising approach to this issue but most are special-purpose with fixed physical and visual appearance. This chapter provides an overview of recent work to add haptic feedback to interactive surfaces, including haptic and tactile displays, tangibles on tabletops, general-purpose controls, and typing on multi-touch tables. The focus of the chapter is Silicone Illuminated Active Peripherals (SLAP). SLAP Widgets are physical translucent general-purpose controls, such as buttons, knob, sliders, and keyboards, that can be used to manipulate virtual objects on interactive tabletop surfaces. They combine benefits of physical and virtual controls, providing the strong affordances and haptic feedback of physical controls and enabling the dynamically changeable appearance possibilities of virtual controls. SLAP Widgets are particularly promising for tasks in which eyes-free manipulation is advantageous and their plasticity encourages development of context sensitive controls and exploration of alternative interface forms.

Introduction

Interactive multi-touch surfaces have recently emerged as an interesting extension to the established direct manipulation graphical desktop metaphor. Direct manipulation [1, 2] provides a natural way of interacting with graphical user interfaces (GUIs). On interactive multi-touch surfaces, objects can be manipulated by directly touching and dragging them, allowing interaction without the indirection of keyboard or mouse. Furthermore, while traditional graphical interfaces enable an individual user to manipulate dynamic digital data, interactive tables facilitate collocated collaborative work, allowing multiple people to interact simultaneously

M. Weiss (✉)
Media Computing Group, RWTH Aachen University, 52074 Aachen, Germany
e-mail: weiss@cs.rwth-aachen.de

C. Müller-Tomfelde (ed.), *Tabletops – Horizontal Interactive Displays*,
Human-Computer Interaction Series, DOI 10.1007/978-1-84996-113-4_7,
© Springer-Verlag London Limited 2010

with the same computer. Tables are a common and familiar meeting space for all types of conversational exchanges among small groups of people. Interactive table-top surfaces are especially well suited for presenting shared visual information without designating one person as the owner of the information. The horizontal surface of a table affords spreading, sharing, and manipulating a variety of materials. Tables provide a common working environment and direct manipulation ensures that users are aware of each other's operations. In terms of Ubiquitous Computing [3], multi-touch tabletops move users away from desktop computers to interactive systems that hide technology and accentuate direct natural interaction.

As interactive tabletops become more widely available and users have more experience with multi-touch applications on smart phones and other devices there is increasing motivation to design tabletop applications that can assist users with common everyday tasks. However, the direct transfer of conventional desktop applications to multi-touch tables is problematic. This is due to the fact that neither operating systems nor applications were designed with an expectation of multiple simultaneous inputs or gestural interaction. In addition, virtual controls, such as on-screen buttons, suffer from absence of haptic feedback, requiring visual attention during operation. Without visual monitoring input problems can result because of inability to feel a virtual control's boundary or current state. This is particularly troublesome for typing. Although most applications require typing, it is inconvenient and error-prone on virtual keyboards. In addition, the size of a finger in comparison to a mouse cursor can make precise interaction difficult and cause occlusion problems when operating small controls [4].

Since their introduction in 1997, Tangible User Interfaces [5], or in short *tangibles*, have proven to be useful interface components that provide natural haptic feedback during interaction. They allow users to manipulate data with real physical interface objects. However, most tangibles are either restricted to a specific purpose, e.g., the composition of a music piece, or have specific physical affordances associated with particular domain objects. Thus, bringing *conventional* general physical widgets, such as buttons, sliders, knobs, etc., to tabletops is a logical next step. They provide compelling physical affordances, guide users' actions, enable tactile feedback, and can be used in an eyes-free fashion. However, unlike easily changeable graphical widgets they have a fixed visual appearance. Moreover, they are usually expensive and tethered which restricts their use and is especially troublesome for tabletop interaction.

We propose a new class of interface objects that combine properties of both graphical and physical interfaces: translucent general-purpose tangibles. Silicone Illuminated Active Peripherals (SLAP) are a first instance of this new class. They consist of translucent general-purpose physical controls, such as buttons, knobs, sliders, and keyboards, that can be used to manipulate and display the state of virtual objects. Users can place SLAP Widgets on a multi-touch table and use them to interact with virtual objects, e.g., to change the brightness of a photograph or to navigate in an audio file. Like other tangibles they provide haptic feedback to aid interaction without requiring visual attention. An image for each widget, e.g., the label of a button or the state of slider, is back-projected onto the translucent widget and is thus visible to users. The projected image can be dynamically changed to indicate state. For example, the layout of the SLAP Keyboard can be visually altered on the fly between language specific layouts, and its keycaps can be changed to aid entering mathematical or other special symbols. SLAP Widgets do not require any electronics or tethering and can be positioned wherever needed on the tabletop. When no longer required they can be placed aside and out of the way.

In this chapter, we (1) provide an overview of recent work to add haptic feedback to interactive surfaces, (2) address issues with haptic displays and tangibles on tables, (3) discuss benefits and tradeoffs involved in combining the strong affordances and haptic feedback of physical controls with the dynamic visual appearance changes of virtual objects, (4) present SLAP widgets as a first instance of this new class of translucent general-purpose tangibles, and (5) discuss future research directions for exploring tangible controls on interactive multi-touch tables.

Background

In this section, we present an overview of current research on adding haptic feedback to multi-touch tables. We cover haptic and tactile displays, tangibles on tabletops, general-purpose controls, transparent tangibles for dynamic relabeling, and typing on touch surfaces.

Haptic and Tactile Displays

Haptic and tactile displays, as defined by Poupyrev et al., are interactive devices that simulate the haptic sensation of physical objects and textures [6]. We refer to [6, 7] for a general overview.

Pin displays (e.g., [8, 9]) employ a small 2D array of pins that rise out of the surface when actuated to create a physical texture to, for example, simulate a button and its boundaries. Shape Memory Alloys (SMAs) that can assume specific shapes at different temperatures (e.g., [10]). Harrison and Hudson [11] use pneumatics to realize deformable areas on a multi-touch display. Other approaches add tactile feedback by using vibration [12] when virtual controls are triggered, e.g., by using linear vibrotactile actuators. The technologies employed to create haptic and tactile displays currently provide only limited physical affordances and feedback. Complex controls, such as knobs or sliders, cannot yet be realized. In addition, existing approaches are expensive and not applicable for use with large surfaces.

Tangibles on Tabletops

In their seminal *Bricks* paper [13], Fitzmaurice et al. highlighted advantages of the rich affordances of physical objects and introduced the concept of *Graspable User*

Interfaces, interfaces that allow interaction with physical handles as virtual controls. Users can place small physical blocks, called *bricks*, onto virtual objects on a surface and move, rotate, and scale the associated objects by manipulating the bricks. Ishii and Ullmer extended the bricks concept in their pioneering work on Tangbile Bits. Inspired by earlier notions of Ubiquitous Computing [3] and the affordances of physical artifacts [13], they introduced *Tangible User Interfaces (TUIs)* [5, 14]. These interfaces give physical form to digital data [15], exploiting users' haptic abilities to assist manipulation of digital information.

Since tangibles expose strong physical affordances, they have been used in many tabletop applications to enhance interaction metaphors and improve haptic feedback. *Illuminating Light* [16] was an early system that explored use of tangibles on an interactive surface. In one sample tabletop application, users could place tangibles that represented specific optical artifacts, e.g., laser sources, mirrors, and beam splitters, onto a rear-projected tabletop display. Virtual beams, simulated and projected onto the tabletop, radiated from the laser sources and appeared to be reflected or refracted by the tangible elements placed in their paths on the surface. By adding tangibles representing mirrors, beam splitters, and lenses, users could simulate various optical phenomena (Fig. 7.1a). Due to the constant visual feedback, the system created the illusion that the input channel (placing and manipulating physical objects) and output channel (the display of the optical simulation) were the same, providing what has been termed *inter-referential input/output* [1, 2].

In a succeeding project called *Urp* [17], the same authors created a prototype to support architects in planning and designing urban areas. By placing models of buildings on a workbench, physical effects such as winds and shadows were simulated and could change depending on the time of day and placement of models (Fig. 7.1b). In addition to facilities similar to those in Illuminating Light, Urp provided tangibles to change the digital properties of other tangibles, e.g., a wand that switched the opaque facade of a building to glass that in turn resulted in changes to shadow simulation. Tangible tools were also introduced to, for example, measure distances between buildings.

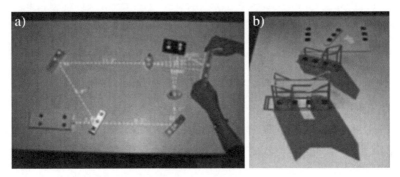

Fig. 7.1 Tangible interfaces on tabletops. (a) Illuminating Light. (b) Urp. Courtesy of Underkoffler and Ishii [16, 17]

Fig. 7.2 The reacTable.
Courtesy of Jordà et al. [18]

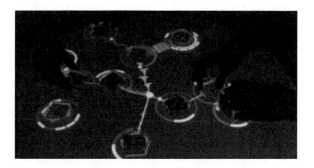

In the above projects, tangibles are geometric representations of their real-world counterparts. This limits the scalability and complexity of these systems. The *reacTable* by Jordà et al. [18] confronts these issues by using acrylic square plates for musical creation. Users are provided with six types of tangibles, including sound generators, filters, and audio mixers, that can be linked to each other (Fig. 7.2). Complex sounds are created by putting the tangibles close to each other. In allusion to real sound mixers, properties such as frequency and speed can be set by turning the specific tangibles. Volume is changed by finger dragging. The table's back projection gives visual feedback about the state and the connectivity of the tangibles.

The idea of synthesizing complex data with tangibles has more recently been explored as a form of tangible programming. In [19], Horn et al. present a tangible version of the *Scratch* programming language that aims to help children learn a programming language by putting building blocks together. They found that tangibles and virtual blocks were equally well understood but tangibles were more motivating and led to increased probability of group participation.

Actuated Tangibles

One inherent problem of all the aforementioned tangible systems is that data can only be manipulated by the user. The system itself cannot change a physical value, such as the position of a building in Urp. It can only reflect the consequences of users' changes and is therefore one-directional. In response to this, actuated tangibles have been developed. We refer to [20] for a detail overview of actuated tangibles.

The *Planar Manipulator Display* by Rosenfeld et al. [21] uses mobile wireless robots which can be freely positioned on a workbench by both the user and the software. The authors propose several applications, including an interior architecture planner: a user can move a piece of furniture to a desired position on the tabletop. Accordingly, all other pieces arrange themselves according to certain constraints, such as moving furniture away from windows to provide most light in the room.

In [22], Pangaro et al. presented the *Actuated Workbench*, which uses an array of electromagnets to freely position tangible "pucks" on an interactive surface. They authors highlight several potential applications, such as undo of tangible operations, remote control of tangibles, and teaching. In a later paper [20], Patten and Ishii enrich the interaction by adding mechanical constraints, like rubber bands or collars. They present an application that automatically arranges telephone towers on a map, which are represented by tangible pucks. The algorithm ensures an efficient distribution of towers, however, by adding mechanical constraints to the tangibles the user can manually override decisions of the underlying algorithm to correct minor mistakes. For example, an oval-shaped ring around two pucks enforces a maximum distance between two telephone towers.

General-Purpose Controls

Most tangible interfaces are special-purpose, and their generality beyond a particular application domain is limited. Conventional controls, such as buttons, sliders, knobs, and keypad, are not only general but have strong physical affordances and well-known natural mappings. In this section, we review work on providing general-purpose controls to improve interfaces for interactive surfaces.

Block et al. developed VoodooSketch [23] (Fig. 7.3a), a system that allows users to design custom interactive palettes to complement multi-touch surfaces. Users can plug real physical controls (e.g., buttons, sliders, knobs, etc.) into the palette and edit parameters of objects on the surface, e.g., the thickness of a drawn line. Functions are mapped to controls by simply drawing labels next to them. For example, the word "opacity" written next to a slider enables users to set the opacity of an object on the surface by dragging the slider. Furthermore, a user can sketch controls using a special pen. For example, a drawn rectangle with the label "Save file" next to it acts as save button and is triggered when the user touches it with the pen. The interactive palette is based on VoodooIO, a flexible substrate material with embedded conductive layers [24] that identifies and monitors widgets when pushed into the surface. A paper with an imprinted dot pattern is bonded on top of this layer.

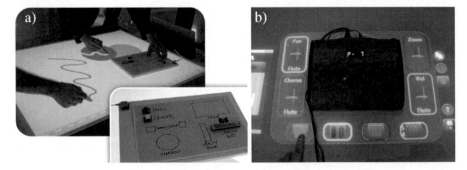

Fig. 7.3 General-purpose controls for tabletops. (a) VoodooSketch represents flexible interactive palettes. Courtesy of Block et al. [23]. (b) Portable device with physical controls provides haptic feedback when manipulating virtual objects. Courtesy of Fiebrink et al. [4]

A special digital Anoto[1] pen captures the drawing of controls and their labels by reading the dot-pattern printed on the paper. In a subsequent study [25], the authors demonstrated that handwritten labels are easy to learn, effective, and more efficient for assigning functions to widgets than conventional approaches, such as selecting a function from a pop-up menu. Physical components can just be removed when not needed anymore whereas drawn widgets remain on the paper. The latter does provide a natural way of saving a palette by just keeping the sheet of paper. A user can then place the interactive palettes anywhere on the surface. However, the palettes consume real estate on the interactive surface and they are tethered which limits mobility and interaction.

Fiebrink et al. point out that interaction with virtual controls lacks precision and propose the integration of physical control devices for tabletop environments [4]. They developed an audio mixer application that allows editing different tracks of a musical piece using a physical device containing four buttons and four knobs. As in VoodooSketch, users can dynamically map functions to the controls (Fig. 7.3b). Controls are surrounded by a visual interface, the "aura", that exposes the function mappings of the controls and represents virtual counter-parts to the physical controls. Accordingly, values such as the volume or speed of a track can be set using both modalities, direct touch and physical controls, providing users with choices that can be matched with particular tasks. In order to map a function to a control, the user first touches a "Copy" icon in the aura. Changeable values in the mixer application are then highlighted and can be moved to the "clipboard" of the device by touching them. By touching the value in the clipboard and selecting a control in the aura the function is finally mapped to it. Due to this serialization, mappings cannot be performed in parallel. The authors comment that this might be desirable if group awareness and communication are critical. The devices allow saving and loading of mappings. In their studies, Fiebrink et al. found that users prefer physical devices when setting continuous values that require high precision while direct touch interaction is used for discrete values. The devices are tethered and opaque.

Similar to conventional tangibles, a major drawback of conventional electronic controls like sliders and knobs is that their physical state is fixed and decoupled from subsequent internal changes to the associated virtual object. For instance, a slider initially mapped to a virtual object does not change as the system changes the virtual object's state. One solution is to employ motorized controls such as the Force Feedback Slider presented by Shahrokni et al. [26] and Gabriel et al. [27]. When first mapped to a virtual object, the physical position of the slider could be set to the current value of the object by using motors. Then a new value could be set by operating the physical control manually. However, motors require additional space on the device (and therewith on the table) and such controls are typically expensive and challenging to manufacture.

---

[1] http://www.anoto.com/

Transparent Tangibles for Dynamic Relabeling

Although general-purpose tangibles provide haptic feedback for tabletop applications, they share the drawback that the visual appearances of the physical controls are fixed. They are opaque and additional graphics around the controls are required to denote their state. A top projection of current state onto the controls is one approach. However, this requires additional hardware, sensing of positions, and the projection will be on a user's hand when the tangible is manipulated. This can break the tight perceptual coupling of physical and virtual state [15]. In this section, we present projects that use transparent tangibles and rear-projection to provide dynamic relabeling while maintaining perceptual coupling.

Schmalstieg et al. enrich a virtual environment with transparent controls called *props* [28]. A table displays a virtual environment providing a stereoscopy view and user-centered projection. The user is equipped with two tracked tangibles, a transparent Plexiglas pad (about 20×25 cm) in the non-dominant hand and a pen in the form of a plastic tube in the dominant hand. The pad displays graphics depending on the task: it can represent a graphical tool palette, a see-through window to show different layers of a rendered landscape, or a volume tool to select objects in 3D space. Even though the pad is held above the table, the actual graphics are rendered on the tabletop using the table's projector, by tracking the user's head and the pad. This creates the illusion that the pad renders the graphics while keeping the tangible lightweight and low-cost.

DataTiles [29] combine the advantages of graphical and physical interfaces by providing transparent, acrylic tiles that can be placed on a *tray*, a flat-panel display enhanced with sensors. Tiles can, for example, represent applications (e.g., weather forecast), portals (e.g., to show webcam streams or printer status), and parameter controls (e.g., to navigate through the video on another tile). Tiles are automatically activated when placed on a grid on the panel and can be composed by putting them next to each other. Similar to props [28], each tile relies on back-projection when placed on the table. In addition, tiles may also expose printed high-resolution content which is then combined with the projected graphics. Users can manipulate a tile's content by using a pen and some tiles contain grooves to guide the user's motion. For example, a parameter tile with a circular groove can be used to navigate through the video on a tile next to it. The tangibles are detected using RFID technology and pen position is sensed by a pen table behind the display.

Tangible Tiles by Waldner et al. [30] extends these interaction ideas. In contrast to DataTiles, transparent tiles are visually tracked using tags that allow them to be freely positioned and orientated on the interactive surface (Fig. 7.4). Virtual objects, such as images, are shown on the table and can be manipulated by placing and moving tiles on the table. The authors provide two kinds of tiles: *container tiles* are used to move, copy and reference objects on the table and *function tiles* allow manipulating objects, e.g., to delete or magnify them. Each tile is labeled with its specific function. Although both DataTiles and Tangible Tiles represent general-purpose tangibles that can be relabeled dynamically, the tile concept, as Waldner et al. point out, provides only limited physical affordances.

Fig. 7.4 Tangible tiles. Courtesy of Waldner et al. [30]

Typing on Touch Surfaces

Typing is one of the most frequent input methods for desktop computers. As multi-touch surfaces find their way into everyday applications, the issue of typing text becomes increasingly crucial. Many researchers have explored typing on small touch displays but only recently have studies started to examine typing on large interactive surfaces. Hinrichs et al. [31] were one of the first to examine text-entry for tabletop displays. They evaluated devices according to visual appearance and performance factors such as their space requirements, rotatability, interference with direct-touch interaction and mobility, and ability to support multi-user interaction. They compared external text-entry methods like physical keyboards and speech recognition with on-screen methods such as handwriting.

While physical keyboards are a highly efficient and optimized text entry method for desktop applications, they are less appropriate for large interactive surface since they require users to switch between direct-touch and typing on a separate external keyboard. Furthermore, they require considerable space, cannot be moved and stored easily, typically are tethered, and, with few exceptions like the Optimus Maximus keyboard,[2] have a fixed keyboard layout. Mobile physical keyboards can be used for text-entry on tabletops but they have many of the same difficulties of other physical keyboards and still require switching between interacting with the surface and the keyboard. Speech recognition allows hands-free input but is error prone and for most users slower than typing. Furthermore, speech input can be disruptive when multiple users are present.

On-screen keyboards on mobile devices have been extensively explored and optimized. They can be dynamically relabeled and displayed where needed. However, lack of haptic feedback results in typing errors, "a general sense of uncertainty when

---

[2]http://www.artlebedev.com/everything/optimus/

typing" [32], and can be a problem for touch typists who rely on the sense of touch to guide text input. In addition, they require visual attention. Handwriting on table-tops is a potential alternative for text input. It is a mobile approach, only requiring a pen or stylus, and supports multi-user interaction. However, it is considered a slow input technique, and accurate handwriting recognition remains a challenging research problem. Gestural alphabets increase speed and accuracy of handwriting on touch-sensitive surfaces. They have similar advantages to handwriting but involve the cost of increased time and effort to learn as well as recognition challenges.

Hinrichs et al. conclude that there is no "perfect" text input method for interactive tabletops and the selection of an appropriate method depends on the specific task. Further empirical studies, especially on tabletops, need to be conducted. We expect text input to remain an important area of research.

SLAP Widgets

In this section, we introduce SLAP Widgets, transparent general-purpose widgets that can used to manipulate virtual objects on interactive tabletops. Our current widget set contains keyboards, keypads, knobs, and sliders. They not only provide tactile feedback but their visual appearance can be dynamically altered. At first, we introduce the multi-touch infrastructure and the SLAP widget set. We then describe the gesture-based pairing mechanism to link SLAP widgets to virtual objects. We conclude with usage scenarios and user studies that compare performance of SLAP widgets with on-screen virtual controls. For more details about the design of SLAP Widgets also see our paper [33].

Multi-touch Table

A multi-touch table as shown in Fig. 7.5 provides the basic infrastructure for sensing physical SLAP Widgets as well as for displaying application graphics such as virtual objects (e.g., photographs, movies, text documents) that users can interact with and modify. The tabletop consists of three layers: an acrylic panel, a layer of foamed sili-cone film, and a diffuse matte. Our system uses a combination of two infrared-based sensing technologies. IR light is projected into the edges of the acrylic panel and changes in surface pressure are detected by an IR camera position below the table surface as users touch the table at various points. This sensing technology is known as FTIR (Frustrated Total Internal Reflection) [34]. Additional infrared LEDs under the table provide Diffuse Illumination (DI) as explained in [35]. The combination of FTIR and DI sensing technologies leads to robust detection of contact pressures from fingertips as well as placement of physical objects on the tabletop. For the later, we employ DI to sense markers on objects placed on the tabletop. FTIR is used for the detection of regular touches, keystrokes on the keyboard, and interactions with other widgets. A short-throw projector beneath the table renders the graphics onto the diffusor.

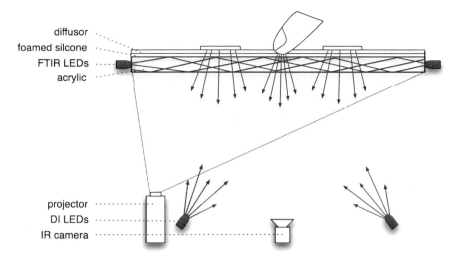

Fig. 7.5 Our multi-touch table combines FTIR and DI to detect both, finger touches and lightweight objects

Widget Set

As shown in Fig. 7.6, all widgets are constructed from transparent acrylic and silicone. This enables the underlying graphics to shine through (Figs. 7.8 and 7.9). Reflective markers of foam and paper mounted beneath each widget create identifying "footprints", which are placed to minimize occlusion of the graphics. As illustrated in Fig. 7.7a, the arrangement of the markers in each footprint determines the widget's type, provides a unique id, and indicates its current state (e.g., the rotation angle of the knob). Figure 7.7b shows example widget footprints as seen by the table's camera. SLAP Widgets are registered by the distinctive arrangement of reflectors and the projected visual representations of widgets are aligned with these reflectors. Touches and moving parts such as the slider's handle (I) and the knob's arm (II) are tracked to update the widget state.

Keyboard – A keyboard is arguably the most necessary computer input device. The SLAP Keyboard adopts the dynamic relabeling advantage of virtual keyboards but unlike virtual keyboards its tangible surface and keys provide haptic feedback. It can be positioned anywhere on the surface and after pairing with an application can be used to enter text as if using a traditional keyboard. In addition, the keyboard layout can be modified on the fly, e.g., in order to show shortcuts (Fig. 7.8) or language-specific layouts.

The SLAP Keyboard is based on a flexible iSkin[3] silicone keyboard cover (Fig. 7.6a). It is mobile and easy to collapse (see requirements in [31]). PVC caps glued onto each key and two rigid strips cemented on the edges of the keyboard

[3]http://www.iskin.com

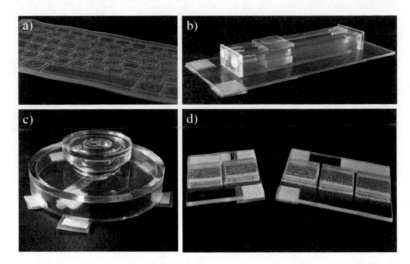

Fig. 7.6 The SLAP widget set. (a) Keyboard. (b) Slider. (c) Knob. (d) Keypads

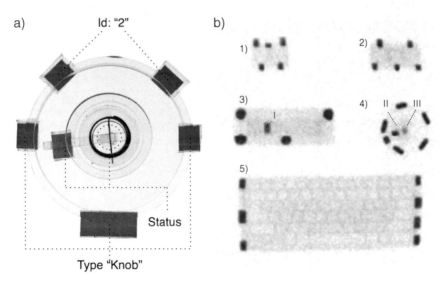

Fig. 7.7 Footprints of SLAP widgets. (a) Knob footprint. The arrangement of markers encodes type, id, and status (rotation angle, press/release state). (b) Footprints as recorded by camera (inverted for better perception). 1–2) Keypad with two and three buttons. 3) Slider with sliding knob (I). 4) Knob with angle indicator (II) and push indicator underneath the rotation axis (III). 5) Keyboard

increase tactile feedback and structural stability. Keycap labels and graphics are dynamically registered as the location of the SLAP Keyboard is tracked. Fingertip forces are conveyed directly through the keys onto the multi-touch surface making use of the FTIR effect, detected as blobs in particular key regions, and interpreted

Fig. 7.8   Dynamic relabeling of SLAP keyboard

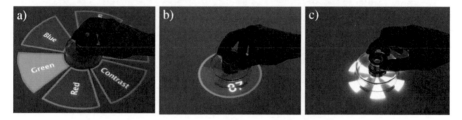

Fig. 7.9   SLAP Knob user interface. a) Selecting image property from menu. b) Setting continuous value. c) Relative navigation for frame stepping in videos

as keystrokes. The IR camera in the table provides a high frame-rate for reliable sensing of key presses.

Keypads – Some applications frequently do not require a full keyboard. For example, a video player may need only a few buttons for playing/pausing, rewinding, and fast-forwarding. Fewer buttons are easier to locate than arbitrarily assigned keys on a full keyboard. For these situations, we designed the SLAP Keypad. We have built keypads with two and three keys. A typical application for a three-keypad would be the video navigation we just mentioned.

A keypad's base is rigid, and only the actual buttons are made of silicone (Fig. 7.6d). At 20 × 15 mm, its keys are also much larger than those of the SLAP keyboard. Otherwise it is similar; fingertip force is conveyed directly and labels/graphics are displayed dynamically. Multiple two- and three-button widgets can be aggregated to create larger tool palettes.

Knob – The SLAP Knob physically enables turning and pushing. These two simple functions are mapped onto different virtual representations depending on the virtual object to which it is linked. The acrylic knob rotates on a clear acrylic base

(Fig. 7.6c). It is vertically spring loaded and can be pressed as a button. An internal reflector arm orbits the axis and indicates an angular position to the camera. A transparent silicone tip in the center of the widget exposes the push state of the knob to the camera: When released, the center is invisible in the camera image. When pushed down, the tip touches the tabletop and causes a FTIR spot in the center, which is detected by the camera (Fig. 7.7b-4). When paired to time-based media, e.g., a video or audio object, the knob can be used to intuitively navigate through the video or adjust volume (Fig. 7.9b, c). However, by using the push mechanism, more complex interactions are possible. When the knob is linked to an image object, pushing it displays a properties menu. By rotating the knob, the user shuffles through a circular menu of properties (Fig. 7.9a). To select a property, such as image brightness or saturation, the user pushes the knob once again. The current value is then displayed underneath it and can be changed with a high degree of precision by turning the knob (Fig. 7.9b). A final push confirms the new value and lets the user choose another property.

Slider – Slider bars are quite common in graphical user interfaces (e.g., scrollbars, parameter adjustment bars). A slider can be used for any interaction in which a continuous value needs to be set. For example, it could be used as a physical timeline for fast navigation in a video, or as an analog slider for setting the size of text characters. As with all SLAP widgets, the possibilities are numerous and depend solely on the virtual object. Just as the knob, the slider is made entirely of acrylic (Fig. 7.6b). Two engraved sides act as rails guiding the linear motion of the sliding knob. For stabilization the slider is mounted onto an acrylic sheet.

Pairing

Widgets must be explicitly linked to virtual objects before they can manipulate them. We refer to this as *pairing*. Inspired by Mayrhofer and Gellersen [36], we implemented a synchronous double tapping gesture: a user simultaneously taps twice next to the widget and onto the virtual object. We used this gesture to avoid recognition problems when multiple users might touch the surface at the same moment.

When first placed on a surface, a widget displays a pulsing blue halo around itself to provide feedback that it has been detected successfully. In this state the widget is not associated with any object. By performing the pairing gesture with a virtual object, an association is attempted. A green flashing halo around both objects and a connecting line between them indicate a successfully established pairing. If a virtual object refuses the association, i.e., if the widget cannot manipulate the particular object, a red halo indicates this problem.

If a previously associated widget is removed and returned to a surface, it will automatically restore its previous association. This permits collaborators to toss controls back and forth without loss of configuration. Pairings are released by repeating the synchronous double tapping gesture. Multiple widgets may be associated with a single virtual object and vice versa.

Usage Scenarios

SLAP Widgets offer versatility and ease-of-use. Having no electronic parts, they are simple, affordable, flexible, and robust. Users can literally slap a widget onto the multi-touch surface and it is immediately ready for use. Versatility is provided by pairing and dynamic relabeling. Although each widget has a specific physical structure, cast from silicone or built from acrylic, its functionality can vary significantly based upon the application used with it and the resulting dynamically changeable visual display.

SLAP Widgets can be used in any application that requires parameter changing functionality, expert shortcuts, or text entry. Since it is often desirable to have a large number of virtual objects on the touch surface but not to have a multitude of physical controls cluttering the surface, SLAP fades controls into view when they are required on a virtual surface, and lets them disappear when they are physically removed from the table. This simplifies interaction, maximizes use of display space, and decreases cognitive load. SLAP supports flexible interaction by providing a small number of controls to interact with an arbitrary number of virtual objects. The following usage scenarios are designed to communicate and emphasize the flexibility of SLAP Widgets.

Collaborative Usage Scenario – One primary advantage of multi-touch tables is to support collaborative group work. Situated around a multi-touch table, several collaborators can work together. One individual can be typing annotations with a SLAP keyboard while a second person is simultaneously interacting with other components of the application or even using another SLAP keyboard to also be entering text. This is very different from the normal situation in which one keyboard must be shared and the cable can restrict easy access. Even with only one SLAP keyboard sharing becomes a much more trivial matter. The flexible silicone keyboard can be tossed between users with no fear of damage and no cable restrictions.

Video Ethnography Scenario – Video ethnographers often need to analyze immense amounts of video data. Typically they work on desktop workstations using existing tools, such as video players and spreadsheets, to do their analysis. Multi-touch tables pose an alternative to the current ethnographic working environment, presenting users with much larger screen space, providing a collaborative space, and enabling new methods for interacting with the data.

We are developing an application for video ethnography. A major task that all ethnographers require is fine-scale video navigation. To assist navigation, we are implementing frame-by-frame navigation using the SLAP Knob. Alternatively, we anticipate using a SLAP Slider for rough navigation. For annotations related to video clips or images, the SLAP Keyboard will be used. Linked with the object, the table projects the keyboard layout, and then the user can quickly enter relevant notes or rapidly switch to another layout for easily coding specific attributes or bookmarking frames of interest. The keypad buttons can change to small thumbnails of the bookmarked frames to assist navigation and a SLAP slider can be used to browse through the bookmarked scenes.

Image Editing Scenario – Editing images represents another interesting scenario for using SLAP Widgets. The SLAP Knob provides an intuitive facility for browsing and modifying image properties. We implemented a menu to cycle through parameters like brightness, contrast, saturation, etc. (Fig. 7.9a). This eliminates the need for complicated menus and submenus that often mask useful features from the novice user. When pushing down the knob, the user can change the specific parameter (Fig. 7.9b). Pushing again returns to the menu selection. A crucial benefit of SLAP Widgets for image editing is that the user can focus visually on the image as a property is adjusted since tactile feedback removes the need to visually attend to the control.

Interface Designer Usage Scenario – Our widget framework can also serve as a toolkit for interface designers working on tabletop applications. They can take advantage of the available widgets and develop a SLAP-based facility for their work. For instance, a designer fashioning an audio mixing application may want to place sliders to represent volume and equalizer levels, knobs to represent gain and fader settings, and keypads for playback controls. In fact, designers may even choose to use SLAP Widgets on a table to cooperatively prototype a traditional application for the desktop.

User Studies

In this section, we present user studies that evaluate the SLAP Widgets. We first describe a quantitative study that compares specific SLAP Widgets with their virtual counterparts and then provide results from a qualitative study.

Knob Performance Task

In our first experiment, a video navigation and annotation task, users were asked to navigate to specific video frames and tag them. This task required users to manipulate controls while visually attending to the video. Since purely virtual controls typically require visual attention, we anticipated that the SLAP Knob would result in faster and more accurate performance because it can be manipulated in an eyes-free fashion. Specifically we hypothesized the following:

- *Hypothesis* 1: Navigation times with SLAP Widgets will be less than with virtual controls.
- *Hypothesis* 2: Navigational overshoots with SLAP Widgets will be less frequent than with virtual controls.
- *Hypothesis* 3: Task completion times with SLAP Widgets will be less than with virtual controls.

The experiment consisted of two conditions that differed only in the use of SLAP Widgets or virtual controls. All controls were placed at the same positions and orientations.

- *"SLAP" Condition:* All controls, two keypads and a knob, were SLAP Widgets with their respective rear-projections.
- *"Virtual" Condition:* All controls were virtual, that is, no widgets were placed on the table, but the graphics were the same as in the SLAP condition.

The keypad buttons were triggered by regular touches. The virtual knob used the standard method of tracking as commonly used by today's desktop applications: When the user holds down her (index) finger in the knob area, the knob rotation follows the finger until it is released, even if dragged outside the area. Each condition involved four trials, and each trial consisted of three instances of navigating to a frame in a video and marking it. Eight video clips were randomly sequenced for each participant; four for the first condition and four for the second. Each participant was randomly assigned to a condition.

Volunteer participants were recruited from a university campus using a general posting in a cafeteria and at a presentation on multi-touch technology. A total of 21 volunteers participated, 19 male and 2 female, between the ages of 22 and 36 with an average age of 25.7. Three were left-handed, 18 right-handed, and none reported any color vision deficiency.

Participants were presented with a multi-touch table with a video window, a bookmark pad, a control pad, and a navigation knob (Fig. 7.10). Depending on the condition, SLAP widgets were or were not in place. The goal of finding and tagging three frames in a video clip was explained. The task was to navigate using a knob and keypad, locate tinted frames, and tag them using a bookmark keypad. Frames tinted in red were to be tagged with a red bookmark, similarly for green and blue. A host computer recorded all actions in a time-coded log file for later analysis.

Typically, a participant would press the *Play* button to start the video, press the *Stop* button when a tinted frame was noticed, navigate frame by frame using the navigation knob until the exact tinted frame was displayed, press a bookmark button to tag it, and press *Play* to continue searching for any remaining tinted frames.

Fig. 7.10 Quantitative test setup. (a) Tabletop layout. (b) Fine-navigation using the SLAP Knob

Video navigation to specific target frames was significantly faster using the SLAP Knob compared to virtual graphics, and it also resulted in fewer overshoots. Moreover, it took participants less time to complete a task using SLAP Widgets than with their virtual counterparts. The study reveals that navigation using virtual knobs required more time and produced more overshoots of the target keyframe compared to the SLAP Knob. We believe the reason for this difference to be that the virtual knob lacks tactile feedback and thus requires visual attention. Participants needed to look to position their fingers at the virtual knob and when their finger drifted away from the central point, the irregular scrolling speed of the video that resulted forced participants to correct their finger position. The SLAP Knob instead was grabbed and turned mostly without visual attention, leading to fewer overshoots and shorter interaction times.

Qualitative Evaluation

Are SLAP Widgets easy to associate and manipulate? What do people like, dislike, or want to change about them? These are questions we addressed in a set of tasks designed to familiarize participants with SLAP Widgets.

Participants were presented with a multi-touch table displaying a video window, an image window, and a text field. The SLAP Widgets were described in a 5-min demonstration of their use including synchronous pairing gestures. Participants were requested to perform the following series of control, navigation, and editing tasks followed by an interview to provide feedback. The tasks and interview were recorded and reviewed.

- *Video Control:* Place a keypad widget on the table, associate it with the video window, and control the video using Play and Pause buttons of the keypad widget.
- *Video Navigation:* Place a SLAP Slider and SLAP Knob on the table, associate them with the video window, scroll through the video using the slider for gross navigation and the knob for fine steps between frames.
- *Image Editing:* Re-associate the SLAP Slider and SLAP Knob to the image window, adjust brightness with the slider and saturation with the knob.
- *Text Editing:* Place a SLAP Keyboard on the table, associate it with the text field, type your name, re-associate the knob to the text field, and modify text color with the knob.

All participants were expert computer users experienced with graphical user interfaces and recruited from a university campus. Seven male and three female participants, between ages of 21 and 28, volunteered to participate and consented to video recording.

Most (9/10) participants declared manipulating the SLAP Widgets was intuitive and self-evident. One participant emphasized that widgets map well-known physical control elements to their virtual equivalents and may be particularly well adapted for people not familiar with virtual controls. Another participant commented on how the widgets permitted resting her hands on them while not using them (something not possible with virtual keyboards and controls).

The pairing gesture was immediately understood by all participants and used readily. Comments indicated that it felt similar to setting a foreground GUI window. Some (4/10) participants suggested alternative pairing gestures such as placing a widget on a virtual object and sliding it to a comfortable position not occluding any virtual objects ("grasp and drag" of control properties), but also felt that synchronous double-tapping was particularly appropriate for the keyboard. Some (4/10) participants felt the SLAP Widgets were too quiet and could benefit from auditory feedback, particularly the keyboard.

Feedback on the keyboard was mixed, some participants suggested improvements. It was felt that the making it easier to feel the edges and keycap contours as well as providing a more traditional tactile response would improve the keyboard. Although participants appreciated the concept of the haptic SLAP Keyboard, most still felt more comfortable typing on the virtual keyboard. This may have resulted from the fact that the DI interface at times created false positives due to hover effects and it appeared difficult for participants to know how hard they had to press the silicone keys. We plan to address both issues in future iterations of SLAP keyboard prototypes.

Future Trends

Interactive surfaces become increasingly common and available to be used in everyday applications. Future operating systems will support multi-touch interaction by default and enable more interface designers to think beyond the current concept of single cursor interaction. Tabletop applications will rapidly move from the simple proof-of-concept prototypes (e.g., photo sorting) that we see currently to practical applications. Interactive multi-touch tabletops will play an crucial role in computer supported collaborative work applications. General-purpose tangibles are particularly valuable in such applications since they not only provide haptic feedback but allow users to be aware of all actions on the table in a variety of domains.

We expect that the emerging trend of organic interfaces [37, 38] will evoke actuated deformable tabletop controls that actively reflect the current system state. Furthermore, we assume that future tangibles will not only be limited to the tabletop, but also the space above and around the table will be incorporated into the applications by making use of gestures and dynamic tangibles whose representations reach beyond the tabletop projection. Multi-touch systems using switchable diffusors, as in SecondLight [39], that allow projection onto the surface as well as on tangibles above represent a particularly promising research direction.

These new interaction modalities require enhanced technologies. Currently, vision is the only way for reliable detection of objects, patterns, and markers on tabletops but we assume that new ways for object detection, maybe similar to RFID chips as in DataTiles [29], will continue to be explored. In terms of transparent tangibles, it is likely that visual markers for position and orientation detection will be completely hidden in the future, as is already being investigated in recent research [40, 41]. However, the development of tabletop applications is still constrained due to technical limitations. Text input using handwriting requires a high camera resolution, fast typing with tangible keyboards, such as the SLAP keyboard, demands a high camera frame rate. Collaborative tabletop interaction naturally takes place on large surfaces, but this requires a high display resolution or multiple synchronized displays. An interdisciplinary development, including Human-Computer Interaction, Computer Science, and Electrical Engineering, will be essential to face these challenges.

Conclusion

Interactive multi-touch horizontal surfaces have considerable potential to become a common part of everyday computing applications. Tabletops provide a natural environment for collaboration and multi-touch tables allow direct manipulation of digital data while supporting the awareness of other users at the table. They are likely to become a crucial part of the overall interactive computing ecology and as with other technologies will need to be carefully integrated into that increasing complex of mobile and distributed ecology.

References

1. Hutchins EL, Hollan JD, Norman DA (1985) Direct manipulation interfaces. Human-Computer Interaction 1(4):311–338
2. Hutchins EL, Hollan JD, Norman DA (1986) Direct manipulation interfaces. In: User centered system design: New perspectives on human-computer interaction, Lawrence Erlbaum Associates, Hillsdale, NJ and London, pp 87–124
3. Weiser M (1991) The computer for the 21st century. Scientific American 265(3):94–104
4. Fiebrink R, Morris D, Morris MR (2009) Dynamic mapping of physical controls for tabletop groupware. In: CHI '09: Proceedings of the 27th international conference on human factors in computing systems, ACM Press, New York, pp 471–480
5. Ishii H, Ullmer B (1997) Tangible bits: Towards seamless interfaces between people, bits and atoms. In: CHI '97: Proceedings of the SIGCHI conference on human factors in computing systems, ACM Press, New York. pp 234–241
6. Poupyrev I, Nashida T, Okabe M (2007) Actuation and tangible user interfaces: The Vaucanson Duck, Robots, and shape displays. In: TEI '07: Proceedings of the 1st international conference on tangible and embedded interaction, ACM Press, New York, pp 205–212
7. Benali-Khoudja M, Hafez M, Alex J, Kheddar A (2004) Tactile interfaces: A state-of-the-art survey. In: Proceedings of the international symposium on robotics, Paris, France, pp 721–726
8. Craig IS, Chanter CM, Southall AL, Brady AC (2001) Results from a tactile array on the fingertip. In: Eurohaptics, Birmingham, UK, pp 26–28
9. Yang GH, Kyung KU, Srinivasan MA, Kwon DS (2006) Quantitative tactile display device with pin-array type tactile feedback and thermal feedback. In: Proceedings of the IEEE international conference on robotics and automation, Orlando, Florida, USA, pp 3917–3922
10. Oelho M, Maes P (2009) Shutters: A permeable surface for environmental control and communication. In: TEI' 09: Proceedings of the 3rd international conference on tangible and embedded interaction, ACM Press, New York, pp 13–18

11. Harrison C, Hudson SE (2009) Providing dynamically changeable physical buttons on a visual display. In: CHI '09: Proceedings of the 27th international conference on human factors in computing systems, ACM Press, New York, pp 299–308
12. Hoggan E, Brewster SA, Johnston J (2008) Investigating the effectiveness of tactile feedback for mobile touchscreens. In: CHI '08: Proceeding of the twenty-sixth annual SIGCHI conference on human factors in computing systems, ACM Press, New York, pp 1573–1582
13. Fitzmaurice GW, Ishii H, Buxton WAS (1995) Bricks. Laying the foundations for graspable user interfaces. In CHI '95: Proceedings of the SIGCHI conference on human factors in computing systems, ACM Press/Addison-Wesley Publishing Co, New York, pp 442–449
14. Ishii H (2008) The tangible user interface and its evolution. Communications of the ACM 51(6):32–36
15. Ishii H (2008) Tangible bits: Beyond pixels. In: TEI '08: Proceedings of the 2nd international conference on tangible and embedded interaction, ACM Press, New York. pp xv–xxv
16. Underkoffler J, Ishii H (1998) Illuminating light: An optical design tool with a luminous-tangible interface. In: CHI '98: Proceedings of the SIGCHI conference on human factors in computing systems, ACM/Addison-Wesley Publishing Co., New York, pp 542–549
17. Underkoffler J, Ishii H (1999) Urp: A luminous-tangible workbench for urban planning and design. In: CHI '99: Proceedings of the SIGCHI conference on human factors in computing systems, ACM Press, New York, pp 386–393
18. Jordà S, Geiger G, Alonso M, Kaltenbrunner M (2007) The reacTable: Exploring the synergy between live music performance and tabletop tangible interfaces. In: TEI '07: Proceedings of the 1st international conference on tangible and embedded interaction, ACM Press, New York, pp 139–146
19. Horn MS, Solovey ET, Crouser RJ, Jacob RJK (2009) Comparing the use of tangible and graphical programming languages for informal science education. In: CHI '09: Proceedings of the 27th international conference on human factors in computing systems, ACM Press, New York, pp 975–984
20. Patten J, Ishii H (2007) Mechanical constraints as computational constraints in tabletop tangible interfaces. In: CHI '07: Proceedings of the SIGCHI conference on human factors in computing systems, ACM Press, New York, pp 809–818
21. Rosenfeld D, Zawadzki M, Sudol J, Perlin K (2004) Physical objects as bidirectional user interface elements. Computer Graphics and Applications. IEEE 24(1):pp 44–49
22. Pangaro G, Maynes-Aminzade D, Ishii H (2002) The actuated workbench: Computer controlled actuation in tabletop tangible interfaces. In: UIST '02: Proceedings of the 15th annual ACM symposium on user interface software and technology, ACM Press, New York, pp 181–190
23. Block F, Haller M, Gellersen H, Gutwin C, Billinghurst M (2008) VoodooSketch: Extending interactive surfaces with adaptable interface palettes. In: TEI '08: Proceedings of the 2nd international conference on tangible and embedded interaction, ACM Press, New York, pp 55–58
24. Villar N, Gellersen H (2007) A malleable control structure for softwired user interfaces. In: TEI '07: Proceedings of the 1st international conference on tangible and embedded interaction, ACM Press, New York, pp 49–56
25. Block F, Gutwin C, Haller M, Gellersen H, Billinghurst M (2008) Pen and paper techniques for physical customisation of tabletop interfaces. In: Horizontal interactive human computer systems, 2008. TABLETOP 2008: Proceedings of the 3rd IEEE International Workshop on 2008, Amsterdam, The Netherlands, pp 17–24
26. Shahrokni A, Jenaro J, Gustafsson T, Vinnberg A, Sandsjö J, Fjeld M (2006) One-dimensional force feedback slider: Going from an analogue to a digital platform. In: NordiCHI '06: Proceedings of the 4th Nordic conference on human-computer interaction, ACM Press, New York, pp 453–456

27. Gabriel R, Sandsjö J, Shahrokni A, Fjeld M (2008) BounceSlider: Actuated sliders for music performance and composition. In: TEI '08: Proceedings of the 2nd international conference on tangible and embedded interaction, ACM Press, New York, pp 127–130

28. Schmalstieg D, Encarnação LM, Szalavári Z (1999) Using transparent props for interaction with the virtual table. In: I3D '99: Proceedings of the 1999 symposium on interactive 3d graphics, ACM Press, New York, pp 147–153

29. Rekimoto J, Ullmer B, Oba H (2001) DataTiles: A modular platform for mixed physical and graphical interactions. In CHI '01: Proceedings of the SIGCHI conference on human factors in computing systems, ACM, New York. pp 269–276

30. Waldner M, Hauber J, Zauner J, Haller M, Billinghurst M (2006) Tangible tiles: Design and evaluation of a tangible user interface in a collaborative tabletop setup. In: OZCHI '06: Proceedings of the 18th Australia conference on computer-human interaction, ACM Press, New York, pp 151–158

31. Hinrichs U, Hancock M, Collins C, Carpendale S (2007) Examination of text-entry methods for tabletop displays. In: Horizontal interactive human-computer systems, 2007. TABLETOP '07: Proceedings of the 2nd annual IEEE international workshop on 2007, Newport, Rhode Island, pp 105–112

32. Hirche J, Bomark P, Bauer M, Solyga P (2008) Adaptive interface for text input on large-scale interactive surfaces. In: Horizontal interactive human-computer systems, 2008. TABLETOP '08: Proceedings of the 3rd annual IEEE international workshop on 2008, Amsterdam, Netherlands, pp 153–156

33. Weiss M, Wagner J, Jansen Y, Jennings R, Khoshabeh R, Hollan JD, Borchers J (2009) SLAP Widgets: Bridging the gap between virtual and physical controls on tabletops. In: CHI '09: Proceedings of the 27th international conference on human factors in computing systems, ACM Press, New York, pp 481–490

34. Han JY (2005) Low-cost multi-touch sensing through frustrated total internal reflection. In: UIST '05: Proceedings of the 18th annual ACM symposium on user interface software and technology, ACM Press, New York, pp 115–118

35. Matsushita N, Rekimoto J (1997) HoloWall: Designing a finger, hand, body, and object sensitive wall. In: UIST '97: Proceedings of the 10th annual ACM symposium on user interface software and technology, ACM Press, New York, pp 209–210

36. Mayrhofer R, Gellersen H (2007) Shake well before use: Authentication based on accelerometer data. In: Pervasive Computing, Springer, Heidelberg, pp 144–161

37. Co E, Pashenkov N (2008) Emerging display technologies for organic user interfaces. Communication of the ACM 51(6):45–47

38. Holman D, Vertegaal R (2008) Organic user interfaces: Designing computers in any way, shape, or form. In Communication of the ACM 51(6):48–55

39. Izadi S, Hodges S, Taylor S, Rosenfeld D, Villar N, Butler A, et al. (2008) Going beyond the display: A surface technology with an electronically switchable diffuser. In: UIST '08: Proceedings of the 21st annual ACM symposium on user interface software and technology, ACM Press, New York, pp 269–278

40. Koike H, Nishikawa W, Fukuchi K (2009) Transparent 2-D markers on an LCD tabletop system. In: CHI '09: Proceedings of the 27th international conference on human factors in computing systems, ACM Press, New York, pp 163–172

41. Kakehi Y, Hosomi T, Iida M, Naemura T, Matsushita M (2006) Transparent tabletop interface for multiple users on lumisight table. In: TABLETOP '06: Proceedings of the 1st IEEE international workshop on horizontal interactive human-computer systems, IEEE Computer Society, Washington, DC, pp 143–150

Chapter 8
Active Tangible Interactions

Masahiko Inami, Maki Sugimoto, Bruce H. Thomas, and Jan Richter

Abstract This chapter explores active tangible interactions, an extension of tangible user interactions. Active tangible interactions employ tangible objects with some form of self automation in the form of robotics or locomotion. Tangible user interfaces employ physical objects to form graspable physical interfaces for a user to control a computer application. Two example forms of active tangible interactions are presented, Local Active Tangible Interactions and Remote Active Tangible Interactions. Local Active Tangible Interactions (LATI) is a concept that allows users to interact with actuated physical interfaces such as small robots locally. The Remote Active Tangible Interactions (RATI) system is a fully featured distributed version of multiple LATI's. The underlining technology Display-Based Measurement and Control System is employed to support our instantiations of Local Active Tangible Interactions and Remote Active Tangible Interactions.

Introduction

Active tangible interactions [1, 2] are an extension of tangible user interactions [3] that employ tangible objects with some form of self automation in the form of robotics or locomotion. Tangible user interfaces (TUI) are graspable physical interfaces that employ physical objects such as blocks, miniature models, and cardboard cut-outs for controlling a computer system. A TUI does not have the user manipulate GUI control elements on a display, such as buttons or sliders, through a traditional mouse and keyboard combination. Instead a TUI encourages users to manipulate physical objects that either embody virtual data or act as handles for virtual data. Such physical interactions are very natural and intuitive for users for the following reasons:

M. Inami (✉)
Graduate School of Media Design, Keio University, Yokohama, Kanagawa 223-8526, Japan
e-mail: inami@computer.org

C. Müller-Tomfelde (ed.), *Tabletops – Horizontal Interactive Displays*,
Human-Computer Interaction Series, DOI 10.1007/978-1-84996-113-4_8,
© Springer-Verlag London Limited 2010

1. they enable two-handed input and
2. provide us with spatial and haptic feedback that aids our understanding and thinking [4, 5].

The physical objects that construct a TUI are referred to as tangibles, and can be categorized as *passive* or *active*. TUI's have a natural relationship with tabletop systems [6–11]; if for no other reason than the objects require a surface to set them upon. The interaction with the surface and other objects on the table is an active area of current investigation [12–16]. The ability to track the physical objects and to provide these objects with computer controlled self-locomotion is the main research goal presented of this chapter.

Tangible user interfaces feature many benefits over traditional GUIs. Fitzmaurice, Ishii and Buxton [4] identified the following TUI advantages:

1. they allow for more parallel user input, thereby improving the expressiveness or the communication capacity with the computer;
2. they leverage our well developed, everyday skills of prehensile behaviours for physical object manipulations;
3. they externalize traditionally internal computer representations;
4. they facilitate interactions by making interface elements more "direct" and more "manipulable" by using physical artefacts;
5. they take advantage of our keen spatial reasoning skills;
6. they offers a space multiplex design with a one to one mapping between control and controller; and
7. they afford multi-person collaborative use.

As previously mentioned, active tangible interactions are concerned with tangible objects that have some form of self propulsion. A good example of support for active tangible interactions is the Display-based Measurement and Control System (DMCS) [2] is a tabletop robot/tracking technology. This system provides a suitable research platform for an active tangible user interface. DMCS has the following advantages: easily scalable, control of orientation, requires minimal calibration, robust tracking system, allows tangibles to be lifted up to 20 cm off the table while still allowing for reliable tracking, and supports both top and rear-projected environments (so occlusion by top-projection can be avoided if need be).

This chapter will provide an overview of the existing active tangible interactions research concerned with tabletop surfaces. In particular the DMCS technology will be explored. Two main forms of active tangible interactions are presented, Local Active Tangible Interactions and Remote Active Tangible Interactions. We have built a number of systems based on these technologies, and this chapter will explore these systems in detail. Finally the chapter will conclude with a discussion of this user interaction paradigm and future directions.

Background

There are main two concepts that underpin our investigations. The first as previously mentioned is tangible user interfaces. The second is TUI's employed for distributed collaboration. This section provides an overview of these concepts.

Tangible User Interfaces

An early example of TUI is the Active Desk [4]; an application supporting interaction through simple Lego^{TM}-like bricks on a table surface that act as grips for manipulating graphical objects. The application merges space-multiplexed I/O (every input device has just has one function) and time-multiplexed-I/O (a single input device has multiple functions at different points in time).

Other earlier work on TUI's include Ullmer and Ishii's metaDESK [17] and Rauterberg et al.'s BUILD-IT system [18]. The metaDESK goal is to complement (not substitute) conventional GUIs with physical interactions. These interactions enable users to shift two building models to navigate, zoom and warp a map. The map orients and positions itself so that the two building models always correspond with their location on the map. BUILD-IT is a comparable TUI, where users manipulate bricks as handles to layout a factory plant. Both system are not appropriate for active tangible interaction, as the bricks are passive (have no means of self propulsion). Furthermore, the bricks cannot be moved automatically by a controlling system.

A useful extension to tangible user interfaces is to couple them with augmented reality (AR) [19] or mixed reality (MR) [20]. Kato et al. [21] combine TUI's with AR (called tangible augmented reality (TAR)) to overlay tangibles with virtual images. A TAR removes the need for users to remember which tangibles represent which set of digital data.

TUI's in Distributed Collaboration

The connected rocking chairs developed by Fujimura, Nishimura and Nakamura [22] share rocking motions with each other, allowing the users rocking the chairs to feel connected. The two networked rocking chairs are controllable via a linear motor attached to the base of the chairs. Equally the connected rocking chairs and the inTouch system of Brave, Ishii and Dahley [23] concern themselves with the concept of distributed haptics. The synchronization of physical interfaces has a similar motivation to active tangible interactions; however they vary in that the above mentioned systems do not concentrate on maintaining remote TUI's synchronization. Their main purpose is providing haptic feedback over remote physical interfaces.

Brace, Ishii and Dahley [23] initially purposed the concept of distributing a TUI. An early exploration is their PSyBench, developed to substitute conventional video/audio conferencing with tangible interfaces. With the use of Synchronized Distributed Physical Objects (SDPO), PSyBench provides the user with the impression that they are sharing matching objects even though they are remote. The PSyBench is based on two networked motorized chessboards. A major limitation of the hardware is the incapability of controlling the orientation of the tangibles.

A comparable concept is Rosenfeld et al.'s [5] bidirectional UI, where tangibles can be employed for both input and output, and can be controlled equally by the computer and the users. Rosenfeld et al.'s Planar Manipulation Scale (PMD) implements "dumb robots" to produce a bidirectional user interface. The two wheel motorized robots can freely move around a table surface. Two pulsing LED's (for position and orientation) underneath each robot enable tracking. To evaluate their investigations, the authors developed a furniture layout application, where seven robots depicting furniture automatically and simultaneously move to form one of a number of pre-set room layouts. The PMD is not implemented in a distributed TUI, but is a suitable technology.

One of a small number of tangible interfaces that supports duplex input and output (IO) is the actuated workbench project [24]. Magnetic pucks (or non-magnetic objects outfitted with magnets) operate on a table surface with a built-in array of electromagnets that are energized to shift the objects. Users can manually slide the magnetic pucks, and these pucks are fitted with infrared (IR) LED's that are sensed with an IR vision system. The quantity of pucks concurrently movable is restricted due to the intricate magnetic array required to move them, and puck orientation is not presently controllable. The objective of the actuated workbench is to allow computer control of the tangibles.

Everitt et al. [25] explicitly investigated the practicability of tangible user interfaces for distributed collaboration activities. They employ networked smart boards onto which Post-it™ notes can be fixed for design intentions. A high resolution camera captures the information on any of the newly added notes, and stores this as an image on a central server. The other client then displays the image with a projector on its smart board. Users can reorganize equally tangible and digital notes, by physically moving them or through computer interaction via a pen or mouse. As the physical notes are not electronic (a limitation), faint grey shadows are projected under each physical note. These annotations turn red when a physical note is required to be shifted to a new position. Fresh notes can be added in parallel, but existing notes can only be moved one at a time. Simple but elegant shadow silhouettes supply a sense of distributed presence while decreasing bandwidth required for complete video-conferencing.

Display-Based Measurement and Control System

The Display-Based Measurement and Control System (DMCS) [2] system is a perfect enabling technology for implementing active tangible interactions. The DMCS

Fig. 8.1 Example robot

removes the need for an external tracking system of the robots in a projection space. The system uses a display device as a dynamic ruler to track the robot. Rather than implementing the tracking and controlling of the robots as disconnect systems (traditionally via a separate camera and data communications to the robot respectively), the DMCS combines both concepts and encapsulates them inside the robot. Communication with the robot is two-way. DMCS is a close-loop solution, thus ensuring the robots are in the correct position on the table. Each robot is fitted with five phototransistors to sense the light intensity, see Fig. 8.1. A unique fiducial marker featuring a gradient from black to white is centred over the set of phototransistors, see Fig. 8.2. The fiducial marker is designed to measure relative positions and directions between the marker and robot independently. Each robot transmits the brightness values of the phototransistors back to a central computer that employs this data to maintain the fiducial marker's position centred over each robot's phototransistors, see Fig. 8.3. Controlling the robot is performed by sending signals to the robot via a cable or radio.

The DMCS's tracking system is closed-loop, as the phototransistors determine the relative position compared to the marker and is self adjusting to have them overlap dynamically [26]. The tracking algorithm continuously employs feedback from each robot to adjust the coordinates of that robot's fiducial tracking marker. The attribute of the DMCS system that is critical for active tangible interactions is that it enables input and output via the robot. The robot can be manipulated by a human to adjust the system's internal state, while at the same time the alteration of information inside the system can be visualized in the physical world by automatically moving the robots. Each robot is fixed with two separately controlled wheels for this function. Figure 8.4 depicts our new robot with retractable wheels for easier manipulation and an integrated sound system. The range of robot sizes is shown in Fig. 8.5. The robots can be augmented with additional features, such as grasping pincers as shown in Fig. 8.6.

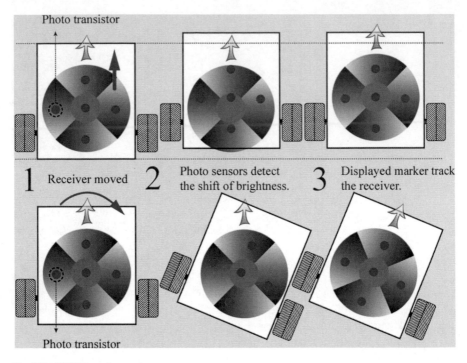

Fig. 8.2 DMCS marker system

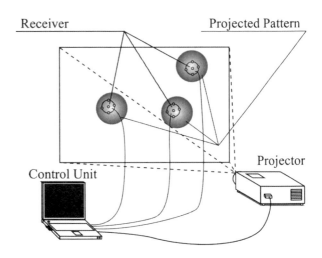

Fig. 8.3 Overall layout

Fig. 8.4 New robot with sound and retractable wheels

Fig. 8.5 Example of two different sizes of tabletop robots

Local Active Tangible Interactions

Local Active Tangible Interactions (LATI) is a concept that allows users to interact with actuated physical interfaces such as small robots locally [2]. This section describes the concept of LATI, and provides an example application Augmented Coliseum.

LATI

LATI brings dynamic physical expressions, haptic feedback and intuitive manipulation to the interactions between the users and the interfaces. We employ DMCS

Fig. 8.6 A robot with a
grasping device on the front
to move physical objects

as a useful technology to develop these kinds of interactions. This technology
can control the actuated interfaces by just drawing fiducial makers on a computer
display. Examples of using Adobe Flash[1] to control robots have been developed,
such as a set of robots in synchronised motion dancing to music. These Flash
controlled robot applications do not require any knowledge of the underlining technology. Just move and rotate the markers on the display, and the robots follow. This
concept is extended to combine TUI's and dynamic changing virtual environments.

The input/output nature of DMCS makes it a natural technology for LATI.
Furthermore, graphics can contribute to dynamic expressions with the actuated
physical interfaces. Movements within the interfaces are able to be enhanced by
animated background graphics. When the background graphics move with TUI's,
the users can perceive movements in both real and virtual environments. Relative
Motion Racing [27] is one example of this effect, see Fig. 8.7. The system controls
small robots and background graphics simultaneously. It can express high velocity
motions of the robots by using combination of slow robot motions and large magnitude graphics motions. This method can expand the virtual size of workspaces in
active tangible systems.

Augmented Coliseum

The input and output via the same physical object nature of a LATI is demonstrated
in an AR game, Augmented Coliseum [28]; a game based on the Display-Based
Measurement and Control System. The game environment employs AR technology
to enable virtual functions for playing a game with small robots, similar to how

---

[1]http://www.adobe.com/products/flashplayer/

Fig. 8.7 Relative motion racing

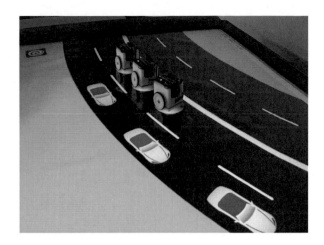

children can use their imaginations to transform a normal room into the sky for playing games with toy airplanes. Augmented Coliseum embodies this concept of imagination virtually by superimposing computer graphics onto toys (in the form of robots) in the physical world. Playing with toys such as small robots and vehicles is improved and enhanced by projecting images to the areas corresponding to the actual positions and directions of the toys. In addition, objects are able to express the phenomena of this augmented reality world by controlling actuators according to the results of simulations. In the environment that we propose, the games are played with small robots and vehicles that can be treated as actual toys of the real world.

The example game *Augmented Coliseum* is played with two users interacting with standard games controllers to move (see Fig. 8.8) and fire on opponents (see Fig. 8.9). Two robots are connected to the same projector/computer [29] system and each is operated by a human player. Each user attempts to "blow up" their opponents' robots, see Fig. 8.10. The robots represent physical battle tanks, which can shoot virtual missiles and lasers at each other. The projectiles are represented visually in the virtual world. Each robot is driven by the human players, which embodies the input in the form of the battle tank's placement in the game space. The playing area (see Fig. 8.11) can be tabletop size or quite large, approximately 3 by 4 m. A novel feature of the use of virtual and physical representations is the robots react to both physical and virtual interactions on the game board. The black circles are regions the robots cannot enter. A simple physics model detects collisions between the robots and other virtual objects inside the game, and these collisions are physically represented by making the robot rock as they collide. This represents output in the form of physical feedback. The concept of input and output via the same physical object is missing from a TUI, but a LATI adds this extra sensation of interaction to the system.

Fig. 8.8 Example robot
moving in the game

Fig. 8.9 Example of one
robot firing on another

Remote Active Tangible Interactions

The Remote Active Tangible Interactions (RATI) [1] system extends the concept of
LATI to a fully remote distributed system. This section first highlights the major
components the RATI. The section finishes with explanation an interior design
application developed with a RATI.

RATI

The RATI system is an extension of the original DMCS system. The DMCS system was extended to allow multiple displays, each with their own application, to

Fig. 8.10 Example of an
explosion on a robot

Fig. 8.11 Overview of the
game space

communicate and synchronise other over a network with a custom XML messaging protocol. The original RATI consisted of two connected DMCS clients with two robots paired together (one on each table). Our latest version of RATI has been tested on three tables with six robots on each table, see Fig. 8.4. The robots on any table could be translated and/or rotated while maintaining a common state between both clients. A set of virtual obstacles and collision-avoidance techniques were developed to prevent robots from colliding with other robots or the obstacles.

For reasons of scalability, an elegant client/server architecture was chosen over P2P as the method to unite the DMCS systems together. The server permits essential data to be stored; such as obstacle coordinates for virtual objects to be shared by all clients. In addition, data on all clients connected (number of robots connected, the physical screen size, resolution, etc) is also stored.

XML was selected to support the protocol because messages are plaintext, platform independent, and extendable. The present protocol defines message structures for sending and receiving translate and rotate commands, querying any client's environment data (e.g. screen resolution, number of robots connected), and querying exact data about any robot (e.g. coordinate, orientation). The server understands each XML message and transmits it accordingly; queries are delivered to the appropriate client, while translate and rotate commands are broadcasted to all other clients.

The DMCS clients are synchronized by sending a *movement* XML message to the server for each occasion a robot/tangible is moved by a user. Three distinctive movement modes are integrated into the RATI system. The selected mode determines when a movement structure should be available. The first mode only publishes the end coordinate of a move. DMCS clients synchronizing the state of their tangibles ignore the path along which that tangible was moved, and simply move to the target coordinate in a straight line. In this mode the client is required to calculate a path that avoids and virtual or physical obstacles. The second mode publishes the exact path of the tangible that was moved. This is realized by publishing the tangible's coordinates in a real-time succession of data packets. In mode three a finite number of waypoints from a tangible's path are supplied. This mode can be used to approximate the path that the robot traversed. The spacing of the waypoints is left to the client, and will be dependent on how often the coordinates are published.

The selection of modes is application specific. For example, if the tangibles represent individual sessions in a schedule, then the tangible's position is important, not how the tangible moved to that position. On the other hand if the tangibles are deployed as an action game, then the exact path of each tangible is very important.

Physical and virtual obstacle avoidance is included in the system to increase the functionality of the system. The obstacles are assumed to be static (i.e. fixed location) when the collision avoidance algorithm is executed so that it would only have to be executed for one instance of each robot move. Obstacle avoidance is determined by the breadth first search (BFS) algorithm, which operates on a graph that defines the robot and all obstacles. The graph is constructed by dividing the screen into a grid. All robots and obstacles are associated with their closest grid node, which is then connected together to form an undirected cyclic graph. This graph is given to the BFS algorithm. The resulting BFS path is pruned to remove any obsolete nodes, after which the robot can be driven along the obstacle-free path.

Furniture Application

An interior design application is described as an example of the suitability of the DMCS technology for remote active tangible interactions. The furniture placement application supports users to visualise the layout of a room of furniture, see Fig. 8.12. The furniture application depicts on a tabletop display six pieces of

Fig. 8.12 Furniture layout
application

furniture as a birds-eye view of a floor plan. The following six furniture items are
represented: chair, couch, fish tank, lamp, table, and TV.

Furniture selection is supported by moving the robot on top of the appropriate
image, upon which the image would snap to the robot and the furniture movement
is slaved to the robot's movement. Only one piece of furniture can be attached to a
robot at a time. A small threshold is included, to avoid any unwanted snapping that
could occur while moving the robot around during normal interaction. This threshold only allows a furniture image to snap to a robot, if the robot was within 10 pixels
of the centre of the representation of the piece of furniture. This threshold is easily
adjustable for different applications. Once a piece of furniture is selected, the robot
takes on the role of that piece of furniture and can be moved around and oriented as
if it was a physical model of that furniture item. This embodies a costume metaphor,
in which a robot can represent different pieces of furniture at different points in time.
The costume metaphor was forced by the limited availability of robots of our original system, which only allowed one tangible per environment. We have overcome
this limitation in our new version of RATI.

Ideally one robot would be available for each piece of furniture, and be permanently bound to that identity for the duration of the application. This is referred to
as space multiplexed input and output (IO), because each device is dedicated to a
single task only. The alternative time multiplexed IO "uses one device to control
different functions at different points in time" [30]. Another appropriate metaphor
for the interface could be a bulldozer metaphor by implementing robots fitted with
forklift arms, see Fig. 8.6. In a bulldozer fashion, a single robot could move all the
passive furniture models, albeit one at a time.

A real-time 3D view of the furniture arrangement provided a third person perspective for users, on a vertical screen across the table from the user. The 3D
visualization provided the users with a front-on perspective of the room. Figure 8.12
depicts the 3D view of an example layout. Each DMCS client is connected to the

server using TCP/IP. The 3D visualization is rendered by a separate computer, which received a continuous stream of data via UDP.

Future Trends

An interesting future trend is an asymmetric use of the robots in a RATI enhanced application. The Hand of God (HOG) is an indoor system to provide an intuitive means for providing a wider bandwidth of human communication between indoor experts and users in the field [31]. Figure 8.13 depicts an indoor expert employing the HOG by pointing to locations on a map. The indoor and outdoor users have a supplementary voice communication channel. An outdoor field worker employing an outdoor AR wearable computer can, for example, visualizes a 3D model of the indoor expert's hand geo-referenced at a point on the map, as depicted in Fig. 8.13. The indoor expert is able to promptly and naturally communicate to the outdoor field operative. As depicted in Fig. 8.13, the indoor expert is able to point to a precise location on a map and give the outdoor user a visual waypoint to navigate to, see Fig. 8.14. Physical props may be placed onto the HOG table; an example is the placement of a signpost onto a geo-referenced point, as shown in Fig. 8.15. These props currently operate as TUI, but the outdoor user is able to virtual move the signpost. The use of active tangible interactions will enable the physical signpost in the HOG tank to move and reflect the new location the outdoor user has placed the virtual signpost. This would enable the physical signpost and virtual signpost to be synchronized. Breaking the RATI one-to-one relationship will open a number of interesting possibilities. Having physical representation of virtual worlds such as Second Life[2] would be possible.

Fig. 8.13 An indoor expert employing the Hand of God interface

---

[2]http://secondlife.com/

Fig. 8.14 Head mounted display view seen by the outdoor participant

Fig. 8.15 Physical props as signposts for the outdoor user

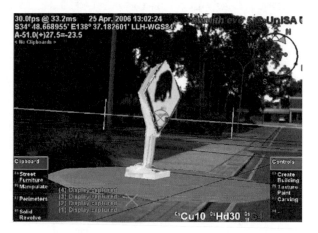

Conclusion

This chapter explored active tangible interactions that are an extension of tangible user interactions. Active tangible interactions employ tangible objects with some form of self automation in the form of robotics or locomotion. Tangible user interfaces (TUI) are graspable physical interfaces that employ physical objects. Two example forms of active tangible interactions were presented, Local Active Tangible Interactions and Remote Active Tangible Interactions. Local Active Tangible Interactions (LATI) is a concept that allows users to interact with actuated physical interfaces such as small robots locally. The Remote Active Tangible Interactions (RATI) system supports fully featured distributed active tangible interactions. The underlining technology Display-Based Measurement and Control System to support our instantiations of Local Active Tangible Interactions and Remote Active

Tangible Interactions was presented. Two applications exploring the concepts are given, Augmented Coliseum (a LATI game) and a RATI enhanced furniture layout application.

References

1. Richter J, Thomas BH, Sugimoto M, Inami M (2007) Remote active tangible interactions. In: Proceedings of the 1st international conference on tangible and embedded interaction (TEI '07), ACM Press, New York, pp 39–42, doi: 10.1145/1226969.1226977
2. Sugimoto M, Kodama K, Nakamura A, Kojima M, Inami M (2007) A display-based tracking system: Display-based computing for measurement systems. In: Proceedings of the 17th international conference on artificial reality and telexistence (ICAT 2007), IEEE Computer Society, Los Alamitos, CA, pp 31–38, doi: 10.1109/ICAT.2007.50
3. Ishii H (1999) Tangible bits: Coupling physicality and virtuality through tangible user interfaces. In: Ohta Y, Tamura H (eds) Mixed reality: Merging real and virtual worlds, Ohmsha Ltd, Tokyo, pp 229–247
4. Fitzmaurice GW, Ishii H, Buxton WAS (1995) Bricks: Laying the foundations for graspable user interfaces. In: Proceedings of the SIGCHI conference on human factors in computing systems (CHI '95), ACM Press, New York, pp 442–449, doi: 10.1145/223904.223964
5. Rosenfeld D, Zawadzki M, Sudol J, Perlin K (2004) Physical objects as bidirectional user interface elements. IEEE Computer Graphics and Applications 24(1):44
6. Kato H, Billinghurst M, Poupyrev I, Imamoto K, Tachibana K (2000) Virtual object manipulation on a table-top AR environment. In: Proceedings of the international symposium on augmented reality (ISAR 2000), IEEE Computer Society, Los Alamitos, CA, pp 111–119, doi: 10.1109/ISAR.2000.10013
7. Dietz P, Leigh D (2001) DiamondTouch: A multi-user touch technology. In: Proceedings of UIST '01, ACM Press, New York, pp 219–226, doi: 10.1145/502348.502389
8. Hachet M, Guitton P (2002) The interaction table: A new input device designed for interaction in immersive large display environments. In: Proceedings of the workshop on virtual environments 2002 (EGVE '02), Eurographics Association, Aire-la-Ville, pp 189–196
9. Shen C, Vernier FD, Forlines C, Ringel M (2004) Diamondspin: An extensible toolkit for around-the-table interaction. In: Proceedings of the SIGCHI conference on human factors in computing systems (CHI 2004), ACM Press, Vienna, pp 167–174
10. Chen F, Close B, Eades P, Epps J, Hutterer P, Lichman S, Takatsuka M, Thomas B, Wu M (2006) ViCAT: Visualisation and interaction on a collaborative access table. In: Proceedings of the 1st IEEE international workshop on horizontal interactive human-computer systems (TABLETOP '06), IEEE Computer Society, Adelaide, pp 59–60, doi: 10.1109/TABLETOP.2006.36
11. Yang F, Baber C (2006) Maptable: A tactical command and control interface. In: Proceedings of the 11th international conference on intelligent user interfaces (IUI '06), ACM Press, New York, pp 294–296, doi: 10.1145/1111449.1111515
12. Fjeld M, Voorhorst F, Bichsel M, Lauche K, Rauterberg M, Krueger H (1999) Exploring brick-based navigation and composition in an augmented reality. In: Proceedings of the 1st international symposium on handheld and ubiquitous computing (HUC '99), Springer-Verlag, London, pp 102–116
13. Raskar R, Welch G, Chen WC (1999) Table-top spatially-augmented reality: Bringing physical models to life with projected imagery. In: Proceedings of the 2nd IEEE and ACM international workshop on augmented reality (IWAR '99), IEEE Computer Society, Washington, DC, p 64
14. Jacob RJK, Ishii H, Pangaro G, Patten J (2002) A tangible interface for organizing information using a grid. In: Proceedings of the SIGCHI conference on human factors in computing systems (CHI '02), ACM Press, New York, pp 339–346, doi: 10.1145/503376.503437

15. Kurata T, Oyabu T, Sakata N, Kourogi M, Kuzuoka H (2005) Tangible tabletop interface for an expert to collaborate with remote field workers. In: Proceedings of the 1st international conference on collaboration technology (CollabTech 2005), Tokyo, pp 58–63
16. Toney A, Thomas BH (2006) Considering reach in tangible and table top design. In: Proceedings of the 1st IEEE international workshop on horizontal interactive human-computer systems (TABLETOP '06), IEEE Computer Society, Adelaide, pp 57–58, doi: 10.1109/TABLETOP.2006.9
17. Ullmer B, Ishii H (1997) The metaDESK: Models and prototypes for tangible user inter faces. In: Proceedings of the 10th annual ACM symposium on user interface software and technology (UIST '97), ACM Press, New York, pp 223–232
18. Rauterberg M, Fjeld M, Krueger H, Bichsel M, Leonhardt U, Meier M (1997) BUILD-IT: A computer vision-based interaction technique for a planning tool. In: HCI 97: Proceedings of HCI on people and computers XII, Springer-Verlag, London, pp 303–314
19. Azuma R, Baillot Y, Behringer R, Feiner S, Julier S, MacIntyre B (2001) Recent advances in augmented reality. IEEE Computer Graphics and Applications 21(6):34–47
20. Milgram P, Colquhoun H (1999) A taxonomy of real and virtual world display integration. In: Mixed reality – merging real and virtual worlds, Springer Verlag, Berlin, pp 1–16
21. Kato H, Billinghurst M (1999) Marker tracking and HMD calibration for a video-based augmented reality conferencing system. In: Proceedings of the 2nd IEEE and ACM international workshop on augmented reality (IWAR '99), IEEE Computer Society, Washington, DC, p 85
22. Fujimura N (2004) Remote furniture: Interactive art installation for public space. In: ACM SIGGRAPH 2004 emerging technologies (SIGGRAPH '04), ACM Press, New York, p 23, doi: 10.1145/1186155.1186179
23. Brave S, Ishii H, Dahley A (1998) Tangible interfaces for remote collaboration and communication. In: Proceedings of the ACM conference on computer supported cooperative work (CSCW 1998), ACM Press, New York, Seattle, WA, pp 169–178
24. Pangaro G, Maynes-Aminzade D, Ishii H (2002) The actuated workbench: Computer-controlled actuation in tabletop tangible interfaces. In: Proceedings of the 14th annual ACM symposium on user interface software and technology (UIST '02), Paris, pp 181–190
25. Everitt KM, Klemmer SR, Lee R, Landay JA (2003) Two worlds apart: Bridging the gap between physical and virtual media for distributed design collaboration. In: Proceedings of the SIGCHI conference on human factors in computing systems (CHI '03), ACM Press, New York, pp 553–560, doi: 10.1145/642611.642707
26. Bajura M, Neumann U (1995) Dynamic registration correction in video-based augmented reality systems. IEEE Computer Graphics and Applications 15(5):52–60
27. Inami M, Tomita M, Nagaya N (2007) Relative motion racing. The National Museum of Emerging Science and Innovation, Tokyo
28. Kojima M, Sugimoto M, Nakamura A, Tomita M, Nii H, Inami M (2006) Augmented coliseum: An augmented game environment with small vehicles. In: Proceedings of the 1st IEEE international workshop on horizontal interactive human-computer systems (TABLETOP '06), IEEE, Adelaide, vol 1, pp 3–8
29. Bimber O, Raskar R (2005) Spatial augmented reality: Merging real and virtual worlds, A K Peters, Wellesley, MA
30. Hauber J, Regenbrecht H, Hills A, Cockburn A, Billinghurst M (2005) Social presence in two- and three-dimensional videoconferencing. In: Proceedings of the 8th annual international workshop on presence, London, pp 189–198
31. Stafford A, Piekarski W, Thomas B (2006) Implementation of god-like interaction techniques for supporting collaboration between outdoor AR and indoor tabletop users. In: Proceedings of the 5th IEEE and ACM international symposium on mixed and augmented reality (ISMAR '06), IEEE Computer Society, Washington, DC, pp 165–172, doi: 10.1109/ISMAR.2006.297809

Chapter 9
Interaction on the Tabletop: Bringing the Physical to the Digital

Otmar Hilliges, Andreas Butz, Shahram Izadi, and Andrew D. Wilson

Abstract Current tabletop applications, which go beyond mouse-like input, mostly use gestures and/or tangible objects. Gestures are mostly recognized by matching input to a given set of predefined (scripted) gestures, and tangible input is implemented by recognizing shapes or markers. While this allows exactly the interactions foreseen by the programmer, it can be observed in the real world, that physical artefacts are used much more flexibly and often in unforeseen ways. We describe two of our explorations into tabletop interaction styles, discuss their respective strengths and shortcomings, and then derive a new model for tabletop interaction based on a physics simulation and rich multi touch input. Interaction with this model achieves a very high fidelity to the physical world and allows appropriation of the interface, i.e., the development of individual and unforeseen interactions with the system. We have evaluated our model in different variations and believe that it holds a strong promise for future, highly flexible tabletop interfaces.

Introduction

In recent years interactive surfaces have become more and more widespread in research and as commercial products [1–6]. Users of these systems often comment on the unique user experience. Being able to directly touch digital information in combination with rich interactive applications, providing direct coupling of input and output, is often described as intuitive or natural. Many compelling scenarios have been proposed, such as browsing and sharing of digital photographs, interacting with maps and other geographical information and strategic planning applications. Most state of the art interaction techniques however, are typically limited to 2D movements and rotations within the surface plane.

O. Hilliges (✉)
Microsoft Research Cambridge, CB3 0FB Cambridge, UK
e-mail: otmarh@microsoft.com

C. Müller-Tomfelde (ed.), *Tabletops – Horizontal Interactive Displays*,
Human-Computer Interaction Series, DOI 10.1007/978-1-84996-113-4_9,
© Springer-Verlag London Limited 2010

Both single-user [7] and multi-user [8] scenarios have been investigated on inter-active tabletops with one or several discrete input points from each person, typically simulating pointing with mice. Others have explored using multiple contact points together (multiple fingers or both hands) to enrich interaction, such as scaling and rotating objects [9, 10], or enabling precise selection [11]. Many of these pro-posed interaction techniques rely heavily on two-dimensional pointing and selecting similar to mouse-based interaction in WIMP interfaces. We call this the "finger-as-cursor" model. Recently hardware has become available that allows for much richer sensing than simply identifying multiple fingertips as cursors. These interactive sur-faces can sense whole hands, and physical objects placed on them. This allows for the creation of much richer and expressive interaction techniques unlocking the users' manual dexterity and motor skills accrued through lifelong experiences with the real world.

Alongside novel hardware developments, many different approaches to interac-tion design in this space have been proposed including pen based, multi-touch and tangible interaction. Many of these interaction styles have similar properties (e.g., directly coupled input and output, physical interaction quality, support for biman-uality). However, interaction techniques have often been designed in an ad-hoc manner and studied in isolation. We offer an early exploration into various of these interaction styles in order to gain a better understanding of the design space as a whole.

Based on the findings from these initial explorations we propose a new model for tabletop interaction aimed at improving the realism of interaction with such systems and affording a variety of fine-grained ways to manipulate virtual objects akin to manipulating real objects. This model harnesses the capabilities of emerging multi-touch hardware as well as game physics simulations. It affords a richer, more open interaction than previously possible by removing application logic and scripted behavior from the system. In consequence, this interaction model enables users to apply manipulation strategies from the real world to virtual objects through the exer-tion of friction and collision forces, thus allowing for skill transfer, experimentation and appropriation.

Background

Sensing fingers and other objects on an interactive surface is a fairly non-trivial task. This has led researchers to experiment with various techniques. While research into multi-touch enabled surfaces started over two decades ago [12], recent hard-ware advances [4, 1, 13, 14, 2] have sparked a new surge of interest surrounding both the hardware and software for large surface, multi-touch interaction [15, 16]. While hardware options are still in flux, they currently offer a variety of possibilities including recognition of multiple touch points [1, 17], recognition of identifiable touch points [4], and simultaneous recognition of tangible objects and multiple touches [13, 14, 5, 2].

Most state of the art interaction techniques however, are limited to (scripted) 2D movements and rotations within the surface plane. Both single-user [7] and multi-user [8] scenarios have been investigated on interactive tabletops with one or several discrete input points from each person, typically simulating pointing with mice. A particularly popular design alternative for tabletop interfaces are *gesture-based* interfaces, which define hand postures or movements to carry some meaning or express an idea. In order to be used in GUIs, these gestures need to be sensed and interpreted in order to trigger some event or perform a command. They may be simple pointing gestures that invoke a command in combination with an on-screen tool, heuristically recognized drawings or traces of more or less abstract glyphs, or they may be some sort of symbolic gesture following a real-world metaphor.

Gesture-based interfaces have been explored in a variety of tabletop contexts such as the architectural domain [18] or the sharing [19, 20], searching [21] and tagging [8] of digital photos. Morris et al. [22] extend the gesture concept to cooperative gestures – multi-user gestural interactions for single display groupware (SDG) applications. Many gestural interfaces are designed relatively ad-hoc and their gestures need to be learned and memorized by users. Although recent work by Wobbrock et al. [23] has yielded interesting results from user-defined gestures on tabletop computers, it remains debatable whether statically defined gestures and scripted gesture-command mappings are a good fit as an interaction style, especially when compared to the rich, flexible and often dynamically adaptive ways in which we engage with real-world objects and how we use these to solve problems.

On regular tables we often store, view and manipulate a variety of objects such as paper, books or cups. Given their natural support for physical objects it is not very surprising that the integration of physical objects (sometimes in combination with direct-touch input) has been explored in various forms. Inspired by Fitzmaurice's seminal work [24] a raft of tangible user interfaces (TUI) in different forms and application domains have been presented. Some TUI examples are literal instantiations of metaphors [25, 26] where the physical and the digital are tightly coupled. Other variations allow for more generic mixed physical and graphical interaction [27]. Often, the use of the tangible paradigm is motivated by the goal to support co-located collaboration, for example TViews [28], and URP [26].

Several hardware advances have made TUIs possible on tabletop displays. Wilson [2] demonstrates a vision-based system capable of tracking physical objects through visual barcodes, hands and sheets of paper using IR-illumination and an off-axis camera equipped with an IR cutoff filter. A similar technique is used in the reacTable [14] to track objects that serve as input to a virtual musical instrument.

TUI and gesture-based interaction have often been studied in isolation even though they share many characteristics. To better understand the differences and commonalities of these two approaches we discuss explorations into both interaction paradigms in the following sections. We then analyze their suitability, strengths and shortcomings for tabletop interaction. Based on this analysis we propose a new model for tabletop interaction that allows for richer human-computer interaction more akin to the flexible and continuous ways in which we manipulate objects in the real world.

Exploring Tabletop Interaction Styles

Both interaction paradigms discussed above show appealing characteristics for tabletop computing. They promise more intuitive manipulations and a better integration between the digital and the physical space. Often systems applying one of these interaction paradigms have been evaluated in formal user studies, but within the context of their application domain. In this section we perform a meta analysis of two systems we have built and evaluated. We want to take a step back and use the opportunity to revisit the results and observations we made while studying our prototypes in order to be able to judge the potential of the interaction styles as generic paradigms for tabletop computing.

In the following section we discuss our exploration into gesture-based interfaces for interactive surface computing. In order to gain a better understanding of this interaction paradigm we built and studied a prototypical application – called Brainstorm – for collaborative problem solving in an environment enhanced with several interactive surfaces. The system uses gestures to invoke almost every single command in the system. We designed several gestures ranging from literal real world metaphors to more abstract gesture to interact with a graphical user interface. The UI itself draws many clues and inspirations from the real world to increase discoverability and ease of use. We reflect on our observations from a formal evaluation and informal system use.

Brainstorm: A Case Study

Brainstorm is a system built using several interactive surfaces including a digital tabletop and several wall-mounted displays. The system is intended for supporting co-located collaborative problem solving. Collaborative problem solving requires knowledge and information to be exchanged among team members; different skills have to be coordinated and the information communicated by others needs interpretation, so that new ideas can be created and new solutions can be found [29].

We designed the Brainstorm socio-technical system to explore the possibility of merging the physical and social qualities of a traditional face-to-face collaborative creative environment with the benefits of digital technology, such as persistent data storage, distributed information access, and the possibility to review previous processes or to undo actions. This section discusses the challenge of embedding digital technology in a collaborative creative process. Our goal was to take advantage of some of the qualities of Electronic Brainstorming Systems (EBS) without causing communication breakdowns.

Designing the Brainstorm System

Building on these considerations we have developed a system that spans across several interactive displays embedded into tables and walls. The displays used in

Fig. 9.1 Overview of the
physical setup in Brainstorm.
Smartboards embedded into
the table and wall function as
primary input surfaces

Fig. 9.1 Overview of the physical setup in Brainstorm. Smartboards embedded into the table and wall function as primary input surfaces

this system are commercially available Smartboards^{TM} in case of the table and the center display of the interactive wall (see Fig. 9.1). The wall display is extended by two additional, back-projected displays. In addition to the contact reporting by the Smartboard, the entire wall is turned into an interactive surface by a custom-built finger tracking system [30]. This allows an almost seamless information transfer from one display to another. The utilized Smartboards sensing is limited to two simultaneous points of contact. Therefore, our system was designed with only two users in mind.

The design of the user interface builds metaphorically on paper post-its, on the ways in which they are socially used, as well as on their manipulation vocabulary in the physical world in order to suggest ways in which ideas can be generated and manipulated as information units in the EBS appliance. Studies of paper in work practice, in fact, show that paper continues to be widely used [31], some of the reasons including its spatial flexibility (it can be quickly arranged in the physical space), sociability (it facilitates face-to-face communication by being passed on), and tailorability (it is easily annotated). The Brainstorm interface was designed around the paper-based brainwriting technique. Interaction happens via pen-trace gestures, and the system provides immediate visual feedback by rendering the recognized path and a prediction of the area enclosed by the drawn path (see Fig. 9.2a).

Additional mechanisms, such as dragging and flicking of post-its were implemented to support the passing of ideas by physical metaphors. All of these interactions, however, were individually scripted and had to be used as designed. To this end, the design of Brainstorm implements a limited manipulation vocabulary and relies on simple marking gestures for direct manipulation such as drawing a square, writing text, and stroking for moving, whose direct feedback is augmented by the coincident spatial mapping of input and output (i.e., there is no such device as a pointer or a remote controller). This creates a transparent causal relationship between gestures and output, and supports visibility of gestures. More design details

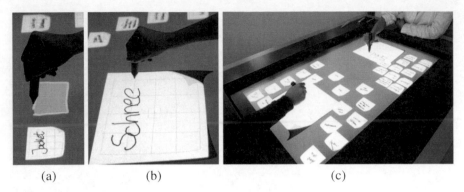

(a)   (b)   (c)

Fig. 9.2 (**a**) Creating a post-it by drawing a rectangular closed path. (**b**) Writing on an enlarged post-it. Handwriting is recognized and stored for later retrieval. (**c**) Two users interacting with the system at the same time

and interface mechanisms are discussed in [32], but their description here would not add much to the discussion in this chapter.

Evaluation

In order to assess these design choices with respect to their underlying motivations, the Brainstorm EBS was compared to the paper-based brainstorming process. The detailed results on the comparative study are published in [32]. There the goal was to understand the implications of blending such an EBS in the physical space, in comparison to a traditional paper-based brainstorming technique. However, in the context of this exploration we will focus on discussing results and observations relevant to the analysis of the chosen gesture-based approach as interaction style for tabletop computing.

Participants stated that they found the interface of the system very easy to learn. We credit this to the close resemblance of each interface element to the real world (e.g. post-it notes). These elements are also manipulated in similar ways as they would be in the real world (e.g., writing on paper with a pen). This allows users to build on knowledge they gathered from a lifelong learning experience with the real world and the objects in it. Touch sensitive interfaces and fluid gestures make using the technology more continuous and analog. This allows users to apply strategies they already use in the real world to both implicitly and explicitly convey information about the objects in the environment (e.g., territoriality) (Fig. 9.3).

Even if the close resemblance of virtual items to real world artifacts is beneficial to the ease of learning the interface, it is worth exploring the specific and different affordances of digital media. These can augment physical actions, providing effects which are only possible in the digital realm (e.g. the automatic re-orientation and appearance on the wall of virtual post-its). As long as objects have a clearly distinct and explainable behavior, users seem to be willing to accept and use a technique

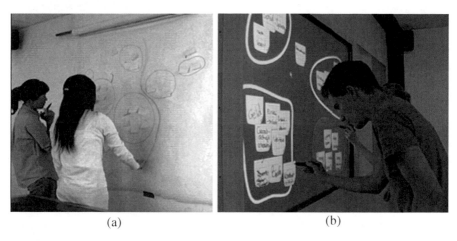

(a)   (b)

Fig. 9.3 Applying different strategies to semantically sort post-its. (**a**) Background annotations; various stroke patterns and region (sub)-division in the paper condition. (**b**) Spatially arranging post-its to convey meaning in digital condition

even if it is unrealistic in the strict sense. For example, the participants reacted very positively to the possibility to skid post-its across the table, even if this is not as easily achieved with real paper (due to its weight and friction). Although the system does not provide an accurate simulation of the physical world it clearly benefits from borrowing visual and behavioral metaphors from the real world. However, this type of physicality also possesses some limitations. They become apparent when paying close attention to the differences in interaction strategies applied by participants in the digital vs. the physical realm when organizing ideas into clusters in the structural phase of the brainstorming process.

An obvious advantage of the digital version is that many objects can be moved, copied or deleted at once and we could observe how participants made frequent use of this feature. In fact in the digital condition spatially arranging post-its was the predominant strategy and was preferred even to clustering. The other features such as connecting clusters and especially annotating clusters were only rarely used. In harsh contrast participants showed a variety of strategies to work around the more laborious task of physically moving clusters of post-its in the traditional conditions. For example, they labeled clusters, created sub-clusters or divided existing clusters into semantically disjunct areas by using differently stroked lines or background patterns (Fig. 9.3). Of course these functionalities could be implemented in the digital as well but a fundamental difference exists: In general the users showed great aptitude in appropriating the available materials to work around the *absence of features* (e.g., copying, mass moving) by exploiting the *available physical properties* of objects. For example, scribbling onto various parts of the background, annotating connecting lines or sticking several post-its on top of each other. This clearly shows the much higher flexibility of the physical version with respect to unforeseen uses of the available artifacts. The fully scripted digital interface simply didn't lend itself to this kind of appropriation, which is a very general problem with these types of interfaces.

Tangible and Hybrid Interaction on Tabletops

One of the main advantages of interactive surfaces over tangible interfaces is their flexibility. Because the interface is purely virtual, it can be dynamically reconfigured to serve different purposes. However, touch sensitive surfaces do not offer the same tactile feedback which traditional (non touchscreen) interfaces provide through physical buttons, knobs and switches. This feedback is important for motor learning and the automation of repetitive tasks such as touch typing on a QWERTY-keyboard (text entry is a task still notoriously difficult on direct-touch interfaces (cf. [33]). Using physical controls in combination with interactive surfaces promises to combine the best of these two worlds. In this section we will report our earlier findings from developing and studying a hybrid application designed for co-located sharing of digital photos, the PhotoHelix . Interestingly, recent efforts by Weiss et al. [34, 35] have further elaborated on the hybrid principle and a study confirmed some of our findings.

Photohelix [34] (see Fig. 9.4) uses the notion of time and events to organize photo collections. Events are represented as image piles on a helix-shaped calendar (Fig. 9.4b). Events and pictures are accessed, manipulated and inspected using a hybrid, bi-manual interaction technique. One hand operates a physical handle to position and control the calendar view (rotation adjusts the current time setting). The other hand is used to inspect and modify events as well as individual pictures for browsing and sharing purposes. The results from our evaluation suggest that the current design provides several benefits for browsing, organizing and sharing (as in storytelling) digital photo collections. For a discussion of issues in the particular context of photo handling please refer to.

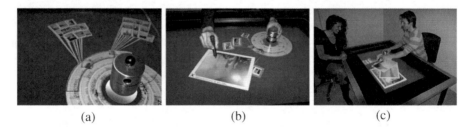

(a)   (b)   (c)

Fig. 9.4 (**a**) Photohelix overview: a physical handle is used to position and control a spiral-shaped calendar. Pictures are loosely grouped into events. (**b**) Users can (re-)arrange event structure as well as individual photos using a set of lightweight interaction techniques to facilitate dialogue about the photos. (**c**) Two users engaged in photo-talk using the Photohelix

Observations and Implications

In addition to our findings from the user study discussed in [34] we have collected much more data from users interacting with the Photohelix over the span of two additional experiments. One user study was performed to learn more about particular differences and commonalities between direct-touch and tangible interaction. A third user study investigated a particular conversational aspect, called sidetracking, that we observed frequently in participants engaging in photo-talk [36]. When launching into our exploration we had a set of expectations motivating the use of a physical handle for interaction. Some of them could be confirmed, while some require further study.

First, we wanted to unlock manual dexterity and exploit physical affordances to create a richer interaction vocabulary. Although the virtual manipulations in Photohelix are limited, we could observe how users exploited their fine-grained motor skills and the mechanical properties of the device in order to accomplish their current task. Figure 9.5 illustrates a typical learning process. Initially the user is touching the dial with great care and attempting to figure out its mechanics (Fig. 9.5a). Later, both hands are used, for control of the object. Eventually, the participant reverts to one-handed operation of the device and also a more relaxed posture (Fig. 9.5b) and finally uses the device without spending much visual attention (Fig. 9.5c).

Another question was whether the physical handle in Photohelix would encourage bi-manual interaction. Given the possibility to operate the device without paying much visual attention we did expect users to simultaneously interact with photos using their fingers or the pen and operate the device using the non-dominant hand. Figure 9.6 illustrates various degrees of bi-manual interaction. We did observe both symmetric and asymmetric bi-manual interaction. Users interacted with both hands in a coordinated effort to accomplish one task (e.g., scaling a photo with one hand, while moving the entire helix away to avoid overlap of visual elements as in

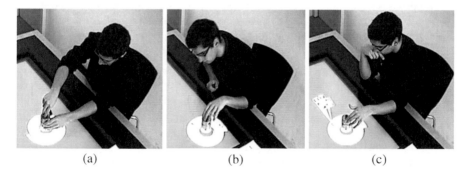

           (a)   (b)   (c)

Fig. 9.5 Evolution of manipulation style over time. (**a**) Careful, two-handed manipulation of physical object, full visual attention. (**b**) One-handed manipulation, full visual attention. (**c**) One-handed manipulation, shared visual attention

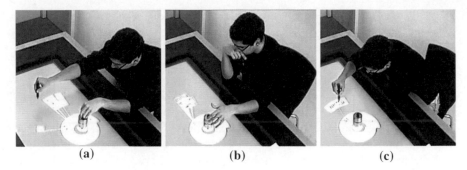

(a)   **(b)**   **(c)**

Fig. 9.6 Various degrees of bi-manuality when interacting with the Photohelix. (**a**) One-handed manipulation of individual photos. (**b**) One-handed manipulation of physical interaction handle. (**c**) Simultaneous manipulation of physical handle and individual photos

Fig. 9.6c), or they used their two hands simultaneous but with separate concerns (e.g., closing open photos while beginning to scroll and search for new images). However, the majority of interactions with PhotoHelix did not happen in a bi-manual fashion – or at least hands were not used in parallel very often. Predominantly participants would use the dominant hand to manipulate individual images while resting the non-dominant on the table's edge (Fig. 9.6a) or use the non-dominant hand to operate the physical device to access particular events (Fig. 9.6b).

We close our discussions with a few remarks on the general design of such hybrid interfaces and their suitability as a general tabletop interaction model. Because we are using tangible input devices (physical objects and touch surfaces) to manipulate virtual things, people bring with them many experiences from the physical world. Due to the almost unconstrained freedom of interaction we have in the real world, it is easy to frustrate or confuse users through a disparity of performed action and system response. To clarify, one should consider the following example often observed during our user studies. Participants often raised the complaint that the arrangement of photos on the calendar is fixed and linear (sometimes causing manual effort to reach chronologically distant events) they also expressed the wish for some sort of zooming mechanism many times simultaneously lifting the handle off the table to indicate how this could be implemented. When using tangibles as input devices it is practically impossible to anticipate all possible expected (ab)-uses of the device.

Consequently, it is easy to generate an unexpected or confusing system response. It is necessary to consider these physical experiences and to try and match the effect of a person's actions with their expectations. Although more studies would be necessary to further investigate this issue, the authors intuition is that consistency and externalization of rules is a key issue here. For example, participants responded well to limitations through mechanical constraints, possibly because they understood certain manipulations are impossible with this particular device. Other interactions that are mechanically possible (such as lifting the device or tilting it), but were not sensed, could be observed repeatedly. Often complemented by user comments on what event the particular manipulation should trigger in the virtual interface.

A New Model for Tabletop Interaction

In our earlier explorations we could observe how the more physically inspired gestures such as flicking of post-its were received more favorable (and memorized better) than the iconic, abstract gestures. We have also experienced how the scripted nature of these "pseudo-physical" interactions can be problematic. Users that were under the assumption that virtual objects behave according to the laws of physics or at least similar to real world objects often tried to perform other physical manipulations – these had not been anticipated by the developer in advance and as a result were not possible. Therefore we developed an interaction model that allows for interactions with the virtual realm through manipulations similar to those performed on real world objects without the limitations imposed by scripted or pre-defined behavior of on screen objects.

Recently, very sophisticated physics simulation packages have become accessible and found widespread use in many 3D computer games. These physics simulations are capable of modeling complex mechanical structures and model their behavior realistically in 3D graphical applications. In our interaction model we make use of the capabilities of these physics simulations and explore the intersection of rich surface input data and virtual worlds augmented by realistic, open-ended and non-scripted behavior of virtual objects. Modeling rich 2D sensor data within a 3D physics simulation is non-trivial and we highlight and discuss several of the challenges we encountered when developing our interaction model. Based on our previous experiences we wanted our model to support the following aspects:

- Enable rich physical gestures through manipulations similar to the real world.
- Using sophisticated physics simulations to add real world dynamics to virtual objects and enable users to interact through the exertion of forces such as friction and collisions.
- Support of multiple simultaneous contact points and areas (not just fingertips) and also real (tangible) objects.
- A technique that works within the bounds of the physics simulation and makes use of the sophisticated constraint solver built into many available software packages.
- A generic model that works with different virtual objects irrespective of their shape or material (e.g., boxes, spheres, cloth)

This enables a variety of fine-grained and casual interactions, supporting finger-based, whole-hand, and tangible input. We will demonstrate how our technique can be used to add real-world dynamics to interactive surfaces such as a vision-based tabletop, creating a fluid and natural experience. Our approach hides many of the complexities inherent in using physics engines from application developers, allowing the creation of applications without preprogrammed interaction behavior or gesture recognition. In order to achieve all this, the key idea is to utilize physics engines designed for computer games that simulate Newtonian physics, thus enabling interaction with digital objects by modeling quantities such as force, mass, velocity, and friction. Such engines allow the user to control and manipulate virtual objects through sets of parameters more analogous to those of real-world interactions.

While physics engines are comprehensive, they are also complex to master. Many coefficients and parameters are exposed to application developers, and controlling the simulation via user input is non-trivial, particularly when considering more than a single contact point. We present a simple yet powerful technique for modeling rich data, sensed from surface technologies, as input within the physics simulation. Our approach models one or more contact points, such as those sensed from a multi-touch surface [4, 1], and also scales to represent more sophisticated shapes such as outlines of the whole hand or tangible objects on the surface [5, 2, 6]. This allows the user to interact with objects by friction forces and collisions, but avoids exposing users and application programmers to the complexities of the physics engine.

Finally, we demonstrate the applicability of the technique using a commercially available games physics engine and a prototype vision-based interactive surface. We highlight some of the interactions such an approach affords, for example gathering multiple digital objects or fine control of a virtual ball using friction and collision forces, as shown in Fig. 9.7. Our system creates natural and fluid physics-based interactions "for free" – i.e., without the need either to explicitly program this behavior into the system or to recognize gestures. We also demonstrate the ability of advanced physics simulators to enable user interaction with more complex materials such as soft bodies and cloth, as shown in Fig. 9.7.

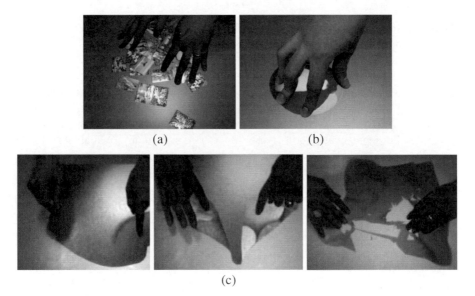

(a)   (b)

(c)

Fig. 9.7 Some examples of physics-enabled interactions supported by our technique. (**a**) Gathering and moving multiple objects using both hands and multiple fingers simultaneously. (**b**) Interacting with a ball through collision and friction forces. (**c**) Folding a cloth-like 3D mesh and tearing it apart

Interactive Surface Input

A contact on an interactive surface (e.g., a fingertip touching the surface) is most easily represented as a discrete 2D point. In the case of vision-based interactive surfaces, neighboring sensor pixels are usually grouped into continuous regions or connected components [37], with the idea that each component corresponds to a contact. The center of the component is then easily calculated. This approach thus reduces each contact to a point-based representation, regardless of shape.

This point representation of contacts allows application developers to think in terms of familiar point/rectangle hit testing algorithms typical of traditional cursor-based systems, but it imposes significant limits on interaction. First, point based hit testing may fail to catch the user touching a virtual object if the contact is not compact, as when the user places a large part of their hand on surface. In this case, the center point may lie outside the target object. Secondly, tracking point-based contacts to deduce motion can lead to difficult problems related to correspondence. For example, consider two fingers that move so near to each other that they now appear as a single contact. The choice of which of the original contacts to eliminate can result in very different motion interpretations. Finally, reducing contacts to points prevents users from drawing on the full spectrum of manipulation styles found in everyday life. Consider the multiple grasping strategies illustrated in Fig. 9.8, for example. Each gives a different feeling of control in the real world. Ultimately, it seems that point-based systems encourage the exclusive use of index fingers on interactive surfaces.

One approach for preserving more information about contact shape is to determine the bounding box of the contact, or the major and minor axes of an ellipse model that approximately fits the shape. These approaches work well for compact contacts (e.g., fingertips) and certain hand poses [18], but less so for complex shapes and their motion. Alternatively, the shape may be represented more precisely as a polygon mesh by calculating each contact's contour, represented as a closed path [38]. Another technique is to take pixels lying near the contour by computing the spatial gradient using a Sobel filter.

Fig. 9.8 Different grasping strategies to rotate an object such as a book resting on a surface

Physics Simulations

Today's physics engines enable the creation of real-world mechanics and behavior in graphical applications while hiding computational complexity. They employ many physics concepts such as acceleration, momentum, forces, friction, and collisions. In addition to rigid bodies, many systems model particles (for smoke, dust, and so forth), fluids, hair, and clothes. Virtual joints and springs give "rag doll" characters and vehicles appropriate articulation, and materials can be programmed with specific properties so that ice is slick, for example. The present work primarily concerns contact forces, such as those due to collisions and friction between simulated bodies.

The handling of collisions is typically divided into collision detection, the determination of whether two rigid bodies are in contact, and collision response, the application of appropriate forces if they are in contact. For example, the collision of a cube falling on the floor may be detected by considering the intersection of the faces defining the cube with those of the floor. The change in motion of the cube as a result (the response) is a function of mass, inertia, velocity, the point of contact with the floor, and other factors. Friction forces resist motion when the surface of one body stays in contact with the surface of another. If two surfaces are moving with respect to each other, kinetic friction opposes the forces moving the bodies. If two surfaces are at rest relative to each other, static friction opposes forces that would otherwise lead to the motion of one of the bodies.

Surface Input Within a Physics Simulation

In order to interact appropriately with virtual objects in a physics engine, surface contacts must be represented within the simulation. The major strategies to achieve this are as follows:

- Direct forces: A force is applied where a contact point touches a virtual object. The force direction and magnitude is calculated from the contact's velocity and size if available.
- Virtual joints and springs: Each contact is connected to the virtual object it touches by a rigid link or spring, so that the object is dragged along with the contact.
- Proxy objects: Contact points are represented as rigid bodies such as cubes or spheres. These bodies are an approximation of the contacts, and interact with other virtual objects by collisions and friction forces.
- Particles: Where additional information about a contact's shape is available, multiple rigid bodies – or particles – are combined to approximate the shape and motion of the contact more accurately. This allows for better modeling of interaction with the whole hand or other contacts such as tangible objects.

At first sight, it remains open, which strategy enables the most realistic interaction with advanced physics simulations. We describe our rationale and experiences in implementing and evaluating all the above alternatives. The main contribution is the development of a novel interaction technique that retains a high fidelity of interaction to the physical world, but can be implemented quite efficiently.

Applying Forces Directly

A typical strategy for moving an object on an interactive surface in response to touch is to continually update its position to match the touching contacts position. We will refer to this manner of moving objects by setting their position and orientation directly as kinematic control.

Within a physics simulation, the most common way for an application to control the movement of a rigid body is to apply one or more forces to it. From a programmer's point of view, this approach is very different from moving an object by setting its position. To effect kinematic control within a physics simulation, we must calculate the precise force and torque required to move the object into its target position (Fig. 9a). This ensures correct collision response with other bodies in the simulation. In comparison, directly setting the position of the body within a simulation can lead to unstable and unpredictable results. Absolute positioning might be analogous to teleporting a real object from one location to another, potentially causing interpenetration of objects or other physically absurd situations. A natural strategy for moving an object to follow a contact on an interactive surface is therefore to consider that each contact imparts a friction force to the body it touches according to the contact's motion (and presumed mass). Unfortunately, to calculate the forces necessary to match a contact's movement, all other external forces acting on the body must be taken into account and counteracted (Fig. 9.9b, c). These may include friction forces and collision responses that are difficult or impossible for application developers to obtain.

This difficulty extends to considering forces corresponding to surface contacts. In the case of multiple contacts, the correct friction forces corresponding to each

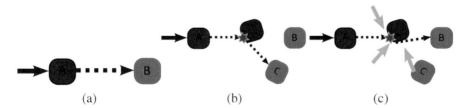

                    (a)   (b)   (c)

Fig. 9.9 Applying forces directly. (**a**) To move an object from A to B we must apply a force of correct magnitude to the object. (**b**) Hidden (from the developer) forces such as collisions with other objects can lead to unwanted results. (**c**) To calculate counteracting forces all other external forces need to be taken into account. This can be very complex and sometimes force values are difficult to obtain

contact must be determined simultaneously. In fact, at the heart of any physics engine is a sophisticated constraint solver that addresses this very problem. Without essentially constructing a new solver within the physics engine, or without access to internals of the existing solver, it would seem impossible to correctly apply contact forces directly. One possible solution is to treat all frictions as kinetic. But this poses a problem if the user wants to statically pin one point of the object while moving another. Because kinematic friction forces only act in the presence of relative motion, the counteracting force that keeps the "pinned" part of the object stationary must first move. Thus, this approach results in a somewhat viscous and slightly unpredictable feel when moving objects.

Connecting to Objects with Joints and Springs

Another kinematic approach, used in systems such as BumpTop [39], is to connect virtual objects and an input contact using a joint. Think of this as an invisible piece of rope of predefined length that is tied to the object at a particular anchor point. The object is then pulled along using this rope. By attaching a joint off-center, the object is subject to both force and torque – allowing the object to move and rotate using a single connection. In our earlier pinning example, one joint attaching a stationary contact point to one corner of the object would serve as a pivot point. A second joint attaching a second moving contact point to an opposing corner would cause the object to spin around the first contact point.

This approach is not well suited for multiple simultaneous contact points, particularly those pulling in opposite directions. While in the real world, multiple contacts pulling in opposite directions on an object would result in the fingers sliding or the object deforming or tearing, neither behavior is supported by joint constraints on a rigid body. It is thus easy for multiple rigid constraints to overconstrain the simulation, resulting in numerical instability and unpredictable behavior. Springs can in part alleviate some of these issues by providing more flex in the connection. However, a trade-off exists between the elasticity of the spring and how responsive the connected object is to contact motion (springs should be fairly short and rigid to allow for a faster response). Problems of numerical stability and uncontrolled oscillations are likely [10]. Another approach is to allow the joint or spring to break in these situations, but this can easily lead to situations where objects fly out of the user's reach.

Development of a New Technique

We have so far described two techniques that one would typically employ in single-point physics-enabled applications, and discussed the limitations of both in terms of modeling multiple contacts. The modeling of such input is challenging but only part of the story with respect to the limitations of these approaches. First, as we described earlier, contacts are not always discrete 2D points, and it may be desirable to match the shape of the contact input closely. It is unclear how one would model more sophisticated shapes and contours with either of these initial approaches. Second, the above techniques address the case where the user touches the object directly, thereby moving the object by friction forces. Neither of these approaches addresses the movement of objects by collision forces, i.e., from contact forces applied to the side of the object (as in Fig. 9.8b). The next section presents a technique which handles friction and collision forces in the same framework and is easily extended to handle shapes of arbitrary contour. In doing so, it addresses many of the difficulties of the previous techniques.

Discrete Proxy Objects

The idea of proxy objects is to incorporate into the physics simulation a rigid body for each surface contact. These bodies are kinematically controlled to match the position of the surface contacts and can be thought of as incarnations of contact points within the physics simulation. Because they are regular rigid bodies, they may interact with other rigid bodies in the usual ways: either by collision or friction. The proxy approach carries various benefits such as hiding the complexity of force calculations (in fact, hiding almost all physics aspects) from the programmer, while avoiding the difficulties of the previously described approaches. It leverages collision as well as friction forces (both static and kinetic) to model rich interactions such as pushing, grabbing, pinching, and dragging. Proxy objects interact with other objects in the simulation through the means provided by the engine. Finally, this approach avoids unnecessary strain on the solver (e.g., inserting extreme force values) and resulting unstable simulation states.

Proxy objects are created and positioned for each point of contact. Most simply, a single shape primitive such as a cube or sphere may be used for each contact. When a contact initially appears, a ray casting calculation is performed to determine the 3D position of the proxy so that it touches the underlying object, as shown in Fig. 9.10. An interesting alternative to using a sphere or cube as a proxy shape is to create a thin capsule, box, or cylinder which stretches from the 3D camera near plane to the surface of the touched object (see Fig. 9.11). This kind of proxy will collide not only with objects resting on the same plane as the touched object (or "floor"), but also objects that are in mid-air, or stacked on other objects. Such behavior may correspond more closely to user expectations.

As the sensing system provides updates to a contact position, the corresponding proxy object is kinematically controlled to match the updated position. This is done, as described earlier, by applying the necessary forces to bring the proxy object (of known mass) to the updated position of the contact. This scheme allows users to leverage collision forces to push objects around or grab objects by touching them from two opposing sides.

A small change in the kinematic control enables the proxy object to exert friction forces when it lies on top of another rigid body (as when the user touches the top surface of a virtual object, for example). In particular, only forces tangential to the touched object are applied to match the contact position. As with regular dynamic bodies, gravity is still included as an external force. In the case where gravity is

Fig. 9.10 Positioning of proxy objects works as follows: (**a**) For each surface contact a discrete proxy object is created. (**b**) A ray-casting operation returns intersection points with other virtual objects or the ground plane. (**c**) Proxy objects are positioned at these intersections. Surface motion is mapped to lateral motion of the proxy objects. Proxy objects interact with other virtual objects through collision and friction forces

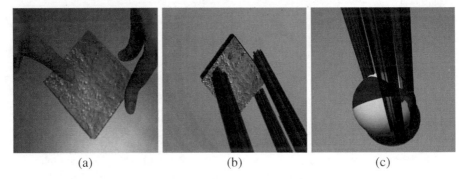

(a)   (b)   (c)

Fig. 9.11 Particle proxies approximating the shape of various objects: (**a**) Interaction on the surface; applying friction from the top and collisions from the side to grip a virtual block. (**b**) Screenshot of the 3D scene. *Long red* objects are multiple particle objects approximating the shape of the surface contact. (**c**) Particle proxies accommodate arbitrarily shaped objects including non-flat objects such as this sphere

directed into the surface, the proxies thus exert downward force onto other objects and cause friction forces. This hybrid kinematic-dynamic control of the object can be implemented by direct addition of forces to the proxy rigid body, or by a prismatic joint constraint on the body's motion. The simulated weight of the finger on the object may be adjusted by changing the mass of the proxy object, while the material properties of the virtual objects may be adjusted by changing static and kinetic friction coefficients.

The main advantage of the proxy object technique is that it leverages the built-in capability of the physics engine to simulate both friction and collision contact forces. Most significantly, because the calculation of contact forces is handled entirely by the built-in physics engine solver, the combined effect of simultaneous static and kinetic friction forces due to multiple proxy objects is handled correctly. These friction forces enable users to translate and rotate objects (through opposing forces) that they touch directly.

Particle Proxies

Thus far we have approximated each touch point as a single proxy object. This permits a simple, fast implementation, and lends itself to sensing systems that report only contact position and no shape information, as well as applications that favor interaction with the fingertip or stylus.

Some interactive surfaces provide shape information, such as an oriented ellipse, bounding box, or full polygonal contour. The idea of the particle proxy is to model the contact shape with a multitude of proxy objects ("particles") placed along the contour of the contact (see Fig. 9.11). Particles are added and removed as contours change size and shape. A practical implementation involves creating a new set of proxy objects for the contour at the beginning of each simulation frame, and destroying all proxy objects after the physics simulation has been updated. Even though the proxies will be destroyed after the physics update, each enacts collision and friction forces during the update.

The advantage of the particle proxy approach is twofold. First, collisions appear to be more correct because they more closely follow the shape of the contact. This is particularly important when using the flat or side of the hand, tangible objects, or generally any contacts other than fingertips (see Fig. 9.12). Similarly, the distribution and magnitude of friction forces on the top of an object are more accurately modeled. For example, the flat of the hand may exert more friction than the tip of a finger (Fig. 9.8c) by virtue of having more particles assigned to it. Likewise, a single contact turning in place can exert friction forces to rotate an object. Unlike the single proxy model, each particle is placed (ray cast) separately, so that a contact can conform to irregularly-shaped 3D virtual objects (Fig. 9.11).

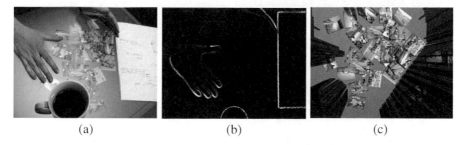

(a)   (b)   (c)

Fig. 9.12 Particle proxies method overview. (**a**) Photograph of user interaction; shown are two hands a notebook and a cup. (**b**) Sobel image shows contours of surface contacts. (**c**) For each pixel on the contacts' contour a particle (*red*) is projected into the scene. Particles interact with virtual objects through friction and collision forces

As in the single proxy object model, each particle is kinematically controlled to match the movement of the contact to which it belongs. Generally, the velocity of a point on the contour can be computed by examining the contact's contour in the previous frame. This calculation may be simple, as with an ellipse model, or more complex, as with a polygonal contour.

From Tracking to Flow

One difficulty in basing velocity calculations on tracked contacts is that tracking can fail, particularly when the user is using less constrained grasping postures such as the edge or flat of a hand rather than the more cursor like index finger. In these cases, components can split and merge in ways that do not correspond to how we see the physical input, leading to erroneous velocity calculations, and ultimately in the case of our physics simulation to unpredictable motion. An alternative approach is to calculate the motion of the particle independently of any tracked contact information. For example, local features of the image may instead be tracked from the previous frame to calculate velocity. Simple block matching of the sort used in optical flow [40] is one such technique (see Fig. 9.13). In short, two subsequent images are compared and a least squares approximation is computed for a transformation that matches the current frame to the previous one with the best possible overlap. This transformation then yields the movement vector of each single pixel between frames. When using local motion estimates, the tracking of discrete contact objects and exact contours may then be avoided altogether by placing proxy particles at image locations with high spatial gradient (e.g., Sobel filter [38]). These pixels will lie on contact contours. They are sufficient to realistically move objects

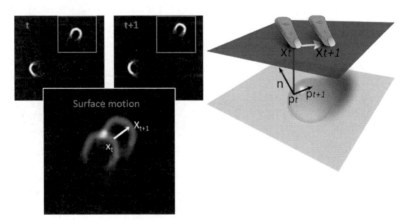

Fig. 9.13 Computing flow of a particle. Surface motion at point x_t is computed by comparing successive edge images. Corresponding tangential motion in the scene is calculated by projecting image point x_t into the 3D scene, to obtain point p_t. Point p_{t+1} is found by projecting image point x_{t+1} onto tangent plane formed by normal n and point p_t. For brevity only one particle is shown while a fingertip in contact with surface would be approximated by many

larger than the contact area, but at the same time eliminate many proxy objects from the inner area, thus increasing efficiency considerably. The particle proxy technique is summarized as follows:

```
compute Sobel image from surface input
for each pixel with high spatial gradient:
    ray cast into scene to determine initial particle position
    add particle rigid body to physics simulation
    compute contact motion at particle (e.g., from flow)
    compute corresponding tangential motion in scene
    apply force to particle to match scene motion
    apply downward force (gravity) to particle
update physics simulation
destroy all particle rigid bodies
```

The instantaneous, piecewise nature of the shape and motion calculations of the flow-based particle proxy method possesses important advantages. First, the friction and contact forces lead to more stable physics simulation results than the calculation of shape and motion from discrete tracked objects. Second, because the technique makes few assumptions regarding the shape or movement of contacts, it imposes few limits on the manipulations a user may perform, whether leading to collisions, friction forces, or combinations thereof.

New Physics-Based Interactions

Our goal in introducing more detailed surface input types into a physics simulation is to enable a wide variety of manipulation styles drawn from real-world experience. While we have only begun to explore some of the possibilities that these techniques afford, here we consider a few which we believe are noteworthy.

Manipulation Fidelity

The ability to exploit detailed shape and motion information has broad consequences when considering the manipulation of even the simplest objects. Free moving virtual objects can be moved by any one of a variety of strategies that combine collisions against the contours of hands and fingers with static and kinetic frictions. Because all three kinds of forces can be employed simultaneously, the overall impression is one of unusually high fidelity. An interesting example is the manipulation of a ball that is free to roll on the surface: it may be compelled to roll, spin, stop, or bounce in a surprisingly precise fashion, using a single light touch, multiple touches, or the flat of the hand for stopping power (Fig. 9.7). Physical objects can also be integrated at no cost, allowing a variety of interesting tangible behaviors (see Fig. 9.7 for some examples).

The ability to sense and process contours, as well as distribute friction forces piecewise across the virtual space, enables the manipulation of many objects at once, just as one might move a group of small objects spread across a table (see Fig. 9.7a). Users may use the edges of their hands (or even arms) to collide against many objects at once, or use the flats of multiple hands to apply friction forces. For interactive surfaces able to sense physical objects, an interesting possibility is to use a ruler to move and align multiple objects.

3D Manipulations

Modeling virtual objects and input in 3D enables interesting yet familiar interactions. For example, a flat object resting on a larger flat object may be moved by tapping its side or applying friction. Depending on the masses and frictions involved, it may be necessary to hold the larger object in place. It is thus important for the designer to tune masses, frictions, and appearances to match user expectations. If the interaction is limited to collision forces from the side and friction forces from the top, however, the manner in which a user may place the smaller object on top of another is unclear. Ramps, seesaws, and other constructions are possible, if somewhat contrived. In certain cases it may be possible to flip one object onto another through the application of sufficient friction forces to one side of the object.

When the objects to be stacked are thin, such as cards representing documents [41, 39], one approach is to give the top and bottom surfaces of each object a cambered shape that allows the user to raise one side by pressing down on the other. The user may then move another like-sized card under the tilted card (Fig. 9.14a). This behavior corresponds to our awareness that in the real world even "flat" objects such as cards and paper have some 3D shape that is often intuitively exploited to manipulate them.

Cloth and Soft Bodies

We have used rigid bodies such as boxes and spheres to explain our interaction techniques. However, in the real world many objects are not rigid but are instead soft,

(a) (b) (c)

Fig. 9.14 Interactions enabled by our model. (**a**) Sliding cambered cards on top of each other by pushing on by the side and holding the other in place. (**b**) A physical card is used to gather several pieces at once. (**c**) Pinning down a virtual cloth with a real wooden torus

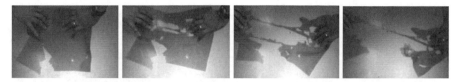

Fig. 9.15 Tearing a cloth apart by applying forces in opposing directions

malleable, and can deform or dissolve when forces are exerted on them. Examples include rubber, cloth, and paper. In addition to rigid body dynamics, most available physics simulations offer some form of support for soft body, cloth, and fluid simulation. As all interactions in our model are mediated through collision or friction forces, the model can be applied to arbitrary virtual objects. For example, it is possible to crumple a piece of cloth with a grasping interaction using all the fingers of one hand. The crumpled cloth can then be straightened by pushing down with the flat hand. One can even tear paper like objects apart by applying forces in opposing directions on two corners (Fig. 9.15).

Another possible application would allow soft volumetric bodies to be squished so as to fit into cavities or compressed so as to slide underneath other objects. Soft materials could also be used for terrains; deformation could be triggered by users digging their fingers into the terrain, using their whole hands to form valleys, or using a cupping gesture to create elevations. These interactions, would, of course, greatly benefit from force sensing. More open-ended and free-form interactions with particle systems (e.g., simulating sand) and fluids can be imagined in a gaming context.

User Study

To further understand and evaluate the utility of the techniques described in this paper, an exploratory experiment was performed. The following questions were addressed:

- Are users able to comprehend and exploit the openness of interaction that the physics model affords?
- Is the interaction of sufficient fidelity?
- Is it discoverable and predictable?
- Do users notice and value the added fidelity, or do they just expect kinematic control?
- Ultimately, how do users express their expectations in the physics-enabled manipulation?

The study exposed 6 participants to 3 simple physics-enabled tasks (as shown in Fig. 9.16), and analyzed various behavioral and experiential aspects of interaction

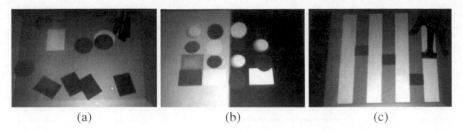

(a)   (b)   (c)

Fig. 9.16 (**a**) Task 1: Exact positioning of boxes and spheres. (**b**) Task 2: Sorting by color. (**c**) Task 3: Steering a cylinder (*red*) across narrow bridges (*blue*)

during task completion. The 3 male and 3 female participants came from a range of backgrounds, and all had normal (or corrected to normal) vision and no mobility impairments. The experiment was conducted on an early prototype of Microsoft Surface [5], using the Nvidia PhysX gaming physics engine.

The experiment utilized a $3 \times 3 \times 2$ within-subjects (repeated measures) design. Each participant worked through the three puzzles in each of three interaction techniques: Joints, Proxies, and Particles. Pilot testing included a fourth condition, Direct Forces, but this was dropped during further testing (as explained below). For techniques that do not intrinsically support collisions, a simple collision model based on kinematic objects was applied, allowing interactions from the top and the sides of an object. In addition, we hypothesized that the presence of visual feedback showing users precisely where their input is applied might improve the discoverability of each technique. Visual feedback of Joints was represented as red lines drawn from the contact point to the anchor point on the object (these disappeared if the joint was broken); Proxies as red cubes at each center point where contact was sensed; and Particles as smaller red cubes per pixel in the contour image. We ran each technique with and without visual feedback as our third independent variable. The task setup (see Fig. 9.16) was as follows.

- In Task 1, each of four spheres and rectangles were placed exactly on matching targets; each object disappeared upon proper placement.
- In Task 2, an assortment of objects of different shapes, sizes, and masses were sorted onto the left or right portions of the screen depending on their color.
- In Task 3, a cylindrical object was steered from a set starting position (far top right of photo) to a target (shown in red) by passing several waypoints (shown in blue) without dropping the object from a platform (which caused the task to restart).

The tasks were presented in the same order to each participant, whereas the order of interaction techniques was counterbalanced across participants using a Latin-square design. Experimentation occurred in two main phases (with visual feedback of the input and without), presentation of which was, again, counterbalanced across participants. During the experiment, participants were not given any direct instruction, but had several attempts to try out each new puzzle. Participants performed each task twice (excluding any training), under experimental conditions, to provide an average completion time for each condition. Participants were interviewed informally after completing their session.

Early Issues with Direct Forces

Initially, the Direct Forces technique was implemented by applying a smooth velocity at a given contact point on the object, computed as a measure of the displacement between the contact's current and last positions (i.e., kinetic friction). This seemed a fair approximation for modeling surface input as direct forces. However, our pilots questioned the efficacy of this technique. Specifically, users found it difficult to complete tasks that involved accurately positioning objects; i.e., moving and then stopping an object at the target location. Moving the object could be performed reasonably, but to stop it the user needed to counteract the motion in the opposite direction. This often led to excessive velocity applied in the reverse direction, causing objects to "overshoot" the target. Consequently, performance with this technique was so poor that we felt it needed no further evaluation. Based on these issues and feedback from the pilots, we excluded this technique from analysis.

Initial Results and Observations

Although this was only an initial exploration, we observed many promising interactions and forms of gesture within the study. Users seemed aware of the potential of this new type of environment and exploited the physics-based system's facilitation of experimentation, and we observed many new interaction strategies.

Kinematic Control and the Curse of the Single Finger

Figure 9.17 shows the completion times for all tasks. Joints provide kinematic control that closely mimics drag-and-drop behavior, and thus facilitate easy positioning of objects. This is reflected in the results. After some experimentation, there was a moment when users discovered that the object was under familiar kinematic control. Users commented that "my hands are like magnets" or "I can press hard and stick my fingers." Of course, pressure and magnetism were not factors at play here (in fact, post study interviews revealed that participants were unsure of the general principle behind the Joints technique). Nevertheless, users performed the task rapidly after discovering the object was somehow fixed to their fingers.

However, the quantitative results tell only part of the story. During the study we also observed many limitations with the kinematic approach. The discovery of this type of essentially drag-and-drop behavior in the Joints condition led users to predominately interact with a single finger and with a single object at a time. Even rotations of an object were predominantly undertaken using a single finger [9].

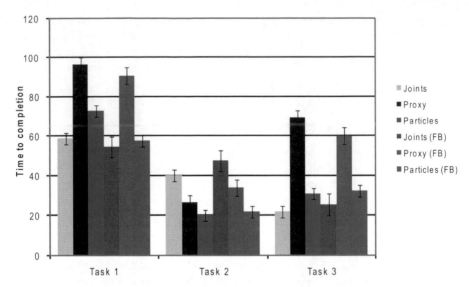

Fig. 9.17 Task completion times. *FB* denotes conditions in which feedback of user's input was provided

Experimentation with multi fingered or bimanual techniques was therefore rare in the Joints condition. During informal interviews, users commented that the condition was "limited" and "less satisfying" than the other techniques even though they performed the tasks rapidly. Although it is too preliminary to draw significant conclusions, it does suggest the need to measure more than task completion time when evaluating such physics-based techniques.

Users also had a poor understanding of how collisions were supported in a kinematic approach such as Joints. We observed many instances where accidental collisions caused by hit testing on the side as opposed to the top of the object would cause an object to move away from the user and cause a great deal of confusion. This makes us revisit whether a kinematic plus collision model makes any sense to the user at all: Why indeed should an object only be sticky when you touch its top as opposed to its sides? This actually led some users to infer that objects were magnetized in a way that supported both attraction (when touching the top) and repulsion (when colliding with the sides).

Using Feedback to Go Beyond Kinematic Control

As shown in the results, feedback did not play a significant role in the Joints condition, as one might expect given the familiarity of the approach. Feedback played a more significant role for Particles in Task 1. After some training time, users discovered they could interact with more than just their fingertips. Bimanual "cupping" and "throwing and catching" techniques were devised to rapidly move objects to target positions (Fig. 9.18). These strategies, and the general level of fine control,

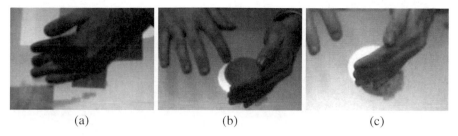

(a)   (b)   (c)

Fig. 9.18 Using contours of the hand to move (**a**) multiple boxes. (**b**) Providing a barrier to smoothly change direction of a sphere over the target area. (**c**) Fine-grained manipulations to complete sorting task

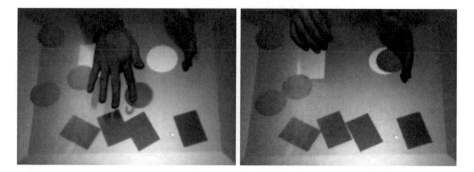

Fig. 9.19 Throwing and catching an object from a greater distance using both hands

enabled users in the Particle condition to obtain completion times comparable to more kinematic approaches. During interviews, users reflected positively about the interactions Particles afforded.

However, these types of contour based bimanual interactions could not be utilized with Proxy objects – although participants did try. In fact, in many cases, a hand gesture on the surface would be poorly approximated as a single proxy (the center of mass of the contact shape), causing objects to slip through a hand or causing other peculiar hit testing behavior. Multiple fingers were used to reorient boxes effectively, but overall, bimanual control was rare (Fig. 9.19).

While the "drag and drop" nature of Task 1 clearly favored kinematic control such as that offered by the Joints approach, Task 2 offered a clear advantage to concurrent manipulation of multiple objects for rapid sorting. As might therefore be expected, use of both Proxy and Particles techniques, which seemingly promoted multi-touch interaction, led to faster completion times in this task (Fig. 9.20).

Coming to Grips with Non-planar Objects

Another specific trade-off in our design was that the rigid body cubes in the Proxy condition only provided an effective means for interacting with flat objects. They

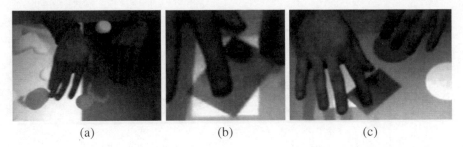

(a)   (b)   (c)

Fig. 9.20 Two-handed and multi-fingered strategies adopted in the proxy and particle conditions.
(**a**) Coarsely moving objects using both hands. (**b**) Two-fingered rotation by applying torque to
align a box. (**c**) Fine-grained movement of two objects using a single finger of each hand

provided little grip of spherical objects (or more complex 3D meshes). This was
clearly evident in the final task where the Proxy cubes struggled to keep the cylindrical object under control, as shown in Fig. 9.16. In this task, we found users often
reverted to point-based interaction to control the small non-planar object; the use
of contours was infrequent. However, our initial results suggest that Particles still
outperform Proxy objects for these purely point-based interactions. This suggests
that for scenarios where touch-only input is available, the Particle model subsumes
the single Proxy object model.

Observations and Implications

The results of the user study and general experimentation suggest that while the
more familiar kinematic approaches (somewhat inevitably) offer more predictable
control in some situations, the particle proxy approach can offer comparable performance while providing new modes of interaction (such as cupping the ball in
Fig. 9.18). That our study participants were able to devise new manipulation strategies from limited feedback and training is encouraging. With more time, we expect
users to further draw on their experience with real-world manipulations. There
are a number of ways in which our interactive surface simulation does not match
the physics of the real world. In suggesting that we abandon familiar, kinematic
point-based control in favor of strongly physics-based techniques, an important
consideration is whether users are able to negotiate these differences.

First, while in the real world one might apply more or less force to control friction, our system has no sense of how hard the user is pressing. When using particle
proxies, the amount of friction applied is instead proportional to the number of proxies applied to the object, which itself is related to the surface area of the touch. For
example, a single finger moving across an object will apply less friction than multiple fingers. Not surprisingly, this distinction was generally lost on study participants,
who often tried to press harder to bring an object under their control. Similarly, our

users would sometimes apply multiple fingers to an object when they wanted precise movement. Because of the inevitable imprecision of the simulation, the object would move too unpredictably for very fine control. In many of these cases, it would have been better to use a light (small) touch rather than a full grip.

Second, grasping a virtual object by placing contacts on either side can be difficult if not impossible in many of our techniques. Such manipulations require persistent resting contacts to be placed on virtual objects. The particle-based approach, in which each proxy is created every frame, places the proxy corresponding to a grasping finger on top of the object, thus defeating attempts to grasp it. The single proxy object approach uses persistent proxies, and so allows grasping of an object resting on the floor. It may be possible to extend the particle approach to allow proxies to persist at a given depth when it seems appropriate, or to explore a hybrid approach in which both the particle and single proxy techniques are used simultaneously.

Grasping may be difficult to replicate for more fundamental reasons. Virtual objects exert no counteracting force against the fingers, so it is difficult to know how "hard" the fingers are pressing on an object. Grasping an object in order to lift it out of the plane may be challenging to depict directly on an interactive surface with a 2D display. Similarly, the sensation of moving the hand across an interactive display surface is the same regardless of the simulated material, and whether the contact exerts static or kinetic friction.

Clearly, there is no need to completely replicate the physics of object manipulation in order to construct useful applications exhibiting physics-inspired behavior. The appropriate degree to which the techniques in this paper are applied depends on the application. A game might naturally exploit detailed physics throughout, while a graphical layout application might be very selective. Joint constraints provided by physics engines may be used to constrain motion, for example, to ease alignment tasks. While joints can be used to simulate the real-world counterparts of traditional GUI sliders, dials, buttons, and the like (as suggested by [38]), some aspects of traditional interactions do not naturally lend themselves to a physics implementation. Changing the size of an object dynamically, for example, does not lend itself to rigid-body simulation.

Conclusion

We have introduced a number of techniques to incorporate interactive surface input primitives into a real-time physics simulation. Our techniques take advantage of the fidelity of sensing provided by vision-based interactive surfaces, with the goal of enabling in a virtual domain the range of object manipulation strategies available to us in the real world. Thereby forming a new model for tabletop interaction that incorporates the physical aspects often accredited to direct-touch interaction and successful in other interaction styles with a flexibility and open-ended nature not possible with previous approaches. Our model allows for and encourages rich interactions with virtual objects, using not only multiple fingertips but novel, often in-situ designed interactions such as the cupping, throwing and raking gestures discussed above. Our user study and general observations have revealed that users are receptive for this new model of interaction. In general they had little problems in interacting with the virtual realm. However, kinematic more traditional interaction styles were still prevalent especially during initial contact with the system. We expect that users, as they become more familiar with the capabilities of the approach, will further draw on their real world knowledge and thus develop richer interaction strategies. However, this requires further study possibly in a long-term field study.

Of course the approach has several limitations and issues such as the lack of tactile feedback and collision response. Novel materials might be able to mitigate this problem through passive tactile feedback [42] or novel, active (actuated) displays providing dynamic, computer controllable tactile feedback in addition to vision based multi-touch input [43]. Another issue and possibly a more important issue is the mismatch of input and output fidelity. Even though the input data from vision-based interactive surfaces is rich, it is, in most cases, limited to 2D – sometimes augmented with a narrow band of hover [44] or pressure sensitivity [45, 46]. In contrast, in our interaction model the virtual world we interact with is three-dimensional. Our mapping (especially the particle approach) allows for coarse 3D interactions but these interactions are severely limited because scene motion is constrained to two dimensions. Virtual objects can be manipulated in various ways (see Fig. 9.8) but these manipulations are limited to interacting with objects by touching them on their sides or touching them from top to drag them. On real tables we routinely pick objects up flip them around and put them into containers, all of which are interactions not possible with our current model. Therefore, interacting with the 3D scene sometimes can feel as if interacting with objects protected by a layer of transparent film while poking objects with fingers or chop-sticks.

References

1. Han JY (2005) Low-cost multi-touch sensing through frustrated total internal reflection. In: Proceedings of the 18th annual ACM symposium on user interface software and technology (UIST '05), ACM Press, New York, pp 115–118, doi: 10.1145/1095034.1095054
2. Wilson AD (2005) PlayAnywhere: A compact interactive tabletop projection-vision system. In: Proceedings of the 18th annual ACM symposium on user interface software and technology (UIST '05), ACM Press, New York, pp 83–92, doi: 10.1145/1095034.1095047
3. Wilson AD (2004) Touchlight: An imaging touch screen and display for gesture-based interaction. In: Proceedings of the 6th international conference on multimodal interfaces (ICMI '04), ACM Press, New York, pp 69–76, doi: 10.1145/1027933.1027946
4. Dietz P, Leigh D (2001) Diamondtouch: A multi-user touch technology. In: Proceedings of the 14th annual ACM symposium on user interface software and technology (UIST '01), ACM Press, pp 219–226, doi: 10.1145/502348.502389
5. Microsoft (2008) Microsoft Surface. http://www.microsoft.com/surface/, accessed 19.09.2008
6. Rekimoto J (2002) Smartskin: An infrastructure for freehand manipulation on interactive surfaces. In: Proceedings of the SIGCHI conference on human factors in computing systems (CHI '02), ACM Press, New York, pp 113–120, doi: 10.1145/503376.503397

7. Wigdor D, Penn G, Ryall K, Esenther A, Shen C (2007) Living with a tabletop: Analysis and observations of long term office use of a multi-touch table. In: Proceedings of the second IEEE international workshop on horizontal interactive human-computer systems (TABLETOP '07), IEEE Computer Society, Los Alamitos, CA, pp 60–67, doi: 10.1109/TABLETOP.2007.33

8. Morris MR, Paepcke A, Winograd T, Stamberger J (2006) TeamTag: Exploring centralized versus replicated controls for co-located tabletop groupware. In: Proceedings of the SIGCHI conference on human factors in computing systems (CHI '06), ACM Press, New York, pp 1273–1282, doi: 10.1145/1124772.1124964

9. Kruger R, Carpendale S, Scott SD, Tang A (2005) Fluid integration of rotation and translation. In: Proceedings of the SIGCHI conference on human factors in computing systems (CHI '05), ACM Press, New York, pp 601–610, doi: 10.1145/1054972.1055055

10. Moscovich T, Hughes JF (2006) Multi-finger cursor techniques. In: Proceedings of the conference on graphics interface (GI '06), Canadian Information Processing Society, Toronto, ON, pp 1–7

11. Benko H, Wilson AD, Baudisch P (2006) Precise selection techniques for multi-touch screens. In: Proceedings of the SIGCHI conference on human factors in computing systems (CHI '06), ACM Press, New York, pp 1263–1272, doi: 10.1145/1124772.1124963

12. Lee SK, Buxton W, Smith KC (1985) A multi-touch three dimensional touch-sensitive tablet. In: Proceedings of the SIGCHI conference on human factors in computing systems (CHI '85), ACM Press, New York, pp 21–25, doi: 10.1145/317456.317461

13. Hodges S, Izadi S, Butler A, Rrustemi A, Buxton B (2007) Thinsight: Versatile multi-touch sensing for thin form-factor displays. In: Proceedings of the 20th annual ACM symposium on user interface software and technology (UIST '07), ACM Press, New York, pp 259–268, doi: 10.1145/1294211.1294258

14. Jordà S, Geiger G, Alonso M, Kaltenbrunner M (2007) The reacTable: Exploring the synergy between live music performance and tabletop tangible interfaces. In: TEI '07: Proceedings of the first international conference on tangible and embedded interaction, ACM Press, New York, pp 139–146, doi: 10.1145/1226969.1226998

15. Hinckley K, Sinclair M (1999) Touch-sensing input devices. In: Proceedings of the SIGCHI conference on Human factors in computing systems (CHI '99), ACM Press, New York, pp 223–230, doi: 10.1145/302979.303045

16. Morris MR, Cassanego A, Paepcke A, Winograd T, Piper AM, Huang A (2006) Mediating group dynamics through tabletop interface design. IEEE Computer Graphics & Applications: Special Issue on Interacting with Digital Tabletops 26(5):65–73, doi: 10.1109/MCG.2006.114

17. SMART (2009) SMART Technologies, SMART Table. http://www2.smarttech.com/st/en-US/Products/SMART+Table/, accessed 21.01.2009

18. Wu M, Balakrishnan R (2003) Multi-finger and whole hand gestural interaction techniques for multi-user tabletop displays. In: Proceedings of the 16th annual ACM symposium on User interface software and technology (UIST '03), ACM Press, New York, pp 193–202, doi: 10.1145/964696.964718

19. Shen C, Lesh N, Moghaddam B, Beardsley P, Bardsley RS (2001) Personal digital historian: User interface design. In: Extended abstracts on Human factors in computing systems (CHI '01), ACM Press, New York, pp 29–30, doi: 10.1145/634067.634090

20. Shen C, Lesh N, Vernier F (2003) Personal digital historian: Story sharing around the table. Interactions 10(2):15–22, doi: 10.1145/637848.637856

21. Morris MR, Paepcke A, Winograd T (2006) Teamsearch: Comparing techniques for co-present collaborative search of digital media. In: Proceedings of the first IEEE international workshop on horizontal interactive human-computer systems (TABLETOP '06), IEEE Computer Society, Washington, DC, pp 97–104, doi: 10.1109/TABLETOP.2006.32

22. Morris MR, Huang A, Paepcke A, Winograd T (2006) Cooperative gestures: Multi-user gestural interactions for co-located groupware. In: Proceedings of the SIGCHI conference on human factors in computing systems (CHI '06), ACM Press, New York, pp 1201–1210, doi: 10.1145/1124772.1124952

23. Wobbrock JO, Morris MR, Wilson AD (2009) User-defined gestures for surface computing. In: Proceedings of the 27th international conference on human factors in computing systems (CHI '09), ACM Press, New York, pp 1083–1092, doi: 10.1145/1518701.1518866

24. Fitzmaurice GW, Ishii H, Buxton WAS (1995) Bricks: Laying the foundations for graspable user interfaces. In: Proceedings of the SIGCHI conference on human factors in computing systems (CHI '95), ACM Press/Addison-Wesley Publishing Co., New York, pp 442–449, doi: 10.1145/223904.223964

25. Ullmer B, Ishii H (1997) The metaDESK: Models and prototypes for tangible user interfaces. In: Proceedings of the 9th annual ACM symposium on user interface software and technology (UIST '97), ACM Press, New York, pp 223–232, doi: 10.1145/263407.263551

26. Underkoffler J, Ishii H (1999) Urp: A luminous-tangible workbench for urban planning and design. In: Proceedings of the SIGCHI conference on human factors in computing systems (CHI '99), ACM Press, New York, pp 386–393, doi: 10.1145/302979.303114

27. Rekimoto J, Ullmer B, Oba H (2001) DataTiles: A modular platform for mixed physical and graphical interactions. In: Proceedings of the SIGCHI conference on human factors in computing systems (CHI '01), ACM Press, New York, pp 269–276, doi: 10.1145/365024.365115

28. Mazalek A, Reynolds M, Davenport G (2006) Tviews: An extensible architecture for multiuser digital media tables. IEEE Computer Graphics & Applications: Special Issue on Interacting with Digital Tabletops 26(5):47–55, doi: 10.1109/MCG.2006.117

29. Amabile TM (1996) Creativity in context: Update to "the social psychology of creativity". Westview Press, Boulder, CO

30. Boring S, Hilliges O, Butz A (2007) A wall-sized focus plus context display. In: Proceedings of the fifth annual IEEE conference on pervasive computing and communications (PerCom '07), White Plains, New York

31. Sellen AJ, Harper RHR (2003) The myth of the paperless office. MIT Press, Cambridge, MA

32. Hilliges O, Terrenghi L, Boring S, Kim D, Richter H, Butz A (2007) Designing for collaborative creative problem solving. In: Proceedings of the 6th international conference on creativity & cognition, Washington, DC

33. Hinrichs U, Hancock M, Collins C, Carpendale S (2007) Examination of text-entry methods for tabletop displays. In: Proceedings of the second IEEE international workshop on horizontal interactive human-computer systems (TABLETOP '07), pp 105–112, doi: 10.1109/TABLETOP.2007.10

34. Hilliges O, Baur D, Butz A (2007) Photohelix: Browsing, sorting and sharing digital photo collections. In: Proceedings of the second IEEE international workshop on horizontal interactive human-computer systems (TABLETOP '07), IEEE Computer Society, Los Alamitos, CA, pp 87–94, doi: 10.1109/TABLETOP.2007.14

35. Weiss M, Wagner J, Jansen Y, Jennings R, Khoshabeh R, Hollan JD, Borchers J (2009) Slap widgets: Bridging the gap between virtual and physical controls on tabletops. In: Proceedings of the 27th international conference on human factors in computing systems (CHI '09), ACM Press, New York, pp 481–490, doi: 10.1145/1518701.1518779

36. Hilliges O, Kirk D (2009) Getting sidetracked: Display design and occasioning phototalk with the photohelix. In: Proceedings of the 27th international conference on human factors in computing systems (CHI '09), ACM Press, New York, pp 1733–1736, doi: 10.1145/1518701.1518967

37. Chang F, Chen CJ, Lu CJ (2004) A linear-time component-labeling algorithm using contour tracing technique. Computer Vision and Image Understanding 93(2):206–220, doi: 10.1016/j.cviu.2003.09.002

38. Gonzalez RC, Woods RE (2006) Digital image processing (3rd Edition). Prentice-Hall, Inc., Upper Saddle River, NJ

39. Agarawala A, Balakrishnan R (2006) Keepin' it real: Pushing the desktop metaphor with physics, piles and the pen. In: Proceedings of the SIGCHI conference on human factors in computing systems (CHI '06), ACM Press, New York, pp 1283–1292, doi: 10.1145/1124772.1124965

40. Barron JL, Fleet DJ, Beauchemin SS (1994) Performance of optical flow techniques. International Journal of Computer Vision 12(1):43–77, doi: 10.1007/BF01420984
41. Robertson G, Czerwinski M, Larson K, Robbins DC, Thiel D, van Dantzich M (1998) Data mountain: Using spatial memory for document management. In: Proceedings of the 11th annual ACM symposium on user interface software and technology (UIST '98), ACM Press, New York, pp 153–162, doi: 10.1145/288392.288596
42. Harrison C, Hudson SE (2009) Texture displays: A passive approach to tactile presentation. In: Proceedings of the 27th international conference on human factors in computing systems (CHI '09), ACM Press, New York, pp 2261–2264, doi: 10.1145/1518701.1519047
43. Harrison C, Hudson SE (2009) Providing dynamically changeable physical buttons on a visual display. In: Proceedings of the 27th international conference on human factors in computing systems (CHI '09), ACM Press, New York, pp 299–308, doi: 10.1145/1518701.1518749
44. SMART (2003) SMART Technologies DViT. http://www.smarttech.com/DViT/, accessed 12.09.2009
45. Smith JD, Graham TCN, Holman D, Borchers J (2007) Low-cost malleable surfaces with multi-touch pressure sensitivity. In: Proceedings of the second IEEE international workshop on horizontal interactive human-computer systems (TABLETOP '07), pp 205–208, doi: 10.1109/TABLETOP.2007.28
46. Hilliges O, Kim D, Izadi S (2008) Creating malleable interactive surfaces using liquid displacement sensing. In: Proceedings of the third IEEE international workshop on horizontal interactive human-computer systems (TABLETOP '08), pp 157–160, doi: 10.1109/TABLETOP.2008.4660199

Chapter 10
Supporting Atomic User Actions on the Table

Dzmitry Aliakseyeu, Sriram Subramanian, and Jason Alexander

Abstract One of the biggest obstacles that application developers and designers face is a lack of understanding of how to support basic/atomic user interactions. User actions, such as pointing, selecting, scrolling and menu navigation, are often taken for granted in desktop GUI interactions, but have no equivalent interaction techniques in tabletop systems. In this chapter we present a review of the state-of-the-art in interaction techniques for selecting, pointing, rotating, and scrolling. We, first, identify and classify existing techniques, then summarize user studies that were performed with these techniques, and finally identify and formulate design guidelines based on the solutions found.

Introduction

Research into tabletop systems began more than 15 years ago with the DigitalDesk [1], which proposed the idea of a horizontal computationally enhanced interactive surface (aka as a digital table or a tabletop system). Since then, a large portion of research prototypes have aimed at being point-designs (or one-off designs) that highlight the feasibility of the design or promote new opportunities for tabletop systems. In doing so, they also propose different kinds of interaction techniques; for example, The InteractiveDESK [2], introduced the concept of linking physical objects, such as a scrapbook, to digital information, like a computer folder; the use of a three-dimensional space above the table was first proposed within the Responsive Workbench [3]. Active Desk [4] and metaDESK [5] were the first systems to implement the concept of using physical objects to both control and represent digital information.

D. Aliakseyeu (✉)
User Experiences Group, Philips Research Europe, 5656AE Eindhoven, The Netherlands
e-mail: dzmitry.aliakseyeu@philips.com

C. Müller-Tomfelde (ed.), *Tabletops – Horizontal Interactive Displays*,
Human-Computer Interaction Series, DOI 10.1007/978-1-84996-113-4_10,
© Springer-Verlag London Limited 2010

In recent years there has been a growing interest in bringing these various tabletop systems to the market. One of the biggest obstacles that application developers and designers face is a lack of understanding of how to support basic/atomic user interactions. User actions, such as pointing, selecting, scrolling and menu navigation, are often taken for granted in desktop GUI interactions, but have no equivalent interaction techniques in tabletop systems. Recognizing this need, the research community has recently started exploring various techniques to support atomic interactions in different tabletop scenarios. For example, Aliakseyeu et al. [6] proposed and evaluated mechanisms to scroll documents on pen-based tabletop systems while Benko et al. [7] looked at virtual objects selection mechanisms.

Most of these basic interactions are standard for conventional GUI based systems, and have been extensively studied. However, the adaptation of these atomic user actions to the tabletop environment is not straightforward:

- First, tabletop systems offer richer interaction possibilities, therefore simple translation from the standard GUI is unlikely to be optimal;
- Second, the size and horizontal position of the display introduces new challenges such as large reaching distances and range, display occlusion by users' hands and physical objects, lack of precision, the need to orientate objects, the need for sharing, and the lack of tactile feedback.

This chapter offers a structured review of research efforts in supporting atomic user actions. We provide a survey of interaction solutions for tabletop systems and a classification that aims to help designers choose suitable implementations of interaction techniques. We, first, identify and classify existing techniques, then summarize user studies that were performed with these techniques, and finally identify and formulate design guidelines based on the solutions found. When formulating design guidelines, the main measures that we take into account are performance, error rate, user preferences, practical issues and compatibility with other solutions. Later chapters in the book look at other performance measures such as coordination and collaboration.

To keep the chapter focused we only explore selecting, pointing, rotating and scrolling.

Atomic Actions and Chapter Layout

We define the chosen atomic actions as follows:

- *Selecting*. Selection is the process of highlighting a target object on the screen. Examples of this include touching the object with the hand (finger), stylus or physical object and clicking a button on a stylus, physical object or other interaction device.

- *Pointing*. Pointing is the process of moving a cursor from an initial position to a target object on the screen. The cursor reacts to, for example, the hand (finger), stylus, physical object or other interaction device movements. The literature documents four broad categories of pointing techniques: deposit, retrieve, local-operate, distant-operate and combinations of the above.
- *Rotating*. Rotating is the ability to reposition (translate) and reorient (rotate) physical objects, such as printed documents, photos and charts. Rotation forms a vital part of collaboration in tabletop settings. Digital tables offer the potential benefit of bringing together the traditional face-to-face setting with advantages of an electronic information processing unit. Reorienting documents is one such interaction that is important for digital tables but is generally implicit in the screen's orientation in traditional desktop interaction.
- *Scrolling & Panning*. Scrolling is an important interaction technique for supporting many daily tasks within large information spaces. Scrolling actions shift the viewport to content that is of interest and that currently resides off-screen. Usually 1D shifting (scrolling a text document) is referred to as *scrolling,* while 2D shifting (exploring a map) as *panning.* For consistency, in this chapter we will only use the term *scrolling*, and if necessary we will clarify if it is 1D scrolling or 2D scrolling.

Tabletop systems support a large variety of input mechanisms. The choice of a particular input will define how the different atomic actions are performed. There are three common input mechanisms for interacting with a tabletop system:

- Finger(s), and/or hand(s) and other parts of the fore-arms (DigitalDesk [1], DiamondTouch [8], Microsoft Surface ©, Entertaible ©);
- Stylus (pen) (VIP [9, 10]);
- Specific tangible objects, such as game pawns, tool representations, etc. (BUILD-IT [11], metaDESK [5], Microsoft surface ©, Entertaible ©).

Every input method has its pros and cons; for example, selection of an object by simply touching it with your finger is a very intuitive technique used in touch screens, however issues such as occlusion, parallax and reach distance may lead to poor performance of this otherwise simple and straightforward technique. These issues are common among many interaction techniques and can prevent reliable interaction.

Usually, a particular interaction technique addresses one or more of these issues. These issues are highlighted as we discuss each atomic action.

The next four sections describe our four selected atomic actions. Each section is laid out as follows: first, we introduce the atomic action, second, we describe the most relevant existing techniques that perform this action, third, we outline relevant user studies and fourth we provide design recommendations and open questions for the atomic action.

Selecting

We consider selection as a distinct operation from pointing. However, the performance with target selection is commonly studied with pointing and selection as one combined operation [12, 13]. Unfortunately, these two elements are rarely investigated in isolation. However, some evidence suggests that selection alone (i.e. button clicking) without pointing can consume a significant amount of the total target selection time [14, 15]. As a result, enhancing the selection mechanisms on an input device can lead to more efficient interactions. Furthermore, selection techniques differ in their intuitiveness to users, and the accuracy that users can achieve.

Selection Techniques

This section provides an overview of existing selection techniques. Not all techniques that are discussed were specifically designed for tabletop systems; however, many are included as they could equally be applied in a tabletop situation (some techniques were developed for large vertical displays, some for portable pen and touch based devices, and some for desktop systems).

The two most prominent concerns for selection are *occlusion* and *two state input*. Most touch based tabletop systems are two-state devices (Fig. 10.1): (0) out of range and (1) tracking. Conversely, the mouse and some stylus inputs are three-state devices: they additionally support a (2) dragging state when the mouse button or pen-tip is pressed down. This means that pointing and selection may interfere with each other if no measures are taken, as both use the tracking state to initiate the operation [16]. The two state input is therefore is not a concern for selecting "non-movable" objects such as those used for menu selections and text input.

Most of the finger/hand based techniques either address the two-state issue prevalent on touch screen or the issue of covering small targets. Some techniques address both issues.

The **two state** issue is addressed by the following techniques: *Take-off* [17], selection on finger down-up transition within target area; *Tactile* (also referred as

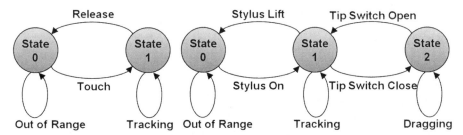

Fig. 10.1 Two state model as applicable in basic interactive tabletop systems (*left*) and three state model as applicable in various stylus based systems [16], such as from Wacom © (*right*)

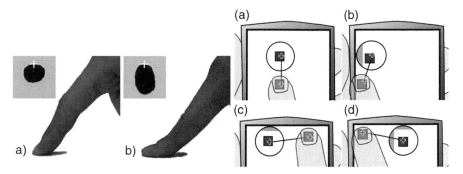

Fig. 10.2 (*Left*) The SimPress press-through technique as implemented by Benko et al. [7]; (*Right*) Shift technique [23]

press-through) [18], selection on changing from low to high finger pressure within target area; *SimPress* [7] a special variant of the press-through technique (Fig. 10.2, left); *Double tap* [19], selection on finger down-up-down-up (tap-tap) within target area; *HoTTop* click gesture [20], selection is done by placing two fingers on the area of interest (document page); *DTMouse* [21]: selection or mode change performed by tapping with the second finger; *SmartSkin mouse press* [22]: selection on hand-surface distance, where a distance between the surface and the palm is used to distinguish between pressed and released states.

In all of the solutions discussed above, the finger covers (part of) the target object, which can lead to issues when selecting small objects. Widgor et al. [24] showed that selection precision can be learned and improved with practice. However, when the user requires visual feedback (e.g. during text selection) and when the user is selecting one object among multiple small closely located objects, alternative solutions might be needed.

The issue of covering is addressed either by creating a cursor offset or by local zooming. Although some of these techniques were developed and evaluated on PDAs only, which have relatively small screens and target objects, this potentially is also an issue for tabletop applications. Offset techniques include: *cursor offset* [7] that places a cursor above the finger, enabling it to select small targets without covering them; *dual finger offset* [7] that places a cursor above the finger, with the offset triggered by placing a second finger; *shift* [23] that creates a callout near the finger with the content that is under the finger (Fig. 10.2, right); *dual finger stretch* [7] that stretches the area of interest, making the selection of small objects simpler; *under the table selection* [25] where the hand of a user is placed under the table, therefore it does not occlude the targets that are projected on top of the table; *rub-pointing* [26], combines zooming and selecting into one movement; *zoom-tapping* [26], employs tapping with the secondary finger for zooming.

With a stylus, users commonly invoke a selection by directly tapping over an object (quickly touching and then releasing the stylus without horizontal movement, similar to a button click). Since tapping does not reflect how people naturally use

Fig. 10.3 Slide touch [27]

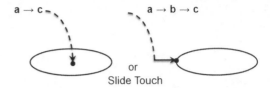

notepads, where writing and making checkmarks is common, designers have developed an alternative referred to as *touching* [27]. Unlike tapping, which requires that a pen touch a screen and be lifted directly over the target to select it, touch interactions only require that the target be touched at some point (Fig. 10.3). As a result, touching supports the selection of targets by crossing them, making checkmarks and even tapping. An example of such a technique is a *slide touch* [27]. With this technique, the target is selected when the pen touches it for the first time – the pen can initially either land on the target or outside of the target (Fig. 10.3).

Results show [15, 27] that touching is a viable alternative to tapping for completing selection, even for the elderly [15]. Other pen-based systems have shown to provide effective selection mechanisms by crossing targets. With *CrossY* [28] the pointing is eliminated and instead selection happens in one fluid motion by crossing an object.

Various stylus based systems use a three state model for selection in a similar manner to the conventional desktop mouse. For example, to select an object with the Wacom© digital pen, touching the object is not enough, the pen must also be pressed against the surface so that the tip switch is activated. This allows pointing and selecting to be differentiated.

Tangible objects require slightly different interactions for selection. Tangible objects must usually be placed on top of a virtual object for selection to take place. The tracking technology will determine the type of mode switch employed for selection to take place. For example, the BUILD-IT system [11] uses tangibles that are active as soon as they are placed on the table. To select a virtual object the tangible (physical object) must be placed on top of the object and to deselect it the tangible needs to be covered by the hand. The VIP system [29], which is also vision based, uses a modified approach: to select or deselect the object, only a specific part of the tangible needs to be covered (leading to a "virtual button").

Comparison of Selection Techniques

Potter et al. [17] compared the following three selection techniques: First-contact, land-on, and take-off. They concluded that *take-off* has the best performance in terms of speed and error rate and it was most preferred by the users.

Benko et al. [7] studied the press-through technique without tactile feedback on a touch screen (SimPress). The authors concluded that SimPress worked only if the user was always approaching the tabletop from the same direction; otherwise the orientation of the hand and arm had to be taken into account.

Ren and Moriya [27] compared six selection strategies for pens. The comparison used a standard Fitts law experiment: participants selected a number of appearing targets as fast and as accurately as possible using different selection strategies. They found that Slide Touch (Fig. 10.3) is the best technique in terms of selection time, error rate, and subjective preference.

Hourcade et al. [15] compared a touching techniques and tap selection techniques. The touch technique was similar to the Slide Touch techniques proposed by Ren and Moria [27]. The study focused on accuracy and age differences. They found that all age groups (18–22, 50–64, 65–84) were more accurate when touching than when tapping circular targets with a diameter of 16 pixels = 3.84 mm.

Design Recommendations and Open Questions

When selecting objects that require only two-sate input (e.g. menus and text input):

- Touch-based techniques should be used when selecting objects. Examples of these techniques include *slide touch* [27], *take-off* [17] and *direct touch*. *Take-off* or *direct touch* should be employed when there is a high density of potential targets.
- For selecting small objects *cursor offset* can be used; *cursor offset* can also be used to remedy the input-output parallax. However, if possible, *cursor offset* based techniques should be avoided since it was shown that they require significantly more time than simple touch techniques and the system needs to know the orientation of the user (which can be either calculated by analyzing the finger surface contact area, or avoided by using midpoint between two fingers) [7]. The choice for cursor offset should be based on a desired performance and error rate.
- As an alternative to *cursor offset* [7] and for selecting very small targets, local zooming (e.g. *dual finger stretch* [7]), or showing a copy of the occluded screen area in a non-occluded location (e.g. *shift* [23]) can be employed. These techniques are the most appropriate both in terms of users' performance and preference.

The corresponding sizes for "small" and "large" targets need to be experimentally determined, however we can safely say that targets larger than the finger tip can be considered large, and targets that are smaller than the input resolution can be considered small.

When selecting objects that require three-state input (e.g. dragging and activating):

- *Bimanual or multi-finger* techniques are the most effective. The object can be selected using one of the techniques described above and then the second hand or another finger can be used to change the object's state. Different users can be discriminated by using a threshold distance between the detected finger positions. Alternatively, single point techniques such as *SimPress* [7] can be employed.

- A three state system (mode switch) can also be implemented using tangible objects. For example, an interactive physical object that is used for both selection and positioning could communicate button presses on the object to the table.

There are still a number of questions that remain unanswered:

- *Universal selection method*. Based on the literature review we can conclude that no single technique can address all aspects of selecting on the tabletop, therefore a hybrid (mixed) technique with several modes is necessary. It is however unclear what combination would be the most efficient, as this is likely to be dependent on the task and context.
- *Three state-input (mode switching)*. Direct touch is the simplest and fastest technique for selection; however, it does not immediately support mode switching. Techniques that support mode switching suffer from either lower performance or a lack of robustness. The problem of mode switching can be addressed both through software solutions (SimPress) or hardware (for example, by making tabletop surfaces pressure sensitive). The universally best solution still requires further research.
- *Occlusion*. Occlusion is addressed by a large number of techniques. However, Widgor et al. [24] found that in many situations occlusion is not a problem, especially if the target size is large. However, as the input and output resolution of tabletop systems continues to grow, occlusion may become a main concern when choosing the most suitable selection technique.

Pointing

Pointing is the process of moving a cursor from an initial position to a target object on the screen, the cursor reacting to the hand (finger), stylus, physical object or other interaction device movements.

The literature documents four broad categories of pointing: deposit, retrieve, local-operate, distant-operate and combinations of the above [30]:

- *Deposit*: These techniques allow users to move an object from within their vicinity to a distant location (e.g. Flick [19, 31]).
- *Retrieve*: These techniques bring distant objects closer to the user for selection (e.g. Drag-and-Pop [32]), but do not support relocation of the cursor to a distant location.
- *Local-operate*: These techniques allow the user to interact with objects that are within their hand-reach. They support cursor-offsetting and/or high-precision

control for local-control of the pointer (e.g. Dispositioned Cursor [33] and Dual-Finger MidPoint [7]).

- *Distant-operate*: These techniques allow users to relocate their cursor to a distant location to facilitating object manipulation in distant locations. Examples include the Perspective Cursor [34] and Push-and-Throw [35].
- *Combination techniques*: These techniques combine two or more of the function-alities described above. For example, Push-and-Pop [35] supports the retrieve and distant-operate functions and Radar Views [36] allow the user to deposit and retrieve.

Another important dimension of pointing techniques is the location of input [37]. The input location can be in the personal space (close to the user – within about one meter) or in the group space (the area between the users, visible to all of them but not always easy to access). Techniques that make use of personal input space are called *indirect* techniques; interaction with objects on the entire table is performed from the personal area. Techniques which make use of group input space are called *direct* techniques, interaction with objects happens directly on the place of the object itself. Mixed techniques are a midway between direct and indirect techniques and thus make use of input from the personal and group space.

Pointing Techniques

This section provides an overview of existing pointing techniques. Techniques will be presented based on the location of input (direct or indirect).

Direct Pointing Techniques

These techniques allow the user to interact with objects that are within their hand-reach. They often support cursor-offsetting and/or high-precision control for local-control of the pointer [37].

The most common techniques in this category are: *drag-and-drop,* an interaction technique where the user selects an object by touching it with a stylus, and deselects it by lifting the stylus from the tabletop [37]; *touch-input,* an interaction technique comparable to drag-and-drop – the difference is that a body part (e.g. a finger) is used instead of a stylus [38]; *pick-and-drop* [39], the user can "pick up" an object by touching it with a digital pen (or finger or any other suitable device), and then "drop" the object anywhere in the workspace by repeating the touch action in the desired location.

Unlike the techniques described above, the following techniques are coupled to a specific input mechanism (finger/hand touch or pen/stylus): *dispositioned cursor* [33]: shows the cursor just above the finger tip, combined with the take-off selection technique; *zoom-pointing* [33]: first the user zooms to a sub area defined by drawing a rectangle, they can then perform direct pointing at a finer scale, combined with the take-off selection technique; *cross-keys* [33]: uses four arrow keys around a visor to finely adjust the cursor, combined with the take-off selection technique; *precision-handle* [33]: uses a virtual pantograph for precise pointing, combined with the take-off selection technique; *dual finger offset* [7] is activated by placing a secondary finger anywhere on the surface, the cursor is subsequently offset above the primary finger by a predefined fixed amount (selection is done via the SimPress); *dual finger midpoint* [7]: positions the cursor exactly halfway between the two fingers, giving the user both a cursor offset as well as a variable reduction of cursor speed (selection is done via the SimPress); *dual finger stretch* [7]: adaptively scales the user interface (selection is done via the SimPress); *dual finger slider* [7]: the right finger (primary) controls the cursor, the left finger (secondary) invokes the invisible slider, with speed reductions modes achieved by moving the secondary finger towards the primary finger (selection is done via the SimPress); *SDMouse* [40]: emulates full mouse functionality through multi-finger input; *bubble cursor* [41]: is an improvement of area cursors [42] that allows selection of discrete target points by using Voronoi regions to associate empty space with nearby targets using hotspot; *DynaSpot* [43]: couples cursor activation area with it speed, the faster cursor is moved the larger the activation area of the cursor.

Indirect Pointing Techniques

Indirect techniques make use of the personal input space. They employ virtual embodiment and local and shared feedback [37].

Radar views [36] are an interaction technique that makes use of a miniature view of the entire workspace which is displayed in front of each user (Fig. 10.4); *bubble-radar* [44] combines radar views and bubble cursor techniques; *pantograph* (also referred as Push-and-Throw) [35] is an interaction technique in which the user moves the stylus in his/her personal space, as with radar, however, there is no workspace miniature; *telepointers* [37] are an interaction technique which is equivalent to the pantograph, but without the line that connects the stylus to the cursor; *drag-and-pop* [32] brings proxies of all potential targets in the direction of movement closer to the user (Fig. 10.5); *throw and flick* techniques [19, 31, 45, 46] use a simple stroke (with the pen or hand) on the table surface to slide an object, mimicking the action used to send physical objects across a table; *superflick* [47] adds an optional closed-loop control step to basic Flick; *HybridPointing* [48] allows the user to quickly switch between absolute and relative pointing thus combining direct and indirect pointing.

Radar

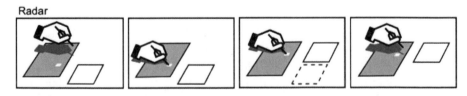

Fig. 10.4 Radar view interaction scenario [37]

Fig. 10.5 In drag-and-pop, each valid target icon in the direction of the drag motion creates a linked tip icon that approaches the dragged object. Dropping onto a tip icon saves mouse travel to distant targets [32]

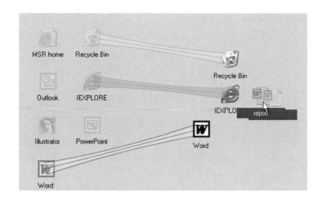

Comparisons of Pointing Techniques

Albinsson and Zhai [33] compared the following high precision selection techniques using Fitts-law tasks: dispositioned cursor (take-off), zoom-pointing, cross-keys, and precision-handle. They concluded that take-off's one-step nature makes it fast when the target is large enough, but hard to operate accurately when aiming at single pixels; zoom pointing performed well on speed, errors, and user preference for all target sizes; cross-keys allowed the users to select small targets with low error rates.

Benko et al. [7] compared a number of dual finger pointing techniques that aimed to improve selection precision. They found that dual finger stretch performed the best on speed, error, and user preference measures. This was the only tested technique that did not provide a cursor offset.

Nacenta et al. [36] compared several pen-based pointing techniques like the Radar View, Pantograph and Pick-and-drop via Fitts-law tasks. Target width W was set at 80 mm and distance D at 25, 50, 80, 140 cm. They concluded that the Radar View was significantly faster than all other techniques in the ranges tested. Reetz et al. [47] compared Flick and Superflick with a Radar view for a variety of placement tasks. They found that flick was faster than Radar Views but it also had lowest accuracy, whereas Superflick was nearly as fast and as accurate as Radar Views.

Design Recommendations and Open Questions

In this section a number of guidelines that address single user pointing are formulated. Based on the analyzed comparisons we can conclude that:

- *Local pointing.* For local pointing or when all parts of the table are within hand reach, direct techniques such as touch input [38] are preferable. To avoid the occlusion problem and for more precise positioning, touch input can be combined with zooming techniques, such as Dual finger stretch [7], or techniques that show a copy of the occluded screen area in a non-occluded location, such as Shift [23].

- *Reaching distant areas.* For reaching distant areas, techniques that bring objects closer to the user, e.g. Radar View (additional visualizations such as a pantograph line that connects input with a cursor can be used to improve the awareness) [36] and Drag-and-Pop [35] are preferable.
- *Quick transfer.* For the quick transfer of objects, throwing techniques such as Flick [19, 31, 45, 46] should be employed.

These guidelines however cannot be directly applied to a multi-user setting. In multi-user settings, speed and accuracy are less relevant performance measures than collaboration and coordination. For example, the high performance Radar View technique might not be the best choice for a collaborative setting. For more details on interaction techniques that foster coordination readers should refer to Chapter 13.

In a similar manner to selection, there are still several questions that remain unanswered:

- *Occlusion and mode switch* issues have a similar impact on pointing.
- *Multi-display.* Tabletop systems are often used in combination with other devices. In such a multi-device, multi display situation pointing becomes a more challenging task. Many techniques described here will not be able to span more than one screen. The scalability of these techniques therefore will need to be investigated further. A discussion on multi-display pointing can be found in Nacenta et al. [30].

Rotation

When people collaborate in face-to-face settings, they often share tools, artefacts and documents. The ability to reposition (translate) and reorient (rotate) content and tools is a vital part of collaboration in the tabletop setting. Tabletop systems like Entertaible © offer the potential benefit of bringing together a traditional face-to-face setting with the advantages of an electronic information processing unit. To make interaction with digital tables as flexible, intuitive and effortless as real tables we need to design techniques that allow the user to interact with a combination of digital and physical content using familiar everyday gestures. Reorienting content is one such interaction that is important for digital tables, but has not been critical for traditional desktop interaction.

In a multi-user environment, the orientation of artifacts on the table becomes even more important, as it functions as a means for communication between users. Reorientation enhances collaborative actions as it helps users to show information to other users who are seated across the table and do not share the same perspective. Further, users can orient objects on the table in such a way that they add information to their story or show whether or not the object is personal (directed towards the user) or shared (oriented towards the other users).

There are a number of challenges in designing systems and interaction techniques for tabletops; one of these is that, unlike vertical displays, tabletops do not have a predefined orientation. Since the users' perspectives change as they move around the table, designers cannot make assumptions about the preferred orientation of artefacts – there is no clear up or down, left or right. Therefore, tabletop applications must allow users to easily move and reorient objects: towards themselves for reading and manipulation, and towards others around the table during group activities.

In many tabletop and non-tabletop systems, these actions have traditionally been considered as two distinct operations (examples to follow in the next section). If one wants to move and rotate an object, one does so sequentially. On *desktop* systems, input is usually restricted to a 2DOF device like the mouse, and so rotation and translation are often divided into two separate gestures or commands. Desktop applications like Microsoft PowerPoint support planar rotation of objects by allowing the user to activate a planar rotation widget and providing rotation handles at the corner of the to-be-rotated object (Fig. 10.6). Users can rotate the object by selecting the rotation handle and moving the mouse in a clockwise or anti-clockwise direction. The object then rotates around an axis located at its centre. The translation actions are usually support via dragging.

Reorientation is an extremely common action in traditional tabletop collaborations. Kruger et al. [49] conducted an observational study of collaborative activity on a traditional table to show that the strategy of automatically reorienting objects to a person's view is overly simplistic. Their studies suggest that reorientation proves critical in how individuals *comprehend information*, how collaborators *coordinate their actions*, and how they *mediate communication*. For more details on coordination readers should refer to Chapter 13 and on collaboration to Chapter 17.

Kinaesthetic studies have demonstrated that rotating and translating are inseparable actions in the physical world [50] and that integrated interaction techniques are more appropriate mechanisms for integrated actions [51]. These studies suggest advantages for interaction methods that integrate rotation and translation to form a class of interaction techniques called *reorientation*.

Here we review various interaction techniques that have been investigated in the literature for *reorienting* content and tools on digital tables.

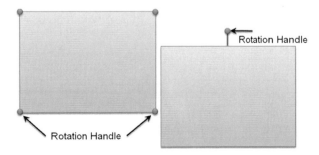

Fig. 10.6 Planar object rotation handles in standard desktop packages like Microsoft PowerPoint

Rotation Techniques

In general, there are three main ways in which orientation of objects can be supported by a tabletop system: (1) rotating the entire workspace (central part of the workspace can sometimes be fixed), (2) automatically reorienting artefacts on the workspace, or (3) allowing users to change the orientation of individual artefacts. An alternative approach is to reduce the necessity to reorient: in some cases, icons, controls and tools could also be designed in such a way that they do not have a clear orientation and can be viewed from different sides (for example, using picture icons as opposed to text labels).

There are several techniques that allow for each of these three mentioned ways of orientating objects on a tabletop [49, 52, 53]:

- *Fixed orientation*;
- *Full reorientation:* the entire physical tabletop could be either manually or electronically rotated;
- *Person-based automatic reorientation:* information is oriented automatically by the tabletop system;
- *Environment-based automatic reorientation:* items are oriented towards the person closest to it, often to the edges of a table;
- *Manual orientation:* the user to orientates the objects by themselves;
- *Multiple copies of information:* copies of information are created that can be rotated separately, so users can have their own perspective on them.

Some examples of rotation techniques are:

Corner-to-rotate. A common implementation of rotation in early tabletop systems is a direct adaptation of the desktop metaphor for 2D rotation and is used to support rotation in several tabletop systems such as DiamondSpin [54], i-LAND [55] and ConnecTables [56]. The rotation is performed by touching one of the object corners, and then turning it around an axis located at the centre of the object.

Rotate 'N Translate (RnT). RnT [57] is a tabletop interaction technique that combines rotation and translation into a single gesture. It is primarily intended for pen, stylus or finger use and uses two degrees of freedom (that correspond to the translational freedom for the input device). In RnT, the virtual object is partitioned into two regions by a circle around the object (Fig. 10.7, left). By clicking within the circular region in the centre of the artefact, the user can drag the artefact around the workspace (translate only). By clicking outside of the circle, the user can rotate and translate the artefact using a single gesture. Translation and rotation begin simultaneously, with artefact translation following the movement of the pointer.

Turn and Translate (TnT). TnT [53] is based on physical surrogates for rotation and translation of digital objects on the table, using three degrees of freedom (two

Fig. 10.7 (*Left*) RnT. A control point is selected in the lower right, and the artefact rotates counter clockwise while it is translated upward [53]. (*Right*) TnT. *Left*: sensor positioned on object. *Right*: object rotated by twisting block [53]

translational and one rotational). The user places a physical prop over the virtual object and manipulates the virtual object using the physical prop. The technique has been used in many tangible tabletop systems such as BUILD-IT [11], metaDESK [5] and Visual Interaction Platform [9], see Fig. 10.7, right.

Cutouts [58]. This technique allows users to interactively create multiple views of the tabletop workspace and move and re-orient these views.

Two finger rotation [19, 22]. This method, combined with simultaneous positioning and sometimes scaling, is the most widely used in multi-touch systems. Some systems [22] allow the user to perform reorientation and scaling using more than two fingers, in this case the system automatically uses a least-squares method to determine the motion (consisting of moving, rotating and scaling) that best satisfies the constraints provided by the fingers.

Comparison of Rotation Techniques

In an experimental study, Kruger et al. [57] compared corner-to-rotate with the RnT technique in a series of tasks that involved *precise targeting* (precise rotation and translation), *document passing* (a less-precise rotation and translation task that attempted to mirror a real-world collaborative activity – the passing of document) and *collaborative document passing* (three participants completing a word puzzle by passing and decoding clues to form a completed sentence). The authors found that RnT was faster than corner-to-rotate, and had fewer touches (but by design RnT requires one touch less than corner-to-rotate). There is no significant difference with corner-to-rotate in terms of error rate and user preference.

In a further study, Liu et al. [53] compared RnT with variations of TnT. The tasks were similar to the first two tasks of the study by Kruger et al. [57]. They found that with TnT users were almost twice as fast and twice as accurate when rotating an object, with participants indicating a greater preference for this technique.

Design Recommendations and Open Questions

The literature provides a number of formulated guidelines for supporting rotation:

- Krueger et al. [52] concluded that free rotations must be supported and the lightweight, orientation of user-positioned items must be maintained.
- Based on evaluations carried out thus far, TnT appears to be the simplest solution available that exploits tangible interaction and requires very little instruction to use.
- There has been no comparison of two-finger rotation with either the single-touch RnT or tangible rotation techniques such as TnT. But on a multi-touch table there is a strong expectation that RnT would still be a good rotation method to include alongside other techniques.
- The potential problem with using tangible objects is that reorientation could end up being an "Always ON or Always OFF" feature. At the moment there seems to be no down-side to this. But it is possible that future applications might need to explore simple ways in which the users can dynamically switch between reorientation and translation only. In this case, TnT may turn out to be no better than the corner-to-rotate technique.

There has been limited investigation into multi-touch solutions for re-orientation. It is also worthwhile to look carefully at how we can use a simple metaphor that translates across multiple input devices, such as the finger, stylus, and tangible objects. Although there have been studies on the importance of reorientation in collaboration and comprehension, most of these studies have been carried out on real tables and there have been no investigation into the effect of digital rotation techniques on collaboration and comprehension.

Scrolling

Scrolling is an important interaction technique that facilitates users' daily tasks with information spaces that are too large to be shown in their entirety, at a single point in time. Scrolling actions shift the viewport to regions that are of interest and that currently reside off-screen. There are a number of factors that influence scrolling performance, namely [6]:

- *Mapping function.* Scrolling mechanisms are driven by a mapping function that performs a translation of the user's manipulation of the input device to the scrolling operation. Various types of mapping functions exist, however most of the current systems can be classified as either a zero-order position mapping or a first-order rate mapping. In a zero-order position mapping system, the relative displacement of the cursor produces a proportional scrolling distance. This type of control is embedded within the classical scrollbar, with users controlling the viewport displacement distance by adjusting the scrollbar thumb. With a first-order rate mapping system, such as in rate-based scrolling, the mapping function translates the displacement of the cursor (or some other value such as force on an isometric input device) to scrolling speed.

- *Input device*. Several multi-stream input devices were designed to support a range of interactive tasks, including scrolling, such as a wheel or an isometric joystick [59] on a mouse.
- *Target distance*. Numerous studies have shown that scrolling mechanisms are affected by various document sizes and target distances [60–62].
- *Visual feedback*. With scrolling tasks, visual feedback typically consists of a smooth or a blurred transition from one part of the information space to another. Researchers have developed a number of alternative visualization techniques to reduce the effect of blurring that occurs at high scroll rates (e.g. [63–65]). Kaptelinin et al. [64] found that transient visual cues, an aid that differentiates the current text and the text that will replace it, can improve reading performance with text-based documents.
- *Target type*. The perceptual characteristics of the target can influence scrolling performance. Particularly at high scrolling rates, targets that are considered as being "more" preattentive facilitate more rapid searches.
- *The user's familiarity with the document*. The level of familiarity a user has with an information space has a direct effect on scrolling performance [60, 62] – users take less time to find an object if its position is known in advance.

There is large number of scrolling techniques addressing one or more of these factors. To provide focus, we limit our discussion to conventional scrolling techniques used on desktop systems, and scrolling techniques designed specifically for tabletop systems.

Scrolling Techniques

Scrolling techniques can be classified into two categories: device independent and pen/touch-based techniques.

Device independent: These scrolling techniques are controlled using a variety of input devices. The *scrollbar* is the most commonly employed interface widget for navigating large information spaces, requiring the user to position a scrollbar "thumb"; *rate-based scrolling* uses a first-order rate mapping, the mapping function translates the displacement of the cursor (or some other value such as force on an isometric input device) to scrolling speed; *panning* (e.g. using Adobe Reader's *hand tool*) facilitates 2D scrolling dragging the face of the content to the required position; *Space-Filling Thumbnails (SFT)* [61] allows users to switch between a normal reading view and a thumbnail view in which all document pages are scaled and tiled to fit the window, providing an overview of all of the document's pages and ultimately eliminates the need for a scrollbar.

Pen/touch-based scrolling: The *scroll ring* (e.g. Apple iPod™) is designed as a doughnut-shaped touchpad that scrolls content in response to a user's circular strokes; the *virtual scroll ring* [66] is a software implementation of the scroll ring, negating the need for additional hardware; the *radial scroll tool* [67] uses a stirrer (a device that converts circular motions of a pen into a series of values that can be used to control the rotation of an object, as studied by Evans et al. [68]) as a tool to determine the direction in which the pen is spinning, feeding the output into scroll direction and velocity; *curve dial* [69] is an improved version of the radial scroll tool, it uses the curvature of the mouse drag (or drag of another pointing device such as pen or finger) to determine the direction of scrolling; *crossbar* [28] allows users to navigate by crossing the pen over a crossbar; *gesture scrolling/panning* [22] is based on a "hand" tool, but is enriched by multi-touch capabilities: in a similar manner to the hand tool, users can start scrolling by sliding a finger along the surface, while the speed of scrolling is controlled by the number of fingers in contact with surface, i.e. scrolling speed increases as the number of fingers increases; *Multi-Flick-Standard* (MFS) [6] maps the pen flick speed to the document scrolling speed, similar to setting a flywheel in motion; *Compound Multi-Flick* (CMF) [6] is a compound technique that combines flicking with a displacement-based control; *Multi-Flick-Friction* (MFF) [6] is similar to MFS but includes an additional friction "factor" that gracefully reduces the document scrolling speed after some time interval.

Comparison of Scrolling Techniques

Smith and Schraefel [67] compared the Radial Scroll Tool with standard scrolling techniques available in touch-based systems. The independent variables were interface type (tablet and large screen touch display), scroll distance (short: targets 5 pages/images apart and long: targets 20 pages/images apart), technique (radial scroll and traditional scroll, namely the scrollbar in combination with software keyboard's arrow and page keys), and task type (find a picture, find a heading). The study showed that for both the tablet and the wall mounted display, with both image and text selection, radial scroll worked better for navigating short distances and traditional scroll worked better for long distances.

Aliakseyeu et al. [6] compared three multi-flick scrolling technique modifications with the standard scrollbar on three pen based devices – a table, a Tablet PC and a PDA. Two experiments were carried out: one that required users to scroll a list of items (names of cities), and another that required scrolling in a standard text document. They concluded that Multi-flick scrolling is an effective alternative to conventional scrolling techniques. They found that Compound-Multi Flick is on average faster than the two other flick modifications and is as effective as using the scrollbar and is most preferred by users.

Design Recommendations and Open Questions

Scrolling short documents (less than five pages):

- In situations where the scrolling distances are short and the user requires good control of the scrolling speed (for example, when reading), techniques similar to Curve Dial [69] are the most appropriate.
- In situations where the document is unknown and the user wishes to explore the information space (for example, browsing a web page) multi-flick [6] based techniques are preferable.

Scrolling long documents:

- When scrolling through a long and unknown document, multi-flick [6] based techniques are a good option. These techniques allow scrolling to start with a single stroke. The user can then remove their hands from the table, avoiding the occlusion problem.
- When scrolling through known documents, the Crossbar [28] is an appropriate choice. It provides the user with information regarding their position within the document, it allows them to quickly jump into a desired location and it is based on a common and well know widget (the scrollbar). However, this technique is only appropriate for 1D scrolling (the introduction of the second bar will break the scrolling into two separate actions: vertical and horizontal scrolling). Alternatives such as multi-flick may be better suited when 2D scrolling is required.
- A standard scrollbar can be used for scrolling though long, but familiar documents. In a similar manner to the crossbar, the scrollbar can only facilitate 1D scrolling.

To provide a complete solution, all three of the techniques mentioned above can be implemented simultaneously. Users can easily discriminate between curve dial and flick and the crossbar provides a separate interface element. This leaves the user to choose the most appropriate or their preferred option depending on their task at hand.

There are still a number of questions that remain unanswered:

- *Mode switch*. Some interaction techniques may require a mode switch to discriminate them from application commands. For example, in a drawing program, a flicking gesture for drawing a line needs to be discriminated from a flicking gesture to pan the canvas. Curve Dial and Multi-Flick may require this type of mode switch.
- *Finger friction*. Curve Dial requires a constant circular movement of the finger, which is potentially a tiring action and should probably only be used for scrolling short distances. Alternatively, tangible objects can be used instead of the finger to reduce the friction between the finger and the table.

- *Screen real-estate and document position awareness.* The scrollbar, while taking up some valuable screen real-estate, provides the user with useful information regarding their location within the document and the current portion of the document on-screen. Even when employing gesture-based scrolling techniques, users still require some awareness of their position. A passive scrollbar (i.e. one that cannot be interacted with) can be employed in this situation; however, it remains to be seen if this is the best solution.
- *Tangible scrolling.* Instead of a finger, an active or passive tangible object can be used for scrolling. For example, a tangible object with a wheel similar to the mouse wheel can be used for this purpose – the location of the object would define the document to scroll and turning of the wheel would perform the scrolling itself (the wheel turn can either be detected by the table – passive tangible, or it can be done electronically within the object and transmitted wirelessly to the table – active tangible).
- *Visual enhancement techniques* (SFT, SDAZ, etc.). A number of techniques have been proposed to allow a higher scrolling speed by using different visualization approaches [28, 63–65]. So far these techniques have been implemented and studied solely on desktop systems, their usability on tabletop systems is unclear and requires further investigation.

Discussion

In presenting the interaction techniques we also identify design factors (or issues) that affect each atomic action. For example, selection is affected by *reaching distance or range, number of states of selection model, occlusions* and *parallax*.

Although each section also identifies how interaction techniques address some of these issues, it is not always clear how well a particular technique deals with each design factor or if any of the factors have a negative impact on the technique.

One further limitation of the techniques documented in this chapter is the lack of evaluation in terms of multi-user coordination, collaboration and comprehension. The most commonly used performance measures are time, error-rate and user preference. However, in a multi-user setting other metrics that relate to group dynamics are just as important. More research is needed to identify design principles and guidelines that take into consideration the above factors (interested readers should refer to Chapter 13 for details).

This chapter focused only on four types of atomic actions – selection, pointing, rotation and scrolling. Actions such as menu navigation, 2D map navigation, and text-entry are equally important although due to space limitations these are not explored within this chapter.

Conclusion

In this chapter we have provided a structured review of the research efforts into supporting atomic user actions. Specifically, we looked at selecting, pointing, rotating and scrolling actions. Our review considered input methods supported by different tabletop systems and also identified challenges faced when designing interaction techniques that support these atomic actions. Despite the large number of interaction techniques that offer different support for atomic actions, there are no clearly preferred techniques or techniques that address all design challenges. Based on this review we identify several open research questions that we hope will stimulate further research in this area.

References

1. Wellner P (1993) Interacting with paper on the DigitalDesk. Communications of the ACM 36(7):87–96, doi: 10.1145/159544.159630
2. Arai T, Machii K, Kuzunuki S, Shojima H (1995) InteractiveDESK: A computer-augmented desk which responds to operations on real objects. In: CHI'95: Proceedings of the conference companion on human factors in computing systems, ACM Press, New York, pp 141–142, doi: 10.1145/223355.223470
3. Krüger W, Bohn CA, Fröhlich B, Schüth H, Strauss W, Wesche G (1995) The responsive workbench: A virtual work environment. Computer 28(7):42–48, doi:10.1109/2.391040
4. Fitzmaurice GW, Ishii H, Buxton WAS (1995) Bricks: Laying the foundations for graspable user interfaces. In: CHI'95: Proceedings of the SIGCHI conference on human factors in computing systems, ACM Press/Addison-Wesley Publishing Co., New York, pp 442–449, doi: 10.1145/223904.223964
5. Ullmer B, Ishii H (1997) The metaDESK: Models and prototypes for tangible user interfaces. In: UIST'97: Proceedings of the 10th annual ACM symposium on User interface software and technology, ACM Press, New York, pp 223–232, doi: 10.1145/263407.263551
6. Aliakseyeu D, Irani P, Lucero A, Subramanian S (2008) Multi-flick: An evaluation of flick-based scrolling techniques for pen interfaces. In: CHI'08: Proceeding of the twenty-sixth annual SIGCHI conference on human factors in computing systems, ACM Press, New York, pp 1689–1698, doi: 10.1145/1357054.1357319
7. Benko H, Wilson A, Baudisch P (2006) Precise selection techniques for multi-touch screens. In: CHI'06: Proceedings of the SIGCHI conference on human factors in computing systems, ACM Press, New York, pp 1263–1272, doi: 10.1145/1124772.1124963
8. Dietz P, Leigh D (2001) DiamondTouch: A multi-user touch technology. In: UIST'01: Proceedings of the 14th annual ACM symposium on User interface software and technology, ACM Press, New York, pp 219–226, doi: 10.1145/502348.502389
9. Aliakseyeu D, Martens J-B, Subramanian S, Vroubel M, Wesselink W (2001) Visual interaction platform. In: INTERACT'01: Proceedings of Interact 2001, IOS Press, Amsterdam, pp 232–239
10. Brandl P, Forlines C, Wigdor D, Haller M, Shen C (2008) Combining and measuring the benefits of bimanual pen and direct-touch interaction on horizontal interfaces. In: AVI'08: Proceedings of the working conference on advanced visual interfaces, ACM Press, New York, pp 154–161, doi: 10.1145/1385569.1385595
11. Rauterberg M, Fjeld M, Krueger H, Bichsel M, Leonhardt U, Meier M (1997) BUILD-IT: A computer vision-based interaction technique for a planning tool. In: Proceedings of the HCI on people and computers XII, Springer-Verlag, London, pp 303–314
12. Balakrishnan R (2004) "Beating" Fitts' law: Virtual enhancements for pointing facilitation. International Journal of Human-Computer Studies 61(6):857–874, doi: 10.1016/j.ijhcs.2004.09.002
13. MacKenzie IS (1992) Fitts' law as a research and design tool in human-computer interaction. Human-Computer Interaction 7(1):91–139, doi: 10.1207/s15327051hci0701_3
14. Bohan M, Chaparro A (1998) To click or not to click: A comparison of two target-selection methods for HCI. In: CHI'98: Proceedings of the CHI 98 conference summary on human factors in computing systems, ACM Press, New York, pp 219–220, doi: 10.1145/286498.286707

15. Hourcade JP, Berkel TR (2006) Tap or touch? Pen-based selection accuracy for the young and old. In: CHI'06: Extended abstracts of the CHI' 06 conference on human factors in computing systems, ACM Press, New York, pp 881–886, doi: 10.1145/1125451.1125623
16. Buxton WAS (1990) A three-state model of graphical input. In: INTERACT'90: Proceedings of the interact '90, North-Holland Publishing Co., Amsterdam, pp 449–456
17. Potter RL, Weldon LJ, Shneiderman B (1988) Improving the accuracy of touch screens: An experimental evaluation of three strategies. In: CHI'88: Proceedings of the SIGCHI conference on human factors in computing systems, ACM Press, New York, pp 27–32, doi: 10.1145/57167.57171
18. MacKenzie IS, Oniszczak A (1998) A comparison of three selection techniques for touchpads. In: CHI'98: Proceedings of the SIGCHI conference on human factors in computing systems, ACM Press/Addison-Wesley Publishing Co., New York, pp 336–343, doi: 10.1145/274644.274691
19. Wu M, Balakrishnan R (2003) Multi-finger and whole hand gestural interaction techniques for multi-user tabletop displays. In: UIST'03: Proceedings of the 16th annual ACM symposium on user interface software and technology, ACM Press, New York, pp 193–202, doi: 10.1145/964696.964718
20. Masoodian M, McKoy S, Rogers B (2007) Hands-on sharing: Collaborative document manipulation on a tabletop display using bare hands. In: CHINZ '07: Proceedings of the 7th ACM SIGCHI New Zealand chapter's international conference on computer-human interaction: Design centered HCI, ACM Press, New York, pp 25–31, doi: 10.1145/1278960.1278964
21. Esenther A, Ryall K (2006) Fluid DTMouse: Better mouse support for touch-based interactions. In: AVI'06: Proceedings of the working conference on advanced visual interfaces, ACM Press, New York, pp 112–115, doi: 10.1145/1133265.1133289
22. Rekimoto J (2002) SmartSkin: An infrastructure for freehand manipulation on interactive surfaces. In: CHI'02: Proceedings of the SIGCHI conference on human factors in computing systems: Changing our world, changing ourselves, ACM Press, New York, pp 113–120, doi: 10.1145/503376.503397
23. Vogel D, Baudisch P (2007) Shift: A technique for operating pen-based interfaces using touch. In: CHI'07: Proceedings of the SIGCHI conference on human factors in computing systems, ACM Press, New York, pp 657–666, doi: 10.1145/1240624.1240727
24. Wigdor D, Penn G, Ryall K, Esenther A, Shen C (2007) Living with a tabletop: Analysis and observations of long term office use of a multi-touch table. In: Tabletop'08: Proceedings of the second annual IEEE international workshop on horizontal interactive human-computer systems, pp 60–67, doi: 10.1109/TABLETOP.2007.33
25. Wigdor D, Shen C, Forlines C, Balakrishnan R (2006) Table-centric interactive spaces for real-time collaboration. In: AVI'06: Proceedings of the working conference on advanced visual interfaces, ACM Press, New York, pp 103–107, doi: 10.1145/1133265.1133286
26. Olwal A, Feiner S, Heyman S (2008) Rubbing and tapping for precise and rapid selection on touch-screen displays. In: CHI'08: Proceedings of the twenty-sixth annual SIGCHI conference on human factors in computing systems, ACM Press, New York, pp 295–304, doi: 10.1145/1357054.1357105
27. Ren X, Moriya S (2000) Improving selection performance on pen-based systems: A study of pen-based interaction for selection tasks. ACM Transactions on Computer-Human Interaction 7 (3): 384–416, doi: 10.1145/355324.355328
28. Apitz G, Guimbretière F (2004) CrossY: A crossing-based drawing application. In: UIST'04: Proceedings of the 17th annual ACM symposium on user interface software and technology, ACM Press, New York, pp 3–12, doi: 10.1145/1029632.1029635
29. Aliakseyeu D, Martens JB, Rauterberg M (2006). A computer support tool for the early stages of architectural design. Interacting with Computers 18(4):528–555, doi: 10.1016/j.intcom.2005.11.010
30. Nacenta M, Gutwin C, Aliakseyeu D, Subramanian S (2009) There and back again: Cross-display object movement in multi-display environments. Human-Computer Interaction 24(1&2):170–229, doi: 10.1080/07370020902819882

31. Geißler J (1998) Shuffle, throw or take it! Working efficiently with an interactive wall. In: CHI'98: Proceedings of the CHI 98 conference summary on human factors in computing systems, ACM Press, New York, pp 265–266, doi: 10.1145/286498.286745

32. Baudisch P, Cutrell E, Robbins D, Czerwinski M, Tandler P, Bederson B, Zierlinger A (2003) Drag-and-pop and Drag-and-pick: Techniques for accessing remote screen content on touch and pen-operated systems. In: INTERACT'03: Proceedings of the Interact'03, Springer, pp 57–64

33. Albinsson P, Zhai S (2003) High precision touch screen interaction. In: CHI'03: Proceedings of the SIGCHI conference on human factors in computing systems, ACM Press, New York, pp 105–112, doi: 10.1145/642611.642631

34. Nacenta M, Sallam S, Champoux B, Subramanian S and Gutwin C (2006) Perspective cursor: Perspective-based interaction for multi-display environments. In: CHI'06: Proceedings of the SIGCHI conference on human factors in computing systems, ACM Press, New York, pp 289–298, doi: 10.1145/1124772.1124817

35. Collomb M, Hascoët M, Baudisch P, Lee B (2005) Improving drag-and-drop on wall-size displays. In: GI'05: Proceedings of the graphics interface 2005, Canadian Human-Computer Communications Society, pp 25–32

36. Nacenta MA, Aliakseyeu D, Subramanian S, Gutwin C (2005) A comparison of techniques for multi-display reaching. In: CHI'05: Proceedings of the SIGCHI conference on human factors in computing systems, ACM Press, New York, pp 371–380, doi: 10.1145/1054972.1055024

37. Nacenta MA, Pinelle D, Stuckel D, Gutwin C (2007) The effects of interaction technique on coordination in tabletop groupware. In: GI'07: Proceedings of the graphics interface 2007, ACM Press, New York, pp 191–198, doi: 10.1145/1268517.1268550

38. Ha V, Inkpen K, Mandryk R, Whalen T (2006) Direct intentions: The effects of input devices on collaboration around tabletop display. In: Tabletop'06: Proceedings of the first IEEE international workshop on horizontal interactive human-computer systems, IEEE, pp 177–184, doi: 10.1109/TABLETOP.2006.10

39. Rekimoto J (1997) Pick-and-drop: A direct manipulation technique for multiple computer environments. In: UIST'97: Proceedings of the 10th annual ACM symposium on user interface software and technology, ACM Press, New York, pp 31–39, doi: 10.1145/263407.263505

40. Matejka J, Grossman T, Lo J, Fitzmaurice GW (2009) The design and evaluation of multi-finger mouse emulation techniques. In: CHI'07: Proceedings of the 27th international conference on human factors in computing systems, ACM Press, New York, pp 1073–1082, doi: 10.1145/1518701.1518865

41. Grossman T, Balakrishnan R (2005) The bubble cursor: Enhancing target acquisition by dynamic resizing of the cursor's activation area. In: CHI'05: Proceedings of the SIGCHI conference on human factors in computing systems, ACM Press, New York, pp 281–290, doi: 10.1145/1054972.1055012

42. Worden A, Walker N, Bharat K, Hudson S (1997) Making computers easier for older adults to use: Area cursors and sticky icons. In: CHI'97: Proceedings of the SIGCHI conference on human factors in computing systems, ACM Press, New York, pp 266–271, doi: 10.1145/258549.258724

43. Chapuis O, Labrune J-B, Pietriga E (2009) DynaSpot: Speed-dependent area cursor. In: CHI'09: Proceedings of the 27th international conference on human factors in computing systems, ACM Press, New York, pp 1391–1400, doi: 10.1145/1518701.1518911

44. Aliakseyeu D, Nacenta MA, Subramanian S, Gutwin C (2006) Bubble radar: Efficient pen-based interaction. In: AVI'06: Proceedings of the working conference on advanced visual interfaces, ACM Press, New York, pp 19–26, doi: 10.1145/1133265.1133271

45. Hascoët M (2003) Throwing models for large displays. In: Proceedings of the British HCI 2003, British HCI Group, pp 73–77

46. Moyle M, Cockburn A (2002) Analyzing mouse and pen flick gestures. In: Proceedings of the SIGCHI-NZ, pp 266–267

47. Reetz A, Gutwin C, Stach T, Nacenta MA, Subramanian S (2006) Superflick: A natural and efficient technique for long-distance object placement on digital tables. In: GI'06: Proceedings of the graphics interface 2006, Canadian Information Processing Society, pp 163–170
48. Forlines C, Vogel D, Balakrishnan R (2006) HybridPointing: Fluid switching between absolute and relative pointing with a direct input device. In: UIST'06: Proceedings of the 19th annual ACM symposium on user interface software and technology, ACM Press, New York, pp 211–220, doi: 10.1145/1166253.1166286
49. Kruger R, Carpendale S, Scott SD, Greenberg S (2003) How people use orientation on tables: Comprehension, coordination and communication. In: CSCW'03: Proceedings of the 2003 international ACM SIGGROUP conference on supporting group work, ACM Press, New York, pp 369–378, doi: 10.1145/958160.958219
50. Yanqing W, Christine LM, Valerie AS, Kellogg SB (1998) The structure of object transportation and orientation in human-computer interaction. In: CHI'98: Proceedings of the SIGCHI conference on human factors in computing systems, ACM Press/Addison-Wesley Publishing Co., New York, pp 312–319, doi: 10.1145/274644.274688
51. Jacob R, Sibert LE, McFarlane DC, Mullen J (1994) Integrality and separability of input devices. ACM Transactions on Computer-Human Interaction 1(1):3–26, doi: 10.1145/174630.174631
52. Kruger R, Carpendale S (2003) Exploring orientation on a table display. Department of Computer Science, University of Calgary
53. Liu J, Pinelle D, Sallam S, Subramanian S, Gutwin C (2006) TNT: Improved rotation and translation on digital tables. In: GI'06: Proceedings of the graphics interface, Canadian Information Processing Society, pp 25–32
54. Shen C, Frédéric DV, Forlines C, Ringel M (2004) DiamondSpin: An extensible toolkit for around-the-table interaction. In: CHI'04: Proceedings of the SIGCHI conference on human factors in computing systems, ACM Press, New York, pp 167–174, doi: 10.1145/985692.985714
55. Streitz NA, Geißler J, Holmer T, Konomi S, Müller-Tomfelde C, Reischl W, Rexroth P, Seitz P, Steinmetz R (1999) i-LAND: An interactive landscape for creativity and innovation. In: CHI'99: Proceedings of the SIGCHI conference on human factors in computing systems, ACM Press, New York, pp 120–127, doi: 10.1145/302979.303010
56. Tandler P, Prante T, Müller-Tomfelde C, Streitz N, Steinmetz R (2001) Connectables: Dynamic coupling of displays for the flexible creation of shared workspaces. In: UIST'01: Proceedings of the 14th annual ACM symposium on user interface software and technology, ACM Press, New York, pp 11–20, doi: 10.1145/502348.502351
57. Kruger R, Carpendale S, Scott S, Tang A (2005) Fluid integration of rotation and translation. In: CHI'05: Proceedings of the SIGCHI conference on human factors in computing systems, ACM Press, New York, pp 601–610, doi: 10.1145/1054972.1055055
58. Pinelle D, Dyck J, Gutwin C, Stach T (2006) Cutouts: Multiple views for tabletop groupware. HCI-TR-06-04, Computer Science Department, University of Saskatchewan
59. Zhai S, Smith BA, Selker T (1997) Improving browsing performance: A study of four input devices for scrolling and pointing tasks. In: Proceedings of the IFIP TC13 international conference on human-computer interaction, IFIP conference proceedings, vol 96. Chapman & Hall Ltd., London, pp 286–293
60. Andersen TH (2005) A simple movement time model for scrolling. In: CHI'05: Extended abstracts of the CHI '05 conference on human factors in computing systems, ACM Press, New York, pp 1180–1183, doi: 10.1145/1056808.1056871
61. Cockburn A, Gutwin C, Alexander J (2006) Faster document navigation with space-filling thumbnails. In: CHI'06: Proceedings of the SIGCHI conference on human factors in computing systems, ACM Press, New York, pp 1–10, doi: 10.1145/1124772.1124774
62. Hinckley K, Cutrell E, Bathiche S, Muss T (2002) Quantitative analysis of scrolling techniques. In: CHI'02: Proceedings of the SIGCHI conference on human factors in computing systems, ACM Press, New York, pp 65–72, doi: 10.1145/503376.503389

63. Cockburn A, Savage J, Wallace A (2005) Tuning and testing scrolling interfaces that automatically zoom. In: CHI'05: Proceedings of the SIGCHI conference on human factors in computing systems, ACM Press, New York, pp 71–80, doi: 10.1145/1054972.1054983

64. Kaptelinin V, Mäntylä T, Åström J (2002) Transient visual cues for scrolling: An empirical study. In: CHI'02: Extended abstracts of the CHI '02 conference on human factors in computing systems, ACM Press, New York, pp 620–621, doi: 10.1145/506443.506513

65. Klein C, Bederson BB (2005) Benefits of animated scrolling. In: CHI'05: Extended abstracts of the CHI '05 conference on human factors in computing systems, ACM Press, New York, pp 1965–1968, doi: 10.1145/1056808.1057068

66. Moscovich T, Hughes JF (2004) Navigating documents with the virtual scroll ring. In: UIST'04: Proceedings of the 17th annual ACM symposium on user interface software and technology, ACM Press, New York, pp 57–60, doi: 10.1145/1029632.1029642

67. Smith GM, Schraefel MC (2004) The radial scroll tool: Scrolling support for stylus- or touch-based document navigation. In: UIST'04: Proceedings of the 17th annual ACM symposium on user interface software and technology, ACM Press, New York, pp 53–56, doi: 10.1145/1029632.1029641

68. Evans KB, Tanner PP, Wein M (1981) Tablet-based valuators that provide one, two, or three degrees of freedom. ACM SIGGRAPH Computer Graphics 15(3):91–97, doi: 10.1145/965161.806794

69. Smith G, Schraefel MC, Baudisch P (2005) Curve dial: Eyes-free parameter entry for GUIs. In: CHI'05: Extended abstracts of the CHI '05 conference on human factors in computing systems, ACM Press, New York, pp 1146–1147, doi: 10.1145/1056808.1056855

Chapter 11
Imprecision, Inaccuracy, and Frustration: The Tale of Touch Input

Hrvoje Benko and Daniel Wigdor

Abstract Touch and multi-touch technologies have generated a great deal of excitement. In this chapter we focus on addressing the fundamental limitations associated with the use of touch as the primary input mechanism. We discuss seven problems facing the users of touch-based interfaces and offer a set of possible solutions from the available research so far. In particular, we address issues such as the lack of haptic feedback and hover, as well as problems with precision, occlusion, capture and physical constraints which plague this technology. We then describe two case studies from our own work, which provide complementary solutions to all of the issues discussed in this chapter. By discussing these projects in detail, we aim to expose the reader to the complexity of the issues at hand, to various design considerations, and to the intricate implementation details necessary for implementing such solutions.

Introduction

Supporting direct and natural interactions with the on-screen content is one of the most frequently cited benefits of touch-based interfaces. However, bypassing the input device and allowing input with the human finger to directly the screen comes with significant problems. These range from the issues of reduced precision, finger occlusion, as well as the lack of clear feedback about the state of interaction.

This can manifest itself in a lack of confidence that any given input is being accurately received by the application, caused by a general inability to properly attribute unexpected results to their actual causes. The reduction in confidence in the device often also manifests itself as an increase in user frustration and confusion across the entirety of the experience. This is exacerbated in multi-user systems, in which the actions of other users add additional variability to the system's response.

H. Benko (✉)
Microsoft Research, One Microsoft Way, Redmond, WA 98052, USA
e-mail: benko@microsoft.com

C. Müller-Tomfelde (ed.), *Tabletops – Horizontal Interactive Displays*,
Human-Computer Interaction Series, DOI 10.1007/978-1-84996-113-4_11,
© Springer-Verlag London Limited 2010

In this chapter, we first describe the set of seven problems facing the users of touch-based interfaces. We discuss each problem in detail and offer a set of possible solutions from the available research so far. We then focus on two case studies that address some of these problems in detail. Our first case study explores the set of bimanual (or two-finger) solutions, called *Dual Finger Selections* [1], to the issues of finger occlusion and precision of touch selection. The second case study presents a comprehensive visualization solution, called *Ripples* [2], which provides visual feedback to reduce the ambiguities with touch-based input. Finally, we summarize the techniques discussed in this chapter in hope of providing concise guidance to researchers and practitioners who are interested in developing their own touch-based solutions.

Human Finger as an Input Device

When interacting with a touch system, there are a number of situations where the user's input will result in an unexpected behaviour. The user might place two fingers onto an object anticipating a particular response, and another is presented, or no response at all. Did the hardware fail to detect the touch? Did their fingers miss the target? Is the multi-finger response not what they believed it to be? Was there a simultaneous accidental activation elsewhere on the device that changed the state of the object? Is the object not enabled for touch interaction?

How the application reacts to the user's input determines how well the user will be equipped to understand the reasons for the unexpected behaviour. However, most applications do not provide an explicit feedback mechanism that can help users to understand why their action was not successful, and the application feedback is usually constrained to responses designed to signal the execution of successful actions only. The result is applications which *respond* to touch input, but do not provide information about the *causes* of those responses. We refer to this as *touch feedback ambiguity problem*, where, in the case of confusing or unsuccessful actions, the user is usually left to deduce the cause of error from very little or no application feedback. Previous research, as well as our own observations, have found that this ambiguity can lead to a disconnection from the system, and frustration, or a loss of sense of control [3–5].

To understand this problem, consider the difference between actuation of an on-screen object with a mouse or a touch screen: with the mouse, the user moves the pointer over an object and clicks the button, and with the touch screen, the user taps directly on the object on the screen. Now, consider what happens when the system does not react in an expected manner.

The user is left to interpret this response using the feedback which has been made available by the system. In the case of a mouse input, feedback provided by the operating system helps the user to quickly isolate the cause. Visual movement of the mouse reassures the user that the system is still working, the physical activation of the mouse button affirms that the input was delivered, and the position of the mouse

Table 11.1 Causes of an unexpected behaviour to input in a mouse-based system and the feedback given by the hardware or operating system (OS) in typical mouse and touch systems to each, or left to applications (app)

	Feedback refuting cause	
Cause of unexpected behaviour	Mouse	Touch
System is non-responsive	OS: pointer movement	(App)
Hardware failed to detect input	HW: activation of button	(App)
Input delivered to wrong location	OS: visible pointer location	(App)
Input does not map to expected function	(App)	(App)

pointer makes it apparent where the input was delivered. In touch-based systems, this is typically not the case [6, 7], and so it is left to the application to provide feedback for all of these potential causes. Table 11.1 describes various possible causes of unexpected behaviour, as well as the source and type of feedback available to dispel that cause in each of a mouse and direct-touch system.

It is possible for application designers to provide visual feedback distinguishing these sources of error or frustration. However, this makes it more difficult to produce touch-based applications than mouse-based ones, which do not require this feedback mechanism. Further, relying on individual applications to provide feedback decreases the likelihood of consistency across applications.

Sources of Touch Input Error and Frustration

To fully understand the issue with touch feedback ambiguity, we must first explain the potential sources of error that contribute to the ambiguity. In addition of defining the problems, we provide a detailed summary of all relevant solutions to these problems from the related research work.

Lack of Activation Notification and Haptic Feedback

When interacting with a WIMP system, users feel a physical "click" when they depress the mouse button. When working with a touch screen, users feel the moment of contact with the display. However, depending on the particular hardware, the moment of activation can vary: with some vision-based systems, for example, activation occurs before the finger reaches the display, which might result in a different initial position of the touch contact than where the user thinks the contact occurred. With some resistive technologies, a degree of pressure is required for activation [8]. There is no consistent physical sensation connected with this transition. A correct feedback should indicate the activation moment, and help the user to be accurate in their touches.

Most input devices provide some feedback to the user to signal the activation event (e.g., mouse clicks, keyboard keys presses, etc.). In many legacy touchscreen systems, the screen is used as a controller for a mouse pointer. The consequence is that, for every touch, the pointer moves to the point of contact providing some feedback of its location. However, providing a clear notification to the user that a touch event has occurred is challenging in a multi-touch or multi-user context. Poupyrev et al. investigated providing haptic feedback by embedding a vibro-tactile actuator underneath the touchscreen; however their method precludes scaling to multi-touch [9]. While not designed for finger input, Lee et al. designed a range of haptic sensations, by embedding a solenoid within a stylus for stylus-based interfaces [10]. Hancock et al. investigated the use of auditory feedback, but point out its limitations in a multi-user system; these problems would no-doubt be amplified in a multi-touch system [11].

An interesting alternative is to provide passive physical widgets on top of touch screens such as transparent knobs, buttons, or keypads (e.g., SLAP widgets [12]). While effective in providing direct feedback, such widgets impose a lot of constraints on the size, shape and layout of the interface elements and reducing the directness of the touch experience by requiring the use of additional objects. Physical widgets can also be integrated within the screen, as is the case with air-actuated deformable buttons [13]; however this rather static approach also suffers from the lack of flexibility when it comes to layout or size of the interface.

Lack of Hover State

Buxton stipulated that most modern interfaces depend on a three-state input model [14] (i.e., for a mouse those states are out-of-range, tracking and dragging). However, most touch-screens are only able to reliably sense two states (out-of-range and in-contact). The ability to sense hover is greatly missed as currently any contact with the interactive surface becomes an instant engagement without the ability to preview one's actions before committing. Figures 11.1 and 11.2 illustrate.

Most interactive surfaces have been designed to disregard the activity in the hover zone above the surface in order to reduce the amount of noise in the touch sensing. However, various methods have been proposed to simulate the hover state. Potter et al. proposed sending an activation on contact *take-off* which effectively made the

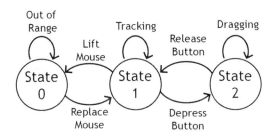

Fig. 11.1 The 3-state model of input as expressed for the mouse (adapted from Buxton [14])

Fig. 11.2 The 2-state model
is more common for touch
devices (adapted from Buxton
[14]). The lack of state 1
means that the user receives
no feedback before the
system is "engaged"

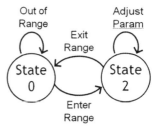

entire contact state a hover state [8]. This behaviour has also been used in more
recent techniques that explored adding more precision to selection (e.g., [1, 15]).
Benko et al. used the change on the contact area to simulate the hover state for a
touchscreen in a technique called SimPress [1]. In principle their technique is equal
to the concept of light and heavy touch as discussed in the Glimpse interaction [16]
or to the behaviour of mapping different levels of pressure on a pressure sensitive
touch screen device [17].

The Fat Finger Problem: Occlusion and Precision Issues

Two fundamental problems with direct-touch finger input are that the user's finger
occludes the target in the critical moment before touching the display (the *occlusion
problem*) and that the touch area of the finger is many times larger than a pixel of
the display (the *precision problem*).Those two issues are most commonly referred
to together as the *fat finger problem* (e.g., [18]).

Touch screens offer good pointing performance for large user interface targets
[19], and save device space while maximizing the visual display area by superimposing the control surface over the screen. This has allowed the creation of devices
such as the Sony Cyber-shot DSC-N1[1] digital camera and, more recently, the Apple
iPhone,[2] in which nearly the entire front surface is occupied by the screen and the
size of the device is limited only by its display.

Because of these two issues, a user is often unable to accurately specify the point
of contact with the display [8]. For small mobile devices, the occlusion problem is
especially drastic because the hand often covers the majority of the display. Previous
solutions to these problems have attempted to provide software or hardware aids.

The first such approach is the offset cursor, described by Potter et al. [8]
(Fig. 11.3a). This technique involves offsetting the interaction point a few millime-
tres from the point of contact with the display, and visualized with a crosshair. Users
make selections within the user interface by positioning the crosshair over an item,
then lifting their finger from the device. The authors note that the result is that users
feel put-off that the system does not respond beneath their finger.

---

[1] http://www.sony.com

[2] http://www.apple.com/iphone

Fig. 11.3 Two offset cursor techniques: (**a**) Potter et al.'s original offset cursor [8]; (**b**) shift offsets both the cursor and the data beneath the finger (adapted from [15])

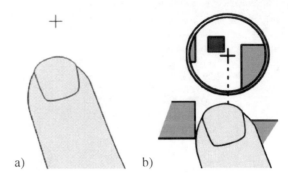

a)   b)

A variation on the offset cursor solution is Vogel and Baudisch's Shift technique [15]. In Shift, the primary interaction is direct touch. When touching on or near small targets, however, the view of the area beneath the finger, along with the touch location, are automatically offset from the user's finger (Fig. 11.3b).

An alternative to offsetting cursors is the use of more complex tools. Albinsson and Zhai [20] presented a pair of widgets to overcome the fat finger problem and to increase precision. Their widgets (e.g., the *cross-keys* widget and the *precision-handle* widget) are designed for single finger operation, and require first that the user coarsely positions the widget, followed by finer-grained movements by touching a separate buttons or areas of the widget.

Another design is the use of touch cursors. This approach was described in the LucidTouch project [21]. In that project, input to the device is moved to the back of the device to remove the effects of finger occlusion (similar to [22–24]), and the device simulates to the user the experience of looking through the device, while maintaining direct touch interactions (Fig. 11.4). When a finger is hovering over the device, the point used for hit testing is shown on a shadow of the user's hands. When the user actually touches the display, the touch cursor changes colour. This technique addresses the issues of both occlusion and touch precision.

Furthermore, several techniques investigated mapping multiple contact points to reduce the fat finger problem. Each relies on mapping multiple input locations onto a

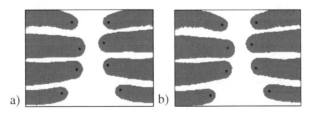

a)   b)

Fig. 11.4 The Lucid touch [21] solution puts the interaction to the back of the device. The images are showing the "virtual shadows" of the user's fingers active in the back of the device: (**a**) all touch-cursors are *red*: no fingers are touching the device, (**b**) the three fingers with *blue* touch-cursors are touching the display. © 2009 ACM, Inc. Included here by permission

single selection. Later in this chapter, we describe a set of five two finger techniques, called *Dual Finger Selections* [1], in detail in the first case study below. Similarly, the *DTMouse* solution [25], enabled placing two fingers on the table, positioning the mouse pointer between them, and then make selections by tapping a third finger. It is also possible to treat multiple contacts as approximations of an area cursor such as envisioned by Moscovich et al. [26].

Accidental Activation and Tabletop Debris

As Ryall et al. point out, with a multi-touch system, "every touch counts", especially with horizontal touch systems, accidental activations are common [3]. Such accidental touches can be due to inadvertent touches by the same or different user (e.g., resting an elbow on the tabletop) or by physical objects left on the surface that trigger accidental activations. When this occurs, users are able to observe only the consequence to the application. As they also point out, some accidental inputs are not noticed by the user, and so sudden changes in the state of the system cannot be properly linked to their cause. A meaningful feedback would make the causes of accidental activations clear to the user.

Accidental touches by additional fingers or parts of the user's arm often cause unsuspected behaviours in touchscreen interfaces. Such unwanted actions can be reduced by placing the interaction on the underside of the surface (e.g., [21–24]) or by specifically modelling the user's touch behaviour and discarding the unwanted touches [27]. An interesting alternative is to create user interface elements that respond not only to touch, but to a touch with a particular shape (e.g., ShapeTouch [28]). This requirement makes such elements harder to invoke accidentally since only touching with a particular hand shape will permit activation.

In addition, users of tabletop systems have been observed to place objects on the surface of the screen (e.g., a long term tabletop use study by Wigdor et al. [29]) and many touch-sensing technologies can and do track objects on the surface. The result can be unexpected behaviour when the system responds to these unintended inputs. In our own internal observations of users, we found that this was particularly problematic when an object would act as an additional contact for an object being manipulated by the user.

When scrolling a list, for example, the Microsoft Surface[3] multi-touch tabletop uses the average distance travelled of all contacts on the list to compute its movement. Because it is interpreted as a stationary contact, a beverage placed on the surface of the table, as reported in [29], has the effect of halving the speed of scrolling of a list. A visualization framework should visualize both that debris on the table is being interpreted as an input, as well as when stationary contacts are placing additional constraints on movement.

---

[3]http://www.microsoft.com/surface

Non-responsive and Captured Content

Invariably, applications will sometimes include elements that are not intended to respond to touch: deactivated controls, background images, etc. Furthermore, elements that are supposed to respond to touch input (such as buttons, etc.) can be unresponsive if they are already *captured* by some other contact.

In a standard WIMP system, user interface controls have two capture states: captured (typically entered when the mouse is clicked on a control), and un-captured. In a multi-touch system, multiple fingers may attempt to capture a control simultaneously. How to deal with multiple, possibly contradictory touches to the same control is an issue decide by framework designers. In the DiamondSpin SDK, "click" events are generated every time a user taps a button, even if another finger is "holding it down" [6]. On Microsoft Surface, "tap" events (equivalent to "click") are generated for buttons only when the last captured contact is lifted from the control. While both approaches have merit, a consequence of the latter is that buttons can be "held down" (captured) by a user.

However, some multi-touch controls can be captured by more than a single contact simultaneously, i.e., *over-captured*. For example, selecting the thumb of a slider with two fingers can mean that it will not track directly under a single finger when moved. When too many contacts have captured a control, its behaviour can be well defined, but inconsistent with the direct-touch paradigm, leading to confusion. Although visual cues should afford inactivation to the user, this state nonetheless adds another source of error in which the user will receive no reaction, requiring correct feedback.

To understand why non-responsive content is particularly problematic for touch systems, consider the difference between actuation of an on-screen object with a mouse or a touch screen. With the mouse, the user moves the pointer over an object and clicks the button, and with the touch screen, the user taps directly on the object on the screen. Now, consider what happens when the system does not react in an expected manner. The user is left to interpret this response using the feedback which has been made available by the system. In the case of a mouse input, feedback provided by the operating system helps the user to quickly isolate the cause. Visual movement of the mouse reassures the user that the system is still working, the physical activation of the mouse button affirms that the input was delivered, and the position of the mouse pointer makes it apparent where the input was delivered. In touch-based systems, this is typically not the case, and so it is left to the application to provide feedback for all of these potential causes.

We provide solutions to the issues of non-responsive content and capture visualization in our second case study, described later in this chapter.

Feedback of Physical Manipulation Constraints

Touch and multi-touch input often rely on the principle of direct manipulation. The principal is that the user places their finger(s) onto an object, moves their finger, and the object changes its position, orientation, and size to maintain the contact points. The direct-touch paradigm is broken when movement constraints are reached. For example, this can occur when attempting to move an object past the bounds of its container, or to resize an object past its size limit.

A rather clever solution to this problem has been seen in some commercial products. In some cases, this has been addressed by "elastic" effects, where the finger is seen to "slip" along the content, which springs-back to its maximum value when the finger is released. This is demonstrated on the Apple iPhone when attempting to scroll past the end of a list.

As manipulation constraints become more complex, it becomes more difficult to illustrate to the user that a constraint has been reached – because so much is moving at the same time, the user simply doesn't notice the content "slipping".

The *metaDESK* system famously addressed rotation constraints between two physical objects with the placement of a physical constraint on their manipulation: a bar that attached to both and prevented each from rotating relative to the other [30].

The use of a physical constraint relies on the presence of physical objects to constrain the interactions. When these are not available, other solutions are needed to address this problem. Nacenta et al. explored the issue of dynamically constraining the degrees of freedom when manipulating on-screen objects [31], e.g., limiting the scaling of an object when rotating it. Such interactions, while providing clear benefits, have an effect similar to the "snapping" behaviour which tends to break the direct manipulation metaphor and tends to cause finger slipping over content (Fig. 11.5).

A problem with snapping is that it does not allow the user to feel as if they are in control of objects, and prevents them from accessing certain values. The authors addressed this with "catch-up zones", as the user of their system slides towards a desired value, the object accelerates towards the "snap" value, and remains there as the finger slides along the screen. When the finger has travelled a sufficient distance, the object begins to slide once again, at an accelerated rate, until it catches-up with the finger. The result is that objects feel as if they "stick" in desirable locations.

Use of controls can also extend beyond the bounds of those controls. For example, in a traditional GUI, the scrollbar can be captured by selecting it with the mouse. At that point, vertical movements of the mouse are applied to the position of the thumb, and horizontal movements are ignored. The result is that the mouse pointer can be moved away from the slider while still controlling it. This is equally necessary in a touch system, but mapping fingers to their controls is a potential

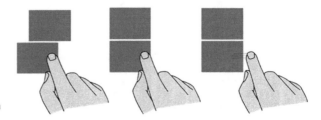

Fig. 11.5 An example physical manipulation constraint: snapping. The lower block stops moving once it aligns with the upper one. The consequence is that the finger slips off the block, giving the user the impression that it was "dropped"

source of confusion with multiple touch-points, controls, and users all interacting simultaneously.

Direct-touch systems rely on the use of a fixed mapping between input location and displayed result. This creates a fun and "natural" feeling, but also significantly limits the potential for "reaching" interaction. *HybridPointing* project did this dynamically, to a great effect, allowing the user to dynamically switch between direct and indirect pointing mode [32].

If not done carefully, mixing direct and indirect touch in the same system can result in user dissatisfaction. In fact, according to Potter et al., the use of indirect in a touch system is undesirable [8]. Additionally, multiple users controlling multiple objects from a distance may become confused as to which objects are under which users' control. Thus, it is important to make it clear which object is responding to which touch at all times.

Case Study #1: Addressing the Fat Finger Problem with Dual Finger Selections

Addressing the fat finger problem implies solving two problems simultaneously: (1) the finger used for selection will partially or completely occlude the target making it difficult to see what is being selected, and (2) it is difficult to perform precise selections since the finger contact is often large when compared with the target. The discrepancy between the finger size and the small target in the standard user interface is best illustrated by the chart in Fig. 11.6. Note that the mean value of 18.3 mm for the right index finger width is derived from the anthropometric data provided by Feeney [33].

| | | Target Width | |
Target Element	Device Space	Visual Space 17" screen 1024×768	Visual Space 39" screen 1024×768
Close Button 	18 pixels	6 mm (32.8% of finger)	10.8 mm (59.0% of finger)
Resize Handle 	4 pixels	1.34 mm (7.3% of finger)	2.4 mm (13.1% of finger)

Fig. 11.6 Comparison of small target widths to an average right hand index finger width at the fingertip (estimated as 18.3 mm for an adult*) (adapted from Benko [34]). Note: Values for the 30'' diagonal screen correspond to the display characteristics used in this case study

We now discuss five different interaction techniques that use two contacts in order to resolve the fat finger problem. These techniques, called *Dual Finger Selections* are part of a larger body of work, previously published by Benko et al. [1].

These techniques assume that the selection does not happen implicitly when landing on or taking off, but rather explicitly. The explicit click event can be facilitated in numerous ways; for example, by using a pressure sensitive device or by using the touch contact area to approximate the hover state (light touch is a hover and heavy touch is click). The adaptation of the later technique called *SimPress* was used in design of Dual Finger Selections [1]. Also, since most touch screens and tabletops cannot identify which of the individual user's fingers or hands is touching the surface without special gloves, for the purpose of these Dual Finger interactions, the first contact with a tabletop surface is always referred to as a *primary finger*, while the second contact is referred to a *secondary finger*.

Dual Finger Offset

The initial and simplest Dual Finger Selection technique, called *Dual Finger Offset*, provides a user triggered cursor offset. The cursor offset is not enabled by default as in [8], but rather invoked on demand. By placing a secondary finger anywhere on the surface, the cursor is subsequently offset with respect to the primary finger by predefined fixed amount. This offset always places the cursor above the primary finger. To accommodate both left- and right-handed users the cursor is placed to the left or to the right of the primary finger based on the relative position of the secondary finger. For example, by placing the secondary finger to the left of the secondary finger to the left of the primary, the cursor appears to the left of and above the primary finger. While providing an on demand offset helps resolve the occlusion problem, this technique does not assist the user in making more precise selections.

Dual Finger Midpoint

Dual Finger Midpoint technique provides variable offset and enables finer control of the cursor speed (Fig. 11.7). This technique is triggered by placing the secondary finger on the surface. The cursor is then offset to the midpoint between the primary and the secondary finger. DTMouse technique [25] is based on a similar premise; however, it required a third finger to actually trigger a selection. A similar behaviour occurs on any resistive touchpad that places the pointer at the midpoint of all touches (e.g., SMART Board Interactive Whiteboard[4]).

While both fingers are in contact, moving either or both fingers controls the movement of the cursor. This technique allows for variable reductions in cursor

---

[4]SMART Technologies: www.smarttech.com

Fig. 11.7 Dual finger midpoint technique positions the cursor at exactly the halfway point between the *two fingers*, giving the user both a *cursor* offset as well as a variable reduction of cursor speed. © 2009 ACM, Inc. Included here by permission

speed: when both fingers are moving in the same direction and the same speed, the cursor follows with the same speed, while when only one finger is moving, the cursor moves with half the speed of that finger.

At best, this method reduces the finger speed by a factor of 2 which yields good results for most targets; but it does not provide enough control for the smallest targets. An additional shortcoming of this technique is that not all locations on the screen are equally accessible. For example, screen corners are not accessible using midpoint selection. Consequently, the utility of this technique is somewhat limited by the fact that in today's user interfaces small targets often are located in the corners of the screen.

Dual Finger Stretch

Dual Finger Stretch allows the user to adaptively scale a portion of the screen with the secondary finger while the primary finger performs the selection. To allow for simultaneous "stretching" and selection, the primary finger provides the initial anchor location around which the user interface is scaled, while the secondary finger identifies the corner of the square area which will be scaled. By moving the secondary finger closer or further away from the primary finger, the square stretching area is reduced or expanded as illustrated in (Fig. 11.8). Lifting the secondary finger from the table resets the interface to its default un-stretched state. Upon this reset, the cursor is offset with respect to the primary finger and is placed where it was located in the stretched state. The cursor offset is reset when all fingers are removed from the table. The extent of control-display ratio manipulation depends on two physical limits: (1) the closest perceptible distance between user's fingers and (2) the largest diagonal of the screen. For most common mid-screen manipulations, Dual Finger Stretch enables control display ratios roughly up to 10. By allowing clutching and repeated zooming, it may be possible to further increase this ratio.

The Dual Finger Stretch technique has several advantages over the related single finger ZoomPointing technique (designed by Albinsson and Zhai [20]) primarily due to the dual finger design. First, zooming and selection are not decoupled into two separate actions. Instead they can happen concurrently which results in a fluid interaction. Second, the interface scales in all directions from the original primary finger's location. This provides an important advantage over traditional rectangle

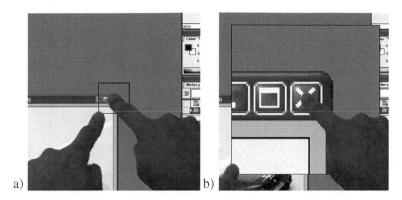

Fig. 11.8 Dual finger stretch technique adaptively scales the user interface: (**a**) the *secondary finger* specifies the *square zooming area* centred at the primary finger's location, (**b**) *primary finger* performs precise selection while, simultaneously, the secondary finger adjusts the level of magnification. © 2009 ACM, Inc. Included here by permission

selection where the two points specify the diagonal corners of the zooming rectangle (also known as bounding box zoom).

With the rectangle selection, the user tends to place the primary finger off target in order to "capture" the target in the zoomed area, while with Dual Finger Stretch, the user places the primary finger directly on target and the interfaces scales underneath in all directions. Placing the finger off-target requires the user's primary finger to traverse an increased distance to perform final selection because the target will appear to move away from the finger as the zoom level increases. By encouraging placement of the primary finger as close to the target as possible, the eventual distance that this finger will need to traverse to acquire the target is minimized.

Dual Finger X-Menu

To allow users to adaptively adjust the control-display ratio as well as obtain cursor offset while looking at an un-zoomed user interface, we have designed the *Dual Finger X-Menu* widget. This circular menu is invoked whenever the secondary finger establishes contact with the surface. It is positioned so that the finger is located at its centre. The user can select a particular assistance mode by moving the secondary finger to any of the desired regions of the menu (Fig. 11.9b). Dual Finger X-Menu has six selection areas shown in Fig. 11.9a. Four areas control the relative speed of the cursor: *normal, slow 4x, slow 10x*, and *freeze*. Normal mode moves the cursor with the same speed as the primary finger; the two slow modes reduce the speed of the cursor by a factor of 4 and 10 respectively, while freeze mode "freezes" the cursor in place, disabling any cursor movement.

The ability to completely stop the cursor from moving has two benefits. First, by freezing the cursor, the user can quickly and easily establish a desired cursor

Fig. 11.9 Dual finger X-menu contains four selection areas for cursor speed control (normal, slow 4x, slow 10x and freeze), and two toggle areas (snap and magnify). Magnify mode presents an integrated magnification widget in the middle of the menu, while snap mode removes the current cursor offset. When freeze mode is selected, the cursor is completely immobile. © 2009 ACM, Inc. Included here by permission

offset. This is accomplished by freezing the cursor temporarily, moving the finger to achieve the desired offset, and then unfreezing the cursor again. Second, when selecting very small targets, even small amounts of noise can cause an error. Such noise can be due to device tracking errors, tremor in the user's hand, or noise due to the clicking motion. By freezing the cursor in place, the user can ensure that the desired selection is successful even in very noisy conditions.

The left two areas on the crossing menu invoke two helper modes: "snap" and "magnify". When snapping is triggered, the cursor offset (if any) is removed and the cursor snaps back to the current location of the primary finger. This mode is useful in repositioning the cursor in the slow movement modes because it is easy to run out of tracked screen space when using the slow cursor modes. Magnify mode presents a small magnification area in the middle of the crossing menu that shows the enlarged area under the cursor. The magnification factor is fixed at 2x.

This mode is particularly useful when the primary finger overlaps the cursor. In this case the magnified image acts as a lens showing the portion of the interface obstructed by the primary finger. A simple cursor notification widget displays which cursor speed level is currently selected, without requiring the user to refer back to the menu. The behaviour of this notification widget can be seen in Fig. 11.10.

Dual Finger X-Menu is not operated by clicking, but rather by "crossing" the finger into a particular area, which enables more experienced users to activate modes by simply performing quick strokes in a particular direction. With practice, this

Fig. 11.10 Cursor notification widget signals the current amount of cursor speed reduction: (**a**) 4x reduction, (**b**) 10x reduction, and (**c**) frozen cursor. © 2009 ACM, Inc. Included here by permission

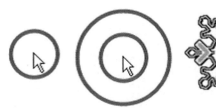

selection can be made without looking, and could therefore allow for an expert mode in which the menu could be completely hidden from the user. Removing the secondary finger from the surface will cause the menu to disappear.

Dual Finger Slider

The different interaction modes of Dual Finger X-Menu offer a palette of options, but tend to distract the user from the task at hand. The *Dual Finger Slider* technique incorporates the menu's most useful features, but simplifies and streamlines the overall interaction (Fig. 11.11). Given that two finger interactions are a very natural way of specifying distance, this interaction uses the distance between fingers to switch between cursor speed reduction modes. This technique does not present an on-screen widget to the user. Instead, it relies completely on the user's ability to gauge the spatial relationship between their fingers. The same cursor notification widget (Fig. 11.10) is used to signal the cursor speed to the user.

Moving the secondary finger towards the primary finger reduces the cursor speed in 3 discrete steps. This allows for the same reductions in cursor speed that is available in Dual Finger X-Menu: *normal*, *slow 4x*, *slow 10x*, and *freeze*. Moving the secondary finger away from the primary increases the speed up to the normal speed. Continuing to move the fingers apart triggers a "snap" which warps the cursor back to the primary finger's location. Snapping is signalled by a distinct sound effect. The distance that the secondary finger traverses in switching speed reduction modes is predefined and is not dependent on the distance between the fingers. The modes are remembered even after the user lifts the secondary finger which allows for clutching in the interaction.

Summary of Experimental Results

In a qualitative comparative study which asked the users to repetitively select small targets (1, 2, 4, 8 pixels wide on a $30''$ 1024×768 pixel screen), the Dual Finger Stretch technique outperformed the others and was also the most preferred technique. Interestingly, Stretch was the only one that did not provide a cursor offset. This clearly demonstrated that the benefit of increased target size successfully compensated for the fingertip occlusion factor. The data from this experiment is consistent with the results from a study by Albinsson and Zhai [20] which also showed that their zooming technique outperformed on-screen widgets that provided cursor speed control.

However, in many applications, scaling may have an undesired effect of losing overview of the interface and there Slider and X-Menu offer appealing alternatives. Both Slider and X-Menu techniques performed comparatively to Stretch in terms of error rate (all three were under 5%), but imposed a 1s penalty in performance.

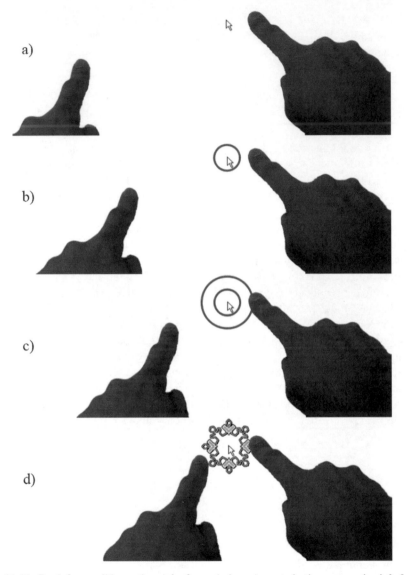

Fig. 11.11 Dual finger slider – the *right finger* (primary) controls the cursor, the *left finger* (secondary) is invoking the invisible slider; speed reductions modes are achieved by moving the fingers closer together: (**a**) normal, (**b**) slow 4x, (**c**) slow 10x, (**d**) frozen cursor mode. © 2009 ACM, Inc. Included here by permission

Selecting really small targets might not be a frequent task in a touch-driven interface.

These five techniques present a useful set of interactions that effectively resolve the fat finger problem. While simple and effective, they require the use of at least two fingers which can be a significant limitation, particularly on a small display where a single finger use would be preferred. Following this work, Vogel and Baudisch, incorporated the offset zoomed region (similar to the X-Menu solution) into the *Shift* interaction technique designed for a single finger use [15]. Shift showed the zoomed offset region with a delay proportional to the size of the target underneath, which makes it appear only when the target was small enough to warrant the zoom and the improved precision.

Case Study #2: Addressing the Feedback Ambiguity Problem

Currently there is no generalized visual language for conveying various error conditions to the user. It is left to the application designer to reflect the state of the contact in some visual property of the application. Even worse, there has been no description of a set of visual states and transitions which, when taken together, address each of these conditions. There are two possible outcomes: either the application fails to provide a visualization, or each application provides its own, independent (and therefore inconsistent) visualization. In either case, the result is that, when system responses do not map to users' expectations, the ambiguity of this feedback makes it impossible to decipher the causes of unexpected behaviour. Further, the burden on designers of applications for direct and multi-touch systems is much greater than for mouse systems, making it difficult to transition from the mouse to the touch world.

Per-contact visuals were selected over other techniques in an attempt to minimize visual overhead: ensuring consistent, unambiguous feedback was available, but not overwhelming. Of course, it would be possible for a designer to fully instrument an application so that every element conveys an individual response that is appropriate to the particular element, rather than having a generalized visualization tool. Were they to do this, a requisite first step would be to identify those states and transitions requiring visualization, ensuring that all sources of unexpected behaviour are identifiable by the user. The contribution of our work, therefore, is threefold. First, we describe the need for this feedback, and describe the various error conditions requiring disambiguation. Second, we describe a spanning set of states and transitions which, if uniquely visualized, results in a touch system free of ambiguity. Finally, we provide a set of application independent, user-tested, and iteratively designed visualizations which illustrate those states and transitions. These designs are ready to be taken-up by system designers, in order to ease the development of effective direct and multi-touch applications.

Ripples, a contact visualization system, was designed to provide a feedback information channel to users, helping them to be more accurate and efficient in their interactions with the system. Ripples consists of a set of 6 visualizations spanning 14 states and transitions that place the information beneath and around users' fingertips. The design of effective contact visualizations is critical as these are intended to be constantly present, sitting atop all applications. In designing contact visualizations, we faced several design challenges:

1. Visualize action sources, alleviate feedback ambiguity
2. Provide clear visual encodings of multiple parameters
3. Maintain visual integrity of underlying applications
4. Build a framework requiring little work from application developers to leverage

   Balancing these requirements required careful blending and balancing of interaction, visual, and system design.

Visual States and Transitions

Ripples' states and transitions of can be divided into two categories: those that apply
to any direct-touch system, and those which apply primarily to multi-touch.

Basic Contact Visualization States

Basic states provide helpful feedback for any touch-system, and address many of
the problems described previously. We determined a need for visualization of several states, and of the transitions between those states. The aim was to establish
a minimum spanning set, providing visualizations only where needed to combat
specific problems (Fig. 11.12).

   State 0 cannot be visualized in most systems, as it precedes detection. The visualizations of transition A and state 1 address the problem of clearly indicating the
activation event. They also help to note *accidental activations*, as unintended contacts receive an individual response, allowing the user to correct their posture. To
help the user to differentiate between *fat fingers* and *non-responsive content*, and
to visualize *selection*, the visual provided for transition A differentiates between
contacts which have successfully captured an object, and those which have not
(Fig. 11.13).

   To address the fat finger problem, we also included an animation for transition D
(Fig. 11.14). This animation emphasizes the hit-testing point, similar to [8, 15, 21].
Unlike this past research, the point is not offset from the contact, maintaining
direct-touch. To overcome occlusion, transition D employs hysteresis, so that it will

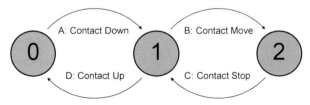

Fig. 11.12 Ripples states and transitions. 0: Not yet touching, 1: stationary contact, 2: moving
contact. © 2009 ACM, Inc. Included here by permission

Fig. 11.13 *Left*: 1 of 2 animations is shown for transition A. If an object is captured, a *circle* shrinks around the contact. If not, it "splashes" outward. *Right*: state 1 is identical for both captured and uncaptured. © 2009 ACM, Inc. Included here by permission

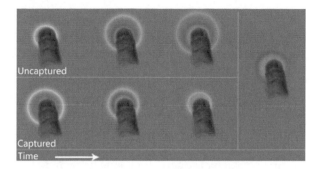

Fig. 11.14 Transition D (see Fig. 11.12): when contact is lifted, the visualization shrinks to the hit testing point. © 2009 ACM, Inc. Included here by permission

continue to be visible for a moment after the user lifts their finger. This effect is similar to the afterglow concept presented in the Phosphor work [35] and it serves to explain the user what action just occurred.

Furthermore, as the contact visualization disappears, it contracts to the hit-test point, so that this point is the last thing seen by the user (Fig. 11.14). Unlike previous work, the goal is not to assist the user in making the current selection, but rather to improve accuracy over time by helping them to learn the point/finger mapping.

The addition of State 2 was made to allow us to address the issue of lag. In our visual rendering, the contact is seen to transition to a trail shown behind the finger, making lag appear to be a design element. State 2 and transitions B and C are shown in Fig. 11.15.

Fig. 11.15 State 2 is shown as a trail, which reduces the perception of lag. 1: Contact is static (state 1), 2: begins to move (transition B), 3: moving (state 2). © 2009 ACM, Inc. Included here by permission

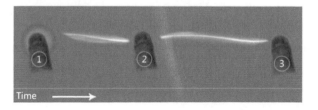

Multi-touch and Advanced Contact Visualization States

In addition to the basic contact visualization, additional states were added to address issues which arise primarily with multi-touch systems. These issues are *multiple capture states, physical manipulation constraints, interaction at a distance,* and *stolen capture.*

In examining these problems, we found that all could be addressed by adding just two states and their associated transitions. These are shown in Fig. 11.16.

State 3 is described earlier as *over-captured*: when the number of contacts captured to a control exceeds the available degrees of freedom of that control, necessitating breaking the direct-touch input paradigm. For example, if two fingers have captured the thumb of a slider, or if three have captured an object enabled for two-finger rotate/translate/scale. As in the basic contact visualizations, this difference is conveyed through the transitions. Transitions F receives the same visual treatment as transition A for an uncaptured contact, and transition G the same as a captured contact. To differentiate these, however, transitions F and G are applied to *all contacts* captured to a control, clearly differentiating states 3 and 1.

State 4 is a condition under which the user has met a constraint on translation, scaling, or rotation of an object. In the Microsoft Surface SDK, these contacts remain captured to the object even though they are no longer touching it. An alternative capture model might cause the contact to lose capture of the object once the finger is no longer touching it. Whatever model is employed, it is critical that a visual be provided to explain why the object is no longer under the user's finger – this addresses the problems of *physical manipulation constraints* and the *interaction at a distance.* To visualize these constraints, we employed a visualization similar to the trails seen in state 2 (see Fig. 11.15). In state 4, the trails become "tethered" to the point at which the constraint was reached, illustrating that the contacts are now "slipping" from their last point of direct-touch (Fig. 11.17).

A purist's interpretation of state 4 would yield tethers when interacting with the majority of controls, since most map multiple degrees of freedom to a single dimension or cannot be moved. What we found, however, was that this could produce what we termed the *Freddy Kruger effect,* where tethers were appearing regularly all over the display. We reduced the frequency of the tethers to the minimal set needed to address specific as sources of error (see above).

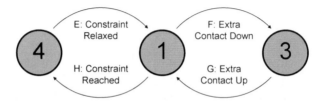

Fig. 11.16 Additional ripples states and transitions for multi-touch. 1: (see Fig. 11.12), 3: object is over-captured, 4: contact operating beyond constraints. © 2009 ACM, Inc. Included here by permission

Fig. 11.17 Ripple tethers indicate that a size constraint has been reached on an item being scaled.
© 2009 ACM, Inc. Included here by permission

The first such situation was the over-constrained scrolling of a list. It was determined through iterative design that, in most cases, the reaction of the list itself matched user intent, and thus did not require visualization of constraints. The remaining case involves tabletop debris, which can cause slower than expected scrolling of a list. In this situation, determined by the presence of a stationary contact, tethers are rendered to demonstrate that the list is scrolling slowly because of that contact (Fig. 11.18).

The final state 4 visualization visually tethers contacts which have slid off of, but are still captured to, controls. Again, to reduce unnecessary visuals, we split

Fig. 11.18 Tethers indicate that slow scrolling of the list is due to the presence of the stationary contact. © 2009 ACM, Inc. Included here by permission

Fig. 11.19 *Left*: contact
controlling the slider is
visually tethered to it at all
times. *Right*: for stationary
controls, such as buttons, the
tether is shown only when
another contact attempts to
actuate the control. © 2009
ACM, Inc. Included here by
permission

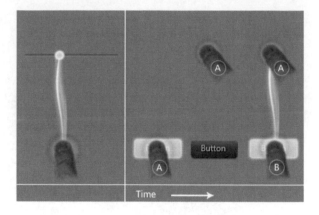

these into two classes: for controls which can be manipulated from a distance, the
visualization is shown from the moment the contact slides off the control. For stationary controls, the tether is shown only when another contact attempts to actuate
the control, addressing stolen capture (Fig. 11.19).

System Design

Key to Ripples' success as a cross-application standardized visualization is its integration into a platform. Those seeking to implement Ripples for their platforms
can do so as a system-level framework which renders the visuals above all applications running on the system. Extensions for various UI toolkits can then be created
which pass contextual information to the rendering layer. The contextual information includes which contacts are captured, whether and to where tether lines should
be rendered for each captured contact, and which colours should be used to provide
the optimal appearance over the application. Once a UI toolkit has integrated with
the Ripples rendering framework, applications using this toolkit automatically get
the benefits of Ripples without any burden on application authors.

Designers of platforms who wish to support application development without a
UI toolkit can provide API's to allow application developers to request the rendering
of Ripples above their application in real time.

We recommend that such a framework include mechanisms to allow modification of Ripples, an extensibility mechanism. This allows UI control developers and
application designers to fine-tune parts of the visualization provided for contacts
captured to their controls and applications. Our system is implemented for modification on a per-control and container basis, similar to pointer customization for
mice in most software development kits. Our goal was to make it easy to modify
the visual appearance without changing the underlying behaviour. An application
can choose to disable visuals entirely, to maintain the functionality but replace the
visualization, to select different colours to better match their application, or leave
Ripples unmodified.

Design Recommendations

Three sets of design recommendations can be gleaned from this work. The first is for system designers: the states and transitions we have identified all require visualization in order to address the litany of problems affecting user confidence in their inputs to touch and multi-touch systems. In some cases, these visualizations can be reused in order to reduce visual overhead. Because of this reuse, we reintroduce moments of ambiguity which we found to be minimal. Also, it should also be noted that the capture models may vary in other toolkits, requiring a different set of visuals.

The second set of recommendations is for application designers. A contribution of this work is that the Ripples system is application independent, and is intended to be generic and equally well suited for use in any platform. As one of our study participants noted, however, not providing visualizations atop applications can be seen as "more like reality". The challenge to an application designer, therefore, is to provide contextual visualizations which provide unambiguous visual representation of the states and transitions we have described, while maintaining visual consistency with their overall design.

The final set of design concerns relate to those seeking to implement a Ripples-like system. Providing visualizations for the states and transitions described above is sufficient to address feedback ambiguity. However, careful consideration must still be made with respect to visual design issues.

Summary and Conclusions

A preponderance of issues affects the user experience with touch displays. System designers have, for the most part, relied on interaction paradigms designed for the mouse, replacing the pointer with the finger. As we have seen, this simple replacement fails to meet the burden of creating a good user experience, leaving users with diminished precision, feedback, increased accidental input, and a variety of other issues. We have also examined a number of techniques intended to address several of these issues.

A challenge for those seeking to implement a platform to enable touch input is understanding the plethora of interaction techniques described by researchers. While each has merit in addressing some aspect of touch, none successfully addresses all of the issues we have described. As an aid to the reader, we have summarized the challenges we have described, plotted against the various techniques intended to address them (Table 11.2).

When implementing a tabletop system, it is essential that interaction techniques be selected which address all of the issues we have described in this chapter. Upon examination, Table 11.2 makes it apparent that none of the techniques described in the literature fully addresses fundamental interaction problems introduced when using a touch-only system. A combination of these techniques,

Table 11.2 This is a summary of different interaction techniques discussed in this chapter. Issues related to touch input that are solved with each technique are denoted with a checkmark. Two sets of techniques highlighted on the bottom were discussed in detail as case studies in this chapter

	Issues						
Interaction techniques	Activation notification and haptic feedback	Lack of hover	Fat finger: occlusion	Fat finger: precision	Accidental activation and debris	Non-responsive and captured content	Physical manipulation constraints
Offset cursor [8]		✓	✓	✓			
Precision handle [20]		✓	✓	✓	✓		
Cross-keys [20]		✓	✓	✓	✓		
SimPress [1]		✓					
Glimpse [16]		✓					
DTMouse [25]		✓	✓	✓			
Shift [15]		✓	✓	✓			
Lucid touch [21]	✓	✓	✓	✓			
Area cursors [26]		✓	✓	✓			
SLAP widgets[12]	✓			✓	✓		
VibroTactile feedback [9]	✓	✓					✓
HybridPointing [32]		✓	✓	✓			✓
ShapeTouch [28]					✓		
Dual finger selections [1]		✓	✓	✓			
Ripples [2]	✓				✓	✓	✓

therefore, is required in order to create an excellent user experience with touch displays.

Ultimately, the scale and scope of the issues we have described will vary depending on context. While each is important, variations in the conditions of use will affect how severely these issues impact the user experience. Those seeking to build effective tabletop systems should carefully consider the context of use of their system, and prioritize the development of solutions those problems that are likely to have a great impact.

Acknowledgments The authors would like to thank various members of Microsoft Research and Microsoft Surface groups for valuable feedback. In particular, we thank Andrew D. Wilson, Patrick Baudisch, Bryan Beatty, Meredith Ringel Morris, and Jarrod Lombardo for their assistance.

References

1. Benko H, Wilson AD, Baudisch P (2006) Precise selection techniques for multi-touch screens. In: Grinter R, Rodden T, Aoki P, Cutrell E, Jeffries R, Olson G (eds) Proceedings of the SIGCHI conference on human factors in computing systems (Montréal, QC, April 22–27, 2006). CHI '06, ACM Press, New York, pp 1263–1272, doi: 10.1145/1124772.1124963
2. Wigdor D, Williams S, Cronin M, White K, Levy R, Mazeev M, Benko H (2009) Ripples: Utilizing per-contact visualizations to improve user interaction with touch displays. In: Proceedings of the ACM symposium on user interface software and technology (UIST '09), ACM Press, New York, pp 1–10
3. Ryall K, Forlines C, Shen C, Morris MR, Everitt K (2006) Experiences with and observations of direct-touch tabletops. In: Proceedings of the first IEEE international workshop on horizontal interactive human-computer systems (January 05–07, 2006). TABLETOP, IEEE Computer Society, Washington, DC, pp 89–96, doi: 10.1109/TABLETOP.2006.12
4. Shen C, Ryall K, Forlines C, Esenther A, Vernier FD, Everitt K, Wu M, Wigdor D, Morris MR, Hancock M, Tse E (2006) Informing the design of direct-touch tabletops. IEEE Computer Graphics and Applications 26(5) (September 2006):36–46, doi: 10.1109/MCG.2006.109
5. Wu M, Shen C, Ryall K, Forlines C, Balakrishnan R (2006) Gesture registration, relaxation, and reuse for multi-point direct-touch surfaces. In: Proceedings of the first IEEE international workshop on horizontal interactive human-computer systems (January 05–07, 2006). TABLETOP, IEEE Computer Society, Washington, DC, pp 185–192, doi: 10.1109/TABLETOP.2006.19
6. Shen C, Vernier FD, Forlines C, Ringel M (2004) DiamondSpin: An extensible toolkit for around-the-table interaction. In: Proceedings of the SIGCHI conference on human factors in computing systems (Vienna, Austria, April 24–29, 2004). CHI '04, ACM Press, New York, pp 167–174, doi: 10.1145/985692.985714
7. Touchlib, A multi-touch development kit, http://nuigroup.com/touchlib/, Accessed 23.09.2009
8. Potter RL, Weldon LJ, Shneiderman B (1988) Improving the accuracy of touch screens: An experimental evaluation of three strategies. In: O'Hare JJ (ed) Proceedings of the SIGCHI conference on human factors in computing systems (Washington, DC, May 15–19, 1988). CHI '88, ACM Press, New York, pp 27–32, doi: 10.1145/57167.57171
9. Poupyrev I, Maruyama S, Rekimoto J (2002) Ambient touch: Designing tactile interfaces for handheld devices. In: Proceedings of the 15th annual ACM symposium on user interface software and technology (Paris, France, October 27–30, 2002). UIST '02, ACM Press, New York, pp 51–60, doi: 10.1145/571985.571993
10. Lee JC, Dietz PH, Leigh D, Yerazunis WS, Hudson SE (2004) Haptic pen: A tactile feedback stylus for touch screens. In: Proceedings of the 17th annual ACM symposium on user interface software and technology (Santa Fe, NM, October 24–27, 2004). UIST '04, ACM Press, New York, pp 291–294, doi: 10.1145/1029632.1029682
11. Hancock MS, Shen C, Forlines C, Ryall K (2005) Exploring non-speech auditory feedback at an interactive multi-user tabletop. In: Proceedings of graphics interface 2005 (Victoria, BC, May 09–11, 2005). GI, vol 112, Canadian Human-Computer Communications Society, School of Computer Science, University of Waterloo, Waterloo, ON, pp 41–50
12. Weiss M, Wagner J, Jansen Y, Jennings R, Khoshabeh R, Hollan JD, Borchers J (2009) SLAP widgets: Bridging the gap between virtual and physical controls on tabletops. In: Proceedings of the 27th international conference on human factors in computing systems (Boston, MA, April 04–09, 2009). CHI '09, ACM Press, New York, pp. 481–490, doi: 10.1145/1518701.1518779
13. Harrison C, Hudson SE (2009) Providing dynamically changeable physical buttons on a visual display. In: Proceedings of the 27th international conference on human factors in computing systems (Boston, MA, April 04–09, 2009). CHI '09, ACM Press, New York, pp 299–308, doi: 10.1145/1518701.1518749

14. Buxton W (1990) A three-state model of graphical input. In: Diaper D, Gilmore DJ, Cockton G, Shackel B (eds) Proceedings of the IFIP Tc13 third interational conference on human-computer interaction (August 27–31, 1990). North-Holland Publishing Co., Amsterdam, pp 449–456

15. Vogel D, Baudisch P (2007) Shift: A technique for operating pen-based interfaces using touch. In: Proceedings of the SIGCHI conference on human factors in computing systems (San Jose, CA, April 28–May 03, 2007). CHI '07, ACM Press, New York, pp 657–666, doi: 10.1145/1240624.1240727

16. Forlines C, Shen C, Buxton B (2005) Glimpse: A novel input model for multi-level devices. In: CHI '05 extended abstracts on human factors in computing systems (Portland, OR, April 02–07, 2005). CHI '05, ACM Press, New York, pp 1375–1378, doi: 10.1145/1056808.1056920

17. Han JY (2005) Low-cost multi-touch sensing through frustrated total internal reflection. In: Proceedings of the 18th annual ACM symposium on user interface software and technology (Seattle, WA, October 23–26, 2005). UIST '05. ACM Press, New York, pp. 115–118, doi: 10.1145/1095034.1095054

18. Siek KA, Rogers Y, Connelly KH (2005) Fat finger worries: How older and younger users physically interact with PDAs. In: Proceedings of INTERACT '05, pp 267–280

19. Schilit, B, Adams, N, Want, R (1994) Context-aware computing applications. In: Proceedings of the 1994 first workshop on mobile computing systems and applications – Volume 00 (December 08–09, 1994). WMCSA, IEEE Computer Society, Washington, DC, pp 85–90, doi: 10.1109/WMCSA.1994.16

20. Albinsson P, Zhai S (2003) High precision touch screen interaction. In: Proceedings of the SIGCHI conference on human factors in computing systems (Ft. Lauderdale, FL, April 05–10, 2003). CHI '03, ACM Press, New York, pp 105–112, doi: 10.1145/642611.642631

21. Wigdor D, Forlines C, Baudisch P, Barnwell J, Shen C (2007) Lucid touch: A see-through mobile device. In: Proceedings of the 20th annual ACM symposium on user interface software and technology (Newport, Rhode Island, October 07–10, 2007). UIST '07, ACM Press, New York, pp 269–278, doi: 10.1145/1294211.1294259

22. Hiraoka S, Miyamoto I, Tomimatsu K (2003) Behind touch, a text input method for mobile phones by the back and tactile sense interface. Information Processing Society of Japan, Interaction 2003, pp 131–138

23. Wigdor D, Leigh D, Forlines C, Shipman S, Barnwell J, Balakrishnan R, Shen C (2006) Under the table interaction. In: Proceedings of the 19th annual ACM symposium on user interface software and technology (Montreux, Switzerland, October 15–18, 2006). UIST '06, ACM Press, New York, pp 259–268, doi: 10.1145/1166253.1166294

24. Baudisch P, Chu G (2009) Back-of-device interaction allows creating very small touch devices. In: Proceedings of the 27th international conference on human factors in computing systems (Boston, MA, April 04–09, 2009). CHI '09, ACM Press, New York, pp 1923–1932, doi: 10.1145/1518701.1518995

25. Esenther A, Ryall K (2006) Fluid DTMouse: Better mouse support for touch-based interactions. In: Proceedings of the working conference on advanced visual interfaces (Venezia, Italy, May 23–26, 2006). AVI '06, ACM Press, New York, pp 112–115, doi: 10.1145/1133265.1133289

26. Moscovich T, Hughes JF (2006) Multi-finger cursor techniques. In: Proceedings of graphics interface 2006 (Quebec, June 07–09, 2006). ACM International Conference Proceeding Series, vol 137, Canadian Information Processing Society, Toronto, ON, pp 1–7

27. Vogel D, Cudmore M, Casiez G, Balakrishnan R, Keliher L (2009) Hand occlusion with tablet-sized direct pen input. In: Proceedings of the 27th international conference on human factors in computing systems (Boston, MA, April 04–09, 2009). CHI '09, ACM Press, New York, pp 557–566, doi: 10.1145/1518701.1518787

28. Cao X, Wilson AD, Balakrishnan R, Hinckley K, Hudson SE (2008) ShapeTouch: Leveraging contact shape on interactive surfaces. In: Proceedings of the IEEE international workshop on horizontal interactive human-computer systems (Tabletop '08), pp 129–136

29. Wigdor D, Perm G, Ryall K, Esenther A, Shen C (2007) Living with a tabletop: Analysis and observations of long term office use of a multi-touch table. In: Proceedings of the IEEE international workshop on horizontal interactive human-computer systems (Tabletop '07), pp 60–67

30. Ullmer B, Ishii, H (1997) The metaDESK: Models and prototypes for tangible user interfaces. In: Proceedings of the 10th annual ACM symposium on user interface software and technology (Banff, AB, October 14–17, 1997). UIST '97, ACM Press, New York, pp 223–232, doi: 10.1145/263407.263551

31. Nacenta MA, Baudisch P, Benko H, Wilson A (2009) Separability of spatial manipulations in multi-touch interfaces. In: Proceedings of graphics interface 2009 (Kelowna, BC, May 25–27, 2009). ACM International Conference Proceeding Series, vol 324, Canadian Information Processing Society, Toronto, ON, pp 175–182

32. Forlines C, Vogel D, Balakrishnan R (2006) HybridPointing: Fluid switching between absolute and relative pointing with a direct input device. In: Proceedings of the 19th annual ACM symposium on user interface software and technology (Montreux, Switzerland, October 15–18, 2006). UIST '06, ACM Press, New York, pp 211–220, doi: 10.1145/1166253.1166286

33. Feeney R (2002) Specific anthropometric and strength data for people with dexterity disability, consumer and competition policy directorate, Department of Trade and Industry, London

34. Benko H (2007) User interaction in hybrid multi-display environments. Ph.D. Dissertation. Department of Computer Science, Columbia University, New York, May 2007

35. Baudisch P, Tan D, Collomb M, Robbins D, Hinckley K, Agrawala M, Zhao S, Ramos G (2006) Phosphor: Explaining transitions in the user interface using afterglow effects. In: Proceedings of the 19th annual ACM symposium on user interface software and technology (Montreux, Switzerland, October 15–18, 2006). UIST '06, ACM Press, New York, pp 169–178, doi: 10.1145/1166253.1166280

Chapter 12
On, Above, and Beyond: Taking Tabletops to the Third Dimension

Tovi Grossman and Daniel Wigdor

Abstract Extending the tabletop to the third dimension has the potential to improve the quality of applications involving 3D data and tasks. Recognizing this, a number of researchers have proposed a myriad of display and input metaphors. However a standardized and cohesive approach has yet to evolve. Furthermore, the majority of these applications and the related research results are scattered across various research areas and communities, and lack a common framework. In this chapter, we survey previous 3D tabletops systems, and classify this work within a newly defined taxonomy. We then discuss the design guidelines which should be applied to the various areas of the taxonomy. Our contribution is the synthesis of numerous research results into a cohesive framework, and the discussion of interaction issues and design guidelines which apply. Furthermore, our work provides a clear understanding of what approaches have been taken, and exposes new routes for potential research, within the realm of interactive 3D tabletops.

Introduction

Horizontal, direct touch tabletops, which overlay large display and input surfaces, have recently been the focus of numerous studies. As the display and interaction surface of the typical tabletop display is 2D, the majority of this increasingly large body of work has focused on 2D applications and 2D interactions. However, the tasks which we carry out on physical tables are commonly three-dimensional in nature. It is thus desirable to consider how such tasks could be carried out and supported by interactive tabletop systems.

Example applications are numerous: A team of doctors could plan a surgery with a 3D virtual representation of a patient's body; an architect could inspect a virtual

T. Grossman (✉)
Autodesk Research, Toronto, ON M5A 1J7, Canada
e-mail: tovi.grossman@autodesk.com

C. Müller-Tomfelde (ed.), *Tabletops – Horizontal Interactive Displays*,
Human-Computer Interaction Series, DOI 10.1007/978-1-84996-113-4_12,
© Springer Verlag London Limited 2010

3D model of a new building and its surrounding area before creating a physical model; a new car model could be displayed and annotated in a design studio before a 1-to-1 scale physical clay model is built. Given the inherent 3D nature of such applications, it would seem appropriate that designers consider 3D display, input, and interaction technologies.

A number of projects have extended the tabletop to the third dimension, using a wide variety of techniques and technologies. However, the majority of these applications and the related research results are scattered across various research areas and communities, such as interactive 3D graphics, virtual reality, augmented reality, and tangible user interfaces. An interface designer creating a 3D tabletop application is thus left with the challenging endeavour of sorting through the previous work to help make appropriate design decisions. In an effort to alleviate this problem, it is our goal to review and classify the previous work in interaction with 3D tabletops, in an attempt to provide insights for future applications and research.

In this chapter, we provide an extensive review of the previous work done with interactive 3D tabletops and present a taxonomy which unifies this research into a single cohesive framework. We then discuss interesting areas of the taxonomy which have yet to be explored, along with a set of general interaction issues and design guidelines which are applicable within this framework.

Interactive 3D Tabletops

While interactive tabletop research tends to focus on 2D applications and interactions, significant research has also examined 3D tabletop systems. Often such systems diverge from the typical tabletop setting, and thus may not be referred to as tabletop systems.

For the purpose of our work, we consider an interactive 3D tabletop system as any system which presents a 3D virtual environment on or above a horizontal surface. Furthermore, we do not limit our considerations to any specific interaction metaphors. While the majority of tabletop systems provide direct-touch interaction, systems using indirect touch and supplementary input devices have also been explored, so we consider similar systems for 3D tabletops.

It is our goal to review and categorize such systems to provide future researchers with a clear understanding of what has been done and what can be done in the realm of interactive 3D tabletops. In the following section we review the 3D tabletop platforms and applications which have been developed. Following this literature review we will categorize the previous systems into a taxonomy of interactive 3D tabletops.

Existing Technologies

In this section we review the existing technologies used to implement 3D tabletop systems.

Two-Dimensional Tabletop Technologies

The most basic implementation of a 3D tabletop system uses a 2D tabletop display. Such systems typically display two-dimensional imagery atop a multi-touch input device (Fig. 12.1). Although the underpinnings of such surfaces stem from the early 1980s [1], there has been a recent slew of technologies employed for multi-touch input on a tabletop [2–7]. While most commonly such systems are used for 2D applications, they can be used for interacting with 3D data. Roomplanner allows users to interact with floor plans, using an orthographic top-view projection [8]. The Active Desk is a large scale drafting table which designers can work in a similar method to a traditional drafting table [9]. More recently, there has been a surge of 3D interaction techniques being developed for 2D tabletop environments. Hancock et al. explored "shallow depth" interactions for 3D using a 2D tabletop [10]. Reisman et al. extended this work by developing a constraint based solution to provide direct 3D manipulation techniques [11]. Wilson et al. implemented a full 3D physics engine within a 2D table top environment to provide physically realistic 3D interactions [12], and later ex-tended this to allow users to pick objects up using a combination of 2D and 3D gestures [13].

Fig. 12.1 The microsoft surface table. A multi-touch input device with a two-dimensional display

Stereoscopic Technologies

With the use of stereoscopic technologies, the imagery presented by a 2D tabletop displays can be perceived as "popping out" of the table, potentially providing the user with a more realistic 3D experience. For example, the ImmersaDesk [14] is a large scale drafting table which provides stereoscopic images (Fig. 12.2). Users wear shutter glasses, and their viewing location is tracked so that the imagery is

coupled with the user's viewpoint, providing a depth cue known as motion parallax. The user interacts with the imagery using a wand tracked in 3D. A similar
platform is the responsive workbench, a virtual working environment that pro-vides
virtual objects and control tools on a physical "workbench" [15, 16]. Users collaborate around the workbench, with shutter glasses and head tracking providing
a non-immersive virtual environment. The virtual workbench is a smaller implementation, which also presents 3D imagery using shutter glasses [17]. However
with the virtual workbench, the display is actually above the perceived location
of the tabletop and facing down. The user looks through and interacts behind a
half-mirror.

Augmented and Virtual Reality

In virtual reality systems, head mounted displays are commonly used to immerse
the user in a 3D environment [18]. While head mounted virtual reality environments tend to be large areas which the user can explore, some systems use head
mounted displays for table centric spaces, such as in surgical procedures [19]. A
less immersive alternative, which allows the user to maintain the context of their
surrounding environment, is to use a head mounted augmented reality display [20].
Such displays have been used for tabletop interactions, such as in VITA, a system
supporting offsite visualization of an archaeological dig [21], which displays 3D
imagery above a direct-touch tabletop. Another method of augmenting a physical

workspace is to place a transparent projection screen between the viewer and the table, as in ASTOR, where virtual labels appeared alongside physical objects [22].

Tabletop Spatially Augmented Reality

The augmented reality systems described in the previous subsection augment the physical world by placing virtual imagery on a viewing plane. In this section we describe systems which augment the physical world by projecting imagery directly on to physical objects (Fig. 12.3). Such systems have been termed "Tabletop spatially augmented reality" [23]. An advantage of such systems is that supplementary hardware devices, such as glasses and head mounted displays, are not required. A disadvantage is that the display space is constrained to the surface of objects.

Fig. 12.3 Raskar et al.'s spatially augmented reality

Illuminating Clay [24] and Sandscape [25] are two examples of tabletop spatially augmented reality systems. In these systems, users interact with physical clay and sand, with the deformations being sensed in real time, and virtual imagery being projected on to the surface. In URP [26], physical architectural placed on a workbench are augmented with dynamic virtual imagery projected on to the scene. With tablescape plus [27], animated objects are projected on to small, vertical planes which can be moved around the table. Raskar introduced Shader Lamps, where dynamic imagery is projected onto physical objects, in a way that gives the illusion that the objects are moving, or the display conditions, such as lighting, are changing [28]. While initially non-interactive, follow-up work demonstrated dynamic shader lamps, which allowed users to virtually paint the physical objects [29].

Three-Dimensional Volumetric Displays

Volumetric displays present imagery in true 3D space, by illuminating "voxels" (volumetric pixels) in midair (Fig. 12.4). Favalora provides a thorough survey of

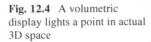

Fig. 12.4 A volumetric
display lights a point in actual
3D space

the various technological implementations of volumetric displays [30]. The true 3D
imagery in volumetric displays has been shown to improve depth perception [31]
and shape recognition [32].

Besides providing true 3D images, the main difference from the other 3D tabletops displays is that volumetric display are generally enclosed by a surface. This
means that users cannot directly interact with the 3D imagery. Balakrishnan et al.
explored the implications of this unique difference to interaction design by using
physical mockups [33]. More recent working implementations have allowed users to
interact with the display by using hand and finger gestures on and above the display
surface [34], and by using a hand-held six degree-of-freedom input device [35].
Although not truly three-dimensional, a similar spherical display was demonstrated
by Benko et al. [36]. With this display, interactions and display were con-strained to
the planar surface of the sphere.

Taxonomy

We have provided an overview of the existing 3D tabletop display technologies.
As discussed, a number of implementations have been explored, each with their
own benefits and drawbacks. However many of these research results are scattered
across various research areas, without any overall organization. Complicating the
matter is that while all of the work fits our description of a 3D tabletop research,
many of the results were not intended to be considered tabletop research. In some
cases the interactive tabletop research area had yet to be recognized. Such work
may be overlooked when tabletop researchers start considering approaches for 3D
applications.

With the outlined previous work in mind, we now define a taxonomy of the
various implementations of interactive 3D tabletops. Our hope is to help future

re-searchers understand the possible design space of interactive 3D tabletops, clarify which aspects of the design space have been explored, and expose possible implementations which have yet to be considered. This taxonomy will also serve as a basis for a discussion of specific interaction issues and design guidelines applicable to the various areas of the taxonomy, which we will provide in section "Interaction Issues and Design Guidelines". Our taxonomy is organized into 3 main areas: display properties, input properties, and physical properties (Fig. 12.5).

Fig. 12.5 Taxonomy of interactive 3D tabletops

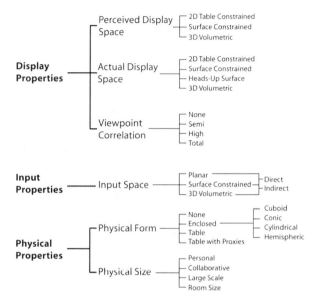

Display Properties

The first main area of the taxonomy is the display properties. We consider the perceived and actual display spaces, along with the correlation between the user's viewpoint and the provided viewpoint of the imagery.

Perceived Display Space

The perceived display space is defined as the spatial location for which displayed imagery is perceived to be based on stereoscopic depth cues.

2D Table Constrained: In a traditional 2D tabletop display, the display space is 2D. Even when 3D imagery is displayed using a perspective projection on the table [10, 13, 12], we still consider the display space to be 2D if no stereoscopic depth cues are provided.

Surface Constrained: In tabletop spatially augmented displays, imagery is projected onto the table surface and physical proxies. An interesting variation is Second light [37], where imagery can be projected through the table by an under-mounted projector, onto objects above the surface. We term the resulting display space as surface constrained. While the displayed imagery exists in 3D space, the imagery itself is 2D.

3D Volumetric: When stereo cues are provided, via a head mounted display, shutter glasses, or a volumetric display, the perceived display space is truly 3D (Fig. 12.6).

Fig. 12.6 The responsive workbench's display was constrained to the table, with false 3D created through shutter glasses

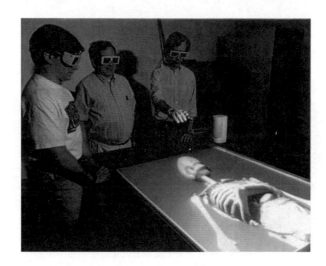

Actual Display Space

The actual display space considers where the actual displayed imagery exists. While this property is not meant to impact the user's perception of the imagery, it has been shown to affect the user's depth perception [31] and performance in three-dimensional tasks [38]. It is also an important property to consider as it will affect overall experiences and interaction affordances [18].

2D Table Constrained: In a tradition tabletop setup, the actual display space is also the 2D table itself. In systems where users wear stereo shutter glasses, the actual display space is also constrained to the table, even through the user perceives 3D imagery.

Surface Constrained: In the spatially augmented reality applications, which project imagery onto physical proxies, the actual display space is constrained to surfaces on and above the table (Fig. 12.7). Although the actual display space exists in 3D, we do not consider it to be truly 3D or volumetric, since imagery cannot exist anywhere in the working volume.

Fig. 12.7 Illuminating clay
projected onto curved
surfaces

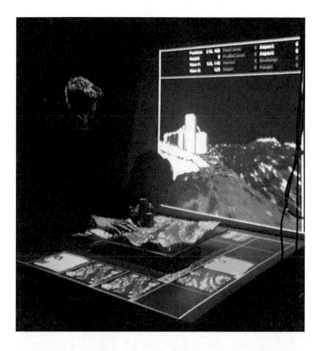

Fig. 12.8 Benko et al.'s
hybrid virtual environments
used a head-mounted display
to insert imagery into the
space between the user and
the table

Heads-Up Surface: When the actual display space is on a transparent surface
between the user and table, we term the display space as Heads-up-Surface. This is
the case when using a head mounted display, or when virtual imagery is projected
on a see-through display plane (Fig. 12.8).

3D Volumetric: When imagery can appear anywhere on or above the display,
the display space is 3D volumetric. Currently, volumetric displays are the only
technology with this capability.

Viewpoint Correlation

When we move our heads in the physical world our viewpoints change, which affects the visual images which we receive. The last property of the display which we consider is the range of viewpoints which can be obtained of the imagery by physically moving around the display. For this property, there are no discrete values; we categorize the technologies based on 4 magnitudes.

None: In a traditional tabletop set up, the user's viewpoint is independent of the displayed imagery. The displayed image is static, regardless of the users viewing location.

Semi: In some systems, such as spatially multiplexed autostereoscopic displays [39], a finite number of viewpoints are provided (Fig. 12.9). With such systems, the transitions from one viewpoint to the next can be choppy, but the basic motion parallax effect is provided.

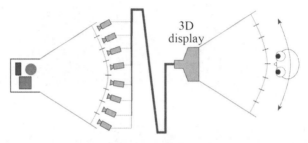

Fig. 12.9 Dodgson described autostereoscopic 3D displays, in which multiple views are available to the user depending on their head position. The set of viewpoints is limited to horizontal position and an assumed vertical position, providing only semi-correlation to the user's viewpoint

High: High viewpoint correlation means that the viewpoint of the virtual imagery continuously changes with the user's viewing location, with limited exceptions. This can be achieved with a standard 2D display and tracking the user's head (Fig. 12.10), or by using a volumetric display. The expectation with such technologies is when the user moves below the horizontal plane of the table. In this case, the user will see the bottom of the table, not the bottom of the imagery on top of the table. This is also the case when working with a physical table.

Total: When using a head mounted display to create a virtual reality tabletop experience, total correlation between the user's viewpoint and the displayed imagery can be achieved. Without the presence of a physical table, users could potentially view imagery from below the horizontal plane of the virtual table.

Input Properties

An important consideration for 3D tabletop displays is how the user interacts with the displayed imagery. A full categorization of input technologies and techniques

Fig. 12.10 The 2-user responsive workbench provided highly correlated views by displaying 4 different images on the screen, and timing shutters worn over the eyes to provide the correct image to each user's correct eye [15]

is beyond the scope of this chapter, and we refer the reader to relevant previous literature [40]. For the purpose of our taxonomy, we only consider the input space.

Input Space

The input space is defined as the physical location where the user can provide in-put. This property is important because it will impact the type of interaction techniques and usage metaphors which must be made available.

As we have seen, in the 2D realm, tabletops typically overlay input and display devices for direct-touch input. When working in 3D, this may no longer be feasible for three reasons: first, virtual objects may be perceived above the display plane, and thus cannot be "touched" by touching the display surface; second, display technologies may impair the ability to reach within the volume; and third, objects may simply not be within reach of the user. Clearly, the adaptation of the direct-touch input paradigm to the third dimension is not a simple one. The following lists input spaces which have been considered:

Direct 2D: The most common form of input with tabletop displays is direct 2D input, where the user can directly touch and interact with the displayed imagery (Fig. 12.11).

Indirect 2D: Indirect 2D input is useful when the display space is larger than the user's reach. Implementations include mapping a small local area of the display as the input space to the entire display surface [41], or by using a mouse or similar supplementary device [42, 43].

Direct Surface Constrained: In the spatially augmented reality systems where the virtual imagery is constrained to the surface of physical objects, interaction could also be constrained to those surfaces. For example, a user could add virtual paint to a physical object by using a physical brush tracked in 3D space [23].

Indirect Surface Constrained: Interaction can be surface constrained and indi-rect if an intermediate interaction surface is present. Such is the case with a

Fig. 12.11 Wu and
Balakrishnan demonstrated
direct-2D input in their
room-planning application [8]

Fig. 12.12 Grossman et al.'s
gestural interaction system
for volumetric displays
included input modes that
were constrained to the
surface of the device, but
which mapped the 2D input
space onto the volume within
[34]

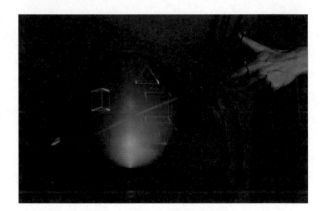

volumetric display, where the display enclosure can act as a touch sensitive surface [34] (Fig. 12.12).

Direct 3D: When the user can directly reach into the virtual imagery and grab objects in 3D space, the interaction is direct 3D. This is a common input metaphor in virtual reality environments, and is also possible in systems using stereo glasses.

Indirect 3D: In some virtual environments, the input is 3D, but indirect interaction techniques are provided. This is necessary when objects are out of the user's reach [44]. Indirect 3D interaction can also be used in volumetric displays, to overcome the physical surface between the user and displayed imagery [35].

Physical Properties

The last area of our taxonomy is the physical properties of the display. This is an important factor as it will affect how the user will interact with the display. Most relevant to the interactions is the physical properties of the actual work area, or perceived display space, and not the display hardware.

Physical Form

The physical form refers to the physical shape of the system. This property may affect possible input spaces, and required input mappings.

None: In head-mounted VR displays, the entire environment is virtual, so the work area has no physical form at all.

Enclosed: Most volumetric displays have an enclosed physical form, to protect the user form the mechanics of the display (Fig. 12.12). Various shapes of this enclosure have been proposed, including cuboid, conic, cylindrical, and hemispheric.

Table: In a typical tabletop setting, or a tabletop using stereo shutter-glasses, the physical form consists of the planar table surface.

Table with Proxies: In spatially augmented tabletops, the physical form is defined by the table and the location and shape of the addition physical proxies (Fig. 12.13).

Fig. 12.13 Tabletscape plus provided physical properties which extended the display [27]

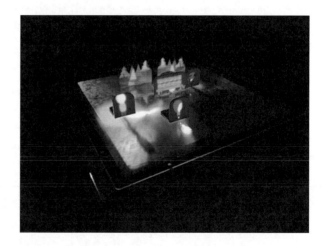

Physical Size

The other important factor relevant to physical properties is the size of the display. The affect of size has been discussed in the 2D tabletop literature [45], and we expect that similar issues will be present in 3D tabletop displays. We categorize sizes by what users can reach and what they can see, as these will be critical factors in the design of interfaces. While the definitions consider the areas within the reach of the user, it does not necessarily imply that the technology actually allows the user to reach into the display.

Personal: A personal sized 3D Tabletop display is small enough that the user can easily reach the entire display area.

Collaborative: With a collaborative sized display, a user can easily reach the center of the display. Such display sizes, for 2D tabletops, are generally meant for multiple users, so that between each user, the entire display space is accessible [45].

Large Scale: We define a large scale 3D tabletop display as being too big for a user to reach the center of the display. This means that even with multiple users, there will be areas inaccessible via direct touch interaction. However the display is small enough that users can easily see and interpret all areas of the displayed imagery.

Room Size: A room sized display would take up the entire space of a room. This means that there will be areas that the user cannot reach, and also areas that the user cannot easily see.

Taxonomy Application

One of the contributions of the taxonomy which we have presented is that it classifies the work which has been done into a cohesive framework. By examining where the existing technologies fall within this taxonomy, we can provide insights on what areas of research have been thoroughly explored, and what areas have been given less attention. Furthermore, by combining the various properties of the taxonomy in different ways, we can propose new and interesting 3D tabletop system implementations which have yet to be explored. Table 12.1 shows one such combination.

Table 12.1 Three parameters of our taxonomy: *Perceived Display Space*, *In-Put Space*, and *Actual Display Space*. *Light grey* cells are unexplored. *Dark grey* cells are impractical

	Perceived display space	Actual display space			
	Input space	2D table	2D heads up	3D surface const.	3D volume
2D	2D planar	#1	#3		
	Surface-const.				
	Volumetric				
3D surface	2D planar			#4	
	Surface const.			#5	
	Volumetric			#6	
3D volume	2D planar	[46, 14]	[21]	#7	#10
	Surface const.			#8	[34]
	Volumetric	#2	[21, 22]	#9	[35]

This particular arrangement of parameters allows us to focus on combinations of technologies, so that we might examine platforms for past and future development. As is immediately evident, some technologies have received more focus than others, while others have received almost no attention. A discussion of all areas is not within the scope of this paper: we will now review a few of the more compelling cells of this view of our taxonomy.

Planar Input to 2D Display (Cells 1, 2)

Cell 1 represents the large collection of 2D tabletop research which has been de-scribed previously [8–10], while cell 2 includes the multitude of 2D tabletop displays which were augmented with stereo viewing [14–17]. This has defined the baseline for research in 3D tabletops, though we hope to expand that focus.

Heads-Up Display of 2D (Cell 3)

Without a tabletop, this cell might describe various augmented reality projects. We are not aware, however, of any use of heads-up displays to augment a tabletop with 2D imagery. Although perhaps not as compelling as some of the 3D uses of this technology (from cell 2), heads-up displays for 2D tabletops might allow for interesting mixes of public and private information [8], and differentiate the view of each user [15], advantageous for reasons described by Matsuda et al. [47].

One system relevant to this area is PenLight, which augments physical paper with virtual imagery, projected from a miniature projector integrated into the pen itself [48]. This system was used to overlay 3D building information onto physical 2D blue prints. In its current implementation, the projected imagery is coplanar with the physical table. One interesting area to explore would be to instead project the imagery onto an intermediate surface, to distinguish between the physical and virtual display layers, or to display virtual cross sections in their true spatial locations.

Surface Constrained 3D (Cells 4–6)

Cells 5 and 6 include a number of projects which project imagery onto 3D surfaces. These projects include methods which limit input to moving objects around on the surface of the table [27] (cell 4), those which constrain it to the surfaces of 3D objects [24, 25] (cell 5), and those that allow unconstrained input [23, 26] (cell 6). The taxonomy allows for a quick distinction between these works, while also identifying an unexplored area (cell 4): the use of planar input to surface-constrained display areas. Such systems could provide interesting mappings between input and display spaces, such as manipulating objects by interacting with their shadows [49].

Stereo Spatial Augmentation (Cells 7–9)

These cells represent an as-of-yet unexplored use of 3D for tabletops. It describes a concept similar to Sandscape [25], Illuminating Clay [24], and Second Light [37] in that it would involve projecting onto the surface of 3D objects. However, with the addition of shutter glasses the system could present imagery which diverges from the structure of the physical proxies. With the current tabletop spatially augmented systems this is not possible. Such systems could be useful for scenarios where users view 3D models, and also want the ability to make minor adjustments to the structure.

Planar Input with Volumetric Displays (Cell 10)

This currently unexplored cell represents interacting with volumetric displays using traditional 2D input methods. This could be interesting to explore, since the input configuration could support standard desktop interactions which users are al-ready familiar with.

Interaction Issues and Design Guidelines

Due to the lack of a unified framework, previously interaction issues related to 3D tabletop systems have been discussed based on specific point designs and implementations. Similarly, the design decisions gone into the development 3D tabletop systems have been made on a one-by-one basis for each technological implementation. An intended contribution of our work is to be able to discuss interaction is-sues, and design guidelines for 3D tabletop systems at a higher level, independent of the specific implementation, based solely on where systems exist within the taxonomy. In this section, we present some of these generalized interaction issues and design guidelines.

Caveats in Increasing Perceived Display Space

In our taxonomy we discuss 3 possible perceived display spaces, with 3D volumetric being at highest level. The motivation to diverge from a 2D perceived display space is to improve the user's perception of the 3D environment, and in some cases to provide a more realistic simulation. While research has shown that introducing stereoscopic cues can improve a user's ability to carry out 3D tasks [38], designers should be careful before deciding upon the display configuration.

First, with the exception of autostereoscopic displays, providing a perceived 3D scene means introducing supplementary hardware, such as shutter glasses or head mounted displays. Such devices can be uncomfortable, reduce the ubiquity of the system (as they will no longer be walk-up-and-use), and can cause the user to lose the context of their surrounding environment or collaborators [18, 31].

Furthermore, when the perceived display space is inconsistent with the actual display space, the depth cues which the human brain receives become inconsistent. Most critical is the discrepancy between the accommodation and convergence cues, as this has been known to cause asthenopia in some users [50]. Symptoms associated with this condition include dizziness, headaches, nauseas, and eye fatigue.

A more subtle issue is that when the actual display space is 2D table con-strained and the perceived display space is 3D volumetric, there is actually a constraint on the perceived display space. Because the user is seeing pixels on the surface of the display, it would be impossible to perceive imagery that is above the user's line of sight to the back of the display. This means that the perceivable display space is actually triangular in shape – the further away the imagery is to the user, to less height it can have. As a result, such a configuration would not be very appropriate for applications where tall objects will appear, such as the architectural design of a high rise building.

The display configurations unaffected by these limitations are 2D tabletop systems, spatially augmented reality tabletop systems, and volumetric displays. These configurations should be considered if the designer foresees the discussed limitations as being problematic.

Losing Discrete Input and Tactile Feedback

Increasing the input space to 3D, whether it is direct or indirect, allows users to directly specify and manipulate objects in 3D space. However, there are a number of drawbacks of this input paradigm.

One problem is that discrete contact-to-surface events, which are typically used to trigger events in 2D tabletop interfaces, do not occur. As such, designers must provide interactions to execute discrete events. One possibility is to use free-hand gestures [51], such as a gun gesture to perform selections [34]. The alternative is to have the user hold an input device which has buttons that can be used to execute the discrete events.

Second, when interacting in midair, the user loses the tactile feedback present when interacting on 2D surfaces. This is problematic as sensory feedback is considered to be essential when interacting in 3D spaces [52]. Some explored solutions include bimanual input, physical proxies, and force feedback devices [52].

We refer the reader to Hinckley's survey paper on "spatial input" for a thorough discussion of other associated difficulties and possible solutions [52]. Due to these difficulties, designers should consider planar or surface constrained input, even if the technological implementation can support a 3D input space.

Mapping 2D Input to 3D Space

If planar or surface constrained input is being used, then the system needs a way to map two degrees-of-freedom interactions into 3D space. An exception is if no three degrees-of-freedom tasks are required in the application, such as the case for shallow depth interactions [10]. Otherwise, with only two degrees-of-freedom in-put, tasks such as moving an object to a point in 3D space must be carried out sequentially. A number of interactions have been developed to support 3D interactions with 2D input, such as three dimensional widgets [53]. Other possible approaches are to use supplementary input streams for added degrees-of-freedom, such as using a mouse scroll wheel [54], mouse tilt [55], or pressure [56] to define depth during interactions. Another way to increase the degrees-of-freedom is to use bimanual interactions [57] and multi-finger gestures [46].

Indirect Interactions May Be Required

While there are tradeoffs to using direct and indirect interactions in 3D tabletop applications, there are some cases where we would strongly suggest that indirect interactions be provided. Obviously if the input space is indirect, then indirect interaction techniques must be provided. Furthermore, when the physical form of the system is enclosed, then the interaction space must be indirect. Lastly, when the physical size is large scale or room size, then indirect interactions are required to make all areas of the display accessible.

One possible indirect interaction technique is to use a virtual cursor, which has a positional offset form the user's hand or handheld input device [44]. Another technique commonly used in VR applications is a ray cursor, which acts like a virtual laser pointer being emitted from the user's hand [58]. This approach has also been used in 2D tabletop systems [43], and studied within volumetric displays [35]. The use of physically "flicking" objects to move them to inaccessible areas has also been investigated [41].

Providing Navigation and Visual Aids

The transition from 2D to 3D necessitates a series of changes in the way navigation is handled and visualized. For example, in systems which lack viewpoint correlation of 3D imagery, a mechanism will be required to allow for the viewpoint to be changed. Conversely, in those systems which do provide some correlation of viewpoint to head position, visualization of the automatic change of viewpoint may be required to overcome orientation effects.

This is equally true as the perceived or actual space grows beyond the tabletop: in room sized displays, mechanisms to allow the user to see distant imagery may be required.

Lessons from 2D

Each of the above guidelines were derived through categorization and examination of efforts already expended in 3D tabletop systems. Here we describe lessons al-ready learned by researchers of traditional tabletops, which may need to be re-examined when moving to 3D.

Common, Shared Display and Input Area

Various research efforts have uncovered behaviours of both individuals and groups using tables and interacting with either physical or virtual objects. These include user territoriality [59], effects of group and table size [45], closeness [47], and the use of orientation for communication [16]. As tables move to 3D, several of these issues may increase in prominence, and new issues may arise.

Varied Point of View

With users seated around all sides of a tabletop, each participant receives a distinctly different view of information on the display. As such, traditional desktop interfaces, which assume a particular orientation, are clearly inappropriate for these displays. A great deal of research has gone into the effects of orientation on group interaction [59–62] and perception [63–65], and interfaces to help overcome or exploit these issues [63, 66]. Naturally, with 3D tabletops, this problem is much more severe, since the rotation of objects can be in any of three orientations, and in fact faces of 3D objects may be completely invisible to some users. Early work describing this issue with text readability found interesting results [67], but further is required.

Conclusions

In this chapter, we have introduced a taxonomy of 3D tabletop systems. This taxonomy categorizes 3D tabletops based on their display, input and physical proper-ties. A contribution of this taxonomy is that it allows us to organize previous research into a single high-level framework. Furthermore, it allows us to identify combinations of the discussed properties which have yet to be explored.

Evident from the large body of work in 3D tabletops is that they are a compelling platform for future development. It is our hope that, through the creation of the taxonomy, we will inspire and aid further development in this domain.

Acknowledgments We thank Andy Wilson, members of the Dynamic Graphics Project at University of Toronto, and members of the Mitsubishi Electronic Research Laboratories.

References

1. Mehta N (1982) A flexible machine interface. M.A.Sc. Thesis, Electrical Engineering, University of Toronto
2. Dietz P, Leigh D (2001) DiamondTouch: A multi-user touch technology. In: Proceedings of the 14th annual ACM symposium on user interface software and technology, ACM Press, New York, pp 219–226, doi: 10.1145/502348.502389

3. Han JY (2005) Low-cost multi-touch sensing through frustrated total internal reflection. In: Proceedings of the 18th annual ACM symposium on user interface software and technology, ACM Press, New York, pp 115–118, doi: 10.1145/1095034.1095054
4. Rekimoto J (2002) SmartSkin: An infrastructure for freehand manipulation on interactive surfaces. In: Proceedings of the SIGCHI conference on human factors in computing systems: Changing our world, changing ourselves, ACM Press, New York, pp 113–120, doi: 10.1145/503376.503397
5. SMART Technologies Inc. Digital Vision Touch Technology. http://www.smarttech.com/dvit/, accessed 05.02.2009
6. Wilson AD (2004) TouchLight: An imaging touch screen and display for gesture-based interaction. In: Proceedings of the 6th international conference on multimodal interfaces, ACM Press, New York, pp 69–76, doi: 10.1145/1027933.1027946
7. Wilson AD (2005) PlayAnywhere: A compact interactive tabletop projection-vision system. In: Proceedings of the 18th annual ACM symposium on user interface software and technology, ACM Press, New York, pp 83–92, doi: 10.1145/1095034.1095047
8. Wu M, Balakrishnan R (2003) Multi-finger and whole hand gestural interaction techniques for multi-user tabletop displays. In: Proceedings of the 16th annual ACM symposium on user interface software and technology, ACM Press, New York, pp 193–202, doi: 10.1145/964696.964718
9. Buxton W (1997) Living in augmented reality: Ubiquitous media and reactive environments. In: Video mediated communication. pp 363–384
10. Hancock M, Carpendale S, Cockburn A (2007) Shallow-depth 3d interaction: Design and evaluation of one-, two- and three-touch techniques. In: Proceedings of the SIGCHI conference on human factors in computing systems, ACM Press, New York, pp 1147–1156, doi: 10.1145/1240624.1240798
11. Reisman J, Davidson P, Han J (2009) A screen-space formulation for 2D and 3D direct manipulation. In: Proceedings of the 22nd annual ACM symposium on user interface software and technology, ACM Press, New York, pp 69–78, doi: 10.1145/1622176.1622190
12. Wilson AD, Izadi S, Hilliges O, Garcia-Mendoza A, Kirk D (2008) Bringing physics to the surface. In: Proceedings of the 21st annual ACM symposium on user interface software and technology, ACM Press, New York, pp 67–76, doi: 10.1145/1449715.1449728
13. Hilliges O, Izadi S, Wilson AD, Hodges S, Garcia-Mendoza A, Butz A (2009) Interactions in the air: Adding further depth to interactive tabletops. In: Proceedings of the 22nd annual ACM symposium on user interface software and technology, ACM Press, New York, pp 139–148, doi: 10.1145/1622176.1622203
14. Czernuszenko M, Pape D, Sandin D, DeFanti T, Dawe GL, Brown MD (1997) The ImmersaDesk and infinity wall projection-based virtual reality displays. SIGGRAPH Computer Graphics 31(2):46–49, doi: 10.1145/271283.271303
15. Agrawala M, Beers AC, McDowall I, Fröhlich B, Bolas M, Hanrahan P (1997) The two-user responsive workbench: Support for collaboration through individual views of a shared space. In: Proceedings of the 24th annual conference on computer graphics and interactive techniques international conference on computer graphics and interactive techniques, ACM Press/Addison-Wesley Publishing Co., New York, pp 327–332, doi: 10.1145/258734.258875
16. Krüger W, Bohn C, Fröhlich B, Schüth H, Strauss W, Wesche G (1995) The responsive workbench: A virtual work environment. Computer 28(7):42–48, doi: 10.1109/2.391040
17. Poston T, Serra L (1994) The virtual workbench: Dextrous VR. In: Virtual reality software and technology, pp 111–121
18. Buxton W, Fitzmaurice G (1998) HMDs, caves, & chameleon: A human centric analysis of interaction in virtual space. Computer Graphics, The SIGGRAPH Quarterly 32(4): 64–68
19. Geis WP (1996) Head-mounted video monitor for global visual access in mini-invasive surgery: An initial report. Surgical Endoscopy, 10(7):768–770
20. Feiner S, Macintyre B, Seligmann D (1993) Knowledge-based augmented reality. Communications of the ACM 36(7):53–62, doi: 10.1145/159544.159587

21. Benko H, Ishak EW, Feiner S (2004) Collaborative mixed reality visualization of an archaeo-logical excavation. In: Proceedings of the 3rd IEEE/ACM international symposium on mixed and augmented reality, symposium on mixed and augmented reality. IEEE Computer Society, Washington, DC, pp 132–140, doi: 10.1109/ISMAR.2004.23

22. Olwal A, Lindfors C, Gustafsson J, Kjellberg T, Mattsson L (2005) ASTOR: An autostereoscopic optical see-through augmented reality system. In: Proceedings of the 4th IEEE/ACM international symposium on mixed and augmented reality, IEEE Computer Society, Washington, DC, pp 24–27, doi: 10.1109/ISMAR.2005.15

23. Raskar R, Welch G, Chen W (1999) Table-top spatially-augmented reality: Bringing physical models to life with projected imagery. In: Proceedings of the 2nd IEEE and ACM international workshop on augmented reality, IEEE Computer Society, Washington, DC, p 64

24. Piper B, Ratti C, Ishii H (2002) Illuminating clay: A 3-D tangible interface for landscape analysis. In: Proceedings of the SIGCHI conference on human factors in computing systems, ACM Press, New York, pp 355–362, doi: 10.1145/503376.503439

25. Wang Y, Biderman A, Piper B, Ratti C, Ishii H (2002) Sandscape. Get in touch, Ars Electronica Center, Linz, Austria 2002

26. Underkoffler J, Ishii H (1999) Urp: A luminous-tangible workbench for urban planning and design. In: Proceedings of the SIGCHI conference on human factors in computing systems, ACM Press, New York, pp 386–393, doi: 10.1145/302979.303114

27. Kakehi Y, Iida M, Naemura T, Mitsunori M (2006) Tablescape plus: Upstanding tiny displays on tabletop display. In: ACM SIGGRAPH 2006 emerging, ACM Press, New York, p 31, doi: 10.1145/1179133.1179165

28. Raskar R, Welch G, Low KL, Bandyopadhyay D (2001) Shader Lamps: Animating real objects with image based illumination. In: Eurographics workshop on rendering (EGWR 2001), London

29. Bandyopadhyay D, Raskar R, Fuchs H (2001) Dynamic Shader Lamps: Painting on movable objects. In: IEEE and ACM international symposium on augmented reality, pp 207–216

30. Favalora GE (2005) Volumetric 3D displays and application infrastructure. Computer 38(8):37–44, doi: 10.1109/MC.2005.276

31. Grossman T, Balakrishnan R (2006) An evaluation of depth perception on volumetric displays. In: Proceedings of the working conference on advanced visual interfaces, ACM Press, New York, pp 193–200, doi: 10.1145/1133265.1133305

32. Rosen P, Pizlo Z, Hoffmann C, Popescu V (2004) Perception of 3D spatial relations for 3D displays. Stereoscopic Displays XI:9–16

33. Balakrishnan R, Fitzmaurice GW, Kurtenbach G (2001) User interfaces for volumetric displays. Computer 34(3):37–45, doi: 10.1109/2.910892

34. Grossman T, Wigdor D, Balakrishnan R (2004) Multi-finger gestural interaction with 3d volumetric displays. In: Proceedings of the 17th annual ACM symposium on user interface software and technology, ACM Press, New York, pp 61–70, doi: 10.1145/1029632.1029644

35. Grossman T, Balakrishnan R (2006) The design and evaluation of selection techniques for 3D volumetric displays. In: Proceedings of the 19th annual ACM symposium on user interface software and technology, ACM Press, New York, pp 3–12, doi: 10.1145/1166253.1166257

36. Benko H, Wilson AD, Balakrishnan R (2008) Sphere: Multi-touch interactions on a spherical display. In: Proceedings of the 21st annual ACM symposium on user interface software and technology, ACM Press, New York, pp 77–86, doi: 10.1145/1449715.1449729

37. Izadi S, Hodges S, Taylor S, Rosenfeld D, Villar N, Butler A, Westhues J (2008) Going beyond the display: A surface technology with an electronically switchable diffuser. In: Proceedings of the 21st annual ACM symposium on user interface software and technology, ACM Press, New York, pp 269–278

38. Ware C, Franck G (1996) Evaluating stereo and motion cues for visualizing infor-mation nets in three dimensions. ACM Transactions on Graphics 15(2):121–140, doi: 10.1145/234972.234975

39. Dodgson NA (2005) Autostereoscopic 3D displays. Computer 38(8):31–36, doi: 10.1109/MC.2005.252

40. Hinckley K (2002) Input technologies and techniques. In: The human-computer interaction handbook: Fundamentals, evolving technologies and emerging applications, pp 151–168
41. Reetz A, Gutwin C, Stach T, Nacenta M, Subramanian S (2006) Superflick: A natural and efficient technique for long-distance object placement on digital tables. In: Proceedings of graphics interface 2006, ACM international conference proceeding series, vol 137, Canadian Information Processing Society, Toronto, ON, pp 163–170
42. Forlines C, Wigdor D, Shen C, Balakrishnan R (2007) Direct-touch vs. mouse input for tabletop displays. In: Proceedings of the SIGCHI conference on human factors in computing systems, ACM Press, New York, pp 647–656, doi: 10.1145/1240624.1240726
43. Parker JK, Mandryk RL, Inkpen KM (2005) TractorBeam: Seamless integration of local and remote pointing for tabletop displays. In: Proceedings of graphics interface 2005, Canadian Human-Computer Communications Society, School of Computer Science, University of Waterloo, Waterloo, ON, pp 33–40
44. Mine MR (1995) Virtual environment interaction techniques. In: Technical report, UMI Order Number: TR95-018, University of North Carolina at Chapel Hill
45. Ryall K, Forlines C, Shen C, Morris MR (2004) Exploring the effects of group size and table size on interactions with tabletop shared-display groupware. In: Proceedings of the 2004 ACM conference on computer supported cooperative work, ACM Press, New York, pp 284–293, doi: 10.1145/1031607.1031654
46. Benko H, Feiner S (2007) Balloon selection: A multi-finger technique for accurate low-fatigue 3D selections. In: Proceedings of the IEEE symposium on 3D user interfaces, Charlotte, NC, pp 79–86
47. Matsuda M, Matsushita M, Yamada T, Namemura T (2006) Behavioral analysis of asymmetric information sharing on Lumisight table. In: Proceedings of the first IEEE international workshop on horizontal interactive human-computer systems, IEEE Computer Society, Washington, DC, pp 113–122, doi: 10.1109/TABLETOP.2006.6
48. Song H, Grossman T, Fitzmaurice G, Guimbretiere F, Khan A, Attar R, Kurtenbach G (2009) PenLight: Combining a mobile projector and a digital pen for dynamic visual overlay. In: Proceedings of the 27th international conference on human factors in computing systems, ACM Press, New York, pp 143–152, doi: 10.1145/1518701.1518726
49. Herndon KP, Zeleznik RC, Robbins DC, Conner DB, Snibbe SS, van Dam A (1992) Interactive shadows. In: Proceedings of the 5th annual ACM symposium on user interface software and technology, ACM Press, New York, pp 1–6, doi: 10.1145/142621.142622
50. McCauley M, Sharkey T (1992) Cybersickness: Perception of self-motion in virtual environments. Presence: Teleoperators and Virtual Environments 1(3):311–318
51. Baudel T, Beaudouin-Lafon M (1993) Charade: Remote control of objects using free-hand gestures. Communications of the ACM 36(7):28–35
52. Hinckley K, Pausch R, Goble JC, Kassell NF (1994) A survey of design issues in spatial input. In: Proceedings of the 7th annual ACM symposium on user interface software and technology, ACM Press, New York, pp 213–222, doi: 10.1145/192426.192501
53. Conner BD, Snibbe SS, Herndon KP, Robbins DC, Zeleznik RC, van Dam A (1992) Three-dimensional widgets. In: Proceedings of the 1992 symposium on interactive 3D graphics, ACM Press, New York, pp 183–188, doi: 10.1145/147156.147199
54. Venolia D (1993) Facile 3D direct manipulation. In: Proceedings of the INTERACT '93 and CHI '93 conference on human factors in computing systems, ACM Press, New York, pp 31–36, doi: 10.1145/169059.169065
55. Balakrishnan R, Baudel T, Kurtenbach G, Fitzmaurice G (1997) The Rockin' mouse: Integral 3D manipulation on a plane. In: Proceedings of the SIGCHI conference on human factors in computing systems, ACM Press, New York, pp 311–318, doi: 10.1145/258549.258778
56. Cechanowicz J, Irani P, Subramanian S (2007) Augmenting the mouse with pressure sensitive input. In: Proceedings of the SIGCHI conference on human factors in computing systems, ACM Press, New York, pp 1385–1394, doi: 10.1145/1240624.1240835

57. Balakrishnan R, Kurtenbach G (1999) Exploring bimanual camera control and object manipulation in 3D graphics interfaces. In: Proceedings of the SIGCHI conference on human factors in computing systems. ACM Press, New York, pp 56–62, doi: 10.1145/302979.302991

58. Liang J, Green M (1994) JDCAD: A highly interactive 3D modeling system. Computers and Graphics 18(4):5499–506

59. Scott SD, Carpendale MST, Inkpen KM (2004) Territoriality in collaborative tabletop workspaces. In: Proceedings of the 2004 ACM conference on computer supported cooperative work, ACM Press, New York, pp 294–303, doi: 10.1145/1031607.1031655

60. Kruger R, Carpendale MST, Scott SD, Greenberg S (2003) How people use orientation on tables: Comprehension, coordination and communication. In: Proceedings of the 2003 international ACM SIGGROUP conference on supporting group work, ACM Press, New York, pp 369–378, doi: 10.1145/958160.958219

61. Tang, JC (1991) Findings from observational studies of collaborative work. In: Greenberg S (ed) Computer-supported cooperative work and groupware, Academic Press Computers and People Series. Academic Press Ltd., London, pp 11–28

62. Shen C, Vernier FD, Forlines C, Ringel M (2004) DiamondSpin: An extensible toolkit for around-the-table interaction. In: Proceedings of the SIGCHI conference on human factors in computing systems, ACM Press, New York, pp 167–174, doi: 10.1145/985692.985714

63. Forlines C, Shen C, Wigdor D, Balakrishnan R (2006) Exploring the effects of group size and display configuration on visual search. In: Proceedings of the 2006, 20th anniversary conference on computer supported cooperative work, ACM Press, New York, pp 11–20, doi: 10.1145/1180875.1180878

64. Wigdor D, Balakrishnan R (2005) Empirical investigation into the effect of orientation on text readability in tabletop displays. In: Proceedings of the ninth conference on European conference on computer supported cooperative work, Springer-Verlag, New York, pp 205–224

65. Wigdor D, Shen C, Forlines C, Balakrishnan R (2007) Perception of elementary graphical elements in tabletop and multi-surface environments. In: Proceedings of the SIGCHI conference on human factors in computing systems, ACM Press, New York, pp 473–482, doi: 10.1145/1240624.1240701

66. Shen C, Ryall K, Forlines C, Esenther A, Vernier FD, Everitt K, Wu M, Wigdor D, Morris MR, Hancock M, Tse E (2006) Informing the design of direct-touch tabletops. IEEE Computer Graphics and Applications 26(5):36–46, doi: 10.1109/MCG.2006.109

67. Grossman T, Wigdor D, Balakrishnan R (2007) Exploring and reducing the effects of orientation on text readability in volumetric displays. In: Proceedings of the SIGCHI conference on human factors in computing systems, ACM Press, New York, pp 483–492, doi: 10.1145/1240624.1240702

Part III
Around and Beyond Tabletops

The last part of the book addresses research topics of Computer Supported Cooperative Work. Collaborators are *around tabletops* using the tabletop as common workspace for interacting and collaborating with digital information. The typical group around a tabletop setting is small in size and can also become distributed across multiple sites in scenarios of *beyond tabletops*. In that case the common workspace on a tabletop becomes shared across multiple sites and possibly accompanied with communication technologies.

Nactenta et al. start this part with an exploration of how different interaction techniques affect individual actions and group processes, and provide a detailed discussion of the design trade-offs of different interaction techniques. In the next chapter Collins and Kay focus on the topic of accessing digital information from personal file stores of users around tabletops and discuss their associative file access mechanism. Scott and Carpendale then present their work on a Theory of Tabletop Territoriality. These empirical and theoretical investigations further the understanding of social interaction practices around tabletop. The authors provide an overview of factors influencing the spatial properties of tabletop territories. In the following chapter Isenberg et al. emphasise the role of tabletop settings for collaborative visualization in work and learning environments as well as in public settings. The last two chapters go *beyond tabletops,* addressing the issue of collaboration around distributed tabletops. Tuddenham and Robinson present their work on remote tabletop interfaces and discuss exploratory studies investigating interaction techniques and work practices. Finally, Müller-Tomfelde and O'Hara discuss the role of tabletop settings in real-world scenarios introducing the notion of *distributed assemblies.* This work explores and discusses links between tabletop research and that in the domains of Ubiquitous Computer and Media Space.

Chapter 13
Individual and Group Support in Tabletop Interaction Techniques

Miguel A. Nacenta, David Pinelle, Carl Gutwin, and Regan Mandryk

Abstract A wide range of interaction techniques have been proposed for digital table systems. These techniques can vary in several ways – for example, some can manipulate objects from afar, whereas others require direct touch; some visually connect the cursor to the position of the user, whereas others simply assign different colours to different users. The differences in the way that these techniques are designed can lead to different experiences for the people around the table – particularly in terms of the support that is provided for either a person's individual actions or the group's overall aims. This chapter explores this issue – the ways that the design of an interaction technique can affect individual and group processes – and provides a detailed discussion of the design tradeoffs seen in selecting interaction techniques for tables. To organize the design space, we identify three perspectives (that of the action, the individual, and the group) that highlight different aspects of an interaction technique's design, and six criteria (performance, power, awareness, coordination, use of space, and preference) that allow assessment of a technique's support for individual and group concerns. We discuss the ways that different designs affect the six criteria, using empirical evidence from our own and others' previous experiments. Through this analysis, we demonstrate that different design decisions can have a large impact on people's experience in a tabletop task, and that designers should assess individual and group needs before selecting interaction techniques for tabletop groupware systems.

Introduction

Users of tabletop groupware manipulate computational artefacts using interaction techniques provided by the application. These techniques can vary in several ways – for example, some use virtual cursors (e.g., [1]), most use direct physical touch

M.A. Nacenta (✉)
Department of Computer Science, University of Calgary, Calgary, AB T2N 1N4, Canada
e-mail: miguel.nacenta@ucalgary.ca

C. Müller-Tomfelde (ed.), *Tabletops – Horizontal Interactive Displays*,
Human-Computer Interaction Series, DOI 10.1007/978-1-84996-113-4_13,
© Springer Verlag London Limited 2010

(e.g., [2]), and others use three-dimensional pointing (e.g., [3]). The way these techniques are designed can provide varying capabilities and limitations for users, and different techniques offer different advantages: some afford improved group awareness, but restrict users' ability to reach across the table; others allow reaching, but compromise awareness and may lead to an increase in the number of conflicts [4]. Ignoring the effects of interaction technique design can lead to systems that are unnecessarily hard to use, or that neglect basic social collaborative processes.

Our research has explored how different aspects of the design of interaction techniques affect collaboration; in this chapter, we summarize our work and present a higher-level analysis of how design decisions can affect both individual and group capabilities in tabletop collaboration. We consider the design of interaction techniques from three perspectives: that of the action itself, where we look at the effects of where input and feedback are located on the table; that of the individual's embodiment on the table (e.g., a virtual cursor); and that of the group, in which we consider the effects of policies governing access to resources. To evaluate and compare different interaction techniques we introduce six criteria that represent the concerns of both individuals and groups: performance, power, awareness, interference, space use and overall preference. We draw from our own work and others' results to present the tradeoffs of the different options and how they affect individual performance and group behaviour. The goal of this chapter is to introduce these important factors of the interaction-technique design space, and summarize how the factors affect both object manipulation and group process in tabletop systems.

Background

Our work was partially inspired by Scott and colleagues' survey of the design of tabletop systems [5]. This chapter extends that work by focusing on the consequences of the design of interaction techniques, which Scott et al. suggested as an area that required more attention. We summarize in this chapter three studies that were previously published [1, 4, 6] but in addition, we identify underlying concepts that are useful for characterizing tabletop interaction techniques, and discuss insights that we have arrived at through an extended investigation of interaction on tables.

Our chapter focuses on the design of interaction techniques for the manipulation of objects in co-located tabletops. Specifically, we are interested in interaction techniques that allow users to change the position of objects on the table, or to select and activate objects that are already on the table. Several other types of techniques exist that allow other actions on tabletops (e.g., selecting files from folders, or scrolling), but these techniques are studied elsewhere (e.g., Chapters 10 and 14), and fall outside of the scope of our studies. In addition, other parameters exist that are relevant to the tabletop scenario; for example, the size of the group and the size of the table. Although these parameters might affect the design of interaction techniques, we make the study of the design space tractable by choosing to focus on intrinsic factors of the techniques. We believe that our results, together with research that focuses on these other variables (e.g., [7, 8]) will be useful in the future to form a more complete picture of tabletop system design.

In our analysis, we also draw from other areas of HCI that are not specific to tabletops. For example, we discuss and analyze interaction techniques that were designed for other environments such as vertical large displays [9] and Multi-Display Environments (MDEs) [10, 11]. Although multi-display environments have specific issues of their own [12], some work that studies behaviour of groups in MDEs is also related to our own work (e.g., [13]). Other related work is brought up in the text where relevant.

An Analytical Framework for Tabletop Interaction Techniques

Our analysis of the design space of interaction techniques on tabletops is centred on the basic trade-off between designing for individuals and designing for groups [14]. This trade-off is further refined into six criteria: performance and power (which affect mostly the individual), awareness, conflict, and space management (which affect mostly groups), and individual preference, which provides a summarizing criterion as perceived by the users.

A Tradeoff Between Individual and Group Benefits

Designers of computer-supported collaborative systems often have to choose between favouring the work of the individual and facilitating group work [14]. This is particularly common in the design of groupware for distributed collaborative work (where people work out of different physical locations). For example, powerful techniques based on text input might provide quick interaction, but might also make it very difficult for users to stay aware of what everyone else is doing.

In co-located collaborative environments (e.g., multi-user tabletop systems) the information available about the group is richer because group members share a common physical space, making actions visible to everyone and making it easier to gather information about the group. This has often led researchers and designers to consider the co-located scenario as the ideal configuration for many collaborative activities.

As we introduce computer support into co-located collaborative settings, we also introduce new interaction possibilities that depart from non-computer-supported collaboration. For example, in a computer-supported environment it is possible to easily replicate a document so that several people can simultaneously manipulate it from separate locations, and it is possible to easily access distant regions of the workspace without having to walk around the room. Although these new possibilities extend the individual's capabilities beyond physical-world limitations, they can also alter the mechanisms that allow for natural coordination between collaborators.

The delicate balance between interaction that is beneficial for individuals and interaction that is beneficial for groups requires careful consideration when designing interaction techniques for tables. In the following subsections, we introduce the main criteria that we use to analyze how a design decision affects the individual and the group.

Individual Criteria for Judging Interaction Techniques

The goal of the individual in an interactive system is to accomplish tasks quickly and easily; individuals are therefore interested in what an interaction technique can do for them in terms of the task at hand, and how efficient and effective the techniques are. We therefore consider two criteria in the design of interaction techniques for object manipulation in interactive tabletop environments: performance and power.

Performance

The performance of an interaction technique is the speed or accuracy with which a user can execute tasks with that technique. Interaction techniques are often compared in the HCI literature using performance measures such as task completion time (speed), accuracy (magnitude and frequency of errors), or a combination of the two. These measures are usually tested in highly-controlled laboratory experiments with many repetitive short trials.

The results of these measures are usually reliable and easy to generalize to real environments because the tasks that are measured (e.g. pointing, steering and dragging) are frequent in real world scenarios. Performance improvement is often the goal of interaction technique design, because gains in accuracy or speed can accumulate over the course of a task and result in dramatically better overall performance, less frustration, and reduced workload.

Power

The power of a technique is determined by the types of actions and manipulations that the technique makes possible for the user [12]. One of the most important manifestations of power for our purposes is *reach*; techniques that can only operate within the physical reach of the user (i.e., within a meter of the user's position [15]) are less powerful than techniques that can access the whole space from any location. As we will see, individual power is also restricted if a user cannot grab objects that other users are manipulating.

The power of a technique is usually clearly defined by the design of the technique. Unlike performance, power can generally be understood by looking at the basic characteristics of a technique, without the need for empirical tests.

Group Criteria for Judging Interaction Techniques

The group as a whole has different requirements in a shared task than a single individual. We characterize the group perspective as being more interested in how well the group can work together, whether people are able to keep track of others' activities, and whether the group can organize itself efficiently. This division follows the idea that concerns in a shared activity can be divided into *taskwork* and *teamwork* [16]. Therefore, we look at three criteria below that have been frequently identified as important issues for teamwork: awareness, interference, and space use.

Group Awareness

Group awareness is the degree to which people perceive and understand others' activities in the shared task. Awareness information includes several elements, including information about *who* is working, *where* they are working (in the task and in the workspace), and *what* they are doing.

Awareness information has been identified as an important element of collaboration, and has been the subject of extensive study in the CSCW literature (e.g., [17, 18]). Group awareness is often difficult to measure and compare across techniques [19]; in our studies we report subjective measures of awareness and some objective measures; however, often we rely on indirect measures (such as conflict, discussed below) to determine how well people can use awareness information to coordinate their actions.

Interference

Interference involves actions that negatively affect the performance of another user [20]. A specific type of interference, which we call *conflict*, is the situation in which two or more people attempt to obtain the same resource. Interference and conflict can be a consequence of the lack of information awareness (previous subsection). Another type of interference is the visual obstruction of content by other users, since this can prevent the access to content or resources that are necessary to perform certain tasks.

Conflicts are relatively easy to detect and measure for certain tasks (e.g., by counting the number of times in a system log that people attempt to obtain the same object); interference can also be measured via subjective reports or observational analysis.

Space Use

The patterns of use of tabletop space can help reveal important aspects of collaboration. For example, it has been suggested that territoriality, (the partitioning of the work space in territories that enable different purposes) helps groups coordinate their actions [21]. In this chapter we do not discuss the nature of territoriality or whether it is a consequence or the cause of coordination (for a specific account of territoriality, see Chapter 15); our goal here is to present results on how space use differs with changes in interaction technique. These results are mostly presented in the form of activity maps that show the location and distribution of users' actions across the table surface.

User Preference as Criterion for Judging Interaction Techniques

The preference of users for a certain technique over another is also a useful criterion. We will generally assume that people report preference for techniques that are
beneficial for them as well as for the group, at least for cooperative tasks. Although
useful, preference is a complement to, and not a substitute for, other criteria because
it is important for us to find out the specific strengths and weaknesses of interaction
techniques, and preference is generally an aggregate variable of many factors.

We recognize that the criteria presented above are not comprehensive; other criteria have been suggested (e.g., equality of participation [22]). However, our criteria
represent phenomena and measures that have been used by several researchers to
better understand the effects of interaction techniques on tabletop collaboration. The
conceptual study of relationships between the criteria (e.g., is territorial space use a
consequence or an enabler of group awareness?), is beyond the scope of this chapter.

Three Perspectives on the Design of Tabletop Interaction Techniques

In addition to the group-centric and individualistic criteria introduced above, it is
important to look at interaction design from multiple perspectives, since different
views often capture and highlight different aspects of the design space. Therefore,
we consider three fundamental perspectives on the design of tabletop interaction
techniques: the action, the person, and the group.

- The action perspective deals with the specifics of the interaction technique and
  the ways that input and feedback are provided and supplied. Even this low level
  can have major effects on group concerns (such as awareness).
- The person perspective considers how interaction is carried out by a person in a
  tabletop system, and focuses on the representations of people in the groupware
  system (i.e., their embodiments).
- The group perspective looks at how overall policies and rules can affect both the
  efficacy of interaction techniques and support for group goals.

Each of these three perspectives corresponds to specific decisions in the design
of interaction techniques. In the following subsections we outline these perspectives
and the main design dimensions that they highlight.

The Action Perspective: Location of Input and Output

At the most basic level, interaction techniques allow individuals to translate their
own physical actions into actions in the virtual space (in our case, the manipulation
and translation of objects on the table). The first set of design decisions have to

do with which areas of the table are used to provide input for the technique, and which areas of the table will display the action's output. We define two regions for this analysis: *local space* and *shared space*. Local space is the area directly in front of the user; this space can be comfortably reached by the user, and it is generally not easy for other users to see or reach. Shared space is the area that is visible and accessible to several users. Note that the area in front of each user can in some cases be part of shared space, if it is used for input and output by other users of the table. The distinction between local space and shared space is therefore not only about distance to the users, but also about whether the table is being used to display a local access space for an individual user or a shared space where everyone can see and interact with task objects.

We assume that tabletop systems will generally be designed to share objects, such that a common set of virtual objects can be manipulated by several users. We also assume that the table is big enough to enable the existence of both local space and shared space.

Combinations of Input and Output Locations

The combinations of locations of input and visual output give rise to different interaction techniques (see Table 13.1). If input and output are in the same space, we have *direct input* techniques (shared input space, shared display space [9, 11, 23–26]). Input and output are also coincident in *world-in-miniature* (WIM) techniques,[1] but these use local input space and local output space [10, 11, 27, 28]. Note that pure world-in-miniature techniques are equivalent to having individual displays for each user, and this organization does not make much sense for tabletops,

Table 13.1 Examples of interaction techniques according to location of input space and feedback space

		Location of Output		
		Local	Local & Shared	Shared
Input space	Local	World-in-miniature	Radar, Vacuum, Drag-and-Pop	Telepointers Pantograph
	Local & Shared			TractorBeam
	Shared			Pick-and-drop Direct-touch MediaBlocks

---

[1] Word-in-miniature techniques could be considered direct-input techniques because the input and the output happen in the same space. However, in this chapter we consider world-in-miniature techniques as a separate category and we will use the term *direct input* to refer to techniques where input and output are both in the *shared* space.

since the majority of the display would not be used. A more meaningful setup with world-in-miniature techniques puts output in the individual areas *and* in the shared space (i.e., local input space, local and shared output space).

In opposition to direct-input techniques we have *indirect-input* techniques, which decouple the input and output spaces. Input is usually placed in local space, but the same output is shared by all. Examples of these techniques include mouse-operated techniques [29, 30], as well as finger- and pen-input extensions [9, 11, 31]. Note that dissociating the space in the opposite way (shared input space, local output space) makes little sense for obvious reasons.

A special type of technique are those that use laser-beam or finger-based pointing [3, 32–34]. These techniques provide a continuum between local input space and shared input space, and they can be used in a range of ways: completely from the user's local space, directly above the objects that users want to manipulate (shared space), or anywhere in between.

The Person Perspective: Embodiments

Embodiments are placeholders for people in shared workspaces [35, 36]. Embodiments are added to interaction techniques to provide users with feedback about their own actions, but they also help people stay aware of others' presence, location, and movement [17].

There are two types of embodiments that are used in tabletop systems, and each is associated with a different type of input. *Physical embodiments* use a person's actual body, and are common in direct-input systems where people manipulate objects by touching them with a pen or fingertip. *Virtual embodiments* show each person using a digital representation on the table surface; these kinds of embodiments are necessary with indirect-input systems, where people manipulate a cursor rather than touching objects directly, and where the virtual embodiment (i.e., the cursor) conveys information about people's actions. We discuss each embodiment type below, and describe design dimensions that can be used to develop virtual embodiments for tabletop systems.

Physical and Virtual Embodiments

Physical embodiments make use of the actual physical body of the user, and direct-input techniques, where both input and output are in the shared space, rely on physical embodiments. One of the main advantages of using direct input is that people can easily stay aware of others' interactions with the table, because they can see them physically reaching into the workspace [13].

In contrast, virtual embodiments are digital representations of users. They are common in distributed groupware, where people must rely on computer-mediated information to track others' actions. Telepointers, the simplest form of virtual embodiment, are widely used in shared-workspace groupware to represent each person's mouse cursor [37].

Virtual embodiments are used with indirect techniques on tabletops because the lack of direct contact makes it necessary to indicate the user's point of action in the workspace. However, virtual embodiments often provide little information about who is controlling each cursor [29, 32, 38], and this can negatively affect group processes. More explicit and better designed virtual embodiments have the potential to help people track others' actions more effectively when indirect techniques are used.

Virtual Embodiment Dimensions

The physical presence of people around the table makes it possible to develop new mappings between cursor and user that are not feasible in distributed groupware. Lines can be drawn from the user to their cursor, or cursor arrows can point directly at the user that controls them. In this section, we propose visual design dimensions that can be used in virtual embodiments for tables. Little previous work has been done in this area, so these dimensions are only an initial set that are based on our experiences working with tabletop embodiments. We discuss five main dimensions in this section: size, realism, line, identity indicator, and profile.

Size. Telepointers used in distributed groupware are small so that they do not occlude content. However, it can be difficult to track small cursors when they are far away in a large display [39].

Realism. Virtual embodiments can be abstract (e.g., telepointers), or can be more realistic and can resemble people's bodies or arms – such as the video arms used on distributed displays [40–42].

Line. User identity can be made more explicit in tabletop embodiments by drawing a line from the user's position to their cursor. This approach has been used in a version of the Pantograph technique (described by Hascoët [9]).

Identity indicator. Visual variables such as colour, texture, orientation, and shape can be used to help identify embodiments [36]; several of these variables have been used in distributed groupware (e.g., [37]). On tables they can be combined in new ways; for example, the orientation of an embodiment can dynamically change so that it always points to the user who controls it.

Profile. The visibility of virtual embodiments can change based on differences in several visual variables. Embodiments can have different levels of transparency, and can be painted on top of or behind digital artefacts on the table. Reducing visibility can help to minimize occlusion and distraction caused by embodiments, but it also can make awareness information harder to perceive.

The Group Perspective: Control Policies

Tabletop systems allow people to work closely together using a common display; however, working in close proximity in a common workspace introduces opportunities for people to interfere with each other, either intentionally or unintentionally. Several researchers have investigated how conflict and interference around tables can arise during collaboration and how it can be dealt with [7, 20, 43]. Others have also looked at how coupling (the degree to which one person's actions are dependent on another's) affects the distribution and use of shared resources among collaborators [38, 41].

Most tabletop systems do not provide support for coordination, leaving it to social protocol and negotiation between users. However, Morris and colleagues [43] found that people often have both "accidental and intentional conflicts" on tabletop systems and that more explicit support for coordination is needed. They concluded that global coordination policies may need to be added to tabletop systems to minimize conflicts between users. They also hypothesized that conflicts will become more common on tables as the number of users increases because it becomes harder to monitor the actions of all users. They proposed several global coordination mechanisms. Notable among these are: (1) making all elements accessible to everyone and relying on social protocols, (2) allowing users to lock objects so that others cannot access them, (3) giving each user a ranking, and allowing higher ranking users to take objects from lower ranking users, and (4) allowing physical measurements, including speed and force applied by the user, to determine who is able to retrieve a contested object.

Other approaches for providing coordination policies are possible. Instead of using deterministic policies, we can implement control policies within the interaction techniques that determine which users can gain control of a shared object in different circumstances. These rules can be based on many different factors; in our initial exploration, we looked at two ways to dynamically assign *control levels*: through explicit control by the user, and according to the distance to their personal territory.

The Effect of Design Decisions on Individual and Group Criteria

In the previous two sections we presented the basic elements of our analysis of the design space: a set of criteria to evaluate the effects of interaction techniques, and three perspectives on the design space that correspond to specific design decisions for interaction techniques. In the rest of the chapter, we will use empirical results from three related studies [1, 4, 6] to investigate how the design decisions affect our criteria.

It is important to note that a given design aspect does not necessarily affect all criteria. For each combination of design factors, Table 13.2 shows the criteria for which our studies can show evidence of effects.

In the following subsections we briefly summarize our studies and present the most important results, organized according to the list of individual and group criteria. For a detailed description of each of the studies, refer to the original papers. Although each of the studies corresponds roughly to one of the design aspects, there is some overlap between study I and II in that both investigate aspects of input/output and embodiments.

Table 13.2 The crossing between design decisions and the criteria they affect

| Design aspect | Criteria | | | | | |
	Power	Performance	Awareness	Interference and conflict	Space use	Preference
Input/output	√	√	√	√	√	√
Embodiments			√	√	√	√
Control policies	√			√	√	√

Study I: Input, Output and Embodiments

In our first study [4], we focused on techniques that differ in the location of input and output, and also introduced limited variation in the type of embodiment (followed up in more detail in study II).

Apparatus

Our tabletop system consists of a large top-projected tabletop surface (125 × 160 cm, 1,024 × 1,536 pixels – see Fig. 13.1) with three magnetically-tracked pens for input (Polhemus Liberty). All software was custom-designed and programmed for the studies.

Fig. 13.1 An image of our tabletop setup

Study Design Summary

For this experiment we designed two collaborative tasks. The first task, a cooperative game, was designed to test coordination, synchronization and possibility of conflict. In the game, participants had to quickly move shapes into bins that were distributed across the table. Individuals all worked together to achieve a high group score (there were no individual scores, and therefore, no encouragement for competition). The rules of the game ensured that cooperation was needed and that being aware of other's actions would result in better scores. Our intention was to gain insight into activities with high time demands and with clear performance goals.

The second task was a storyboarding activity in which participants had to arrange digital pictures to form a story. This task was designed to be similar to open-ended design and planning work that occurs in everyday office settings.

We tested 10 groups of three participants in either of the two tasks (five in the game task, five in the storyboard task). Each group performed the assigned task five times, once with each of five interaction techniques (see also Fig. 13.2):

- Drag-and-drop (shared input space, shared feedback space, physical embodiment). Users select an object by touching it with the pen, and deselect by lifting the pen from the tabletop. Users can move objects by dragging the tip of their pen across the table.

Drag-and-drop

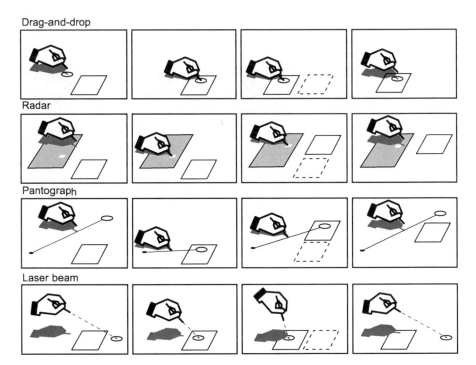

Fig. 13.2 Moving an object with different interaction techniques. The *circle* in rows 1, 3, and 4 represents the cursor; the *grey rectangle* in row 2 is the radar's workspace miniature. Telepointers (not shown) is identical to Pantograph but without the line connecting the cursor to the pen tip

- Radar view (local input, local and shared feedback, no visible embodiment). A miniature of the entire workspace (32×24 cm, 1/5 scale) is displayed in front of each user. Users manipulate the content of the larger tabletop from within the miniature. Others' cursors, each with a different colour, are visible in the miniature, but no representation of users is shown in the shared space.
- Pantograph (local input space, shared feedback space, line embodiment). The user moves the pen in her local input space as with radar; however, there is no workspace miniature. Instead, the cursor position is proportional to the position of the pen (5X) so that the whole table can be reached with little movement. A coloured line is drawn from the cursor to the tip of the pen.
- Telepointers (local input space, shared feedback space, small cursor embodiment). Telepointers are equivalent to the Pantograph but without the line that connects the cursor to the pen.
- Laser Beam (local or shared input, shared feedback, small cursor embodiment). Users hold the pen above the table and point the tip at the desired location. The cursor is shown at the point where an imaginary line extending from the pen's tip intersects with the tabletop plane. To select an object, the user clicks the stylus button; a selected object can be moved by pointing the pen at a new location on the table.

The techniques selected for our study were chosen to represent different design choices of the input/output and embodiments design aspects. Drag-and-drop is the only pure direct-touch technique, where the input and output both take place in the shared space. The Radar technique is a world-in-miniature technique that provides input and output in the local space, although it also provides output simultaneously in the shared area. Telepointers and Pantograph both provide input and output that are dissociated (indirect input). The laser beam is a hybrid technique, since the input can gradually go from local space (pointing from a distance) to direct touch.

In terms of embodiments, Drag-and-drop does not require any virtual embodiment because the embodiment is the physical body of the participant. The Radar lacks a shared-space embodiment; Telepointers rely on the small coloured pointer in shared space. The Pantograph is equivalent to Telepointers, except that its virtual embodiment also connects the physical location of the user with the location of the circular cursor; therefore the Pantograph has a more explicit embodiment than Telepointers. Finally, the Laser Beam's embodiment goes gradually from just a cursor (when the pen is operated from afar), to a physical embodiment (when the pointer is operated near to the manipulated object).

Summary of Findings According to the Criteria

Performance

The highest scores in the game task were obtained with the Drag-and-drop and Radar techniques. For the same techniques we also observed more activity (more frequent object movements). These results confirm previous studies that have found that having input and output in the same place is generally superior in performance [11, 44].

Surprisingly, the performance measures for the laser pointer were similar to the indirect techniques, and not to Drag-and-drop or Radar. Our observations indicate that users definitely prefer to use the pointer from a distance rather than physically move around the table to an object; however, we also saw that distance pointing was cumbersome and that overall performance was reduced, even though participants had the option of using the laser pointer as a Drag-and-drop technique when targets were nearby. This result confirms the findings of a longitudinal study of the Tractor Beam technique [32].

Power

The Power characteristics of our techniques are derived by inspection. It is evident that the only technique that has restricted power is Drag-and-drop because it is the only technique that requires physical reach to access distant parts of the table (shared input and output space). The power of techniques is reflected in the answers of participants to questions related to ease of reach; participants clearly preferred indirect techniques for access to distance areas. Radar was ranked best for this purpose, and Drag-and-drop worst.

Awareness

Although in this study we did not design an explicit measure of awareness, we did ask participants which techniques made it easier to transfer objects to others, which incorporates some elements of awareness. Participants ranked Drag-and-Drop and Pantograph as best for the transfer of objects, and stated that these techniques made it easier to track where people were working in the workspace (i.e., they provided better location awareness information), and therefore facilitated the timely transfer of objects.

Interference

The main measure of interference in this study was the number of conflicts (we defined conflicts as two or more people trying to grab the same object simultaneously). Because our game was collaborative, and since simultaneous touch of an object would prevent the use of the object to obtain points, we can assume that simultaneous touches were always inadvertent conflicts and a source of interference.

We found that people had significantly more conflicts with Radar than they did with any other technique. These results suggest that using local space for input and output weakens people's ability to anticipate and prevent conflicts. While carrying out the experiments, we also observed that with the Radar, participants focused on their miniature maps and tended to ignore the shared space. This result is consistent with studies of collaboration with personal displays, which show that the quality of collaboration is reduced when people are given the opportunity to work separately in private space instead of encouraging the common use of displays [45].

In the subjective measures, users reported that Drag-and-drop and the Pantograph were best to avoid conflicts. The physical embodiment of the Drag-and-drop technique and the virtual embodiment of the Pantograph were perceived as helpful to avoid conflicts.

Space Use

Our experimental application recorded activity maps during the sessions to summarize the amount of activity by different users on different parts of the table. Every time that a user clicked on an object, released an object, dragged the cursor or moved the cursor, it left a trace on the maps (Fig. 13.3). Each participant left traces of a different colour (Red, Green or Blue). These maps allow us to tell how often different parts of the table were used with the different techniques.

The maps show obvious differences in the movement patterns of both the tasks and the interaction techniques. The structure of each task shows up in the activity maps but, most importantly, differences between techniques show up as differences in the distribution of the colours.

The most obvious differences in activity distributions appear between Drag-and-drop, Laser Beam, and the rest of the techniques. Drag-and-drop and Laser Beam exhibit similar spatial distribution; the actions of users are concentrated in certain

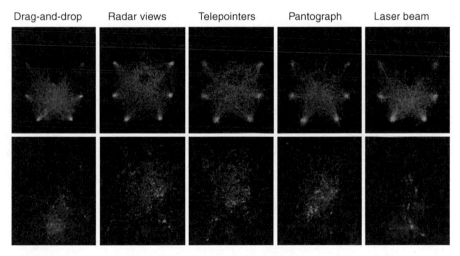

Fig. 13.3 Movement maps for all techniques in the game task (*first row*) and the storyboard task (*second row*). Each map aggregates data across groups. Each of the primary colours (*blue, green, red*) represents the users sitting to the *left, bottom,* and *right* of the image respectively. *Higher colour* intensity represents a higher number of cursor movements in that pixel. *White pixels* are points accessed equally by all users

areas and do not overlap much with the other users' actions. This is not very surprising for Drag-and-drop, because people's reach is restricted with this technique. It is striking, however, that Laser Beam (similar to Radar Views, Telepointers and Pantograph in that it can provide access to the shared space from local input for the whole table), showed a pattern more similar to the confined areas of Drag and Drop. This effect might be due to the increased difficulty of using the Laser Beam at a distance.

The other three techniques that have local input (Radar Views, Telepointers and Pantograph) show more homogeneous maps, which indicates that users take advantage of local input to access all areas of the display. However, the difference in distribution between Telepointers and Pantograph (more concentrated for Pantograph) suggests that the nature of the output (the two techniques only differ in this aspect) affects the use that is made of the space.

Preference

One of the most relevant findings from the preference results is that techniques are valued differently according to the task. In particular, Fig. 13.4 shows clearly that Radar view was a popular technique for the game task, but was considered worse than any other technique for the storyboard task. From the comments of the users, we know that with the storyboard task, the Radar did not provide enough fidelity to adequately see and monitor others' actions and artefacts in the miniature view, forcing users to repeatedly switch their focus from local to shared feedback space. Overall, these results show that the nature of the task plays a fundamental role in the choice of techniques.

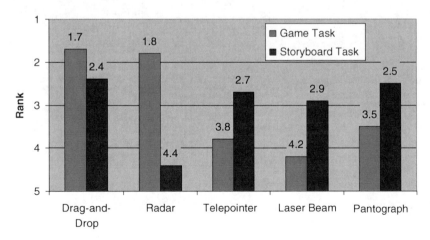

Fig. 13.4 Preferred techniques (*taller bars* are better)

Study II: Physical and Virtual Embodiments

Our second study [1] further investigated the effects of embodiments, both physical and virtual. For virtual embodiments, the study manipulated several variables that change the appearance of the technique. The apparatus was identical to the apparatus described for study I.

Study Design Summary

Study II compared seven embodiment techniques – a direct-touch technique and six indirect-input techniques that used virtual embodiments. The main goals of the study were to determine the differences between physical and virtual embodiments, and to determine the effect of these differences on collaboration and preference.

The six virtual embodiment techniques used in the study cover the embodiment design dimensions described earlier in the chapter. They were implemented as variations of the Telepointers and Pantograph techniques described in the previous study (local input space, shared output space). The embodiments were drawn in a different colour for each of the participants (red, blue, or green). The different variations of the embodiments follow (see also Fig. 13.5):

- *Circle*. Equivalent to Telepointers in Study I.
- *Arrow*. Cursors are represented using an opaque arrow that always points to the user that controls it.
- *Narrow Pantograph*. Equivalent to the Pantograph from study I, but with a translucent line.
- *Wide Pantograph in front*. Equivalent to the narrow Pantograph, except ten times wider.
- *Wide Pantograph in back*. Equivalent to the wide Pantograph in front, except the line is painted behind the objects on the table.
- *Arm*. Similar to the pantograph techniques, except an arm is used to represent the user's cursor. The arm width is the same as that of the wide pantograph techniques, and it is always painted in front of objects.
- *Direct-touch*. Equivalent to Drag-and-Drop in Study I.

We tested seven groups of three participants while they carried out a photo grouping task where they sorted 80 pictures into three different categories. The participants were asked to work together, positioning the pictures so that they did not overlap, and so that they were grouped with other pictures in the category.

We assessed participants' awareness of others' cursor position by freezing the task at random intervals, making the cursors and embodiments disappear, and asking the participants to estimate the table position where each user was working. This measure is based in Endsley's SAGAT [19, 46].

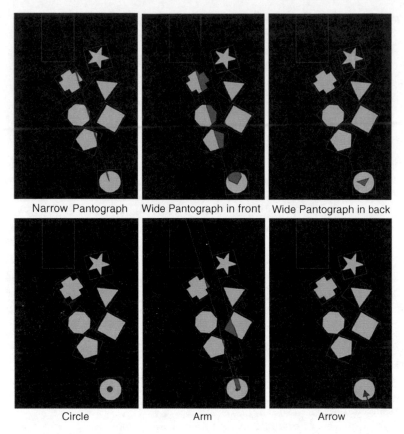

Narrow Pantograph   Wide Pantograph in front   Wide Pantograph in back

Circle   Arm   Arrow

Fig. 13.5 Virtual embodiments. User controlling embodiment sits at the *top*, where the input *rectangle* is shown

Summary of Findings According to the Criteria

Awareness – Objective Differences

People were significantly more accurate in identifying others' locations with Direct-touch than any virtual embodiment by a difference of approximately 12 cm. One possible explanation is that physical arms do, as expected, provide better awareness than virtual embodiments. This is a reasonable explanation, both because people are experienced at interpreting the motions of others' arms, and because arms are obvious physical features that exist in the 3D space above the table (rather than 2D images on the table surface). Another explanation is that the increased accuracy could be due to people's understanding of how far people can reach with direct touch.

Awareness – Subjective Differences

In contrast to the freeze data, people rated all three of the large virtual embodiments (Arm, wide Pantograph in front, and wide Pantograph in back) as easier to keep track of than the physical arms of Direct-touch. It is not clear why these subjective results differ from the results of the freeze test; one explanation is that people rated the visibility of the embodiment instead of their perceived awareness of other's actions.

This could also explain the discrepancy between the low subjective rankings for the small embodiments (Line, Arrow, and Circle) and their equally-accurate freeze test results. However, it might be possible that the freeze method did not accurately measure the effect that we were interested in, or was not powerful enough (in the statistical sense) to detect differences, while the users might have understood the benefits of more visible embodiments.

Interference

We asked people to rank techniques according to how distracting they were, and according to how much the embodiments interfered with their task. We were surprised that no significant differences emerged in the ranking of the techniques, as some embodiments were dramatically larger.

We suggest three explanations for these results. First, it is possible that distraction has more to do with interruption in terms of the task, and less to do with simple visual information. That is, even though some of the embodiments were large, they did not break people's focus on their individual work. Similarly, it may be that large objects are not necessarily distracting if they behave in predictable ways, allowing people to accommodate to, and therefore ignore, the incoming information. This is certainly true with real arms; they are large, but were seen in our study as least distracting. Third, it is possible that small embodiments cause distraction because they make it harder to identify the embodiment's owner, equalizing the distraction caused by the additional visual information of techniques with larger embodiments.

Space Use

The study showed large differences between physical and virtual embodiments and the amount of time spent in others' personal territories. People spent more time in others' territories with virtual embodiments, and it is clear that when people have a virtual embodiment, they do spend more time intruding. As with the objective awareness measure, the simple physical limits of reach explains this difference.

Contrary to the results of Study I, we did not find differences in the spatial distribution of activity between the different virtual embodiment techniques. This result does not refute the earlier finding, however, since the tasks were different, and the strong layout nature of the sorting task might have masked the effects of the line connection.

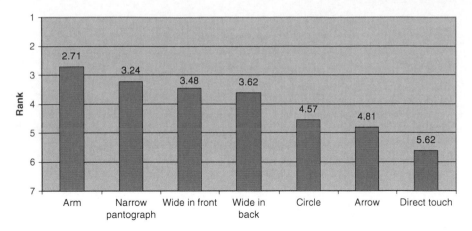

Fig. 13.6 Mean preference ranking by technique (*taller bars* mean better ranking)

Preference

We asked participants to rank the techniques according to overall preference. As can be seen in Fig. 13.6, there are substantial differences in the mean ranks given to the different techniques, with Arm ranked highest (mean rank 2.7 of 7) and Direct-touch ranked lowest (mean rank 5.6 of 7).

Arm had the highest average ranking, and most people (14 of 21) preferred it over the wide Pantograph techniques, which had the same width and transparency levels. People's comments showed that they liked the Arm embodiment because it was more natural, and felt more like an extension of their real arm. The disconnected techniques (Circle and Arrow) both had low average rankings. Several participants stated that they found it difficult to keep track of others with these cursors because there was no visible connection to the person, and that the colour mappings were difficult to remember.

Direct-touch was ranked the lowest by 14 of 21 participants. Comments suggested that people disliked the technique for two main reasons: the limitations on reaching distance, and the physical effort that was required to access objects. These results contradict what was found in the previous study, but the differences are, again, likely the cause of the difference in the task. Nevertheless, the low ranking for the Direct-touch technique in this study is important because it shows that indirect techniques are preferred to direct touch in some situations.

Study III: Control Policies

In our third study [6], we evaluated three new group coordination policies for indirect-input techniques. These coordination policies were designed to preserve the benefits of indirect techniques (e.g., quick access to all areas of the table) while also addressing the issues of decreased coordination and decreased territorial space use that accompany indirect input (as observed in studies I and II).

Study Design Summary

Each coordination policy that we created allows users to protect objects from being taken by others, but the protection is dynamic and is not absolute. All policies operate using the concept of a numeric variable, called a control level, which is set dynamically either by the system or through user input. A user with a higher control level can prevent others from taking an object in her possession, and can also steal objects from others with a lower control level. Each policy uses a slightly different approach for setting the dynamic control level.

The two *automatic* approaches set the control level based on how close the user's cursor is to their personal territory – the closer to their territory that the user operates, the higher her control level. In one version (*automatic object*) the system applies the control level to protect objects currently held by the user's cursor, while in the other version (*automatic territory*), the control level is applied to objects in the user's personal territory. The third approach (*user control*) applies the control level to objects currently held by the user's cursor through real-time user-specified control levels, regardless of the location of their cursor. The apparatus was the same as in the previous two experiments, except that input was provided by four mice with pressure sensors on the left side. The pressure sensor was used to set the control level in the *user control* technique, with more pressure resulting in higher control levels.

We carried out an evaluation of the interaction techniques where six groups of three people used the three techniques as well as a baseline technique where no control levels were applied. Each group used all techniques while playing a competitive tabletop game designed to encourage a high level of interaction between the players, and to encourage players to take objects from each other.

The main goal of the study was to evaluate the effect that the different coordination policies would have on several aspects of group interaction, including conflicts, space use, and access patterns. Note that in this study the task was competitive, and therefore the nature of interference is substantially different (it is good to generate interference for other users). We designed a competitive task because it allowed us to observe many occurrences of conflicts and to assess how the different policies affect behaviour in a controlled environment. Although these results need to be validated with a realistic, non-competitive task, the results are useful as mild competitive scenarios are part of many tasks (e.g., negotiation), and users often need to secure their individual goals even in collaborative scenarios.

Summary of Findings According to the Criteria

Power

The analysis of power in the design of control policies requires subtle distinctions. On one side, techniques with control policies are limited in power, since they do not allow access to every object at all times. On the other side, unrestricted access limits the power of other participants to manipulate objects without interruption of the action. Since not all users can have all power simultaneously, the way in which power is distributed becomes important. In our explorations we mapped power dynamically to a continuous range of distance or user control; this distribution of power is more complex than not regulating power at all or that using binary controls such as those from distributed systems (e.g., [47]). However, our approach can help modulate some aspects of the group behaviour, as indicated through the other measures of our study.

Interference

We logged the number of times people stole objects from other users, and we organized the analysis according to whether the object was being held by another user or whether the object was in another user's personal territory. The automatic territory technique had the fewest thefts in both categories. There was a significant difference in the average number of thefts occurring from users' cursors, with automatic territory having significantly fewer thefts than automatic object (see Fig. 13.7, left; no value is shown for the "no control" condition since these thefts were not possible with this condition). For thefts from others' territories, there was a significant difference between automatic territory and all other techniques (Fig. 13.7, right).

The territorial space use and protection benefits seen in our study show that techniques with automatic control policies have the potential to help overcome some of the conflicts seen with indirect input. Other problems, such as people working in others' territories, are less likely since it is more difficult to take items from others when working far from the home position. Further, the automatic territory-based policies could also prevent other types of disruptive behaviour beyond the movement or theft of objects; for example, continuous reorientation of documents could be avoided.

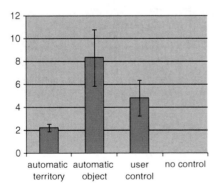 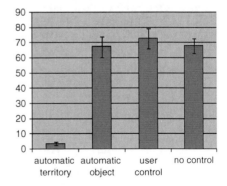

Fig. 13.7 Means (± SE) of the number of objects stolen from users' cursors (*left*) and the average number of objects stolen from users' personal territories by coordination policy (*right*)

Fig. 13.8 Mouse movements
for a representative user
sitting at the *right side* of the
table

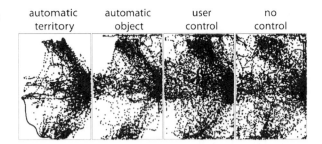

| automatic | automatic | user | no |
| territory | object | control | control |

Space Use

One of the main benefits of indirect techniques is that they allow people to quickly
access all areas of the table. Figure 13.8 shows movement maps that record every
time a user moved their mouse cursor in the study. When people used the "no control" and "user control" techniques, they accessed most areas of the table, and did
not spend the majority of their time working in their personal territories. However,
log results and movement maps show that when people used automatic coordination techniques – which gave them protection advantages when they worked in
close physical proximity to themselves – they spent more time near their personal
territory.

Most users indicated that the automatic techniques supported an increased awareness of territorial use of the table. They stated that they were more aware of their
personal territories, and half of the users indicated that they were more aware of
others' territories as well. Several participants' pointed out that with user control,
they did not pay as much attention to space use. Our results show that automatic
control policies based on personal territories reinforce territorial space use.

Preference

In spite of the more restricted use of space seen with automatic techniques, people
preferred them. People had a strong preference for the automatic territory technique
since it helped them to avoid having objects stolen by others. They strongly disliked
the user control technique because of the extra effort required to constantly set the
control level (by pushing the pressure sensor). The automatic techniques did not
require extra effort, and automatically adjusted the level of protection based on the
location of the user's cursor. Our results suggest that people are willing to accept
restrictions in how much of the table they routinely access in favour of having more
protection over the objects they are using.

General Discussion

In the previous sections we have provided an overview of the results of three studies
on three areas of the design space of interaction techniques for tabletop systems. In

this section we discuss some of the implications of the results in combination with previous research in the area and the limitations of our analyses. The section ends with Table 13.3, which highlights the main results of Study I, II and II organized by criteria.

The Action Perspective: The Location of Input and Output

Our results from studies I and II show how manipulating the input and output locations of interaction techniques can significantly affect many aspects of tabletop use. From the point of view of the individual, the data from our studies suggests that direct input (which usually implies having input and output in the same space) provides superior performance on tabletops. This is confirmed for tabletop settings by other research that focused specifically on performance aspects [44, 11]. From the group's perspective, having input and output in the shared space has advantages for awareness, at least in the collaborators' judgments. Hornecker and colleagues [20] arrived at similar conclusions as our studies: that is, direct input results in higher levels of awareness.

However, placing input and output in the shared space also poses important problems. It often came across in our work that the power of direct input is limited by reach (also discussed in [11, 15]). In addition, the physical presence of arms and hands can make it difficult for people to collaborate very closely due to physical obstruction or occlusion of the content [48].

There are several alternatives to direct input that do not suffer from these same problems. For example, world-in-miniature techniques provide access to the whole table from the local input space, therefore eliminating physical interference; WIM techniques also happen to provide the best individual performance, even superior to direct touch (see the Performance section in Study I, and [11]). However, we have shown that although the Radar (our WIM technique) also provides output in the shared space, it results in many more conflicts, likely due to the lack of useful awareness information. These results are consistent with Haué and Dillenbourg's study [45], which found that using personal spaces for interaction (laptops in their case) impairs coordination.

Between direct input and WIMs are the techniques that operate in the local space but show output in the shared space. These indirect-input techniques are powerful and avoid most of the problems of Direct-touch and WIMs such as occlusion, physical interference and poor awareness information. In fact, participant preferences in study II suggest that, in some cases, indirect input is preferable to direct input.

However, studies I and II indicate that the awareness information is not comparable to that of direct touch. Nevertheless, it might be possible to improve awareness in these techniques and achieve a good balance through the design of embodiments, which we discuss in the next subsection.

The Person Perspective: Embodiments

Studies I and II show that embodiments can change the spatial behaviour of users, their preference towards a technique, and their perceived awareness information. This evidence suggests that the design of interaction techniques should pay close attention to the specific design of the feedback and, more specifically, to how the person is represented in the shared space.

In particular, we found that connecting the physical position of the user with the cursor (for indirect techniques) facilitates the acquisition of information about who is doing what where. Although our second study did not find significant differences between different indirect embodiments in terms of objective awareness, subjective rankings and comments from users show perceived differences.

Changes in the size and visibility of the visually-connected embodiments did not significantly affect most of the criteria (e.g. awareness, space use). However, the arm embodiment was perceived differently, and was preferred by many users, probably because it makes the cursor feel like a more natural extension of the body.

The Group Perspective: Control Policies

Study III looked at how control policies can affect group behaviour. Although we tested a small subset of solutions, our results showed that manipulating control policies can be a useful tool to encourage or discourage certain kinds of group behaviour. Basing the control policy on the region of a user's interaction will promote territorial space use and allow users to more easily protect their artefacts. This region-based approach will likely decrease conflicts and interference as protecting artefacts is easier and users may have to explicitly communicate their need for a shared resource in another user's personal territory. In addition, the control policy choice affects the distribution of an individual's power over the table surface. With a region-based approach, a user has greater power to interact with artefacts close to their personal territory, while a user-controlled approach distributes power evenly to users over the entire table surface.

Our study was the first to investigate dynamic control power at multiple levels and covers only a small set of design options. More work is needed to test other designs, the effects of providing users with multiple levels of control versus the ability to lock or unlock artefacts, and cooperative – rather than competitive – scenarios. We also need to investigate how control policies can be applied beyond the control of shared objects to other aspects of interaction, such as the access of cursors to certain regions of the table.

The Individual Versus Group Trade-Off

As is usually the case in interaction design, most of the choices that we have discussed in this chapter involve tradeoffs. In particular, the tradeoffs between the needs of individual and the group persist throughout our studies. For example, we now know that prioritizing the individual criteria of performance and power when designing the input and output of a technique (i.e., choosing a WIM) can be detrimental to group processes by resulting in increased conflicts and poor awareness. Also, the best embodiment possible for conveying group awareness information (the physical arm) is limited in individual power by the constraints of the real world. Similarly, control policies might limit the power of what a specific user can do, but might help keep conflicts in the group to a minimum.

The existence of a trade-off does not mean that designers face a zero-sum problem in which it does not matter what design is chosen; on the contrary, by understanding the tradeoffs and goals of the particular scenario, a skilled designer can find the best solution for the problem at hand. The main goal of this chapter is to encourage designers and researchers to pay careful attention to the individual's interaction needs on tabletops, as well as the consequences of their designs for group processes. We also suggest elements of the design that can be manipulated to optimize interaction for specific scenarios: the relation between the input and output spaces, embodiments, and control policies.

Table 13.3 Summary of findings by criteria

	Performance	Power	Awareness	Interference	Space use	Preference
Action	• Performance dependent on task • Direct touch best overall	• Direct touch restricted by reach	• Physical embodiment best • Importance of connecting cursor and user	• Radar worst (lack of shared-space embodiment)	• Major differences between direct and indirect	• Direct touch best • Pantograph best of indirect techniques
Person			• Better awareness with direct touch • Subjective differences found for indirect techniques	• No major differences in distraction across any technique	• Differences between direct and indirect • No differences within indirect	• Arm (indirect) best • Direct touch worst
Group		• Policies limit power	• Reduced need for vigilance to avoid conflicts	• Large differences between automatic and manual policies	• Controls increased territoriality	• Automatic territory techniques best

Limitations and Future Work

Our research raises several questions that need to be addressed through additional research, and it also creates design opportunities for those attempting to develop new interaction techniques. In this section, we discuss several future directions for tabletop research and development.

Task dimensions. In study I, we found that the choice of task strongly affected personal preference for interaction techniques. However, this study only raises the issue that task and technique interact; the reasons for this variability are still open to speculation and require further study. Currently, the dimensions that are relevant to selecting and specifying tabletop tasks for experimental purposes (e.g. coupling levels, task structure, cognitive vs. physical demands, etc.) are poorly understood, making it challenging to choose representative tasks and to understand why specific results are found. Future research should work toward developing a deeper understanding of task, and this should allow the interplay between task and design to be considered more extensively.

Group dimension and other factors. The studies discussed in this chapter focused specifically on interaction techniques, and generally kept other factors constant. For example, we included groups that were made up of three or four people. Others have shown, however, that group size has an effect on the group process [7, 8], and increased group size seems to increase the coordination overhead needed to carry out a group activity. In the future it will be important to test group size and other factors (such as work style or group organization) in combination with the design of interaction techniques to extend our understanding to more general settings.

Emerging dimensions and techniques. The frameworks presented in this chapter were based on an analysis of current interaction techniques. However, new tabletop interaction techniques continue to be introduced and show surprising variability. In the future, new dimensions may need to be considered. Further, there is ample opportunity to use the dimensions presented in this chapter, and to recombine them to develop new interaction techniques. Last, although our analysis of input and output variables covers most existing techniques, our work represents only a first step in the coverage of the design space of embodiments and control policies. Additional work is needed to explore the design space further.

Conclusion

In this chapter we investigated the design tradeoffs inherent in selecting interaction techniques for tabletop groupware systems. We discussed three perspectives on the design space: action, person, and group; and identified key design issues that are highlighted by each perspective (input and feedback, embodiments, and group policies). In addition, we identified six criteria that can assess and compare techniques in terms of support for both individual and group concerns. We explored this analytical framework using empirical data from three of our own studies; our experiments evaluated a range of interaction techniques, and provided a comprehensive look at direct and indirect interaction on tables. The information in this chapter can be used by tabletop researchers and developers to select appropriate interaction techniques, to design new interaction techniques, and to motivate future research.

References

1. Pinelle D, Nacenta M, Gutwin C, Stach T (2008) The effects of co-present embodiments on awareness and collaboration in tabletop groupware. In: Proceedings of graphics interface 2008, Canadian Information Processing Society, Windsor, ON, pp 1–8
2. Dietz P, Leigh D (2001) DiamondTouch: A multi-user touch technology. In: Proceedings of the 14th annual ACM symposium on user interface software and technology, ACM Press, Orlando, FL, pp 219–226, doi: 10.1145/502348.502389
3. Parker JK, Mandryk RL, Inkpen KM (2005) TractorBeam: Seamless integration of local and remote pointing for tabletop displays. In: Proceedings of graphics interface 2005, Canadian Human-Computer Communications Society, Victoria, BC, pp 33–40
4. Nacenta MA, Pinelle D, Stuckel D, Gutwin C (2007) The effects of interaction technique on coordination in tabletop groupware. In: Proceedings of graphics interface 2007, ACM Press, Montréal, QC, pp 191–198, doi: 10.1145/1268517.1268550
5. Scott SD, Grant KD, Mandryk RL (2003) System guidelines for co-located, collaborative work on a tabletop display. In: Proceedings of the eighth conference on European conference on computer supported cooperative work, Kluwer Academic Publishers, Helsinki, Finland, pp 159–178
6. Pinelle D, Barjawi M, Nacenta M, Mandryk R (2009) An evaluation of coordination techniques for protecting objects and territories in tabletop groupware. In: Proceedings of the 27th international conference on human factors in computing systems, ACM Press, Boston, MA, pp 2129–2138, doi: 10.1145/1518701.1519025
7. Ryall K, Forlines C, Shen C, Morris MR (2004) Exploring the effects of group size and table size on interactions with tabletop shared-display groupware. In: Proceedings of the 2004 ACM conference on computer supported cooperative work, ACM Press, Chicago, IL, pp 284–293, doi: 10.1145/1031607.1031654
8. Inkpen K, Hawkey K, Kellar M, Mandryk R, Parker K, Reilly D, Scott S, Whalen T (2005) Exploring display factors that influence co-located collaboration: Angle, size, number, and user arrangement. In: Proceedings of HCI international 2005, Las Vegas, NV
9. Hascoët M (2003) Throwing models for large displays. In: Proceedings of HCI 2003, British HCI Group, pp 73–77
10. Baudisch P, Cutrell E, Robbins D, Czerwinski M, Tandler P, Bederson B, Zierlinger A (2003) Drag-and-pop and drag-and-pick: Techniques for accessing remote screen content on touch- and pen-operated systems. In: Proceedings of interact 2003, vol 3, pp 1–5
11. Nacenta MA, Aliakseyeu D, Subramanian S, Gutwin C (2005) A comparison of techniques for multi-display reaching. In: Proceedings of the SIGCHI conference on human factors in computing systems, ACM Press, Portland, OR, pp 371–380, doi: 10.1145/1054972.1055024
12. Nacenta MA, Gutwin C, Aliakseyeu D, Subramanian S (2009) There and back again: Cross-display object movement in multi-display environments. Human-Computer Interaction 24(1):170–229
13. Ha V, Inkpen K, Mandryk R, Whalen T (2006) Direct intentions: The effects of input devices on collaboration around a tabletop display. In: Horizontal interactive human-computer systems, 2006. TableTop 2006. First IEEE international workshop on, p 8, doi: 10.1109/TABLETOP.2006.10

14. Gutwin C, Greenberg S (1998) Design for individuals, design for groups: Tradeoffs between power and workspace awareness. In: Proceedings of the 1998 ACM conference on computer supported cooperative work, ACM Press, Seattle, Washington, DC, pp 207–216, doi: 10.1145/289444.289495

15. Toney AP, Thomas BH (2007) Modeling reach for use in user interface design. In: Proceedings of the eight Australasian conference on user interface, vol 64, Australian Computer Society, Inc., Ballarat, VIC, pp 27–30

16. Salvador T, Scholtz J, Larson J (1996) The denver model for groupware design. SIGCHI Bulletin 28(1):52–58, doi: 10.1145/249170.249185

17. Gutwin C, Greenberg S (2002) A descriptive framework of workspace awareness for real-time groupware. Computer Supported Cooperative Work 11(3):411–446

18. Schmidt K (2002) The problem with 'awareness': Introductory remarks on 'awareness in CSCW'. Computer Supported Cooperative Work 11(3):285–298

19. Endsley MR (1995) Measurement of situation awareness in dynamic systems. Human Factors: The Journal of the Human Factors and Ergonomics Society 37(1):65–84, doi: 10.1518/001872095779049499

20. Hornecker E, Marshall P, Dalton NS, Rogers Y (2008) Collaboration and interference: Awareness with mice or touch input. In: Proceedings of the ACM 2008 conference on computer supported cooperative work, ACM Press, San Diego, CA, pp 167–176, doi: 10.1145/1460563.1460589

21. Scott SD, Sheelagh M, Carpendale T, Inkpen KM (2004) Territoriality in collaborative tabletop workspaces. In: Proceedings of the 2004 ACM conference on computer supported cooperative work, ACM Press, Chicago, IL, pp 294–303, doi: 10.1145/1031607.1031655

22. Marshall P, Hornecker E, Morris R, Dalton NS, Rogers Y (2008) When the fingers do the talking: A study of group participation with varying constraints to a tabletop interface. In: Horizontal interactive human computer systems, 2008. TABLETOP 2008. 3rd IEEE international workshop on, pp 33–40, doi: 10.1109/TABLETOP.2008.4660181

23. Vernier F, Lesh N, Shen C (2002) Visualization techniques for circular tabletop interfaces. In: Proceedings of advanced visual interfaces, ACM Press, 2002, pp 257–263

24. Wu M, Balakrishnan R (2003) Multi-finger and whole hand gestural interaction techniques for multi-user tabletop displays. In: Proceedings of the 16th annual ACM symposium on user interface software and technology, ACM Press, Vancouver, BC, pp 193–202, doi: 10.1145/964696.964718

25. Shen C, Everitt K, Ryall K (2003) UbiTable: Impromptu face-to-face collaboration on horizontal interactive surfaces. In: UbiComp 2003: Ubiquitous Computing, pp 281–288

26. Rekimoto J (1997) Pick-and-drop: A direct manipulation technique for multiple computer environments. In: Proceedings of the 10th annual ACM symposium on user interface software and technology, ACM Press, Banff, AB, pp 31–39, doi: 10.1145/263407.263505

27. Swaminathan K, Sato S (1997) Interaction design for large displays. Interactions 4(1):15–24, doi: 10.1145/242388.242395

28. Bezerianos A, Balakrishnan R (2005) The vacuum: Facilitating the manipulation of distant objects. In: Proceedings of the SIGCHI conference on human factors in computing systems, ACM Press, Portland, OR, pp 361–370, doi: 10.1145/1054972.1055023

29. Brignull H, Izadi S, Fitzpatrick G, Rogers Y, Rodden T (2004) The introduction of a shared interactive surface into a communal space. In: Proceedings of the 2004 ACM conference on computer supported cooperative work, ACM Press, Chicago, IL, pp 49–58, doi: 10.1145/1031607.1031616

30. Rekimoto J, Saitoh M (1999) Augmented surfaces: A spatially continuous work space for hybrid computing environments. In: Proceedings of the SIGCHI conference on human factors in computing systems: The CHI is the limit, ACM Press, Pittsburgh, PA, pp 378–385, doi: 10.1145/302979.303113

31. Geißler J (1998) Shuffle, throw or take it! Working efficiently with an interactive wall. In: CHI 98 conference summary on human factors in computing systems, ACM Press, Los Angeles, CA, pp 265–266, doi: 10.1145/286498.286745

32. Parker J, Mandryk R, Inkpen K (2006) Integrating point and touch for interaction with digital tabletop displays. IEEE Computer Graphics and Applications 26(5):28–35, doi: 10.1109/MCG.2006.110

33. Myers BA, Bhatnagar R, Nichols J, Peck CH, Kong D, Miller R, Long AC (2002) Interacting at a distance: Measuring the performance of laser pointers and other devices. In: Proceedings of the SIGCHI conference on human factors in computing systems: Changing our world, changing ourselves, ACM Press, Minneapolis, MN, pp 33–40, doi: 10.1145/503376.503383

34. Vogel D, Balakrishnan R (2005) Distant freehand pointing and clicking on very large, high resolution displays. In: Proceedings of the 18th annual ACM symposium on user interface software and technology, ACM Press, Seattle, WA, pp 33–42, doi: 10.1145/1095034.1095041

35. Benford S, Bowers J, Fahlén LE, Greenhalgh C, Snowdon D (1995) User embodiment in collaborative virtual environments. In: Proceedings of the SIGCHI conference on human factors in computing systems, ACM Press/Addison-Wesley Publishing Co., Denver, CO, pp 242–249, doi: 10.1145/223904.223935

36. Stach T, Gutwin C, Pinelle D, Irani P (2007) Improving recognition and characterization in groupware with rich embodiments. In: Proceedings of the SIGCHI conference on human factors in computing systems, ACM Press, San Jose, CA, pp 11–20, doi: 10.1145/1240624.1240627

37. Greenberg S, Gutwin C, Roseman M (1996) Semantic telepointers for groupware. In: Proceedings of sixth Australian conference on computer-human interaction, 1996, pp 54–61, doi: 10.1109/OZCHI.1996.559988

38. Pinelle D, Subramanian S, Gutwin C (2006) Designing digital tables for highly integrated collaboration. Technical report. HCI-TR-06-02, Computer Science Department, University of Saskatchewan, Saskatoon, SK, http://hci.usask.ca/publications/view.php?id=34

39. Nacenta MA, Sallam S, Champoux B, Subramanian S, Gutwin C (2006) Perspective cursor: Perspective-based interaction for multi-display environments. In: Proceedings of the SIGCHI conference on human factors in computing systems, ACM Press, Montréal, QC, pp 289–298, doi: 10.1145/1124772.1124817

40. Tang JC, Minneman S (1991) VideoWhiteboard: Video shadows to support remote collaboration. In: Proceedings of the SIGCHI conference on human factors in computing systems: Reaching through technology, ACM Press, New Orleans, LA, United States, pp 315–322, doi: 10.1145/108844.108932

41. Tang A, Tory M, Po B, Neumann P, Carpendale S (2006) Collaborative coupling over tabletop displays. In: Proceedings of the SIGCHI conference on human factors in computing systems, ACM Press, Montréal, QC, pp 1181–1190, doi: 10.1145/1124772.1124950

42. Tang A, Neustaedter C, Greenberg S (2007) VideoArms: Embodiments for mixed presence groupware. In: People and computers XX, Engage, pp 85–102

43. Morris MR, Ryall K, Shen C, Forlines C, Vernier F (2004) Beyond "social protocols": multi-user coordination policies for co-located groupware. In: Proceedings of the 2004 ACM conference on computer supported cooperative work, ACM Press, Chicago, IL, pp 262–265, doi: 10.1145/1031607.1031648

44. Forlines C, Wigdor D, Shen C, Balakrishnan R (2007) Direct-touch vs. mouse input for tabletop displays. In: Proceedings of the SIGCHI conference on Human factors in computing systems, ACM Press, San Jose, California, USA, pp 647–656, doi: 10.1145/1240624.1240726

45. Haué J, Dillenbourg P (2009) Do fewer laptops make a better team? In: Interactive artifacts and furniture supporting collaborative work and learning, pp 1–24

46. Endsley MR, Kiris EO (1995) Situation awareness global assessment technique (SAGAT) TRACON air traffic control version user guide. Technical report, Texas Tech, Lubbock, TX

47. Greenberg S, Marwood D (1994) Real time groupware as a distributed system: Concurrency control and its effect on the interface. In: Proceedings of the 1994 ACM conference on

computer supported cooperative work, ACM Press, Chapel Hill, NC, pp 207–217, doi: 10.1145/192844.193011
48. Müller-Tomfelde C, Schremmer C, Wessels A (2007) Exploratory study on concurrent inter-action in co-located collaboration. In: Proceedings of the 19th Australasian conference on computer-human interaction: Entertaining user interfaces, ACM Press, Adelaide, pp 175–178, doi: 10.1145/1324892.1324925

Chapter 14
File System Access for Tabletop Interaction

Anthony Collins and Judy Kay

Abstract The diverse and fast changing hardware for tabletop interaction has created exciting opportunities for new software interfaces that will enable people to exploit the potential of tabletops. This chapter describes our exploration of such software for the fundamental and important task of accessing digital information from people's personal file stores. We explain how our novel associative file access mechanism was created in response to the particular challenges of tabletop interaction design, notably support for collaboration, effective use of each individual's personal stores of digital information, accounting for the context of use, addressing the challenges of varying orientation of users around the table, and limited input. We illustrate the lessons we have learnt from a series of evaluations of our software interface and link these to future trends for supporting people in being able to collaborate on tasks that make use of personal files at tabletops.

Introduction

We envisage tabletops as pervasive interfaces, facilitating a new means of collaboration, around a tabletop, on tasks that people would naturally wish to do at a table. These include both social and workplace interaction in tasks such as planning and sharing of information, which are commonly done by small groups of people seated around a table. To realise the potential of tabletop interaction, one of the challenges that must be addressed is provision of interfaces that make it easy for people to access their personal stores of files so that these can be used for the collaborative tasks.

Support for file system interaction is a fundamental facility for existing desktop interaction. This means that we can build from the foundations provided by the existing file system interfaces. However, the tabletop imposes several distinctive

---

A. Collins (✉)
School of Information Technologies, University of Sydney, Sydney, NSW 2006, Australia
e-mail: anthony@it.usyd.edu.au

C. Müller-Tomfelde (ed.), *Tabletops – Horizontal Interactive Displays*,
Human-Computer Interaction Series, DOI 10.1007/978-1-84996-113-4_14,
© Springer-Verlag London Limited 2010

interaction challenges. One important class of these follows from the importance of collocated collaboration at tabletops. Unlike the conventional desktop, the table-top needs to support a small group of people working together on a task. In many classes of such collaboration, it is helpful if the tabletop users can draw upon and share relevant files that are stored on their personal computers. With the trend towards powerful carried devices, such as laptops, Personal Digital Assistants (PDAs) and smartphones, the individuals may need files held on these. Importantly, the collaboration may require access to the files of multiple users at the same time.

Existing file system access mechanisms do not support such collaboration well. This is primarily due to their evolution as a means for an individual to work with their own files in a hierarchical structure. Even on desktops, this poses problems, as reflected in an important body of research into new file system mechanisms. The limited support for multiple classifications makes it cognitively demanding to organise and later retrieve files that cannot be easily classified. The retrieval of a file is based on its storage location, instead of its content, and large hierarchies are time consuming to reorganise. Another important limitation is that they provide no support for dynamic reorganisation depending on the task. For example, consider two people who are planning a holiday. They may have files about hotels and tourist attractions each stored in separate sub-hierarchies in their personal file systems. At one time, they may need to access hotels that are near particular attractions. Later, they may need to view the attractions near each interesting hotel. It would require tedious reorganisation (including copying across file systems) to easily access the files in the desired ways. Such limitations have driven research to create new file system interfaces overcoming the limitations of hierarchies. The demands of tabletop collaboration exacerbate these limitations, making that work even more important.

In addition to the issues of hierarchical structuring, the design of the file access interface must take account of issues that are quite different from desktop interfaces. These include the need to allow for the different orientation of the people around the table, as tabletops should support face-to-face and around-the-table collaboration. Another characteristic of tabletop interaction is that it should be possible to achieve effective interaction without the use of a keyboard and mouse; there is generally just finger or pen-based touch as the main means of user input. This creates very different interface challenges from those driving design of desktop interaction. Tabletop research has highlighted other interface challenges, notably that of clutter, which is particularly important when supporting multiple people working together on a shared workspace.

Combining these new demands, there is a real need for new, collaborative file system interfaces that support multiple users accessing their files and personal information around a tabletop. The goal of our research is to develop and evaluate a new file system access mechanism that takes careful consideration of these key table-top design challenges. This chapter describes the drivers for our approach, and the series of studies that have informed its design and assessed its effectiveness. The remainder of this chapter is organised as follows. We first provide the related work on tabletop file access as well as novel file access mechanisms more broadly. Next, we introduce our new collaborative file system interface for tabletops, followed by a description of the drivers that have informed its design. Then, we report results from a series of user studies, showing how they informed the design and their implications for future trends in tabletop file system interaction.

Background

This section reviews the two keys areas of previous research that have informed our work. First, we describe the exploration of tabletop information access. Then, we overview the broader work on novel user interfaces to files and personal information.

The importance of tabletops as a medium for users to navigate through a collection of information is reflected in a variety of research. For example, tabletops have the potential to support people sharing and telling stories about their digital photograph collections, as reflected in *SharePic* [1] and *Photohelix* [2]. Both cluster photographs into *chronological events* for rapid navigation of large collections, so that people can retrieve relevant photos based on the dimension of *time*. For the case of large collections of heterogeneous information, Shen et al.'s *Personal Digital Historian (PDH)* [3] provides a faceted browsing interface for historical information, via the dimensions of *who*, *what*, *where* and *when*. They conducted a qualitative evaluation with 14 participants working with 1,250 documents, with positive outcomes. However, participants highlighted "clutter" and "over crowding" within groups of information as key issues in the interface. The PDH project also explored other visualisation and interaction techniques, including hierarchical [4].

Morris et al.'s *TeamSearch* [5] took a search-based approach to tabletop information access, enabling small groups to either individually or collectively search for digital media on a tabletop by arranging *tokens* to form Boolean queries. Their evaluation highlighted the benefits of *collective* information search at a tabletop – a greater sense of awareness of each group member's activity compared to individual searches. Participants also favoured collective search to complete the retrieval tasks.

Another key area of tabletop research is *micro-mobility* of electronic documents between tabletops and other devices in a computer augmented environment. Through this, users can transfer documents to a tabletop in order to interact with them. *MultiSpace* [6] supports document mobility between a number of devices in a room, such as a tabletop, an interactive whiteboard, and multiple personal devices such as PDAs. It aims for visible transfer of objects between devices using *portals*, similar to earlier work looking at smooth interchange of digital information among devices in a hybrid computer environment [7]. While MultiSpace demonstrates the usefulness of supporting movement of digital documents between a tabletop and other devices, it requires users to manually transfer the information between these devices. This makes it tedious for navigation of larger file systems from a tabletop. It requires *DocuBits* and *Containers* [8] to select either portions of a screen, or small collections of documents to be moved between devices.

Work on accessing *personal file systems* from a tabletop has been limited. *UbiTable* [9] allows users to conduct spontaneous, unplanned tabletop collaboration where the participants share chosen files from their laptop computer. Users sit at the tabletop, using their laptop to select particular files for public display. *Public, private* and *personal* spaces are used to control what is visible and selectable by others at the tabletop. Each person's desktop environment (and file system) is kept completely private, except for specific files that have been explicitly shared. This affords privacy, though the relationships and similarities between each person's file system are not highlighted. Each user must also have an understanding of exactly what information is available on the computer that might be relevant for the collaboration.

In more recent work on sharing personal files on a tabletop, Hartmann et al.'s tangible drawers [10] enable each user to plug-in a USB flash drive and view their personal files in a virtual drawer shown in front of them on the tabletop. The drawer can be activated and navigated by pulling a physical handle out of the table. This interface allows classical file system interaction on a tabletop. However, users must individually *copy* information onto the table from their drawer, and the presentation of files within the drawer is unstructured – users must navigate their files by rotating a physical knob that scrolls though the entire file system. Consequently, this approach is potentially limited to a small collection of documents as it only presents a flat, unstructured view of the file system, with no way of quickly retrieving specific information.

Overall, the literature just reviewed explored several important research questions related to collaborative interaction with information collections at tabletops. The issue of access to broader file systems, that may be carried, local and remote, is an important area to explore further for tabletops. It is particularly important to place emphasis on *collaboration* – there is much to explore looking at how to support people collaborating with their file systems. We now review work on other novel file and personal information interfaces designed for traditional desktop interaction.

The hierarchical file system – first popularised by the UNIX operating system [11] – has become ubiquitous in personal computing. Despite its limitations for file organisation, and various attempts to explore alternatives, hierarchies have a strong legacy in modern computing. It is often argued that the use of a strict hierarchy to organise a computer file system (where files can only be stored in a single directory) is not efficient for an average computer user, as it may be difficult to store and retrieve files that cannot be easily categorised, and a knowledge of where files are stored is required for retrieval [12–14]. Malone [15] found that the difficulty in deciding how to classify information can cause cognitive difficulties in using a file system. More importantly, when a file system has several hierarchical levels, the difficulty of creating new categories is a barrier in maintaining the file system. Malone proposes that computers can help with this problem by supporting multiple classification, deferred classification, and automatic classification.

Unconventional file access interfaces have been explored in an attempt to address these limitations of hierarchical file access. Attribute-based file system interfaces enable powerful searching that hides the underlying hierarchical file organisation. The *Semantic File System* [16], for example, automatically extracts attributes from files (such as author, creation date, and the file content itself), and creates dynamic virtual directories containing all files matching a user's search criteria. Similarly, *Presto* [17] allows attribute-based document management, with little regard for the underlying storage location of documents. Users can attach arbitrary attributes to express "features" of the documents that will be meaningful for later retrieval. Marsden et al.'s *Attribute Browser* [12] took a relational database approach, where a user can browse their files starting with a broad query that is progressively refined by specifying attributes (such as creation date and size) of the files they are searching for. Attribute-based file system browsing does not address the fact that users may want to find *collections* of information related to a particular task, but with each file having unique attributes and meta-data (such as differing titles and authors). Users must also explicitly search for files that they require, instead of being presented with all files related to a particular task automatically.

A trend in desktop computer operating systems is the inclusion of content-indexed file system search to simplify the process of locating documents in a large hierarchy. For example, *Apple Spotlight* and *Windows Vista Instant Search* allow users to search their computer as if it were a single information-space, with relevant information presented together regardless of its type and where it is stored. These tools focus on the integration of *personal information* – managed by *Personal Information Management (PIM)* tools – and a heterogeneous file system.

Taking a different approach, Jones et al. [18] highlight the importance of the folder metaphor, arguing that folders are information in their own right because they help decompose information and make it easier to understand. An ethnography study was conducted to understand the role of folders in the organisation of project-related information. Participants stated they would not trust a search tool to find all required information, and that a search tool would not provide enough control to ensure all required items are in one place at all times. This is a key issue to address when replacing existing file system interaction with search-based navigation facilities.

A large body of work aimed to achieve *unified* PIM, where files and personal information are accessible regardless of their type or the tools used to manage them. *Stuff I've Seen (SIS)* [19] and *Phlat* [20] both provide a unified index to all files and personal information that a user has seen on their computer, combining separate information-spaces (such as e-mail, the computer file system, calendars, and visited web pages) into a single interface that does not rely on a hierarchical organisation structure. They use contextual cues (such as dates and people) to facilitate information retrieval. This is similar to *Lifestreams* [21], and *MyLifeBits* [22], where the information a user has seen is ordered in a timeline for later retrieval. *Haystack* [23] is another unified PIM tool with a similar approach, though it also allows users to create arbitrary, meaningful relationships between the stored information to aid retrieval. Karger et al. [23] discuss the concept of presenting "similar items" alongside user-selected items, in order to support iterative query refinement, which is similar to ideas explored in the *Implicit Query (IQ)* prototype [24], where information relevant to the user's current context is presented in a peripheral interface. At a tabletop, this technique could be particularly useful for suggesting similar items across each person's file collection.

This range of approaches is important in informing the design of tabletop file access mechanisms. We drew inspiration from them, even though they were designed for use by a single person, with a keyboard and mouse, seated before an upright display. Notably, they fail to deal with the key tabletop issue of collaboration, or the challenge of enabling interaction with multiple sets of files and personal information.

Collaborative File System Access for Tabletop Interaction

We now introduce our approach to facilitating collaborative file system *access* at tabletops. At its core, our approach aims to provide associative, content-based access to file systems. As we must support multiple people around the tabletop accessing their files at the same time, and given that these people are likely to have organised their file system hierarchies differently, a content-based approach to file system access is highly desirable. There is also the opportunity to explore new mechanisms for file access that exploit the fact that people are sharing information with each other for a particular task. For example, when people are working together on a project around the tabletop, it is likely that they will need to discuss *similar* files across their file systems, but these are unlikely to be stored in the same location and structure in all the file systems.

It is becoming increasingly common for people to have their files distributed across multiple devices, each with their own separate file system. These devices can range from laptop and desktop computers to flash memory cards and mobile phones. Some files may also be stored "in the cloud" on a remote web server. When multiple people meet together and need to share their files, these files may need to be retrieved from multiple places at once (both local and remote), making the retrieval problem even more complex. As we envisage tabletops as a hub for social collaboration, there is a real need for the tabletop to automatically *pull* the required information from multiple sources for discussion and collaborative work.

The tabletop, while offering many benefits for collaborative interaction, imposes new challenges over those already present in conventional interface design. In particular, supporting multiple users sitting at different positions around the tabletop creates new challenges that existing file system interfaces do not face.

Bringing together these key goals of providing *content-based access*, retrieving *similar information from multiple sources*, and *designing within the constraints of tabletop interaction*, we now describe *Focus*, our collaborative file system interface for tabletops. We begin by illustrating the *user view* of our approach, followed by a discussion of the key design aspects that address the salient tabletop and file system interface design challenges.

User View

Focus, shown in Fig. 14.1, is an *associative* file system interface for tabletop collaboration. Focus retrieves all files related to the current *focus file*, across each computer

Fig. 14.1 People using
Focus to share and discuss
their personal files at a
multi-user tabletop

of the users at the tabletop. This *focus file* navigation technique enables fast retrieval
of *similar* information across the connected file systems. To make their files accessible at the table, users run the *Focus Exporter* application on their personal computer:
this allows them to make their whole file system, or specific parts of it, available for
access at the table.

In Focus, files look like objects placed on top of the tabletop surface, as there are
no borders or other markings on them. When a file is touched, subtle lines appear on
it to indicate its selection areas. A file can be *moved* by selecting it inside the main
area and dragging it. When moving files, they have a realistic momentum so they
can be *flicked* around the tabletop. Files can be rotated and resized (in a combined
rosize action) by selecting the file at one of its corners and dragging the corner. A file
can be *flipped* by selecting it within an indicated area (in the centre of each edge),
and dragging across to the opposite edge. Once flipped, the filename appears written
on the back.

When first launched, Focus displays a broad start view (shown in Fig. 14.2) with
the first file (alphabetically) in each exported directory, of each remote file system,
presented in a radial layout to support people sitting at different orientations around
the tabletop. From the start view, file navigation is based on the notion of a focus
file. Once a user selects a focus file, all other similar[1] files across the file systems are
loaded and displayed on the tabletop immediately. The retrieved files are presented
as a single file-space, regardless of their kind or which file system they are stored in.
The initial display size of each retrieved file is used to indicate its similarity to the
focus, and irrelevant files are automatically hidden after each focus selection in order
to reduce clutter on the tabletop. If a file was previously displayed on the tabletop, it
is presented at its last screen position to provide spatial consistency between focus
selections, and to allow users to create arbitrary spatial groupings of documents (as
in [25]).

---

[1] Based on any textual file content and other available meta-data, such as keywords and filename.

Fig. 14.2 *Top*: a screen-shot
of Focus showing the start
view, with files presented in a
spiral. *Bottom*: Focus
showing similar files from
multiple file systems. Files
have been rearranged by
users, and are sized according
to their similarity to the focus
file

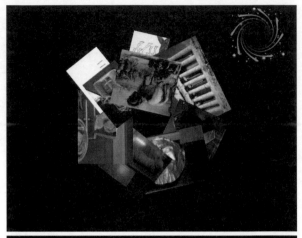

Focus provides additional widgets with special functionality to support common
file access tasks. The *History Browser* (shown in the top middle of Fig. 14.2 bottom)
supports "back" and "forward" operations through focus selections, and allows users
to return to the start view of the file systems. The *Black Hole* (top right of Fig. 14.2)
provides the functionality of a temporary "trash can," but it is also designed to
address some of the challenges of tabletop interaction design – objects can be *flicked*
to the Black Hole in cases where a user cannot reach it, and it gives visual feedback
that an object is about to be hidden (the object shrinks as it moves closer to the
centre of the Black Hole). *Storage Bins* are provided as special container objects
on the tabletop that show thumbnails of items dragged into them, similar to [26].
A space-filling thumbnail layout accommodates the thumbnails. Files placed in a
Storage Bin are unaffected by future focus selections, and so remain visible on the

tabletop until explicitly removed by a user. All these widgets can be moved, rotated and resized on the tabletop just like the files.

Similarity and Implementation Overview

With its associative file access mechanism, it is essential that Focus will correctly retrieve the relevant information after each focus selection. People use a variety of tools to mange their personal information, and they employ a variety of different organisation strategies both within and across different tools [27]. Furthermore, different tasks require very different sets of files. Accordingly, we have created a mechanism for users to define the meaning of similarity for the files on their machine – users can adjust (on a scale of 0–10) the importance of each meta-data attribute (see Fig. 14.3). For example, if the user deems files by the same author(s) as closely related, the user increases the weighting on the "authors" attribute. These settings can be tuned depending on the task at hand. For example, a user might remember certain keywords about a document, so they may wish to adjust the sliders to place high importance on the "keywords" meta-data field in the similarity calculation. Alternatively, users can "set and forget," by assigning values that broadly represent their file system organisation. The similarity settings are set independently on each remote computer to suit the semantics and organisation of that computer's files.

Focus has been developed using the *Cruiser* tabletop platform [28], a multi-user, gestural, collaborative tabletop system. It uses the *Mimio Interactive* whiteboard pen system, but is independent of the hardware (a version called *SharePic* [1] used the *DiamondTouch*). Focus currently supports a range of information types,

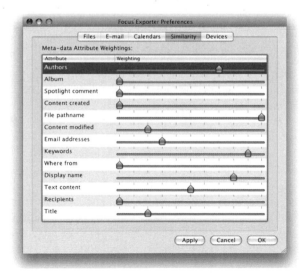

Fig. 14.3 The Focus Exporter desktop interface for defining the meaning of similarity (on each user's machine)

including images, PDF documents, stored web-pages, and documents from many popular applications such as those bundled in Microsoft Office and Apple iWork. E-mail is supported from any e-mail client that supports the *mbox* or *Maildir* formats.

Focus Exporter is a separate application that builds on the Apple *Spotlight* search framework to perform content search of a user's file system. The Focus Exporter applies additional calculations, based on the user-assigned weights, to determine the level of similarity between files. The tabletop communicates with the exported file systems using a *Transport Layer Security (TLS)* protected HTTPS connection. The communication protocol uses *JavaScript Object Notation (JSON)*, facilitating creation of Focus clients for other platforms.

Key Design Aspects

In this section, we explain how Focus addresses several key distinguishing and interrelating challenges that impact on tabletop file system interface design.

Collaboration: A key goal of tabletops is to support collocated collaborative interaction. As tables fit the normal way that small groups of people often choose to socialise or work together, tabletop interfaces should support small groups of people working at the table. Some tasks may involve users working together as a group, requiring designers to place a strong emphasis on facilitating interpersonal interaction, and other tasks may involve users working individually on different areas of the table. Therefore, tabletops must support natural *transitions* between personal and group work [29].

Focus is designed primarily as a collaborative interface, supporting multiple people accessing their file collections simultaneously at the tabletop. The similarity-based file retrieval mechanism is designed to exploit the fact that people who are working together are likely to be sharing related information. Importantly, the design makes it natural for one person to perform a focus selection on other people's files. A user can also choose to work individually on particular parts of the tabletop, as we do not assume a fixed position or orientation for file access tasks. While files are initially presented in the middle of the tabletop in a radial layout, files can be arbitrarily grouped on the tabletop depending on the task, with their position retained between focus selections.

Context of Use: The usefulness of tabletops for collaboration suggests that they will often be located in shared spaces, rather than in private. The shared context of use of tabletops also makes it unlikely that users will choose to work on them exclusively. This makes it important to support people in easily moving their information between devices with natural transitions, as recommended in [29]. Thus, it is essential that people can easily locate and view their digital information at the tabletop, without distracting shifts of focus and effort, such as needing to convert and copy information to the tabletop first. As such, our approach avoids the need for any explicit transfer of information. Rather, files are automatically retrieved when they are deemed similar to a new focus selection.

For shared use, the issues of file privacy and user control over the similarity calculation mechanism are particularly important. In Focus, users are able to control these away from the tabletop, thereby providing additional privacy. It is critical that users can control the release of their files to the tabletop. Users are given complete control over this, and are able to export either their whole file system or only specific parts of it. The similarity calculation mechanism is customised on a per-machine (per-user) basis, allowing the search mechanism to operate differently for each user of the tabletop.

Orientation and Table Use: A fundamental facility of a collaborative tabletop interface is to support people sitting face-to-face and around-the-table, and so tabletop interfaces must support arbitrary orientation of interface elements [30]. Interface elements must also be orientation independent when presenting information, as a key concern is state ambiguity induced by viewing the table from different angles.

In Focus, all interface elements are easily rotatable, and have no state ambiguity when viewed from different orientations. Files are presented in a radial layout in the middle of the tabletop, so that no particular orientation is favoured. Furthermore, it draws each user's attention to the centre of the tabletop while viewing the files, which we believe will foster workspace awareness, leading to improved collaboration. Files can be easily moved and rotated from the initial positions as desired, and any spatial groupings of files will be retained between focus selections.

Clutter: The combination of table size, display resolution, and multiple users makes clutter a critical problem to address. Clutter may arise from the need to present large amounts of information [3], or the need to replicate information for multiple people [31]. In a multi-user setting, where people are creating and interacting with files on the tabletop simultaneously, management of clutter becomes challenging – existing methods in conventional desktop interfaces, such as a "taskbar" to control active windows, were designed for single-user interaction at a fixed position on the screen. Also, the management of clutter by one user could have unintentional and adverse effects on other users of the tabletop. For example, a user might hide or close a file that other users of the tabletop still need.

Clutter is a particularly challenging issue for a tabletop file system interface – people need to retrieve information from potentially large file systems, and multiple people may be working around the tabletop at the same time. This calls for approaches to file system access that show only relevant information, and only when it is needed. A key design decision in Focus is that it clears the table after each focus selection, and so it only loads a small set of files related to the selected focus file. Files can be kept on the tabletop, if desired, by placing them in Storage Bins.

Limited Input: It must be natural to interact with the tabletop using input with special constraints not present in desktop computer interaction. A keyboard and mouse is typically not present in a multi-user tabletop setting, and so interface selection targets must be sufficiently large for direct-touch interaction, which potentially contributes to interface clutter. While providing a virtual keyboard on the tabletop is possible, this contributes to screen clutter (particularly when multiple keyboards are required), and provides no tactile feedback when pressing keys. Physical keyboards are an option, though these would impact on users' flexibility to move to different parts of the tabletop, particularly when there are multiple people sitting around it. Indeed, design should avoid reliance on text input, with careful attention to interface target sizes.

One potential approach to enabling access to file systems from a tabletop would be a text-based search interface, such as those found in modern operating systems. However, this requires users to enter search terms for each query (which may be tedious at a tabletop depending on what kind of text input is available), and people typically only use search as a last resort for retrieving their files – *navigational* interfaces to file systems are clearly preferred [32]. Thus, the approach taken in Focus is to provide a content-based *browsing* interface that avoids reliance on any textual input to locate information. The Focus interface is designed to be usable by pen or finger, providing sufficiently large input targets for all interface elements, and it uses a simple *dwell* gesture to perform the core action of the interface – locating similar files across each user's file system.

Research Findings

An essential part of our iterative design approach has involved a series of observational studies that informed our understanding of the way that people access files at tabletops with different file system interfaces.

We explored the following research questions:

1. Usability – can people achieve tasks effectively with Focus?
2. Collaboration – does Focus facilitate collaboration, compared with a conventional hierarchical file system interface?
3. Unified access – can people access broad, unified personal information collections with Focus, without reliance on the underlying file hierarchy?

This section describes a series of user studies – both individual and collaborative – to address these important research questions for tabletop file system access.

Studies of Hierarchical and Associative Access

Our first study [33] compared use of our associative access and a hierarchical tabletop file interface, specifically addressing the *usability* and *collaboration* research questions. The hierarchical interface, the *Browser*, was developed to provide a *spatial* file browser that operates effectively within the same tabletop interaction constraints – it is orientation independent, allows people to work collectively or individually at any position around the tabletop, provides graphical representations of files and folders, and has large selection targets (for touch or pen input). The Browser represents the familiar hierarchical navigation mechanism used in conventional file system interfaces. We compared *OnTop* (an earlier version of

Focus) with the Browser to examine what impact our associative access approach has on people's usage of their files and the tabletop workspace. This evaluation was exploratory and mostly qualitative: using observations of *success* in task completion, number of *errors* made and *user recovery*, and *affective aspects*. The experiment was within-subjects double-crossover – the participants completed the tasks with both conditions (associative and hierarchical) with the ordering balanced between trials.

Ten participants worked in pairs on five collaborative file access tasks. They were given a scenario of working together to create a set of information about ancient Greek history, for a museum exhibition. One participant was allocated text documents related to the project, while their partner had photographs and e-mails. They had to meet at the tabletop and share specific information with each other and make decisions about what to use for the exhibit. The tasks required regular cross-hierarchy and cross-file system access amongst the users (see [33] for more details). The results gave us a valuable sense of the relative strengths and weaknesses of the two approaches to file system interaction. Two main themes emerged in the results: collaboration and clutter.

Beginning with collaboration, participants were private with their file system interactions when using the Browser due to a high sense of ownership, and they never interacted with their partner's file system, unless a file was passed to them first. By contrast, participants were more social and co-operative when completing tasks using OnTop – participants often helped their partner to complete the tasks by suggesting possible focus files in their own file system to retrieve similar information belonging to their partner. We observed that OnTop appeared to give better support for users to collaborate on the access process when working to complete a joint task, due to the combined view of the users' file-spaces. By contrast, the hierarchical Browser has the tendency to make each user take charge of accessing their own files. With the Browser, clutter posed a problem for users and they needed to systematically clean-up, usually with no help from their partner (following from an increased sense of ownership affecting interaction with the objects on the tabletop). OnTop's automatic "pruning" (showing only relevant information for the current focus file) proved helpful for reducing clutter, particularly when the file collection size was doubled as part of the experiment.

The qualitative feedback for both file access interfaces was positive – participants considered the tabletop to be an important collaborative medium, and seamless access to personal file systems on a tabletop was considered to be an exciting feature. All participants noted the familiarity of the Browser's hierarchical mental model, making it easier to understand initially. However, participants embraced the unfamiliar idea of associative access. Questionnaires indicate that participants found OnTop consistently easier to use, and eight participants considered OnTop to be more efficient for this collaborative task.

A second study [34] was conducted to gain a deeper, more quantitative understanding of collaboration with hierarchical and associative file system interfaces. At this early stage of exploring tabletop file system access, one natural starting point is the widespread *Windows Explorer* because it is so familiar, being very similar to all commonly used desktop file system interfaces. So, to leverage people's familiarity and compare the key differences in interaction, we compared Focus with Windows Explorer. Following from the key emerging themes of our first study [33], we identified two main dimensions to analyse: collaboration and screen use (notably clutter and its management, and general strategies for organising tabletop space).

In this study, twenty participants worked in pairs on a collaborative holiday planning task. Participants were told they were holidaying with their partner in London, England and Florence, Italy, and they needed to work with their partner to choose which tourist attractions they would visit and which hotels they would stay in. The study was again within-subjects double-crossover, where participants repeated the same planning task using each interface, but with a different holiday destination (either London or Florence). Participants were first asked to complete an individual organisation task that involved them viewing and organising the provided files (with a desktop computer) before collaborating at the tabletop, enabling them to gain enough familiarity with the files first.

In the results, the two interfaces exhibited important differences in terms of the amount of information viewed, and the level of interaction participants had with each other's files. For speed of task completion, nine out of ten trials were faster[2] completing the tasks with Explorer than with Focus. However, participants viewed files at the same rate (i.e. viewed the same number of files per minute) with both interfaces. Thus, significantly more files were viewed and considered in the collaboration when using Focus. Furthermore, participants interacted significantly more with *each other's files* using Focus than with Explorer, which contributed to the larger number of files viewed. Using Explorer, it was rare that a participant would reach over to their partner's files or folders to interact with them. We observed the opposite with Focus – participants freely interacted with all objects on the tabletop, with no perceived ownership boundaries affecting the interaction. Consequently, Focus encouraged *semantic* grouping of information in the workspace more than with Explorer. Ownership partitioning of the workspace (where files and folders were kept on separate halves of the tabletop, in front of the corresponding owner) occurred significantly more with Explorer than Focus. The semantic partitioning that was dominant in Focus provided an important way of dealing with clutter. For example, by grouping all files based on the part of the task for which they were needed (such as by forming a group of attractions and a group of hotels of different criteria), participants were able to see a subset of files relevant to the discussion. This lead to more efficient use of the tabletop space, as participants spread-out their files to different areas of the tabletop instead of keeping them directly in front of them.

Broadly, the study indicated that collaboration was richer with Focus because it helped participants consider each other's files more and to consider multiple issues at once (i.e. considering hotels and attractions together instead of deciding on one before the other). With Focus, we also observed *serendipitous* file discoveries in

---

[2] Note that participants were not put under any time pressure to complete the tasks.

four of the ten trials. These were cases when the similar files returned by Focus produced something that a participant liked, but did not explicitly retrieve or expect to be retrieved, causing them to include it in their decision making (for example, including a nearby hotel they discovered while discussing their favourite tourist attraction).

The study showed that existing hierarchical file access has a place, particularly for an individual accessing their own files in a structure they know well. At the same time, the study points to the benefits of an associative multi-machine file access mechanism for improving collaboration, its capacity to overcome the silos of hierarchical file organisation and the ways that its characteristics facilitate greater depth of interaction for tasks such as planning. The Focus style of interface supported better management of the large display, encouraging semantic, rather than pure ownership clustering of files, and the improved management of clutter.

Accessing Broader Personal Information Collections

While the preceding studies dealt with collaboration, a single-user-study [35] addressed the research questions of *usability* and *unified access*. It examined the issue of navigating broader collections of personal information – including a hierarchical file system, e-mail and visited web-pages – with Focus. The evaluation was qualitative to study whether users are able to effectively navigate diverse kinds of personal information (that would typically be organised with different applications) using associative access, where a *unified* view of the information is presented. The evaluation was a single participant study to analyse the usability with one participant interacting with Focus.

Six participants worked individually on three access tasks related to a travel planning scenario. The participant had to organise certain information at the tabletop related to the tasks that they were going to complete during the day, based on the contents of an e-mail inbox, and various files and web-pages stored in the provided file system. Each task involved retrieving items related to a particular group of e-mails, and placing them in Storage Bins.

The participants were able to effectively access and organise the personal information using Focus, employing a variety of techniques to navigate the information on the tabletop. E-mails were used extensively as focus items by all users to navigate through the information, and were preferred in many cases when they could have selected other items instead (such as photos or PDF documents). For all participants, digital photographs, web-pages and PDF documents that contained pictures and business logos were faster to identify on the tabletop (as participants always interacted with them first), and so they were used as focus items more often. When asked about using associative access, one participant stated that "it felt natural having all of the different items appear on the table – it made finding things related to a topic easier." Another participant stated that Focus was "easier to use than a conventional interface – especially for things that are stored in different ways (e.g. e-mail and photos)." Other valuable usability suggestions and general feedback were also given by participants (for more detail, see [35]).

A key issue emerging from the questionnaire responses was that of personal information privacy. Four participants explained that if they were to use such an interface for accessing their information with a friend or colleague they would need complete control over the search scope. One participant stated that they would only use Focus to connect to a machine that did not store private and sensitive information, but would be comfortable using it with a work machine.

Discussion

Our studies have highlighted several interesting properties of the different interfaces evaluated. We now discuss our research findings in terms of the key design aspects for our approach (outlined in an earlier section).

Collaboration: Our two comparative evaluations [33, 34] have shown that the mechanisms for file access at a tabletop can have a significant impact on the amount and style of interaction with information on the tabletop. A hierarchical interface is predictable if a user remembers the organisation, and is efficient for retrieving specific files for which their location is well-known. For collaboration, each user must access their own files individually and present this to others on the table-top. Associative access is less predictable, but can automatically retrieve similar information across each person's file collection. We have seen this encouraging interaction with each other's files, resulting in people viewing and discussing more information while working together at the tabletop. However, it is clear that a hierarchical approach is more appropriate in situations where ownership boundaries on the tabletop are desirable (for example, when users are discussing sensitive information that they want to maintain control over).

Context of Use: Our study of access to broader personal information collections [35] evoked interesting feedback from participants regarding privacy of their personal information. It is clearly an important area of exploration for tabletop file system interfaces. In our approach we have assumed that a user has exported a set of files to the tabletop that they wish to collaboratively access. Further studies are required to understand if people can sufficiently control the release of their files with the Focus Exporter tool, and to understand the implications of such control on the collaboration. It is particularly important that each user can tune the similarity calculation mechanism to suit their files and the task at hand. The feedback obtained in all three studies points to the importance of helping users better understand (and better exploit) how the similarity calculation mechanism works. Indeed, it is important that users can scrutinise and control the retrieval system, if it is to be as predictable as hierarchical access.

Orientation and Table Use: The study of Windows Explorer and Focus [34] has shown that the file access mechanism can have a significant impact on how people use the tabletop workspace. Hierarchical access encourages people to keep their folders and files directly in front of them, leading to greater control and some privacy over those files, though this potentially limits the use of the tabletop space. Due to the combined view of the file systems in Focus, people chose to employ semantic partitioning more frequently, resulting in a greater utilisation of the tabletop space. This improved support for forming spatial groupings of information with Focus is a valuable feature for tabletops [29].

Clutter: It is clear from our experiences that clutter is a key challenge in tabletop file system interfaces. A hierarchical interface requires users to regularly "clean-up" (i.e. close any folders/files that are no longer needed) in order to make space for other users of the tabletop. Our studies have indicated that the associative access approach has the potential to manage clutter better than a hierarchical interface, due to its automatic clearing of the tabletop when a new focus item is selected. The semantic partitioning encouraged by Focus led to people grouping information on the tabletop to manage clutter [34].

Limited Input: Focus was designed to address the limited input of a tabletop by not relying on users to enter search queries to locate their information. The approach has been to enable content-based *browsing* of multiple file systems with a single dwell gesture, which performs a focus selection, retrieving all similar files for display on the tabletop. The feedback in our studies to this approach has been positive. Participants found it particularly useful for integrating personal information that would otherwise be separated on a desktop computer [35], such as e-mail and the file system. For collaborative use, Focus has shown clear benefits for supporting people accessing similar information distributed across multiple file systems.

Collectively, these results show associative access to be a valuable direction for future tabletop file system interfaces that must foster collaboration. However, it is clear that users need hierarchical access when desired (or as a fallback when the associative access fails to locate the desired information). There are several key challenges to research further, including user control and understanding of the associative access mechanism, and studies with larger groups of participants. In our studies so far, participants have been provided with a set of authentic tasks and associated files to ensure comparability between experiments. Future studies will look at having users access their own files at the tabletop, as part of a larger group task.

Future Trends

The tabletop medium brings exciting new opportunities for enabling natural, highly collaborative interaction with digital information. There are several emerging directions that we believe are important to consider in future tabletop research.

The limitations of hierarchies for storing and retrieving files are well understood. We believe *tagging* is a powerful direction for file systems. Tagging has the advantage that it is relatively simple to access information without knowledge of its storage location. In particular, a set of related information can be easily retrieved from multiple devices at once. However, tagging requires input of additional meta-data for storage, so file storage interfaces should be designed to encourage this. As people carry increasingly sophisticated small devices with them, the need to access personal information that is distributed across these will be common. It is also clear that "cloud" (web-based) file storage will play an important role in the future, fur-thering the need to explore ways for users to integrate their local and remotely-stored information. Tagging may simplify this process, as retrieval of the needed informa-tion does not require locating each file in a particular part of the hierarchy on each device. Of particular importance is the research into techniques for bringing all of this information together for use on whichever device the user chooses, whether it be a desktop, wall display, tabletop or smartphone.

We have made considerable progress in understanding how to support file access on tabletops; complementary research must explore how people can *store* what they have done at the tabletop. It is unclear how this should operate at a tabletop, par-ticularly when people have been working with files retrieved from many devices – where should the result go and who should it belong to? It is important to sup-port transitioning from collaborative work at a tabletop back to individual work at a conventional desktop interface.

Another potential trend is the *carried personal server*. As computer storage becomes even cheaper and smaller, people will have the opportunity to carry large amounts, perhaps *all*, of their digital information with them, wherever they go. Being carried, these devices are likely to be limited to very small screens, or they may lack a visible interface entirely. Tabletops and other large display devices will serve an important role as "walk-up and use" terminals, where people can easily access and work with any of their digital information with no prior configura-tion. Arising in this scenario are important challenges of user interaction, privacy, security, software and hardware.

Conclusion

Tabletops are a promising medium for supporting people accessing and collabo-rating with their file systems and broader personal information collections. Our work has addressed the important question of how this fundamental functionality should operate at a multi-user tabletop. Our coverage of the topic has been focused on *access*, as we have not explored the implications of associative file access on management and storage.

This chapter has several key contributions. The first is our progress on interac-tion design for the fundamental tabletop facility of file access. This has particular importance for tabletops, the motivator of our work, but it also has a potential role for other classes of Single Display Groupware, such as wall-sized interac-tive displays. Another important contribution is the new focus-based associative file access mechanism: although this was designed in response to the particular demands of tabletops, we believe it has broader applicability both on desktops and on carried devices, particularly those with touch interaction. A third contribution is the results from studies we have conducted both to inform our interface design work and to evaluate the learnability and effectiveness of our file access interface approach.

Our studies have provided insight into new ways to support tabletop file system access. Hierarchical interfaces are well understood and efficient for retrieving specific information from a *known* location in one user's file system. However, for collaborative tabletops that must support access to multiple file systems concurrently, associative file system interfaces provide important benefits for helping people access their files together, and this can contribute to the collaboration around the tabletop.

Acknowledgments   This work is partly funded by the Smart Services CRC.

References

1. Apted T, Kay J, Quigley A (2006) Tabletop sharing of digital photographs for the elderly. In: Proceedings of CHI '06, ACM Press, New York, pp 781–790
2. Hilliges O, Baur D, Butz A (2007) Photohelix: Browsing, sorting and sharing digital photo collections. In: Proceedings of TABLETOP '07, IEEE Computer Society, Los Alamitos, CA, pp 87–94
3. Shen C, Lesh NB, Vernier F, Forlines C, Frost J (2002) Sharing and building digital group histories. In: Proceedings of CSCW '02, ACM Press, New York, pp 324–333
4. Vernier F, Lesh N, Shen C (2002) Visualization techniques for circular tabletop interfaces. Technical report TR2002-001, Mitsubishi Electric Research Laboratories
5. Morris MR, Paepcke A, Winograd T (2006) TeamSearch: Comparing techniques for co-present collaborative search of digital media. In: Proceedings of TABLETOP '06, IEEE Computer Society, Washington, DC, pp 97–104
6. Everitt K, Shen C, Ryall K, Forlines C (2006) MultiSpace: Enabling electronic document micro-mobility in table-centric, multi-device environments. In: Proceedings of TABLETOP '06, IEEE Computer Society, Washington, DC, pp 27–34
7. Rekimoto J, Saitoh M (1999) Augmented surfaces: A spatially continuous work space for hybrid computing environments. In: Proceedings of CHI '99, ACM Press, New York, pp 378–385
8. Everitt K, Shen C, Ryall K, Forlines C (2005) DocuBits and containers: Providing e-document micro-mobility in a walk-up interactive tabletop environment. Technical report TR2005-053, Mitsubishi Electric Research Laboratories
9. Shen C, Everitt K, Ryall K (2003) UbiTable: Impromptu face-to-face collaboration on horizontal interactive surfaces. In: Proceedings of UbiComp 2003, 5th international conference on ubiquitous computing, Springer, Berlin/Heidelberg, Lecture Notes in Computer Science, vol 2864, pp 281–288
10. Hartmann B, Morris MR, Cassanego A (2006) Reducing clutter on tabletop groupware systems with tangible drawers. In: Adjunct proceedings of UbiComp 2006, ubiquitous computing. Orange County, CA
11. Ritchie DM, Thompson K (1974) The UNIX time-sharing system. Communications of the ACM 17(7):365–375
12. Marsden G, Cairns DE (2003) Improving the usability of the hierarchical file system. In: Proceedings of SAICSIT '03, South African institute for computer scientists and information technologists, Republic of South Africa, pp 122–129
13. Quan D, Bakshi K, Huynh D, Karger DR (2003) User interfaces for supporting multiple categorization. In: Proceedings of INTERACT 2003, the 9th IFIP TC13 international conference on HCI, IOS Press, Amsterdam, pp 228–235

14. McGee K, Foo J (2004) DocPlayer: Why doesn't your desktop play this way?, http://www.ida.liu.se/˜kevmc/pubs/mcgee-docplayer.pdf , retrieved April 1, 2006
15. Malone TW (1983) How do people organize their desks? Implications for the design of office information systems. ACM Transactions on Information Systems 1(1):99–112
16. Gifford DK, Jouvelot P, Sheldon MA, O'Toole Jr JW (1991) Semantic file systems. In: Proceedings of the 13th ACM symposium on operating systems principles, ACM Press, New York, pp 16–25
17. Dourish P, Edwards WK, LaMarca A, Salisbury M (1999) Presto: An experimental architecture for fluid interactive document spaces. ACM Transactions on Computer-Human Interaction 6(2):133–161
18. Jones W, Phuwanartnurak AJ, Gill R, Bruce H (2005) Don't take my folders away! Organizing personal information to get things done. In: Proceedings of CHI '05, ACM Press, New York, pp 1505–1508
19. Dumais S, Cutrell E, Cadiz J, Jancke G, Sarin R, Robbins DC (2003) Stuff I've seen: A system for personal information retrieval and re-use. In: Proceedings of SIGIR '03, ACM Press, New York, pp 72–79
20. Cutrell E, Robbins D, Dumais S, Sarin R (2006) Fast, flexible filtering with Phlat – personal search and organization made easy. In: Proceedings of CHI '06, ACM Press, New York, pp 261–270
21. Freeman E, Gelernter D (1996) Lifestreams: A storage model for personal data. SIGMOD Record 25(1):80–86
22. Gemmell J, Bell G, Lueder R, Drucker S, Wong C (2002) MyLifeBits: Fulfilling the Memex vision. In: Proceedings of MULTIMEDIA '02, ACM Press, New York, pp 235–238
23. Karger DR, Bakshi K, Huynh D, Quan D, Sinha V (2005) Haystack: A customizable general-purpose information management tool for end users of semistructured data. In: Proceedings of CIDR '05, pp 13–27, http://www-db.cs.wisc.edu/cidr/cidr2005/papers/P02.pdf
24. Dumais S, Cutrell E, Sarin R, Horvitz E (2004) Implicit queries (IQ) for contextualized search. In: Proceedings of SIGIR '04, ACM Press, New York, pp 594–594
25. Robertson G, Czerwinski M, Larson K, Robbins DC, Thiel D, van Dantzich M (1998) Data mountain: Using spatial memory for document management. In: Proceedings of UIST '98, ACM Press, New York, pp 153–162
26. Scott SD, Carpendale MST, Habelski S (2005) Storage bins: Mobile storage for collaborative tabletop displays. IEEE Computer Graphics and Applications 25(4):58–65
27. Boardman R, Sasse MA (2004) "Stuff goes into the computer and doesn't come out": A cross-tool study of personal information management. In: Proceedings of CHI '04, ACM Press, New York, pp 583–590
28. Apted T, Kay J, Assad M (2005) Sharing digital media on collaborative tables and displays. In: Proceedings of the spaces in-between: Seamful vs. seamless interactions (in conjunction with UbiComp 2005), Tokyo
29. Scott SD, Grant KD, Mandryk RL (2003) System guidelines for co-located collaborative work on a tabletop display. In: Proceedings of ECSCW '03, Springer, Netherlands, pp 159–178
30. Shen C, Vernier FD, Forlines C, Ringel M (2004) DiamondSpin: An extensible toolkit for around-the-table interaction. In: Proceedings of CHI '04, ACM Press, New York, pp 167–174
31. Morris MR, Paepcke A, Winograd T, Stamberger J (2006) TeamTag: Exploring centralized versus replicated controls for co-located tabletop groupware. In: Proceedings of CHI '06, ACM Press, New York, pp 1273–1282
32. Bergman O, Beyth-Marom R, Nachmias R, Gradovitch N, Whittaker S (2008) Improved search engines and navigation preference in personal information management. ACM Transactions on Information Systems 26(4):1–24
33. Collins A, Apted T, Kay J (2007) Tabletop file system access: Associative and hierarchical approaches. In: Proceedings of TABLETOP '07, IEEE Computer Society, Washington, DC, pp 113–120

34. Collins A, Bezerianos A, McEwan G, Rittenbruch M, Wasinger R, Kay J (2009) Understanding file access mechanisms for embedded ubicomp collaboration interfaces. In: Proceedings of UbiComp 2009, ACM Press, New York, pp 135–144
35. Collins A, Kay J (2008) Collaborative personal information management with shared, interactive tabletops. In: Proceedings of personal information management 2008 (a CHI 2008 Workshop), http://pim2008.ethz.ch/papers/pim2008-collins-etal.pdf, accessed 12.03.2010

Chapter 15
Theory of Tabletop Territoriality

Stacey D. Scott and Sheelagh Carpendale

Abstract This chapter discusses empirical and theoretical investigations of the practice of tabletop territoriality in order to understand how to exploit such social interaction practices that people have developed over years of collaborating in traditional tabletop environments in the design of digital tabletops. These investigations reveal that collaborators at traditional tabletop workspaces use three types of tabletop territories to help coordinate their interactions within the shared tabletop workspace: personal, group, and storage territories. These tabletop territories facilitate collaborative interactions on a table by providing commonly understood social protocols that help people to share a tabletop workspace by clarifying which regions are available for individual or joint task work, to delegate task responsibilities, to coordinate access to task resources by providing lightweight mechanisms to reserve and share task resources, and to organize the task resources in the workspace.

Introduction

Few existing technologies provide the rich, fluid interactions that occur during co-located collaboration on traditional tables with traditional media, such as paper and pens. In hopes of leveraging the collaborative benefits of traditional tabletop workspaces researchers have begun to develop tabletop systems that enable access to digital media during a variety of collaborative activities, such as photo sharing, layout design, and educational games. Yet there are many open issues related to the design of collaborative tabletop systems, such as whether these systems should automatically enforce ownership of workspace content. This chapter discusses a set

S.D. Scott (✉)
Department of Systems Design Engineering, University of Waterloo, Waterloo, ON N2L 3G1, Canada
e-mail: s9scott@uwaterloo.ca

C. Müller-Tomfelde (ed.), *Tabletops – Horizontal Interactive Displays*, Human-Computer Interaction Series, DOI 10.1007/978-1-84996-113-4_15, © Springer-Verlag London Limited 2010

of empirical studies that investigated tabletop territoriality as manifested on traditional tables to better understand these open issues and to learn how to leverage the interaction skills people have developed over years of collaborating at traditional tables in digital tabletop interaction. The findings from these studies reveal that collaborators use three types of tabletop territories to help coordinate their interactions within the shared tabletop workspace: personal, group, and storage territories. These tabletop territories facilitate collaborative interactions on a table by providing commonly understood social protocols that help people organize and share the tabletop workspace.

In this chapter, we will explore the theoretical meta-understand that can be developed by examining these studies and ongoing application of these study results to digital tabletop interaction through the lens of the extensive more general research on human territoriality. The goals of this chapter are:

- To describe the empirical studies (both ours and others) that have informed the theory of tabletop territoriality,
- To provide background on the theoretical underpinnings of tabletop territoriality in the broader human territoriality literature,
- To describe the theory of tabletop territoriality and its implications for the design of digital tabletops, and
- To discuss possible future directions for this research, especially related to developing further knowledge of how territoriality manifests in digital tabletop settings.

Background

In the late 1980s and 1990s, several foundational studies occurred in the Computer-Supported Cooperative Work (CSCW) research community that focused on understanding collaborative interaction practices at a shared tabletop workspace [1–3]. Although these studies were conducted to inform the design of distributed groupware systems involving shared virtual workspaces, such as virtual whiteboards used during desktop conferencing, their findings provided the first detailed evidence of collaborative use of a tabletop workspace. This evidence provides an initial foundation for developing collaborative interaction theory that can be used, in turn, to develop design requirements for collaborative digital tabletop systems.

A key collaborative work practice identified by these early studies was workspace partitioning. In a study of collaborative tabletop design sessions, Tang [2] observed that workspace partitioning was a key resource for mediating group interactions. A subsequent study by Kruger et al. [4], which investigated the role of orientation in collaborative tabletop use, identified similar partitioning behaviour. Both Tang and Kruger et al. observed that people use proximity and orientation to establish personal and group spaces while collaborating at a table. Tang observed that during design activities, people establish a personal space in close proximity to them on the table to explore ideas on their own before presenting them to the group. Kruger et al. observed similar establishment of personal spaces during collaborative puzzle solving activities. In their study, participants' personal spaces were used to reserve pieces for their own use. Kruger et al.'s study also revealed that items located in someone's personal space were typically oriented towards themselves.

Although these studies provide a good starting point in understanding the practice of workspace partitioning, they offer limited insight into how or why partitioning facilitates collaboration. As such details may influence the design requirements of systems developed to support this work practice, we decided to conduct additional observational studies specifically designed to investigate tabletop interaction practices for the purpose of informing tabletop system design.

Our studies indicate that the partitioning behaviour reported in the literature is part of a more complex practice of establishing *tabletop territories* on a tabletop workspace, akin to the broader human behavioural practice of establishing *territories* in our physical environments (e.g., a roommate's "side of the room"). Taylor [5] defines human territoriality as:

> An interlocking system of attitudes, sentiments, and behaviors that are specific to a particular, usually delimited, site or location, which, in the context of individuals, or a small group as a whole, reflect and reinforce, for those individuals or group some degree of excludability of use, responsibility for, and control over activities in these specific sites (p. 81).

Taylor further specifies that territories "range in size from chairs, seats, or sides of a table, to street blocks" [5, p. 89]. Our observational data support Taylor's theory that territorial behaviour occurs during human interaction at a table. Our research also confirms Tang's [2] claim that workspace partitioning (or tabletop territoriality) can provide collaborative benefits, including task and group facilitation. These findings are consistent with research on human territoriality, which asserts that territories help mediate social interactions [5–7].

Facilitating task and group interactions on a digital tabletop system seems a worthwhile design goal, as it would allow people to focus on completing their task activities rather than expending time and effort coordinating their actions in the workspace. The remainder of this chapter describes our efforts to understand how to address this design goal.

Territoriality on Traditional Tabletop Workspaces

To further understand the potential task and collaborative benefits of the practice of tabletop territoriality and to elucidate how digital tabletop systems could be designed to support this collaborative practice, we conducted new observational studies of traditional tabletop collaboration. Evidence gathered from these studies was then synthesized with report findings from prior tabletop studies. This synthesis provided a broad view of collaborative interactions practices on a shared tabletop workspace over a wide variety of tasks and user groups. The theoretical human territoriality literature was used to interpret the meaning and generalizability of these empirical findings.

To address the inherent tradeoff between realism (ensuring ecologically valid scenarios and behaviour) and precision (being able to experimentally control extraneous influencers of behaviour and to accurately record behaviours) in existing (and ethical) research methods [8], we conducted two observational studies that were carefully designed to complement the existing studies of tabletop collaboration and to enable data triangulation and concept generalization [8].

The first study focused on observing spatial tabletop interaction in a casual usage setting where a variety of tabletop games were available for individual and group use. The study occurred in an open, public location (a university lounge and café area), where participants could come and go as desired. This created a relaxed, friendly atmosphere where people felt comfortable joining ongoing games or starting new ones. This setting provided opportunities to observe a wide variety of tabletop interaction practices, including patterns of individual and group tabletop use, usage patterns across different types of tabletop gaming activities (e.g. puzzles, boards games, card games), and interaction patterns across tables of different size and shape and across groups of different sizes and interpersonal dynamics.

While these observations provided significant insights into participants' broad patterns of spatial interaction practices, including workspace partitioning, their interactions could not be recorded in precise detail due to the study protocol used. To establish the relaxed atmosphere described above, and engender realistic individual and social behaviour that is difficult to reproduce in a laboratory setting, information posters that established implicit consent to study participation upon interaction with the study materials were used (see Scott [9] for details). As informed consent cannot be guarantee with such protocols, only handwritten observer field notes were used to record participants' spatial interactions. To supplement this broad view of tabletop interaction practices, a laboratory-based study was then conducted that enabled participants' spatial interactions during a collaborative tabletop design activity to be captured in fine detail using a video camera.

The specifics of these two studies are described below, along with the findings from the spatial interaction analyses conducted on each data set.

Study 1: Tabletop Territoriality in a Casual Setting

Several activity tables were set up in an open area adjacent to a lounge and café area where students, staff, and faculty often congregated at Dalhousie University in Halifax, NS, Canada. Observations were made during a consecutive, 5-hour period, during which 18 students participated in the various activities, for various lengths of time (10 min to several hours). A casual, "drop-in" style procedure was used. An implied method of subject consent was used whereby large signs were posted that advised people that by interacting at the activity tables they were consenting to be observed by the researcher.

Basic instructions were provided to explain each activity. Three activity tables were set-up: a puzzle table, a Pictionary® table, and a LEGO® table. The puzzle table consisted of two adjoining tables (76 cm² each), containing several puzzles: Tangram, a word puzzle, and a jigsaw puzzle. The Pictionary® table consisted of a round table (94 cm diameter) containing the Pictionary® game, in which teams competed to advance around a game board by identifying target phrases drawn by teammates. The LEGO® table consisted of one rectangular table (61×153 cm) containing a variety of Lego® blocks and instructions suggesting re-designing the university's Computer Science building, though participants were free to build whatever they wished. An opportunity also arose to observe (with their consent) several students playing the Magic™ card game (these students often played near the observational area). While primarily a card game played in the hand, the Magic™ game also involves placing cards and small game pieces on the table. Participants' tabletop interactions were recorded in observational field notes.

Data Analysis

Based on preliminary data analyses that indicated that tabletop collaborators tend to establish three types of tabletop territories, personal, group, and storage territories, the Study 1 field notes (textual notes and sketches of participants' tabletop interactions) were first reviewed to identify any overall interaction patterns that appeared to correspond to each type of tabletop territory. Next, the *affinity diagramming* analysis method [10] was applied to the field notes to help reveal the particular characteristics of each type of tabletop territory. To prepare the data for this process, each tabletop activity or interaction that appeared to correspond to a tabletop territory was recorded separately (duplicates were made if an activity or interaction appeared to correspond to multiple territories). The recorded observations were then separated into three groups–one for each type of tabletop territory–and then each group was used to create a separate affinity diagram.

Results and Discussion

The field note review and the affinity diagramming process revealed many interesting characteristics of personal, group, and storage territories, including what purpose each territory served for task and group interactions, typical activities that occurred in each territory, and the spatial properties of each territory. The following sections provide the details of these characteristics for each type of tabletop territory.

Characteristics of Personal Territories

Personal territories correspond to the "personal spaces" or "personal areas" that others have reported tabletop collaborators using for individual activities such as note-taking, reading, or writing (e.g., [2, 4]). The characteristics of personal territories revealed by the data analysis are summarized in Table 15.1. Personal territories were

Table 15.1 Characteristics of personal territories

Purpose
- Working on main task activities, by individuals alone at the table
- Working individually on same task that the group is working on in group space (e.g. exploring a tangram solution)
- Temporarily holding group resources
- Monitoring a collaborator's activities (sometimes used as a reference area for others)
- Assistance from other group members (e.g., counting cards in Magic^{TM})

Typical activities
- Reading, writing, and drawing (e.g. Pictionary^{TM}, word puzzle)
- Comparing items
- Assembling task products (when alone at the table) (e.g. puzzle, tan silhouette)
- Placing task items (e.g. cards in Magic^{TM})
- Searching of task items (e.g. puzzle pieces)
- Sorting task items (e.g. puzzle pieces)
- People leaned on the table in these spaces

Spatial properties
- Generally located in front of each person at the table
- Fluctuates as people come and go from the table
- Individuals use larger personal territories when working alone than when working in groups

used by participants working alone at the table to perform their main task activities, such as assembling the jigsaw puzzle or sorting puzzle pieces. Participants also used their personal territories to temporarily disengage from the group to perform independent activities, such as exploring an alternative solution to a tangram or word puzzle, or to reserve a task resource.

In addition to being useful for their respective "owners", personal territories were also a useful resource for other group members at the table. People occasionally monitored the activities and task items within their collaborators' personal territories. In an example from the tangram task, shown in Fig. 15.1, a participant, P$_B$, used his personal territory to explore an alternate solution to a tangram problem while the rest of the group continued to work on the problem in the group territory. When he thought he had the solution, he returned to the group territory to try out the idea with the actual tangram pieces (called tans). The other group members referred to the drawing located in his personal territory to help them understand his actions in the group territory.

On occasion, people offered assistance in someone else's personal territory. In an example from the Magic^{TM} game, shown in Fig. 15.2, the player P$_3$ assists another player, P$_4$, in P$_4$'s personal territory. Throughout the game P$_3$ offered P$_4$ (who appeared to be the least skilled Magic^{TM} player in the group) suggestions, instructions, and clarification of the rules. In this episode, P$_3$ helps P$_4$ count the game cards located in P$_4$'s personal territory. Though this space was typically reserved for P$_4$'s use, P$_3$, in the role of "tutor", appeared to be welcome to assist P$_4$ in this area.

These two episodes both illustrate the importance of allowing group members to view, and sometimes access, other members' personal territories. The ability to

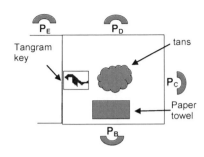

Fig. 15.1 Tangram table configuration

TRANSCRIPT EXCERPT:

P_E watches P_C put tangram together [tangram key is facing P_C]

P_B gets paper towel and pen and tries to draw the tans on a piece of paper towel to solve the current tangram.

...

P_B continues to draw on paper towel. Next, he moves 2 tans together in the middle of table, then returns to paper towel.

P_B says "Ok." He moves the tans around on the table. The other players are all looking at his paper.

P_D says "Now you need to get that inside."

P_E says "How many did you solve so far?" [to the group]

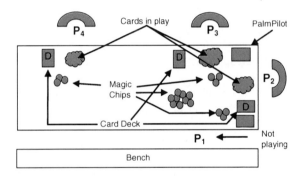

TRANSCRIPT EXCERPT:

P_3 & P_4 put game chips on cards in play on the table.

P_2 slides game chips towards himself when he wins a hand – keeping them on the table, he
   slides them one by one with his fingers.

P_2 has a card with 2 white chips sitting on top of it.

P_3 reaches over, touches all P_4's cards on the table while he counts out loud [appears to be counting points]

P_4 rotates his cards on the table 90 degrees.

P_1 is dealt into the game.

Fig. 15.2 Magic™ card game table configuration

monitor the artefacts and the interactions of others in their personal territories helps group members anticipate when assistance may be needed and helps them to understand their collaborators' motivations for actions that they perform in the group territory.

Typical actions within the personal territories included: reading, writing, and drawing; searching and sorting task artefacts; comparing task items; and placing, arranging, rotating, and moving items. It is important for tabletop systems to provide access to tools and functionality to support these tasks in or near each group member's personal territory to enable them to work independently in these territories and to provide enough space to accommodate these activities.

People typically established personal territories directly in front of them on the table. Group members also tended to restrict their personal territories to smaller areas than a person alone at a table. Additionally, the size and shape of personal territories tended to vary, expanding and contracting as the number of people at the table varied as people transitioned between working independently or in concert with the group. In general, people easily accommodated changes in group membership through fairly slight adjustments to the orientation and location of the task resources. This accommodation typically occurred with no accompanying verbal remarks related to the availability of task resources, yet people appeared to implicitly understand these actions to be an invitation to join the task interactions.

Characteristics of Group Territories

Group territories correspond to the "group spaces" or "shared areas" that others have reported tabletop collaborators using when cooperatively creating designs, playing games, or sharing tabletop objects (e.g., [2, 4]). Not surprisingly, our analysis revealed that group territories only emerged when there was more than one person at the table. Individuals performed tabletop activities using personal and storage territories only.

The characteristics of group territories revealed by the data analysis are summarized in Table 15.2. The group territory appeared to be available for use by all members of the group to perform the main task activities, such as assembling a tangram silhouette or interacting with the Pictionary® game board. People working in their personal territories sometimes also referred to items located in the group territory to assist with their individual task activities. Thus, it is important for a tabletop system to allow people to simultaneously view their personal territory and the group territory to facilitate quick glances between these two territories. Moreover, as illustrated in Fig. 15.1, people often transition quickly between using personal and group territories; thus, easy access to both territories should be provided.

Although assistance from other group members occasionally occurred in the personal territories, it typically occurred in the group territory. Assistance often resulted from one group member explicitly asking for help on a task activity. Unsolicited assistance was also observed, often after someone noticed a collaborator was having difficulty with a task activity. An example of unsolicited assistance is shown in Fig. 15.3, from the tangram task. In this episode, the participant, P_D, assists his partners, P_B and P_C, as they assemble the tangram silhouette in the group territory. As P_D watches his collaborators work in the group territory, he offers verbal suggestions, accompanied by gestures above the table surface.

People tended to establish one main group territory which was located in the central area of the table and extended to the areas between group members' seating positions. When sub-groups were present, multiple sub-group territories tended to be established on the table. These sub-group territories were typically located

Table 15.2 Characteristics of group territories

Purpose
- Working on group product or task by several members of the group
- Working on group product or task by an individual, while others in group discuss the problem (e.g., tangram)
- Placement of reference items for individual work when task is offloaded to personal territory to try new ideas (e.g., tangram)
- Assistance from other group members (e.g., tangram, moving a game piece out of the way)

Typical activities
- Assembling task product (e.g., tangram)
- Sorting
- Displaying group-related information (e.g., game board in Pictionary™)

Spatial properties
- Generally located in a central area on the table, easily accessible by all members (not all members can easily reach all of the group territory, but typically everyone can reach most of the space)
- Existence of sub-group territories when there are sub-groups working at the table (e.g., Pictionary™ and at the puzzle table, there were different groups working on different things at once – jigsaw, tangram, and word puzzles)
- Fluctuate in size, shape, and location in response to changes in personal territories, group size, and current task needs

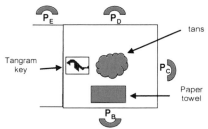

TRANSCRIPT EXCERPT:
They switch the tangram key to a new silhouette. In the middle of the table, P_B and P_C slide, pick up, replace, and arrange tans. P_D points and suggests moves but does not interact with tans.

P_D says "What about the small triangle?"

P_B says "You had it right the first time." Points to the tans with the pen. He draws on the paper towel again.

P_D says "You had the neck right before."

Fig. 15.3 Tangram table configuration

along the table edge between sub-group members' seating positions. Therefore, tabletop systems being used for activities that lend themselves to the formation of sub-groups, should enable such task interactions along the table edge between users. Placing fixed interface components in this area may hinder such interactions.

A more subtle example of unsolicited assistance in the group territory was observed during the Pictionary™ game. At one point during the game a player, P_H, noticed that a player from the opposing team, P_J, intended to flip the game timer. With no explicit request from P_J, P_H moved the game deck to create more space for the timer. This action provides an example of a commonly observed behaviour: group members accommodating the actions of others in the group territory. Group members frequently monitored what others were doing in the group territory, which enabled them to anticipate the needs of their collaborators and helped them coordinate their interactions in this shared space.

Typical actions in the group territories included assembly of the task product (e.g., moving, rotating, sorting, comparing, and arranging puzzle pieces) and displaying information relevant to all group members. Since this study only involved tabletop games, other types of interactions would likely be necessary for completing other tabletop activities. In general however, the activities necessary to complete the main task activities need to be supported in the group territory, as well as any support tools that the system may provide for facilitating these activities.

Characteristics of Storage Territories

Storage territories are areas on the table used for storing and organizing task resources and non-task items (e.g. food, drinks, and books). The characteristics of storage territories revealed by the data analysis are summarized in Table 15.3. Storage territories served as a place to store task resources (e.g., loose puzzle pieces, spare paper or pencils), reference items (e.g., the tangram key), and non-task items (e.g., food and drinks). Establishing storage territories appeared to help participants organize task and non-task items in the workspace.

Typical storage territory activities related to organizing stored task resources. Participants often piled, searched, and sorted items within these territories. Items were often moved between storage territories and the other tabletop territories, sometimes one item at a time and sometimes groups of items at a time. The contents within storage territories were typically very loosely arranged: little effort was made to keep the storage areas strictly organized. For example in the jigsaw puzzle task, participants created separate piles of items in the storage territories for various

Table 15.3 Characteristics of group storage

Purpose
- Place to store task resources (e.g., puzzle pieces, pencils, spare paper)
- Placement of non-task items (e.g., bowls, cups, etc.)
- Placement of reference items (e.g., puzzle key in tangram, box lids in jigsaw puzzle)

Typical activities
- Searching, when brought closer (e.g., puzzle)
- Loose arrangement of items
- Piling
- Storing items
- Movement of items in "bunches" to personal territory (e.g., a group of puzzle pieces were piled/spread out for use)

Properties
- Often located at the periphery of the personal and group territories
- Multiple storage areas
- Moveable storage areas (e.g. puzzle box lid)
- Full and partial storage areas – some appear to be more "temporary" than others
- Can be piled (e.g. jigsaw puzzle box lids)

---

classes of puzzle pieces. The box lids, turned upside down to act as make-shift trays, were often used to store loose piles of puzzle pieces.

The ability to loosely arrange items in the storage territories allowed people to exert only the necessary amount of effort to organize the workspace as the task evolved. For example as one participant assembling the jigsaw puzzle came across each corner piece in a pile of pieces in the box lids, he added them to a pile of corner pieces beside the partially assembled puzzle. At the time of discovery, he was not ready to add them to the assembled edge. Storing them in this pile allowed him to separate them from the other, non-classified, pieces and access them more efficiently when needed. As the task evolved and became more organized, people spent more time arranging items in the workspace; yet before those final stages of the task, people tended to want more casual access to task resources. Tabletop systems should support varying levels of resource organization by allowing casual storage of items in the workspace.

The above example also illustrates some of the spatial properties of storage territories. Multiple storage territories were often kept on the table. Participants also established temporary storage territories that contained artefacts that were quickly reincorporated into the main activity. In general, storage territories typically emerged on the periphery of the personal and group territories, but were also located on other convenient surfaces, such as table edges, nearby chairs, box lids, people's laps, and the floor.

In summary, the analysis of Study 1 revealed that personal, group, and storage territories all play an important role in both task and group interactions. Personal territories provide a space for people to perform task activities (e.g., reading, writing, and sorting resource items), and also appear to serve an important collaborative role by providing a visible, accessible area for other group members to keep track of a teammate's independent activities. The group territory provides a space for collaborators to work together on the task product and to assist each other in task activities. Finally, storage territories provide a space for organizing resource items on the table, and can be created on auxiliary surfaces that can be moved around the table.

Study 2: Tabletop Interactions in a Formal Setting

The second study involved three small groups (2–3 participants each) performing a layout planning activity on a table using traditional media in a laboratory setting. Seven university students from a variety of academic backgrounds were paid to participate in the experiment. Participants performed the experimental task seated at a round table (94 cm diameter) located in a usability laboratory at Dalhousie University.

Each group was asked to create a furniture layout plan for a reading room in a library, which adhered to a set of design requirements. The layout plan was to be created on a white, circular cardboard Floor Plan (61 cm in diameter) located on the experiment table. Participants were given paper supplies to create the furniture layout, including paper icons of furniture and Post-it[TM] notes, pens, and scissors to make custom items. At the beginning of the activity, piles of related furniture items were located in the middle of the Floor Plan and other resources were piled on the table edge. The task took between 30 and 45 min to complete. Participants' activities were videotaped and observational field notes were collected.

Data Analysis

To help understand the significance of participants' interactions within the table-top workspace a new video analysis method was developed, called *spatial action analysis*. This analysis method involved first partitioning the tabletop workspace into various interaction zones. Because the interactions occurred on a round table, a compass-style partitioning was used, along with a centre-to-table edge partition-ing. That is, the table was divided into 16 *directional zones* (Fig. 15.4) and 4 *radial zones* (Fig. 15.5). Participants' tabletop activities were then transcribed from the video data and coded according to their directional and radial zone locations.

Fig. 15.4 Directional zones

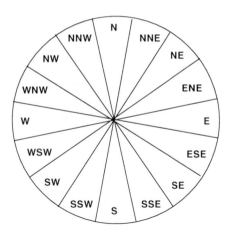

To help interpret the results of the spatial action analysis, an *activity plot* was created for each study participant (Fig. 15.6). Each activity plot summarized the tabletop activity that one group member performed in each tabletop zone during their entire collaborative session. The tabletop activity performed in each zone is represented by a dot centred in the corresponding zone. The size of the dot in each zone corresponds to the *relative* amount of activity the participant performed in that zone, as compared to the maximum amount of actions that occurred in any one tabletop zone. The amount of activity is mapped to six dot sizes (smallest to largest): 1–9, 10–29, 30–49, 50–69, 70–89, and 90–100%. The absence of a dot corresponds to an absence of activity by that participant in that zone. The location of the participant who performed the actions is indicated beside the plot with a silhouette icon.

Fig. 15.5 Radial zones

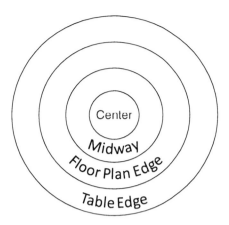

Results and Discussion

The results of the spatial action analysis confirm that participants made use of tabletop territories to help coordinate their actions during the layout planning activity.
The analysis reveals that participants in Study 2 also established personal, group,
and storage territories during their collaborative sessions. The analysis also provides
a more precise understanding of some of the characteristics of tabletop territories
revealed by the analysis of Study 1. For example, the fine-grained observations
enabled by the video data suggest that storage territories sit atop the group and personal territories in the workspace and are not separate partitions in the workspace.
The results of the spatial action analysis in conjunction with the video transcripts
clarify who interacted where on the table and what they were doing when interacting
at those locations.

Personal Territories

Participants' spatial interactions during their collaborative sessions are shown in
the activity plots in Fig. 15.6. These plots demonstrate that tabletop activity was
strongly influenced by the participants' seating positions. Across all three groups,
participants dominated the activity in the *table edge* zones directly in front of them
(87–100% of the actions that occurred in these zones). Participants used the *table
edge* zones nearest them for keeping furniture items they used frequently, for writing
on Post-it[TM] notes, for reading instruction sheets, and for cutting items into custom
shapes. Thus, it appears that participants used the *table edge* zones directly in front
of them on the table as their personal territories.

Personal territories appeared to provide each person with dedicated space on the
table for performing independent activities. When participants wanted to modify
Floor Plan items they would typically remove the item from its position on the
Floor Plan, modify it in their personal territories, and then replace it on the Floor

Activity Plots

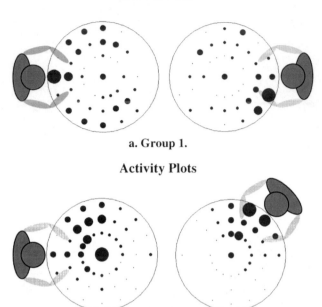

a. Group 1.

Activity Plots

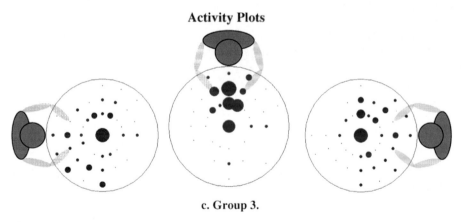

b. Group2. [†] This person spent 5 minutes at N then moved to NE.

Activity Plots

c. Group 3.

Fig. 15.6 Activity plots for each group: (**a**) group 1, (**b**) group 2, and (**c**) group 3. Each plot indicates the relative amount of activity that each person performed in the various regions on the shared tabletop workspace throughout the entire collaborative session

Plan. This behaviour facilitated both the interactions of individual group members and of the group as a whole.

Ergonomically, the proximity of the personal territory eased such tasks as reading, writing, and manipulating items. Also, by moving an item into their personal territory, the person implicitly communicated their intentions to use the item, effectively reserving it for their own use. Furthermore, while this person was interacting in their person territory, there was more space available in the group territory for their collaborators to work on other parts of the task. These benefits illustrate the importance of allowing people to easily move items between the group and personal territories in a digital tabletop workspace, as well as the importance of providing access to support tools, such as item editing and manipulation tools, within the personal territory.

Though no group explicitly discussed reserving these areas for anyone's personal use, participants performed very few, if any, actions in their collaborators' personal territories (0–13% of any actions that occurred in these zones), even in the group of three participants where multiple participants could easily reach the area in front of other group members. It appears that social norms dictate that the tabletop area directly in front of someone is reserved for use by that person.

In general, when a group member wanted an item that was located in someone else's personal territory, they would ask that person to pass them the item. In the few cases where someone did interact in someone else's personal territory, they were always retrieving a task resource. These interactions occurred quickly and fluidly with little to no disruption to the actions of the "owner" of the personal territory. Often, these actions were accompanied by changes in body language which appeared to signify the owner giving permission to the collaborator for interacting in that area. For example, the owner would often sit back a little when they noticed their partner reaching for something in their personal territory, and would often stay in that position until their partner was done. Alternatively, people would also just move their arms to the left or right as their partner accessed items in their personal territory, while continuing to interact with items on the table. Sometimes the owner would more actively accommodate their partner's interactions by helping them find a resource item, and then returning to their previous activities once the desired resources were found.

Group Territories

Figure 15.6 indicates that personal territories were the only areas consistently avoided by others. Thus, it appears that the remaining tabletop workspace was generally considered available for all group members to use. To varying degrees, all participants utilized most of the Floor Plan and table edge locations between participants. It appears, then, that the group territory covered the entire table to the exclusion of the areas occupied by personal territories.

The group territory was primarily used for assembling furniture arrangements in the Floor Plan. It was also used to discuss layout ideas and to assist others in creating or modifying furniture arrangements. Moreover, it served as a place to share task resources. Participants would often pass each other resource items via the group territory.

All groups used a divide-and-conquor approach to perform the layout task, spending the majority of their time working independently on different furniture arrangements in separate regions of the group territory, essentially partitioning up the group territory (Fig. 15.6). Unlike the personal territories though, no area of the group territory appeared to be exclusively reserved for use by any one group member. The partitioning of the group territory appeared to help group members avoid conflicts while sharing the workspace by clarifying who should work where. This partitioning occurred with little to no verbal negotiation. Participants typically discussed what type of arrangements should be made in the workspace rather than who should be working where.

Generally, participants took the initiative for creating and maintaining arrangements in the Floor Plan directly in front of them, as illustrated by participants' dominance of the actions performed in the group territory nearest them. In the two pair groups, participants were responsible for well over half of the interactions in the group territory zones nearest them (70–94% of the actions[1]). In the group of three, participants performed well over one third of the actions in the group territory nearest them (48–70% of the actions[1]).

This implicit delegation of responsibility of the workspace areas in close proximity to each group member appeared to clarify each member's role in the collaborative task, helping them to coordinate their workspace activities. However, there appeared to be more ambiguity as to who was responsible for areas farther away from any group member. In general, interaction in these areas was much less dominated by any particular person and involved more verbal negotiation. Similarly, the activity plots and video data revealed that there was also less exclusivity of use and more verbal negotiation in areas that were equally close to several people. For example, participants in Group 3 (who were seated closer together than participants in the other groups), spent less time working independently in the group territory and more time negotiating their furniture arrangements as compared to the other 2 groups. It appears, that the ease with which group members can divide up responsibility for the group territory partially depends on the amount of space each individual group member alone can easily reach: the more "overlap" areas or "out of reach" areas there are, the more explicit coordination will likely be needed. Thus, both the size of the table and the seating arrangement of collaborators can potentially impact the ease of coordinating activities in a tabletop workspace.

One observed event suggests that the proximity of items in the group territory influenced how responsible group members felt for those items. About 30 minutes into Group 2's session, the participants rotated the Floor Plan. The rotation was initiated by the participant seated at West, who wanted to work on an area of the Floor Plan located across the table from her. Together, she and her partner carefully rotated the Floor Plan about 110° counter-clockwise on the table. After the workspace rotation, the area she wanted to work on was located closer to her (in the N direction) and another fairly unfinished area was in front of her. She spent the remainder of the

---

[1]This represents the activity in the three directional zones directly in front of each person. For example for participants at W, the *floor plan edge* and *midway* activity is reported in the WSW, W, and WNW zones.

session working mostly in these areas, as indicated by the concentration of actions in the NW to N directions in her activity plot (Fig. 15.6b).

Before the rotation, the participant at NE (pNE) expressed his concern that an arrangement his partner (pW) had created on the table in front of her was too cluttered. At the time, pNE made some minor adjustments to it, but pW immediately readjusted the arrangement, almost back to its original state. After the rotation, this arrangement was located near pNE (in the E direction). He soon began removing items from the arrangement and readjusting it. pW helped him a little, readjusting the arrangement while pNE removed items, but in the end, they agreed on a final arrangement that contained much fewer furniture items. pW seemed much more open to pNE's input on "her" arrangement once it had moved closer to him (or farther from her) on the table. pNE also appeared more comfortable taking charge of the arrangement in its new position. Interestingly, pNE appeared to be the less dominant team member. Throughout their session, pW appeared more comfortable interacting on pNE's "side" of the table, as illustrated by the four times as many actions that she performed in his half of the workspace (220 actions) as he did in hers (53 actions).

This episode suggests that there may be positive benefits to enabling rotation of the main work area on a digital tabletop workspace. It may allow less dominant members of the group to more freely contribute their ideas to the workspace. Such functionality may be particularly appropriate for moderated collaborative settings where a facilitator (e.g., a teacher in a classroom) can initiate a workspace rotation, especially since a less dominant team member may not be assertive enough to initiate such a global action. However, caution should be taken in providing workspace rotation functionality in a digital workspace since such an action would likely affect all content in the workspace and, thus, may be disruptive to the group activity if other members are not expecting the action to occur.

Storage Territories

Throughout their sessions, participants stored the task resources in storage territories at various locations on the table. These storage territories were relocated in the workspace at different stages of the task, depending on where participants were currently working and what task resources they currently needed. Storage territories often contained loosely arranged individual items, piles of items, or a mix of both. Using storage territories to casually store workspace items appeared to help collaborators organize their task resources during the layout planning task.

At the beginning of each layout session, all of the furniture icons were contained in several piles located in the centre of the Floor Plan. By the end of each session, all spare furniture icons had been moved to the table edge. How quickly these resources migrated from a large storage territory in the centre of the table to several storage territories along the table edge, however, depended on the organizational preferences and working style of each group. In general, the mobility of the storage territories enabled groups to access task resources where they needed them, when they needed them.

Similar to the behaviour observed in Study 1, participants in this study appeared to maintain only loose organization of task resources within each storage territory. This loose organization often provided certain benefits to completing the layout task. It provided a cognitively lightweight mechanism for storing resource items. The process of searching through items in a loosely organized store of task resources also appeared to benefit the layout task by prompting discussions about the current state of furniture arrangements. For example, during one of Group 3's discussions of what type of chairs to use in a specific furniture arrangement, one participant asked the group the difference between two types of chairs he had noticed while browsing through a pile of chairs on the Floor Plan. The group discussed the two types of chairs, eventually deciding to use the "comfortable chairs". They then continued working on the furniture arrangement.

The location of a storage territory appeared to influence who utilized the resources contained within it. Stored resource items were often shared among participants, especially when the storage territory was located along the table edge between participants or in the *midway* or *central* zones. Participants often moved these storage territories around the group territory as they shared these resources. In contrast, when a storage territory was located in or near someone's personal territory, that person often became responsible for distributing those resources. For example, the participant at NE in Group 2 became responsible for creating and distributing customized items using the Post-it^{TM} notes located on the table edge to his left (in the E-ENE direction). Relative to his activity on the rest of the workspace, he made frequent use of the table edge directly in front of and adjacent to him (44% of his total tabletop actions occurred on the table edge between N and E). Delegating responsibility for task resources appeared to facilitate the divide-and-conquer strategy used by all groups to perform the layout task, a strategy commonly used in collaborative activities [11, 12]. Similar to delegating partitions of the group territory, having one group member responsible for distributing certain resources allowed the other group members to focus on other aspects of the group task.

Interaction Between Territories

Each type of tabletop territory played an important role in helping participants share the tabletop workspace while performing the layout planning task. Based on the activity patterns discussed above, though, it appeared that all three tabletop territories did not exist as mutually exclusive partitions of the workspace. Personal and group territories appeared to be separate partitions, with associated accessibility properties, defined and controlled through social norms. Personal territories appeared to be extensions of group members' personal spaces [13]; thus, a personal territory existed in the tabletop workspace directly adjacent to each person and was generally reserved for use by that person. The group territory covered the remaining tabletop workspace, including the areas in the centre and along the table edge between participants. In general, items in the group territory appeared to be available to all group members. However, responsibility for task items in areas of the group territory within close proximity to a particular group member appeared to be implicitly delegated to that person, at least in tasks that afford a divide-and-conquer strategy.

Storage territories, on the other hand, appeared to exist atop these other two territories and were mobile in the workspace. Furthermore, they took on the accessibility property of the territory on which they were currently located. For example, the activity plots and video data revealed that when a storage territory was located in the group territory, all participants tended to utilize the resources it contained. Whereas, when a storage territory was located on the table adjacent to someone, that person typically became the sole or dominant user of its resources. Simply moving a single resource item (or an entire group of resources) from the group territory to someone's personal territory and vice versa provided a lightweight mechanism for changing the availability of an item (or items), helping collaborators coordinate their use of the available resources.

In summary, the spatial action analysis of Study 2 clarifies our understanding of personal, group, and storage territories. Personal territories tend to be used almost exclusively by their "owner", while the group territory tends to be shared by group members. The analysis also reveals that when a task lends itself to a division of labour, partitions emerge within the group territory. These partitions appear to clarify the responsibilities of each group member in the workspace, helping group members coordinate their use of the workspace. However, the findings also suggest that such partitioning may restrict the contributions of less dominant group members who have ideas for the portion of the group activity being performed in someone else's partition. Rotating the workspace may help mediate this situation. Such workspace actions should be done with caution, however, as they might introduce ambiguity as to the responsibilities of each group member in the workspace, which may increase the need for explicit coordination and verbal negotiation.

The study findings also indicate that storage territories appear to sit atop the group and personal territories, rather than existing as separate partitions in the workspace. Storage territories appear to take on the accessibility property of whichever territory over which they are currently positioned. The ability to move storage territories in the workspace appears to provide a lightweight, commonly understood, mechanism for collaborators to change the availability of resource items – either to reserve them for personal use or to make them available to other group members.

Figure 15.7 shows a conceptual diagram of the relationship between the three types of tabletop territories. In general, when group members arrive at a table, the table surface is available for sharing and, thus, forms the group territory. A personal territory is then established in front of each group member at the table, expanding and contracting as necessary, and moving with the person's tabletop location. Storage territories, on the other hand, are established in a variety of locations on the table and appear to sit atop the personal and group territories. Storage territories are also moved around the tabletop workspace to suit the current task needs.

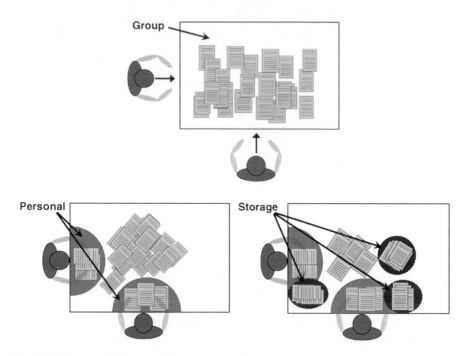

Fig. 15.7 Conceptual diagram of the three types of tabletop territories

Theoretical Perspective from the Human Territoriality Literature

To help us understand the practice of tabletop territoriality in the broader context of human interaction, this section discusses the more general phenomenon of *human territoriality*. Over our lifetime we develop many strategies to mediate our interactions with the people we encounter and work within our homes, in our workplaces, on the street, at a table, and so on. One such strategy is human territoriality. Territoriality helps mediate people's social interactions [5, 14–16]. Fisher et al. [7] state that, in contrast to territorial behaviour in animals, for humans, "many of the purposes territoriality serve are not as closely related to survival, and they may be seen primarily as 'organizers' on a variety of dimensions (e.g., they promote predictability, order, and stability in life)" (p. 178).

There is little agreement in the literature on a precise definition of territoriality (Table 15.4 provides several examples); however, most researchers agree that territoriality involves the use of or access to a physical space and "ownership" or "rights to" that space, and may also involve the concepts of defence, exclusivity of use, personalization, and identity (e.g., [5, 7, 14, 15–17]). Gifford [17] explains the lack of agreement on a precise definition as a "matter of emphasis" (p. 137). As

Table 15.4 Sample definitions of human territoriality

Territoriality as a means to assert some level of control or ownership over a space:

Human territoriality can be viewed as a set of behaviours and cognitions an organism or group exhibits, based on perceived ownership of physical space [7, p. 176]

Territoriality is a pattern of behavior and attitudes held by an individual or group that is based on perceived, attempted, or actual control of a definable physical space, object, or idea and may involve habitual occupation, defence, personalization, and marking of it [17, p. 137]

Territorial functioning refers to: an interlocking system of attitudes, sentiments, and behaviors that are specific to a particular, usually delimited, site or location, which, in the context of individuals, or a small group as a whole, reflect and reinforce, for those individuals or group some degree of excludability of use, responsibility for, and control over activities in these specific sites [5, p. 81]

Territoriality as a means of maintaining a desired level of personal space and privacy:

Territorial behaviour is a self/other boundary-regulation mechanism that involves personalization of or marking of a place or object and communication that it is "owned" by a person or pup. Personalization and ownership are designed to regulate social interaction and to help satisfy various social and physical motives. Defense responses may sometimes occur when territorial boundaries are violated [14, p. 107]

Territoriality as a means to control or influence people, phenomena, or relationships:

Territoriality is "the attempt by an individual or group to affect, influence, or control people, phenomena, and relationships, by delimiting and asserting control over a geographical area. . . . [Territories] are the results of strategies to affect, influence, and control people, phenomena, and relationships." [16, p. 19]

shown in Table 15.4, some researchers emphasize the "control" aspect of territoriality (e.g., over a space or a person), while others emphasize the "preservation" aspect of territoriality (e.g., the ability to maintain personal space in a crowded place).

Taylor's definition of territoriality was given in earlier in the chapter (and also appears in Table 15.4) to establish the complexity of human territoriality: how territoriality manifests in our behaviour changes over place and time and is highly context dependent. As this definition suggests, and as our analyses show, the level of territorial behaviour exhibited in a tabletop workspace is context dependent: the available table space, the group size, the task activities, and other factors that are detailed below influence people's territorial behaviour during tabletop collaboration.

For the purposes of the remaining discussion, though, the simpler, operational definition of territoriality offered by many environmental psychologists will suffice. Fisher et al. [7] state that:

Human territoriality can be viewed as a set of behaviours and cognitions an organism or group exhibits, based on perceived ownership of physical space (p. 176).

This definition highlights an important aspect of territoriality that our investigations reveal to be a key aspect of the territorial behaviour exhibited on a table: the notion that territorial behaviour stems from the "perceived ownership" of space.

This view of territoriality is also reflected in Altman's [14], Gifford's [17], and Taylor's [5] discussions of human territoriality. As our studies show, when people interact in a shared tabletop workspace, they exhibit more territorial behaviour (i.e., more exclusivity of use) in areas of the table where the "ownership" (or sense of "responsibility for") those areas is implicitly understood by all group members.

Primary, Secondary, and Public Territories

Many environment psychologists distinguish between three main types of territories used by humans: primary, secondary, and public (e.g., [7, 14, 17]). These territories differ across a number of dimensions, including the associated level of perceived ownership, how serious an intrusion by another person or group is perceived to be, and the typical duration of use or occupancy of the space in question [7]. Examples of primary territories include a house or a dorm room. These places have a fairly permanent level of perceived ownership and are likely to be defended if an intrusion from a "non-owner" occurs. A classroom, on the other hand, is an example of a secondary territory. This territory has a moderate level of perceived ownership, whereby students and teachers using the classroom are perceived to be one of a number of "qualified" users. Finally, an area on the beach, a restaurant table, and seats on a bus are all examples of public territories. These territories are characterized by low perceived ownership of the space, short duration of use, and generally being available to a large number of possible users.

With respect to these three types of human territories, work tables are likely somewhere between a secondary and a public territory, depending on the context. For example, whether a table is located in someone's personal office, in a communal meeting room, or in a cafeteria may affect the perceived level of ownership of the table space and the resulting level of territoriality exhibited. Whether the contents of the table are owned by a particular group member may also affect the level of territoriality exhibited. However, for "peer" collaborations where group members have come together for a shared purpose, it is likely that group members would perceive a fairly equal level of ownership of the shared table space. Thus, for our purposes we will consider work tables as public territories. Taylor [5] asserts that people exhibit "minimal territorial functioning" in public territories, which helps in "facilitating usage and minimizing conflict" (p. 222).

Design Can Affect Territorial Behaviour

Poorly designed public territories can hinder people's ability to exhibit their preferred level of territorial behaviour, sometimes leading to social discomfort and disorder. Altman [14] claims that:

> The occupant of a public territory is at the mercy of a culture or spatial designer. For example, the crowded elevator and the crowded subway or bus do not really allow very much

space per person ... and restaurants sometimes seat different parties overly close to one another. Thus if the design of a public territory is bad, there may not be efficient boundary-control mechanisms. One might expect, therefore, that people will often have to rely heavily on other mechanisms, such as nonverbal and verbal behaviors, to assist in regulation of privacy in public settings (p. 120).

While Altman speaks about territoriality as a means of maintaining a desired level of personal space and privacy (which is the focus of his research), it is also reasonable to assume that other aspects of territoriality, such as the role it plays in mediating people's social interactions, will be affected by poor spatial design. The findings from our studies support this supposition: in situations where collaborators had a compromised tabletop workspace (e.g., the table was small or people were seated close together) they exhibited less territorial behaviour, and required more explicit verbal and non-verbal negotiation to share the workspace.

It must be noted that most research in human territoriality focuses on how people can effectively avoid conflict, maintain personal space and privacy, protect their homes and possessions, and so on. However, in collaborative situations, especially among peers, people are often willing to make personal compromises, such as being willing to maintain a smaller personal space and being willing to share their possessions, in order to gain the benefits of working with others. The primary goal of our investigations is to uncover precisely how territorial behaviour can help people *work together* on a tabletop workspace. Our hope is that this knowledge will enable the design of digital tabletop workspaces that effectively support people's social and task interactions.

Implications for the Design of Digital Tabletop Systems

Consistent with Taylor's assertion that territoriality in public territories is context dependent, our findings indicate that the social meaning attributed to tabletop regions was derived from the current context of tabletop activities and often changed over time. We observed that the size, shape, and sometimes location, of tabletop territories often changed as a tabletop activity evolved. Within the human territoriality literature a location, or partition of space, and a territory are often considered equivalent. Yet, our findings revealed that tabletop territories are not necessarily mutually exclusive partitions in the workspace. Considering a tabletop territory as a unique combination of its *spatial properties* (i.e. size, shape, and location), its *purpose,* and the *interactions* it supports provides a deeper understanding of how these territories contribute to the collaborative process. This knowledge can then be used to guide the design of digital tabletops to support the practice of tabletop territoriality.

Table 15.5 summarizes these three aspects of group, personal, and storage territories. This table synthesizes our findings with related findings from the literature to provide a broader picture of tabletop territoriality. The spatial properties listed in this table represent the general spatial properties of tabletop territories. In practice, the

Table 15.5 Design aspects of personal, group, and storage territories

	Personal territories	Group territories	Storage territories
Purpose	• Provides space for independent activities away from the main group interactions [2, 4], enabling various levels of participation in group activity • Provides "semi-private" space to explore alternate ideas that may later be integrated into main group activity [2]	• Provides space to perform main task activities [2, 4], including: - working together on the task - working independently the task [3] - sharing task resources [3] - discussing ideas [2, 1] • Provides space to assist others [1]	• Provides place to store task resources (e.g., tools, reference materials) • Organizes tabletop items • Enables people to access task resources *where* they need them, *when* they need them • Enables reservation of task resources
Spatial properties	• Typically established directly in front of each group member, within immediate reach [4] • Typically stationary while the person remains at the same tabletop location	• Typically one central group territory [2, 4] • Occupies areas available for sharing, typically within reach of group members (e.g., centre of table and table edges between group members) • Sub-group territories are sometimes established between adjacent team members	• Sit atop the other tabletop territories • Mobile in the workspace • Often positioned near the edges of personal or group territories
Interactions	• Typical task interactions, such as reading, writing, and manipulating items • Items tend to be oriented toward the territory "owner" [4] • Task items often smaller here than in group territory; proximity makes items easy for "owner" to see [2]. Small items helps create "semi-private" space [2]	• Often mix of tightly-coupled and loosely-coupled interactions [2, 1] • People sometimes partition the group territory, assuming responsibility for proximate regions [18] • People tend to use larger task objects (when available), enabling sharing of objects [19] • "Compromised orientation of items used to accommodate most group members [4]	• Organizational activities, including: - adding and removing items - reorganizing individual and piled items - searching and comparing items • Items are added or removed, one at a time or in groups of items at a time

size and shape of these tabletop territories often fluctuate during collaborative tabletop interaction, again, depending on the context. Factors that influence this dynamic behaviour are discussed in the box below.

Factors Influencing the Spatial Properties of Tabletop Territories
Our investigations revealed several distinct factors that can influence the spatial boundaries of tabletop territories:

Group size and seating arrangement. People easily accommodate others at the table by altering the size of their personal territories. When people are close together, they generally use small personal territories. This provides extra space for the group territory and for other people's personal territories.

Size of the table. Small tables force people to sit close together, influencing the establishment of tabletop territories as discussed above. A small table may prevent group members from simultaneously establishing personal, group, and storage territories. It may also compromise the group's ability to share the table space. A larger table enables people to sit at a comfortable distance and establish tabletop territories within reach. However, an overly large table may force group members to sit far apart, which may hinder people's ability to access shared items in the group territory.

Visible barriers. A visible demarcation of tabletop regions can restrict people's perceived personal space [7]. Such visible barriers in the tabletop workspace may create a psychological barrier to expanding a tabletop territory across it. For instance, the edge of the cardboard Floor Plan in Study 2 appeared to restrict peoples' personal territories from this edge to the table edge.

Task activities. Tabletop territories often change shape and size as a task activity evolves. People expand and contract their personal territories based on whether they are working independently or in concert with the group. These spatial changes to the personal territories lead to corresponding spatial changes to the group territory. Also, storage territories are often expanded when someone is searching for a stored item.

Task materials. Larger task items will necessarily need more space for manipulating and sharing than smaller task items. For instance, a group sharing a large map will need a larger group territory than a group sharing a few Post-it^{TM} notes. Having a large task item covering the table (e.g., an architectural schematic) may also restrict people's ability to establish personal territories.

Overall, the spatial properties of tabletop territories reflect people's opportunistic use of table space: they tend to use whatever space is available. At the same time these spatial properties are strongly influenced by social protocol that requires people to accommodate others at the table. People typically restrict their personal activities to "socially appropriate" areas on the table. They generally refrain from using the table space directly in front of others and try to accommodate their collaborators as well as they can given the available table space.

One of the most important findings revealed by our investigations is that providing fixed visible partitions in the workspace may in fact hinder natural territorial behaviour during tabletop collaboration. The above discussion illustrates that the size, shape, and location of tabletop territories typically fluctuate over the course of a collaborative activity. Moreover, partitioning the digital workspace into personal and group areas, as done in several existing collaborative tabletop systems [20–22] may in fact present a visible barrier to collaborators that may hinder optimal usage of table space. Supporting the practice of tabletop territoriality in digital tabletop workspaces appears to need a more subtle approach.

The spatial properties, purpose, and interactions supported by each type of tabletop territory described in Table 15.5 can be used to develop collaborative tabletop workspaces that support a variety of usage scenarios. A key theme revealed by the tabletop studies discussed in this chapter is that traditional tabletop workspaces enable appropriation of a single workspace for a wide variety of uses and users. The same table can support different individual and collaborative working styles, task materials (large and small, and few and many task items), individual and collaborative task activities (games, design, planning, reading, writing, conversations, etc.), and fluctuations in group membership.

Such multipurpose capability is enabled, to a large degree, by the fact that traditional tabletop workspaces and tools place few constraints on what parts of the table can be used, on where materials must be located, on where interaction must occur, or on who must perform those interactions. This flexible use of the workspace and available tools enables group members to use adaptable protocols, such as territoriality, to guide the collaborative work process. When changes in individual or collaborative activities are necessary or desired during the task progression, group members are free to change their use of the space and tools appropriately.

Future Trends

This chapter focused on territoriality on traditional, non-digital tabletop workspaces. Our own [9] and others' research [18, 23] have confirmed that territorial behaviour is also exhibited when people collaborate at a digital tabletop workspace. However, this practice has not yet been studied in detail in technology-augmented environments. Studies of new digital tabletop interaction techniques, for example, which enable people to access distant workspace objects, indicate that, although territorial functioning occurs, it may manifest in different ways [24]. To understand the impact of such new interface and interaction designs, more in-depth investigation of territoriality in digital environments is needed.

Digitizing the workspace also enables workspace configuration possibilities such as multi-display systems that provide a shared tabletop workspace connected to multiple mobile personal workspaces displayed on tablets or smartphone devices, and distributed tabletop systems (see Chapter 17). Investigations by Tuddenham and Robinson [25] of group work on a distributed tabletop system indicate that territoriality tends to be more subtle. Remote collaborators still partition the (virtually) shared workspace, but the partitions in their study tended to resemble a "patchwork rather than a strict left-right arrangement" (p. 2142).

This patchwork partitioning was often structured by the task itself: while performing a furniture arrangement, individuals' workspace interactions tended to be bound by "the 'walls' in the floor plan ... or new 'walls' created by the participants during the task" (p. 2143). Similar task-structured workspace partitioning was observed by Tse et al. [26] in an investigation of collaborative drawing activities on a desktop single display groupware system where pairs of people used multiple mice to draw on a shared desktop computer. They found that by default a proximity-based partitioning of the shared workspace (similar to the group territory partitioning found in Study 2) was adopted by their participants, yet when the task structure suggested a more efficient partitioning of the workspace, people tended to adopt the task-based partitioning will little to no discussion. The furniture arrangement task studied by Tuddenham and Robinson provided a fairly complex room layout structure that did not offer an obvious "split" in task structure. Thus, not surprisingly, they observed significantly more explicit verbal coordination (as compared to their co-located tabletop collaboration condition), such as "'I'll do the common room now' ... 'You can start on the secretary's room'" (p. 2146). We found similar explicit verbal coordination Study 2 when ownership of particular areas of the table was ambiguous because multiple people could easily (or with similar levels of effort) reach these areas (e.g., in centralized areas).

Interestingly, Tuddenham and Robinson concluded that the presence of patchwork partitioning "suggest[s] that remote tabletops do not support the work practice of territoriality" (p. 2146). Insights from the human territoriality literature discussed above, however, provide an alternative interpretation: that territorial functioning was still present, but that it was less spatially bound due to the lack of physical constraints normally placed on co-located collaborators. Recall Gifford's [17] definition of territoriality provided in Table 15.4 that states that territorial behaviour is "based on perceived, attempted, or actual control of a definable physical space, *object*, or *idea*" (p. 137, emphasis added). An alternative explanation of the non-proximity based partitioning behaviour exhibited by collaborators using a distributed tabletop system is that they were, through verbal communication, establishing *perceived control* of an *object* or *idea*, such as "the common room." Once such control is established, and commonly understood, their partners will then concentrate on other objects/ideas within the task. This is a different manifestation of territorial behaviour than the primarily proximity-based partitioning behaviour discussed in this chapter, but it likely served the same purpose: to help people maintain order in their shared interactions. Providing a task structure than can easily be divvied up, even conceptually, may help reduce the need for explicit verbal coordination in remote collaborative situations.

Designing tasks or shared workspaces that lend themselves to implicit, or minimally explicit, assignment of responsibility across group members needs further investigation. Such knowledge could inform the design of distributed collaboration systems (tabletop-based or potentially otherwise) that exploit natural territorial behaviour to gain the collaborative benefits this social practice provides.

Conclusion

This chapter carefully examines the practice of tabletop territoriality. This practice involves the establishment and maintenance of various tabletop territories on a shared tabletop workspace. In particular, people tend to establish three types of tabletop territories: personal, group, and storage territories. Careful analyses of territorial behaviour from two observational studies reveal that the three types of tabletop territories have dynamic spatial properties that fluidly change as task activities evolve. The analyses also indicate that tabletop territoriality facilitates task and group interactions on a table by providing commonly understood social protocols that help people:

- share the tabletop workspace by clarifying which regions are available for joint task work, for assisting others, and for performing individual activities separate from the group,
- delegate task responsibilities,
- easily coordinate access to task resources by providing lightweight mechanisms to reserve and share task resources, and
- organize the task resources in the workspace.

This work also indicates that enabling the practice of tabletop territoriality in a digital tabletop workspace requires careful application of the nuances of tabletop territoriality discussed in this chapter to the design of digital tabletop systems. The insights gained from this research provide a knowledge base which can be used to inspire the design of new digital tabletop workspaces, as well as to help predict the impact of potential interface and interaction designs on collaborators' territorial behaviour and on their collaborative interactions in general.

References

1. Bly SA (1988) A use of drawing surfaces in different collaborative settings. In: Proceedings of CSCW '88, conference on computer supported cooperative work (Portland, OR, 1988), ACM Press, pp 250–256
2. Tang JC (1991) Findings from observational studies of collaborative work. International Journal of Man-Machine Studies 34(2):143–160
3. Gutwin C, Greenberg S, Roseman M (1996) Workspace awareness in real-time distributed groupware: Framework, widgets, and evaluation. In: Sasse RJ, Cunningham A., Winder R (eds) People and computers XI (Proceedings of the HCI' 96), Springer-Verlag, conference held August 20–23, 1996, London, pp 281–298
4. Kruger R, Carpendale MST, Scott SD, Greenberg S (2004) Roles of orientation in tabletop collaboration: Comprehension, coordination and communication. Journal of Computer Supported Collaborative Work 13(5–6):501–537
5. Taylor RB (1988) Human territorial functioning: An empirical evolutionary perspective on individual and small group territorial cognitions, behaviors, and consequences. Cambridge University Press, New York
6. Aiello JR (1987) Human spatial behavior. In: Stokols D, Altman I (eds) Handbook of environmental psychology, John Wiley & Sons, Toronto, ON, pp 389–505

7. Fisher JD, Bell PA, Baum A (1984) Environmental psychology, 2nd ed. Holt, Rinehart and Winston, Toronto, ON

8. McGrath J (1984) Groups: Interaction and performance. Prentice-Hall, Englewood, NJ

9. Scott SD (2005) Territoriality in collaborative tabletop workspaces, Department of Computer Science, University of Calgary, Calgary, AB

10. Holtzblatt K, Jones S (1993) Contextual inquiry: A participatory technique for system design. In: Namioka A, Schuler D (eds) Participatory design: Principles and practice. Lawrence Earlbaum Publishers, Hillsdale, NJ, pp 180–193

11. Cockburn A, Greenberg S (1996) Children's collaboration styles in a Newtonian microworld. In: Conference companion of CHI'96: ACM conference on human factors in computing systems (Vancouver, BC), pp 181–182

12. Scott SD, Mandryk RL, Inkpen KL (2003) Understanding children's collaborative interactions in shared environments. Journal of Computer-Aided Learning 19(2):220–228

13. Sommer R (1969) Personal space: The behaviour basis of design. Prentice-Hall, Englewood Cliff, NJ

14. Altman I (1975) The environment and social behavior. Brooks/Cole Publishing Company, Monterey, CA

15. Edney JJ (1976) Human territories: Comment on functional properties. Environment and Behavior 8:31–47

16. Sack RD (1986) Human territoriality: Its theory and history. Cambridge University Press, Cambridge

17. Gifford R (1987) Environmental psychology. Allyn & Bacon, Inc., Boston, MA

18. Ryall K, Forlines C, Shen C, Ringel-Morris M (2004) Exploring the effects of group size and table size on interactions with tabletop shared-display groupware. In: Proceedings of CSCW' 04: ACM conference on computer-supported cooperative work (Chicago, IL), ACM Press, pp 284–293

19. Rogers Y, Hazlewood W, Blevis E, Lim Y-K (2004) Finger talk: Collaborative decision-making using talk and fingertip interaction around a tabletop display. In: Extended abstracts of CHI'04: ACM conference on human factors in computing systems (Vienna, Austria), pp 1271–1274

20. Shen C, Everitt KM, Ryall K (2003) UbiTable: Impromptu face-to-face collaboration on horizontal interactive surfaces. In: Proceedings of UbiComp' 03: 5th international conference on ubiquitous computing (Seattle, WA), pp 281–288

21. Shen C, Ryall K, Forlines C, Esenther A, Vernier FD, Everitt K, Wu M, Wigdor D, Morris MR, Hancock M, Tse E (2006) Informing the design of direct-touch tabletops. IEEE Computer Graphics and Applications 26(5):36–46

22. Omojola O, Post ER, Hancher MD, Maguire Y, Pappu R, Schoner B, Russo PR, Fletcher R, Gershenfeld N (2000) An installation of interactive furniture. IBM Systems Journal 39(3&4):861–979

23. Pinelle D, Barjawi M, Nacenta MA, Mandryk RL (2009) An evaluation of coordination techniques for protecting objects and territories in tabletop groupware. In: Proceedings of the ACM conference on human factors in computing systems (CHI '09), ACM Press, Boston, MA, pp 2129–2138

24. Pinelle D, Gutwin C, Nacenta MA (2008) The effects of co-present embodiments on awareness and collaboration in tabletop groupware. In: Proceeding of GI '08: graphics interface conference, Canadian Information Processing Society, Windsor, ON, pp 1–8

25. Tuddenham P, Robinson P (2009) Territorial coordination and workspace awareness in remote tabletop collaboration. In: Proceedings of CHI 2009: ACM conference on human factors in computing systems, ACM Press, Boston, MA, pp 2139–2148

26. Tse E, Histon J, Scott SD, Greenberg S (2004) Avoiding interference: How people use spatial separation and partitioning in SDG workspaces. In: Proceedings of the 2004 ACM conference on computer supported cooperative work, ACM Press, Chicago, IL, pp 252–261

Chapter 16
Digital Tables for Collaborative Information Exploration

Petra Isenberg, Uta Hinrichs, Mark Hancock, and Sheelagh Carpendale

Abstract There is great potential for digital tabletop displays to be integrated in tomorrow's work and learning environments, in which the exploration of information is a common task. In this chapter, we describe the stream of research that focuses on digital tabletop collaborative visualization environments. We focus on two types of interfaces: those for information exploration and data analysis in the context of workplaces, and those for more casual information exploration in public settings such as museums.

Introduction

Groups of people often form decisions or gain knowledge about a topic by coming together in physical environments to discuss, learn, interpret, or understand information. These groups often make use of tables to view, share, and store visual information. This information work is common in meeting rooms, research labs, classrooms, museums, and other public settings. Tabletop displays can augment information exploration in physical spaces. They can support the collaborative and interactive exploration of digital information beyond the possibilities that printed paper, projected slide shows, or non-interactive media such as posters, blackboards, or bulletin boards can offer.

We discuss the role of tabletop displays for collaborative information exploration in two specific contexts: work environments and public spaces. In work environments, such as meeting rooms or research labs, teams of analysts bring a vast amount of domain-specific knowledge to the table, while in public spaces, such as museums or art galleries, people bring with them a large variety of knowledge that is difficult to predict or expect. Nonetheless, both contexts invite the possibility of

P. Isenberg (✉)
Department of Computer Science, University of Calgary, Calgary, AB T2N 1N4, Canada
e-mail: petra.isenberg@ucalgary.ca

C. Müller-Tomfelde (ed.), *Tabletops – Horizontal Interactive Displays*,
Human-Computer Interaction Series, DOI 10.1007/978-1-84996-113-4_16,
© Springer-Verlag London Limited 2010

gaining insight through the process of exploring information. By looking at existing examples of information exploration in work environments and public settings, we discuss their commonalities and differences in order to arrive at practical considerations for designing tabletop interfaces to support information exploration in each context.

In both contexts, information exploration is a broad task that can consist of several possible sub-tasks, including browsing through data, understanding the data, or searching for particular information, with a variety of goals, including answering specific questions, confirming and defining hypotheses, or making decisions. Throughout this chapter, we focus on the role that visualization plays in facilitating these tasks and goals. Visualization is a field of research that is concerned with designing interactive representations of data to amplify human cognition [1]. It has been recognized that not only the design of the visual representation but also the design of appropriate mechanisms to interact with the data are critical to the success of a visualization tool. The design of visualizations for collaborative use on tabletops in a workplace as well as in a public setting, therefore, requires special design considerations both for representation as well as interaction. This chapter is meant to provide an overview of this emerging research area and provide initial considerations for the design of information representations on tabletops.

Information Exploration in the Workplace

In many areas, domain experts perform data analysis on a daily basis. For example, molecular biologists frequently analyze huge datasets from lab experiments, business analysts look at trends in financial data, or historians explore large document databases to bring historical events into context. Visualizations of such data can help their work in several ways. Studies have shown that visual representations of information can improve the detection of anticipated and unanticipated patterns in data, reduce search times, help people to make inferences about data, form hypotheses, as well as improve data exploration by providing a manipulable medium [1]. Recently, these benefits of visualizations have led to increasing adoption of single-user analysis and information exploration systems in the workplace.

With the rapid growth of the complexity and size of datasets in many work scenarios, however, the need to support multiple people simultaneously viewing and manipulating these visualizations is increasing. This growth means that domain experts from different disciplines and with different skill sets are often required to collaborate, to make informed decisions about a dataset, and to improve the quality of an analysis result. Datasets on which decision and discoveries are based may not only be too large to handle by a single analyst but may also be susceptible to a variety of interpretations, in which case experts may need to discuss and negotiate their interpretations of the data.

Digital tables offer great potential to support this type of work. In the near future digital tabletops may be installed in offices, meeting rooms, or research labs where today's domain experts already meet to discuss, interpret, and analyze data. One of the great advantages of tabletop displays in the workplace is their ability to support such collaborative work. Analysis systems that use digital tables can enable in-situ discussion, exploration, and interpretation – in close contact with the data and its visualization. Team members can work independently while being able to spontaneously react to findings in the data and to resolve data conflicts as a group.

The design of interfaces, visualizations, and interaction techniques for visual analysis by teams of domain experts around tabletops is an active research area. We first give an overview of existing systems and research approaches for data analysis in the workplace. At the time of this writing, examples of systems for exploring information at a tabletop display in the workplace have been limited mostly to research prototypes. As the cost of such systems goes down, we expect to see more commercial examples arise. Nonetheless, the research prototypes demonstrate the viability of tabletop systems for improving people's ability to collaboratively explore information.

3D Scientific Visualization

The 3D Responsive Workbench is an early digital tabletop information exploration system [2] for 3D scientific data analysis. It had the goal to replace computer desktops and provide a work situation more similar to those encountered in an architect's office, in surgery rooms, or in scientific research labs. The Responsive Workbench uses a horizontal surface to display stereoscopic 3D information through shuttered glasses. These glasses are synchronized so that more than one person can view the same 3D scene from different perspectives. For instance, a person at one side of the table can see the front (ventral) side of a human skeleton and a person at the other side of the table can see its back (dorsal) side. Moreover, if one person were to point at the 3D model (e.g., at the skeleton's right elbow), the view is corrected for the other viewer so that they can see what they are pointing to as though it were in physical space. Interaction in the system is made possible through tracked gloves that each viewer must wear. This early virtual reality prototype demonstrates one of the first instances of coordinated views for multiple people analyzing visualizations at a tabletop display. Several visualization applications were proposed for similar environments including simulation and visualizations in fluid dynamics [3], virtual wind tunnels [3], or medical visualization [4].

Tools for Collaborative Information Exploration

The DT Lens [5] system demonstrates how tools can be used for the exploration of geospatial visualizations on an interactive tabletop. This system addresses a number of important issues for collaborative information explorations systems. It provides multiple people with the ability to geometrically deform, annotate, and explore the visual information simultaneously. The system uses a DiamondTouch [6] to provide input simultaneously for up to four people to control lenses that enable detailed views of information within a larger context. For example, a lens can be used to zoom into a map in a small portion of the display, while maintaining the context around that zoomed in area. Thus, each person can focus on a portion of interest, without hindering another person's ability to focus on something else within the same dataset. Interaction techniques with the lenses were designed to encourage rapid exploration.

Workspace Organization for Collaborative Information Exploration

Some previous systems have focused on the question of how information should be organized and presented on a tabletop display to enable exploration and analysis of data. Isenberg and Carpendale [7] built a collaborative tabletop visualization system for the comparison of hierarchical data (Fig. 16.1). The system is implemented on a high-resolution tabletop from SMART Technologies which uses a DViT overlay supporting two concurrent inputs. The system is a research prototype designed to explore early work on guidelines for tabletop design (e.g., [8, 9]) and information visualization design [1]. The system breaks with the standard design of information visualization interfaces for this type of work. Representations of hierarchical datasets are put on movable planes which can be freely repositioned, resized, and oriented to facilitate coordination and collaboration. Comparison between multiple hierarchical datasets is possible by moving different representations in close proximity to one another. When visualizations are close to each other, meta-visualizations are added to highlight similar and different branches in the representations.

Fig. 16.1 System for collaborative comparison of hierarchical data [7]

Information Visualization Design for Coordinated Information Exploration

Tobiasz et al. [10] explore how work with multiple views of the same data can be coordinated on a tabletop display through Lark (Fig. 16.2). The system is designed on a large high-resolution tabletop from SMART Technologies, capable of capturing two concurrent and independent inputs. With Lark, teams of experts can create multiple views of the same hierarchical dataset and individually explore the data using a number of different types of exploratory interaction: filtering, annotation, color coding, and changes of data encoding (e.g., from a TreeMap to a node-link diagram). Lark allows team members to coordinate their interaction with views and representations through a meta-visualization that connects the different views. Through the meta-visualization the scope of interaction with the data can be set, which allows team members to share or restrict how others observe their interaction with the data. This meta-visualization lets collaborators explore different parts of the data while remaining aware of the history of their exploration and see at the same time how current views relate to those of their partners.

Cambiera [11] is a multi-user Microsoft Surface application for the joint exploration and analysis of large text document collections (Fig. 16.3). The system is designed on a Microsoft Surface for use with up to four people. The goal of this system is to provide visual mechanisms to help people remain aware of their joint interaction with data items. Each person can concurrently search for interesting documents and is then presented with visual representations of the documents returned by a search. Techniques from information visualization are used to augment the search results with meta-information about the joint interactions. Documents can, for example, be pulled from a search result and opened up to read. The representation of this document is then automatically augmented with glyphs that represent who read a specific document and darker document backgrounds show that a document has been read more frequently. Representation of search results also show which documents both collaborators have found in common. These specific types

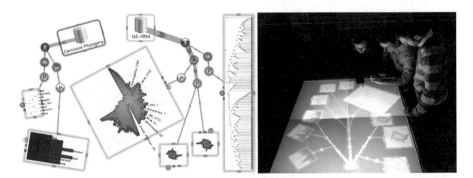

Fig. 16.2 Lark: meta-visualization for the coordination of interaction with views of the same data [10]

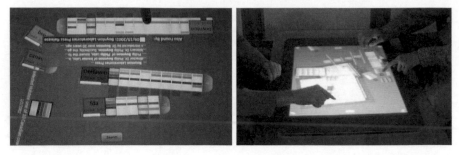

Fig. 16.3 Cambiera: collaborative information exploration through text document collections [11]

of meta-visualization are meant to help the group remain aware of each others' work and are called *collaborative brushing and linking* techniques.

Multi-display Environments for Information Exploration

Tabletops have also been integrated into multi-display environments (MDEs) to support information exploration work. Forlines et al. showed two projects in which a tabletop serves a coordinating function in a setting with several vertical displays and a tablet PC. In the first project, Forlines et al. [12] retrofitted Google Earth to allow multiple people to explore geospatial information. In the second project, a single-user visualization application for protein visualization (Fig. 16.4) was retrofitted to be used collaboratively in an MDE [13]. In both projects, the tabletop is the primary input device to coordinate different views of the visual information on all connected displays. These projects raise the interesting question of how current visualization systems can be sufficiently retrofitted to support group work around visualizations and how multiple displays can be effectively used for data analysis in an MDE.

Similarly, the project WeSpace [14] uses a tabletop in a walk-up-and-use environment for collaborative research. Visualizations from connected laptops can be shared to a tabletop and large displays for joint discussion and analysis. Again, the

Fig. 16.4 Visualization in a multi-display environment [13]

tabletop serves a coordinating function for views sent from the different laptops. WeSpace received enthusiastic feedback from the domain experts using the system for their data analysis.

Information Exploration in Public Spaces

Tabletop displays have started to become more common outside of research labs and work environments. For instance, we can find them in museums and art galleries where they are used to convey information to people in an interactive and potentially engaging way. The use of horizontal digital surfaces to present interactive data visualizations has several advantages, especially for more casual public settings where people gather in their spare time. Information visualizations presented on digital tabletops can turn abstract data into interactive exhibits that evoke attention and curiosity and entice visitors to take a closer look. The physical setup of tabletop displays enables visitors to approach the presented information from all sides; several groups or individuals can collaboratively explore, share, and discuss the data visualization. The ultimate goals of large horizontal information displays in public spaces are to attract people's attention, draw them closer to the installation, and promote lightweight information exploration that leads to serendipitous discoveries, some reflection on the presented data, and/or active discussion of this data with peers.

One of the first tabletop systems designed to support casual exploration of information is The Pond [15]. The objective for developing this tabletop system was to enable collaborative data exploration. Along these lines, conveying a rich experience was one of the key design objectives. The tabletop workspace resembles a virtual pool where information elements float around, like creatures in a shoal. A wooden, wavy shaped frame around the table surface allows people to casually lean over and explore the information floating by. Interaction techniques for exploring information and starting queries to bring up new information are intentionally kept simple to allow for walk-up-and-use interaction. Visual aesthetics and simplicity of interaction were emphasized to make the installation accessible by broad and diverse audiences and to facilitate focusing on information instead of learning how to interact with the system.

While The Pond was only installed in a laboratory setting, several similar systems can now be found in public spaces. There are several examples of tabletop systems that have appeared in both museums and art galleries.

Tabletop Installations in Museums

In recent years, tabletop systems with similar objectives to The Pond have been installed in museums. floating.numbers by ART+COM, for instance, is a tabletop installation that was developed for the Jewish Museum in Berlin, Germany

[16]. The installation enables visitors to interactively explore the meaning of numbers in Jewish culture. Information elements in the form of numbers are floating in a water-like stream across the tabletop surface. Dragging a number out of the stream reveals its meaning in the form of textual information and images. People can simultaneously interact from all sides of the table.

Another example is the "Tree of Life" [17] – an interactive tabletop installation developed for the Museum of Natural History in Berlin, Germany, to make information about the evolution of species interactively explorable (Fig. 16.5). Questions about species and corresponding answers are presented through text and images. The background of the tabletop interface consists of a tree visualization resembling the hierarchical relationships between different species. This background visualization, however, is not based on real data but has mostly decorative purposes. While the tree visualization reacts to people's interaction with visual effects, exploring the information hinted at within the tree is not possible. A study at the museum [18] revealed that visitors were intrigued by the tree visualization, visible in their immediate attempts to interact with it and explore it further.

The interface of the Tree of Life table is divided into four quadrants. Each of the quadrants reveals different questions and can be explored independently from each other. In this way, the table enables parallel information exploration. However, the support of collaborative information discovery is limited, since a question and its corresponding answer can only be controlled by one person at a time. Furthermore, information exploration is limited to scrolling through textual information. Hornecker [18] found that, while people actively discussed the content of other exhibits within the museum, they mostly talked about the technology and interaction techniques when mingling around the tabletop installation.

Other information installations have been developed using different form factors of horizontal surfaces. EMDialog [19] is an interactive information installation that was developed to enhance an art exhibition showing paintings from the artist Emily Carr (see Fig. 16.6). The installation presents two linked information visualizations that invite museum visitors to explore the extensive discourse about Emily Carr along temporal and contextual dimensions. EMDialog consists of a large display tilted by a 45° angle. In addition, a large wall projection next to the digital table shows a clone of the tabletop interface.

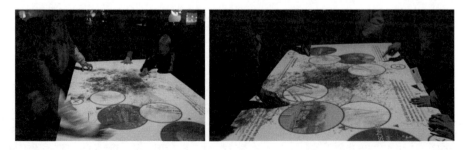

Fig. 16.5 The tree of life table by ART+COM [17] (photo courtesy of Eva Hornecker)

Fig. 16.6 EMDialog: an interactive museum installation for exploring information about the artist Emily Carr [19]

This form of physical setup makes interaction with the display widely visible across the exhibition floor and enables collaborative and social data exploration. Visitor statements from questionnaires revealed that the physical setup of the installation created curiosity and drew people toward the visualizations. Visitors were able to watch other people interact with the display, which enabled them to preview information that the visualization contained and to learn how to interact with it by observation. However, this visibility of interaction also made some visitors feel uncomfortable. Some felt shy about interacting in front of other people. Others did not want to take control of the visualization, being aware that other visitors might be in the middle of reading certain information. These observations show that while the combination of tabletop displays with large wall displays might have some potential for attracting the attention of visitors, physical setups like this need to be carefully designed to not have the opposite effect.

Tabletop Installations in Art Galleries

Tabletop installations have also been built in the context of art galleries. In contrast to tabletop exhibits in museums that usually have an educational intent, tabletop information installations in art galleries often aim to trigger experiences and emotions. The interaction of visitors with the horizontal display and their active experience of content becomes an integral part of the art installation.

memory [en]code (Fig. 16.7) is a tabletop system that visualizes the dynamics of human memories in an interactive way [20]. This system differs from other tabletop visualization systems, as the visualization is not based on a predefined dataset but dynamically evolves through the active participation of gallery visitors.

Visitors are invited to type their own thoughts or memories into the system. These text snippets are transformed into organic-looking cell creatures which start to float on the tabletop surface in a seemingly autonomous manner. Visitors can browse

Fig. 16.7   memory [en]code, a tabletop exhibit in an art gallery [20]

through the cells by touching a cell's nucleus to reveal the thoughts they are holding. While the content of existing cells cannot be edited directly, cells can be merged
together to create a new cell containing content from both parent cells. Cells have
a certain lifetime determined by the length of their content and how often visitors
interact with them. Old or unpopular cells slowly fade away until they disappear
completely from the surface. Over time, a collection of different memories and
thoughts takes form on the tabletop. The participatory aspect of memory [en]code
positively influences people's engagement with the installation. The fact that all
information is created by other visitors and the ability to leave personal traces adds
a personal touch to the installation. People often came back several times to see if
cells they had created were still in the system.

Designing for Information Exploration on a Tabletop

When designing visualization systems for collaborative information exploration, we
are faced with a number of challenges in common with other tabletop work: the
need to support awareness and common ground formation, perceptual problems, as
well as collaborative interaction issues. However, the nature of collaborative information exploration tasks with visual data representations requires that the analysis
and understanding of the represented information, as well as the social interaction
around the data, be guaranteed. In this section, we discuss these challenges in the
context of visual information exploration and point out the differences that need to
be considered when designing for workplace and public settings.

Contextual Challenges

One of the main differences to consider when designing tabletop applications for
workplace or public settings is the context in which the information is being
explored. While the context for workplace systems often goes hand-in-hand with

well-defined tasks and goal-oriented analysis, the context for public settings can vary dramatically. We discuss design challenges for both situations next.

Work Environments: Domain Experts typically perform information exploration and analysis in small groups whose members are already acquainted. There are typically well defined analysis goals, for example, to find a specific answer in the data, to confirm or derive a hypothesis, or to form decisions. These goals must be supported by the tabletop software and, hence, the development of specific software may be necessary when datasets and tasks change.

In contrast to tabletop systems designed for public spaces, the expectations about interaction techniques and data representations differ in the workplace. The questions in work scenarios are typically quite complex and difficult. Also, the data analysis results might be vital to make important (sometimes time-critical) decisions with many variables to consider. Information visualization interfaces, therefore, typically have a large number of parameters to manipulate. Work teams are often prepared to invest time in learning, and tabletop interfaces designed for these settings can, therefore, often include new interactions and visual designs if they might improve the efficiency and quality of collaborative information exploration. Work teams also often may spend considerable time using an interface, making the effort to learn new techniques worthwhile.

Several information exploration sessions are often necessary to come to a common understanding of a particular dataset in the workplace. Tabletop software for collaborative information exploration should, therefore, support capturing of interaction histories with the information in order to allow groups to interrupt their analysis and continue at a later stage. At the same time, it is often the case that individual group members may drop in and out of a running collaborative information exploration session. For these group members it may also be useful to implement history and summarization mechanisms to show what has been missed. First approaches are incorporated in Lark and Cambiera [10, 11] (see above).

Public Spaces: The audience gathering around a tabletop in a public space can be highly diverse. Visitors of museums and art galleries, for instance, not only differ in age but also in social and cultural background, knowledge, and interests [21]. Furthermore, people often visit exhibitions without clearly defined questions or goals in mind, but explore them serendipitously based on spontaneous interest [21, 22]. Interaction with exhibits tends to be brief and usually only occurs once per visitor. This means that tabletop interfaces for information exploration in public settings need to be designed differently from workplace systems in terms of interaction techniques and information design.

Interaction techniques need to be designed with a walk-up-and-use scenario in mind. Visitors of public spaces are not likely to read elaborate instructions on how to interact with the system but will try to figure out exploration techniques and capabilities of the visualization on the fly. Interaction with the tabletop system therefore should be accompanied by direct feedback mechanisms that encourage further interaction or lead visitors to try different interactive mechanisms.

The diversity of people visiting public spaces is often reflected in a variety of interaction times and exploration styles. Some people will only interact with

the tabletop installation for a few moments, while others will explore information in detail for a longer amount of time. Therefore, the design of information
visualizations on public tabletop systems should reward both short- and long-term
exploration. Furthermore, some people prefer guided exploration, while others like
to follow their personal interests using more open exploration techniques. Both
techniques should be supported [19].

Technological Challenges

In both workplaces and public spaces, hardware challenges exist for the setup of
information exploration environments. These challenges relate to size and resolution
of the table but also its spatial placement, robustness, and form factor.

Workplace Environments: Domain experts often have to do fine-grained analysis
of large and detailed datasets. For the visualization of this data, the size and resolution of a tabletop is critical. As datasets increase in size, it becomes more and more
difficult to display them in their entirety. Large and high-resolution tables allow
more data to be displayed and support several people working together – either with
multiple copies of a data representation or with different parts of a shared visualization. However, detailed and large datasets may require the rendering and reading
of small textual labels and other data items. With growing resolution, the displayed
information items can become physically smaller resulting in selection difficulties.
Using fingers or pens may no longer be sufficient to select small data items and
alternative selection techniques may have to be used or designed (e.g., [23]). Also,
when large datasets have to be rendered on high-resolution tabletop screens, combined with several simultaneous inputs, response time may become very important.
It is necessary to develop algorithms that can support multi-person interaction on
tables with very high resolution.

Groups of domain experts may also often meet around a digital table to perform long analysis sessions. Therefore, the form factor of the table should be such
that it supports comfortable seating positions similar to current meeting spaces in
conference rooms or offices.

Public Spaces: Similar to the workspace, public settings can benefit from the
availability of large and high-resolution tabletop displays. In public settings, the size
of a group wanting to access a table may be much larger than in a workplace. For
example, it is not unusual for school classes to gather around a tabletop to interact
with and explore information in a museum. In such situations, it is critical that the
whole system remains responsive and that the software does not crash, even if 40
hands are touching the table at the same time or even issue conflicting information
exploration commands.

Tables for public settings also need to be robust in their physical design,
spill-proof and resistant to scratching or pushing. In contrast to domain expert information exploration sessions, one, cannot expect children or large groups of adults to
treat a public tabletop display with care. It is important to consider that the physical

setup of the display (size, orientation, and location) can influence the group size and number of different groups of people interacting with it.

Perceptual Challenges

The environment suggested by a tabletop display is particularly unique to computing systems. In particular, the display has a horizontal orientation and affords multiple people standing at different sides of the table. These properties are compelling for a variety of reasons, but also introduce some unique perceptual challenges. Specifically, the assumption common to desktop computing that there will be one viewer directly in front of the display is no longer valid. For example, Wigdor et al. [24] performed a study that suggests that visual variables (e.g., angle, length, shape) are perceived differently on a horizontal surface than on a vertical one. In 3D, the problem is exacerbated, as the projection from 3D onto the 2D surface requires an assumption about the point of view of the (one and only) observer. Thus, a projected image may appear drastically different to observers standing at opposite sides of the table. Several systems have explored solutions to the problem of multiple points of view [2, 25, 26] but the degree of this problem on digital tables has still been largely unexplored.

Some visual elements in both 2D and 3D are particularly sensitive to changes in orientation (e.g., text). Some studies have shown that people are still capable of reading short bits of text at non-zero orientations [27], but they are still slower, and so larger bits of text are best to read in the correct orientation. Other research suggests that the act of orienting visual elements is often used to communicate with others [28] and a variety of methods to perform this act have been introduced to tabletop display environments [28–31]. Thus, perception of visual elements that have an intrinsic orientation may play an important role in the collaboration that occurs in a tabletop display environment. These perceptual challenges exist in both workplace as well as public settings, but the types of problems that may arise vary somewhat.

Work Environments: In work environments, the perception of the visual information may be relevant for a variety of reasons. The visual variables used to represent the information may need to precisely depict a value to be judged by the observer, or it may be important to compare two (or more) visual elements. A person on one side of the table may also need to be able to trust that someone across the table can perceive a visual variable in a predictable way (i.e., that their view is not warped in some way). At present, there is little work to suggest how to design systems that address these issues. However, the current work points to the fact that the simple solution of using the same design criteria for vertical displays may not suffice for horizontal ones [24].

Public Spaces: In more artistic or learning environments found in public spaces, the precise value of a particular visual element may not be as important as in systems designed for domain expert analysis in the workplace. Instead, it may be more important for the designer to consider the fact that the perceptual *experience* of two observers standing at opposite sides of the table will differ. This difference in experience can be thought of as an additional challenge for the designer; the system can be made to either mitigate these perceptual differences, or to take advantage of them in order to create a unique experience for the observers. Nonetheless, the consideration of the orientation of the visual elements can be particularly important in a public space. Grabbing the attention of someone passing by will involve the consideration of how the display looks from both far away and from close proximity. Orientation-sensitive elements, such as text, may play an important role in drawing attention, indicating a suitable viewpoint, or to help encourage communication between multiple simultaneous observers.

Collaborative Challenges

Several previous studies of collaborative information exploration, both for work environments [32, 33] as well as public spaces [19], suggest a need to support a wide range of collaboration styles. People may be interested in exploring parts of the information by themselves without interfering with other people, but may at any given time switch from this parallel work to a phase in which they work more closely together, sharing information items, and discussing them closely.

Despite these initial similarities, the information exploration goals and contextual exploration scenarios for information visualization in work environments and public spaces are quite different and, hence, different design challenges arise.

Work Environments: Global changes to views and encodings of data are fairly common in single-user visualization systems and if one is interested in re-designing such an application for tabletop use, the re-design of these features for synchronous group work is critical [11]. One option is to design visual representations that support synchronous interaction (as, for example, in the DTLens system [5]); another is to allow for the ability to create several interactive views of the same dataset (as, for example, in the collaborative tree comparison system from [7]).

Since the datasets used in expert systems are often large, complex, uncertain, and subject to different interpretations, people have to pay close attention to the data they may be working with in order to keep their exploration context and intermediate findings in memory. Thus, for information exploration tasks, the physical cues naturally available in a co-located environment only provide limited support for awareness and common ground formation. Team members may still be able to see each others' hand and arm movements, gestures, and hear their incidental comments about data, but when the complexity of the information visualization requires increased concentration, these awareness cues may be missed. For example, a person may be pointing to a specific data item in a visualization and make a comment about it, but another person may be too focused to pay attention to which item it is, what its context is within the dataset, or even to which dataset it belongs. When designing interfaces and visual representations for collaborative information exploration, we thus need to ensure that people can simultaneously concentrate on the complex data and maintain an awareness of each others' work and activities. Mechanisms may have to be put in place to support better contextual understanding for the reference of data items. In the Cambiera system [11], for example, this problem was addressed by including meta-visualizations of the interactions with the data on a visualization in order to show which information items others had read, referenced, or found.

Large and complex datasets place a high cognitive load on the viewers. It is, therefore, important that collaborators can externalize some of their findings easily and, for example, annotate the data to mark a finding or to rate the reliability, trustworthiness, or certainty of a data item. This externalization is particularly important for collaborative data analysis because individuals may, on a momentary notice, switch context, work with another person, and then have to return to their previous work. Keeping an integrated exploration history together with data annotations could greatly support this type of expert information exploration.

Public Spaces: Museum studies have found that people often visit public exhibitions in groups. The studies conducted by Hinrichs et al. [19] and Hornecker et al. [18] confirm this finding for tabletop installations within museum settings.

The physical setting of a tabletop display allows different visitor groups to approach the installation from all sides. When several people interact with a tabletop display at the same time, however, it is hard to maintain awareness of who is exploring what part of the visualization. In a public setting, this awareness is even more compromised since it is less likely for visitors who do not know each other to communicate or pay attention to each other and, hence, the possibility of interaction conflict is high. The public tabletop systems described earlier deal with this problem in different ways. floating.numbers [18] and memory [en]code [23] both involve visualizations that consist of independent information objects. People can interact with different objects without interfering with each other. Since the visualization in EMDialog [22] was not designed to support several people exploring it in parallel, the physical setup of the installation was designed not to invite parallel information exploration among unacquainted people. As a third example, information presented on the Tree of Life table is divided in four quadrants [19, 21] to allow four different groups of people to explore it without interfering with each other. These examples show that there is a variety of ways to enable parallel independent information exploration.

The character of collaborative interactions with information displays in public settings, however, differs from work settings. Group interaction in public settings is less focused around maximizing insights from the visualization and more about experiencing information collaboratively in a social way. When collaboratively exploring a museum exhibit, social interaction and information sharing can play an important role. Parents, for instance, often use information exhibits to explain causalities within the information to their children [18, 34]. While in this situation often only one person is interacting at a time, the process of information exploration is still highly collaborative. Similar forms of collaboration can be observed among adults when they are still unclear of what an installation has to offer and how to interact with it [19]. Groups also explore visualizations in parallel and periodically share their insights through discussion, whereas others go through all information together [19].

Future Trends

What will our world be like 20 years from now? It is likely that technology will become even more ubiquitous in our environments and that it will come in many different form factors. Humans have considerable experience and expertise working together on physical tables, making this form factor a particularly promising one to promote. At the same time, we are collecting more diverse sets of information than ever before. This data can range from the experimental datasets in biology, where millions of data items have to be analyzed, to social datasets about our interactions with the world around us: data about our consumption of electricity, our social networks on Facebook, or about the environments we live in. All of this information is being collected for the purpose of being explored. Due to our familiarity with working on physical tables, digital tabletops are a promising medium for working with information. They combine the benefits of a large display area for information, enough space for several people to share, and a seating or standing arrangement that allows for easy discussion and interaction among group members. Supporting collaborative information exploration will become an extremely important task for future systems in a large number of different settings.

Tabletop displays have recently found their way into public installations in museums or other public spaces. However, their use as information exploration devices in these casual settings – characterized by a diverse audience with different motivations and interests – is still highly under-explored. Future systems will likely explore different approaches to initiate collaboration and discussion around the presented information. In particular, the combination of tabletop technology and personal mobile devices seems promising, since it could enable visitors to explore exhibits individually and collaboratively. Therefore, multi-display scenarios that incorporate both large horizontal and vertical displays as well as small personal mobile devices such as cell phones and PDAs are likely to be incorporated into public information exhibits. Information visualizations will have to be tailored toward these multi-display environments involving both individual and collaborative information exploration.

As tabletop technology becomes cheaper, larger, and higher in display resolution, we also expect to see more tabletop installations in workspaces emerge. In these situations the expected benefit for the use of tabletops is great. Imagine a future meeting room being equipped with a large digital table and other large displays. Instead of the currently common static slideshow presentation, groups could interactively explore information together, discuss it, change it, and call up meta-information, additional views and data as needed. Such a setting promises not only to produce analysis results of higher quality through the combined input of several different domain experts, but also a more enjoyable and creative data analysis environment. However, to realize such a future workspace a lot more research on systems, tools, and methods for collaborative data analysis are needed. Important research directions are the design of visual representations, their joint manipulation, and the issue of awareness in collaborative information exploration. Others are the design of appropriate multi-person interaction techniques and gestures for touch-sensitive displays to explore information.

Conclusions

In this chapter we have summarized, discussed, and explained a number of issues arising when designing information exploration environments in two different spaces: workplace settings, where we expect domain experts in an area to gather, explore, and analyze often large and complex datasets, and public spaces, where the design has to support a much more diverse set of people, tasks, and goals. Table 16.1 gives a high-level description of the issues we discussed in the previous sections. However, design requirements for every tabletop installation will differ and further research on collaborative information exploration systems is needed to refine these design considerations.

Table 16.1 Issues for the design of information exploration systems in workplace and public settings

	Workplace settings	Public settings
Contextual challenges		
Group size	Small	Small–large
Group familiarity	Acquainted	Unacquainted–intimate
Group background	Same–different	
Exploration goals	Well-defined	Undefined–well-defined
Usage patters	Repeated use	One-time–repeated use
Exp. time investment	Hours–weeks	Minutes–hours
Willingness to learn interface	Medium–high	Low
Information representation	Must convey many data dimensions and parameters	Must be easy to read, understand, and explore
Technological challenges		
Table size and resolution	Large	
Table form factor	Comfortable for sitting around	For standing or sitting, highly robust
Perceptual challenges		
Perceptual focus	Data readability	Exploration experience
Collaborative challenges		
Collaboration styles	Parallel–joint	
Exploration history	High need	Low–medium need
Awareness of others' data exploration activities	High need	Low–medium need
Focus of visualization use	Analytical, group insight, discovery	Social experience, insight, discovery

References

1. Card S, Mackinlay JD, Shneiderman B (eds) (1999) Readings in information visualization: Using vision to think. Morgan Kauffman Publishers, Inc., San Francisco, CA
2. Agrawala M, Beers AC, McDowall I, Fröhlich B, Bolas M, Hanrahan P (1997) The two-user responsive workbench: Support for collaboration through individual views of a shared space. In: Proceedings of computer graphics and interactive techniques (SIGGRAPH), ACM/Addison-Wesley, New York, pp 327–332
3. Wesche G, Wind J, Göbe M, Rosenblum L, Durbin J, Doyle R, Tate D, King R, Fröhlich B, Fischer M, Agrawala M, Beers A, Hanrahan P, Bryson S (1997) Application of the responsive workbench. Computer Graphics and Applications 17(4):10–15
4. Choi YJ, Choi SM, Rhee SM, Kim MH (2005) Collaborative and immersive medical education in a virtual workbench environment. In: Knowledge-based intelligent information and engineering systems, Spinger Verlag, Berlin/Heidelberg, pp 1210–1217
5. Forlines C, Shen C (2005) DTLens: Multi-user tabletop spatial data exploration. In: Proceedings of user interface software and technology (UIST), ACM Press, New York, USA, pp 119–122
6. Dietz P, Leigh D (2001) Diamondtouch: A multi-user touch technology. In: Proceedings of user interface software and technology (UIST), ACM Press, New York, pp 219–226
7. Isenberg P, Carpendale S (2007) Interactive tree comparison for co-located collaborative information visualization. IEEE Transactions on Visualization and Computer Graphics 13(6):1232–1239
8. Scott SD, Grant KD, Mandryk RL (2003) System guidelines for co-located collaborative work on a tabletop display. In: Proceedings of the European conference on computer-supported cooperative work (ECSCW), Kluwer Academic Publishers, Dordrecht, pp 159–178
9. Ryall K, Morris MR, Everitt K, Forlines C, Shen C (2006) Experiences with and observations of direct-touch tabletops. In: Fjeld M, Takatsuka M (eds) Proceedings of horizontal interactive human-computer systems (TABLETOP), IEEE Press, Los Alamitos, CA, pp 89–96, doi: 10.1109/TABLETOP.2006.12
10. Tobiasz M, Isenberg P, Carpendale S (2009) Lark: Coordinating co-located collaboration with information visualization. IEEE Transactions on Visualization and Computer Graphics 15(6):1065–1072
11. Isenberg P, Fisher D (2009) Collaborative brushing and linking for co-located collaborative visual analytics of document collections. Computer Graphics Forum 28(3): 1031–1038
12. Forlines C, Esenther A, Shen C, Wigdor D, Ryall K (2006) Multi-user, multi-display interaction with a single-user, single-display geospatial application. In: Proceedings of user interface software and technology (UIST), ACM Press, New York, pp 273–276
13. Forlines C, Lilien R (2008) Adapting a single-user, single-display molecular visualization application for use in a multi-user, multi-display environment. In: Proceedings of advanced visual interfaces (AVI), ACM Press, New York, pp 367–371
14. Wigdor D, Jiang H, Forlines C, Borkin M, Shen C (2009) WeSpace: The design development and deployment of a walk-up and share multi-surface visual collaboration system. In: Proceedings of human factors in computing systems (CHI '09), ACM Press, New York, pp 1237–1246
15. Ståhl O, Wallberg A, Söderberg J, Humble J, Fahlén LE, Bullock A, Lundberg J (2002) Information exploration using the pond. In: Proceedings of collaborative virtual environments (CVE), ACM Press, New York, pp 72–79
16. ART+COM (2004) floating.numbers. Website: http://artcom.de, accessed March 2008
17. ART+COM (2007) Tree of life. Website: http://www.artcom.de, accessed April 2009
18. Hornecker E (2008) "I don't understand it but it is cool": Visitor interactions with a multi-touch table in a museum. In: Proceedings of tabletops and interactive surfaces (TABLETOP), IEEE Computer Society, Los Alamitos, CA, pp 121–128

19. Hinrichs U, Schmidt H, Carpendale S (2008) EMDialog: Bringing information visualization into the museum. IEEE Transactions on Visualization and Computer Graphics 14(6):1181–1188

20. Schmidt H, Hinrichs U, Dunning A, Carpendale S (2007) memory [en]code – Building a collective memory within a tabletop installation. In: Proceedings of computational aesthetics in graphics, visualization, and imaging (CAe), Eurographics Association, Aire-la-Ville, Switzerland, pp 135–142

21. Screven CG (2000) Information design in informal settings: Museums and other public spaces. In: Jacobson RE (ed) Information design. MIT Press, Cambridge, MA

22. Allen S (2004) Designs for learning: Studying science museum exhibits that do more than entertain. Science Education 88(S1):S17–S33

23. Benko H, Wilson AD, Baudisch P (2006) Precise selection techniques for multi-touch screens. In: Proceedings of human factors in computing systems (CHI), ACM Press, New York, pp 1263–1272

24. Wigdor D, Shen C, Forlines C, Balakrishnan R (2007) Perception of elementary graphical elements in tabletop and multi-surface environments. In: Proceedings of human factors in computing systems (CHI), ACM Press, New York, pp 473–482

25. Hancock M, Carpendale S (2007) Supporting multiple off-axis viewpoints at a tabletop display. In: Proceedings of horizontal interactive human-computer systems (TABLETOP), IEEE Computer Society, Los Alamitos, CA, pp 171–178

26. Kitamura Y, Nakayama T, Nakashima T, Yamamoto S (2006) The illusionhole with polarization filters. In: Proceedings of virtual reality software and technology, ACM Press, New York, pp 244–251

27. Wigdor D, Balakrishnan R (2005) Empirical investigation into the effect of orientation on text readability in tabletop displays. In: Proceedings of the European conference on computer-supported cooperative work (ECSCW), Kluwer Academic Publishers, Dordrecht, pp 205–224

28. Kruger R, Carpendale S, Scott SD, Tang A (2005) Fluid integration of rotation and translation. In: Proceedings of human factors in computing systems, ACM Press, New York, pp 601–610

29. Liu J, Pinelle D, Sallam S, Subramanian S, Gutwin C (2006) TNT: Improved rotation and translation on digital tables. In: Proceedings of graphics interface, Canadian Information Processing Society, Mississauga, ON, pp 25–32

30. Shen C, Vernier FD, Forlines C, Ringel M (2004) DiamondSpin: An extensible toolkit for around-the-table interaction. In: Proceedings of human factors in computing systems (CHI), ACM Press, New York, pp 167–174

31. Hancock MS, Vernier FD, Wigdor D, Carpendale S, Shen C (2006) Rotation and translation mechanisms for tabletop interaction. In: Proceedings of horizontal interactive human-computer systems (TABLETOP), IEEE Computer Society, Los Alamitos, CA, pp 79–86

32. Tang A, Tory M, Po B, Neumann P, Carpendale S (2006) Collaborative coupling over tabletop displays. In: Proceedings of human factors in computing systems (CHI), ACM Press, New York, pp 1181–1190

33. Isenberg P, Tang A, Carpendale S (2008) An exploratory study of visual information analysis. In: Proceedings of human factors in computing systems (CHI), ACM Press, New York, pp 1217–1226

34. vom Lehn D, Heath C, Hindmarsh J (2001) Exhibiting interaction: Conduct and collaboration in museums and galleries. Symbolic Interaction 24(2):189–216

Chapter 17
Coordination and Awareness in Remote Tabletop Collaboration

Philip Tuddenham and Peter Robinson

Abstract Remote collaboration technologies frequently provide a shared visual workspace of the task at hand, but often lack support for the visual cues and work practices of co-located collaboration. This is particularly acute in design tasks, in which the shared workspace is the focus of collaboration. Lately there has been growing interest in *remote tabletop interfaces*: large horizontal interactive surfaces that provide shared workspaces for remote collaboration. These interfaces may afford some of the cues and beneficial work practices associated with collaboration at conventional tables. If so, they may offer benefits over other remote collaboration technologies. However, while a number of remote tabletop interfaces have been constructed, there are few empirical findings around these interfaces in practice. This chapter reviews current work in remote tabletop interfaces and then presents an exploratory study investigating two work practices in remote tabletop collaboration.

Introduction

Effective support for synchronous remote collaboration has long proved a desirable yet elusive goal for computer technology. Consumer videophone technology was unveiled in 1964, amid forecasts of replacing standard telephony by the early 1970s [1]. Forty years later, video conference technology is more widely available yet remains largely unused, and so perhaps little has changed in practice. Researchers have discussed a variety of problems, most notably poor reproduction of the visual cues, such as eye gaze, that mediate face-to-face conversation [2], and the inability to initiate and conduct the informal collaborative interactions

P. Tuddenham (✉)
Computer Laboratory, University of Cambridge, Cambridge CB3 0FD, UK
e-mail: philip.tuddenham@cl.cam.ac.uk

C. Müller-Tomfelde (ed.), *Tabletops – Horizontal Interactive Displays*,
Human-Computer Interaction Series, DOI 10.1007/978-1-84996-113-4_17,
© Springer-Verlag London Limited 2010

that occur outside of formal scheduled collaboration [3]. Both problems may soon be solved. The falling cost and commoditisation of large displays, camera equipment, and network bandwidth are making always-on remote "video windows" between spaces more feasible in practice, while novel techniques faithfully reproduce visual cues that were absent or distorted in previous technologies [4, 5]. These advances are currently making their way into commercial meeting-room systems.

Technologies that provide a shared visual workspace of the task at hand, rather than of the other remote collaborators, remain rather less advanced. Researchers have demonstrated large-format remote whiteboards to support fixed sketching [6]. However, remote collaboration for other workspace-based activities is largely confined to collaborative versions of conventional desktop-computer applications. These systems lack support for the visual cues and work practices that underpin visual workspaces in co-located collaboration, leading to well-documented problems [7]. The problems are particularly acute in tasks, such as collaborative design, in which a shared visual workspace is a natural focus [8]. A shared visual workspace is also important in a number of other prevalent collaborative tasks such as document review, data analysis and information-gathering.

Recent developments in technology to support co-located collaboration may offer opportunities to address these problems of remote work. The increasing size and resolution of affordable display technologies have led to predictions of ubiquitous large displays [9]. Researchers investigating co-located collaboration have consequently constructed large horizontal interactive displays around which co-located collaborators can sit and interact using their hands. These tabletop interfaces present interactive shared task artefacts that appear on the display and mimic real-world task artefacts such as photos or puzzle pieces.

Scott [10] and Morris [11] argue that conventional tables are prevalent in work environments because they are well-suited to many collaborative two-dimensional information tasks, such as planning, scheduling, brainstorming, design, and layout. Their size and orientation enables collaborators to sit around, and to spread out and spatially-organise the task artefacts. Tabletop interfaces aim to enable access to interactive content during such tasks, and in a way that affords established collaborative work practices. They have been demonstrated for tasks including planning [12] and design [13], and can afford beneficial work practices observed at conventional tables, such as fluid switching between individual and group work [14], and territorial partitioning as a coordination mechanism [13].

A tabletop approach might similarly offer benefits to shared workspaces for remote collaboration. A number of research projects have used large horizontal interactive surfaces to present a shared visual workspace to support remote collaboration [15–22]. Figure 17.1 shows a representative example of these *remote tabletop interfaces*.

However, there has been little consensus among researchers on how to design these remote tabletop interfaces. Moreover, many remote tabletop projects have concerned themselves with constructing remote tabletop interfaces, rather than characterising the extent to which they support remote collaboration. This has

Fig. 17.1 Representative example of a remote tabletop interface. Two tabletop interfaces are linked to provide a large shared workspace with purple remote arm "shadows". From [47]; © 2009 ACM, Inc. Included here by permission

been necessary because the interfaces present technical challenges. Nevertheless, motivations of supporting remote collaboration have often not been developed into well-grounded claims, and there has been little evaluation to determine whether such claims would hold in practice.

In particular, the design of remote tabletops is based in part on an untested assumption: *that a tabletop design will afford for remote collaborators the beneficial work practices of co-located tabletop collaboration, such as fluid transitioning between individual and group work, and coordination based on spatial partitioning.* Conventional groupware suffers from limited support for the work practices and visual cues of co-located collaboration [23]. Accordingly, if this assumption holds, then remote tabletop interfaces may provide a more effective remote collaboration medium. However, the assumption has not been tested in practice, and in contrast to co-located tabletop collaboration, we know little about the work practices afforded by remote tabletops.

The aims of this chapter are threefold: (i) to review work in this area, (ii) to identify key areas of exploration, and (iii) to present a study that begins to explore these areas.

We begin by presenting a review of remote tabletop interfaces, which details the prior systems and discusses their origins and the empirical findings. Based on the review, we identify work practices as a key area of exploration for remote tabletop interfaces. We then present a study that compares work practices in co-located and remote tabletop collaboration. We conclude with a discussion of future trends and a summary.

Background: From Remote Sketching to Remote Tables

Remote Tabletop Interfaces

This section adopts a fairly narrow definition of remote tabletop interfaces: remote horizontal interactive surfaces linked together to create a shared workspace in which the task artefacts are composed of computer-generated imagery. Large shared workspaces for whiteboard-style fixed remote sketching are discussed later (see "Large Format Remote Sketching"). Similarly, remote augmented reality interfaces, in which some task artefacts are physical rather than computer-generated, again have different design issues and are discussed later (see "Remote Augmented Reality Surfaces").

Escritoire [24, 16] was one of the earliest remote tabletop interfaces by this definition. Instead of real paper, it used projected light to create "virtual sheets of paper" in a large horizontal shared workspace for remote collaboration. Two projectors were arranged to create a large (A0 size) low-resolution peripheral area, for storing virtual sheets, surrounding a smaller high-resolution foveal area, into which virtual sheets could be dragged for manipulation or reading. This arrangement was partly a product of the available display technology, and was inspired by the use of space on desks in offices rather than collaborative work practices. Remote collaborators used styluses and bimanual techniques to move and annotate "virtual sheets of paper", and to gesture to each other with telepointer traces.

RemoteDT [17] presented a large horizontal shared workspace containing a Windows XP desktop. Remote collaborators used direct-touch input to interact with legacy applications, to sketch, and to gesture to each other with telepointers. Multiple co-located collaborators could interact concurrently. TIDL [18] provided similar functionality for legacy Java applications using multiple mice. Regenbrecht et al. [19] demonstrated a remote tabletop system in which remote collaborators could move and rotate photos using touch input. The system did not provide a remote gesture representation such as a telepointer or arm shadow, and did not allow multiple co-located collaborators to interact concurrently.

VideoArms [20] enabled remote collaborators to use touch input to move task artefacts, such as photos, and to sketch. Each collaborator's arms were captured using a camera and presented to remote collaborators as an image overlaid on the workspace. The system supported group-to-group collaboration since each surface was large enough for multiple co-located collaborators to stand around, though the touch input system did not allow co-located collaborators to interact concurrently. Distributed Tabletops [25] and Digitable [21] provided similar functionality and remedied this problem using multiple styluses and multi-touch surfaces respectively.

Lastly, C-Slate [22] provided a shared workspace in which remote collaborators could use touch input to reposition task artefacts, such as virtual sheets of paper, and could annotate using a stylus. Like VideoArms, Distributed Tabletops and Digitable, each collaborator's arms were captured using a camera and presented on the surface to remote collaborators. The image of the arm became translucent as the arm was lifted from the surface. The surface was not sufficiently large for co-located collaborators to work side-by-side.

In summary, although the systems all provide large horizontal interactive surfaces, they differ in design: some use indirect mouse input whereas others use direct stylus or touch input devices; some provide remote representations of collaborators' arms whereas others use telepointers or traces; some use interaction techniques such as rotation that favour around-the-table interaction, whereas others focus on support for legacy applications; and some use surfaces sufficiently large for collaborators to work side-by-side while others do not.

Large Format Remote Sketching

Remote tabletop interfaces have their origins in large-format remote sketching interfaces, which in turn were motivated by studies of co-located collaborative design work.

Tang [26] studied the use of shared paper drawings in design meetings on conventional tables. He observed that the process of creating and discussing drawings is often more important than the resulting drawings themselves. He notes that collaborators fluidly interleave drawing and writing with gestures that not only express ideas but also mediate interaction by negotiating turn-taking and focusing attention. Tang's study was preceded by a similar study by Bly [8], and prompted several further studies of co-located collaborative design [27, 28].

The work prompted a shift in remote collaboration technologies away from conventional monitor and mouse interaction and towards larger direct-input remote collaboration interfaces that could afford interleaved sketching and gesturing, unmediated remote representation of hand gestures, and space to mediate interaction.

Commune [29] and VideoDraw [30] linked horizontally-mounted monitors to provide a shared workspace for remote design work. The systems supported simultaneous sketching using styluses, gesturing, and instant visual updates to all sites as users sketched. Commune used a digital stylus system for drawing and gesturing using a cursor, whereas VideoDraw used video links to enable whole-hand gesturing. In an evaluation of Commune using a two-person design task, the authors observed three novel aspects of the system: both collaborators shared the same orientation of the horizontal workspace; both collaborators were able to mark and point to exactly the same place in the workspace without interference from each other's hands; and collaborators were able to switch seamlessly between writing, drawing and gesturing. They also observed that cursors convey only pointing gestures rather than the rich variety of gestures observed in co-located collaboration, and that the drawing space provided by a monitor was too small.

VideoWhiteboard [6] linked large vertical projected displays to support remote sketching. As with VideoDraw, collaborators could sketch simultaneously and see instant visual updates as others sketched. Instead of whole-hand gestures, collaborators now saw the shadows of their remote collaborators' entire bodies. The authors observed that the larger display now allowed collaborators to work side by side at each site. Although the shadows conveyed many of the gestures used in white-board interaction, they observed problems when pointing to precise locations, when conveying subtleties such as head-nods from a distance, and when collaborators' shadows overlapped. This may have been exacerbated by the lack of local feedback of the shadows presented to remote collaborators.

Ishii [31] later demonstrated ClearBoard, which provided the remote sketching task space of VideoDraw, combined with a head-and-shoulders video view of the remote collaborator presented on the same surface. The design imitated collabora-tion through a clear glass board on which collaborators could draw. The camera at each site was positioned behind the surface in order to achieve greater spatial fidelity.

Remote Augmented Reality Surfaces

Following the early remote sketching systems, researchers created various large-format remote collaboration systems that augmented tangible task artefacts with visual information. Double DigitalDesk [32, 15] was one of the earliest such sys-tems. Each collaborator sat at his or her own desk and interacted with their own paper copy of the same page of information. The system augmented this paper with a video image showing annotations made by the remote collaborator, and an image of the remote collaborator's hands.

Double DigitalDesk followed TeamWorkStation [33], which provided similar functionality but displayed the shared workspace on a conventional vertical monitor, rather than augmenting the paper on the desk itself. Double DigitalDesk inspired a number of later projects that pursued the approach of augmenting physical paper with remote annotations, such as Tele-Graffiti [34], LivePaper [35], Agora [36], and PlayTogether [37]. Kirk et al. [38] demonstrated a similar system for remote physical assembly tasks on horizontal surfaces.

Augmenting tangible artefacts to create a shared workspace tends to lead to prob-lems maintaining consistency across the two remote sites. It is not clear how Double DigitalDesk, for instance, addresses the problem of one collaborator moving their copy of a shared document in the workspace, or turning the page of a multi-page document; the remote annotations would then project onto the incorrect page. Some interfaces, such as PlayTogether, have addressed this by opting not to replicate tan-gible task artefacts at each site. Instead, they have presented each collaborator with a projected image of tangible task artefacts that are not physically present at their own site. In such systems, only the collaborator who is co-located with a given task artefact can manipulate it; the other collaborators can only see it (typically at a low display resolution) and gesture to it. This asymmetry is inherent in tasks such as remote surgery, and advantageous in tasks such as remote bomb disposal. It may, however, be problematic for the kinds of information tasks traditionally performed on tables, in which collaborators share task artefacts by passing them among themselves. Remote tabletop interfaces avoid the issues of asymmetry and consistency by using computer-generated imagery instead of tangible objects.

Empirical Findings

There have been relatively few empirical studies of remote tabletop interfaces. In contrast to the wealth of knowledge about collaboration around conventional tables and tabletop interfaces, we know relatively little about remote tabletop collaboration.

The majority of findings relate to the design of the remote arm representation. Firstly, Kirk et al. [39] conducted a number of experiments using an instructor-follower remote physical assembly task and a remote augmented reality surface. The follower participant sat at a table and assembled physical components on the table by following instructions from the instructor participant. The instructor sat at a different table and saw a video image of the follower's workspace. A video image of the instructor's arms was projected onto the follower's table, allowing the instructor to gesture to the follower. The authors found that this unmediated video representation of hands could convey a variety of complex gestures [38]. Furthermore, Kirk et al. [39] showed that this representation yielded performance benefits over a video-only condition with no gesturing. Their analysis of language showed that gesturing enabled deictic utterances that may have replaced lengthier descriptive utterances, and that gesturing enabled turn-taking. A further study using a similar task [40] compared this unmediated video representation of the hands with an alternative in which the instructor could sketch on the follower's workspace, but could not gesture with their hands. The hand gesture representation yielded faster task completion than the sketching approach or a combination hands and sketch approach, with no loss of accuracy.

Secondly, Tang et al. [20] hypothesised that high-fidelity remote arm representations in the shared workspace enable collaborators not only to gesture to each other but also, when combined with direct input devices, to infer the actions being generated by the movement of the arm. Impoverished, indirectly-controlled representations such as telepointers do not, for instance, allow collaborators to see each other reaching with their hands for a task artefact or tool, or retracting their arms from the display to think. In an exploratory study of design and puzzle tasks using remote arm representations and direct input devices, they observed that remote collaborators spent considerable periods of time watching each other work, which supports this hypothesis.

A number of further studies relate to remote tabletop interfaces more generally, but do not address the issue of work practices. Escritoire [16] was trialled using a laboratory study involving three pairs. In questionnaire responses, they all agreed strongly that the shared workspace was useful, and were less sure that a video view showing the remote collaborator's face was also useful. Hauber et al. [41] investigated a decision-making task and compared three conditions: co-located tabletop collaboration; a conventional GUI remote collaboration interface with a shared workspace and a head-and-shoulders view of the remote collaborator; and remote tabletop collaboration, sat at opposite ends of the table, with a vertical screen showing the head-and-shoulders view of the remote participant. Participants in the remote tabletop condition talked more about the technology, took longer to complete the task, reported being more aware of their remote partner, and reported feeling more like they were in the same room.

Pauchet et al. [42] used Digitable to compare remote and co-located tabletop collaboration using a puzzle task. Remote collaborators again were provided with head-and-shoulders video of each other using vertical screens. They reported faster task completion times in the remote interface, though it is not clear whether this generalises to other tasks.

Work Practices in Remote Tabletop Collaboration

The works reviewed in the previous section establish that remote tabletop interfaces are technically feasible, and suggest that high-fidelity remote arm representations may help remote collaborators to gesture and to remain aware of each other's actions.

However, it remains unclear whether they support collaborative activities to the same extent as the conventional tables and tabletop interfaces that they mimic. In particular, tabletop interfaces have been found to be successful at supporting collaboration in part because they can afford some of the beneficial work practices observed in collaboration at conventional tables. It is not clear from the prior work whether it is possible to design remote tabletop interfaces to afford these work practices.

We suggest this is a key topic for further exploration in this area. With this in mind, we review two collaborative work practices that have been observed in collaboration at conventional tables and at tabletop interfaces, and discuss whether they may also be afforded by remote tabletop interfaces.

Workspace Awareness

The ability to maintain an awareness of other collaborators' actions in the workspace is central to many collaborative tasks, and underpins a number of beneficial work practices. Co-located collaborators use a variety of visual and auditory cues to maintain awareness, whereas remote collaborators are reliant on the cues conveyed by the system. Gutwin and Greenberg [7] describe how "[poorly-designed remote collaborative systems] often seem inefficient and clumsy compared with face-to-face work". Consequently, the generation, presentation and use of awareness cues are important factors in the design of a remote collaboration system.

More formally, Gutwin and Greenberg define workspace awareness as "the up-to-the-moment understanding of another person's interaction with the shared workspace" [7]. They argue that workspace awareness underpins a number of beneficial collaborative work practices. One such work practice is *collaborative coupling*, the way in which collaborators move regularly between working individually and working closely together as part of a shared task. These changes tend to be opportunistic and unpredictable [43]. For instance, collaborators may switch from working individually to working closely together in order to discuss a decision or because one collaborator needs the other's involvement in order to make progress with their work. Gutwin and Greenberg argue that supporting this work practice is important, but difficult to achieve in practice. The system must provide awareness cues so that each collaborator remains aware of the state of their peers and of the task in order to be able to instigate discussion or individual work at appropriate points, and to identify when their peers are trying to do so. Workspace awareness therefore underpins collaborative coupling. A number of other work practices also rely on workspace awareness, such as coordinating intricate actions when working closely together; anticipating the actions of collaborators; and identifying appropriate times to offer assistance [7].

Gutwin and Greenberg [7] suggest that collaborators not only maintain awareness by conversing and gesturing, but also by directly and peripherally watching each other work. In particular, they gain awareness through *consequential communication* (watching a collaborator's arms) and from *feedthrough* (watching changes in task artefacts as they are manipulated).

In an observational study of a group design task at a conventional table, Tang [26] observed how peripheral awareness enables collaborators to coordinate intricate actions and switch appropriately between working individually and working closely with others. Similar behaviour has been observed in studies of tabletop interfaces, for a variety of tasks including information-gathering and planning [12], photo-layout [13], and route-planning [14]. This suggests that, like conventional tables, tabletop interfaces can afford high levels of workspace awareness and so the practice of collaborative coupling.

Workspace awareness principles have been applied to the design of remote arm representations in remote tabletop interfaces. As described earlier (see "Empirical Findings"), Tang et al. [20] suggest that remote arm representations can help collaborators watch each other work, and hence aid consequential communication. However, in order to design for awareness we must consider not only the arm representations but interaction more generally. For example, in conventional groupware, consideration of awareness cues when collaborators manipulate task artefacts and navigate the workspace is also important [44]. It is unclear how remote tabletop interaction techniques impact workspace awareness, and so we do not understand how to design remote tabletops to afford the desirable work practices that depend on it.

Territorial Coordination and Seating Arrangement

A number of studies have shown that collaborators at conventional tables partition the workspace into regions. When sat around a conventional table, each collaborator has a distinct area of table in front of them in which they carry out individual work as part of the task. Tang [26] observed a collaborative design task using paper on a conventional table, and noted that designs sketched in this area were "within a personal boundary and not intended for others to perceive". Scott et al. [45] observed a similar task and observed that participants moved task artefacts, such as paper or scissors, into this personal territory to reserve them for themselves, and would later return them to the table centre to indicate their availability to the group. Collaborators also implicitly partitioned space in the centre of the table so that each adopted responsibility for the nearest region. Similar territorial behaviour was observed in a tabletop interface using a collaborative photo-layout task [13]. Collaborators would, for instance, move a virtual container of digital photos to the table centre when working together, and when working individually would move containers into and out of their personal work area as necessary, without disrupting their partner. Territoriality is therefore a prominent coordination mechanism in tabletop collaboration.

However, it is unclear whether remote tabletop interfaces will afford this practice. Territoriality among remote tabletop collaborators may depend upon seating arrangement. They can arrange themselves either around the table, as if co-located, or alternatively can both sit at the same place relative to the workspace. This second, *overlaid*, arrangement is unlikely to afford territoriality since collaborators' personal areas will overlap, and so may lead to coordination difficulty.

Seating preferences in remote tabletop collaboration are unclear. Kirk and Stanton-Fraser [40] compared overlaid and non-overlaid arrangements in a remote instructor-follower physical-assembly task. They found a non-significant trend that the overlaid arrangement was easier and led to more task progress. However, the instructor-follower character of the task meant that territorial coordination was not possible. By contrast, co-located collaborators often prefer to interact at a distance that preserves their personal space [46].

Exploratory Study

Having identified work practices as a key area of further exploration for remote tabletop interfaces, we now present an exploratory study that investigates this area. The full results are described in our previous publication [47].

This study seeks to understand:

- Whether remote tabletops afford the coordination mechanism of territoriality, and whether this is affected by seating arrangement.
- How the design of remote tabletops impacts workspace awareness and the work practices that depend on it.

Method

Technology

The study used the Distributed Tabletops system [25] (Fig. 17.1). The system provides a large shared workspace in which co-located or remote collaborators can move, reorient, and otherwise manipulate task artefacts using digital styluses. All collaborators may interact concurrently. Collaborators' arms are displayed using a translucent remote "shadow" representation. Each collaborator's shadows are also shown locally in order to provide local feedback of the remote representation. The system runs at 60 fps with a latency of around 100 ms. Arm shadows are captured at 15 fps. Sites were also linked using a speakerphone.

Study Design

The study compared three conditions (Fig. 17.2):

- *Co-located-adjacent* (CA): Collaborators sat at adjacent corners of the same table. Each had their own stylus, and both could interact concurrently.
- *Remote-adjacent* (RA): Collaborators sat in separate rooms at tables which were linked using the system and using a speakerphone. Collaborators were again positioned at adjacent corners. Again, both collaborators could interact concurrently.
- *Remote-overlaid* (RO). As remote-adjacent, except that collaborators were positioned in the overlaid arrangement.

Fig. 17.2 Study conditions. From [47]; © 2009 ACM, Inc. Included here by permission

| Co-located-adjacent (CA) | Remote-overlaid (RO) | Remote-adjacent (RA) |

The study followed a within-subjects design. Each pair of participants tested each of the three conditions, and the presentation order was counterbalanced across pairs using a Latin square. Pairs attempted each of three design briefs in turn using the system; one in each condition. The presentation order of design briefs was counterbalanced across the conditions and pairs. Data was captured using system log files and video recordings. Post-condition and post-study questionnaires asked about preferences and difficulties; these were further explored in semi-structured interviews.

Task and Interaction

The study used a furniture layout task in which participants were asked to work together to fulfil a design brief by arranging diagrammatic furniture on a floor plan.

For example, one such brief asked participants to design a communal space for a new library and to provide, among other things, as much seating as possible, and areas for photocopying. The other briefs were similar and asked for designs for a common room and for a research lab. Participants were asked to colour furniture items to illustrate the different parts of the brief. After each task, participants were asked to give a short joint presentation and to answer questions about their solution.

This task is representative of various tabletop design tasks. It requires discussion and manipulation of 2-D task artefacts in order to explore different approaches and tradeoffs. Participants were also instructed to apply their own prior knowledge of communal spaces. This led to implicit constraints which, along with the tradeoffs and joint presentation, ensured that collaborators had to maintain an awareness of each other's actions and to coordinate if they were to produce a mutually-satisfactory design.

The shared workspace presented a 75 × 75 cm blue square containing an empty white floor plan, "piles" of diagrammatic furniture nearest the participants, a task brief, and a key explaining the furniture representations (Fig. 17.1). At the task outset, the floor plan was empty except for lines marking room boundaries.

Each participant had a stylus with which they could move any of the task artefacts (including the plan). The system used the popular Rotate 'N' Translate interaction technique [48], which uses a pseudo-physics model to enable task artefacts to be rotated and translated simultaneously in a single stylus stroke. Once moved onto the floor plan, furniture would snap orientation to multiples of 45° and would "stick" to the floor plan if the plan were moved. The colour of an item of furniture could be changed by tapping twice with the stylus to open a colour menu, and then tapping on the appropriate menu item.

Participants and Procedure

Eighteen paid participants aged 20–39 were recruited from a Computer Science department to form 9 pairs (16 males; 2 mixed-sex pairs). Participants in each pair reported having met previously. Two participants were left-handed. One had limited experience with tabletop interfaces; the others had none.

Each pair was first given a short tutorial about interacting with the system, after which each participant practiced individually until comfortable. Once the experiment structure had been explained, the pair completed each condition in turn. In each condition, the participants were arranged appropriately and asked to stay in their seats and not to move the seats. Participants practiced together until comfortable using a practice brief, to minimise learning effects during the recorded sessions. All pairs took about 10 min before their first condition, and about 2 min thereafter. The session workspace was then loaded. Participants were instructed to work together to arrange the task artefacts to fulfil the brief to the best of their abilities. They were advised that it might take between 15 min and half an hour, and that at the end they should make a short presentation and answer questions on their finished design.

After the presentation and questions, each participant completed a post-condition questionnaire. Once all three conditions were complete, each participant individually completed a post-study questionnaire, and the pair took part in a semi-structured interview.

Results: Initial Observations

Pairs in each condition worked for an average of 21 min. Participants often used their prior experiences (for example, that photocopiers should be situated away from working areas because of the noise). This led them to explore different layouts and adjust their design as they proceeded, to produce an outcome that was most appropriate in the context of their own prior experience. We observed both individual and group work, and both turn-taking and concurrent work.

Pairs in all three conditions appeared to have few difficulties interacting with the system. The post-condition questionnaire used 7-point Likert scales to ask about ease of task completion, ease of communication, and the extent to which the pair worked together (Table 17.1). Friedman rank tests for repeated-measures ordinal data did not yield significant differences among conditions.

Table 17.1 Mean (standard deviation) Likert scale responses. From [47]; © 2009 ACM, Inc. Included here by permission

Question	CA	RO	RA
"We worked together throughout the task."	2.0	2.1	2.1
(1=strongly agree, 7=strongly disagree)	(0.8)	(1.2)	(0.9)
"How easy or hard was the task to complete using this technology?"	2.5	2.2	2.4
(1=very easy, 7=very hard)	(0.9)	(0.9)	(0.8)
"How did you find communicating this way?"	1.7	1.9	2.3
(1=very easy, 7=very hard)	(0.8)	(0.6)	(0.8)

At the end of the study, participants were asked individually which of the remote conditions they preferred. Eleven preferred overlaid, 6 preferred adjacent, and 1 had no preference. A chi-squared test yielded no significant overall preference.

Results: Territorial Coordination

System log files were used to generate *activity maps*. Each map shows the locations of one pair's interactions with furniture in the workspace in a single session [45]. Figure 17.3 shows activity maps for a single representative pair. The black and white marker distributions in the co-located-adjacent conditions show a trend for partitioning the floor plan and surrounding space according to proximity, so that each participant worked broadly in the half of the table nearest themselves. By contrast, the marker distributions in the remote cases suggests that participants broadly partitioned the workspace into regions in which they worked, but the partitioning forms a patchwork rather than a strict left-right arrangement.

Fig. 17.3 Activity map
showing interactions of one
pair in the workspace. Each
marker corresponds to a task
artefact being picked up or
dropped. Colour indicates the
person interacting. From [47];
© 2009 ACM, Inc. Included
here by permission

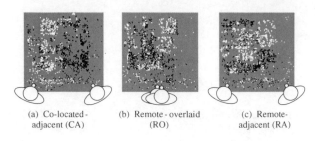

(a) Co-located-   (b) Remote-overlaid   (c) Remote-
adjacent (CA)   (RO)   adjacent (RA)

Such a quasi-naturalistic open-ended task inevitably leads to variations in partitioning, depending on how activity unfolded at the time, and so it is difficult to make
inferences from the visual data alone. Accordingly, a quantitative statistical analysis of the extent of left-right partitioning was performed on the underlying location
data. We began by quantifying the extent to which participants' interactions were
partitioned to the left and right.

Following the approach of Scott et al. [45], we calculated the proportion of interactions carried out by each participant on each side of the table to find, for instance,
that the left side was 30% participant A and 70% participant B. However, we cannot
use this figure to infer partitioning because B may have been more active than A on
both sides. Similarly, we may calculate that, for instance, 80% of B's interactions
were on the right-hand side of the table, but again we cannot infer partitioning since
80% of A's interactions may also have been on that side.

Instead, we desire an alternative metric to measure the extent of partitioning
between collaborators. We calculate the *left-right partitioning index* by first taking the proportion of A's interactions that lie within the left half of the table, and
then the same for B's, and then taking the absolute difference between the two figures. For example, if 80% of A's interactions fell on the left side, and 30% of B's,
the resulting index would be $|0.8-0.3| = 0.5$. If A's interactions were entirely on
the left, and B's entirely on the right, the index would be $|1.0-0.0| = 1.0$. If both
participants interacted to the same extent on the left, the resulting index would be 0.
Accordingly, this metric is an aggregate measure that we can use quantitatively to
highlight differences in partitioning.

The partitioning indices across different conditions are shown in Fig. 17.4 (left).
The trends are consistent with the patterns observed in the activity maps. The mean

Fig. 17.4 Left-right
partitioning index and rate of
coordination utterances for
each condition. Error bars are
95% confidence intervals and
indicate variation within pairs
(i.e. the error considered by a
repeated-measures ANOVA).
From [47]; © 2009 ACM, Inc.
Included here by permission

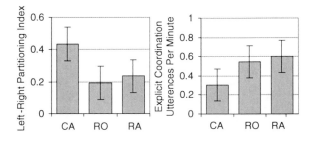

index for the co-located-adjacent condition is 0.4, corresponding to a 70%:30% split between sides of the table. The mean index in both remote conditions is 0.2, corresponding to a 60%:40% split. This is perhaps surprising: the extent of partitioning in the remote-adjacent case is quantitatively indistinguishable from the remote-overlaid case, in which participants were overlaid and hence could not partition by proximity.

The difference among the conditions was significant using a one-way repeated-measures ANOVA ($F(2,16)=7.02$, $p<0.01$). Pairwise t-tests found significant differences between CA and RA ($t(8)=3.64$, $p<0.01$), and between CA and RO ($t(8)=2.83$, $p=0.022$).

The activity maps shown in Fig. 17.3 show the location of interactions relative to the shared workspace. Figure 17.5 shows the marker locations transformed to appear relative to the participants' final furniture layout. This provides some insights as to how the remote participants spatially partitioned the task into the patchwork arrangement: the markers are often partitioned according to either the "walls" on the floor plan at the task outset, or to "islands" of furniture or new "walls" created by the participants during the task.

That participants in the remote conditions did not partition based on proximity, as is the social norm, suggests that they may have worked to explicitly coordinate their activities. Although much of the coordination seemed implicit in the activities of the participants, they sometimes coordinated with explicit utterances to make clear to each other the activities they had completed or were about to start (e.g. "I'll do the common room now", "I've finished doing the windows", "You can start on the secretary's room"). We coded the dialogue and found that such explicit coordination utterances were twice as frequent on average in the remote conditions (Fig. 17.4, right). The difference between conditions was significant using a one-way repeated-measures ANOVA with the conservative Greenhouse-Geisser sphericity correction

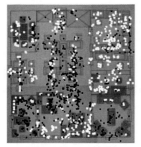
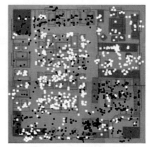

Remote - overlaid   Remote - adjacent

Fig. 17.5 Interactions of one pair overlaid on their final furniture layouts. Furniture layouts and "walls" are shown as *lines* and coloured areas under the markers; participants themselves coloured the furniture during the task. Each marker corresponds to a task artefact being picked up or dropped. Marker colour (*black or white*) indicates the person interacting. From [47]; © 2009 ACM, Inc. Included here by permission

$(F(2,16)=6.142, p=0.03)$. Pairwise t-tests identified significant differences between CA and RO ($t(8)=4.25$, $p<0.01$), and between CA and RA ($t(8)=2.40$, $p=0.04$).

Results: Workspace Awareness

We now consider workspace awareness, and the beneficial work practices that rely on it. As described in the review of empirical findings, prior research has investigated intentional gesture in detail, and so we focus on the remaining sources of workspace awareness, namely consequential communication and feedthrough. We begin by examining the work practice of collaborative coupling, which relies on workspace awareness (described in the review of work practices).

Coupling Styles

We iteratively refined a coding scheme for the coupling styles observed in the present study. Randomly-selected segments of video data from each condition were repeatedly analysed using a similar approach to prior exploratory studies of co-located collaboration [45, 14]. The initial coding categories were informed by field notes and by the co-located tabletop coupling styles identified by Tang et al. [14]. This initial analysis yielded four distinguishable coupling styles that exhaustively and mutually-exclusively classify the coupling arrangement at any time:

- *Simultaneous work on the same problem (SWSP)*: the partners are actively working together to solve the same problem, such as both creating a wall.
- *View engaged*: As Tang et al. [14]. Though the partners are working together, one is watching closely while the other manipulates the display, for instance while taking turns or demonstrating ideas to each other.
- *Discuss*: the partners are discussing ideas together and neither is manipulating the display
- *Independent work*: the partners are working independently while either manipulating or looking at the workspace. Partners may be conversing or working in silence.

We explored whether the different conditions affected the ability to work in the different coupling styles. We used the above scheme to code the entire video of every session to calculate the proportion of time spent in each coupling style (Fig. 17.6). There was large variation among different pairs: some tended to be predominantly closely-coupled throughout; others tended to work independently. This is to be expected in a quasi-naturalistic task. Nevertheless, large differences among conditions in the proportion of time spent in each style were not apparent, and analysis using repeated-measures ANOVAs found no significant differences.

This result is perhaps surprising: working remotely did not seem to have a practical impact on collaborators' behaviour at this aggregate level, in a fairly

Fig. 17.6 The proportion of time spent in each coupling style in each condition. *Error bars* indicate variation within pairs and show 95% confidence intervals. From [47]; © 2009 ACM, Inc. Included here by permission

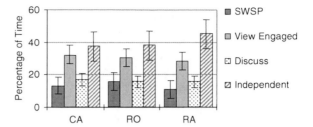

representative design task. Participants seemed able to work independently and closely coupled to the same extent regardless of whether co-located or remote.

Coupling Transitions

Our observations of the video record suggest that participants in all conditions were able to change fluidly between different coupling styles. The changes seemed swift and opportunistic and were often preceded not by explicit gestures or conversation but instead by one collaborator watching another's arm movements (consequential communication) or another's manipulation of task artefacts (feedthrough).

Figure 17.7 shows a representative example. The collaborators L and R are working independently, and in different parts of the workspace (Fig. 17.7a). L notices R working in the corner and starts to watch (view engaged, Fig. 17.7b). L then begins to help R by moving a piece of furniture into position, while ensuring that his arm does not block R's activity (simultaneous work on the same problem, Fig. 17.7c). At this point, the collaborators begin to talk. The video also revealed similar instances of anticipation and assistance, such as by watching closely and then instigating discussion, or taking turns to demonstrate different ideas to each other.

Support for different coupling styles and fluid transitions between is desirable and suggests high levels of awareness. Yet it is not clear how this arose as a result of the design of remote tabletop interfaces. However, the video also revealed that two occasionally-used interaction techniques tended to cause awareness problems. The use of the techniques by one partner tended to be unanticipated by the other, and in contrast to the otherwise-fluid transitioning between coupling styles, this resulted in confusion that had to be resolved verbally. Though undesirable, these techniques offer an opportunity to gain insights by exploring how they impaired workspace awareness while the remainder of the system afforded the otherwise-high awareness level.

The first occasionally-used problematic technique was the movement of the large floor plan. Like the furniture items, the plan could be simultaneously translated and rotated by touching any part of it with the stylus and then dragging, using the popular Rotate 'N' Translate technique [48]. Observations of the video suggest that movement of the large floor plan by a collaborator was often unanticipated by their partner. Figure 17.8 shows a representative example. L states his intention to spin the

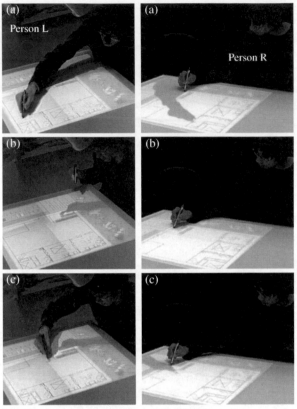

(L and R work independently. L glances at R's work.) (a)

(L stops work and watches R.) (view engaged) (b)

L: eh it's good need a door

(L assists R by adding a door to the room that R is arranging.)

(simultaneous work on the same problem) (c)

Fig. 17.7 A series of coupling transitions. From [47]; © 2009 ACM, Inc. Included here by permission

floor plan while R begins to reach towards the top of the plan to interact (Fig. 17.8a). However, as R's hand nears the top of the plan, L begins to spin it (Fig. 17.8b). R stops the reaching action, retracts his hand (Fig. 17.8c) and says "oh I see yeah".

Though the participants quickly recovered, this sequence contrasts with the smooth coupling transitions observed throughout the majority of the sessions as participants moved furniture (for example, Fig. 17.7). This is curious because both the movement of the furniture and the movement of the floor plan used the same Rotate 'N' Translate interaction technique. The difference may result from the large size of the floor plan. Because furniture items are small, a collaborator has to reach towards a furniture item in order to interact with it. This reaching motion can be peripherally observed by their partner, either in the motion of the arm (if co-located) or the shadow (if remote). This consequential communication enables them to anticipate

Fig. 17.8 Deliberate movement of the floor plan by one participant was unanticipated by their collaborator. From [47]; © 2009 ACM, Inc. Included here by permission

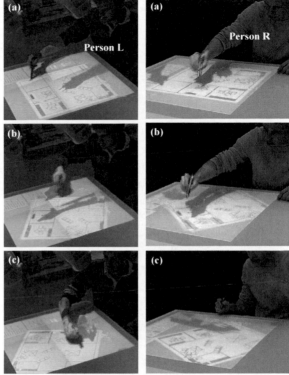

L: do you want to spin the plan so you can get at it more easily
(R reaches towards the top of the plan start working (a)
(L starts to rotate the plan. R has not anticipated this and has to abort the reaching action.) (b)
(L still rotates the plan. R backs off looking puzzled.) (c)
R: oh I see yeah

the action. By contrast, the movement of the floor plan can be instigated from any point within its large area. Because it does not require reaching to a particular point, the action is likely harder to anticipate. In Fig. 17.8a, for example, R cannot infer from his view that L is about to rotate the plan. The large size of the floor plan may also impact negatively in a second way. Furniture items are small and so any movement of them is localised to the vicinity of the interacting arm or arm shadow. A collaborator can safely assume that if their partner's arm or arm shadow is far from their own then their actions will not interfere. This is not the case for the large floor plan, since it is so large that its movement is not localised near to the hand causing the movement.

The second problematic interaction technique was the colour menu, which opened when a participant tapped twice on a furniture item. Like the movement of the floor plan, this action often seemed unanticipated by the instigator's partner. Figure 17.9 shows a representative example. L has opened a colour menu (Fig. 17.9a) but as she presses on it to choose a colour, R opens another colour

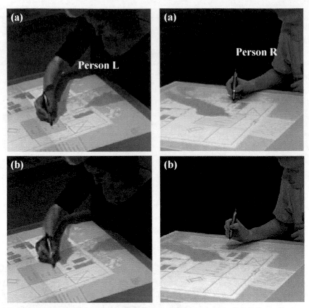

(L has opened a menu and is about to press on it.) (a)
(R opens a menu as L presses, causing L to press on this
new menu instead of her own menu. Consequently, the
wrong item of furniture changes colour.)(b)
L: oh?

Fig. 17.9 Opening of a menu by one participant was unanticipated by their partner. From [47];
© 2009 ACM, Inc. Included here by permission

menu that overlaps the original. L unintentionally presses on the overlapping menu
instead. This selects the wrong colour and the wrong furniture item. The collaborators are confused and discuss what happened (Fig. 17.9b). Again, though quickly
resolved, this contrasts with the fluid coupling switches observed when moving furniture (Fig. 17.7). Like the movement of the floor plan, this problem may again be
explained using the awareness framework. Figure 17.9a illustrates that the tapping
action by R to open the menu is not obvious from the arm shadow seen by L, and
so the action provides no consequential communication. Furthermore, there is no
feedthrough as the action unfolds because the menu appears instantly once the tapping action is complete. By comparison, the movement of the furniture is continuous
and so is perceptible as the action unfolds, providing feedthrough. Furthermore,
the furniture moves with the shadow of the dragging arm, providing consequential
communication.

Discussion

Territorial Coordination

The study condition significantly affected the collaborators' partitioning of the
workspace. Participants in the co-located-adjacent condition partitioned the floor

plan and surrounding space broadly according to who was nearest. This proximity partitioning is consistent with the territoriality findings of Scott et al. [45]. Their study observed two pairs at conventional tables. The left-right partitioning indices from their data can be calculated as 0.51 and 0.42, which is consistent with our results.

Participants in the remote-overlaid condition were not able to partition and delegate by proximity since their personal regions overlapped. Nevertheless, each pair partitioned the floor plan into a patchwork of areas in which one or the other participant worked. The partitioning followed the boundaries visible at the start of the task, and new boundaries created using the task artefacts.

Participants in the remote-adjacent condition behaved much as those in the remote-overlaid condition; the adjacent seating arrangement did not lead to the proximity-based partitioning observed in the co-located-adjacent condition. This indicates that territorial coordination may arise from more than seating arrangement alone.

Video observations of participants reaching may help explain this difference between the co-located-adjacent and remote-adjacent conditions. Participants in the co-located-adjacent condition seemed to avoid reaching across their partners, perhaps because this would block them from working. Before reaching they would often wait for an opportune moment, and sometimes asked permission (Fig. 17.10). In the remote conditions, by contrast, partners would unhesitatingly work directly

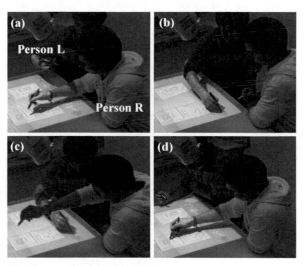

Fig. 17.10
Co-located-adjacent collaborators have difficulty working across each other. From [47]; © 2009 ACM, Inc. Included here by permission

(R and L are working independently.) (a)
L: yeah I'll start doing pigeon holes
R: okay
(R leans back and L leans across and takes a bookshelf.) (b)
L: um boodshelves are pigeon holes can I just steal like loads?
(L leans across to take more and R tries to work.) (c)
(L finishes taking and R leans forward to work again.) (d)
L: cheers

across each other, work within the arm shadows themselves, and reach to take furniture from immediately in front of each other (Fig. 17.7). This blocking hypothesis helps explain the differences in partitioning and is supported by recent findings in the literature. Nacenta et al. [49] found that action-at-a-distance techniques (like "tractor beams"), that avoid blocking problems, lead to less proximity-based partitioning in co-located tabletop collaboration than when using conventional techniques like Rotate 'N' Translate. Similarly, Ha et al. [50] found that when using a mouse (which avoids blocking problems), a majority of participants reported being more likely to interact with objects on their partner's side of the table than when using a stylus.

These results suggest that, unlike co-located collaboration at conventional tables and tabletop interfaces, remote tabletop collaboration does not afford the work practice of territorial coordination. As described earlier, social norms dictate that space immediately in front of a collaborator is reserved as an area in which they can try ideas away from the group, and can move task artefacts to reserve them for their use [45]. This cannot be the case in the remote-overlaid condition, because these regions are overlaid. That remote-adjacent collaborators unhesitatingly took task artefacts from immediately in front of others, suggests that this condition also does not afford personal territories.

We have described two further results. Firstly, like Kirk [40], there was a nonsignificant trend for remote collaborators to prefer the overlaid arrangement. Ten of the 11 who expressed this preference reported having difficulty reaching parts of the table when remote-adjacent. However, this difficulty was not reported when co-located-adjacent, despite the participants being sat in the same positions relative to the workspace. Video observations suggest this effect may be caused by a limitation of the remote gesture system. Co-located participants would point to the far corner of the table, using the 3-D trajectory of their finger or hand to avoid having to reach. The remote arm representation did not convey these 3-D depth cues and so remote collaborators would instead gesture by reaching out and hovering their hands over the far corner. This problem was most acute in the remote-adjacent condition because participants were seated to one side, and may have led to the preference for remote-overlaid.

Secondly, we showed that the patchwork partitioning in the remote cases coincided with more frequent explicit coordination utterances. This suggests that the lack of support for social norms may require greater formal coordination effort.

Workspace Awareness

Our investigation of workspace awareness began by examining collaborative coupling. As discussed in the review of work practices, this is a beneficial work practice that relies on a high level of workspace awareness and is afforded by co-located tabletop collaboration. We identified four coupling styles and found no significant differences among conditions in the proportion of time spent in each style. Furthermore, the confidence intervals on these proportions indicate that moving among experiment conditions impacted little on collaborators' abilities to work in the different styles. This contrasts with Tang et al. [14], who observed a fifty percentage-point difference in the proportion of time spent in similar coupling styles as a result of manipulating the design of a tabletop interface. We would not claim that the condition has no impact on ability to work in different styles in general; an alternative task may result in a more pronounced difference. Nevertheless, for this fairly representative design task, the conditions seemed to have relatively little impact at an aggregate level.

Collaborators' abilities to switch fluidly between coupling styles seemed dependent on the interaction techniques. In particular, two techniques used occasionally tended to impair workspace awareness and to lead to confusion that was resolved verbally. Though the collaborators recovered quickly, these instances provide insights into how the design afforded the otherwise-high level of awareness. Firstly, the movement of the floor plan lacked consequential communication because the action could be instigated from any point without having to reach first, and so was hard to anticipate. Secondly, the opening of the menu lacked consequential communication because the instigating double-tap action was not conveyed by the arm shadow; and lacked feedthrough because the menu appeared instantly and at the end of the action.

By comparison, most coupling changes seemed smooth and opportunistic, mediated by consequential communication and feedthrough as collaborators moved furniture items. Partners also offered each other assistance at appropriate times and closely-coordinated their actions when working in the same part of the floor plan, providing further indication of a high level of workspace awareness. The movement of a furniture item provided consequential communication because the collaborator had to reach towards an item in order to move it, and because the movement of the item was then coupled to that of the interacting hand. The action further provided feedthrough via the continuous movement of the item, which could be observed by collaborators as the action unfolded.

Implication #1: Visual Boundaries to Aid Coordination

Whereas co-located tabletop collaborators coordinate based on proximity, remote tabletop collaborators partition the task in a patchwork arrangement based on visual boundaries. Furthermore, our observations suggest that neither remote arrangement affords a personal territory in which to try ideas away from the group and to reserve task artefacts. Applications and techniques designed for co-located tabletop collaborators may therefore encounter coordination difficulties if applied naively in a remote tabletop setting. One way to address this problem may be to provide flexible visual boundaries for remote tabletop collaborators. For instance, each collaborator could be provided with their own moveable coloured palette region to act as a personal territory onto which task artefacts could be placed.

Implication #2: Localised, Continuous Visual Changes

Our observations of interaction techniques suggest that a high level of awareness can be afforded by interaction techniques that:

- localise visual changes to the vicinity of the interacting hand;
- and localise the area in which the action can be instigated;
- and produce continuous visual changes.

We observed how two interaction techniques proved difficult to anticipate, and led to confusion, because they did not satisfy these properties.

Many interaction techniques demonstrated in prior tabletop interfaces satisfy these properties, and the resulting high awareness level may contribute to the effectiveness of these interfaces in affording collaborative activities. For instance, techniques like Rotate 'N' Translate [48], for moving small photos, are localised and produce continuous visual changes, similar to the movement of the furniture items in this study. Similarly, dragging from a pile to create new task artefacts, dragging to a "recycle bin" to remove task artefacts, and using individual movable lenses [14, 51] to view different visualisations all satisfy these properties.

The properties can also be applied to suggest ways of improving the two problematic interaction techniques in the current study. Instead of double tapping to open the menu, for instance, the menu could open gradually while the collaborator drags from a point, so that the movement of the hand and menu are observable as the action unfolds. The menu could alternatively be kept permanently open as a moveable box or a toolglass [52]. Like the furniture items, this permanent menu would lead to visible reaching actions and, when moved, would provide continuous localised visual changes. When dragging a large task artefact like the floor plan, the visual effects can no longer be localised to the dragging hand because of its size. Nevertheless, a small "drag handle" can be attached to the task artefact to localise the area in which the action can be instigated, so that collaborators can see each other reaching towards the handle and so anticipate the action.

Our suggestion that continuous visual changes may improve awareness in tabletop interaction techniques follows a similar proposal of Gutwin and Greenberg [44] for conventional GUI groupware. However, we believe that localising interaction has not previously been explored as a tool to improve workspace awareness. Moreover, just as Gutwin and Greenberg [44] argue that enforcing continuous visual changes in conventional groupware can increase awareness but negatively impact individual power (e.g. by prohibiting fast keyboard shortcuts), so enforcing locality may lead to a similar tradeoff: localising the point at which an action can be instigated may boost awareness through increased reaching, but requires extra reaching effort by collaborators. This may impact productivity and ultimately lead to fatigue. Prior experience suggests that a reasonably balance may exist, because collaborators at conventional tables frequently reach to acquire task artefacts. This is supported by Morris et al. [53], who explored reach in a tabletop interface by comparing a single central shared menu against replicated menus near to each collaborator. When using the central shared menu, participants were concerned not by the ergonomics of reaching, but by the socially-awkward proximity of their hand to others' hands. This physical proximity arose perhaps because the task required frequent menu use by different collaborators, but would not occur in remote tabletops.

Future Trends

There are considerable opportunities for further research in this area. Firstly, the limitations of the exploratory study offer a number of opportunities to broaden the findings. Further work could establish the effects of collaborating remotely for tasks where a lack of spatial partitioning is particularly disadvantageous, and investigate the effectiveness of the proposed visual boundaries and coloured palettes. Further work could also explore whether the findings extend to larger groups of mutually-remote collaborators and to group-to-group collaboration.

Secondly, further work could also explore further the proposed awareness inter-action techniques (such as dragging from a point to create a menu). The properties of localised and continuous visual changes may also be applied to boost workspace awareness in other kinds of remote collaboration interface, such as conventional GUI groupware. Novel 3-D display technologies may enable 3-D depth cues in remote arm representations and hence address the problem of leaning to gesture, in remote tabletops and other large-format interfaces.

Thirdly, future work may begin to consider how to combine the shared workspace of remote tabletops with a head-and-shoulders video view. Such an addition may offer benefits in tasks, such as negotiation tasks, that rely on social cues. However, the person-space technology must faithfully convey spatial cues such as eye gaze, body orientation, and arm location, to avoid impairing the accurate spatial cues conveyed by the remote tabletop task-space technology. Some systems, for instance, use an overlaid remote tabletop arrangement yet present a video view of the remote collaborator on a vertical display on the far side of the table [22]. Such systems may present conflicting spatial cues because a user sees the remote arm reaching away from them on the table but towards them in the video view.

Finally, perhaps most importantly, as the cost of large displays decreases, and remote tabletop interfaces become easier to construct over time, there may be an opportunity to move away from laboratory-based work and towards field studies of long-term installations and real-world tasks.

Conclusion

This chapter began by reviewing work in remote tabletop interfaces, an emerging class of interfaces for remote collaboration in a shared workspace. We showed that there has been little empirical work in the area, and in particular that the work prac-tices afforded by remote tabletop interfaces are not well understood. As a starting point to explore this area, we presented a study of two work practices in remote tabletop collaboration. The study compared co-located and remote tabletop col-laboration using two remote seating arrangements. Neither of the remote seating arrangements led to territorial partitioning of space in the way observed in the co-located arrangement. We propose that this difference was caused by differences in reaching. All three conditions afforded individual and group work as part of a shared task. However, two interaction techniques impaired workspace awareness in the remote cases, and so impaired the ability to transition fluidly between working styles. We propose that these problems were caused by a lack of localised interaction, and a lack of continuous visual changes. The results yield implications for the design and further study of these interfaces.

Acknowledgments We gratefully acknowledge Mark Ashdown, Alan Blackwell, Darren Edge, Cecily Morrison, and the anonymous referees, for feedback on drafts; and the EPSRC and Thales Research and Technology (UK), who funded this work.

References

1. Egido C (1988) Video conferencing as a technology to support group work: A review of its failures. In: CSCW'08: Proceedings of the 1988 ACM conference on computer-supported cooperative work, ACM Press, New York, pp 13–24
2. Okada KI, Maeda F, Ichikawaa Y, Matsushita Y (1994) Multiparty videoconferencing at virtual social distance: Majic design. In: CSCW '94: Proceedings of the 1994 ACM conference on Computer supported cooperative work, ACM Press, New York, pp 385–393
3. Bly SA, Harrison SR, Irwin S (1993) Media spaces: Bringing people together in a video, audio, and computing environment. Communicaton of the ACM 36(1):28–46
4. Nguyen D, Canny J (2005) Multiview: Spatially faithful group video conferencing. In: CHI '05: Proceedings of the SIGCHI conference on Human factors in computing systems, ACM Press, New York, pp 799–808
5. Nguyen DT, Canny J (2007) Multiview: Improving trust in group video conferencing through spatial faithfulness. In: CHI '07: Proceedings of the SIGCHI conference on Human factors in computing systems, ACM Press, New York, pp 1465–1474
6. Tang JC, Minneman S (1991) Videowhiteboard: Video shadows to support remote collaboration. In: CHI '91: Proceedings of the SIGCHI conference on Human factors in computing systems, ACM Press, New York, pp 315–322
7. Gutwin C, Greenberg S (2002) A descriptive framework of workspace awareness for real-time groupware. Computer Supported Cooperative Work 11(3):411–446
8. Bly SA (1988) A use of drawing surfaces in different collaborative settings. In: CSCW '88: Proceedings of the 1988 ACM conference on computer-supported cooperative work, ACM Press, New York, pp 250–256
9. Weiser M (1999) The computer for the 21st century. SIGMOBILE Mob Comput Commun Rev 3(3):3–11
10. Scott SD (2005) Territoriality in collaborative tabletop workspaces. PhD thesis, University of Calgary, Calgary, Alberta, Canada
11. Morris MR (2006) Supporting effective interaction with tabletop groupware. PhD thesis, Stanford University
12. Rogers Y, Lindley S (2004) Collaborating around vertical and horizontal large interactive displays: Which way is best? Interacting with Computers 16(6):1133–1152
13. Scott SD, Carpendale MST, Habelski S (2005) Storage bins: Mobile storage for collaborative tabletop displays. IEEE Computer Graphics and Applications 25(4):58–65
14. Tang A, Tory M, Po B, Neumann P, Carpendale S (2006) Collaborative coupling over tabletop displays. In: CHI '06: Proceedings of the SIGCHI conference on human factors in computing systems, ACM Press, New York, pp 1181–1190
15. Wellner P (1993) Interacting with paper on the DigitalDesk. Communication of the ACM 36(7):87–96
16. Ashdown M, Robinson P (2005) Escritoire: A personal projected display. IEEE MultiMedia 12(1):34–42

17. Esenther A, Ryall K (2006) RemoteDT: Support for multi-site table collaboration. In: Proceedings of the CollabTech'06: International conference on collaboration technologies (CollabTech)

18. Hutterer P, Close BS, Thomas BH (2006) Supporting mixed presence groupware in tabletop applications. In: TABLETOP '06: Proceedings of the 1st IEEE international workshop on horizontal interactive human-computer systems, IEEE Computer Society, pp 63–70

19. Regenbrecht H, Haller M, Hauber J, Billinghurst M (2006) Carpeno: Interfacing remote collaborative virtual environments with table-top interaction. Virtual Reality 10(2):95–107

20. Tang A, Neustaedter C, Greenberg S (2006) VideoArms: Embodiments for mixed presence groupware. In: HCI 2006: Proceedings of the 20th British HCI Group annual conference, Springer, London, pp 85–102

21. Coldefy F, dit Picard SL (2007) Digitable: An interactive multiuser table for collocated and remote collaboration enabling remote gesture visualization. In: Proceedings of the PROCAMS'07: IEEE workshop on projector-camera systems, pp 1–8

22. Izadi S, Agarwal A, Criminisi A, Winn J, Blake A, Fitzgibbon A (2007) C-Slate: A multi-touch and object recognition system for remote collaboration using horizontal surfaces. In: Proceedings of the TABLETOP'07: Second annual IEEE international workshop on horizontal interactive human-computer systems, pp 3–10

23. Gutwin C, Greenberg S (1999) The effects of workspace awareness support on the usability of real-time distributed groupware. ACM Transactions on Computer-Human Interaction 6(3):243–281

24. Ashdown M (2004) Personal projected displays. PhD thesis, University of Cambridge Computer Laboratory

25. Tuddenham P, Robinson P (2007) Distributed tabletops: Supporting remote and mixed-presence tabletop collaboration. In: Proceedings of the TABLETOP'07: Second annual IEEE international workshop on horizontal interactive human-computer systems, pp 19–26

26. Tang JC (1991) Findings from observational studies of collaborative work. International Journal of Man-Machine Studies 34(2):143–160

27. Olson GM, Olson JS, Carter MR, Storrøsten M (1992) Small group design meetings: An analysis of collaboration. Human-Computer Interaction 7:347–374

28. Bekker MM, Olson JS, Olson GM (1995) Analysis of gestures in face-to-face design teams provides guidance for how to use groupware in design. In: DIS '95: Proceedings of the first conference on designing interactive systems, ACM Press, New York, pp 157–166

29. Bly SA, Minneman SL (1990) Commune: A shared drawing surface. SIGOIS Bulletin 11(2–3):184–192

30. Tang JC, Minneman SL (1991) Videodraw: A video interface for collaborative drawing. ACM Transactions on Information Systems 9(2):170–184

31. Ishii H, Kobayashi M (1992) Clearboard: A seamless medium for shared drawing and conversation with eye contact. In: CHI '92: Proceedings of the SIGCHI conference on human factors in computing systems, ACM Press, New York, pp 525–532

32. Wellner P, Freeman S (1993) The DoubleDigitalDesk: Shared editing of paper documents. Technical Report EPC-93-108, Xerox Research Centre, Cambridge

33. Ishii H (1990) Teamworkstation: Towards a seamless shared workspace. In: CSCW '90: Proceedings of the 1990 ACM conference on computer-supported cooperative work, ACM Press, New York, pp 13–26

34. Takao N, Shi J, Baker S (2003) Tele-graffiti: A camera-projector based remote sketching system with hand-based user interface and automatic session summarization. International Journal of Computer Vision 53(2):115–133

35. Robinson JA, Robertson C (2001) The LivePaper system: Augmenting paper on an enhanced tabletop. Computers & Graphics 25(5):731–743

36. Kuzuoka H, Yamashita J, Yamazaki K, Yamazaki A (1999) Agora: A remote collaboration system that enables mutual monitoring. In: CHI '99: CHI '99 extended abstracts on human factors in computing systems, ACM Press, New York, pp 190–191

37. Wilson A, Robbins DC (2006) PlayTogether: Playing games across multiple interactive table-tops. In: IUI'06 workshop on tangible play: Research and design for tangible and tabletop games
38. Kirk D, Crabtree A, Rodden T (2005) Ways of the hands. In: ECSCW'05: Proceedings of the 9th conference on European Conference on Computer Supported Cooperative Work, Springer-Verlag Inc., New York, pp 1–21
39. Kirk D, Rodden T, Fraser DS (2007) Turn it this way: Grounding collaborative action with remote gestures. In: CHI '07: Proceedings of the SIGCHI conference on human factors in computing systems, ACM Press, New York, pp 1039–1048
40. Kirk D, Fraser DS (2006) Comparing remote gesture technologies for supporting collaborative physical tasks. In: CHI '06: Proceedings of the SIGCHI conference on human factors in computing systems, ACM Press, New York, pp 1191–1200
41. Hauber J, Regenbrecht H, Billinghurst M, Cockburn A (2006) Spatiality in videoconferencing: Trade-offs between efficiency and social presence. In: CSCW '06: Proceedings of the 2006 20th anniversary conference on computer supported cooperative work, ACM Press, New York, pp 413–422
42. Pauchet A, Coldefy F, Lefebvre L, Picard SLD, Perron L, Bouguet A, Collobert M, Guerin J, Corvaisier D (2007) Tabletops: Worthwhile experiences of collocated and remote collaboration. In: Proceedings of the TABLETOP'07: Second annual IEEE international workshop on horizontal interactive human-computer systems, Newport, RI, pp 27–34
43. Dourish P, Bellotti V (1992) Awareness and coordination in shared workspaces. In: CSCW '92: Proceedings of the 1992 ACM conference on computer-supported cooperative work, ACM Press, New York, pp 107–114
44. Gutwin C, Greenberg S (1998) Design for individuals, design for groups: Tradeoffs between power and workspace awareness. In: CSCW '98: Proceedings of the 1998 ACM conference on computer supported cooperative work, ACM Press, New York, pp 207–216
45. Scott SD, Carpendale MST, Inkpen KM (2004) Territoriality in collaborative tabletop workspaces. In: CSCW '04: Proceedings of the 2004 ACM conference on computer supported cooperative work, ACM Press, New York, pp 294–303
46. Hall ET (1966) Distances in man: The hidden dimension. DoubleDay, Garden City, NY
47. Tuddenham P, Robinson P (2009) Territorial coordination and workspace awareness in remote tabletop collaboration. In: CHI'09: Proceedings of the 27th ACM SIGCHI conference on human factors in computing systems, ACM Press, New York, pp 2139–2148
48. Kruger R, Carpendale S, Scott SD, Tang A (2005) Fluid integration of rotation and translation. In: CHI'05: Proceedings of the 2005 SIGCHI conference on human factors in computing systems, Minneapolis, MN, pp 601–610
49. Nacenta MA, Pinelle D, Stuckel D, Gutwin C (2007) The effects of interaction technique on coordination in tabletop groupware. In: Proceedings of the Graphics Interface 2007, ACM Press, New York, pp 191–198
50. Ha V, Inkpen KM, Mandryk RL, Whalen T (2006) Direct intentions: The effects of input devices on collaboration around a tabletop display. In: Proceedings of the TABLETOP 2006, Adelaide, South Australia, pp 177–184
51. Forlines C, Shen C (2005) DTLens: Multi-user tabletop spatial data exploration. In: UIST '05: Proceedings of the 18th annual ACM symposium on user interface software and technology, ACM Press, New York, pp 119–122
52. Bier EA, Stone MC, Pier K, Buxton W, DeRose TD (1993) Toolglass and magic lenses: The see-through interface. In: SIGGRAPH '93: Proceedings of the 20th annual conference on computer graphics and interactive techniques, ACM Press, New York, pp 73–80
53. Morris MR, Paepcke A, Winograd T, Stamberger J (2006) Teamtag: Exploring centralized versus replicated controls for co-located tabletop groupware. In: CHI '06: Proceedings of the SIGCHI conference on human factors in computing systems, ACM Press, New York, pp 1273–1282

Chapter 18
Horizontal Interactive Surfaces in Distributed Assemblies

Christian Müller-Tomfelde and Kenton O'Hara

Abstract In recent years we have seen a huge growth of interest in tabletop research and technologies. Apart from the increasing research into underlying hardware technologies and interaction mechanisms, there has also been a significant interest in the dynamics of collaboration that happens "on" and "around" interactive tabletop surfaces. Most of this work has focussed on collocated interaction, exploring issues such as equity of participation, territoriality, orientation and coordination. This body of work has highlighted several important aspects of tabletop settings, particularly in terms of impact on the dynamics of collaboration. Much less attention, though, has been given to collaborative work practices happening around interactive horizontal surfaces in the presence of other media, technologies and artefacts, and especially in the context of remote collaboration. This chapter presents research and findings of interactive tabletop settings in environments that include various other artefacts and devices. We label these settings with the term "assemblies" to describe and emphasises the real-world character of settings that draws on the concepts of Ubiquitous Computing and Media Space, as well as everyday objects such as pen and paper. We conclude this chapter by highlighting important aspects of distributed assemblies with respect to the boundaries of interactivity and the orientation of these environments.

Introduction

Interactive tabletops have been under investigation over a decade. Research effort has concentrated on appropriate technologies for the tabletop hardware, as well as the software for interacting with the displayed information. In addition, research has been conducted to further our understanding of collocated collaboration at tabletops

C. Müller-Tomfelde (✉)
CSIRO ICT Centre, Marsfield, NSW 2122, Australia
e-mail: Christian.Mueller-Tomfelde@csiro.au

C. Müller-Tomfelde (ed.), *Tabletops – Horizontal Interactive Displays*,
Human-Computer Interaction Series, DOI 10.1007/978-1-84996-113-4_18,
© Springer-Verlag London Limited 2010

and how to best support users in these settings. The tabletop interface has unique characteristics that differentiate it from others, such as desktop computers, handheld devices or electronic white boards. For example, with tabletops, the notions of "top" or "down" as observed on traditional vertical desktop computer displays do not exist in the same ways. Together with the use of direct touch and gesture interaction, these properties have crucial consequences for the design of tabletop interactions and technologies. Placing objects on the interactive tabletop is another example where new avenues for tangible interaction research are opened. Traditional applications with a graphical user interface designed for use with mouse and keyboard need to be refined when interaction is by direct touch input devices. Similarly, the ability to rotate objects such as application windows or digital documents, imitating some of the handling of paper documents has become another important issue. Another uniqueness of the tabletop interface is the computer display and interaction space no longer belong to an individual. Due to its size and horizontal layout, the interface is considered semi-public rather than private. Consequently, the tabletop interface is highly suitable for small group collaboration, whether seated or standing around tabletops.

Office based applications, entertainment and domestic applications have emerged, as well as the use in public spaces such as cafes and museums. The most valuable research on tabletop settings has focussed on the tabletop display and how to interact with information and digital artefact on it. However, more work is necessary to advance understanding of the role of tabletops in the real-world application scenarios. We assume that today's real-world collaborations neither consist of solely using tabletops for interaction nor are they limited to only co-located joint activities. Laptops, netbooks, and mobile phones amongst others have become increasingly used for collaboration while applications may run in a computing cloud or data centres. Collaboration across multiple sites beyond traditional phone and video conferences has also becomes more important when it comes to teamwork using groupware applications on high-speed networks. These scenarios may involve the use of high definition video mediated communication with shared interactive workspaces. In addition, today's hybrid work environments consist of digital workspaces as well as real spaces with users fluidly selecting and switching between them effortlessly as they carry out their work. An interactive tabletop combines aspects of these real and digital workspaces. The table is a physical surface around which a small team can work together, while the horizontal interactive display provides team members access to any digital information, documents, and applications.

In the following, we will provide a brief background of the role of tabletops in combination with other information and communication artefacts – both digital and physical. We introduce the term "assemblies" within our research context and, in particular explore "distributed assemblies" that incorporate interactive tabletops. We provide an overview of our related studies targeting aspects of interactive tabletops in distributed assemblies. Finally, we discuss and summarise the results of our findings.

Background

Consider office workers in typical everyday settings: besides having their own standard desktop computers, they utilise a variety of other devices and artefacts that constitute and contribute to their work environments. These devices and artefacts are either directly or indirectly related to the desktop computer, such as attached portable digital storage units, laptops, mobile phones or a collection of data CD-ROMs on the shelves. Even more traditional media exist and are still used in today's offices, such as books, folders, pens and paper documents. White boards and pin-up boards are still useful to quickly support discussions in ad hoc face-to-face meetings, jot down notes, or to sketch out ideas. Often, interactions with applications on the desktop computer or laptop are complemented by using paper and pen, e.g., for note taking. During a presentation of electronic slides to a small group, a traditional flip chart might be used to capture minutes or topics, or discuss side ideas. In other words, nowadays work environments still draw on traditional media and technologies for everyday work practices. What holds true for today's work environments for individuals may not be different when small groups gather around interactive tabletops or to collaboration environments in the domestic domain.

Tabletops in Scenarios of Ubiquitous Computing

Integrating tabletop settings into everyday environments, whether in the work place, public spaces, or domestic environment, relates to scenarios described and envisioned by Mark Weiser in the early 1990s [1]. He introduced the paradigm of Ubiquitous Computing (Ubicomp) in which computing was embedded into everyday objects and environments. Tabletop settings fits neatly within these envisioned scenarios of Weiser. What is important here though is the need to consider the tabletop in the context of the broader ecology of interactive devices and everyday objects that comprise the scenarios of the Ubicomp vision. Early research works have explored how interactive tabletops can be integrated into an office environment with other enhanced room elements [2, 3] or with a set of laptops [4]. Research continues into recent times using hand held devices (e.g. [5]) or mobile phones (e.g. [6, 7]). Further research is necessary to articulate other aspects of artefact assemblies with respect to group work in tabletop settings.

Tabletops in Media Spaces

Although an interactive tabletop is well suited for the work of a small collocated group, tabletops can also be considered for distributed collaboration scenarios. When accepting slightly tilted interactive displays to be classified as tabletops, the ClearBoard System from 1992 by Ishii and Kobayashi [8] can be regarded as an important landmark research publication. The ClearBoard can be considered as one of the first examples of a distributed collaboration using tabletops. Interaction on shared displays was accompanied by audio/video link between two sites to provide eye contact amongst collaborators.

In the same year, the Hydra desktop video conferencing system was presented by Sellen et al. [9]. Their work explored the possibility of maintaining the correct spatial configuration of the conference partners. The Hydra system was combined with the Active Desk [10], also a slightly tilted interactive display, to showcase the use in video conferencing application with shared applications. In the late 1990s the Agora system [11] was developed to study mediated remote collaboration around a shared desktop. The system was designed to allow up to four participants to collaborate by monitoring each others' activity naturally. Similarly, the aim of the t-Room project [12] was to allow users in multiple t-Rooms feel as if they were in the same room. In the centre of the enclosed space was a worktable that was captured with a video camera, replicating the surface of the worktable on the horizontal display of the tables at remote sites. Recent studies have investigated implications for the distributed collaboration "around" shared workspaces on interactive tabletops (see e.g., [13, 14]), while some of these works are in the tradition of the ClearBoard system, where a video link was integrated, others rely on audio communication only (see also previous Chapter 17).

Distributed Assemblies

The focus of this chapter is to discuss tabletops in the presence of other media, technologies, devices, and artefacts. We use the term *assembly* to refer to an environment or space for interaction and collaboration consisting of multiple devices and artefacts with a wide range of properties. Devices and artefacts may be large interactive displays, standard desktop computers, laptops, netbooks, smart and mobile phones and also includes other technologies, e.g., for audio and video communication. Further possible elements of assemblies are white boards, flipcharts, books, folders, paper and pen, as well as other room elements such as tables, chairs etc. This definition of assemblies strives to comprise not only scenarios of Ubiquitous Computing and of Media Spaces, but eventually also those of Tangible User Interfaces, Multi-Display Environments (MDE), as in [15, 16] and Roomware [3], amongst others. Not only does the term attempts to integrate the above listed devices, scenarios and approaches, but it also highlights the heterogenic and hybrid character of everyday interaction and collaboration environments. The concept of *distributed assemblies* then refers to scenarios of distributed collaboration where artefacts and devices in multiple remote spaces form assemblies for users to work with.

Studies in Distributed Assemblies

In this section, we also offer reflections on issues arising from tabletops in distributed assemblies. In particular, we explore the relationship between *interactivity* and *non-interactivity*, and the some implications of video mediated communication in distributed settings using tabletops. These are presented through a number of studies. We first look at a field study of an interactive table deployed in the public setting of a café bar. The notions of interactivity and non-interactivity are raised. Related to these notions, we then present a second study which offers an examination of the role of a table rim in managing artefact assemblies in collocated use. Following this we report on a field study of distributed meetings in an office environment in which an interactive horizontal surface is used to interact with shared vertical displays. Finally, we report observations from a more formal investigation into distributed collaboration around tabletops. These studies highlight and emphasise the boundaries of interactivity as well as the influence of shared workspace and video mediated communication on the perceived orientation of the setting in distributed assemblies.

Collocated Tabletop Interaction

The focus of the majority of the tabletop research is on the interactive horizontal display area and on understanding how best to support interaction and collaboration at tabletops. Research has been conducted to gauge the physical reach at tabletops in terms of ergonomics [17], and the use and organization of the space on tabletops during collaboration [18] (see also Chapter 14). These concepts need careful examination when designing tabletop interfaces for successful deployment in real-world settings. Little attention so far has been paid to the fact that most horizontal interactive displays still require a physical support base or frame around the display area, which we refer to as the rim around the tabletop. The rim usually frames the entire interactive display area, and we can assume that the rim can be reached without much effort and used very easily. Therefore, it is very likely that the rim, though non-interactive, can serve specific needs of users, for example, to physically lean upon, to rest arms, or to place and work with artefacts such as paper. Of additional interest is the rim that exists in the area and can be characterised as the individual's "personal space" [18] used exclusively by a single user when considering group collaboration. Upon realising the concept of personal space in digital tabletop settings, it is apparent this personal space includes both a non-interactive area on the rim and an interactive area on the horizontal display.

Unsurprisingly, tabletop research has so far focused exclusively on issues of interactivity with tabletops, from different sensing mechanisms to application design and social studies of tabletop usages (e.g. see [19–21]). Little explicit attention has been given to understand the role of non-interactive areas on tabletops and the relationship between interactivity and non-interactivity. Actions in the interactive area may constrain actions in the non-interactive area and vice versa and this could impact and shape the ways interactivity is managed.

In this subsection, we offer reflections on the relationship between interactivity and non-interactivity in the context of artefact assemblies in tabletop settings. These are presented through a number of studies. The first is a field study of an interactive table deployed in a café bar, while the second is a more formal experiment that explicitly looks at the role of a table rim in managing artefact assemblies in tabletop use.

Café-Bar

The relationship between interactivity and non-interactivity is both dynamic and complex. At times it is clearly delineated through design (e.g. a rim around a table) while at other times the relationship is fluid – something negotiated by actors in the accomplishment of social action. As Crabtree argues, this accomplishment and organisation of social action relies upon the spatial and material arrangement of artefacts [22]. In any setting and with any technology, these arrangements comprise both interactive and non-interactive elements and the relationship between them. In any particular engagement with an interactive table people will move fluidly between interactive and non-interactive intentions or actions with a continual negotiation of the regions and boundaries where interactivity and non-interactivity should occur. In this respect we can draw some parallels with Palen and Dourish's [23] discussion of how people continuously negotiate boundaries of public and private dissemination and the work of Bellotti et al. [24] in their discussion of sensing systems where inherent ambiguities exist between intentional and non-intentional interactions and where there is a need to continuously negotiate the boundaries between them.

The field study involved the deployment of an interactive table in a café-bar. The interactive table was situated in a room in the bar with a large sofa and wooden bench arranged for sitting around the table (see Fig. 18.1a). The rest of the room consisted of several small coffee tables each with 3–4 chairs arranged around them (see Fig. 18.1b). The interactive table consisted of a PC and a horizontal touch screen display housed in a low coffee-table format style casing. The touch screen display was a 40-inch plasma with a screen resolution of 1280 768. A wooden rim of approximately 11 cm surrounded the screen on all sides. The touch screen was

Fig. 18.1 Images of (**a**) the interactive table in the café-bar; (**b**) the room in which the table was situated – two guests had a meeting at one of the standard coffee tables

single touch only. The content on the display consisted of home page with graphical links to a range of short films, interactive installations and games from *dShed* (www.dshed.net) the Watershed's online showcase of creative digital media.

To set the context for discussion of interactivity and non-interactivity, we begin an analysis of the relationship between people and standard table surfaces in the room without interactive consequences. The spatial properties of the tables are of significance here because they essentially position people at particular physical distances from each other and in particular postures with respect to other social actors on the table. Physical distance, being related to zones of social distance has bearings on the way the table surfaces are used and touched under different social circumstances. We illustrate this by examining an episode where two young women were having a meeting at one of the coffee tables depicted in Fig. 18.1b. On the table they had separate paper documents for discussion arranged on the table among their drinks. At different points during the conversation the girls engaged with and touched the surface in different ways. One of the girls rested her elbows as she leant over the document on the table to read it. The other girl then leant into the table with her arms touching the surface as a way of signaling her interest and attention. Through the conversation they leant in and out of the table in a carefully choreographed manner. Where and how the surface was touched during the ongoing course of these encounters are intimately bound by the unfolding action, in-the-moment social action the relationship with the material arrangements of artefacts on the table and the relationship with table itself. The spatial properties of where and how the surface was touched were something continuously negotiated by all parties. It was highly contingent and something done unknowingly without awareness. It was done with great social significance but importantly, as we shall discuss later, without interactive consequence. In other conversations we observed, there was similarly choreographed use and touch of the table surface but with different spatial properties reflecting the different social relationships, artefact configuration and unfolding conversational trajectories of the particular episodes.

The significance of this dynamic use and touch of the non-interactive surfaces becomes apparent when we place these issues within the context of the interactive table where interactive and non-interactive intentions in relation to the horizontal surface come together. Let us consider an episode where the non-interactive intentions and actions impacted on subsequent interactive opportunities with the table. In this episode a woman arrived at the interactive table. She was struggling to carry a large handbag, several packets of crisps and peanuts and a glass of red wine in both hands. She dumped them all down together on the glass surface of the interactive table, without initial concern for the arrangement of the objects. With her hands free she was able to then arrange things properly on the interactive surface as she settled down.

In this episode, as the woman arrived at the table, its primary function was as a physical surface onto which an awkward-to-carry group of objects needed to be rested. At this point in her encounter, the interactive properties of the table were of secondary concern. In performing this activity, though, the non-interactive placement of objects then rendered the interactive properties of the table inaccessible. This was not simply through obscuring the information on the table but rather that this particular touch screen technology did not gracefully deal with touch detection in the context of other objects on the table. By doing these non-interactive actions at the beginning of her encounter with the table, further uses of the interactive properties were blocked.

What is apparent in this episode is the multi-faceted nature of the table surface and actor intentions within the context of the café environment. We have highlighted here the behaviour on arrival but of further significance here is how encounters such as these unfold over time during the visit [25]. For example, other people arrived to join the woman at the table later on in the encounter and they too placed drinks and objects on the surface that inhibited interactive use. Similarly, bar staff brought plates of food to the table and placed them down on the surface. During a typical café episode, then, the points at which there was a clash between non-interactive intentions and interactive potential were many. More importantly, these points involved other parties. Any management of the boundaries between non-interactive and interactive use was then something to be dealt with collaboratively within the context of other well-established social and behavioural schemata for café episodes.

In managing the boundaries between interactive and non-interactive intentions, we observed a number of notable behaviours. In the first instance, we saw some placement of bottles and glasses on the rim of the table in order to allow interaction with the content on the display. Important to this strategy is the clear delineation in the design of interactive and non-interactive properties of the table – the wooden rim being understandably non-interactive in these instances and thus affording placement of objects in the context of interactive intent. For some people though, the rim was too narrow and raised, leading to concerns about precarious placement of drinks at the edge of the table and the potential to spill onto the table and damage the technology. For these people, while there was clear delineation, the particular dimensions of the design created hindrances to such a strategy.

Exploratory Rim Study

A rim around an interactive display can be found in various settings and in different combinations of display technologies and interaction devices. Apart from the interactive table in the café-bar, we consider now first research tabletop systems that showcase patterns of use of the rim and then commercial tabletop systems to investigate how the rim is configured and used.

Collaboration scenarios around the UbiTable [26] include personal laptops for ad-hoc meetings around the coffee table-like interactive surface. The multi-touch device [27] rests on a real table and comes with an approximately 5 cm rim elevated several centimetres from the real table. Possibly due to reasons of stability, laptops are placed on the rim and partially occlude the personal interactive display area, while the group space in the centre remains visible for both collaborators. In recent research about the equity of interaction participation [28], the same multi-touch device is used in a similar setting. The physical table under the touch device serves as an area to lean on, place sheets of paper and operate with computer mice. In other research work however, the rim is explicitly introduced to support the comfortable use of mice and for leaning on the table while standing around it [29, 30].

For the tabletops used in the Augmented Surface system [4] no explicit rim is realised since the whole surface of a table is used for top-down data projection. However, the laptops in the collaboration scenario are placed on the edges of the physical table within reach of the users leaving a central space on the table for group usage.

Most commercially available tabletop systems using display technology such as rear projection come with a rim around the interactive display area [31, 32]. The predominant design of the tabletop systems we examined comprises a non-interactive rim around the interactive display area that is smaller at the long side of the display than at the short side. This holds for the design of table systems with a 4:3, as well as with a 16:9 screen ratio. The analysis of technical specifications reveals the rim at the long side of the table systems varies from 11, 18 and to 28 cm, respectively. The short side of the table has a rim of 18, 25 and 55 cm (see Fig. 18.2). We considered also two other tabletop systems that come with a uniformly sized rim: the DiamondTouch DT107 [33] and the reacTable* [34]. With this is mind, one can assume this is a frame for physical support of the technology rather than a rim designed deliberately for users (see Fig. 18.2). While the small tabletop systems [31, 32] are designed for sitting around, the InteracTable [35] with its larger rim is designed for small groups standing around the table [3].

To further understanding of how the rim around a digital tabletop is used with an assembly of artefacts, we conducted an exploratory study collecting quantitative and qualitative data through questionnaires, objective measures and observations. We configured a 46-inch diagonal LCD display (ratio 16:9) as a multi-touch tabletop. The height of the tabletop was 73.5 cm, chosen to accommodate comfortably seated positions around it. The table had a non-interactive rim of 25 cm on the long side, and 31 cm on the short side, of the interactive display (see fourth table shape from the left in Fig. 18.2). This design was guided by those of commercially available tabletop systems and by the form factors of a standard laptop (footprint of 33 cm by 23 cm), a wireless keyboard (44 cm by 16 cm) and the A4 paper size

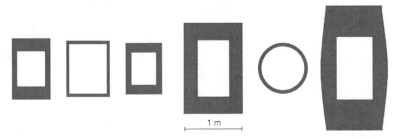

Fig. 18.2 Rim designs around horizontal interactive display spaces. The available systems depicted are (LTR): Microsoft Surface [31], DiamondTouch DT107 [33], Smart Table Model 230i [32, 36], table rim shape used in our study, reacTable* [34] and InteracTable [35]

(21 cm by 29.7 cm). We decided to have one side of the rim slightly thinner than a standard laptop's width and the other side shorter than the height of an A4 page. The aim was to elicit participant preferences regarding the placement of items on either interactive or non-interactive areas.

A group of three participants worked collaboratively on the interactive tabletop sorting task with 18 magazine covers (electronic copies of cover pages only) by defining two categories and organising the pages on the digital multi touch tabletop. Additionally, the group was provided with one set of spiral bound print outs of the 18 cover pages, one laptop with digital copies of the cover pages to flip through, and a wireless keyboard/ mouse set to control the pages on the tabletop (see Fig. 18.3).

After the participants filled out an initial questionnaire, we briefed them on the task. The participants were asked to come to an agreement as to who would take each of the three items to the tabletop area. We informed them they could change their seating position, swap the selected items with their colleagues and use multi-touch surface at any time. The participants were then asked to bring their selected item to the table, take a seat, and make themselves comfortable, awaiting further instructions. The tabletop display showed electronic cover pages in a pile, rotated at various angles. We captured the seating positions of the participants, and the location of the items each placed on the table, before they began the task. When asked to begin, the group worked on the task (see Fig. 18.3) until the pages were organised to the group's satisfaction. Finally, they filled out a post-task questionnaire.

We collected data from 12 participants (4 groups). They were on average 26.6 years old (standard deviation (SD) = 3.1), 3 were female and 10 reported to know the other group members. With respect to the participant's experience of using display technologies, 8% reported having no experience with large screens, compared to 50% having some, 34% regular and 8% daily experience. Regarding their experience of using horizontal computer displays, over a quarter of the participants had no experience, while 75% were somewhat experienced, due to their participations

Fig. 18.3 Team of participants completing the classification task using an assembly of artefacts such as laptop, keyboard, mouse and set of printouts

in similar studies before. Most of the participants had some or regular experience with touch interaction. We asked the participants also about the assembly of artefacts they usually bring into their meetings. Among the most mentioned were pens (100%), note paper (67%) and mobile phones (67%). Other items brought into meetings are print outs (92%) and laptops (50%). However, 25% reported to always bring their laptops into meetings.

Our observations revealed that 75% of the participants sat on the long side of the table. The predominant group seating arrangement had one participant sitting at each long side and the third sitting at the short side of the table (see, e.g., the group in Fig. 18.3). Only in one trial, two participants sat side-by-side at one long table side facing the third colleague on the opposite long side. Furthermore, we observed that participants who brought the laptop to the table sat down exclusively at the long side. Twenty five percent of the participants with the keyboard and 50% with the print outs sat at the short side. The participants positioned keyboard and print outs predominantly in front of them, while they placed the laptop on the side and slightly oriented the laptop display towards them. One participant explained that the laptop "screen prevented seeing the [horizontal display]. So it had to be sideways." The participants aligned the items with the border of horizontal display so as to not obscure the display, though they were not instructed to do so. During the course of the task they neither changed their initial seating position significantly, nor did they swap the items they brought to the table. In one trial, a participant with the laptop quickly rearranged her initially selected seating position at the short side and moved to a long side of the table to sit side-by side with a colleague. When asked about the motivation for this, she suspected that she would have better access to the pages on the table in her new position. In all trials, the participants occasionally used the items they placed on the table, while in the final phase, the interaction on the multi-touch table dominated.

In the post-questionnaire, we captured basic ergonomic factors of the tabletop setting. Nearly all of the participants (11) reported having good reachablity of the digital cover pages on the horizontal display. Seven participants agreed they had enough visibility of the pages, but 4 participants raised issues on this point. Three of these four participants were sitting at a short side of the table. One participant explained after the trial his strategies to cope with this shortcoming: he compensated for the poorly visible cover pages on the opposite side of his seating position by looking up and investigating them in his print outs in front of him. Almost all participants assessed the size of the rim to be appropriate and reported that they had enough space to place their items. Concerns were raised as to whether the small rim at the long side of the table is sufficient for supporting the laptop. One participant rated the rim to be a "[g]ood size but too small for laptop" and another criticized that "the [long] sides are too small for A4 to fit."

Distributed Collaboration

Our concerns in this section are in understanding the role, value of and behavioural practices with paper documents and other artefacts in the context of distributed tabletop settings. We would also like to understand the impact of the orientation of the setting on the ways distributed tabletop collaboration is carried out.

In everyday work, it is well established that paper plays a vital role in the ways work practises are conducted (e.g. [37]). Given the particular affordances of the paper medium, it is likely paper will continue to form a part of the artefact assemblies within which tabletop-based work interactions will be done. While there have been efforts within tabletop research to accommodate paper artefacts in the interaction, this has typically involved an explicit attempt to provide computational links between the physical and digital worlds (e.g. [38]). However, there has been little effort in looking at the behavioural practices of everyday paper documents in the context of tabletop settings (though see recent work by Ruiz et al. [39]), in real-world settings and in particular in distributed environments.

Collaboration Appliance Meeting Wizard

In articulating these concerns, we draw in particular on observational studies of a distributed collaboration appliance called Meeting Wizard. With Meeting Wizard, a large vertical projected display is used to present information to a group of users. To interact with this display surface, multiple interactive tablets are placed on a horizontal surface used by the group members to simultaneously point to, navigate through and mark up the information on the vertical display (see Fig. 18.4). Using this arrangement, the pointing and marking technology is decoupled spatially from the viewing surface providing the benefits of both vertical display and the configuration of the group around a horizontal interaction surface. As we shall see in the fieldwork, this arrangement has particular implications for how shared interactivity is managed and the clear demarcation of personal versus shared resources.

From our fieldwork observations of Meeting Wizard use in distributed collaboration, a notable feature was how individuals in the meeting would often have their

Fig. 18.4 A distributed meeting in which personal paper resources are marshalled around the tablet while interacting with the large shared projected surface

own paper version of the digital document being shared over Meeting Wizard. While the fact that paper documents are brought into a meeting is of course not a new phenomenon, the distribution of activities across the same document together in digital and paper form is nevertheless worth some commentary in light of our concerns with distributed media assemblies. In particular, the role they play in the management of ongoing individual and collaborative activities. The key here is the distinction in the shift between personal and shared use of information.

If we consider the documents presented on the shared surface, these are essentially visible and "owned" by all those present in the distributed meeting. Changing the view or marking up the document is in essence something that has to be achieved collaboratively; something that has to be negotiated with other present parties. Typically then, people would use some form of conversational device or signal in order to negotiate changing page or view. While this shared view works for coordinating attention, individuals may also want to look at different parts of the document at different times to support a particular cognitive strand they were taking. For example, in response to an ongoing conversation, a particular issue might have been evoked in an individual's mind that relates to another part of the document. They might use their own paper version of the document to go to that page and explore the relationship without disrupting the current conversation flow around the shared view. This is an important way of, for example, fluidly managing conversational threads and introducing new topics. The important point here is that as a personal resource, the paper version can be controlled and manipulated without incurring the social cost associated with negotiating over a shared resource. An example of this can be seen in a tele-meeting between one group in London and another group based in Hong Kong. One of the junior members of the meeting, J, was examining a printout of the photographs currently being displayed on the Meeting Wizard and currently being discussed. Having examined the paper version of the photographs, J leaned over towards PK sitting to the left of him, orienting the printout in PK's direction. While pointing to the printout J had a short discussion with PK. A few moments later when appropriate and when the other thread was completed, PK used the Meeting Wizard display to draw everyone's attention to the point that was raised in the prior side discussion. So the paper, in this example, as a personal resource had supported some individual cognition and then transformed fluidly into a conversational resource for a parallel side discussion in preparation for a new thread while the main discussion over the shared document continued. This illustrates an example of using multiple surfaces were to support the parallel analysis and threads in a very fluid manner.

> It was useful to have paper copies in front of us as well as on the screen so that two separate discussions could happen at the same time in the same meeting area (PK, facades, London)

The public personal boundary is not fixed but something that can be negotiated according to different circumstances [40, 23]. Indeed, when it comes to introducing new technologies, the delicacy of this negotiation is often underestimated in many tasks and many organisational activities (e.g., [37]). The tangibility and micromobility of the paper document allowed them to be managed fluidly making it clear exactly who should view the document. Another way to allow information to move from a personal resource to a shared resource is when the projected version of the document was pointed to the same page as on the paper version of the document. For opening up to the larger group, the paper version was less useful in their ability to bring the information more into the collaborative domain for shared visual reference. It was only by combining it with the electronic version that the shift could be made but this was indirect. Having separate spaces (paper and electronic) was important in creating a clearer permission management as well as allowing these personal and shared uses of the document to happen simultaneously.

Paper versions of the document were also important in providing and managing multiple surfaces. As O'Hara and Sellen [41] and O'Hara et al. [42] have argued, concurrently viewable multiple surfaces are an important part of the cognition underlying reading. Quick-glance access to information on different pages allows the information to be assimilated together in ways that is difficult without concurrent visibility. Observations were made of people moving attention between their paper printouts and the shared display in support of information processing and communication activities. This behaviour applied more broadly to marshalled information in the table space immediately in front of the individual. Indeed one of the key values demonstrated was the ability to interact with the shared conversational resource within the context of documents that had been brought the meeting and personally marshalled around the tablet (see Fig. 18.4).

Having a single shared horizontal collaboration surface, as in standard tabletop setting would only be part of the solution in the way real-world distributed collaboration gets managed. Having information distributed across multiple media surfaces (in this instance paper and projected displays) plays an important part in how activity fluidly moves from individual, to loosely coupled collaboration onto more tightly coupled collaboration during the course of a typical distributed meeting.

However, there were times to when such distributed assemblies across paper and digital surfaces created difficulties within distributed setups. In some of observations of Meeting Wizard in use during a distributed collaboration, we saw a local group begin to use a flip chart as shared visual resource. The work being done on the flip chart needed to be displayed as well as the information on the meeting wizard – again an example of the need for multiple surfaces. But conversational attention of the collocated group was then focused around the activities occurring on the flip chart. As this paper part of the assembly was not available to the remote group, i.e., not part of the distributed assembly it was more difficult for them to maintain involvement in the conversation. In this sense the asymmetry of distributed assemblies (see, e.g. [43]) resulted in certain presence disparities.

Negotiating Study at a Shared Tabletop

Another more formal study we carried out provides us with further insights into the use of distributed assemblies. Rather than focusing on the formal approach and methods of the study, we concentrate in particular on observations and findings of the whole setting to further understanding on the use of tabletops in distributed assemblies. The study was designed to capture effects of the input device and the workspace orientation of the shared tabletop on various objective and subjects parameters. However in this subsection, we emphasise the observations and findings during and after the experiment that were not directly under scrutiny of the main experiment. To understand the context of these observations we begin by describing the setting and task the participants worked on.

The study was conducted on the Braccetto research platform [44, 45] composed of a horizontal tabletop unit and a vertical unit for teleconferencing. On the horizontal LCD, participants could manipulate the presented digital content using direct touch or mouse devices as used in prior studies such as [30, 29]. Two rooms were set up with these workstations and connected via a computer network. The vertical display showed the video image of remote participants. Two participants per site worked collocated and also remotely together. The experimental setup at one site is shown in Fig. 18.5. Only a few controlled experiments exist that use a complex problem solving tasks for the investigation into distributed team collaboration. We aimed to create a task that was complex and quasi-realistic, relevant and interesting for participants to ensure their engagement, and which addresses both external and internal representations of the artefacts in the workspace. We chose a bushfire survival scenario [46] that functioned as a subject of a negotiating task: group members were asked to rank several items based on their value in surviving a bushfire. Due to the fact that Australia, where the experiment was conducted, is highly affected by bushfires, it was assumed that this topic might stimulate their engagement.

Participants in groups of four were introduced to the task by viewing a video describing the following hypothetical situation: Their group in a cottage in the Australian bush received news of a nearby bushfire approaching their location. They were then presented with a set of 12 items (woollen blankets, cell phone, map of area, etc.) found nearby. After viewing the video scenario the participants were randomly assigned into two groups and separated into two rooms. Each participant received an A4 page with a written description of the scenario presented in the video. This gave them the opportunity to review some of the facts. The task was completed in two steps: First, participants ranked individually the items based on their survival

Fig. 18.5 Setup of the experiment: participants are interacting in a shared workspace on the horizontal display (**a**) with their remote collaborators (seen on vertical display). A participant reads the printed description of the bushfire scenario (**b**)

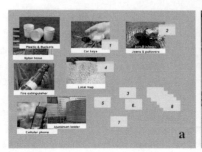 

Fig. 18.6 The detailed view on the workspace (**a**). The participants can attach and remove the numbered yellow cards like digital post-its on the items to mark their rankings. The participants used either direct touch or an optical mouse device to manipulate the artefact (**b**)

value (priming activity), and second, they ranked the items as a group (consensus activity). The participants ranked sets of digital images of the 12 items by attaching digital post-it notes with ranked numbers on the items (see Fig. 18.6a). In the individual ranking, each participant had their own set in the workspace. In the group ranking, a single set of items and post-it notes were available to all participants, i.e., shared across the sites.

With respect to the topics of this chapter, we observed the following behaviour that shed more light on the integration of the tabletop in the distributed assemblies consisting of paper and shared digital artefacts. Participants used the written description of the scenario on the sheet of paper to recall some of the facts. They did this during the individual as well as the group ranking part of the study. In most cases, the participants retreated from the actual group activity to find further hints to improve the ranking (see Fig. 18.5b). When not used, the paper was placed at the side of the table on the rim.

The rim around the interactive tabletop also had the function of allowing standing participants to lean against or rest their forearms on. Since the tabletop was raised higher than a standard table for sitting, they acted more like at a bistro table. Although the trial lasted about 30–40 minutes each, no participants complained about the fact that they had to stand during the trial. For those participants that were asked to use the mouse to control the software artefact, the rim around the tabletop also served as the location where they placed the mouse to operate with it. The setting used in this study was different to that described before with the Meeting Wizard. In the field study the vertical display space was used to provide a shared information space and audio conference call was used to communicate. In the study a rich audio and video link between the sites was established and the horizontal interactive surface was used to display and access shared information.

While this seems to be a major difference between the distributed settings, we can observe commonalities in the way the settings are used with respect to orientation and direction. To further investigate this aspect, we draw on the results of a follow-on mock-up study [47]. This study was conducted after subjects had participated in the previous experiment. The preceding activity can be seen as a primer for this mock-up study where we captured their preferences for alternative platform-setups and configurations. The subjects were asked to work on the following design task. They were given a set of small scale models of the basic elements of the platform, such as displays in landscape and portrait layout and workspace platforms with different tilts. The models were created from thick foam and we provided blu-tack, e.g., to place "screens on the wall".

The important outcome of the study was that over 70% of the participants tilted the horizontal workspace in the mock-up design. Asked for their preference the users clearly showed that they conceptualized basic ergonomic issues of the interactive horizontal tabletop in front of them with regard to visibility of information on the display and reachability of elements when using direct touch input devices. One subjects stated that

> Tilted table allows a better view [. . .] of the pictures stuck onto it" and other subject stated that "A small slope for a touch screen would be more natural for me because I could reach all parts of the touch screen easily in this case.

Although the results of the mock-up study are highly relevant since the participants had a thorough experience of the experiment stetting, some issues were not conceptualised. Tilting the whole tabletop including the rim implies the lost of the affordance of the rim to place objects such as paper and the mouse device on it. While tilting the tabletop has no implication of the interactive digital side of the boundary of interactivity, the properties in the non-interactive area changes significantly.

Discussion

Our field studies and findings from the more formal experiments revealed two important aspects regarding deployment of interactive tabletops in distributed assemblies. First, whether addressing collocated or distributed collaboration, the use of paper and other artefacts of the everyday environments such as offices and semi public spaces plays an important role. Given this, we identified the importance of the boundaries of interactivity of tabletop settings, i.e, the interplay of interactive and non-interactive areas on a horizontal surface. Second, our investigation into distributed collaboration emphasises that presence of vertical shared workspaces or video mediated communication shape the way collaboration is organised and carried out around tabletops. This has implications on how the horizontal interaction surfaces are used in distributed assemblies.

Boundaries of Interactivity

Our concerns with respect to interactivity and non-interactivity are not with the specifics of the particular interactive tabletop deployed in the field study or used in experiments. We recognise some of the specific issues discussed here may not be manifest with other systems, such as multi-touch interactive surfaces. We recognise too, that there may be design solutions for the difficulties highlighted in the café-bar study. However, our intent was to show a demonstrable relationship between the interactive and the non-interactive areas and to provide early insights while conducting the exploratory rim study. In light of this, we would argue that this relationship should be given further attention in the context of emerging interactive surface solutions and distributed assemblies. As we have seen from the findings, this relationship between interactivity and non-interactivity is a complex and dynamic one that is continuously managed and evolved within the context of the different social settings.

How we design for this is an important question. While there were times when the clear delineation between interactive and non-interactive elements was important (e.g. rim vs. touch screen), this is only a small piece of the design puzzle, and the relationship goes beyond a simple static specification of interactive areas and non-interactive areas. This is because spatial arrangement of interactive vs. non-interactive regions was shaped by multiple and dynamic factors, including dimensions of the table surface (e.g. height, length, width, diameter), number of actors around the table, the relationship between them, particular topics of conversation and arrangement of artefacts on the table. With many of these factors continuously changing, the movement between interactive and non-interactive is ultimately a social accomplishment collaboratively achieved by a group of actors. In designing for this relationship then, it is important to go beyond the static delineation of interactive and non-interactive regions on the surface. Rather, the focus should be on supporting social mechanisms that enable and manage fluid transition between interactive and non-interactive.

Directionality

In the field study with the Meeting Wizard as well as in the experiment in the shared workspace it became clear that both the shared vertical display in the Meeing Wizard study and the video display in the Bushfire experiment imposed *directionality* on the local settings. Addressing artefacts that are not part of the distributed assembly, e.g., working on flip charts may interrupt flow of the conversation and collaboration. In the mock-up study we saw users' preferences for tilted workspaces. This may be based on their intuition of what constitutes a more effective work environment that has more comfortable reach and better viewing angles. However, tilting the interaction surface has implications for its orientation. Observers of a vertical display perceive displayed information in the same orientation from any position in front of the display (i.e., position independent orientation). The perceived orientation around a horizontal surface on the other hand, depends entirely on the position of each observer relative to the display. Attributes such as top, down, left or right do not exist. Any tilt angle as suggested by the participants reintroduces directionality, i.e., the notion of top, down, left and right to the tabletop display.

This might encourage users to situate themselves in front of the lowest side of a tilted tabletop. In this arrangement, the viewing angle on the horizontal workspace is optimal for all participants. Since users stand or sit at the tilted tabletop side-by-side, the size of the group will be directly proportional to the width of the screen. The participants may not have realised the ramifications of tilting a fully horizontal tabletop leading to the loss of the affordance of placing and supporting objects on the surface.

The important aspect of our findings is that artefacts in the distributed assemblies have the potential to provide directionality to a setting. The directionality of the horizontal surface, for instance, may become aligned with the directionality of the work environment imposed by a vertical video display of remote collaborators. This holds true for vertical as well as horizontal shared workspace and may be a key convention to facilitate the collaboration in distributed settings. Having too many shared displays in a distributed setting may lead to ambiguous situations where participants of the meeting address different areas in the shared environment.

Conclusion

We presented our work on horizontal interactive surfaces in distributed assemblies. With the term distributed assemblies we want to emphasis that real-world tabletop setting may not be considered isolated points of interaction, but rather as part of an assembly of artefacts with which users can interact. The boundaries of interactivity of tabletop settings have been identified as an important aspect for future research. The non-interactive rim around the interactive area on the surface provides the affordance to place other, possibly interactive artefacts of the assembly. The observations our studies in distributed settings show how a shared vertical display or a video mediated communication display has a tendency to impose directionality on the settings toward the remote parties. Implications for tabletop setting have been discussed such as tilting the horizontal interactive surfaces for better ergonomics. The success of future deployments of tabletop systems in real-world applications for collocated and distributed group work depend on the comprehensive understanding of tabletop collaboration in today's distributed assemblies.

Acknowledgments This research was conducted within the HxI Initiative [45], an Australian research initiative led by the Commonwealth Scientific and Industrial Research Organisation (CSIRO), the Defence Science and Technology Organisation (DSTO) and National Information and Communications Technology Australia (NICTA) [48]. The authors thank the participants of the studies for allowing us to collect and publish the presented data. We thank Gregor McEwan for his initial contribution to this chapter and Kelvin Cheng for his thoughtful comments, suggestions and contributions. We also thank Anja Wessels, Claudia Schremmer and Anastasia Bezerianos for their work on the Bushfire experiment and the mock-up study. Furthermore, we thank Alex Krumm-Heller for his programming assistance for the experiment setup and software. Finally, we thank Kelvin Cheng, Natalie Ruiz and Steve Broadhurst for their work and help in the exploratory rim study.

References

1. Weiser M (1991) The computer for the 21st century. Scientific American 265(3):94–104, http://www.ubiq.com/hypertext/weiser/SciAmDraft3.html
2. Rauterberg M, Fjeld M, Krueger H, Bichsel M, Leonhardt U, Meier M (1998) BUILD-IT: A planning tool for construction and design. In: Proceedings of the SIGCHI conference on human factors in computing systems (CHI '98), ACM Press, New York, pp 177–178, doi: 10.1145/286498.286657
3. Streitz NA, Geißler J, Holmer T, Konomi S, Müller-Tomfelde C, Reischl W, Rexroth P, Seitz P, Steinmetz R (1999) i-LAND: An interactive landscape for creativity and innovation. In: Proceedings of the SIGCHI conference on human factors in computing systems (CHI '99), ACM Press, New York, pp 120–127, doi: 10.1145/302979.303010
4. Rekimoto J, Saitoh M (1999) Augmented surfaces: A spatially continuous work space for hybrid computing environments. In: Proceedings of the SIGCHI conference on human factors in computing systems (CHI '99), ACM Press, New York, pp 378–385, doi: 10.1145/302979.303113
5. Sugimoto M, Hosoi K, Hashizume H (2004) Caretta: A system for supporting face-to-face collaboration by integrating personal and shared spaces. In: Proceedings of the SIGCHI conference on human factors in computing systems (CHI '04), ACM Press, New York, pp 41–48, doi: 10.1145/985692.985698
6. Olwal A (2006) Lightsense: Enabling spatially aware handheld interaction devices. In: Proceedings of the 2006 5th IEEE and ACM international symposium on mixed and augmented reality (ISMAR '06), IEEE Computer Society, Washington, DC, pp 119–122, doi: 10.1109/ISMAR.2006.297802
7. Kray C, Rohs M, Hook J, Kratz S (2008) Group coordination and negotiation through spatial proximity regions around mobile devices on augmented tabletops. In: Proceedings of the 3rd IEEE international workshop on horizontal interactive human computer systems (TABLETOP '08), pp 1–8, doi: 10.1109/TABLETOP.2008.4660176
8. Ishii H, Kobayashi M (1992) ClearBoard: A seamless medium for shared drawing and conversation with eye contact. In: Proceedings of the SIGCHI conference on human factors in computing systems (CHI '92), ACM Press, pp 525–532, doi: 10.1145/142750.142977
9. Sellen A, Buxton B, Arnott J (1992) Using spatial cues to improve videoconferencing. In: Proceedings of the SIGCHI conference on human factors in computing systems (CHI '92), ACM Press, New York, pp 651–652, doi: 10.1145/142750.143070
10. Fitzmaurice GW, Ishii H, Buxton WAS (1995) Bricks: Laying the foundations for graspable user interfaces. In: Proceedings of the SIGCHI conference on human factors in computing systems (CHI '95), ACM Press, New York, pp 442–449, doi: 10.1145/223904.223964
11. Kuzuoka H, Yamashita J, Yamazaki K, Yamazaki A (1999) Agora: A remote collaboration system that enables mutual monitoring. In: CHI '99 extended abstracts on human factors in computing systems (CHI '99), ACM Press, New York, pp 190–191, doi: 10.1145/632716.632836
12. Hirata K, Harada Y, Takada T, Aoyagi S, Shirai Y, Yamashita N, Yamato J (2006) The t-Room – Toward the future phone. NTT Technical Review 4(12):26–33
13. Pauchet A, Coldefy F, Lefebvre L, Louis Dit Picard S, Perron L, Bouguet A, Collobert M, Guerin J, Corvaisier D (2007) TableTops: Worthwhile experiences of collocated and remote collaboration. In: Proceedings of the second annual IEEE international workshop on horizontal interactive human-computer systems (TABLETOP '07), IEEE Computer Society, Newport, RI, pp 27–34, doi: 10.1109/TABLETOP.2007.35
14. Yamashita N, Hirata K, Aoyagi S, Kuzuoka H, Harada Y (2008) Impact of seating positions on group video communication. In: Proceedings of the ACM 2008 conference on computer supported cooperative work (CSCW '08), ACM Press, New York, pp 177–186, doi: 10.1145/1460563.1460591

15. Jiang H, Wigdor D, Forlines C, Shen C (2008) System design for the wespace: Linking personal devices to a table-centered multi-user, multi-surface environment. In: Proceedings of the 3rd IEEE international workshop on horizontal interactive human computer systems (TABLETOP '08), pp 97–104, doi: 10.1109/TABLETOP.2008.4660191

16. Biehl JT, Baker WT, Bailey BP, Tan DS, Inkpen KM, Czerwinski M (2008) Impromptu: A new interaction framework for supporting collaboration in multiple display environments and its field evaluation for co-located software development. In: Proceeding of the twenty-sixth annual SIGCHI conference on human factors in computing systems (CHI '08), ACM Press, New York, pp 939–948, doi: 10.1145/1357054.1357200

17. Toney A, Thomas BH (2006) Considering reach in tangible and table top design. In: Proceedings of the first IEEE international workshop on horizontal interactive human-computer systems (TABLETOP '06), IEEE Computer Society, Adelaide, pp 57–58, doi: 10.1109/TABLETOP.2006.9

18. Scott SD, Carpendale ST, Inkpen KM (2004) Territoriality in collaborative tabletop workspaces. In: Proceedings of the 2004 ACM conference on computer supported cooperative work (CSCW '04), ACM Press, New York, pp 294–303, doi: 10.1145/1031607.1031655

19. Hodges S, Izadi S, Butler A, Rrustemi A, Buxton B (2007) Thinsight: Versatile multi-touch sensing for thin form-factor displays. In: Proceedings of the 20th annual ACM symposium on user interface software and technology (UIST '07), ACM Press, New York, pp 259–268, doi: 10.1145/1294211.1294258

20. Rogers Y, Lim Y, Hazlewood W, Marshall P (2009) Equal opportunities: Do shareable interfaces promote more group participation than single users displays? Human-Computer Interaction 24(2):79–116

21. Wigdor D, Jiang H, Forlines C, Borkin M, Shen C (2009) Wespace: The design development and deployment of a walk-up and share multi-surface visual collaboration system. In: Proceedings of the 27th international conference on human factors in computing systems (CHI '09), ACM Press, New York, pp 1237–1246, doi: 10.1145/1518701.1518886

22. Crabtree A (2000) Remarks on the social organisation of space and place. Journal of Mundane Behavior 1(1):25–44, http://mundanebehavior.org/issues/v1n1/crabtree.htm

23. Palen L, Dourish P (2003) Unpacking "privacy" for a networked world. In: Proceedings of the SIGCHI conference on human factors in computing systems (CHI '03), ACM Press, New York, pp 129–136, doi: 10.1145/642611.642635

24. Bellotti V, Back MJ, Edwards WK, Grinter RE, Lopes C, Henderson A (2002) Making sense of sensing systems: Five questions for designers and researchers. In: Proceedings of the SIGCHI conference on human factors in computing systems (CHI '02), ACM Press, New York, pp 415–422

25. Laurier E, Whyte A, Buckner K (2001) An ethnography of a neighbourhood café: Informality, table arrangements and background noise. Journal of Mundane Behavior 2(2):195–232, http://mundanebehavior.org/issues/v2n2/laurier.htm

26. Shen C, Everitt K, Ryall K (2003) Ubitable: Impromptu face-to-face collaboration on horizontal interactive surfaces. In: Proceedings of the 5th international conference on ubiquitous computing (UbiComp 2003), Lecture Notes in Computer Science, vol 2864, pp 281–288

27. Dietz P, Leigh D (2001) DiamondTouch: A multi-user touch technology. In: Proceedings of the 14th annual ACM symposium on user interface software and technology (UIST '01), ACM Press, New York, pp 219–226, doi: 10.1145/502348.502389

28. Marshall P, Hornecker E, Morris R, Dalton NS, Rogers Y (2008) When the fingers do the talking: A study of group participation with varying constraints to a tabletop interface. In: Proceedings of the 3rd IEEE international workshop on horizontal interactive human computer systems (TABLETOP '08), pp 33–40, doi: 10.1109/TABLETOP.2008.4660181

29. Müller-Tomfelde C, Schremmer C (2008) Touchers and mousers: Commonalities and differences in co-located collaboration with multiple input devices. In: Proceeding of the twenty-sixth annual SIGCHI conference on human factors in computing systems (CHI '08), ACM Press, New York, pp 1149–1152, doi: 10.1145/1357054.1357234

30. Müller-Tomfelde C, Schremmer C, Wessels A (2007) Exploratory study on concurrent interaction in co-located collaboration. In: Proceedings of the 2007 conference of the computer-human interaction special interest group (CHISIG) of Australia on computer-human interaction: Design: Activities, artifacts and environments (OZCHI '07), ACM Press, New York, pp 175–178, doi: 10.1145/1324892.1324925
31. Microsoft Surface (2009) http://www.microsoft.com/SURFACE, accessed 05.02.2009
32. SMART Technologies (2009) SMART Table. http://smarttech.com/table, accessed 05.02.2009
33. Circle Twelve (2009) DiamondTouch. http://www.circletwelve.com/, accessed 05.02.2009
34. Jordà S, Kaltenbrunner M, Geiger G, Bencina R (2005) The reacTable*. In: Proceedings of the international computer music conference (ICMC 2005), Barcelona, Spain
35. Wilkhahn (2001) InteracTable. http://www.roomware.wilkhahn.com/, accessed 10.03.2007
36. SMART Technologies (2009) Specifications SMART Table model 230i. http://www2.smarttech.com/NR/rdonlyres/6095CFE4-ED8F-4C0D-900C-C5C31E4357EF/0/SpecSmartTable230iv20Jan09.pdf, accessed 10.02.2009
37. Harper R, Sellen A (2000) The role of paper in the knowledge economy. PIRA International Yearbook 2000, PIRA, Leatherhead, pp 278–80
38. Everitt KM, Morris MR, Brush AJB, Wilson AD (2008) DocuDesk: An interactive surface for creating and rehydrating many-to-many linkages among paper and digital documents. In: Proceedings of the 3rd IEEE international workshop on horizontal interactive human computer systems (TABLETOP '08), pp 25–28, doi: 10.1109/TABLETOP.2008.4660179
39. Ruiz N, Cheng K, Rittenbruch M (2009) Exploring manual interaction and social behaviour patterns in intensely collaborative teamwork. In: Gross T (ed) Proceedings of the 12th IFIP TC13 conference in human-computer interaction (INTERACT '09), Lecture Notes in Computer Science, vol I, pp 578–581
40. Altman I (1975) The environment and social behavior: Privacy, personal space, territory and crowding. Brooks/Cole Publishing Co., Inc., Monterey, CA
41. O'Hara K, Sellen A (1997) A comparison of reading paper and on-line documents. In: Proceedings of the SIGCHI conference on human factors in computing systems (CHI '97), ACM Press, New York, pp 335–342, doi: 10.1145/258549.258787
42. O'Hara K, Taylor A, Sellen A, Newman W (2002) Understanding the materiality of writing while reading from multiple sources. International Journal of Human-Computer Studies 56:269–305
43. Heath C, Luff P (1992) Media space and communicative asymmetries: Preliminary observations of video mediated interaction. International Journal of Human-Computer Interaction 7:315–346
44. Schremmer C, Krumm-Heller A, Vernik R, Epps J (2007) Design discussion of the [braccetto] research platform: Supporting distributed intensely collaborating creative teams of teams. In: Jacko JA (ed) Human-computer interaction, Springer, LNCS, vol 4553, pp 722–734
45. HxI Initiative (2008) http://www.hxi.org.au, accessed 05.01.2008
46. Human Synergistics (2005) Bushfire survival situation leader's guide. Human Synergistics Inc., Plymouth, MI, accessed 05.09.2008
47. Müller-Tomfelde C, Wessels A, Schremmer C (2008) Tilted tabletops: In between horizontal and vertical workspaces. In: Proceedings of the third annual IEEE international workshop on tabletops and interactive surfaces (TABLETOP '08), pp 53–60, doi: 10.1109/TABLETOP.2006.36
48. Schremmer C, Müller-Tomfelde C (2008) HxI: Research down under in distributed intense collaboration between teams. In: CHI '08 extended abstracts on human factors in computing systems (CHI '08), ACM Press, New York, pp 3645–3650, doi: 10.1145/1358628.1358906

Index

C. Müller-Tomfelde (ed.), *Tabletops – Horizontal Interactive Displays,*
Human-Computer Interaction Series, DOI 10.1007/978-1-84996-113-4,
© Springer-Verlag London Limited 2010